Papua
New Guinea
a travel survival kit

Tony Wheeler
Jon Murray

P9-APL-355

Papua New Guinea – a travel survival kit

5th edition

Published by
Lonely Planet Publications
Head Office: PO Box 617, Hawthorn, Vic 3122, Australia
Branches: PO Box 2001A, Berkeley, CA 94702, USA
12 Barley Mow Passage, Chiswick, London W4 4PH, UK

Printed by
Singapore National Printers Ltd, Singapore

Photographs by
Jon Murray (JM)
Tony Wheeler (TW)
Richard Everist (RE)
Yvon Perusse (YP)
Ann Jelinek (AJ)
Air Niugini
Front cover: Sing-sing participant (Blackstar, Scoopix Photo Library)

First Published
April 1979

This Edition
August 1993

Although the authors and publisher have tried to make the information as accurate as possible, they accept no responsibility for any loss, injury or inconvenience sustained by any person using this book.

National Library of Australia Cataloguing in Publication Data

Wheeler, Tony
Papua New Guinea – a travel survival kit.

5th ed.
Includes index.
ISBN 0 86442 190 7.

1. Papua New Guinea – Guidebooks.
I. Murray, Jon. II. Title.
(Series : Lonely Planet travel survival kit).

919.5304

text & maps © Lonely Planet 1993
photos © photographers as indicated 1993
climate charts compiled from information supplied by Patrick J Tyson, © Patrick J Tyson, 1993

Tony Wheeler

Tony was born in England but spent most of his youth overseas. He returned to England to do a university degree in engineering, worked as an automotive design engineer, returned to university to complete an MBA, then dropped out on the Asian overland trail with his wife Maureen.

They've been travelling, writing and publishing guidebooks ever since, having set up Lonely Planet Publications in the mid-70s. Travel for the Wheelers is now considerably enlivened by their daughter Tashi and their son Kieran.

Jon Murray

Jon Murray took a year off university a long time ago and, after various adventures, ended up working in the Lonely Planet office, Melbourne, Australia. He left to go cycling in Asia but found himself updating guidebooks instead. His computer lives in Melbourne, and Jon manages to visit it from time to time. It has helped him update Lonely Planet's *Bangladesh – travel survival kit*, and contribute to the *Australia – travel survival kit*, *Sydney city guide* and *Africa on a shoestring*. He is also the co-author of LP's *South Africa, Lesotho & Swaziland – travel survival kit*.

From Jon Murray

It's not easy to produce a guidebook for Papua New Guinea (PNG) – the expenses are high and the market is small. I'm particularly grateful to Air Niugini who sponsored flights to and from PNG and around the country. Generous help was also given by Traditional Travel, Haus Poroman Lodge, Malagan Lodge, Loloata Island Resort, Trans Niugini Tours and the Koki Salvation Army Hostel.

Many individuals also gave freely of their time, expertise, information and hospitality. Warm thanks to Ken Ah Chee, Wallace Andrews, John Atkins, Bill Bates, Bernard Choulei, Warren Daniels, Peter van Fleet, Barry Franks, Moana Gangloff, Judy Gordon, Kalamendi the Famous, Mike Kanin, Joseph Kone, Nigel Lang, Noah Lurang, Bruno Letong, Cletus Maiban, the staff at the Malolo Plantation Resort, Tabo Meli, Thomas Molis, Glen Peia, Ian Poole, the Popondetta Cowboys, Bill Rudd, Elijah Saun, Ralph Stüttgen, John Vail, Jennifer Varssilly, Barry Walker, Liz Wright, Kieth Wilson and Maggie Wilson – and a host of other friendly and informative people.

Some of Peter Campbell's drawings from earlier editions of this book have been used once again in this edition. The section on PNG's parks was almost entirely written by Murray D Bruce and Constance S Leap Bruce.

The travellers I met along the way were also of great assistance. Thanks to Lenore Block (AUS), Judy Brealey (AUS), Jean-Jacques Braun (T), David Cooper (C), Debbie (Sin), Vilma Draperi (I), Leo Emans (Holland), Arec Fennes (Holland), Jürg Furrer (CH), Alessandro Guadagni (I), Guedo Knavel (Holland), Amit Lifschitz (Isr), Julian Loader (J), Ulrike Mahler (D), Michael & Angela (UK), Jan Roberts & husband (AUS), Elsa Wagner (PNG) and everyone else.

Thanks also to all the travellers who wrote in – they are listed at the back of the book on page 372.

From the Publisher

At the Lonely Planet in Melbourne, Australia, this edition was edited by Sharan Kaur and Simone Calderwood. Thanks to Sharon Wertheim for compiling the index.

Glenn Beanland was responsible for the design, layout and maps. Margaret Jung designed the cover and contributed to the mapping and Glenn Beanland and Ann Jeffree did the illustrations.

Producing this Book

Tony Wheeler researched and wrote the first two editions of *Papua New Guinea – travel survival kit*. Mark Lightbody, the author of Lonely Planet's *Canada – travel survival kit* researched the third edition and Richard Everist updated the fourth edition. This edition was updated by Jon Murray.

Warning & Request

Things change – prices go up, schedules change, good places go bad and bad places go bankrupt – nothing stays the same. So if you find things better or worse, recently opened or long since closed, please write and tell us and help make the next edition better.

Your letters will be used to help update future editions and, where possible, important changes will also be included in a Stop Press section in reprints.

We greatly appreciate all information that is sent to us by travellers. Back at Lonely Planet we employ a hard-working readers' letters team to sort through the many letters we receive. The best ones will be rewarded with a free copy of the next edition or another Lonely Planet guide if you prefer. We give away lots of books, but, unfortunately, not every letter/postcard receives one.

Contents

Map Legend

BOUNDARIES

—··—··—··—	........International Boundary
—··—··—··—	................Internal Boundary
·+·+·+·+·+·+·	....National Park or Reserve
— — — — — —	.... The Equator
·················	.... The Tropics

SYMBOLS

◉	NATIONAL	........................National Capital
●	PROVINCIAL	........Provincial or State Capital
●	Major	................................Major Town
●	Minor	................................Minor Town
■		..........................Places to Stay
▼		............................Places to Eat
⊠		................................Post Office
✈		....Airport
i		......................Tourist Information
⊖		............Bus Station or Terminal
66		...........Highway Route Number
☪†⌂✝		...... Mosque, Church, Cathedral
∴		........................Temple or Ruin
✚		......................................Hospital
✳		......................................Lookout
⬟		.... Camping Area
⋈		................................Picnic Area
⌂		............................Hut or Chalet
▲		.... Mountain or Hill
⊢■⊣		.... Railway Station
⩵		.... Road Bridge
+++++		.......................Railway Bridge
⇒ ⇐		............................Road Tunnel
⇥ ⇤		.........................Railway Tunnel
⏜		....................Escarpment or Cliff
⏝		....Pass
⊓⊓⊓⊓		.............Ancient or Historic Wall

ROUTES

—————	.......Major Road or Highway
-------------	.... Unsealed Major Road
—————	.... Sealed Road
- - - - - - -	..... Unsealed Road or Track
═════	.... City Street
+++++++++++	.............................Railway
⊷─◉─⊶	.... Subway
··················	.....................Walking Track
- - - - - - -	.... Ferry Route
╫╫╫╫╫╫	.... Cable Car or Chair Lift

HYDROGRAPHIC FEATURES

	.....................River or Creek
	..................Intermittent Stream
	........Lake, Intermittent Lake
	..........................Coast Line
	....................................Spring
	...............................Waterfall
	...............................Swamp
	.... Salt Lake or Reef
	...............................Glacier

OTHER FEATURES

	Park, Garden or National Park
	.... Built Up Area
	... Market or Pedestrian Mall
	.... Plaza or Town Square
	...........................Cemetery

Note: not all symbols displayed above appear in this book

Introduction

Papua New Guinea (PNG) is truly the 'last unknown' – it was virtually the last inhabited place on earth to be explored by Europeans and even today some parts of the country have only made the vaguest contact with the West.

It's also a last unknown for travellers and tourists. Yet it can be a fascinating and rewarding experience and not at all difficult to visit, although it takes a little ingenuity to avoid some of PNG's steep prices. But where else in the world can you riverboat down a waterway famed for its dynamic art and its equally dynamic crocodiles? Climb a smoking volcano and in the same afternoon dive on what a keen scuba diver told me was the best reef he'd seen anywhere in the world?

A Highland sing-sing can be a sight you'll never forget, a flight into one of PNG's precarious 'third level' airstrips is likely to be a fright you'll never forget. It's an amazing country and one that, as yet, is barely touched by the modern tourist trade.

A Visit to PNG

You're visiting a country with a tourist trade in its infancy so you'll have to put up with a few associated expenses and problems along the way. To get the most out of PNG, I think you have to approach it in one of two ways – which I call 'tight' and 'loose'.

By 'tight' I mean having everything arranged and sorted out beforehand. PNG is not a country where you can simply arrive and expect it all to happen – and waiting around can be frustrating and very expensive.

So a package deal, which whisks you from place to place with the minimum of fuss and with everything packed in as tightly as possible, can save a lot of time and frustration. Very careful planning can stitch things up almost as tightly as a package tour, for a lot less money.

On the other hand it is possible to do PNG 'loose' – if you're the sort of experienced shoestringer who can find places to stay in

villages, doesn't mind hanging around in a port waiting for that elusive boat to come by, and can sit patiently waiting for things to happen.

Facts about the Country

HISTORY

The history of Papua New Guinea prior to the arrival of European colonists in the 19th century is only starting to be pieced together. The task is daunting. The highly fragmented indigenous cultures left no written records and the marks they made on the landscape have almost been completely erased; their houses, fields and artefacts have been swallowed by the tropical environment.

The incredible capacity the vegetation has for swallowing history is clear when you look for the scars of WW II. Although you still don't have to search far, whole bases have been completely engulfed by jungle. If you don't know precisely where to look, you can walk straight past bunkers, railways and bomb craters that are less than 50 years old. Little wonder there are few relics of the hunter/gatherers who are now believed to have settled on the island at least 50,000 years ago.

The First Arrivals

It is believed that humans reached PNG and then Australia by island-hopping across the Indonesian archipelago from Asia, perhaps more than 50,000 years ago.

The migration was probably made easier by a fall in the sea level caused by an ice age. At no time was PNG completely joined to island South-East Asia but it was joined to Australia, probably until about 6000 years ago. As a result PNG shares many species of plants and animals (including marsupials) with Australia, but not with Indonesia. The Wallace Line, named after a 19th-century naturalist, marks the deep water between Bali and Lombok, and Kalimantan and Sulawesi (in Indonesia) that formed a natural barrier to animals and humans. In order to reach PNG, people had to cross open water on canoes or rafts.

There have been several waves of people from Asia, and this may be reflected in the

---

What's in a Name?

Few countries have such a long and confusing name as Papua New Guinea. When the first Portuguese explorers came along they named it Ilhas dos Papuas – Island of the Fuzzy-Hairs – from the Malay word *papuwah*. Later Dutch explorers called it New Guinea, because they were reminded of Guinea in Africa.

Then, towards the end of the 19th century, the country was divided up between the Dutch, the Germans and the British. The western half became Dutch New Guinea, the north-eastern quarter became German New Guinea and the south-eastern quarter became British New Guinea. When Australia took over from the British in 1905 they renamed the south-eastern quarter the Territory of Papua.

At the start of WW I, the Australians captured the German section and after the war this was assigned to Australia as a League of Nations Trust Territory. Australia had to run the two parts as separate colonies or, more correctly, a colony and a Mandated Trust Territory. After WW II, the two were combined and administered as the Territory of Papua & New Guinea, sometimes written as Papua-New Guinea or Papua/New Guinea.

Finally, with independence, the country became simply Papua New Guinea. A search for a less cumbersome name for the country has produced Niugini, but this has not gained much favour and, so far, has only been applied to the national airline.

Meanwhile, across the border, the Dutch half of the island went on as Dutch New Guinea into the '60s when Indonesia started its push to take it over. In a last ditch attempt to keep it out of Indonesian hands, the Dutch renamed it West Papua, but it was too late.

In 1962 the Indonesians took over and renamed it Irian Barat (West Irian) then later changed it to Irian Jaya (New Irian). ■

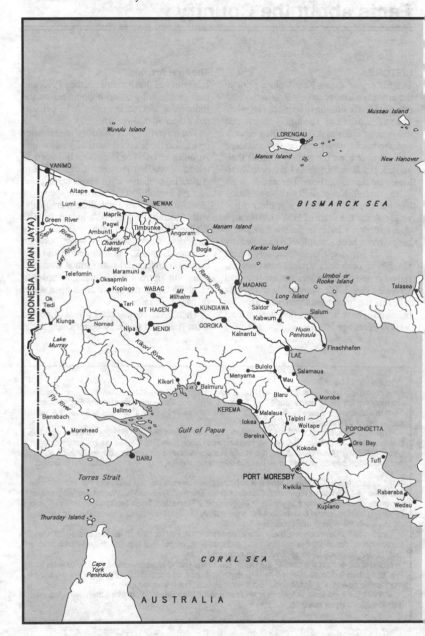

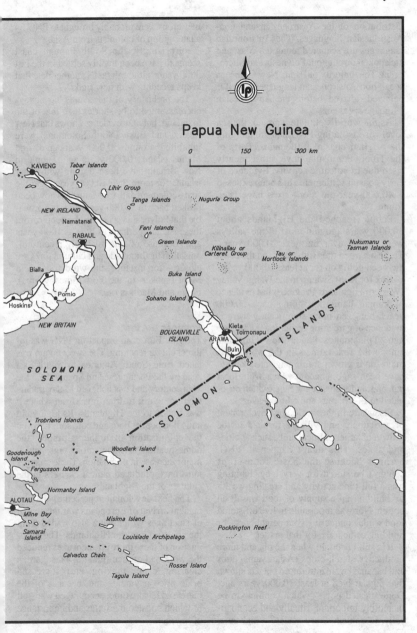

Papua New Guinea

0   150   300 km

distribution of the Austronesian and non-Austronesian languages. The Austronesian languages are scattered along the coast and are spoken throughout Polynesia and Micronesia. The majority of Papua New Guineans speak non-Austronesian languages and, it is believed, arrived before the Austronesian language speakers.

As the world's climate warmed, the sea level rose isolating PNG and submerging the original coastal settlements. Parts of the Huon Peninsula have subsequently risen due to volcanic activity. Evidence of early coastal settlements has been exposed – 40,000-year-old stone axes have been found.

People reached the Highlands about 30,000 years ago and most of the valleys were settled over the next 20,000 years. Trade between the Highlands and the coast has been going on for at least 10,000 years.

Kuk (or Kup) Swamp in the Wahgi Valley (Western Highlands Province) has evidence of human habitation going back 20,000 years, but even more significantly there is evidence of gardening beginning 9000 years ago. This makes Papua New Guineans among the first farmers in the world. The main foods grown at this stage are likely to have been sago, coconuts, breadfruit, local bananas and yams, sugar cane (which originated in PNG), nuts and edible leaves.

Elsewhere in the world, the development of agriculture and villages resulted in the growth of larger political units, such as cities and states. This didn't happen in PNG, perhaps because the basic food crops couldn't be stored for very long. Farming was a full-time activity and creating wealth by building up a supply of food wasn't an option. Nor was it possible to live off stored food while conquering your neighbours – or building cathedrals, for that matter.

It is still uncertain when the pig and more productive starch crops (Asian yams, taros and bananas) were introduced but it is known that pigs arrived at least 10,000 years ago. Domesticated pigs – which continue to be incredibly important, ritually and economically, in contemporary society – and these

new crops were probably brought to PNG by a later group of colonists from Asia.

Surprisingly, the South Papuan coast seems to have been mainly settled in the last 3000 years, although that's another date that keeps receding with new finds.

The prehistory of the islands has always been assumed to be shorter than that of the mainland, but new evidence shows that New Ireland and Buka (North Solomons) were inhabited around 30,000 years ago, and Manus Island 10,000 years ago. People in New Britain have been trading with other islands for more than 10,000 years, and the first-settlement date for Manus has now been pushed back to 10,000 years ago. It's probable that Polynesia was settled by people from these islands, perhaps as little as 1000 years ago. Because of this relatively recent colonisation the linguistic and cultural links are closer – for instance, the word for two in Motu (spoken in the Port Moresby area), Fijian and Maori is *rua*.

Potatoes & Axes

The first European impact on PNG was indirect but far reaching. The sweet potato was taken from South America to South-East Asia by the Portuguese and Spaniards in the 16th century and it is believed Malay traders then brought it to Irian Jaya, from where it was traded to the Highlands. Its high yield and tolerance for poor and cold soils allowed the colonisation of higher altitudes, the domestication of many more pigs, and a major increase in population. These changes must have produced radical changes in the cultures of the Highlands.

The next development preceding the permanent arrival of Europeans was the arrival of steel axes which were also traded from the coast up into the Highlands. The introduction of these more efficient axes reduced the workload of men (making axes, garden clearing, canoe making, etc), increased bride price payments and, because of the increased leisure time, encouraged war – all of which boosted the status and importance of big men.

European Contact

PNG's history of real European contact goes back little more than a century, although the island of New Guinea was known to the European colonial powers long before they came to stay.

The first definite European sighting of the island took place in 1512 when two Portuguese explorers sailed by. The first landing was also Portuguese: Jorge de Meneses landed on the Vogelkop Peninsula, the 'dragon's head' at the north-west corner of the island. He named it 'Ilhas dos Papuas' and got his name in the history books as the European discoverer of New Guinea.

In the following centuries various Europeans sailed past the main island and its smaller associated islands, but the spreading tentacles of European colonialism had far richer prizes to grapple with. New Guinea was a big, daunting place, it had no visible wealth to exploit, but it most definitely did have some rather unfriendly inhabitants. It was left pretty much alone.

Only the Dutch made any move to assert European authority over the island and that was mainly to keep other countries from getting a toehold on the eastern end of their fabulously profitable Dutch East Indies Empire (Indonesia today). They put their claim in by a roundabout method.

Indonesian and Malay traders had for some time carried on a limited trade with coastal tribes for valuable items like bird-of-paradise feathers. So the Dutch simply announced that they recognised the Sultan of Tidor's sovereignty over New Guinea. Since in turn, they held power over the island of Tidor, New Guinea was therefore indirectly theirs – without expending any personal effort. That neat little ploy, first put into action in 1660, was sufficient for over 100 years, but during the last century firmer action became necessary.

The British East India Company had a look at parts of western New Guinea back in 1793 and even made a tentative claim on the island, but in 1824 Britain and the Netherlands agreed that Holland's claim to the western half should stand. In 1828 the Dutch

made an official statement of their claim to sovereignty and backed it up by establishing a token settlement on the Vogelkop.

Nothing much happened for 50 or so years after that, although the coastline was gradually charted and Australia, now evolving from a penal colony towards independence, started to make noises about those foreigners claiming bits of land which were rightfully theirs.

A whole series of British 'claims' followed; every time some British ship sailed by somebody would hop ashore, run the flag up the nearest tree and claim the whole place on behalf of good Queen Vic. The good queen's government would then repudiate the claim and the next captain to sail by would go through the whole stunt again.

In 1883 the Queensland premier sent the Thursday Island police magistrate up to lay yet another unsuccessful claim, but the next year Britain finally got around to doing something about their unwanted would-be possession. At the time the British population consisted of a handful of missionaries and a solitary trader.

There was still very little happening over on the Dutch side of the island, but on the north coast of the eastern half, a third colonial power – Germany – was taking a definite interest. When Britain announced, in September 1884, that they intended to lay claim to a chunk of New Guinea, the Germans quickly raised the flag on the north coast. A highly arbitrary line was then drawn between German and British New Guinea. At that time no European had ventured inland from the coast and it was nearly 50 years later, when the Germans had long departed, that it was discovered that the line went straight through the most densely populated part of the island.

New Guinea was now divided into three sections – a Dutch half to keep everybody else away from the Dutch East Indies, a British quarter to keep the Germans (and anybody else) away from Australia, and a German quarter because it looked like it could be a damn good investment.

The Germans were soon proved wrong;

Cargo Cults

The recurrent outbreaks of 'cargo cultism' in New Guinea are a magnetic attraction for assorted academics.

The arrival of the first Europeans in New Guinea must have had much the same impact that a flying saucer landing would have on us. Like something from the film *Close Encounters of the Third Kind*, local history is divided up into the days of 'pre-contact' and 'post-contact'.

To many people the strange ways and mysterious powers of the Europeans could only be described by supernatural means. In religious systems where it is necessary to invoke the help of spirits to ensure, say, a good yam harvest, it is logical that the same principles be applied if you want manufactured goods. Some of the cult leaders can be regarded as early nationalists and in several cases the cults developed into important political movements.

Cult leaders theorised that the Europeans had acquired their machines and wealth from some spirit world and that there was no reason they too could not acquire similar 'cargo'. Some went further and insisted that the Europeans had intercepted cargo that was really intended for the New Guineas, sent to them by their ancestors in the spirit world. One cultist even suggested that the whites had torn the first page out of all their Bibles – the page that revealed that God was actually a Papuan.

If the right rituals were followed, said the cult leaders, the goods would be redirected to their rightful owners. Accordingly, docks were prepared, or even crude 'airstrips' were laid out, for when the cargo arrived. Other leaders felt that if they mimicked European ways they would soon have European goods – 'offices' were established in which people passed bits of paper back and forth. But when people started to kill their pigs and destroy their gardens (as a prerequisite for the better days to come) or to demand political rights, the colonial government took a firm stand. Some leaders were imprisoned. However arresting cult leaders simply confirmed the belief that an attempt was being made to keep goods rightfully belonging to the New Guineans, so some cultists were taken down to Australia to see with their own eyes that the goods did not arrive from the spirit world.

The first recorded cargo cult outbreak was noted in British New Guinea in 1893. A similar occurrence in Dutch New Guinea dates back to 1867. Cargo cult outbreaks have occurred sporadically ever since. One of the largest took place in the Gulf area just after WW I; it was known as the 'Vailala Madness' and was considerably spurred on by the arrival of the first aeroplane in the region – as predicted by one of the cult leaders.

The cults took another upswing after WW II when the people witnessed even more stunning examples of Western wealth. Seeing black American troops with access to the goods had a particularly strong impact. A more recent example was the Lyndon Johnson affair on the island of New Hanover (see the New Ireland Province chapter). No doubt there will be new events to keep academics happy for some time yet. ■

for the next 15 years the mosquitoes were the only things to profit from the German New Guinea Kompagnie's presence on the north coast. In 1899 the Germans threw in the towel, shifted to the happier climes of the Bismarck Archipelago and quickly started to make those fat profits they'd wanted all along.

Over in the Dutch half nothing was happening at all and the British were trying to bring law and order to their bit.

In 1888 Sir William MacGregor became the administrator of British New Guinea and set out to explore his possession and set up a native police force to spread the benefits of British government. He instituted the policy of 'government by patrol' which continued right through the Australian period. In 1906 British New Guinea became Papua and administration was taken over by newly independent Australia. From 1907 Papua was the personal baby of Sir Hubert Murray who administered it until his death in 1940.

European Exploration

Exploration was one of the most interesting phases of the early European development of PNG. This was almost the last place to be discovered by Europeans and the explorers were only too happy to put their daring deeds down on paper. Gavin Souter's book *The Last Unknown* is one of the best descriptions of these travels.

At first, exploration consisted of short trips in from the coast, often by parties of early mission workers. Later the major rivers were used to travel further into the forbidding inland region. The next phase – well into this century – was trips upriver on one side, over the central mountains and down a suitable river to the other coast. Crossing the tangled central mountains often proved to be the killer in these attempts.

It is interesting to note that more than one early explorer commented on how the curiosity and even awe with which they were met on a first trip turned to outright antagonism on a second. It's more than likely that a lot of this was due to the extreme trigger-happiness of some visitors. The final death count from the exploration of New Guinea undoubtedly showed that the head-hunters had more to fear from the European explorers than vice versa.

From the time of the Australian takeover of British New Guinea, government-by-patrol was the key to both exploration and control. Patrol officers were not only the first Europeans into previously 'uncontacted' areas but were also responsible for making the government's presence felt on a more or less regular basis.

The last great phase of exploration took place in the 1930s and was notable for the first organised use of support aircraft. This last period included the discovery of the vast Highlands region. By 1939 even the final unknown area, towards the Dutch New Guinea border, had been at least cursorily explored.

Since the war there have been more exploratory patrols and the country is now completely mapped, although previously 'uncontacted' peoples have been found recently and it's possible that there are more Highland clans yet to discover the outside world.

WW I & II

Almost as soon as WW I broke out in Europe,

New Guinea went through a major upheaval. Australian troops quickly overran the German headquarters at Rabaul in New Britain and for the next seven years German New Guinea was run by the Australian military. In 1920 the League of Nations officially handed it over to Australia as a mandated territory.

It stayed that way right up until WW II and this split government caused more than a little confusion for the Australians. In the south they had Papua, a place where they had to put money in to keep it operating and where the major purpose was to act as a buffer to an unfriendly state which was no longer there. In the north they had New Guinea, run by Germany as a nice little money spinner and continued in much the same way under the Australians. The discovery of gold at Wau and Bulolo, in the New Guinea half, only compounded the difficulties since the northern half became even more economically powerful in comparison to the south.

During WW II all the northern islands and most of the north coast quickly fell to the Japanese. The Japanese steam-rollered their way south and soon Australia only held Port Moresby. The Japanese advance was fast but short-lived and by September 1942, with the Pacific War less than a year old and Port Moresby within sight, they had run out of steam and started their long, slow retreat.

It took until 1945 to regain all the mainland from the Japanese, and the islands – New Ireland, New Britain, Bougainville – were not recovered until the final surrender, after the atom bombing of Hiroshima and Nagasaki.

The End of Colonialism

There was no intention to go back to the prewar situation of separate administrations and in any case Port Moresby was the only major town still intact after the war, so the colony now became the Territory of Papua & New Guinea. The territory entered a new period of major economic development with a large influx of expatriates, mainly Australians. When it peaked in 1971 the expatriate population had expanded from the 1940 total of about 6000 to over 50,000. Since then it has fallen to closer to 20,000 and is still declining.

The postwar world had an entirely different attitude towards colonialism and Australia was soon pressured to prepare Papua & New Guinea for independence. A visiting UN mission in 1962 stressed that if the people weren't pushing for independence themselves then it was Australia's responsibility to do the pushing. The previous Australian policy of gradually spreading literacy and education was supplemented by a concentrated effort to produce a small, educated elite to take over the reins of government.

Irian Jaya Meanwhile, things were not going nearly so smoothly in the Dutch half of the island. Indonesian resistance to Dutch rule had been simmering, or occasionally flaring up, almost from the moment the Dutch arrived. During WW II the Japanese released the political prisoners held by the Dutch and used them to form the nucleus of a puppet government.

When the war ended, Sukarno, leader of the prewar resistance to Dutch rule, immediately declared Indonesia independent and the British forces who arrived in Indonesia to round up the Japanese troops met with stiff Indonesian resistance. Britain quickly got out of that sticky mess, but the Dutch were not so sensible. For the next few years the Dutch East Indies was racked by everything from minor guerrilla warfare to all out battles. Eventually Dutch military superiority got the upper hand, but politically the Indonesians out-manoeuvred them and in 1949 the Republic of Indonesia came into existence.

Dutch New Guinea was the final stumbling block to a Dutch-Indonesian agreement. The Indonesian argument was that it was part of the Dutch East Indies therefore it should be part of Indonesia. The Dutch were determined to hold on to it as a small face-saving gesture, so right through the '50s it continued as a Dutch colony, while

the Dutch searched desperately for something to do with it.

Obviously a political union with PNG would have been the most sensible thing. At that time, however, the Australians were not considering the prospect of an independent PNG and the problem of confronting Indonesia would have become an Australian problem, not a Dutch one, if the colonies were amalgamated.

The Dutch decided on a quick push to independence; in the late '50s they embarked on a crash programme to develop an educated elite and an economic base – a policy that predated by some years similar moves by Australia. The Dutch started to pour money into their colony, an expensive scheme that soon had to be followed by Australia.

Unfortunately for the Dutch, things were not going too well in Indonesia. The economy there was falling apart, Sukarno's government was proving to be notoriously unstable and his answer to these serious internal problems was simple – look for an outside enemy to distract attention. Holland proved an ideal target and the effort to 'regain' Dutch New Guinea became a national cause.

As Sukarno started to flirt with Russia, the Americans became more and more worried and eventually opted for their long running policy of bolstering up corruption and inefficiency wherever it looks like falling on its face (or into the hands of Communists). The Dutch were politically out-manoeuvred at the UN once again and in 1963 the Indonesians, with support from the USA, took over.

Indonesia's economic collapse was rapidly accelerating by this time and it was in no shape to continue the massive investment projects the Dutch had initiated. By the time Sukarno fell from power in 1965, Irian Barat (west hot land), as it was renamed, had suffered an asset stripping operation with shiploads of Dutch equipment being exported and local businesses and plantations collapsing right and left. Relations with Australia were none too good; perhaps

Sukarno's habit of referring to PNG as Irian Timor (East Irian) and Australia as Irian Selatan (South Irian) didn't help.

After Sukarno's departure, relations rapidly improved; the Indonesian half of the island was renamed Irian Jaya (New Irian) and Australians and Indonesians cooperated on accurately mapping the border between the two halves. Part of the Dutch handover agreement was that the people should, after a time, have the right to vote on staying with Indonesia or opting for independence. In 1969 this 'Act of Free Choice' took place. The 'choice' was somewhat restricted by Indonesia's new President Suharto stating that: 'There will be an act of self-determination, of free choice, in West Irian but if they vote against Indonesia or betray or harm the Indonesian people, this would be treason.' When the 1000 'representative' voters made the act of free choice there was not a treasonable voice to be heard.

Independence

In PNG the progress towards independence was fairly rapid through the '60s. In 1964 a House of Assembly with 64 members was formed; 44 were elected in open competition, 10 were appointed and 10 were elected Australians. Internal self-government came into effect in '73, followed in late '75 by full independence.

At this time, PNG still had a very low rate of literacy and in many parts of the country contact with government officials was still infrequent and bewildering. It is quite probable that the first time many people knew of a central government was when they were told to vote for their parliamentary representative!

A country divided by a huge number of mutually incomprehensible languages, where intertribal antipathy is common and where the educated elite accounts for such a small percentage of the total population would hardly seem to provide a firm base for democracy. Yet somehow everything has held together and PNG works fairly well, especially by new-nation standards. Papua New Guineans have generally dealt with the

problems of nationhood with a great deal of success.

The Free Papua Movement

After independence, PNG's most immediate problem appeared to be relations with its powerful neighbour Indonesia. Following Indonesia's takeover of Irian Jaya, the indigenous Papuans, who had been sold out so badly by the rest of the world, began to organise a guerrilla resistance movement – the Free Papua Movement, which is widely known as the OPM (Organisasi Papua Merdeka). Since its inception, it has fought with varying degrees of success against tremendous odds.

Each time violence has flared, PNG has found itself squeezed between a practical need for good relations with Indonesia and an obvious sympathy for the racially-related Papuan rebels. In balance, practicality has prevailed and PNG has done nothing to assist the rebels – even, on several occasions, handing alleged rebels back to the Indonesian authorities.

Indonesia has maintained tight control over news coming from Irian Jaya and since the late '70s the OPM has been dogged by factionalism, so it is difficult to separate fact from fiction in the fragmented accounts of the struggle that reach the press.

On a number of occasions the OPM has been declared a spent force, only to reappear, seemingly undaunted. The OPM has attracted scant overseas support, but armed with traditional weapons and small numbers of outdated guns and captured rifles the rebels continue to operate.

The border itself is one of those arbitrary straight lines European bureaucrats were so fond of drawing, which have since caused so much misery. Poorly patrolled, until recently badly surveyed, and crossing some of the most isolated and rugged country on the island, it is not likely to hinder the rebels' movements. The Indonesians have claimed they come and go with impunity.

Over the years the OPM has announced it has killed hundreds of Indonesian soldiers and that many thousands of Papuans have been killed in indiscriminant retaliatory attacks. The Indonesian figures are much lower. There were major clashes in 1978, 1981 and 1983 – a number provoked by Indonesia's ambitious transmigration scheme. Irian Jaya has a total population of around 800,000 Papuans and 220,000 Indonesians and the Indonesian government plans to move in still more, although it's very unlikely that the original target of 800,000 will be met.

In 1984 over 100 Melanesian soldiers in the Indonesian Armed Forces deserted to the OPM, sparking a major Indonesian operation which in turn drove over 10,000 Papuans into PNG. Years later these refugees, and those that have come both before and since, remain a political football. Few have shown any interest in returning to Irian Jaya so the PNG government has belatedly decided to resettle them permanently.

Since 1985 the flow of refugees has virtually stopped, indicating a quieter level of activity on the part of both the Indonesians and the OPM, and the relations between Indonesia and PNG have improved. However, it seems unlikely the real grievances of the Papuan people in Irian Jaya have been met, so the problems of the past are likely to recur.

Law & Order

The most publicised problem that faces PNG today is one that can go under the general heading of 'Law & Order'. The worst affected areas are the larger cities (Port Moresby, Lae, Madang and Mt Hagen) and parts of the Highlands. Also, see the Safety section in the Facts for the Visitor chapter.

The problem encompasses everything from traditional tribal wars and modern corruption, to personal violence. When you hear talk of *rascals* and the *rascal problem* this is what is being referred to – not schoolboy pranks.

As you travel around PNG and especially when you speak to white expats you will be hard put to keep this problem in perspective. Extreme paranoia is contagious and crime is a favourite topic of conversation. What you

must continue to ask yourself is: How does it compare with home (think of the Sunday newspapers in your home city) and how does it relate to the friendliness and hospitality I meet everywhere I go?

Although the statistics are unreliable they do not suggest that the law and order situation in PNG is worse than in many other developing or, indeed, some Western countries.

The law and order label has a tendency to obscure a complex question that involves a variety of related issues. The kneejerk response is 'more police and tougher sentencing' but this is unlikely to be a full answer – the problem would not have proved to be so intractable if it was. The real issues that must be looked at are some of the traditional attitudes, the impact of Westernisation, the success or failure of economic development and education, and questions of economic justice, as well as the efficiency and relevance of the political system, police force and judicial system.

It is useful to remember that it is very easy to apply inappropriate Western criteria, and what appears to be uncontrolled anarchy is often nothing of the sort. For instance, tribal war is not necessarily regarded by the Highlanders as a breakdown of law and order but as the process by which law and order is re-established. A case that appears to be straightforward assault may well be a community sanctioned punishment. Looting a store may be in lieu of the traditional division of a big man's estate.

Perhaps the greatest problem is that PNG is not yet a cohesive state, so rules of behaviour that will be strictly upheld within a community will not necessarily be upheld outside it. A man who would never dream of cheating someone in his village might be proud of robbing someone from a rival tribe and feel similarly free from constraints in a strange city.

Clan loyalties also make police work extremely difficult. A village will not necessarily cooperate in the arrest of one of its members – if the rascal's actions have not affected the village negatively, they will often not be seen as wrong. To avoid police becoming involved in their own clan's disputes they are transferred to other areas where they don't know the terrain or the intricacies of local politics. Police and their families are also vulnerable to the threat of payback attacks – which, of course, are *justified* if the policeman has arrested an *innocent* relative.

In the rush for independence, Australia was forced to concentrate on developing an elite who was capable of running the country, and perhaps inappropriately, the model that was used as the basis for development was Australia. Big men were encouraged to develop cash crops, often permanently (mis)appropriating their follower's lands when they did so. The educated few took well-paid positions in a centralised bureaucratic structure that had been transplanted from Canberra.

This had a number of unfortunate side effects. The big men who were encouraged and protected by the Australian administration are now very wealthy and powerful, far outstripping the general populace. Although by Asian standards the problem is not acute, in the Highlands there is a genuine shortage of land, especially of land that is suitable for the development of coffee. The Port Moresby bureaucracy has continued to grow, creating a prosperous middle class and a city that draws the hopeful, the curious and the ambitious – only to surround them with unattainable goodies and dump them in shanty towns without work.

Although people rarely starve in PNG and the village or clan can nearly always meet most simple needs, there is a growing cash economy. People need money to pay tax; to buy second-hand clothes, beer, tobacco, rice and tinned fish; and to send their kids to school. This demand for cash and the limited opportunity most people have to make money obviously creates pressures. There is also a growing number of people who are alienated from their traditional villages (for instance, a family may be driven away because a member has broken a traditional taboo) and these people are completely dependent on the limited opportunities in the cities.

Young men, even those with minimal educational standards, aspire to the status and material wealth that was achieved by the small elite the Australians developed. These ambitious young men, usually unmarried and between about 18 and 30 years old, are drawn to the cities. Once there they take advantage of *wantoks* (relatives) who, under Melanesian tradition, are responsible for feeding and housing them. Unfortunately sufficient jobs just do not exist, so these bored young 'have-nots' wander the town, play cards and pool, drink beer and...

Whatever the reasons, it's hard to pretend you're governing things well if people insist on impaling their neighbours with spears, the well-off middle class (including both local people and expats) are forced to live in razor-wire fortresses, economic development is threatened by corruption and disorder, schools are closed because the safety of teachers cannot be guaranteed, and people (especially women) cannot walk the streets at night.

On several occasions the army has been called in, a state of emergency has been declared and strict controls have been placed on beer sales. The positive effects of these crackdowns have been short term at best. The rascals melt into the bush, or relocate to terrorise some other community, and are back as soon as the heat is off. The longer term solutions are much more difficult, requiring shifts in public attitudes, and long-term restructuring of the economy, the educational and political systems, the police and judiciary.

The changes required present a serious challenge to the country. The government's own INA/IASER 'Report on Law & Order in Papua New Guinea' (the 1984 Clifford Report) observed:

With 62% of the population under the age of 24 (85% in the towns), and with enormous numbers of them being half-educated, unemployed, under-employed, without any social role and very much frustrated, the danger of forceful (maybe violent) political change is near.

Bougainville

There was a real possibility of PNG falling apart when military action by secessionists on Bougainville closed the giant Panguna mine in 1989. The national government withdrew completely from the island, leaving it in the hands of the Bougainville Revolutionary Army (BRA). With such a diverse society, PNG struggles to maintain a sense of nationhood at the best of times, and when the BRA began what amounted to a civil war, there were nervous glances around the rest of the country. That threat seems to have diminished, but the problems on Bougainville remain and the island is off-limits. See the North Solomons Province chapter for more information.

GEOGRAPHY

PNG lies barely south of the equator, to the north of Australia. It is the last of the string of islands spilling down from South-East Asia into the Pacific and really forms a transition zone between the two areas. After PNG you're into the Pacific proper – expanses of ocean dotted by tiny islands. PNG occupies the eastern end of the island of New Guinea.

Additionally, there are a collection of islands, some large, around the main land mass. Manus, New Ireland and New Britain are all provinces of PNG, as are the eastern islands in Milne Bay and the North Solomons group. To the south, the Torres Straits Islands are part of the Australian state of Queensland. Some of these tiny islands are a mere stone's throw from the PNG coast.

PNG's remote and wild character is very closely tied to its dramatic geography. The place is a mass of superlatives – the mountains tower, the rivers rush, the ravines plunge – name a geographical cliche and PNG has it. These spectacular features have much to do with the country's diverse people and its current state of development. When a mighty mountain range or a wide river separates you from your neighbouring tribe you're unlikely to get to know them very well.

The central spine of PNG is a high range of mountains with peaks over 4000 metres high. It's unlikely that a permanent road across this daunting natural barrier will be completed until the end of this century although temporary tracks were attempted during WW II. Meanwhile, travel between the south and north coasts of PNG still means flying – unless you care to walk.

Great rivers flow from the mountains down to the sea. The Fly and the Sepik rivers are the two largest: the Sepik flowing into the sea in the north, the Fly in the south. Both are navigable for long distances and both are among the world's mightiest rivers in terms of annual water flow.

In places the central mountains descend right to the sea in a series of diminishing foothills, while in other regions broad expanses of mangrove swamps fringe the coast – gradually extending as more and more material is carried down to the coast by the muddy rivers. In the western region there is an endless expanse of flat grassland, sparsely populated, annually flooded and teeming with wildlife.

PNG is in the Pacific volcano belt but, apart from a few exceptions along the north coast such as Mt Lamington (Oro Province) which erupted unexpectedly and disastrously in 1951, the live volcanoes are not on the main land mass. There are a number of volcanic islands scattered off the north coast and in Milne Bay plus the active region on the north coast of New Britain. Earthquakes, usually mild, are more widespread.

One of the most interesting features of the geography of PNG is the central Highland valleys. As the early explorers pushed inland the general conclusion was that the central spine of mountains was a tangled, virtually uninhabited wilderness. In the '30s, however, the Highland valleys were accidentally discovered and the wilderness turned out to be the most fertile and heavily populated region of the country. The best known valleys are around Goroka and Mt Hagen, but there are other more remote places right across into Irian Jaya.

PNG is endowed with striking coral reefs making it a paradise for scuba divers. There

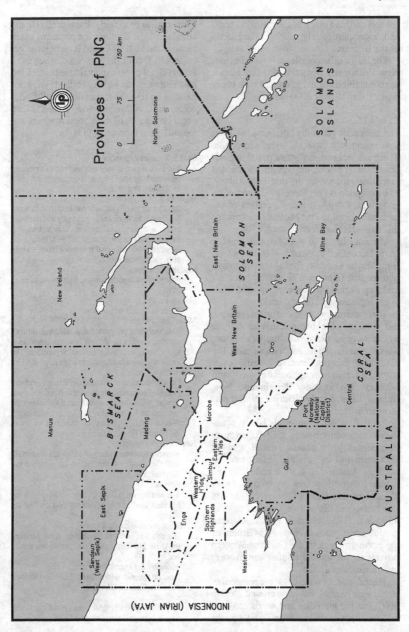

are reefs around much of the mainland coast and, more particularly, amongst the islands of the Bismarck Sea and Milne Bay areas.

The major offshore islands – New Ireland, New Britain and Bougainville – are almost as mountainous as the mainland with many peaks rising to over 2000 metres.

CLIMATE

The climate is generally hot, humid and wet year round, but there are some exceptions. There are wet and dry seasons, but in practice, in most places, the wet just means it is more likely to rain, the dry that it's less likely. The exception is Port Moresby where the dry is definitely dry – the configuration of the mountains around Port Moresby account for this two-season characteristic.

In most places the wet season is roughly from December to March, the dry season from May to October. During the two transition months (April and November), it can't make up its mind which way to go and tends to be unpleasantly still and sticky.

There are many variations on this pattern, the most notable being Lae and Alotau, where May to October is the *wet* season. Some places, such as Wewak and the Trobriand Islands, receive a fairly even spread of rain throughout the year, and others, such as New Britain and New Ireland, have sharply differing rainfall patterns in different areas.

Rainfall, which is generally heavy, nonetheless varies enormously. In dry, often dusty Port Moresby the annual rainfall is about 1000 mm (40 inches) and, like places in northern Australia, it is short and sharp and is then followed by long dry months. Other places can vary from a little over 2000 mm (80 inches) in Rabaul or Goroka, to over 4500 mm (175 inches) in Lae. In extreme rainfall areas, such as West New Britain or the northern areas of the Gulf and Western provinces, the annual rainfall can average over six metres a year.

Temperatures on the coast are reasonably stable year round – hovering around 25°C to 30°C, but the humidity and winds can vary widely. As you move inland and up, the temperatures drop fairly dramatically. In the Highlands, the daytime temperatures often climb to the high 20°Cs but at night it can get quite cold. During the dry season, when there is little cloud cover to contain the heat, Highland mornings can be very chilly. If you keep moving up into the mountains you'll find it colder still. Although snow is rare, it can occur on the tops of the highest summits and ice will often form on cold nights.

Gulf & Western Provinces
> The Gulf region is very wet year round – peaking between May and October. It can also be very wet in Western Province.

Highlands
> In most of the Highlands the rain comes from November to April but is generally not unpleasant. It is cooler and drier from May to October. In the southern Highlands the wet lasts a bit longer at both ends and it is more likely to rain at any time year round.

Madang Province
> Rainy, often thunderstorms, from November to May.

Manus Province
> There is no real wet season.

Milne Bay Province
> This maritime province has a wide variation of weather conditions. Alotau is wetter from April to October, with most rain in September. The Trobriand Islands have fairly even rainfall.

New Britain
> On the north side (including Rabaul and the Gazelle Peninsula), November to April is the wet season, while on the south side of the island the wet season is from May to October with much heavier rainfall. There is no fixed wet season in the Gazelle Peninsula's mountains.

New Ireland Province
> Kavieng receives a fairly even spread of rainfall, and the south of the island is wetter from November to May.

Oro Province
> The wet season is from October to May with the heaviest rain at the beginning and end of the season.

North Solomons Province
> It's the wet and cooler season from January to April; November and December are pretty hot.

Port Moresby & Central Province
> Dry, dusty and windy from May to October; wetter and cooler inland.

Sepik
> July to November is the dry season and the wettest time is between December and April.

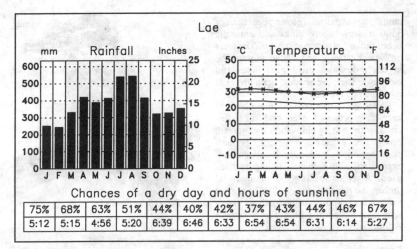

Lae

J	F	M	A	M	J	J	A	S	O	N	D
75%	68%	63%	51%	44%	40%	42%	37%	43%	44%	46%	67%
5:12	5:15	4:56	5:20	6:39	6:46	6:33	6:54	6:54	6:31	6:14	5:27

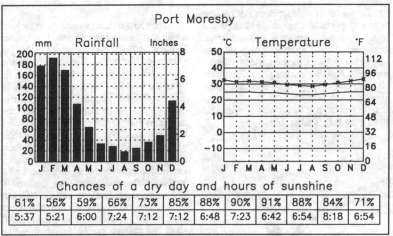

Port Moresby

J	F	M	A	M	J	J	A	S	O	N	D
61%	56%	59%	66%	73%	85%	88%	90%	91%	88%	84%	71%
5:37	5:21	6:00	7:24	7:12	7:12	6:48	7:23	6:42	6:54	8:18	6:54

Morobe Province

In Lae, it's hot and humid from November to February, wetter but cooler from May to October with the heaviest rain in June, July and August. In Wau and Bulolo it is the exact opposite.

FLORA & FAUNA

Flora

The major mountainous region forming part of the backbone of New Guinea and its rugged terrain of high peaks and deep valleys is home to the many and varied highland communities which have come to be the best known attraction for visitors. Here, too, you can find the greatest wealth of PNG's animals and plants.

Of about 9000 species of plants, over 200 are tree-size, mostly found in the lowlands rainforest, but extending to an upper limit of 3500 metres, where pines and antarctic beech thrive (more reminiscent of Tasmania or New Zealand), and above this on the higher mountains are alpine lakes and meadows. There are orchids; again PNG has more than its fair share.

Rainforest enthusiasts will find plenty to keep them occupied. Most of PNG is forested, with shifting cultivation widespread, even in areas where it is very steep. Commercial logging is generally localised, but expanding, often with clear felling methods used. After extracting the commercial timber, the remainder may often be burned for farming purposes. In the south are extensive savannas similar to those of northern Australia.

Fauna

PNG's wealth of wildlife does not contain large and spectacular animals, like elephants or tigers, but is interesting in many ways. There are about 250 species of mammals, mostly bats and rats, including about 60 marsupials and notably tree kangaroos. There are also two kinds of egg-laying echidnas (spiny anteaters).

It is for its 700 or so bird species that PNG's wildlife is most renowned.

Kingfisher

A keen bird-watcher should try to include a visit to a swampy area like the Blackwater Lakes near the Sepik (for water birds) the Highlands (for birds of paradise) and the islands (for sea birds). PNG is the home of 38 of the world's 43 spectacular and gaudy species of bird of paradise, with their bizarre displays and mating rituals. Also numerous in species in PNG, the closely related bower birds may lack incredible feathering in their males, but more than make up for it in their skill in building not only bowers but elaborate maypoles and gardens, complete with a well-kept lawn and flower arrangements.

Among more familiar birds, PNG can boast more parrot, pigeon and kingfisher species than anywhere else in the world. All sizes and colours can be found, from the world's largest, such as the crowned pigeons, to the world's smallest, such as the pygmy parrots, which scurry along small branches and feed on lichens.

Many other groups are represented, with a general similarity to Australian bird life, but often more colourful. Perhaps the most notable of all are the giant cassowaries. Related to the Australian emu, they are stockier birds adapted to forest areas and with a large, horny casque for crashing

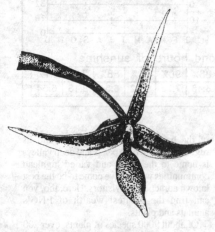
Common Orchid

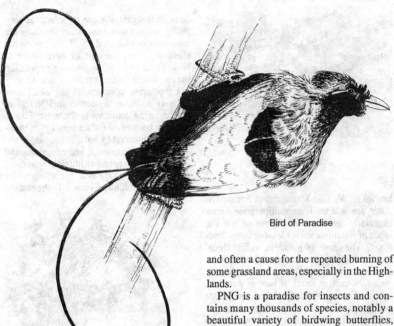

Bird of Paradise

through the undergrowth. Like the bird of paradise, cassowaries are of great ceremonial significance to many of PNG's tribal groups.

My favourite birds are *kokomo* (hornbills). They are of impressive size and seem to be intelligent. Their flight is wonderful. If you're in the jungle and you hear what sounds like a small steam engine approaching, it's a kokomo skimming along like an elegant sculler. The big palm cockatoos are also impressive: with their black feathers, sharply curved beak and spiky crest, they look like they belong in one of the Grimms' nastier fairytales.

Also represented in PNG are about 200 species of reptiles, including two crocodiles and 13 turtles, as well as about 100 snakes, which are much feared by the local people

and often a cause for the repeated burning of some grassland areas, especially in the Highlands.

PNG is a paradise for insects and contains many thousands of species, notably a beautiful variety of birdwing butterflies, including the world's largest butterfly, Queen Alexandra Birdwing. Some insects, such as the brilliant green scarab beetles, are used as body ornaments although the most famous ornaments, of course, are the bird-of-paradise plumes, seen at their best at the Highland shows. They are very valuable not only for sing-sings, but as bride prices, and are carefully stored for use over many years.

National Parks

Conserving the diversity of PNG's natural resources is complicated by the ancient customs of traditional land holdings and the government's reluctance to alienate the people concerned. Totally protected areas are few. Prior to independence only two national parks were established, and only two since, but others have been proposed. A compromise concept is Benchmark Reserves protecting small parts of exploited areas.

The National Parks Board also recognises provincial parks and local parks, better

Stag Beetle

known as Wildlife Management Areas. The latter are intended as multipurpose areas, especially for the management of specific types of wildlife used for food or other functions. They are popular in aiding local communities to prevent over-exploitation, such as of the eggs of scrub turkeys (megapode), or certain kinds of bird of paradise, and are the responsibility of the local groups using the areas. An advantage with this arrangement is that for any commercial exploitation in a particular area, the rights of the people living in the affected area are given priority and the guidelines are clearly established in local Land Use Management Plans.

Also important is the concept of Protected Species, in which all wildlife belongs to the traditional landowners, but the same restrictions apply as in Wildlife Management Areas. The list originally began in the 1920s to protect the bird of paradise and egret from extensive commercial exploitation for their valuable plumes. Added later were most of the birdwing butterflies, the long-nosed echidnas and others. Since independence many more have been added to the list as part of PNG's cooperation with international conservation objectives.

There seems to be a growing awareness of the necessity to conserve forests and wildlife, but traditional landowners are often torn between the rich rewards offered by foreign logging and mining companies and the destruction of their environment. The prob-

lems on Bougainville can be seen as at least partly due to a new generation choosing the environment over cash. Still, the traditional slash-and-burn method of agriculture is widespread and with a growing population the remaining forests are under threat.

Large-scale commercial exploitation is unlikely to be as disastrous in PNG as in neighbouring countries to the west. This is not only because of the recognition of traditional landownership, but also because of the serious social, economic and environmental problems which are resulting right next door. Indonesian Irian Jaya is now coming under serious exploitation pressures. To the east the

Death Adder

same pressures are found in the Solomon Islands. The long-term future in PNG remains uncertain, but the current developments in conservation awareness are very encouraging.

For the latest information on national parks, you can write to the National Parks Service, PO Box 5749, Boroko. For information on Wildlife Management Areas contact the Wildlife Conservation Section, Department of Environment & Conservation, PO Box 6601, Boroko.

No Wildlife Management Areas are listed here, but there are now a fair number scattered through the country and it is best to find out the details for any particular province through the Wildlife Division.

Varirata National Park This 1063-hectare park is 42 km by road from Port Moresby and protects the western escarpment of the Sogeri Plateau, extending to the Astrolabe Mountains. There are upland rainforests and savanna areas here, with several walking trails. There is a good variety of birds and other wildlife here, and it offers an excellent opportunity to see birds of paradise. The reddish plumed raggiana bird of paradise is common here, but the resplendent adult males may be hard to find although its characteristic 'wah-wah' call is a feature of the forests. At over 600 metres elevation, the cooler plateau is a popular escape from Port Moresby. A trip to the park can be combined with other activities, such as visiting the junction of the Kokoda Trail.

McAdam National Park This 2076-hectare park is between Wau and Bulolo with one of its boundaries along the Bulolo River. The stream-dissected areas centred on the Bulolo River Gorge are found here. The park includes lowland rainforest to about 1000 metres, then submontane oak-dominated forests to about 1800 metres and above this are beech-dominated forests with dense bamboo to about 2000 metres. The wildlife includes a large variety of mid-montane species. Echidnas, cuscuses, cassowaries and birds of paradise are some of the highlights.

If you stay at the Wau Ecology Institute, you will hear about other places worth visiting as a result of the extensive surveys they have conducted over many years. The most accessible of these areas is Mt Kaindi (2362 metres). While the lower slopes have been cut over, an exploration from the summit offers the opportunity to explore the forests and see some of the wildlife of the upper vegetation zones. To make it even easier the institute has published a guidebook to the mountain, which is also intended to be an introduction to general New Guinea montane ecology.

Lake Kutubu A national park has been recently declared in the Lake Kutubu area of Southern Highlands Province.

GOVERNMENT

PNG has a three-tiered system of democratic government (national, provincial and local) based on the Australian and Westminster models. There is a ceremonial head of state, the governor general, who is elected by parliament and an independent judiciary and public service.

The most important political forum is the National Parliament and all citizens have voting rights in elections that are held every four years. The parliament elects the prime minister, who in turn appoints ministers from members of his party and/or coalition. The national parliament has ultimate control over the lower levels of government, including the administration of the national budget and the right to veto laws proclaimed by lower levels of government that it feels are not in the national interest.

The decentralised provincial government was introduced in 1976 when nineteen provinces and a separate national capital district were formed, each with an elected provincial assembly, an executive council and premier. The national parliament retains ultimate control and a number of provincial governments have been suspended for mismanagement. Each of these governments has wide powers over education, health and the economy, and the right to levy certain taxes and fees. Finally, there are over 150 local councils.

The provincial government system has been attacked as wasteful, and the national government elected in 1992 has been making noises about abandoning it. This will meet opposition from vested interests and perhaps cause more serious problems. Provincial governments were originally introduced to quell secessionist murmerings from some of the islands and these might again flare up if provincial government is abolished.

National Politics

National politics is a world of shifting alliances. No single party has ever governed in its own right – each successive government has been dependent on shaky, unreliable coalitions. Party discipline is also loose and party members are prone to act independently, changing allegiances overnight and voting as it suits them and, sometimes, their bank balances.

The national parliament is elected on a first-past-the-post system, where the candidate with the highest number of votes is successful and there is no limit to the possible number of candidates. In practice this means that MPs are frequently elected with less than 10% of the total vote. This not only leads to considerable disenchantment on the part of the majority but also, it is sometimes argued, corruption and tribalism. For instance, it is possible for a candidate to split the electorate's vote along tribal lines by encouraging representatives of each tribe in a constituency to stand. Our theoretical candidate would then concentrate on ensuring the loyalty of his own tribe, and perhaps picking up a few votes here and there by spreading a little bit of financial goodwill. The total number of votes that it is necessary to attract can then be very small.

Such unstable arrangements also mean that very few MPs survive more than one electoral term, leaving the parliament short of experience and continuity. There has been considerable criticism of this situation, but as yet no sitting parliament has had the political courage to challenge the status quo.

The political parties themselves are not distinguished so much by ideology as by the personality of their leaders and their regional bases. Generally, there appears to be a remarkable degree of consensus about the kind of society that should be created. All parties basically favour a mixed economy, with governments overseeing and, sometimes, operating alongside private enterprise. Only the details and emphases differ: To what extent should government be decentralised? What controls should be placed on multinationals and expatriates? What emphasis should be placed on rural development?

The country's first prime minister, Michael Somare (The Chief), proved to be a remarkably astute politician with the ability to forge working compromises between diverse groups of people. In 1980, however, Somare's government finally fell to a no-confidence vote and Sir Julius Chan, an equally astute politician from New Ireland, became prime minister. Earlier, when Chan's People's Progress Party (PPP) was in coalition with Somare's Pangu Party, Chan had been deputy prime minister to Somare.

After his fall from power, Somare proved to be just as adept in his role as leader of the opposition and when elections were held in 1982 he and the Pangu Party were returned to power, ahead of an opposition led by Sir Iambakey Okuk's National Party. This government shattered in 1984 when Paius Wingti, Somare's deputy, defected to the opposition and, in 1985, won a no-confdence motion and became the new prime minister.

Wingti formed a coalition which was led by his new People's Democratic Movement (PDM), made up largely of Pangu defectors, and his deputy was Sir Julius Chan. Wingti won the 1987 elections but in 1988 was toppled in a no-confidence motion led by Rabbie Namaliu, the new leader of the Pangu Party. Namaliu survived until the 1992 elections, when Wingti regained power, with Sir Julius Chan once again deputy prime minister.

The instability in government created by the shifting alliances of small parties and opportunistic MPs has been partly curbed, as motions of no confidence are now banned for 18 months after a government is formed.

Wingti's new government is the first to have this breathing space, and it will be interesting to see how it is used. An emphasis on rural development and a tougher line with foreign investors seem to be the main plans, and several foreign mining companies have already had their feathers ruffled. For visitors this is a little double-edged: local-level tourism projects should be boosted, hopefully leading to more and better village accommodation, but immigration procedures have been toughened, making visas more difficult to obtain.

Because there are so many small parties and independents whose support is vital to a party wanting to form a government, the post-election 'lock up' has become a feature of PNG politics. The leaders of the two main groups lure newly elected MPs to a secure place and try to keep them there until their support is promised. Ministries and perks are the bait. Whichever leader hooks a majority of MPs forms a government, becoming prime minister. In 1992 Wingti's lock up was on Doini Island in Milne Bay and Namaliu's was at Loloata Island Resort near Port Moresby. Perhaps it's coincidental, but the less easily 'defended' Loloata failed to produce a government, whereas the remote and inaccessible Doini did.

ECONOMY

Until recently the economy was said to rest on copper, coffee, cocoa and copra. This ignored the fact that most people lived within a successful subsistence economy (growing a small part of the total coffee, cocoa and copra crops) and the contribution made by Australian grants. Since the mid-1980s copper has been overtaken by gold as the single largest item on the export account, the value of copra exports and the Australian grant have declined markedly, but at least 85% of the population are basically still subsistence farmers.

PNG is in the enviable position of having a booming and increasingly diversified mineral sector and largely untapped forestry and fishing resources. Further reserves of gold, copper, silver, nickel, oil and gas are being discovered, virtually daily. In most regions there is sufficient arable land to both produce agricultural surpluses and ensure that people do not starve. The relatively

small population and this natural wealth means that PNG has tremendous economic potential and in terms of the Pacific's island states it is a giant.

There is very little squalor in PNG, and beggars are effectively nonexistent. There are nutritional problems in some parts of the country (a shortage of protein is an age-old difficulty) but virtually everybody is fed and clothed, even if they are unemployed in the cities. This is due in large part to the wantok system, a unique Melanesian system of clan responsibility. Wantok, literally means 'one talk', or common language, signifying a shared origin. Under the system, members of a clan look after one another and share the clan's wealth. This system continues to be tremendously influential and has worked well in situations where only one family member earns a wage – a single wage will often be distributed among dozens of people.

All is not perfect however, and these very advantages can be seen as a two-edged sword. As many other countries have discovered, overseas controlled capital-intensive primary industries, can seriously distort development, aside from the risks of depending on unstable commodity prices. Also, the geographical features which are in some ways so bountiful also mean that there are tremendous transport and communication difficulties.

Even the wantok system has its negative side. It encourages unemployed youths to venture to cities, and some argue that it can sap individual initiative and put a considerable strain on individuals who have to reconcile traditional responsibilities with the demands of a modern economy.

There is also an increasing gap between the expectations of those with an education and available jobs, and between the growing need for cash and the opportunity to make it. As yet, discontent has not manifested itself as a significant political force but it does show itself in the urban shanty towns with their associated crime problems, and disputes over land ownership, especially in the Highlands.

The most significant characteristic of the

economy, however, is that the vast majority of the population is still entirely dependent on semi-traditional agriculture. The remaining minority are almost all involved in either government services (on the Australian model), mining (basically controlled by multinational companies), large-scale plantations (often owned by local capitalists), or the service industries. The clichéd juxtaposition of a traditionally-dressed tribesman standing beside a jet aircraft accurately reflects the startling schism between the two groups.

There is virtually no manufacturing industry, because of a shortage of skilled labour, high wages and the small size of the market. PNG imports include almost all manufactured goods and many basic foodstuffs, not a few of which could be produced locally (fish and rice in particular).

Perhaps the most critical problem is that there is insufficient local capital to establish import replacement industries.

Australian Grant

In the first year after WW II the annual Australian grant was only about half a million kina, but it grew steadily and rapidly through the '50s and '60s and reached around A$200 million a year in the late '70s, representing about 50% of the PNG budget. The Australian government is gradually cutting the annual grant back and it will fall to less than 5% by the mid-1990s. Australia has a huge trade imbalance with PNG, so even in its heyday the level of the grant was less generous than it looked. Also, much of the grant went into funding the cumbersome administrative system, itself a legacy of Australian rule.

Mining

The drop in Australian aid has in large part been offset by the income derived from mining. In the early 1970s the giant Panguna copper mine on Bougainville generated nearly a third of the national income. Panguna was closed by the Bougainville secessionists in 1989, but while this has been a major blow to the economy, new mines

have prevented disaster. Mining now contributes close to 60% of PNG's export income, and, through taxes and government-owned shares, around 40% of internal revenue.

Ok-Tedi, in the remote Star Mountains of Western Province, was the largest gold mine outside South Africa until the Mt Kare mine near Porgera in Enga Province came on stream. At current prices Mt Kare alone earns well over US$300 million worth of gold a year. Mines on Misima Island in Milne Bay Province and the Lihir Group in New Ireland Province will be on a similar scale. To complete the picture, add oil in the Gulf of Papua and the Highlands, more gold mines, particularly on the islands, and the fact that exploration is far from complete.

The cost of developing mines in the difficult climate and geography of the country is enormously high and remains the province of multinational companies. The PNG government has bargained shrewdly with these companies, however, to ensure both government and local shareholdings, and significant compensation for displaced traditional landowners. The Wingti government plans to invest the profits from this mineral bonanza in rural development.

Agriculture

Agricultural exports are dominated by coffee which accounts for around 20% of total exports. Its importance is greater than this because it is one of the most important sources of cash income for the most populous area of the country – the Highlands. It is largely controlled by local capitalists who own the large plantations, but a significant proportion of the total crop comes from small clan holdings. The population density of the Highlands and the unequal distribution of suitable coffee-producing land is arguably the source of considerable friction.

Unfortunately, like most other crops, coffee is subject to major fluctuations in price and to disease. Coffee rust, a largely preventable disease, is currently threatening the industry, particularly the small growers who are not aware of the techniques that limit its damage.

After coffee, cocoa is the most important export crop. Tea has not been the great success once expected although Highland tea is quite pleasant. Rubber production has grown slowly but steadily.

Copra (dried coconut kernels which are processed into vegetable oils and other coconut products) was the backbone of the economy for many years but has now slipped far behind coffee and cocoa. Production is something of a political football as the copra plantations were looked upon as a colonial relic that did not fit with PNG's independent status, but the main problem was, and is, very low prices on the world commodity markets. Since independence there has been a dramatic drop in output and a major fall in plantation employment – the work is simply too unrewarding.

Oil palms are partly responsible for the decline in the copra price as they are a considerably more efficient source of vegetable oils. There are now huge oil palm plantations in Oro, Milne Bay and West New Britain provinces.

The huge, inaccessible timber resources have begun to be exploited, but the industry has already suffered from corruption and environmental abuse.

The enormous potential of fishing around the coast is also beginning to be appreciated – the implementation of the 322-km fishing zone has prompted Asian countries to involve themselves in fishing projects with PNG. Unfortunately, tinned fish remains a major import – even on islands surrounded by fish. There have been attempts at setting up canning plants in PNG, but the financial necessity for them to be at least partly foreign owned has caused problems. At least one foreign company has taken advantage of the tax breaks offered, set up a trial plant, fished out the nearby sea, declared the trial a failure and gone home.

Tourism

PNG would be one of the most popular tourist destinations in the world, were it not for its isolation, high costs and the bad press it receives. Although the number of visitors dropped disastrously in the early '90s, a new international airport in an attractive area (Madang, Rabaul, Milne Bay...almost anywhere but Port Moresby) might put PNG on the big-time resort trail. However, the government's vacillating attitude to foreign investment (which would be required to build Club Med-style facilities) is a disincentive to this.

Many people, both nationals and expats, are ambivalent about mass tourism. Some hotel managers say that a few more visitors would be welcome, but not too many. This cautious attitude might mean that PNG survives the perhaps inevitable flood of tourists with its dignity and charm intact. Meanwhile, visitors are made welcome and treated as individuals rather than just another unit.

POPULATION & PEOPLE

The population is approaching four million, with more than one in three people living in the Highland provinces. Some authorities divide the people into Papuans, predominantly descended from the original arrivals, and Melanesians, who are more closely related to the peoples of the Pacific. Additionally, some people, particularly in outlying islands, are closer to being pure Polynesian or Micronesian. The dividing line between these definitions is a very hazy one.

Politically, four regional groupings, reflecting cultural and historical links, have developed: Papuans (from the south), Highlanders, New Guineans (from the north) and Islanders.

There is a wide range of physical types, from the dark Buka people of the North Solomons, who are said to have the blackest skins in the world, to the lighter, more Polynesian people of the south Papuan coast.

After a spell in PNG you'll soon learn to recognise the shorter, often bearded, Highland men and many other distinct groups of people. Diversity of languages goes along with this diversity of racial characteristics. The same rugged terrain that kept physical features from mixing also kept their languages and cultures separate. It has been estimated that there are over 700 languages spoken in New Guinea.

Who's Who

Western residents are almost always known as expats and the indigenous people are frequently referred to as nationals – never ever natives. The term 'national' is increasingly out of favour; many Papua New Guineans prefer, where a label is necessary at all, to be described by their tribal or regional name or as Papua New Guineans. In more remote areas Westerners will still occasionally find themselves referred to as *masta* or *missus*, but most people, especially in the cities, now find this offensively colonial. The colonial era is still sometimes referred to as the *taim bilong masta*.

A Highlander

Grassroots

Grassroots is a slang term which has entered the language, and refers to, roughly, 'the people'; a grassroot lives in a village or in town on a low income. Given the enormous diversity of cultures and their mutual suspicion ('there are too many different people here' is how Port Moresby's problems are summed up) the development of this unifying concept is a healthy sign for PNG.

Grassroots was also a successful comic strip, now sadly defunct. You can see many examples of *Grassroots* cartoons on the walls of Agnes's Cooking Pot restaurant in Port Moresby.

Expatriates

There is still a considerable expatriate population, although it has fallen considerably from its 1971 peak of around 50,000 to a current figure closer to 20,000. The expatriate population today is made up of a wide variety of nationalities. Although Australians are still in the majority, there are Germans, English, Chinese and Filipinos, amongst many others.

More than half the expatriates live in Port Moresby and many of them are in the country on short-term, lucrative contracts with international companies. Often they lead lives that are totally divorced from reality, commuting between air-conditioned offices, their company-provided houses (invariably surrounded by razor wire) and some sort of club. Partly as a consequence of this isolation their attitudes to, and perceptions of, the country are sometimes quite inaccurate.

You'll also meet expats who have been in PNG since before independence, including ex-*kiaps* (patrol officers), and their attitudes are more realistic. The network of long-term expats can be a handy one to lock into.

The expats who have been in the country for years are a diverse group with an amazingly varied outlook on life in general, and their position in PNG in particular. Someone once said if you come to PNG you've got to be a missionary, a mercenary (one after money, not a shoot-and-kill type) or a misfit.

Sometimes you seem to be talking to all three types at once. The Bible thumpers seem to thump Bibles harder than anywhere else, the 'in it for what it's worth' brigade seem to be in it deeper than anywhere else, and the 'my world is falling apart' gang can be seen propping up the bar and taking solace in the bottle.

Although some mission workers have been criticised for their blinkered attitudes and destructive impact on traditional culture others have done extremely valuable work setting up schools, farms, airports, hospitals, shipping companies, and working among the hapless people lured by the 'big city' aura of towns like Port Moresby. They continue to have a very strong influence on the country. There's also a large and diverse volunteer contingent including Peace Corps, Cuso and VSO workers among others. Most work for low wages and have jobs teaching, nursing, researching or helping with development projects.

At independence many Australian and Chinese residents were eligible for PNG citizenship, but only on the condition that they renounced their original citizenship. Many did so and some now hold positions of considerable political and economic importance. Ex-Australians regularly win seats in parliament.

EDUCATION

About 70% of children at least begin school, although the figure varies widely between provinces, and about 30% of those who make it through to sixth grade go on to high school.

Government community (primary) schools provide basic education and there are some government high schools – so few that most pupils come from far away and have to board at the school. The government system comes under a lot of criticism for raising expectations which the economy can't meet. It's hard to go back to a village and grow yams for the rest of your life after you've been taught about the world and have been exposed to materialism. On the other hand, many people criticise government schools because their standards are too low.

Government schools charge fees, although one of Paius Wingti's 1992 election promises was to provide free education.

The churches run many primary and some secondary schools.

The system of 'international schools' was set up for the children of expats, but now anyone with enough money can attend – they ain't cheap! These schools often have foreign teachers and follow Australian syllabuses. Wealthy nationals and expats send their children to boarding schools in Australia; short-term expats often have this paid for by their employer.

Most provinces have at least one tertiary college and there are two universities, the University of Technology in Lae and the University of PNG in Port Moresby.

ARTS

Papua New Guinea's arts & crafts have been recognised as the most vital in the Pacific. The art is amazingly varied for the same reason as there are so many languages – lack of contact between different villages and groups of people. Particularly on the Sepik, where art is so important and so energetic, you'll find villages only a few km apart with styles that are totally distinct. At the Chambri Lakes, for example, the people in Aibom express themselves purely through clay pots – which no other Sepik village makes. Only minutes away at Chambri, the people specialise in masks and spears of a very distinctive and easily recognised style.

The Sepik is easily the best known area for artefacts; in fact, there's a temptation to think of all PNG art in terms of the Sepik when actually there is far more to be found.

The strength of Sepik art is largely due to its spiritual significance. Every Sepik village has to have its haus tambaran, the men's spirit house. In this men-only club are stored the carvings that represent the various spirits. Since carvings have to be replaced fairly frequently or produced for special ceremonies, it is a living and continuous craft. Today much of the spiritual significance may be lost, although certain ancient pieces are still zealously protected, but the craft continues – for the benefit of collectors and tourists.

Elsewhere the pattern may not be so instantly recognisable as in the Sepik, but the crafts are there. You'll find pottery in many areas, ritual Hohoa boards in the Gulf region, island carvings and shell money, or more recently introduced crafts like the attractive, coarse weavings of the Highlands.

See also the Things to Buy section in the Facts for the Visitor chapter for details of some widely available arts & crafts.

CULTURE

The people of PNG belong to many different cultures and it's difficult to make generalisations. You'll find more information about arts and cultures in the various parts of this book, but understanding even one of the cultures is a lifetime's work – hence the number of anthropologists in the country. However, nearly all Papua New Guineans are Melanesian and have some things in common.

Melanesian Society

PNG is changing fast, but the vast majority of people remain dependent on subsistence agriculture and live in small villages. Many aspects of life are still carried out traditionally, and the social structure and an individual's responsibilities and privileges remain significantly unchanged.

In traditional PNG societies, despite sophisticated agriculture and, in some areas, extraordinary maritime skills, the main tools and artefacts were made of wood, bone, pottery or stone. There was no metal working, no domestic animal power and the wheel was unknown. Extensive trading networks existed, especially along the southern coast and among the eastern islands, but also along the navigable rivers and between the coast and the Highlands. Shells were highly valued and in some places were used as a kind of currency, but other trade items included pottery, stone tools, obsidian, dyes, salt and sago.

The responsibility for the day-to-day work of gardening and caring for animals lay, most usually, with women, who were also responsible for the household. Men were concerned with the initial clearing of the bush, hunting,

trade and warfare. Young men also worked for older men.

The social units were generally small, based on family, clan and tribe, the most important being the extended family. Some observers have described these communities as democratic Edens, where ownership was communal and everyone's basic needs were met. In reality, there was no universal franchise for voters, and village elders, or a 'big man' could hold virtually dictatorial powers. In some places, for instance Bougainville and the Trobriand Islands, hereditary chiefs and clear-cut classes developed.

Individual ownership did not exist in the same way as it does in Western societies, but the accumulation of wealth and its display was often a vital prerequisite for prestige and power. Ownership was vested in the household, which was controlled by a male elder. Within and between the households of the village there were complicated networks of responsibility, which did provide a kind of social security.

Fundamental to the society were notions of reciprocity and family obligations: help, whether it be labour, land, food or pigs, was often given out of duty, or in the expectation of some kind of return (perhaps loyalty in time of war, assistance in organising some future feast). Surplus wealth was not traditionally accumulated for its own sake, but so it could be given away, creating prestige for the giver and placing obligations on the receiver.

In most cases a big man did not create a dynasty. Although a big man's son had a head start in life he still had to demonstrate qualities of his own: hard work, bravery, leadership, trading skill, magical knowledge. Different societies sought different characteristics in their leaders but economic ability was common to all. Wealth was necessary in order for a man to develop dependents and supporters.

The creation of wealth required hard work, and since women were largely responsible for agricultural production it was essential for a man with any ambition to get married. And it was the big men who monopolised the supply of female labour. Big men would sometimes 'give' assistance to young men to help them meet the bride price. Polygamy was often a feature of leadership.

In many areas warfare and ritual cannibalism were commonplace and 'payback' killings perpetuated an endless cycle of feuding. Each small group was virtually an independent nation – so any dealings with the next door tribe were international relations. Although alliances were common, they tended to be shifting and expedient, rarely developing into large, long-term federations.

The world for most Papua New Guineans was closely proscribed: beyond their own clan they were surrounded by hostile or suspicious neighbours who often spoke a completely different language. Although no quarter was ever given in war, and women and children were not in any way exempt from attack, fighting usually occurred in highly ritualised battles – and only after negotiations had failed. Bows and arrows and spears were the weaponry, and there were generally few casualties.

Traditional Wealth

Although the country has shifted to a cash economy to a great extent, traditional forms of wealth are still very important, particularly in the Highlands and on the Milne Bay islands. A wad of banknotes can never have the same impact as kina shells, cassowaries or pigs. A large sow might be worth around K600, but many Papua New Guineans would rather have the pig. Another sign of wealth that is now displayed at paybacks and at ceremonial exchanges in the Highlands is a good stack of beer.

Kina shells are large half-moons cut from the gold lip pearl shell – they are worn as personal embellishment, particularly for ceremonial occasions in the Highlands. The kina coin (there is no one kina note) has a large hole in the centre, probably with the idea that it too could be worn round the neck. They are the most tangible reminder of the centuries-old trade links across the country.

In the Highlands, another traditional display of wealth is the *aumak*, a chain of tiny bamboo rods worn around the neck. Each rod indicates that the wearer has lent out 10 or so kina shells. A long row of these little lengths of bamboo is an indication of great wealth.

In New Britain, shell money is still commonly used alongside the modern paper version, but only for small purchases: tiny shells strung along a piece of bamboo are worth about K0.10 a dozen. In Milne Bay *doba* or leaf money is made out of a bundle of etched and dried banana leaves and grass skirts are also negotiable currency (K5 to K10). *Bagi*, the elaborate shell jewellery that is ritually traded around the islands, is the most important mark of prestige and wealth.

Avoiding Offence

Melanesian society has some pitfalls for outsiders. You'll find tips on polite behaviour throughout this book. See especially the Film & Photography and Safety sections in the Facts for the Visitor chapter.

Sport

Rugby is the most popular game, although physical contact sports are potentially dangerous for people who suffered from chronic malaria in childhood. Soccer is also played and, to a lesser extent, cricket. Rugby matches sometimes end in tear gas, so while it's worth seeing one (the season is the same as Australia's winter sport season, roughly May to August), you should find out the likelihood of trouble before you go.

RELIGION

Traditional religions certainly exist in PNG but drawing a dividing line between traditional beliefs ('superstition') and religion is all but impossible. As with all religions, the myriad beliefs in PNG have developed over tens of thousands of years, and are primarily concerned with making sense of the world. For example, people who live in danger of crocodile attacks are likely to give crocodiles an important place in their culture; the weather is important to farming communities (and the people of PNG were perhaps the world's first farmers), which often celebrate fertility and harvest.

Most people, especially in the Highlands, traditionally lived in very small, independent communities, surrounded by communities which spoke different languages and could attack at any time. It isn't surprising that many traditional beliefs revolve around fear of the unknown and suspicion of difference. Placating the spirits of ancestors is a common theme in traditional beliefs, as is a fear of evil influences and of sorcery/witchcraft.

Does a collection of interests, beliefs and rules of conduct (such as the payback requirement of an eye for an eye) constitute a religion? The Christian missionaries certainly didn't think so, and have been responsible for the destruction of much traditional culture. Whether you see this as beneficial (stopping tribal wars and getting a better deal for women) or vandalism (the burning of carvings and spirit houses on the Sepik and elsewhere) depends on your own, foreign, value system.

In most areas of PNG traditional life continues, but all over the country the various arms of the Christian church are extremely influential. Most people in PNG regard themselves as Christian (the country's constitution states its belief in Christian principles), but most are also very proud of their cultural heritage. The older churches seem to be able to cope with this dichotomy, concerning themselves with education, health and development issues, but there are plenty of hell-fire fundamentalists, mainly American, up to who knows what in remote areas.

The largest churches are the Catholic, Evangelical Lutheran and United churches.

The Catholic church I visited was holding a first communion, but the participants were wearing the same traditional costumes I'd seen the day before at a very 'pagan' sing-sing.

Emma Lucas

LANGUAGE

It is calculated that there are 740 languages in PNG, a third of all the languages in the world. With this amazing basis for mutual incomprehension it's not surprising that there has long been a search for a common linking language.

During the early days of British New Guinea and then Australian Papua, the local language of the Port Moresby coastal area, Motu, was slightly modified to become 'Police Motu', and spread through Papua by the native constabulary. It is still quite widely spoken in the southern Papuan part of PNG, and you can easily pick up a Motu phrasebook in Port Moresby.

In the northern German half of the country the German planters were faced with exactly the same communication difficulties as the British. Their solution was *Pisin* (corrupted to Pidgin) – a term used today to define any trade language, a sort of mid-way meeting point between two languages. The PNG version of Pidgin is now sometimes known as Neo-Melanesian, but more frequently just as Papua New Guinean Pidgin. It is very close to the Pidgin spoken in Vanuatu and the Solomons.

PNG Pidgin has taken words from many languages, including German, but it is primarily derived from English. Since it first came into use around Rabaul during the German days the Melanesian words used in Pidgin are mainly from the languages of East New Britain. There are, however, a number of words indicating other foreign influences. Milk, for example, is *susu* as in Indonesia, although in Pidgin *susu* can also mean breasts.

Many educated people would prefer that you spoke to them in English, as crude Pidgin is the hallmark of the bullying expat. Uneducated people are often shy about talking to an English-speaker (especially on the telephone) but even if you don't speak Pidgin they often unfreeze if you throw a few Pidgin words into an otherwise English sentence.

Pidgin has at times been damned and condemned by everybody from the UN down. It's been called 'baby talk', 'broken

English', 'demeaning' and much worse. There were a number of attempts to discourage its use, but the language has proven to be vigorous and effective, supplanting Motu even in Port Moresby.

In some ways, particularly because of its limited vocabulary, Pidgin is not an ideal language. There are only about 1300 words in Pidgin and they have to cover the same territory covered by 6000 English words. This frequently results in very roundabout and wordy descriptions.

An absurd example of this is the word for cow. There is no separate word for bull or cow; they're described collectively as a *bulmakau* (bull-and-a-cow). *Meri* is the word for woman or female so a cow is described as a female-bull-and-a-cow or a *bulmakau meri*. Despite this disadvantage the language is easily learnt and is often very evocative.

Learning Pidgin can be a hell of a lot of fun. Many words or phrases make perfect sense if you just read them out slowly and thoughtfully, although spoken rapidly they're not easy to follow. I saw a sign outside a cinema in Madang announcing that the film showing was a *piksa bilong bigpela man/meri tasol*. That is, it was a 'picture for big-fellow men and women only', in other words it was for adults only. Who was that uniformed Englishman at the independence day celebrations? None other than the *nambawan pikinini bilong misis kwin*, that is to say the 'eldest child of the Queen' – er Prince Charles! A public library? That's a *haus buk bilong ol man/meri*.

There are quite a few Pidgin words and phrases that have crept into everyday English in PNG. You can always recognise somebody who has spent some time in PNG by the way they say *tru* instead of 'really', 'that's right' or 'you don't say'.

No expat leaves PNG when their work is completed, they *go pinis*. It's never dinner time, always *kai* (food) time, which is followed not by dessert but by *sweet kai*. You'll also be told *maski* which means 'don't bother'. If something is totally unimportant or doesn't matter at all, then it's *samting*

nating (something-nothing). And a private problem, your own affair, is *samting bilong yu*. Nobody gets fired in PNG, they're *raused* from *rausim* or 'thrown out' – that one dates right back to German days.

Conversely, modern English expressions, especially of Australian origin, are keeping Pidgin lively, such as *naiswan*, an expression of approval or congratulations – 'nice one'!

If your Pidgin is less than perfect, it is wise to append *yu save?* or *nogat?* (you understand or not?) to just about any sentence. *Save* is pronounced 'savvy'.

Note that *p* and *f* are pronounced (and often spelled) virtually interchangeably, as are *d* and *t*, and *j* and *z*; *qu* is spelled *kw*; *u* is pronounced like a short *oo*.

Greetings & Civilities

Good morning.	*Moning.*
Good afternoon.	*Apinun.*
See you later.	*Lukim yu bihain.*
How are you?	*Yu stap gut?*
I'm fine.	*Mi stap gut.*

Questions & Phrases

May I take a photo?
  Inap my kisim poto?
Show me.
  Soim me.
Stop here!
  Stap! [1]
Is it far?
  Em i longwe?
near, close by
  klostu
a very long way
  longwe tumas
I would like to buy...
  Mi laik baim...
Where is the...?
  We stap wanpela...?
How much does that cost?
  Em i hamas? [2]
I want something to eat.
  Mi laikim sampela kaikai.
That is mine.
  Em bilong mi.

Be careful!
Lukautim gut!
Go away!
Yu go! [3]
Don't touch! (or) Put it down!
Lusim!

1 The word *stap* has many functions including to stay or to be present or to indicate the progressive form – *em i kaikai i stap* (he is eating).
2 Many townspeople add *kostim* (*Em i kostim hamas?*) but it is better Pidgin not to.
3 It is very impolite to say *raus*, it means 'leave (the house)' more than simply 'go away'.

Small Talk

What is your name?
Wanem nem bilong yu [1]
Where are you from?
Ples bilong yu we?
I don't understand.
Mi no klia gut.
I don't know.
Mi no save.
Speak slowly.
Tok isi.

1 Although this is correct Pidgin it would be very much against the custom to ask somebody their name, although things are changing in the big towns. Even people who know each other's names will not use them and at meetings they will go on for hours without the chairperson calling one person's name. They might call somebody *kona* – the one in the corner, or *hagen* – somebody from around Hagen, or *mausgras* – the one with the beard, or even *grinpela kolsiot* – the one with the green sweater. Anything to avoid using their real name.

Some Useful Words

yes	*yes*
no	*nogat*
please	*plis*
thank you	*tenkyu*
a little	*liklik*
plenty	*planti*
big	*bikpela*
aircraft	*balus*
airport	*ples balus*
bathroom	*rum waswas*
bedroom	*rum slip*
toilet	*liklik haus*
child	*pikinini*
decorations, uniform	*bilas*

forbidden	*tambu*
man/woman	*man/meri*
hospital	*haus sick*
police station	*haus polis*
letter, book, ticket	*pas* [1]
luggage	*kago*
newspaper	*niuspepa*
photo	*poto*
towel	*taul* [2]
relative	*wantok* [3]

1 Anything with writing on it.
2 A towel used to be a *laplap bilong waswas* but that is now rather old-fashioned.
3 Literally means 'one-talk', somebody who speaks the same language – the *ples tok*, language of the place.

Pronouns

I	*mi*
you	*yu*
he/she/it	*em* [1]
they	*ol*
we (including the person spoken to)	*yumi*
we (excluding the person spoken to)	*mipela*
you (plural)	*yupela*
everybody	*olgeta* [2]

1 Note that *em* is followed by *i* to introduce the verb as in *em i kaikai i stap* or *em i no sing-sing*. Similarly after they *ol i wokabout i go*.
2 Note that *ol* indicates the plural as *ol haus* (houses) while *olgeta haus* means 'all the houses' – each of them.

Verbs & Tenses

Tenses are all the same except you append *pinis* (finish) to make it past tense: *mi kaikai pinis* means 'I have eaten'. Two common verbs:

bring, give or take	*kisim*
fasten, shut or lock	*fasim* or *pasim*

Finally, some Pidgin confusion. My brother is my *brata* and my sister is my *susa* but Maureen's brother is her *susa* and her sister is her *brata*. In other words your *brata* is always the same sex, your *susa* always the opposite. Today *sista* is also in common use, however, and that has the same meaning as in English. Note that *kilim* just means to hit (but hard), to kill somebody (or something) you have to *kilim i dai*.

Careful of the sexual phrases – *pusim* means to copulate with, not to push! And while you can *ple tenis* (play tennis), *ple* is also a euphemism for intercourse. A man's trunk or suitcase may be a *bokis*, but a women's *bokis* is her vagina. And a *blak bokis* is not a black suitcase but a flying fox or bat! You'll love the standard reply to 'how far is it?' – *longwe liklik*. It doesn't actually mean a long way and not a long way, it translates more like 'not too near, not too far'.

Food

food	*kaikai* [1]
restaurant	*haus kaikai*
menu	*pas bilong kaikai*
tea	*ti*
coffee	*kopi*
eggs	*kiau*
sugar	*suga*
meat	*abus*
unripe coconut	*kulau*
water	*wara*
drink	*dring*
breakfast	*kaikai bilong moning*
lunch	*kaikai bilong belo*
dinner	*kaikai bilong apinun*

1 Shortening it to simply *kai* is really Australian Pidgin.

Books

Like any language it takes a lot of study to understand Pidgin fully, but you can be communicating on at least a basic level with remarkable speed. Lonely Planet publishes the pocket-sized *Papua New Guinea Phrasebook* that includes grammatical notes, many useful phrases and a vocabulary.

There are a number of alternative phrasebooks and dictionaries that are easily available. The best places to look are the Christian Bookshops in PNG; there is usually one in every town and they have all sorts of literature in Pidgin, including, needless to say, a Pidgin Bible.

It's well worth while buying the *Wantok* weekly newspaper, written entirely in Pidgin. As well as being a decent newspaper, reading it is a good way to learn the language. There are also comic strips, which are easy to follow even for beginners.

There is no substitute for actually hearing the language and if you want to get a head start there is an excellent language course that includes two tapes and an exercise book. It is only available in PNG.

For more information contact the Summer Institute of Linguistics (☎ 77 3544, PO Box 413, Ukarumpa via Lae), PNG.

Facts for the Visitor

VISAS & EMBASSIES

The story on visas has made a number of abrupt about faces over the years, so it is wise to check the regulations with a PNG consular office before you depart. In countries where there is no PNG consular office apply to the nearest Australian office.

The latest change to the visa system has been the re-instatement of the one-month 'easy visa', granted to tourists on entry. You pay K10 and you must have onward tickets.

However, don't rely on this, it's better to get a visa before you leave home. Your passport must have at least six months validity, even if you plan to visit PNG for only a few weeks.

A tourist visa obtained outside PNG requires one photo, costs the equivalent of K10 and permits a stay of up to 60 days. Since they seem to give you what you ask for, ask for the maximum time rather than have to face the problem of extending. There are heavy penalties for overstaying your visa. The most lightly you're likely to get off is paying a K250 fee for 'late application for visa extension'.

You may be asked to show your inward and outward ticketing, that you have sufficient funds and that you have made some sort of accommodation arrangements when applying for your visa. Usually you will only have to show tickets.

People coming in by yacht pay K100 for a visa (which now must be obtained in advance) and possibly a K100 customs clearance fee when they leave.

In Australia there is a PNG High Commission in Canberra, a Consulate-General in Sydney and a Consulate in Brisbane. Although many travellers fly from Cairns in northern Australia visas cannot be obtained there. The Sydney office issues visas only to residents of New South Wales and the Brisbane office only to residents of Queensland. Allow at least a week for the process.

Jayapura in Irian Jaya is another relatively common exit point to PNG and there is now a PNG consul there.

PNG Embassies

Australia
High Commission, Forster Crescent, Yarralumla, PO Box 572, Manuka, ACT 2603 (☎ 273 3322, fax 273 3732)
Consulate-General, Somare Haus, 100 Clarence St, GPO Box 4201, Sydney, 2001 (☎ 299 5151, fax 290 3794)
Consulate, Estates House, 307 Queen St, Brisbane, PO Box 220, Brisbane, 4001 (☎ 221 7915, fax 229 6084)

Belgium
Embassy, 17-19 Rue Montoyer, 1040 Brussels (☎ 512 3126, fax 512 8643)

Fiji
Embassy, 6th floor, Ratu Sukuna House, Suva, PO Box 2447, Government Buildings, Suva (☎ 30 4244, fax 30 0178)

France
Embassy, Apartment 272, Flatotel International Coenson, 14 Rue du Theatre, 75015 Paris (☎ 457 56220, ext 272; fax 405 81222)

Germany
Embassy, Gotenstrasse 163, 5300 Bonn 2, Germany (☎ 37 6855/6, fax 37 5103)

Indonesia
Embassy, 6th floor, Panin Bank Centre, Jalan Jendral Sudirman 1, Jakarta 10270 (☎ 720 1012, fax 73 4562)
Consulate, Jalan Serui No 8, PO Box 854, Jayapura, Irian Jaya (☎ 31250, fax 31898)

Japan
Embassy, Mita Kokusai Building, 3rd floor, 313, 4-28 Mita 1-Chome, Minato-Ku, Tokyo (☎ 345 47801/4, fax 345 47275)

Malaysia
High Commission, 1 Lorong Ru Kedua, off Jalan Ru, Ampang, Kuala Lumpur (☎ 457 4202/4, fax 456 0998)

New Zealand
High Commission, 11th floor, Princes Towers, 180 Molesworth St, Thorndon, Wellington (☎ 473 1560, fax 471 2942)

Philippines
Embassy, 2280 Magnolia St, Dasmarinas Village, Makati, Metro Manila (☎ 810 8456/7, fax 817 1080)

Solomon Islands
High Commission, PO Box 1109, Honiara (☎ 20561, fax 20562)

UK
  High Commission, 14 Waterloo Place, London SW1R 4AR (☎ 930 0922/6, fax 930 0828)
USA
  Embassy, 3rd floor, 1615 New Hampshire Ave NW, Washington DC 20009 (☎ 659 0856, fax 745 3679)
  Permanent Mission to the UN, Suite 322, 866 United Nations Plaza, New York 10017 (☎ 832 0043, fax 832 0918)

Visa Extensions

Tourist visas can be extended for one month for a fee of K10. The Immigration & Citizenship Office in the Central Government Offices in Waigani, Port Moresby, is the only place in the country where you can extend visas and the procedure is slow and frustrating – worth avoiding if you can.

The Immigration section (☎ 27 1170, PO Wards Strip, Waigani) for the Department of Foreign Affairs is on the ground floor of the Central Government Office at Waigani. The office is open only from 8 am to noon, and you'll have to battle hordes of agents who are on first-name terms with the staff. Extending a visa takes at least a week, officially, but one fortunate traveller reports managing it in a day.

Travellers who have tried extending their visas by mail from other parts of the country have generally found it impossible, and have had to trek back to Port Moresby to retrieve their passports. If you do intend to do this, use a courier rather than mail. The address is: Immigration & Citizenship Division (☎ 27 1698, fax 25 4467), Department of Foreign Affairs, PO Wards Strip, Waigani, NCD. If you are having problems it might be a good idea to talk to an agent – see the Yellow Pages under Visa Services.

Foreign Embassies in PNG

Most embassies are in Port Moresby. It's worth making a phone call if you plan to visit between noon and 2 pm – some, including the Indonesian Embassy, close completely for two hours. Consulates, embassies and high commissions in Port Moresby include:

Australia
  Independence Drive, Waigani, PO Box 9129, Hohola (☎ 25 9333, fax 25 9183)
France
  9th floor, Pacific View Building, 1/84 Pruth St, Korobosea, PO Box 1155, Port Moresby (☎ 25 3740, fax 25 0861)
Germany
  2nd floor, Pacific View Apartments, 1/84 Pruth St, Korobosea, PO Box 3631, Boroko (☎ 25 2988)
Indonesia
  1 & 2/410 Sir John Guise Drive, Waigani, PO Box 7165, Boroko (☎ 25 3116)
  Consulate in Vanimo (Sandaun Province)
Italy
  Spring Gardens Rd, Hohola, PO Box 6330, Boroko (☎ 25 3183)
Japan
  4th & 5th floors, ANG House, Cuthbertson St, Port Moresby, PO Box 1040, Port Moresby (☎ 21 1800)
New Zealand
  Waigani Crescent, Waigani, PO Box 1144, Boroko (☎ 25 9444, fax 25 0565)
Philippines
  Islander Village, Wards Rd, Hohola, PO Box 5916, Boroko (☎ 25 6414)
UK
  Kiroki St, Waigani, PO Box 4778, Boroko (☎ 25 1677, fax 25 3547)
USA
  Armit St, Paga Hill, Port Moresby, PO Box 1492(!), Port Moresby (☎ 21 1455, fax 21 3423)

To/From Indonesia

The visa situation for people travelling to or from Indonesia is tricky. Regulations can change overnight, and the left hand rarely knows what the right hand is doing. We quite regularly receive tales of woe from travellers, so it pays to be flexible in your plans if you want to incorporate both Indonesia and PNG in your itinerary.

Although you can get a two-month tourist pass for Indonesia on arrival at certain international ports, if you have an onward ticket and your passport is valid for a minimum of six months, it's much better to get a visa before you arrive – the pass is actually distinct from a visa. Jayapura is *not* one of the ports where passes are issued, although there have been reports that some lucky EC (European Community) citizens have been given 14-day Indonesian transit passes on arrival in Jayapura from PNG, and that these were converted to two-month tourist passes in Biak. Don't count on this.

The two-day-only transit pass requirement no longer applies to visits to Irian Jaya, and it's possible to move fairly freely (with the appropriate police permits) around parts of Irian Jaya these days.

One-month visas to Indonesia are issued at the Indonesian Embassy in Port Moresby, and at the new Indonesian Consulate in Vanimo (Sandaun Province), a short hop by air from Jayapura. Apparently these can be extended in Indonesia. Check that the Vanimo office is still operating to avoid having to backtrack to Port Moresby.

The visa usually takes between two and four days to be issued in Port Moresby, a day in Vanimo. You need an onward ticket from Jayapura, a couple of photos and K10. If you don't have an onward ticket from Jayapura (maybe you plan to leave by sea), try buying a return Vanimo-Jayapura ticket and cashing-in the return half after you obtain a visa.

You do not have to present your application in person at the Port Moresby office, so you could use a courier (not the mail) to ferry your passport to and from wherever you happen to be. This system seems risky and if the consulate in Vanimo remains open it should not be necessary, but it's used by many expats in PNG and there seem to be few problems, although sometimes phone calls are needed to hurry things along.

On at least one occasion the Indonesians have expressed their displeasure at PNG attitudes to the OPM rebels in Irian Jaya by halting the issue of visas in PNG. Since it is impossible to predict when or if the OPM issue will once again flare up it may be wise to get your Indonesian visa at home.

If you enter PNG from Indonesia and plan to exit through Indonesia, do not forget to get a new Indonesian visa in PNG – once you have left Indonesia, the original visa or pass is finished whether or not the time has expired.

To/From Australia

All nationalities (except New Zealanders) require a visa for Australia which is issued free at consulates and is usually valid for six months. Extensions beyond the six-month period seem to be somewhat arbitrary – sometimes they will and sometimes they won't. Visitors aged between 18 and 26 from the UK, Ireland, Canada, Holland and Japan can be eligible for a 'working holiday' visa, and you should apply for this in your own country.

In general the Australian High Commission in Port Moresby seems to be pretty cooperative and very quick in issuing visas. Some travellers seem to use PNG as a convenient way of extending their stay in Australia without having to face the hassles of a straightforward extension. They travel round Australia for their initial six months, spend some time in PNG, and come back to Australia for another six months.

DOCUMENTS

The only essential document is your passport. You do not need an International Health Certificate in PNG, but you do for a number of Asian countries (Indonesia for one). One or two places to stay give discounts to members of the International Youth Hostels Federation. A valid overseas licence is all you need to drive a car for up to three months from the day you arrive.

International Student Identity Cards are very useful, especially if you're under 26 years old. Air Niugini offers significant student discounts as do some of the smaller airlines but not, unfortunately, Talair. Airlines sometimes require an International Student Concession Form, which should be available from your school or institution.

CUSTOMS

Visitors are allowed to import 200 cigarettes (or an equivalent amount of tobacco) and one litre of alcoholic drinks duty free. Personal effects that you have owned for a year (this might be difficult to judge!) are also duty free. You won't have any problem with your camera, film and personal stereo. There is sometimes quite a thorough check made of your gear at Jacksons Airport, Port Moresby.

There are also controls on what you can take out of the country – some items of cultural and historical significance are prohibited exports. This includes anything made before 1960, traditional stone tools, some shell valuables from Milne Bay, and any item incorporating human remains or bird-of-paradise plumes. As a tourist you are unlikely to be sold anything of this nature, but if you are in doubt and you don't like the idea of robbing a country of its heritage, you can get your artefact checked at the National Museum in Port Moresby. Stone tools and artefacts should definitely be checked, because they are often of astonishing antiquity and may provide vital clues to PNG's past.

If you plan to buy artefacts, check your home country's import and quarantine regulations. For instance, many artefacts incorporate animal skins or bones from protected animals, and these may be prohibited imports. If you are carrying the artefacts with you, you will also be subject to the regulations of countries you enter on your way home.

If you clear customs you have entered a country even if you are 'transiting' in a couple of days. The fact that you are an American tourist staying in Cairns for two days will not be an adequate defence against Australian regulations. Crocodile skin (it doesn't make any difference if it came from a farm), tortoise shell, some turtle shells, birds of paradise (and their plumes) are all prohibited imports to Australia because they are considered to be, or belong to, endangered species.

Australian quarantine regulations apply to all wooden articles (including all carvings), and all animal products (including bones and skins). If any of these things are judged to be quarantine risks you will have to pay to have them irradiated, a process that may take up to a week. This is a problem if you are catching a plane to the USA in two days, or if you are clearing customs in Sydney and catching a connecting flight to Melbourne.

You can minimise the risk of this by checking potential purchases yourself. Bone will automatically be treated, signs of borer in wood will mean problems, and hair or untanned skin will also require treatment. That's the theory, anyway – my Trobriands lime containers, with tusks in the lids, were waved through.

There are a number of ways around the problem if you simply must have that hairy mask with the boar's tusks. If you have a lot of artefacts consider sending them all directly home. If you are a genuine transit passenger (that is, you will not clear Australian customs) Australian regulations will not apply to you. If you do clear customs you can have your goods kept in a quarantine bond store (controlled storage) for the duration of your stay, although this is not to be recommended for fragile or very expensive items. You can also, at considerable expense, have the artefacts shipped under quarantine bond to your port of departure (if you land in Cairns, say and depart from Sydney).

MONEY

Currency

The unit of currency is the *kina* (pronounced 'keenah') which is divided into 100 *toea* (pronounced 'toy-ah'). Both are the names of traditional shell money and this connection to traditional forms of wealth is emphasised on the notes too. It's not just chance that the K20 note features an illustration of that most valuable of village animals, the pig.

At the time of independence the kina was on a par with the Australian dollar and many expatriates took great pains to ensure that their future salaries should be set in dollars rather than kina. This was a major mistake since the kina zoomed steadily ahead for years after independence. A high value kina can do wonders in keeping the inflation rate down but it does make the country uncomfortably expensive for outsiders.

You aren't allowed to take out of the country more than K200 in notes and K5 in coins, or more than K250 worth of foreign cash.

Exchange Rates

A$1	=	K0.69
C$1	=	K0.78
DM1	=	K0.59
FF1	=	K0.17
Rp 1000 (Indonesia)	=	K0.47
Y100 (Japan)	=	K0.84
NZ$1	=	K0.52
S$1 (Singapore)	=	K0.59
UK£1	=	K1.44
US$1	=	K0.97

Banks

Banks can be found in all the big towns, but off the beaten track you may have trouble finding a place to change money. Most international currency travellers' cheques are acceptable. Don't run short. If you plan to spend time in the villages, make sure you have smaller denomination notes and a supply of coins.

There is one easy way of carrying money around and that is to open a passbook savings account with a Papua New Guinea Banking Corportion (PNGBC) bank. You can then withdraw money from your account at any branch or agency – found on quite a few of the larger government stations – around the country. It's more convenient than changing travellers' cheques and you get interest on your money.

The PNGBC was once part of Australia's Commonwealth Bank and *might* honour passbook savings accounts (with blacklight signatures) held by customers of the Australian Commonwealth Bank. There is some difference of opinion on this between various officials in PNG and Australia, so don't count on it.

The PNGBC and Westpac (an Australian-based bank) are widely represented. Other banks include the Bank of South Pacific (a member of the National Australia Group) and the Australia & New Zealand Banking Group (ANZ). Banking hours are 9 am to 2 pm (3 pm for the PNGBC) from Monday to Thursday and 9 am to 5 pm on Fridays.

It's relatively simple and straightforward to have money transferred to a bank (preferably Westpac) in PNG from overseas.

Credit Cards

Credit cards are beginning to take off but are by no means accepted everywhere. Both American Express and Diners Club are accepted by the ritzier hotels and restaurants and by Air Niugini and Talair. Amex will give cash advances from their office in Port Moresby at Westpac Travel (☎ 25 4066, fax 25 1675) in Ori Lavi Haus on Nita St in Boroko, PO Box 1552, Boroko.

The ubiquitous Australian Bankcard is unknown and while MasterCard is becoming acceptable at some of the more expensive hotels, few places take Visa. That might change, as Westpac is now associated with Visa as well as MasterCard. The main Westpac branches will give a cash advance on MasterCard of up to K75 on the spot but might have to phone Australia (for a fee) before they can give larger amounts. ANZ will probably do the same with Visa.

Costs

PNG is very expensive. Unless you're staying in villages, budget for Australian prices, or higher, *not* Asian prices. The bottom line is that if you don't restrict your travel to a well-planned shoestring expedition, you will find yourself spending a lot of money – and not necessarily getting much for it. 'Shoddy' is a word that can describe quite a few places in PNG, and even those that are not shoddy can rarely be described as good value.

See the Getting Around chapter for some ways of visiting most of the country in relative comfort without breaking the bank.

One of the primary reasons for the high prices is the spectacular geography. Because the country is so mountainous and rugged and includes so many offshore islands, air transport is often the only feasible method of moving goods and people – and this is expensive. Another reason is that many commodities, including basic foodstuffs, are imported. Australia did not encourage the development of industries that would compete with Australian producers and for many years regarded PNG as a captive export market.

There is no tradition of cheap hotels and restaurants (like there is in Asia) because when Papua New Guineans travel, they stay with their wantoks (relatives), or they use their expense accounts and so don't care how much they are charged. No real urban culture has developed (cities are a very new idea), so street life and night life are virtually nonexistent. Cheap, pleasant eating spots are extremely rare – there is no demand for them.

Once you get out of the towns, however, you move into an almost cashless economy where you can live for virtually nothing – there is virtually nothing to buy! The possibilities for shoestring travel are limitless and the rewards are terrific. You can walk through areas where roads don't exist, you can buy canoes and travel down rivers. All you have to do is get to the end of a secondary road and start putting one foot in front of the other. There's always a place to stay – with a family or in village guesthouses, missions, schools or police stations.

You could travel for weeks virtually without spending a toea if you can survive for long periods on sago or sweet potato (we're talking breakfast, lunch and dinner) and enjoy walking and paddling. This kind of travel can be very demanding but there is no better way to see the country or meet the people. And sago for a week is definitely bearable! However, it is essential that you spend *some* money – paying your way is very important. Two to five kina for a night's accommodation and a kina or some trade store food in exchange for a meal is fair.

Melanesian hospitality is based on an exchange system with the aim of cultivating a long-term relationship. The tourist, passing through, has no role in this tradition of hospitality. When you do give or pay something in exchange for hospitality, traditional responsibilities are fulfilled, the village is supported and, hopefully, the next visitor is welcomed. There are villages in the Upper Sepik which have become pissed off with freeloading foreigners and are now wary of all travellers. As one traveller put it, 'if you can afford to come here, you can afford to feed yourself, and maybe someone else as well'.

Bargaining & Tipping

Bargaining is not a natural part of most day-to-day transactions. It is never a game or an integral, enjoyable part of shopping as it is in Asia. Prices in the markets are set and fair (often they are clearly displayed) and prices on PMVs are also set.

The only time you will come across anything approximating bargaining (serious negotiation would be a more appropriate description) is when you are being charged for a photograph, buying artefacts or are hiring a guide or boat. With artefacts you are sometimes offered an outrageous first price and you are expected to ask for the 'second price'. This is normally what the vendor believes goods are worth. It's very unwise to use bargaining strategies such as belittling the artefact or questioning the vendor's honesty. Remember that if the vendor is selling on behalf of someone else (not unusual) he/she might not be *able* to lower the price.

Sometimes negotiations for things like a river trip will take days. Be low key, not aggressive. This is not an Asian game and you could easily offend someone.

Do not tip, it isn't expected.

Consumer Taxes

Most provincial governments set consumer taxes, ranging from 2½% to 7%. Expensive hotels and restaurants are about the only places where the tax is added onto the bill, rather than included in the total price.

WHEN TO GO

The climate is the main consideration in deciding when to visit PNG – see that section of the Facts about the Country chapter. You'll probably want to avoid rainy seasons (although a good tropical downpour is a sight to be seen) but these vary across the country. Airlines run to capacity from before Christmas to early February (with a lull in January), ferrying people home on holidays and expats to and from Australia.

WHAT TO BRING

The best advice, wherever you go, is to take too little rather than too much. Keep in mind that the domestic airlines have a baggage weight limit of 16 kg, although as a tourist you can usually slip by if your bags weigh around 20 kg. The generally warm climate makes things easy – even in the cool Highlands a sweater is all you'll ever need for the evenings. Naturally what you plan to do and how you plan to travel will shape what you need to take. For instance, the only time you'll need a coat is if you go mountain climbing: it snows on top of Mt Wilhelm.

General

Most of the time all you will require is lightweight clothing, T-shirts, sandals and swimming gear. Natural fibres, cotton in particular, will be most comfortable in the sticky, lowlands humidity. Long-sleeved shirts are not necessary except on the most formal occasions, although they can be very useful as sun and mosquito protection. Coats and ties are virtually never required. Men will find Australian-style 'dress' shorts can be worn for almost any occasion, but lightweight trousers are nice to have for restaurants and cool Highlands evenings. A hat, large enough to shade the back of your neck, and sunglasses will also be useful.

Unless you plan to spend all your time in resorts, don't come laden with gaudy T-shirts, boardshorts, and other 'beach culture' clothing. Other than the small rich elite, most people dress conservatively and many buy their clothes from second-hand stores. Flaunting your foreignness will make you stand out and could attract thieves.

Women must dress discreetly; the often scanty styles of traditional dress do not apply to foreigners and mission-influenced people can be very prudish. From a security point of view, it's not a good idea to call attention to yourself with revealing clothes. A below-the-knee dress is the best solution, although where this is impractical, trousers are usually OK, as long as they're not very tight. Shorts are definitely not a good idea – even on men shorts can be too short or tight. A bikini is inappropriate at all but the most Westernised and protected locations.

PNG is not a good place to buy clothes, unless you want to check out the ubiquitous second-hand shops. You can buy all the essentials in the main towns but they aren't cheap. On the other hand, the day-to-day Western commodities that can be difficult to find in Asia (toothpaste, toilet paper, tampons, etc) are easy to obtain. It is worth carrying a roll of toilet paper (handy if you're likely to be using bush toilets) and sunscreen and insect repellent are essential. A medical kit is also necessary – see the Health section in this chapter.

The most flexible and useful items for carrying your baggage are travel backpacks. These are packs whose internal frames and adjustable harnesses can be zipped away into a compartment. You can use them as packs when you're bushwalking or looking for a hotel, and with the harness hidden you don't run into problems with straps snagging on airport conveyer belts or bus seats. A cheaper alternative is a sports bag with a shoulder strap. Unless you're on a tour or can afford taxis, you will have to do some walking, so make sure your baggage can be easily carried. Packing your things in separate plastic bags helps keep everything organised and dry.

A day pack is handy for carrying a camera (remember you have to take care of cameras because of the humidity and dust), a water bottle (essential if you're walking or can't survive on Pepsi) and your travel survival kit! If you don't need your daypack to be waterproof, buy a billum when you arrive. A money belt or pouch is essential. Because of the heat, a pouch or belt and its contents soon become sodden with sweat, so make sure paper items are sealed in plastic.

A mask and snorkel is definitely worth having, as hire shops are few and far between, prices are high, and virtually every beach is a snorkeller's delight. A *laplap* (the PNG sarong) can be used as a dressing gown, a beach towel, an addition to a skimpy bathing suit, a bed sheet and, of course, a laplap. Consider taking some cutlery, a bowl, plate and mug so you can make your own breakfast or lunch. A Swiss Army knife with a can opener, bottle opener and scissors will be invaluable. A small torch is handy for late night toilet expeditions (vital if you're in a village). Some light nylon cord, another all-purpose item, is useful for hanging mosquito nets, shoelaces, a washing line, tying parcels...

If you're not bushwalking don't bother to bring a tent. If you anticipate spending much time in the Highlands, where the nights can get cold, it is worth considering a sleeping bag that is lightweight and compact. In other areas a sleeping sheet is just as useful and is lighter and smaller.

A mosquito net is essential if you're planning to stay in villages, but you can get these in Port Moresby or Wewak. See the Sepik chapter for details of other items you will need on the river.

Walking & Canoeing

Don't underestimate your potential isolation or the extreme conditions the environment can dish out – you must be properly equipped if you plan any serious walking or canoeing. Lonely Planet's *Bushwalking in Papua New Guinea* gives a detailed rundown of what you will need. There are no specialist bushwalking shops so you must bring major items with you. You can get bush knives (machetes), matches, tinned and dried food, torches and batteries and mosquito nets locally, but you'll look long and hard for a good tent or portable stove. A medical kit is also essential – see the Health section in this chapter.

Briefly, you need a mosquito net, sleeping bag, stove and cooking equipment (kerosene and gas are available, methylated spirits can be bought at chemists – you can't bring them from another country on a plane), rope, decent boots, compass and maps, waterproof jacket or poncho, water canister, waterproof matches, a signalling mirror, torch and, possibly, a bush knife.

The value of a tent is debatable – see Camping in the Accommodation section, later in this chapter, for the pros and cons.

TOURIST OFFICES
Local Tourist Offices

There are few outlets for general tourist information in PNG. One of the best sources is Air Niugini. They play a major role in promoting tourism and most offices are helpful and have some printed information.

There is an information office in the international arrivals hall at Jacksons Airport in Port Moresby. Here you can get a visitors' guide and an annual accommodation directory which is useful for fairly up-to-date information on hotel prices.

A number of provincial governments have officials whose responsibilities include tourism, although they don't have a specific department. You would stand a good chance of reaching them if you addressed your query to: Tourist Officer, Department of Commerce, (name of province). There are 'real live' tourist offices in Madang and Rabaul and a number of other provincial boards, bureaus and offices, especially in Manus, Milne Bay and New Ireland.

If you're stuck for information the best thing to do is simply ask around. There'll usually be someone who can help. In small places you'll often find an English-speaker at the airstrip. The main tourist office addresses are:

National

Air Niugini
  PO Box 7186, Boroko, PNG (☎ 25 9000)
PNG Tourist Office
  PO Box 7144, Boroko, PNG (☎ 25 1269)
  Jacksons Airport (☎ 25 8776)

Provincial

East New Britain Tourist Bureau
  PO Box 385, Rabaul, East New Britain, PNG (☎ 92 1813)
Madang Visitors' Bureau
  PO Box 2025, Jomba, Madang, PNG (☎ 82 3302, fax 82 3540)
Manus Tourist Officer
  PO Box 37, Lorengau, Manus Province, PNG (☎ 40 9361, fax 40 9218)
Milne Bay Visitors' Bureau
  PO Box 337, Alotau, Milne Bay Province, PNG (☎ 61 1503, fax 61 1402)

New Ireland Tourist Bureau
    PO Box 103, Kavieng, New Ireland Province,
    PNG (☎ 94 1449, fax 94 2346)

Overseas Reps

Air Niugini offices are the best sources of information (see the Getting There & Away chapter for overseas addresses). Embassies can help (see the Visas & Embassies section in this chapter for addresses) as can the tour operators (see Organised Tours in the Activities section in this chapter for addresses).

BUSINESS HOURS

Most offices are open from 7.45 or 8 am to 4 pm. Shops generally stay open later, especially on Friday nights and they're also open on Saturday mornings. Trade stores and snack bars usually have more liberal hours.

Banks are open from 9 am to 2 pm (3 pm for PNGBC Bank), Monday to Thursday and until 5 pm on Friday. At Port Moresby Airport there's a bank agency which supposedly opens for the arrival of all international flights – but not necessarily for departures.

Post offices are open from 9 am (sometimes 8 am) to 5 pm weekdays and on Saturday mornings. There's generally not much point in visiting government offices between 12.30 and 2 pm even though lunch officially starts at 1 pm and finishes at 1.30 pm.

Alcohol licensing regulations vary from province to province. It's not unusual for a town or even a whole province to be declared 'dry' if there has been trouble.

HOLIDAYS, FESTIVALS & CULTURAL EVENTS

Each of the twenty provinces of PNG has its own provincial government day and these are usually a good opportunity to enjoy *sing-sings* (traditional ceremonies and dances). Generally, however, sing-sings are local affairs with no fixed yearly schedule, so you'll have to depend on word-of-mouth to find out about them.

Shows and festivals are held on weekends, so the dates change from year to year, usually only by a few days. Similarly, the public holiday associated with a provincial government day will usually be on a Friday or a Monday.

If you want to be certain of a festival date before you arrive, try contacting one of Air Niugini's overseas offices.

January
    New Year's Day (1 Jan)
February
    New Ireland Provincial Government Day (22 Feb)
    Kavieng Show (22 Feb – perhaps moving to late July)
April
    Easter – Traditional church services
    Oro Provincial Government Day (20 April)
June-August
    Yam Harvest Festival (Trobriand Islands)
    Queen's Birthday (mid-June)
    Port Moresby Show – traditional and modern events (mid-June)
    Central Provincial Government Day (mid-June)
    Morobe Provincial Government Day (July)
    Milne Bay Government Day (7 July)
    Remembrance Day – mainly Port Moresby (23 July)
    Rabaul Frangipani Festival – commemorating the first flowers to blossom after the 1937 eruption of Matupit (23 July)
    Madang Provincial Government Day (early Aug)
    Maborasa Festival (Madang) – includes dancing, choirs and bamboo bands (early Aug)
    Manus Provincial Government Day (Aug)
    Simbu Provincial Government Day (Aug)
    Southern Highlands Provincial Government Day (Aug)
    Mt Hagen Show – a big gathering of clans with traditional dances and dress (late Aug)
September
    Goroka Show – similar but bigger than Mt Hagen Show. This used to occur on even-numbered years, but may become annual an annual show (early Sept)
    Independence Day – a great time to be in PNG with many festivals and sing-sings all around the country (16 Sept)
    East Sepik Provincial Government Day (16 Sept)
    Hiri Moale, Port Moresby. Big festival celebrating the huge Papuan trading canoes (16 Sept)
    Malangan Festival (Kavieng or Namatanai, in New Ireland) – the two-week festival includes the famous tree-dancers (16 Sept)
    Milne Bay Show (16 Sept)
October-November
    Enga Provincial Government Day (Oct)
    West New Britain Provincial Government Day (Oct)

Tolai Warwagira (Rabaul) – a two-week festival of sing-sings and other events. Currently celebrated on odd-numbered years (Oct or Nov)
Oro Tapa Festival, Popondetta (Nov)

December
Gulf Provincial Government Day (1 Dec)
Western Provincial Government Day (6 Dec)
Christmas (25 Dec)

POST & TELECOMMUNICATIONS
Post

There is no mail delivery service so if you're writing to people within PNG you must address your letters to post office boxes. Box numbers of hotels and useful companies are given throughout the book. Add the name of the relevant town and the province. For example:

Niugini Guest Haus
PO Box 108
Wewak
East Sepik Province

There's a poste restante service at most post offices. Underline the surname and print it clearly if you want the letter to arrive safely. Even then you have to cross your fingers.

The amount of time a letter takes to be delivered varies radically – it can take from three days to three weeks to travel between Australia and PNG. However, if you have a fixed address, mail usually seems to be quite reliable.

The overseas mail service from PNG is generally good. Wrap parcels carefully as surface mail can be very rough. Allow at least three months for parcel post from PNG to North America. If they're packed in cardboard cartons, with paper packing, masks or other purchases should get back OK.

Postal Rates The postal rates are:

Letters within PNG	K0.21
Aerogrammes	K0.45
Airmail letters (up to 20 gm) to:	
Australia/New Zealand	K0.45
Asia	K0.60
Europe/North America	K0.90

Note that postcards are charged at the letter rate, so you can send two aerogrammes to Europe for the price of a stamp for one postcard.

Many of the pilots who land on the 450 or so strips strewn across the country will post letters for you, if they are stamped.

Telephone

The phone system in PNG, although limited to the main centres, is extremely good – another example of how the infrastructure seems totally out of line with the overall economy. You can direct dial between all the main centres, and there are no area codes to worry about, unless you're ringing a radio phone in which case you dial 019 for the operator. You can also direct dial most of the world, even from payphones.

Payphones charge K0.20 for local calls. For long-distance or international calls, feed in more money every time the red light shines. Unused coins are refunded.

Unfortunately, pay phones can be hard to find, particularly in Port Moresby where there are not enough phones to start with and many are vandalised. In Port Moresby, Lae, Mt Hagen and perhaps some other larger towns you'll find payphones which take phone cards – post offices and a few shops sell the cards.

Some big hotels may allow you to use their phones but the cost is much higher.

When wantoks come to stay you have to support them, and that includes letting them use your phone. As they'll be ringing home a lot, this can mean big bills. Luckily, the PTC has introduced a 'local-area only' phone. They've cunningly made the rental on these a little cheaper than on normal phones, so you can tell your wantoks that this was the only phone you could afford.

Fax

Kwik piksa leta (fax) has taken off in a big way in PNG, and many places have one. You can send faxes from post offices for a few kina, and they can be a useful way of making accommodation bookings. Faxing might even save you money, as you can get through a lot of coins in a payphone when the clerk gives up on your Pidgin and goes off to look for an English-speaker. Fax numbers are listed in telephone directories.

TIME

The time throughout PNG is 10 hours ahead of UTC (GMT). When it's noon in PNG it will be also noon in Sydney, 9 am in Jakarta, 2 am in London, 9 pm the previous day in New York and 6 pm the previous day in Los Angeles. There is no daylight saving (summer time) in PNG.

PNG is close to the equator, so day and night are almost equal in duration and it gets dark quickly. The sun rises about 6 am and sets at about 6 pm.

Don't confuse PNG official time with the unofficial Melanesian time. Melanesian time can be very flexible; make sure you roll with it rather than fight against it! The West's clock-watching phobia has not yet infected much of the South Pacific, so you should not assume other people will regard punctuality as a primary virtue – there are other priorities. Although it's as well to remember that things will often be half an hour late, don't forget they can also be half an hour early!

ELECTRICITY

The electric current on the national grid is 240V, AC 50Hz (the same as in Australia). While all the towns have electrical supplies most of PNG does not have power, other than that provided by the occasional privately owned generator.

WEIGHTS & MEASURES

PNG uses the metric system. See the back pages of this book for conversion tables.

BOOKS

There are plenty of books about PNG – all the wild country, the amazing tribes, the fantastic cultures and the glamour of the last frontier has attracted countless writers and photographers. It was one of the last areas for European exploration and developed its own subcategory of literature: 'patrol officers' memoirs'. It had a dramatic role in WW II and the developments leading up to indepen-

dence were also intriguing. The books that follow are a very small selection of the many that have been written.

General

For facts and figures, a good book is *A Fact Book on Modern Papua New Guinea* by Jackson Rannells (Oxford University Press, 1991). It's designed as a school reference, but it concisely covers most things you might want to know.

Sean Dorney, the Australian Broadcasting Corporation's long-time PNG correspondent, has written an interesting and informative book, *Papua New Guinea – people, politics & history since 1975* (Random House, 1990), which makes sense of the country's recent history.

One of the most interesting of the 'wow, look at these pictures' books is *The World's Wide Places – New Guinea*, one of the glossy Time-Life series. This one is by Roy Mackay with photographs by Eric Lindgrom and covers the spectacular terrain and wildlife very well.

Yachties intending to visit should look for *Cruising Papua New Guinea* by Alan Lucas (Horwitz Grahame, Sydney, 1980).

Anthropology

PNG has been a treasure house for anthropologists and from Malinowski to Margaret Mead, they've made their names here. They're still flocking in today. Malinowski's books are covered in the Trobriand Islands section of the Milne Bay Province chapter of this book – they're weighty, academic books yet very readable.

Margaret Mead's *Growing Up in New Guinea* was first published in 1942, but is still available in a paperback Penguin. She conducted her studies on Manus Island and returned there after the war to investigate the dramatic changes that had taken place as a result of the enormous impact on a wartime American base. Her second Manus book was *New Lives for Old* (Morrow, New York, 1956). A good deal of controversy surrounds her observations, but the books are well written and very readable.

Gardens of War – Life & Death in the New Guinea Stone Age by Robert Gardner & Karl G Heider (Random House, New York, 1968 and also in a Penguin large format paperback) describes ritual warfare of New Guinea tribes, dramatically illustrated with many photographs. Fierce inter-village fighting was still common in the remote parts of Irian Jaya which the authors visited in the '60s.

Cargo cults have also come in for a lot of study. They are a fascinating example of the collision between primitive beliefs and modern technology. The classic book on these cults is *Road Belong Cargo* by Peter Lawrence (Melbourne University Press, 1964).

Culture & Arts

Man as Art: New Guinea Body Decoration by M Kirk is a beautiful coffee table photographic book illustrating the extravagant body decoration of the Highlanders.

The Artefacts & Crafts of Papua New Guinea – a Guide for Buyers is a very useful little booklet produced for the Handcraft Industry of PNG. It has over 250 pictures and short descriptions of a very wide variety of PNG artefacts. If you do intend to buy something (if you don't, this book will change your mind!) it will be invaluable. If you can't find it anywhere else, look for it at the University Bookshop.

History & Exploration

It's difficult to find much information about the country before Europeans arrived. The simple truth is that not a great deal is known, although this glaring gap is now gradually being filled.

Gavin Souter's intriguing book on the exploration and development of New Guinea, *The Last Unknown* (Angus & Robertson, Sydney, 1963), is the book to read if you read nothing else on PNG. The descriptions of the early explorers, some of whom were more than a little strange, is positively enthralling. It barely touches on WW II and stops well before the '60s rush to independence, but it is a highly enjoyable read. You

may have to search for a copy since it's out of print.

Papua New Guinea's Prehistory by Pamela Swadling (PNG National Museum & Art Gallery with Gordon & Gotch, Port Moresby, 1981) gives an excellent introduction to the early history of human settlement and the development of agriculture. It shows how painstaking archaeological research is beginning to piece together a picture of ancient PNG societies and is fascinating reading. The Museum Bookshop sells copies.

Probably the most interesting of all the early explorers' stories would have to be Captain J A Lawson's *Wanderings in the Interior of New Guinea* which was published in 1875. Not since his epic visit has Mt Hercules (over a thousand metres higher than Everest) been seen again – or the New Guinea tiger, the waterfalls larger than Niagara or even the giant daisies or huge scorpions.

The patrol officers' memoirs category came into its prime between the wars and some of the books written then, when patrol officers were not only explorers but also the force of government, are classics of their kind. *Across New Guinea from the Fly to the Sepik*, I F Champion (1932), covers Champion's agonisingly difficult traverse of central New Guinea. *The Land that Time Forgot*, Mick Leahy & Mick Crane (1937), tells of the discovery of the Highlands.

Amazingly, Leahy carried a movie camera when he first explored the highlands and his astonishing film of those first meetings forms the core of a highly acclaimed film, *First Contact*. The old film is counterpointed with modern film of the people, on both sides, who took part in that first close encounter. If you get a chance to see the film, don't miss it. It's available on video, in Australia from Arundel Productions in Sydney. There is now a book of *First Contact*, by Bob Connolly and Robin Anderson (Viking Penguin), with many stills from the film and a lot of additional information. It is definitely worth buying. It's published in both hardback and paperback.

There are also some much more recent reminiscences of those exciting days on patrol. J K McCarthy's *Patrol into Yesterday* (Cheshire, Melbourne, 1963) is another book recommended for exciting reading.

If you're interested in the OPM's struggle in Irian Jaya and the attitudes of the Indonesian and PNG governments, the best book to read is *Indonesia's Secret War – The Guerrilla Struggle in Irian Jaya* by Robin Osborne (Allen & Unwin, Sydney, 1985). It gives a fascinating and sometimes depressing insight into modern imperialism and politics.

Because the history of European contact is so recent it has been well documented in photographs. You'll find a lot of interesting pictures in *A Pictorial History of New Guinea* by Noel Gash and June Whittaker (Jacaranda, Brisbane, 1975). *Taim Bilong Masta* is the book companion to an Australian Broadcasting Corporation oral history of the Australian period. It's extremely readable and full of interest; recommended.

WW II

For a very readable account of the decisive fighting on the Kokoda Trail, culminating in the bitter struggle to recapture Buna and Gona from the Japanese, look for *Bloody Buna* by Lida Mayo. Originally published by Doubleday, New York, in 1974, it is also available in cheap paperback.

The amazing courage of the coast watchers, who relayed information from behind the Japanese lines, knowing that capture would mean a most unpleasant death, is also well documented. Look for Walter Lord's *Lonely Vigil – The Coastwatchers of the Solomons* (Viking Press, New York, 1978). Peter Ryan's *Fear Drive My Feet* (Angus & Robertson, Sydney, 1959) recounts some nerve-racking adventures behind the Japanese lines around Lae.

Some people find poking around the rotting relics from the war an interesting exercise – *Rust in Peace* by Bruce Adams (Antipodean Publishers, Sydney, 1975) tells you where to look, not only in PNG but also in other parts of the Pacific. *Battleground*

South Pacific, photos by Bruce Adams, text by Robert Howlett (Reeds, Sydney, 1970), also has much interesting material on the war. *Pacific Aircraft Wrecks & where to find them*, by Charles Darby (Kookaburra, Melbourne, 1979), is mainly devoted to WW II wrecks in PNG and has many fascinating photographs of these aircraft.

Wildlife

PNG's exotic and colourful bird life has inspired many equally colourful books. For the amateur bird-watcher, the best field manual is *Birds of New Guinea* by Beehler, Pratt & Zimmerman (Princeton University Press, 1986).

A little more down to earth, in price at least, are two books you can find in Port Moresby. *Birds in Papua New Guinea* by Brian Coates (Robert Brown & Associates, Port Moresby, 1977) and *Wildlife in Papua New Guinea* by Eric Lindgrom (Robert Brown & Associates, Port Moresby or Golden Press, Sydney, 1975) provide an interesting introduction with plenty of excellent photographs.

Odds & Ends

If you visit Rabaul, you'll no doubt develop an interest in Queen Emma's highly colourful life which is described in *Queen Emma* by R W Robson (Pacific Publications, Sydney, 1965). A novel based around her life is *Queen Emma of the South Seas* by Geoffrey Dutton (Macmillan, Melbourne, 1976).

The Crocodile, by Vincent Eri, was the first published novel by a Papuan (Jacaranda, Brisbane, 1970 – available in a Penguin paperback). It provides an interesting look at the contact between Europeans and locals from the rarely seen, other side of the fence. *My Mother Calls Me Yoltep* (Oxford University Press, 1980) is by an ex-Governor General of PNG, Sir Ignatius Kilage.

The Visitants by Randolph Snow (Picador paperback, 1981) won the 1979 Patrick White Award. It's a novel set on a remote island in 1959 and deals with the meeting of two very different cultures. *Something in the Blood*, by Trevor Shearston (University of

Queensland Press) is a collection of short stories. *The Snail Race* and *The Talking Pig* are two children's books from Robert Brown & Associates.

For the full story of the Ok Tedi project and its environmental effects look for *Ok Tedi, Pot of Gold* by R Jackson (University of PNG).

Into the Crocodile Nest, by Benedict Allen (Paledin, 1989) is an account of travels and initiation ceremonies on the Sepik. Finally, *In Papua New Guinea*, by Christina Dodwell (Oxford Illustrated Press, Yeovil, England, 1983) is a delightful recent account of an enterprising young Englishwoman's adventures through PNG on foot, by horse and a four-month solo trip down the Sepik by dugout canoe. It also proves, once again, that the facility the English have for producing superbly eccentric travellers is far from dead!

Bookshops

You won't find a great selection of books on the country except in Port Moresby, although Mt Hagen, Goroka, Madang and Lae also have shops with reasonable selections. Probably the best bookshop in the country is the University Bookshop in Port Moresby.

Every major town has a Christian bookshop, and although they stock plenty of books proving Darwin was wrong, and more of that ilk, they also have more general titles. They all stock various Pidgin dictionaries and grammar guides and a range of books written in Pidgin, which are useful if you are making a serious attempt to learn the language.

MAPS

The whole country is covered by topographic maps down to the 1:100,000 scale; there is not yet a complete series for scales larger than that, for example, 1:25,000. The National Mapping Bureau in Waigani (☎ 27 6465, fax 25 9716, PO Box 5665, Boroko, NCD) keeps a complete inventory of the country's 1:100,000 and 1:250,000 topographic map series. They cost about K4 a sheet. In addition to these a wide range of

other maps, including the available 1:50,000 and 1:25,000 topographic maps, are available from the Bureau. You can order from overseas.

Some of the provincial Lands & Survey departments also sell these maps but the office in Port Moresby is the most likely to have complete stocks.

The best easily-available general maps are the *Tourist Guide to Papua New Guinea* (which includes city maps) produced by Shell and the PNG Office of Tourism, and the excellent little map produced by Air Niugini. Look for the Sepik River map available in Wewak.

MEDIA
Newspapers

It's often said that one of the best ways to understand a small place is to read the papers – from cover to cover, classified ads and all. As well as a few skimpy local papers, there is one national daily, the *Post Courier*; it's a tabloid but is more serious than that format usually indicates. If you buy nothing else, it is worth buying *The Times of PNG*, a good-quality weekly review produced by Word Publishing, a Christian outfit. It gives excellent background on current issues and some interesting and provocative columns. The paper is rarely 'churchy', that is, apart from the amazing Bishop David Hand's column.

The same people also publish a weekly newspaper in Pidgin – *Wantok*. If you doubt the vitality and utility of the Pidgin language make sure you buy a copy. The standard of reporting in this paper is high, and reading the centre spread of comics is a good way to begin to learn Pidgin.

Radio & TV

The National Broadcasting Commission operates an AM and FM radio station in Port Moresby, as well as a number of provincial services, including shortwave. One service which is produced in all regional centres is the Toksave ('talk-savvy' – information) programme. This bulletin board means that

The Phantom

The Phantom – you know, the 'ghost who walks', the guy in the tight-fitting one-piece suit who lives in the Skull Cave and runs around righting wrongs and never marrying Diana – is immensely popular in PNG. The strip was translated into Pidgin, and featured great lines, like these written to the Phantom by his greatest admirer: 'Lewa bilong mi, longtaim tumas mi no bin lukim yu. Wataim bai me lukim yu gen? Mi krai long yu. Mi Diana.'

He has been used to advertise the virtues of everything from using a toothbrush to eating peanuts, but I doubt that the latest campaign would meet with Mr Walker's approval: the Phantom features on *laki tikets*, which might *win moni*, although most, like the one pictured, win *nating*. ∎

even the remotest villages are in touch with community events.

EMTV is the sole local TV station, but almost everyone can pick up QTV, the northern Queensland franchiser of Australia's Nine Network. CNN, Indonesian and Malaysian programmes are also widely received on satellite dishes.

Videos are widespread and popular throughout the country – you'll see them in hotels, trade stores and kai shops. Unfortunately, the films they show are often low-quality and extremely violent – it's just like being at home.

There was a great deal of debate before TV started up in PNG: Does the country need TV? What controls should there be? What effect will there be on the local culture? A quick glance through a newspaper TV guide will show the critics' fears were justified.

FILM & PHOTOGRAPHY

PNG is very photogenic and you can easily run through a lot of film, particularly if you happen on some event like a big Highland sing-sing. Bring more film than you'll need and then more again. Film is easily available in the major towns, but it is fairly expensive,

even by Australian standards. Maybe I was unlucky, but both rolls of film I bought in PNG jammed in the camera.

Protect your film and your camera from the dust, humidity and heat as much as you can. It is worth taking a small cleaning kit, and spare batteries. You're unlikely to have your luggage X-rayed before you get into a Sepik canoe, but a lead-lined film bag will help to keep your film cool.

Allow for the high intensity of the tropical sun when making your settings. Between mid-morning and late afternoon you might want to use a filter to avoid washed-out colour. Even on bright sunny days, however, it can be surprisingly dim in the jungle or a shady village so you'll also need long exposures, especially if you're taking photos of dark-skinned people. I found I used a lot of ASA (ISO) 400 film; a flash can also be useful.

Etiquette

Never take a photograph in or of a *haus tambaran* (or any other spirit house) without asking permission. These are holy places and you could quickly find yourself in trouble if you do not respect the wishes and feelings of their guardians. It's best to ask several of the male elders first, to make sure you do actually speak to someone who has the authority to grant your request. Even if you just glance through your viewfinder people will assume that you have taken a photo, so be careful.

You'll find people are generally happy to be photographed, even going out of their way to pose for you, particularly at singsings. It is absolutely essential to ask permission before you snap. At the very least, remember the standards of privacy you would expect at home, although this is not fail-safe – you cannot assume your standards are appropriate until you ask. Don't, for instance, take a photo of someone washing in their bathroom, even if the bathroom is a jungle stream.

You'll rarely have to pay for photographing somebody, but some people, usually men dressed in traditional style, do request payment – about K0.50 to K1 is average but it can be a lot more. People are aware that Western photographers can make money out of their exotic photos and see no reason why they shouldn't get some of the action. If you've gone ahead and taken a photo without getting permission and establishing a price, you may well find yourself facing an angry, heavily-armed Highlander who is demanding K20 in payment. It would take some nerve to argue.

HEALTH

Travel health depends on your predeparture preparations, your day-to-day health care while travelling and how you handle any medical problem or emergency that does develop.

While the list of potential dangers can seem quite frightening, with a little luck, some basic precautions and adequate information few travellers experience more than upset stomachs – and even these are much less common than in other developing countries.

If you are travelling with children, remember that they are likely to be harder hit than you by many diseases (especially dehydra-tion caused by diarrhoea). Lonely Planet's *Travel with Children* gives some basic advice.

No vaccinations are necessary unless you are coming from a country where yellow fever or cholera is a problem. An International Health Card is not required. With the exception of malaria, there are no serious health problems. It is, however, a rugged country where the environment demands respect and the medical services are often overstretched.

Each provincial capital has a hospital and the quality of the staff is apparently good – but they're short of equipment and crowded, so if you did get seriously sick you'd be wise to fly out to Australia, or home.

There are private doctors (they're not cheap) in most main towns and dentists in Port Moresby, Lae and Rabaul.

Travel Health Guides
The following are a number of books on travel health that you might find useful:

Staying Healthy in Asia, Africa & Latin America, Volunteers in Asia, is probably the best all-round guide to carry, as it's compact but very detailed and well organised.
Travellers' Health, Dr Richard Dawood, Oxford University Press, is comprehensive, easy to read, authoritative and also highly recommended, although it's rather large to lug around.
Where There is No Doctor, David Werner, Hesperian Foundation, is a very detailed guide intended for someone, like a Peace Corps worker, going to work in an undeveloped country, rather than for the average traveller.
Travel with Children, Maureen Wheeler, Lonely Planet Publications, includes basic advice on travel health for younger children.

Predeparture Preparations
Health & Travel Insurance Get some! However you're travelling, it's worth taking out travel insurance, both for the loss of valuable possessions and for problems with air travel, such as delays and missed connections. Everyone should be covered against health problems or accidents that will require a flight home or to Australia's medical facil-

ities. It's sensible to buy travel insurance as early as possible. If you buy it the week before you fly, you may find, for example, that you're not covered for delays to your flight caused by industrial action.

There are lots of travel insurance policies available and any travel agent will be able to recommend one. Get one which will pay for your flight home if you are really sick. Make sure it will cover the money you lose for forfeiting a booked flight, and that it will cover the cost of flying your travelling companion home with you.

Note that some policies specifically exclude 'dangerous activities' which can include scuba diving and even trekking. If such activities are on your agenda you don't want that sort of policy.

Health Preparations Make sure you're healthy before you start travelling and get your teeth checked. If you wear glasses take a spare pair and your prescription.

If you require a particular medication take an adequate supply, as it may not be available locally. Take the prescription, with the generic rather than the brand name (which may not be locally available).

Immunisations Malaria prophylactics are essential and have to be taken at least a week before you leave home. See Malaria in the Insect-Borne Diseases section for more details. Make sure that your tetanus cover is up to date: it isn't just rusty nails which cause tetanus, any cut can get infected and the disease is deadly.

Medical Kit There are reasonably well-stocked pharmacies in the main centres but it's a good idea to bring most of your medical needs with you, and definitely a supply of any medication you take regularly. The kit might include:

- Antihistamine (such as Benadryl) – useful as a decongestant for colds, allergies, to ease the itch from insect bites or stings or to help prevent motion sickness
- Antiseptic – mercurochrome and antibiotic powder or similar 'dry' spray – for cuts and grazes
- Aspirin or Panadol – for pain or fever
- Bandages and Band-aids – for minor injuries

- Calamine lotion – to ease irritation from bites or stings
- Kaolin preparation (Pepto-Bismol), Imodium or Lomotil – for stomach upsets
- Rehydration mixture – for dehydration, especially that caused by severe diarrhoea
- Scissors, tweezers and a thermometer (note that mercury thermometers are prohibited by airlines)
- Sunscreen, insect repellent and water purification tablets.

You'll need to give careful thought to your medical kit if you plan to get off the beaten track. The further you get from the towns, in general, the further you will be from medical help. PNG has an impressive system where health workers live in the villages, but there is a shortage of trained people and even if you do find someone, the facilities and drugs they have are often very limited. Take medical advice and do some research on how to treat yourself if you are going to be isolated for any length of time. If you have access to a travellers' medical clinic, use it rather than a general practitioner, and buy a good book. You should be in a position to treat malaria, dysentery, lacerations (it's not hard to hurt yourself with a machete), sprains (it's very rugged country), insect and snake bites (some are highly venomous) and respiratory diseases (colds and even pneumonia are common in the Highlands).

Medical Problems & Treatment
Potential medical problems can be broken down into several areas. First there are the climatic and geographical considerations. Then there are diseases and illnesses caused by insanitation, insect bites or stings, and animal or human contact. Simple cuts, bites or scratches can also cause problems.

Self-diagnosis and treatment can be risky, so wherever possible seek qualified help. Although we do give treatment dosages in this section, they are for emergency use only. Medical advice should be sought before administering any drugs.

Climatic & Geographical Considerations
Sunburn Beware of the tropical sun! Wear a hat that is broad enough to shade the back

of your neck (especially if you're in a boat or a canoe), try to keep your skin covered and apply liberal quantities of an effective sunscreen. Sunglasses are also a good idea, especially if you're on the water.

The sun can be deceptive. If it is overcast you can still get burnt; if you are at any decent altitude (anywhere in the Highlands) you have less atmospheric protection and the fact that you're not hot does not mean you're not cooking. Snorkelling can result in fiendish sunburn. Wear a T-shirt and smother the back of your legs, especially the top of your thighs, with sunblock.

Prickly Heat You may be unlucky enough to suffer from prickly heat when you first arrive. Sweat droplets are trapped under the skin (because your pores aren't able to cope with the volume of water) forming many tiny blisters. Anything that makes you sweat makes it worse. Calamine lotion or zinc-oxide based talcum powder will give some relief but, apart from that, all you can do is take it easy for a few days until you acclimatise.

Heat Exhaustion Make sure you drink enough – don't rely on feeling thirsty to indicate when you should drink. Not needing to urinate or very dark yellow urine is a danger sign. Always carry a water bottle with you on long trips. Excessive sweating can lead to loss of salt and therefore muscle cramping, but taking salt tablets is not a good idea – just add some to your food if you think you're not getting enough.

Dehydration or salt deficiency can cause heat exhaustion. Take time to acclimatise to high temperatures and make sure you get sufficient liquids. Vomiting or diarrhoea further deplete your liquid and salt levels.

Heat Stroke Heat stroke is a serious, sometimes fatal, condition which occurs when the body's heat-regulating mechanism breaks down and the body temperature rises to dangerous levels. Long, continuous periods of exposure to high temperatures can leave you vulnerable to heat stroke. Avoid excessive alcohol or strenuous activity when you first arrive in a hot climate.

The symptoms of heat stroke are feeling unwell, not sweating very much or at all and a high body temperature (39°C to 41°C). Where sweating has ceased the skin becomes flushed and red. Severe, throbbing headaches and lack of coordination will also occur, and the sufferer may be confused or aggressive. Eventually the victim will become delirious or convulse. Hospitalisation is essential, but meanwhile get patients out of the sun, remove their clothing, cover them with a wet sheet or towel and then fan continually.

Fungal Infections Hot weather fungal infections are most likely to occur on the scalp, between the toes or fingers (athlete's foot), in the groin (jock itch or crotch rot) and on the body (ringworm). You get ringworm (which is a fungal infection, not a worm) from infected animals or by walking on damp areas, like shower floors.

To prevent fungal infections wear loose, comfortable clothes, avoid artificial fibres, wash frequently and dry carefully. If you do get an infection, wash the infected area daily with a disinfectant or medicated soap and water, and rinse and dry well. Apply an antifungal powder. Try to expose the infected area to air or sunlight as much as possible and wash all towels and underwear in hot water as well as changing them often.

Cold Not only do you have to worry about getting too hot, but also about getting too cold! Admittedly this is only relevant if you plan to climb the mountains, but if you do, you must be prepared to cope with extreme weather conditions. Even snow is possible on Mt Wilhelm, although that might be preferable to the more likely fog and rain.

Hypothermia (otherwise known as exposure) is a quick and effective killer and once again prevention is better than cure. It's deceptively easy to fall victim to hypothermia through a combination of wind, wet clothing, fatigue and hunger, even if the air temperature is well above freezing. Hypothermia's symptoms include a loss of rationality so people can fail to recognise their own condition and the seriousness of their predicament.

Symptoms are exhaustion, numb skin (particularly toes and fingers), shivering, slurred speech, irrational or violent behaviour, lethargy, stumbling, dizzy spells, muscle cramps and violent bursts of energy. Anticipate the problem if you're cold and tired, and recognise the symptoms early. Immediate care is important since hypothermia can kill its victims in as little as two hours.

First, find shelter from the wind and rain, remove wet clothing and replace with warm dry clothing. The patient should drink hot liquids (*not* alcohol, which can quickly kill the hypothermic patient) and eat some high calorie, easily digestible food. These measures will usually correct the problem if symptoms have been recognised early. In more severe cases it may be necessary to place the patient in a sleeping bag insulated from the ground, with another person if possible, while he/she is fed warm food and hot drinks.

Do *not* rub the patient, place him/her near a fire, try to give an unconscious patient food or drink, remove wet clothes in the wind, or give alcohol.

Altitude Sickness Although you are more likely to be affected by altitude in the Himalaya or the Andes it is quite possible to be affected on a number of PNG's mountains.

Mountain Sickness, Soroche, Altitude Sickness, Acute Mountain Sickness (AMS) – whatever you call it – can in extreme cases be fatal. In all probability however, you will only be lightly affected, although some travellers have experienced real trouble on Mt Wilhelm. You can't predict your susceptibility.

AMS starts to become noticeable at around 3000 metres, becomes pronounced at 3700 metres, and then requires adjustments at each 500 metres of additional elevation after that. The summit of Mt Wilhelm is over 4500 metres high, so if you make a sudden ascent from Lae to Kegsugl, by PMV or plane, and then commence the climb without

giving your body a couple of days to adjust to the new altitudes you are likely to make the expedition unnecessarily difficult, even dangerous. Your body has to undergo a physiological change to absorb more oxygen from the rarefied air and this takes time.

Mild symptoms can be expected over 3000 metres, including headaches and weakness; loss of appetite; shortness of breath; insomnia, often accompanied by irregular breathing; mild nausea; a dry cough; slight loss of co-ordination; and a puffy face or hands in the morning. If you experience a few of these symptoms you probably have a mild case of altitude sickness which should pass. Rest (perhaps for a day or so) until the symptoms subside but if the symptoms become more severe or do not improve you may have to descend to a lower altitude. Monitor your condition carefully and realistically. Increasing tiredness, confusion, and lack of coordination and balance are real danger signs. Any of these symptoms individually, even just a persistent headache, can be a warning.

The only cure for AMS is immediate descent to lower altitudes. When any combination of these severe symptoms occur, the afflicted person should descend 300 to 1000 metres *immediately*, the distance increasing with the severity of the symptoms. When trekking, such a descent may even have to take place at night (responding quickly is vital), and the disabled person should be accompanied by someone in good condition. There's no cure for AMS except descending to lower altitudes, but a pain-killer for headaches and an anti-emetic for vomiting will help relieve the symptoms.

Diseases of Insanitation
Diarrhoea & Dysentery Although these problems are not nearly as severe in PNG as in some of the neighbouring Asian countries it is likely you'll get some kind of diarrhoea when you first arrive. This is the normal lot of travellers whose bodies are adapting to strange food and water and you'll probably recover quickly.

Food, at least in the main cities, is generally problem-free and town water is drinkable. If you plan to rough it in the bush, consider taking some kind of vitamin and mineral tablets to supplement your diet of sago and sweet potato. Outside the towns you are wise to be wary of the water, unless you're sure you know its history. Until you are very high in the mountains, the crystal-clear stream that looks so inviting is likely to have gone through several backyards! Take water purification tablets, preferably iodine based, as the iodine is effective against cysts and other resilient nasties. It doesn't taste great, but that's a small price to pay.

Avoid rushing off to the pharmacy and filling yourself with antibiotics at the first signs of a problem. The best thing to do is eat nothing and rest, avoid travelling and drink plenty of liquid (black tea or sterile water). About 24 to 48 hours should do the trick. If you really can't cope with starving, keep to a diet of yoghurt, boiled vegetables, apples and apple juice. After a severe bout of diarrhoea or dysentery you will be dehydrated and this often causes painful cramps. Relieve these by drinking fruit juices or tea into which a small spoonful of salt has been dissolved; maintaining a correct balance of salt in your bloodstream is important.

If starving doesn't work or if you really have to move on and can't rest, there is a range of drugs available. Lomotil is probably one of the best, though it has come under fire recently in medical literature. The dosage is two tablets, three times a day for two days. If you can't find Lomotil, then try Pesulin or Pesulin-O (the latter includes tincture of opium). The dosage is two teaspoons, four times daily for five days.

Ordinary traveller's diarrhoea rarely lasts more than about three days. If it lasts for more than a week you must get treatment, move on to antibiotics, or see a doctor.

There are two types of dysentery: bacillary, the most common, which is acute and rarely persists; and amoebic, persistent and more difficult to treat. Both are characterised by very liquid faeces containing blood and/or excessive amounts of mucus.

Bacillary dysentery attacks suddenly and is accompanied by fever, nausea and painful muscular spasms. Often it responds well to antibiotics or other specific drugs. Amoebic dysentery builds up more slowly, but is more dangerous, so get it treated as soon as possible. See a doctor. In an emergency, note that tetracycline is the prescribed treatment for bacillary dysentery, metronidazole (Flagyl) for amoebic dysentery.

Giardia This intestinal parasite is present in contaminated water. The symptoms are stomach cramps, nausea, a bloated stomach, watery, foul-smelling diarrhoea and frequent gas. Giardia can appear several weeks after you have been exposed to the parasite. The symptoms may disappear for a few days and then return; this can go on for several weeks. Metronidazole (Flagyl) is the recommended drug, but it should only be taken under medical supervision. Antibiotics are of no use.

Worms These parasites are most common in rural, tropical areas and a stool test when you return home is not a bad idea. They can be present on unwashed vegetables or in undercooked meat and you can pick them up through your skin by walking in bare feet. Infestations may not show up for some time, and although they are generally not serious, if left untreated they can cause severe health problems. A stool test is necessary to pinpoint the problem and medication is often available over the counter.

Diseases Spread by People & Animals
Tetanus This potentially fatal disease, also known as lockjaw, is difficult to treat but is preventable with immunisation. Tetanus occurs when a wound becomes infected by a germ which lives in the faeces of animals or people, so clean all cuts, punctures or animal bites. The first symptom may be discomfort in swallowing, or stiffening of the jaw and neck; this is followed by painful convulsions of the jaw and whole body.

Rabies Rabies is present in PNG but is not at all common. Nevertheless, avoid being bitten or even licked by an animal. If you are, wash and sterilise the site, and if there's a possibility that the animal might be rabid, get help fast.

Sexually Transmitted Diseases PNG might be one of the world's last untouched countries, but AIDS and other STDs are present. Take precautions.

Insect-Borne Diseases

Malaria The most serious health risk in PNG is malaria. It virtually wiped out the early German attempts at colonising the north coast and it's still a very serious problem. Although it is the isolated villagers who suffer the most, the disease kills quite indiscriminately and, sometimes, in spite of medical care.

Prevention is simply a matter of taking a regular dose of the anti-malarial drugs you are prescribed, however malaria has shown a frightening capacity to mutate drug-resistant strains. PNG is now host to malarial strains that can cause cerebral malaria and are resistant to Chloroquine, the most popular anti-malarial drug. Tell your doctor where you are going and he/she will probably prescribe Maloprim, in addition to Chloroquine, unless there is a specific contraindication. Larium is a new drug which is apparently effective against malaria strains in PNG. It's expensive (A$7 for a weekly tablet) but that's cheap compared to what malaria might do to you. You will have no problems getting the appropriate drugs in PNG but the course of medication must be started some weeks before you arrive and continued after you leave.

Fansidar is not recommended. Aside from being dangerous in its own right (it is actually banned as a preventive measure in some parts of the world due to its side effects) it is also used as a last-ditch cure. If a Fansidar-resistant strain develops, a prospect that becomes more likely the more indiscriminately it is used, many people will die.

Whatever prophylactic you use, the only sure way to avoid malaria is to avoid being bitten (yes, this is a bit like a safe-sex pamphlet). Repellent, nets, trousers and long sleeves can all help. The most important time to keep covered is in the evenings and early morning.

Most people who live in PNG for more than a few years come down with malaria, so getting the proper diagnosis and treatment (essential to avoid dangerous complications) is not difficult in towns, but if you're planning to be out of touch for a while you should talk to a doctor about diagnosing and treating yourself.

Prompt diagnosis and treatment could be a problem if you develop headaches and fever after you return home, where you might be told to go away and take a couple of aspirin. If this happens, get a second opinion – fast!

Dengue Fever Dengue fever, also carried by mosquitoes, is another PNG health danger.

There is no prophylactic available for this mosquito-spread disease; the main preventative measure is to avoid mosquito bites. A sudden onset of fever, headaches and severe joint and muscle pains are the first signs before a rash starts on the trunk of the body and spreads to the limbs and face. After a further few days, the fever will subside and recovery will begin. Serious complications are not common.

Cuts, Bites & Stings

PNG isn't a particularly dirty country but it is in the tropics so you should take care that cuts and insect bites don't become infected, otherwise you risk tropical ulcers. These nasty, weeping sores are very difficult to get rid of once they take hold. You might need a course of penicillin.

The number one rule is not to scratch insect bites. That will require a superhuman will if you have been bitten by sandflies and are allergic to them, as many people are. The bastards are tiny and you often don't know you've been bitten until the next day, when an itchiness unlike anything you've ever imagined descends on you. It can cause you a couple of sleepless nights. To make matters worse, sandfly bites often produce tiny sores and if you scratch off the minute scabs they almost invariably become infected. Sand-flies hang out on beaches, but not all beaches, so ask around.

Coral cuts are notoriously slow to heal, as the coral injects a weak venom into the wound. Avoid coral cuts by wearing shoes when walking on reefs, and clean any cut thoroughly. Coral might also cause an existing cut to become infected.

Take some antiseptic powder (better than ointment in a hot, humid climate) to keep cuts clean, and antibiotic powder can stop infections.

Snakes Nearly a hundred different species of snakes are found in PNG but very few of them are dangerous, despite the general hysteria which greets the arrival of any snake in a village.

Trekkers are at risk of being bitten, but it's very unlikely. Most snakes are not aggressive and the sound of you gummocking through the bush should effectively clear the path. Wearing thick socks and being careful stepping over rocks or logs are wise precautions, however. Don't put your hand into holes and be careful when collecting firewood.

If someone is bitten, note that the old treatments of sucking the site and applying a tourniquet are now definitely out. A very tight bandage should be wrapped around the bitten limb, and the patient kept as calm and still as possible – don't carry or, worse, walk him/her to a possible source of medical assistance. Theoretically, immobilisation slows the entry of the poison into the bloodstream to a rate where the body can cope with it.

Jellyfish Local advice is the best way of avoiding contact with these sea creatures with their stinging tentacles. Dousing in vinegar will de-activate any stingers which have not 'fired'. Calamine lotion, antihistamines and analgesics may reduce the reaction and relieve the pain. Spines from sea-urchins can cause deep, painful and easily infected wounds. Take care when walking in water.

Leeches & Ticks Leeches may be present in damp rainforest conditions; they attach themselves to your skin to suck your blood. Trekkers often get them on their legs or in their boots. Salt or a lighted cigarette end will make them fall off. Do not pull them off, as the bite is then more likely to become infected. An insect repellent may keep them away. You should always check your body if you have been walking through a tick-infested area, as they can spread typhus. Vaseline, alcohol or oil will persuade a tick to let go – don't pull them off.

Women's Health

Gynaecological Problems Poor diet, lowered resistance due to the use of antibiotics for stomach upsets and even contraceptive pills can lead to vaginal infections when travelling in hot climates. Keeping the genital area clean, and wearing skirts or loose-fitting trousers and cotton underwear will help to prevent infections.

Yeast infections, characterised by a rash, itch and discharge, can be treated with a vinegar or even lemon-juice douche or with yoghurt. Nystatin suppositories are the usual medical prescription. Trichomonas is a more serious infection; symptoms are a discharge and a burning sensation when urinating. Male sexual partners must also be treated, and if a vinegar-water douche is not effective medical attention should be sought. Flagyl is the prescribed drug.

Pregnancy Most miscarriages occur during the first three months of pregnancy, so this is the most risky time to travel. The last three months should also be spent within reasonable distance of good medical care, as quite serious problems can develop at this time. Pregnant women should avoid all unnecessary medication, but vaccinations and malarial prophylactics should still be taken where possible – ask a doctor. Additional care should be taken to prevent illness and particular attention should be paid to diet and nutrition.

SAFETY

This section on safety is much larger than is usual in Lonely Planet guides, and is a response to fears generated by the bad press that PNG gets, especially in Australia. It's true that travellers are robbed, occasionally with violence, and there have been rapes, but PNG is not the acutely dangerous place it is painted as long as you listen to local advice and, above all, make friends with people who live in the area you are visiting.

One big plus about PNG is that the usual Third-World nightmare of hurtling along in a totally unroadworthy bus with a maniac at the wheel doesn't apply. Most public transport is in reasonable condition and most drivers are aware of the payback and compensation problems they would have if they hit anything – even a chicken or a dog – or injured one of their passengers.

Another plus is that you don't have to fear corrupt and violent authorities.

Background

On the rare occasions when PNG is featured in the outside world's news media, it is likely to be a sensationalist report about some kind of violence. As a result of these reports and the foggy, often inaccurate notions many people have of the past (featuring fierce, head-hunting warriors), PNG is often unjustifiably classified as an extremely unsafe country.

You will get your first taste of these attitudes when you tell your friends your planned destination: 'You're going *where*?' You will get your second taste when you get to Port Moresby, where houses are barricaded like you've never seen them before, and start talking to expats. Everyone will have a favourite gruesome story they will want to tell you. Do not be deterred! If you take reasonable care and use a bit of common sense, you are most unlikely to experience anything other than tremendous friendliness and hospitality.

The expats with the worst stories seem to be the ones who have been in the country only a short time and plan to leave before long. Expats who have been in PNG for years and who have some sort of commitment to the country (such as a spouse and children) are much more relaxed.

You will certainly not get an arrow in the back or have your head hunted. Even looked at historically, this should be seen in perspective.

In the early days of colonisation the local people were fighting white invaders who were often very unsavoury characters. The Highlands were still being opened up in the '50s and until that time there was no indigenous concept of a large Western-style nation; each tribe was, in effect, a sovereign state so its relations with its neighbours or the white invaders were 'foreign affairs'. And foreign affairs often became warfare, although never on a scale to match the conflicts most countries in Europe have witnessed.

Payback squabbles, land disputes and the like, can still develop into full-scale tribal wars, but they are confined to the direct participants.

I heard a reliable story of fighting stopping so a tour group could cross a battlefield, and many expats will tell you of battles they have watched from close at hand. These are not exploits I would recommend unless you are very confident that you know what you are doing, but all reports suggest that as long as you don't put yourself in the firing line at the wrong time (and this will be quite obvious, one way or another) you will be left alone as a complete irrelevance!

In common with many other countries, it is often not safe to wander around at night and this is doubly the case for women. It should be noted that crime is in no way race related and that relations between different nationalities are remarkably good.

Women Travellers

Women should always dress conservatively, even when swimming. Outside the resorts, bikinis do not provide sufficient cover – a laplap (sarong) can come in handy as a wrap. Take your cue from the local women – sometimes you'll notice them washing *fully* clothed. Whether on a beach or in a city, lone women should restrict their movements to

Top Left: Lower montane forest flower (YP)
Bottom Left: Hornbill (AJ)
Top Right: Butterfly (TW)
Bottom Right: Tree Kangaroo (JM)

areas where there are other people around and never go off by themselves.

In many ways Papua New Guinean women have a very hard time and this does affect the situation for visitors. Except in the cities, women are almost always subservient to men and physical abuse is common – the government feels it necessary to produce brochure entitled 'Wife-beating is illegal'. In many parts of the country a women never initiates a conversation with a man, never talks to a male outside her family, never eats at the same table as men, never even sleeps in the same house as any man, including her father or husband.

A lone, Western female traveller has no local parallels and, to a certain extent, a special case will be made of her. Virtually throughout the country, however, it will be difficult for women to have a normal conversation with a man without being misinterpreted as a flirt. Similarly, but in reverse, a Western man who attempts to initiate a conversation with a Papua New Guinean woman can cause embarrassment and confusion.

Public displays of affection are almost unknown, and a Western couple making physical contact in public – even holding hands – is regarded as an oddity and, especially in traditional rural societies, may be regarded with contempt. This can put the woman in danger.

Despite the obvious difficulties, we have received a number of letters from women who have clearly enjoyed travelling around by themselves. And throughout the country you'll find women working as administrators, entrepreneurs, pilots, teachers, nurses, missionaries, adventure travel tour guides, etc, so it definitely can be done! Nevertheless, I would recommend that women do not travel alone in PNG, especially if they haven't travelled before in a highly sexist society.

Many places have women's groups (which sometimes have guesthouses) and these are good places to find out about women's lives in PNG, and to see what is being done to help alleviate their problems.

Note that the Country Women's Association (CWA), which also has guesthouses, is a local branch of a venerable Australian institution, not a grassroots PNG organisation.

Tips

You have to be careful, but without becoming paranoid! Make friends with Papua New Guineans, don't close yourself off. Not only will this add to your enjoyment, but also to your security – you will be identified with a local and have access to first-hand advice and information. There are few places in the world where a smile and a greeting (*Moning*, *Apinun*) are so well received.

You cannot afford to be entirely naive about your popularity, however, because you may well be regarded as a potential source of status, or even wealth. How do you judge whether someone is sincere, or up to no good? There's no easy answer, but you do have to be sceptical and you do have to use your brains. Even if you do decide that someone is all right, don't put yourself in a vulnerable position until you have more than a first impression to go on.

It's not worth considering walking around a big town at night. Even in a group you are vulnerable and there's just no point. There is nothing to see or do on the streets. If you plan to go out to a restaurant or club, catch the last PMV, which normally runs sometime between 6 and 6.30 pm, and get a lift (easy to arrange) or a taxi home. It's worth being especially careful on the fortnightly Friday pay nights – things can get pretty wild.

Take precautions such as concealing some emergency cash and making sure your travellers' cheque numbers are written down somewhere safe. One traveller wrote that while his pack was stolen in a PMV hold-up, a dirty old billum (string bag) he had wasn't touched. You can insure your camera, but not your precious exposed films, so think about mailing film home or to a secure address within PNG. If you lose anything, especially in rural areas, it's worth hanging around for a few days and letting it be widely known that you will offer a reward for the return of your stuff. This probably won't help to get

---

Travellers' Experiences

We have *never* had any problems anywhere in the country and while researching this edition I met only one traveller (as opposed to often-burgled expats) who had been robbed by a Papua New Guinean – two others were robbed by an American! Here are some travellers' comments:

Everywhere I went I met friendly people. I was always the only white person on board PMVs yet people would offer me food and go out of their way to be helpful. I was even invited to spend the night in someone's home in Goroka. Walking along the road to Baiyer River, I had a bloke run up to me and hand me a pineapple. Coming in to Lae after dark, the PMV drove me to the door of the friends with whom I was staying. Meeting people like that, even if I couldn't talk to many of them, really was the high point of my visit to PNG.

As our PMV came around the corner we saw that the road was blocked by a tree, and painted warriors carrying axes ran down the hill towards us. Everyone began to panic, but the warriors stopped and looked sheepish. They had been expecting a police vehicle, and they let us pass and went back to their hiding places. Quite a relief, but on the other hand, someone told me that the reason they wanted to ambush the police was that the police had burned down their village – as punishment for holding up a PMV...

Our PMV was stopped by a big group of men and boys, all carrying what appeared to be weapons. They demanded money from our driver and eventually we got through. However, it wasn't highway robbery but free enterprise. The road was blocked by a bogged truck and people from a nearby village had dug a diversion into the hillside. They were charging a toll for the use of their road. ■

---

you your walkperson back, but your passport and tickets might turn up.

Everything is saner and better away from the towns – the people are friendlier and there are considerably fewer problems. If you are staying in villages, stay with a family rather than in an empty haus tambaran or haus kiap. It's safer and more fun.

In most cases, you'll also be much better off with a guide who speaks the *ples tok* (local language). You won't be so likely to get lost, the guide will know when and who to ask for the various permissions you will need (to camp, to cross someone's land, etc) and you'll have automatic introductions to local people. If you are looking for a guide, start by asking around for someone reliable at missions, government offices, schools or trade stores. Whatever your plans, talk to as many people as you can and listen to their advice.

You are most unlikely to have any trouble from other passengers on a PMV – they're more likely to share their food with you. It isn't particularly common, but there are pickpockets and bag snatchers, so be a little cautious in crowded places like PMVs, bus stops and markets. Don't ever leave valuables unattended in any public place.

The so-called rascal problem is not just one problem and it flares in different areas for different, often predictable, reasons. Port Moresby and Lae are likely to remain dangerous because of the continuing influx of unemployed young men. The same applies to most other large towns. Mt Hagen has this problem, with added trouble because it's the main centre of the volatile Highlands region (people go to town to settle paybacks) and workers from the various mines spend their paychecks there. Most other Highland towns are also edgy. Don't travel after dark in the Highlands. Catch PMVs early in the morning so you will reach your destination in daylight, with plenty of time to get your bearings and find somewhere to sleep before dark. Enga Province sees a lot of tribal fighting and is relatively unsafe.

PMVs are regularly held-up on the Wewak-Maprik road. The Wau area, because of unemployment caused by the closure of a big mine, had a lot of robberies but the situation seems to be settling. Rascals were rampant in Oro Province but in 1992 most of the rascal gangs surrendered in return for some pretty vague promises by politicians. Whether the peace holds remains to be seen.

The safest areas of the country are Milne Bay Province (although yam festival time in the Trobriands can be hectic), New Britain,

New Ireland and Manus provinces. Remember, though, that you can get into trouble anywhere in the world, and that even in the most dangerous areas of PNG most travellers *don't* have trouble.

ACTIVITIES
Bushwalking
For detailed information on walks and walking see the Lonely Planet book *Bushwalking in Papua New Guinea*. Considering the vast areas of rugged, mountainous terrain where the only way to get from village to village is to fly or walk, it is surprising that bushwalking in PNG has not caught on the same way trekking has in the Himalaya.

Some of the walks are tough but, especially on the coast, it's possible to avoid the very steep ascents and descents characteristic of trails in PNG.

Once you're out in the bush you'll find that your expenses plummet. Your major costs will be paying for guides and porters, where they are necessary. Expect to pay a guide between K5 and K10 a day (more like K20 on Kokoda) and a porter about K5 (up to K10 on Kokoda). You'll also have to provide or pay for their food and possibly some equipment.

The best-known walking track in PNG is the Kokoda Trail but there are literally hundreds of other lesser known, but even more interesting walks. The whole country is criss-crossed with tracks, and in most parts of the country there is rarely more than a day's walk between villages. There really is no limit to the alternatives. Listed below are some of the more interesting walks; you'll find others covered in various places throughout this book.

Kokoda Trail (five to seven days) This is a difficult walk over the mountainous spine between the north and south coasts. The trail follows the route that was taken by the Japanese after they landed on the north coast. After almost reaching Port Moresby, they were driven back by Australian and American troops in some of the most bitter fighting

of the war. There are relatively few villages and it isn't a particularly interesting walk from a cultural point of view, but the country is superb and getting from one end to another is a feat to be proud of.

The trail provides an important alternative to flying, as there are no roads between Port Moresby and the north coast or the Highlands. There are other less well-known possibilities, but this is the route most travellers use. See the Port Moresby & Central Province chapter.

Lake Kopiago to Oksapmin (three to four days) This is an extremely difficult but particularly interesting walk. Starting at the very end of the Highlands Highway you cross the Strickland River's spectacular gorge. It is possible to continue on to Telefomin and this would take another six to eight days. From Telefomin you can catch planes to places in the Sepik Basin like April River. See the Highlands chapter.

Mt Wilhelm (three to four days) Mt Wilhelm is the tallest mountain in PNG, and at 4509 metres, it's a serious mountain by any standards. No technical climbing is required and anyone with reasonable fitness should be able to make the summit, if the conditions allow. It can be very cold and even snow on top, and at the higher levels climbers are vulnerable to altitude sickness. The climb is highly recommended; not only do you see traditional Simbu villages on your way to the mountain, but the views from the top are spectacular. See the Highlands chapter.

Mt Wilhelm to Madang (three days) A relatively easy way of getting between the Highlands and the north coast is to follow a 4WD track which takes off the main Mt Wilhelm road just before Kegsugl and goes through Bundi and on to Brahman where, with a bit of luck, you'll find a PMV to Madang. See the Highlands chapter.

Nipa to Lake Kutubu (three to four days) The lodge at Lake Kutubu is one of the better places to stay in PNG. Although you can fly most of the way (from Mendi to Pimaga), it is well worth considering the walk, which goes through a beautiful part of the Southern Highlands, at least one way. See the Highlands chapter.

Wau to Salamaua (three days) This is a fairly tough walk. It is an interesting alternative to the common air hop between Port Moresby and Lae. Wau is in the mountains and is home to the Wau Ecology Institute and Salamaua is a coastal village south of Lae. You could fly from Port Moresby to Wau, spend some time around Wau, walk to Salamaua, relax there, then catch a boat (or walk along the coast) to Lae.

Wedau to Alotau (three to four days) This coastal walk is more a way to cut down on costs, do some swimming and snorkelling and experience village life than a tough slog through the jungle. You don't have to be particularly fit (there is a scramble over a mountain on the last day) and if you find that you're in no hurry to finish, you can extend the walk by another few days. See the Milne Bay Province chapter.

Woitape to Tapini (three days) This is an interesting walk and there are airports at both places and a road runs to Fane, near Woitape. See the Port Moresby & Central Province chapter.

A number of companies offer organised treks. They're not cheap, but they are worth considering if you have limited time. It's hard to guarantee itineraries at the best of times in PNG, but professional companies will probably have a better chance of sticking to them than you will. Some of them also go to places you would be hard pushed to reach yourself, even if you did find out they existed. For addresses see the end of this section.

River Journeys

PNG has some of the world's largest, most spectacular rivers. The Sepik is often compared to the Amazon and the Congo rivers, and the Sepik Basin is an artistic and cultural treasure house.

There are a number of rivers that local people use as 'highways'. These include the Sepik and some of its tributaries (including the April, May and Keram), the Ramu, the Fly and a number of other rivers that flow into the Gulf of Papua. Local people can travel by river between the Irian Jaya border and, virtually, Madang, using the Sepik, Keram and Ramu. On these rivers there is often an assortment of different craft, ranging from dugout canoes to tramp steamers.

If you do want to spend time on a river, there are a number of possibilities: you can buy your own canoe and paddle yourself; you can use 'PMV' boats (unscheduled, inter-village, motorised, dugout canoes); you can charter a motorised canoe and guide/driver when you get to the river; you can go on tours of varying degrees of comfort; and you can sail in a cruise ship with all mod-cons.

All the following options are discussed in some detail in the Sepik chapter.

Canoeing It is possible to buy dugout canoes to paddle yourself. Paddling downstream is the only viable possibility. Accommodation and food are normally available in the villages – meaning floor space in a longhouse and sago and smoked fish in the stomach. In order to survive this happily you have to be prepared to rough it, and be reasonably fit, independent and well equipped. Once you're actually afloat you'll spend very little money, although it is important to pay your way.

This kind of travel is most popular on the Sepik (a few hundred people a year go on these trips) because the reasonably dense population and the fascinating art and culture means there are interesting villages at regular intervals. The river and its flood plain is so large it is not particularly interesting paddling, however, so it is worth considering one of the tributaries.

Motorised Canoes Another alternative, if you are prepared to rough it and live in the villages, is going along as a passenger in an inter-village motorised canoe. The problem with this is that although they are relatively cheap they only run according to demand – there are no schedules. Traffic builds up between Wednesday and Saturday because of people moving around to get to markets, but can be very quiet early in the week and nonexistent on Sundays. Using this method you need plenty of time and patience.

If you are short of time, you can charter a motorised canoe and driver locally. This is, however, very expensive: probably up to K20 per hour of running time (due to the high cost of operating two-stroke engines).

Several Sepik village entrepreneurs are now offering packages of three to five days (or whatever you want) for around K65 a day, including transport, food, accommodation, admittance to haus tambaran, photo fees, etc. These guys tend to be the best guides. There are definite advantages to having a decent guide on the Sepik; you will inevitably miss places, people and things without someone to lead the way, introduce you and explain. See the Sepik chapter for some recommended guides, some of whom can be booked from outside PNG.

The larger tour companies also offer Sepik trips which vary considerably in the degree of luxury they offer. Some are luxuriously based at the Karawari Lodge (eg Trans Niugini Tours), while some are based in the villages (for example, Traditional Travel).

River Boats There are alternatives if you prefer to have something more substantial than a canoe beneath you. Unfortunately, there are no longer regular passenger-carrying cargo boats on the Sepik, but you might get lucky.

The Ok-Tedi mine site near the Irian Jaya border is serviced by barges on the Fly that take ore down to a ship moored off the coast. You may, if you're lucky, be able to get a ride from Daru or Port Moresby to the ship and then a ride on a barge.

Melanesian Tourist Services runs a luxurious cruise boat, the *Melanesian Discoverer*, from Madang to Green River, stopping off in the villages along the way. Trans Niugini Tours has the smaller but also up-market *Sepik Spirit* cruising the Sepik, and Tribal World is planning a less fancy (and less expensive) vessel.

River Rafting Shooting down PNG's turbulent mountain rivers in inflatable dinghies is a sport still in its infancy, but one that has tremendous potential. Not only is rafting great fun, but you also get to see some spectacular country from an unusual perspective. There don't seem to be any regular trips operating from within PNG, but foreign adventure tour operators (such as Raging Thunder in Australia) sometimes have them on their itinerary.

Sea Journeys

If you don't own your own cruising yacht (and when you see PNG's islands and harbours you will wish you did), there are four alternatives left to you: use the regular coastal shipping, take a tour, charter a boat or crew a yacht. All these options are covered in the Getting Around chapter.

Scheduled passenger boats run only between Oro Bay (near Popondetta in Oro

Province) and Wewak, and between Lae and New Britain. There are also some passenger carrying freighters, again only on the north coast and around the islands. However, with time, ingenuity and luck you can travel anywhere by boat.

Traditional Travel sail *wahagas* (traditional outrigger dugouts about 10 metres long) around the untouched islands of the Louisiade Archipelago.

With a dense scattering of beautiful islands, PNG is a great place for sea kayaking. The only company I know which offers regular trips is Raging Thunder in Australia.

Diving

Diving is one of the fastest growing attractions in PNG. If the experts can be believed, this is because PNG is at least the equal of diving meccas like the Red Sea, the Caribbean and the Great Barrier Reef.

Going to PNG and not looking under the water would be like going to Nepal and not looking at the mountains! Snorkelling is the cheapest and easiest way, but there are also a number of dive operators who offer courses, equipment and tours.

There are plenty of excellent places to dive and there is a lot to see. The coast is surrounded by coral reefs, and many are easily accessible to snorkellers. There is, in general, excellent visibility, an abundance of reef and pelagic fish, dramatic drop offs, shells, and soft and hard corals. Those who like diving on wrecks will find the reefs are liberally dotted with sunken ships – either as a result of the reefs or of WW II.

Kavieng New Ireland's excellent diving has as yet attracted little attention. Telita Cruises, based in Milne Bay, cruises here several months of the year. There is also a local operator to contact:

Kavieng Hotel
    PO Box 4, Kavieng, New Ireland, PNG (☎ 94 2199, fax 94 2283)

Kimbe Diving in East New Britain has many people raving about excellent visibility, vol-

canic caves draped in staghorn coral, dramatic drop-offs, sharks, turtles and more. The only operator is based at the Walindi Plantation Resort; the resort is on a huge oil palm plantation, fringed by volcanic mountains and a beautiful bay.

Walindi Diving
    PO Box 4, Kimbe, West New Britain, PNG (☎ 93 5441, fax 93 5638)

Lae Yet another good area.

Niugini Diving
    PO Box 320, Lae, PNG (☎ 42 5692)

Lorengau There are some extremely interesting dives off the barely explored coast of Manus Island.

Ron Knight
    PO Box 108, Lorengau, Manus, PNG (☎ 40 9159, fax 40 9285)

Madang This is probably the most popular location for divers, in probably the most tourist-oriented PNG city. Diving is good all year round. There are superb dives close to town, and Hansa Bay, the resting place for at least 34 Japanese ships, is within striking distance up the coast. All the ships lie in shallow water (less than 25 metres) and are now covered in corals and fish.

Coastwatcher's Motel
    PO Box 324, Madang, PNG (☎ 82 2684, fax 82 2716)
Jais Aben Resort
    PO Box 105, Madang, PNG (☎ 82 3311, fax 82 3560)
Malolo Plantation Resort
    Contact Trans Niugini Tours
Niugini Diving Adventures
    Contact Melanesian Tourist Services

Milne Bay Another superb diving location, with wrecks, reefs and the possibility of whales. Both operators here offer charters and cruises rather than day dives, but you might be able to negotiate something, especially as both have recently added new boats to their fleets.

Milne Bay Marine Charters
    PO Box 176, Alotau, Milne Bay, PNG (☎ 61 1167, fax 61 1291)
Telita Cruises
    PO Box 303, Alotau, Milne Bay, PNG (☎ 61 1186, fax 61 1282)

Port Moresby When people talk about the dry and dusty capital they usually omit to say that there is a magnificent deep-water harbour ringed with coral reefs and dotted with islands. The best diving is in April and May, and between November and January.

The Dive Shop/Diveco
    PO Box 2799, Boroko, NCD, Port Moresby, PNG (☎ 25 4418, fax 25 4466)
Loloata Island Resort
    PO Box 5290, Boroko, NCD, PNG (☎ 25 8590, fax 25 8933)
Tropical Diving Services
    PO Box 1745, Port Moresby, PNG (☎ 21 1768)

Rabaul Built around the massive, flooded caldera of an ancient volcano, Rabaul was a major Japanese base; there are no fewer than 104 diveable war wrecks in the harbour. Visibility is excellent and diving is good all year.

Dive Rabaul
    PO Box 65, Rabaul, East New Britain, PNG (☎ 92 7222, fax 92 4726)
Rabaul Dive Centre
    PO Box 400, Rabaul, East New Britain, East New Britain, PNG (☎ 92 1100)

Wuvulu Island This is acclaimed as one of the great dive sites of the world. Described by James Michener as 'the most perfect atoll', and a favourite place for Jacques Cousteau, Wuvulu rises straight up from an undersea plateau 2000 metres deep. There are no rivers or creeks so the water is unbelievably clear and there are sharks, turtles, manta rays and tuna. There are, however, problems in getting to Wuvulu. See the Manus Province chapter (Wuvulu is north of Wewak but it's part of Manus Province).

There might be other places as well – diving is something of a growth industry. Note that dive courses are available in only some of

these places. See the appropriate chapters for detailed information. Overseas agents who will book some of these dives include:

See & Sea Travel
    50 Francisco St STU 205, San Francisco, CA 94133, USA (☎ 415 434 3400, fax 415 434 3409)
Tropical Adventures
    111 Second North, Seattle, WA 98109, USA (☎ 800 247 3483)
Sea Safaris
    3770 Highland Ave, Suite 102, Manhattan Beach, CA 90266, USA (☎ 800 821 6670)
Sea New Guinea
    100 Clarence St, Sydney 2000, Australia (☎ (02) 267 5563, fax (02) 267 6118)

Surfing & Windsurfing

There is the chance of good surf near Kavieng (New Ireland) from November to February and around Wewak from September to January. Plenty of other places have surf, but finding out about it isn't easy. If you do go exploring, it would be best to avoid June, July and August when the prevailing winds are south-easterly.

The problem is that most accessible PNG beaches are in the lee of reefs or islands and don't open onto the ocean. If you have access to a boat and can get out to the reefs themselves, there are bound to be waves, especially off the eastern coasts of New Ireland and Bougainville, and the unprotected East Sepik coast. This also means that the surf breaks onto coral reefs, so it isn't for the inexperienced.

Diveco (☎ 25 4418, fax 25 4466, PO Box 2799, Boroko) in Port Moresby offers surfing tours.

The very characteristics which make surfing problematical make windsurfing viable: sheltered harbours, strong winds between June and August and, if you're interested, waves outside lagoons. Windsurfing is quite popular, particularly in Port Moresby, Madang and Rabaul. Although you won't always find it easy to get hold of a board, some top-end hotels on the coast have one or two which they hire. The yacht clubs would also be good places to start your inquiries.

Fishing

Sport fishing has enormous potential. Unless they have permission from traditional owners, however, fishers could easily get themselves in trouble. You can't waltz up to a stream, or the edge of the ocean and just cast in a line – everything and every square inch of PNG is owned by someone, including streams and reefs. The fish are definitely there – including trout in the Highlands, reef and pelagic fish offshore – and if you do get permission from the traditional owners, you should have some excellent fishing.

Several tours are offered by Sea New Guinea and Traditional Travel can also arrange tours.

The most famous fishing destination in PNG is the Bensbach Lodge on the Bensbach River near the Irian Jaya border, and the fish is barramundi. It's a beautiful area with superb wildlife, and 20-kg barramundi *are common*. See the Gulf & Western Provinces chapter.

It is possible to hire boats in several towns. The deep water fishing is, allegedly, incredible, with sharks, marlin and other game fish. Most of the dive operators have boats that can be chartered (see the Diving section for addresses), also:

Trans Melanesian Marine
    PO Box 477, Port Moresby, PNG (☎ 21 2039, 23 1074)
Reel Fish Charters
    PO Box 521, Madang, PNG (☎ 82 2572, fax 82 3106)

Bicycling

The lack of roads in PNG makes cycling impractical in most places. However, New Ireland, with good, almost traffic-free roads running along both coasts is a paradise for cyclists. Traditional Travel offers cycle tours of New Ireland, and there might by now be mountain bikes for hire in Kavieng. Namatanai to Kavieng (via the beautiful west coast) takes about four days, more if you take it easy.

The long Highlands Highway probably isn't very safe for cycling because of the risk of robbery (although cycling is so rare that your curiosity value might protect you). The excellent network of roads on the Gazelle Peninsula would be good (if often steep) cycling, but finding a bike to ride is almost impossible.

Caving

Caves in the limestone regions of the Southern Highlands may well be the deepest in the world, but to date they have only been very briefly explored. The Atea Kanada Cave extends for 30.5 km, making it one of the longest caves in the southern hemisphere and Asia.

Bird & Butterfly-Watching

PNG is a paradise for bird life and insects. See the Flora & Fauna section in the Facts about the Country chapter.

Visiting War Wreckages

At the end of WW II the country was littered from end to end with the wreckage of Allied and Japanese aircraft, ships and army equipment. Most of it has been shipped out by bands of scrap dealers, but there is still much to be seen.

There is a national register of aircraft wreckage and from time to time aircraft missing since WW II are still stumbled upon. In *The Hot Land*, John Ryan tells of some of these recently located aircraft and writes of some which are still being searched for. *Pacific Aircraft Wrecks* gives information about wreckage of aircraft all over PNG. See the Diving section for some information about shipwrecks. East New Britain (near Rabaul) is littered with reminders of the war (tunnels, bunkers, landing craft and shipwrecks); there are also many relics at the southern end of Bougainville.

War-buffs can have a fine time poking around debris. Surprisingly, one consistent comment on Japanese aircraft wrecks is that they are generally in better condition than the Allied wrecks due to their superior corrosion protection! Deja vu?

Tour Operators

Air Niugini offices both in PNG and around the world can book most tours and they have

Wrecked Japanese bomber

some packages of their own. See the Getting There & Away chapter for their addresses. Listed below are some of the other major or more interesting operators. Many of the operators listed in the Diving section above also offer tour packages.

Ambunti Lodge
PO Box 248, Wewak; PO Box 83, Ambunti, PNG (☎ 88 1291, 86 2525)
One of the few formal accommodation options on the Sepik; they can prearrange canoe tours.

Grassroutes Ecotravel
PO Box 710, Rabaul (☎ 92 1756)
New Rabaul-based organisation encouraging low-budget treks and accommodation in co-operation with villages in New Britain and New Ireland. Worth checking out.

Haus Poroman
PO Box 1182, Mt Hagen, PNG, (☎ 52 2722, fax 52 2207)
Haus Poroman is one of the best places to stay in PNG, and they also offer Sepik canoe trips, Highlands treks and other packages.

Melanesian Tourist Services
PO Box 707, Madang, PNG (☎ 82 2766, fax 82 3543)
Suite 10B, 302 West Grand Ave, El Segundo, CA 90245, USA (☎ (213) 785 0370, fax (213) 785 0314)
32 Mossville Gardens, Morden, Surrey SM44DG, UK (☎ (081) 540 3125, fax (081) 540 5510)
Alt-Schwanheim 50, 6000 Frankfurt am Main 71, Germany (☎ (69) 35 6667, fax (69) 35 0080)
Via Teulie 8, 20136, Milano, Italy (☎ (02) 837 5892)
Air Niugini, Continental or Qantas offices
Operates the luxury cruise boat *Melanesian Discoverer*, the Madang Resort Hotel and a couple of other up-market lodges. Niugini Diving Adventures is based at the Madang Resort Hotel. Also vehicle tours and some treks.

Mountain Travel – Sobek
6420 Fairmont Ave, El Cerrito CA 94530-3606 (☎ 1-800 227 2384, fax 1-510 525 7710)
Sepik and Trobriand tours

Niugini Tours
100 Clarence St, Sydney 2000, Australia (☎ (02) 290 2055)

Raging Thunder
PO Box 1109, Cairns 4870, Australia (☎ (070) 31 1466, fax (070) 51 4010)
Rafting, sea-kayaking and treks

Traditional Travel
PO Box 4264, Boroko, NCD, PNG, (☎ & fax 25 3966)
Highly recommended. A variety of tours, including canoeing on the Sepik, trekking, fishing in the Gulf, sailing canoes in Milne Bay, bicycling on New Ireland. Although their prices are not in the

shoestring range, they are lower than some other operators'. The best thing about Traditional Travel, though, is that their tours break out of the tourist cocoon and emphasise meeting (and staying with) villagers.

Trans Niugini Tours

PO Box 371, Mt Hagen, PNG (☎ 52 1438, fax 52 2470)

44B Aplin St, Cairns 4870, Australia (☎ (070) 51 0622, (070) 52 1147)

Suite 105, 850 Colorado Blvd, Los Angeles, CA 90041, USA (☎ toll-free 1-800-621 1633 (CA), 1-800-521 7242 (USA & Canada), fax (213) 256 0647)

Suite 433, 52-54 High Holborn, London WC1V 6RB, UK (☎ (071) 242 3131, fax (071) 242 2838)

Blumenstrasse 26, 4000 Dusseldorf 1, Germany (☎ (0211) 80127, fax (211) 32 4989)

Via Ferdinando Galani 25/D 00191 Rome, Italy (☎ (06) 329 3697, fax (06) 328 6261)

This is a large organisation similar to Melanesian Tourist Services. Trans Niugini also operates Sepik cruises (on the *Sepik Spirit*) and has the award-winning Ambua and Karawari lodges and a hotel near Madang. Many tours are offered, including some aimed at those on lower budgets.

Tribal World

PO Box 86, Mt Hagen, PNG (☎ 52 1555, fax 55 1546)

Operates a chain of hotels and offers some tours, including canoeing, trekking and, sometimes, rafting. The group plans a dive boat which will also cruise the Sepik for a much lower fare than the other two boats.

United Touring International

Koyata Building 3F, 2-5 Yotsuya 2-Chome, Shinjuku-ku, Tokyo 160, Japan (☎ (03) 335 52391, fax (03) 335 52438)

HIGHLIGHTS

Most people visit Madang, and it rightly claims the title of the country's tourist centre. There are good accommodation options for all budgets, a relaxed atmosphere and a beautiful harbour. Rabaul (East New Britain) is another pretty town with similar facilities, and the beautiful Gazelle Peninsula offers opportunities for trekking. The Tari Valley (Southern Highlands) is both interesting and beautiful, as is most of the Highlands, and the Mt Hagen and Goroka shows are genuinely spectacular. Floating down the Sepik could be the adventure of a lifetime. New Ireland must be one of the most beautiful and laid-back places in the world, although the

diverse island groups of Milne Bay Province are right up there, too. If you visit Manus you'll probably be the only tourist in the province.

You don't have to be an intrepid traveller to enjoy any of these places, but for those who want to rough it, PNG offers almost unlimited possibilities. You could spend months cruising the islands on small boats, or walking trails in some of the most remote places in the world. Just staying in a village for any length of time will be an introduction to a very different way of life.

ACCOMMODATION

The one unfortunate generalisation that you can make about accommodation is that it is too expensive. Overall the quality is reasonable, although often not worth the price, and in most towns your options are limited.

Booking ahead is a good idea, especially for moderately priced hotels and guesthouses. Most are small and don't take many people before they are full. Spend a few toea to make a booking over the excellent phone system and you could avoid arriving to find the one cheap place is full, and the only alternative is a luxury hotel room. Booking ahead is especially important if there is a festival of some kind. Transport between airports and towns is often nonexistent or exorbitant in price, so most hosts will pick you up, if they know you're coming – another saving. If you're booking by mail remember there is no postal delivery and you must write to a post office box number.

Camping

There are virtually no real camping grounds in PNG, so unless you plan to camp in police station compounds or do some serious hiking, a tent is of little value.

There are a number of problems with camping. Firstly, every square inch of country has a traditional owner whose permission *must* be obtained before you set up occupation. It may look like deserted bush to you, but there will almost always be people coming and going around what are, in fact, their traditional properties. The owner may live just around the corner or kilometres away and when you find him you may well be offered room in a hut anyway. Secondly, there is a problem with security, and you're obviously particularly vulnerable out in the middle of the bush by yourself.

If you are planning to bushwalk, a tent might be useful, although you may find it superfluous until you get into the mountains. At low altitudes you are most likely to be following a reasonably well-travelled route and you will either come across villages or bush shelters at regular intervals. The shelters are built especially for weary travellers, like you, to use. If you are walking with a large group a tent is useful to take the pressure off limited accommodation in villages.

A tent fly can be very useful for helping to waterproof a shelter and a well-ventilated tent inner can be used as a ground sheet, mosquito net, changing room and general insect barricade in huts wherever you are.

The situation does change when you get to higher altitudes because the population density drops, and the weather is much more severe.

Places to Stay – bottom end

You can find somewhere inexpensive to stay in most main towns. 'Inexpensive' is a relative term, though – the cheapest bed in Port Moresby is K20 a night, and elsewhere you'll be paying well over K10 a night for shared accommodation, with a few exceptions.

Most of the cheaper places are mission-run guesthouses and hostels. Lutheran hostels are reliably clean, comfortable and friendly. They usually offer generous servings of fairly plain food in their communal dining rooms, after a blessing. Most hostels exist for the benefit of visiting missionaries and church people, but they are usually happy to take travellers if they have room.

Do not expect to treat these places like a hotel; they're quiet and family oriented. Despite this, all sorts of people use them and they are good meeting places. The mission-

aries can also be helpful with local information and are often very interesting people in their own right. The churches play a very big role in PNG and staying in one of their hostels will give you the opportunity to get a first-hand view of how they operate.

Around the country there are a growing number of provincial women's associations, and some of these have hostels. Not only are they inexpensive (usually) but they provide the rare opportunity to meet politically aware grassroots women. Men can usually stay in women's association hostels.

Although there are a number of YWCA hostels, most cater to permanent residents and are usually full. Still, women in need of somewhere to stay could try them.

Some of the up-market hotels now have backpacker rooms, which cost about the same as a mission guesthouse. Unfortunately, these tend to be in places where there is adequate budget accommodation anyway, like Madang or Mt Hagen. Even if there is no backpacker accommodation, it's sometimes possible to do deals at the more expensive hotels, especially if you arrive at the end of the day.

Out of the main towns you will often find police, district officers, health workers, teachers, mission workers or expats willing to offer you a place to stay but *do not* expect this as a matter of course. Some people may be only too pleased to see you but, equally, there will be many who have no interest in you at all! It is immensely preferable to write or phone ahead, and set something up in advance, if you can. Remember that many of these people are very poorly paid so make sure you pay your way.

The high schools are often quite isolated and they are all boarding schools, so you could get lucky and find a spare bed with them. It's likely you'll have to sing for your supper, or at the very least do a lot of talking! The school headmaster is certain to be a good source of local information. Last but not least, police stations around the country almost always allow you to camp on their grounds, or use a spare room in their barracks, for no charge.

As you'll have gathered, most inexpensive places to stay aren't targeted at budget travellers. There are a few exceptions to this, and it's a real relief to stay somewhere where they understand what you are doing. Some of these places are Haus Poroman near Mt Hagen, the Oro Guesthouse in Popondetta, Ralph's in Wewak, Siar Island in Madang Harbour, Kanai Guesthouse in Rabaul and Koli Guesthouse near Tufi.

There has been spasmodic development of village guesthouses, but with so few travellers passing through, the villagers often get discouraged and allow the guesthouse to fall apart. Some still remain, though, and there are signs that the national tourist authorities are coming to see them as a good way to encourage rural development. If the Grassroutes project in New Britain's Gazelle Peninsula takes off there might be a modest boom in good quality, community-run places to stay in attractive areas.

Staying in Villages If you're willing to rough it a bit and get well off the track, your accommodation costs can be negligible. In most villages you'll find someone willing to take you in.

Remember to pay your way. Two to five kina for a night's accommodation, a kina or some trade store food in exchange for a meal is reasonable. In some areas where they see a lot of travellers you might pay up to K10.

Melanesian hospitality is usually given to foster a long-term relationship and is based on the idea of exchange. As a transient tourist you don't fit into the traditional patterns, but if you do give something in exchange for hospitality, you will be meeting your traditional responsibility, helping the village, and hopefully ensuring a welcome for the next traveller who comes along.

In some villages you might find a *haus kiap* (a house for patrol officers, kiaps) – a council house or some other structure where local people might think you will want to stay. Try to resist this, as not only is staying with a family in their traditional house more enjoyable than sleeping by yourself in a decaying colonial-era structure, but it's

much safer. As soon as you are involved with a community you become, to some extent, the responsibility of that community.

See the Staying in Villages and the Pointers sections in the Sepik chapter for more hints.

Places to Stay – top end

Most of the top-end hotels are relatively recent constructions, often in a motel style with a few carvings tacked on. Prices range from a little to a lot higher than similar places in Australia. Singles range from about K50 to K90 and up. There's quite a wide variety of prices, and you'd be wise to plan ahead carefully. The major centres all have at least one reasonably high-standard (or at least high-price) place. Port Moresby has a Travelodge and several other five-star hotels but the prices are astronomically high.

Some Coral Sea group hotels have set standby rates on rooms still vacant at 5 pm, and many hotels have weekend specials which can be good value.

There are two exceptional luxury hotels, whose nearest equivalents are the famous African safari lodges, and they should not be missed if you have the necessary funds: the Karawari Lodge lies deep in the jungle on a tributary of the Sepik and, best of all, the Ambua Lodge perches at 2000 metres on a ridge in the Southern Highlands overlooking the extraordinary Tari Valley.

Another option combines the virtues of comfort and mobility: the *Melanesian Discoverer* is a well-appointed ship that cruises the Sepik and the north coast as far as the islands of Milne Bay. Trans Niugini Tours' smaller *Sepik Spirit* also cruises the Sepik.

FOOD

While the food is generally uninspiring, you should manage to eat reasonably well, most of the time. Unless you get off the beaten track, however, you probably won't have much opportunity to try local food. To a Western palate that is no great loss since the average diet is made up of bland, starchy foods with very little protein. Western-style PNG food tends to be unimaginative (the roast and three-veg category), although if you're prepared to pay top prices, the food in hotels and restaurants can be good. The big exception to this depressing picture is the magnificent seafood, especially shellfish and crustaceans, available on the coast.

Those on a budget will want to cook for themselves as much as possible, but as most fresh vegetables are flown from the Highlands or even Australia, they are scarce in markets and expensive in supermarkets – except in the Highlands, of course.

Local Food

In much of the low-lying swamp country the staple food is *saksak* (sago) – a tasteless, starchy extract that is washed from the pith of the sago palm. In the Highlands the staple is the *kaukau* (sweet potato), a native of South America that was brought to Asia by the Spanish and Portuguese around the end of the 15th century. Elsewhere, taros, yams and bananas form the starchy basis of subsistence communities' diets. The situation is sometimes a little more inspiring along the coast because there is excellent seafood and the cooking makes heavier use of coconut and even, sometimes, spices like ginger.

Because of the country's limited animal life, protein deficiency has traditionally been a problem. In many regions potential game (reptiles, birds, rodents and small marsupials) is scarce, but hunting is still important. Small boys shooting at birds with slingshots aren't indulging in mindless destruction, they're trying to catch a meal.

Apart from fresh fish, which are only available on the coast and some of the rivers, pigs are the main source of meat protein, although they are not generally eaten on a day-to-day basis, but saved for feasts. Chicken is now quite popular although, strangely, eggs are rarely eaten. New varieties of vegetables are also being introduced and developed for local consumption and as cash crops, particularly in the fertile soil of the Highlands valleys.

The most famous local cooking style is the *mumu*, which is an underground oven. A pit is dug, fire-heated stones are placed in the bottom, meat and vegetables are wrapped in

Taro plant

herbs and leaves and placed on the stones, the pit is sealed with more branches and leaves, and the contents roast and steam. For feasts the pits may be hundreds of metres long, and filled with hundreds of whole pigs.

The most recent staples to be added to the PNG diet are rice and tinned fish or meat. Their importance is clear if you check a smaller trade store's shelves: they often stock nothing more than rice, tinned mackerel, tobacco and salt. Many people who live in the cities, or who don't have access to a garden, have no other affordable choice. In some parts of the country the tinned food helps to alleviate a natural protein shortage.

The tinned food can be pretty awful, especially the meat. '777' brand is supposed to be the best fish. 'Two-minute' noodles are also becoming popular.

Town Food

In all the big towns you'll be able to eat comparatively well in hotels or restaurants. At these places you'll usually find reasonable quality Australian-style food, at prices that are, unfortunately, quite a lot higher than in Australia. Think in terms of K10 to K15 and up. Chinese restaurants are reasonably widespread but they are also expensive.

One possibility that is always worth

checking is The Club. Many towns still have a club – at one time they were havens for white colonialists, but today their memberships are completely open. The drop in the expat population has thrown many of them on hard times and they are generally only too happy to sign in 'out of town' visitors. There will usually be a blackboard menu offering something like steak sandwiches or burgers with salad and French fries for about K7, sometimes less.

The fast food available from kai bars ranges from unthinkably awful to OK. It's usually fried – fish, chicken, lamb chops, rice and chips are the staples, along with things like sheep hearts. Many offer rice and stew, which is cheap and nourishing, although very greasy. You'll find kai bars in every town; bear in mind they usually close by 6.30 pm.

Many larger towns have sandwich bars or cafes and the large Steamships chain stores always have a take-away counter with decent sandwiches. That's about it for prepared food though – nothing exotic, no spices, nothing to write home about.

Mission hostels sometimes supply meals to their guests and these tend to be very good value. In general, however, the shoestring traveller or backpacker will discover that attempting to find something cheap and wholesome is a frustrating experience, and that cooking for yourself is the only way to survive. Some of the hostels have cooking facilities, but even if you don't have a stove handy, it's easy to rustle up a breakfast or a lunch.

Markets sell an inexpensive but often limited range of vegetables and all the main towns have well-stocked supermarkets. There is no bargaining in the outdoor markets; prices are set and fair and are often clearly displayed.

The most ubiquitous food items, stocked by just about every store in the country, are crackers, and it's useful to keep a packet or two with you. The further you get from the main towns, the less likely it is that the crackers on sale will be fresh. Beef crackers are my favourite. They come in packets of four, and the Morobeen brand (K0.33) has

much more flavour than the Paradise Bakery brand (K0.25). Wan-kai is another brand of cracker, and each packet comes with a sachet of peanut butter or other spread.

Vegetarian Food

You might expect a country where protein deficiency is a chronic problem to be a vegetarian's paradise. Wrong. Some of the Chinese restaurants have vegetarian dishes, and you may find reasonable salads at some of the hotel smorgasbords, but in general the pickings are thin (and you will be too, if you are not careful).

The big hotels and restaurants can normally put something together, but in the mission hostels it's a bit more awkward. There's no menu; everyone eats whatever happens to have been cooked and that's that. Again it's possible to organise an exception.

In the bush, I guarantee you'll find it tedious eating sago, yams or sweet potato for breakfast, lunch and dinner. Meat is sometimes produced and, since you're a visitor, a special effort will be made to procure some. It is very difficult to explain the concept of vegetarianism in Pidgin to someone who belongs to a society that revolves around the killing and eating of pigs! You also run the risk of offending a host who has killed something in your honour.

So, make sure you have got cooking equipment, bring vitamin and mineral tablets and, if you are a less than strict vegetarian, you may consider temporarily relaxing your preference!

ALCOHOL & DRUGS
Alcohol

South Pacific is now the only brewery in PNG, but they produce two beers. The everyday drink, which comes in a small bottle (known as a *stubby* to Australians), is known as SP; the more expensive and stronger Export version comes in a colourful can. Wine and spirits are very costly, partly in an attempt to restrict their use.

Betel Nut

All through Asia people chew the nut of the Areca palm known as betel nut or, in Pidgin,

---

Beer Consumption in PNG

The Australian beer culture has been accepted a little too wholeheartedly in PNG. Until 1963, Papua New Guineans were strictly forbidden to consume alcohol; it was for whites only. As the country moved towards self-government, it became obvious that there could not be two laws, one for the locals, one for the expats. Thus, despite some anguished cries that nobody would be safe on the streets, the pubs were opened to all. Twenty-five years later it is clear the effect of beer on PNG has not been a happy one, although you can still walk the streets.

Perhaps there is a connection between the feast-or-famine mentality associated with a pig kill and the consumption of beer: a clan hoards its pigs for months then kills a large number for a feast and embarks on a non-stop orgy of over-consumption. Whatever the reason, some Papua New Guineans have a propensity to keep on drinking until they are either broke or flat on the floor. This is often conducted in depressing, open-air public bars where it's a simple matter of sink another and another and another until they're all gone.

Much of the crime in PNG is caused by drunks or by people looking for money to get drunk.

Various means of fighting the drink problem have been tried – advertising is forbidden, there are heavy taxes and drinking hours are restricted – but none of these measures seem to have much of an effect.

It is worth keeping track of Friday pay nights. If there is going to be trouble, this is the night it is most likely to happen, be it fights, car accidents or robberies. If you're planning to sleep within shouting distance of a bar, forget it! ■

---

buai. Although it's a (relatively) mild narcotic and digestive stimulant and is widely used in PNG, it's unlikely to attract many Western drug fans.

The betel nut is too acidic and slow acting to chew by itself – in PNG, betel nut users generally chew it with lime and seed stalks from a pepper plant. The reaction between the lime and the nut produces the narcotic effect and the extraordinary red stains you'll see splattered along footpaths everywhere. One of the side effects is incredible salivation, which the unpractised find difficult to swallow. The resultant spit can appear to be a most impressive haemorrhage. Prolonged use leads to black teeth, a mouth that is stained a permanent red and, in some cases, mouth cancer.

You'll see the nuts, lime and mustard stalks for sale in every market; sometimes there'll be virtually nothing else. If you decide to try it, take lessons with a local expert. Nuts vary in potency, it is possible to burn yourself with the lime and nausea is a common side effect for the unpractised (remember that first cigarette!).

Marijuana

The Highlands of PNG are the source of reputedly potent marijuana, although for-

eigners are rarely offered any. If you're tempted to look for it, remember that there are heavy penalties for possession and use and that as a foreigner you're much more likely to be busted and harshly punished than a local. Also, some of the people involved in the trade can be pretty heavy. There are persistent rumours that PNG grass is smuggled into Australia in exchange for military hardware.

Tobacco

Tobacco is an important cash crop and, as in many other developing countries, smoking is widespread and guilt-free. International brands are widely available, often in the full-strength version – there's no poring over tar and nicotine ratings in PNG. Locally-made cigars are available in many markets. They look crude but they smell very tempting.

The grassroots' smoke was traditionally tobacco rolled in newspaper (the *Sydney Morning Herald* for preference) but now there are ready-made versions. You puff one of these long cigarettes (the 'ettes' is redundant, they're like thin cigars) for a while then put it behind your ear for later use.

Apparently, when a company began manufacturing these cigarettes they were not allowed to use newspaper because of health regulations, so they made them with pristine rice paper. However, there was market resistance to plain-paper smokes, so they had to print their paper to look like newspaper. This story might be true, as at least one brand of cigarette is wrapped in newspaper that seems to be written in Latin!

THINGS TO BUY

Like everything else in PNG, artefacts are not cheap – particularly if you compare them to the more detailed, but less dynamic, carvings in Indonesia or the Philippines. The price inflation of carvings is also rather astonishing – I've seen prices 600 to 800% higher in artefacts shops in PNG than at source, and there's another huge price jump if you buy them outside the country.

There are a couple of reasons for this (apart from plain, straightforward profit). First of all the channels from the carver to the shops are lengthy and imperfect – long 'buying trips' have to be undertaken for artefact dealers to obtain their stock-in-trade. Secondly, many PNG artefacts are extremely unwieldy or very fragile – there's not a lot of thought given to meeting airline handling requirements and weight allowances, thank God! So transport can be difficult and many items are really only suitable for purchase by museums which can handle major shipping problems. Transporting a Sepik *garamut* drum or orator's stool would just about require a crane.

Arts & crafts anywhere in the world, and in PNG in particular, face two great dangers – lack of interest or too much interest. When the religious or spiritual reasons for an art form have died out – through changes in culture or circumstances – the art can die too unless there is a new reason for it, such as demand from collectors. But it's a two-edged sword, as too much demand can prompt careless, sloppy or lazy work. So if you like a piece – buy it. You'll be doing something to keep the craft alive. But be discerning – better one, more expensive, carefully made item than half a dozen shoddy ones. You'll like it better in the long run too. In the Sepik area in particular watch for hastily done carvings resembling traditional forms but

lacking detail and finesse. Also, some are artificially aged to make them appear more genuine and valuable. Watch for shoe polish used as a stain to disguise wood types and to simulate age.

For more information, see the Arts and Culture sections in the Facts about the Country chapter. Also, see the Customs section in this chapter for a discussion on the possible difficulties with customs regulations.

The descriptions that follow are just a few of the enormous varieties of styles and types of artefacts you may see in PNG; there are far more than this actually available. There are good shops in Port Moresby, Lae and a number of other PNG towns – information on them is in the relevant sections of this book. In some places artefact sellers gather outside hotels; their prices tend to be considerably inflated over what you would pay elsewhere.

The Artefacts & Crafts of Papua New Guinea – a Guide for Buyers is a very useful little booklet produced for the Handcraft Industry of PNG. If you can't find it anywhere else, look for it at the University Bookshop in Port Moresby. If you want to get a preview of New Guinea art in Australia, visit New Guinea Primitive Arts, 6th floor, 428 George St, Sydney.

Pottery

The village of Aibom, near the Chambri Lakes, is virtually the only place on the Sepik to specialise in pottery. Aibom pots are noted for their relief faces which are coloured with lime. They are made by the coil method and are very cheap on the Sepik, but rapidly become more expensive as you move further away because, like other PNG pottery, they are very fragile.

Other interesting pots can be found near Madang, at Zumim near the Highlands Highway from Lae and from the Porebada people in the Central Province. The Amphlett Islanders in Milne Bay also make very fine and very fragile pottery. No pottery is glazed in PNG and it is also often poorly fired so it all suffers from extreme fragility.

Weapons

The Chambri Lake carvers produce decorative spears remarkably similar to their masks. Perhaps with tourists in mind, they can be dismantled and are relatively easy to transport. Bows and arrows are available from a number of places including the Highlands and Bougainville Island. Shields are also popular artefacts as they often have a decorative and spiritual role just as important as their function of protection for a warrior. In the Highlands the ceremonial Hagen Axes are similarly half-tool, half-ritual. Here you will also see the lethal cassowary-claw tipped Huli Picks or on the Sepik, the equally nasty bone daggers.

Spirit Boards, Story Boards & Cult Hooks

In the Gulf Province the shield-like Hohao or Gope boards are said to contain the spirits of powerful heroes or to act as guardians of the village. Before hunting trips or war expeditions the spirits contained in the boards were called upon to advise and support the warriors.

At Kambot, on the Keram River, a tributary of the Sepik, story boards are a modern interpretation of the fragile bark carvings they used to make. The boards illustrate, in raised relief, incidents of village life and are one of my favourite examples of New Guinea art.

Cult hooks – small ones are Yipwons while larger ones are Kamanggabi – are carved as hunting charms and carried by their owners in a bag to ensure success on the hunt, the small ones anyway. Food hooks are used to hang billums of food from the roof to keep it away from the rats, but also have a spiritual significance.

Billums

Billums are the colourful string bags and are made in many parts of the country. They are enormously strong and expand to amazing sizes. Good billums can be rather expensive, particularly in the towns. They are time consuming to make since the entire length of string is fed through every loop. Most billums are now made of plastic or nylon strings rather than natural fibres, which in some ways is a shame; on the other hand, you can hardly mourn the continuing development of such a vital handcraft, especially when the colour and beauty of the new designs are so striking.

Smaller billums make handy daypacks, and when you get home you'll never need a plastic supermarket bag again. The big billums, worn with the strap around the forehead, can carry a staggering amount of stuff, but sometimes just a baby.

Highland Hats

These hats are essential wear for Highlanders. Even down in hot Port Moresby you'll see Highlanders wearing their colourful knitted hats – look at a taxi or PMV driver. You can buy one in Moresby or a Highland market.

Bowls

The Trobriand Islanders are prolific carvers of everything from stylised figures to decorated lime gourds, but my favourites are the beautifully carved bowls. They are generally carved from dark wood and laboriously polished with a pig's tusk. The rims are patterned, often to represent a fish or turtle.

The Tami Islanders near Lae are also renowned for their carved bowls. Further offshore the Siassi Islanders carve deep, elliptical bowls which are stained black and patterned with incised designs coloured with lime. In Milne Bay, the Woodlark Islanders carve bowls somewhat similar to those from the neighbouring Trobriands.

Masks

Masks in PNG are more often intended as decoration than as something to be worn. They are found particularly along the Sepik River, but also in other parts of the country. The Chambri masks from the villages on the Chambri Lakes are the most modern of the Sepik masks – instantly recognisable by their elongated design and glossy black finish with incised patterns in brown and white; colours which are unique to Chambri. They

Sepik spirit mask

make nice gifts because they are smaller than the general run of Sepik masks, easily transportable since they are solid without projecting teeth, horns or other features, and they are very cheap. Small Chambri masks at the village or in Wewak are only one or two kina.

At Korogo, on the Sepik, the masks are made of wood then decorated with clay in which shells, hair and pigs' teeth are embedded. Other distinctive Sepik mask styles are found at Kaminabit and Tambanum. Masks from the Murik Lakes have an almost African look about them. At Maprik the yam masks are woven from cane or rattan. Masks

are also carved at Kiwai Island, near Daru on the southern, Papuan coast.

Musical Instruments

Drums are the main musical instruments in PNG. The predominant drums are the large garamut drums found on the Sepik and made by hollowing out a tree trunk and the smaller kundu drum, which is hour-glass shaped and with a lizard or snake skin head. Trobriand drums are somewhat similar.

Other instruments include the sacred flutes which are always found in male-female pairs and are generally reserved for initiation rites; the bull roarers which are spun round on a length of cord, the pottery whistles of the Highlands and the small, but eerie sounding, Jews harps also found in the Highlands.

Other Handcrafts

Buka baskets, from Bougainville in the North Solomons, are said to be the finest baskets in the Pacific. They are very expensive. Similar, but coarser, baskets are found in the Southern Highlands. Figures of various types are carved on the Murik Lakes, the Yuat River and in the Trobriand Islands.

The Trobriand Islanders also carve very fine walking sticks and some delightful little stools and tables. The walking sticks are often carved from ebony, which is now very rare and found only on Woodlark Island. Tapa cloth, made from tree bark, is beaten and decorated in the Oro Province. Shell jewellery can be found at many coastal towns, particularly Madang and Rabaul.

Getting There & Away

Although there are some wild-and-wonderful ways of getting to PNG, almost everybody comes by air. And the vast majority come by air from Australia to Port Moresby, although there are also direct connections with Singapore, Manila, Honiara (Solomon Islands), Jayapura (Irian Jaya, Indonesia) and Guam. Otherwise, there are a few visiting yachts and the occasional cruise ship.

AIR

Air fares and routes are particularly vulnerable to change. The details given in this section should be regarded as pointers only, and you should do plenty of research before buying a ticket.

Air Niugini, the national airline, operates between Australia and Asia (in conjunction with Singapore airlines). Australian connections are also made by Qantas, Australia's international airline. Continental flies from the USA via Guam. Garuda, Indonesia's national carrier, will get you to Jayapura in Irian Jaya (via Biak), from where you can fly to Vanimo in PNG.

Air Niugini logo

Port Moresby is by far the largest international gateway. From Vanimo you can fly to Indonesia, and there have been direct flights between Mt Hagen and Cairns in Australia, but not currently. There has been talk of opening another international airport in PNG and various local lobby groups are arguing for international airports on Manus Island, at Wewak, Madang, Lae, Rabaul, Alotau...

Air Niugini offices overseas include:

Germany
Raidmannstrasse 45, 6000 Frankfurt 70 (☎ (069) 63 4095, fax (069) 63 13 32)
Hong Kong
Room 705, Century Square, 1-13 Daguilar St, Central (☎ (5) 24 2151, fax 825 526 7291)
Japan
No 2F Ogikubo Kangyo Bldg, 3-2-2 Amanuma Suginami-ku, Tokyo (☎ (03) 539-70678, fax (03) 539-70677)
Malaysia
3rd floor, Pelancongan Abadi Sdn Bhd 79, Jalan Bukit Bintang 55100, Kuala Lumpur (☎ (03) 242 6360, fax (03) 242 1361)
Philippines
G/F Fortune Office Bldg, 160 Legaspi St, Legaspi Village, Makati, Metro Manila (☎ 810 1846, fax 817 9826)
Singapore
No 01-05/06/58 United Square, 101 Thomson Rd (☎ 250 4868, fax 652 533 425)
USA
Suite 3000, 5000 Birch St, Newport Beach, Los Angeles, CA 92660 (☎ (714) 752 5440, fax (714) 752 2160)

Round-the-World Tickets & Circle Pacific Fares

Round-the-World (RTW) tickets are often real bargains, and can work out no more expensive or even cheaper than an ordinary return ticket. Typical prices for South Pacific RTW tickets are from £900 to £1200 or US$2500 to US$3000.

The official airline RTW tickets are usually put together by a combination of two or more airlines, and permit you to fly anywhere you want on their route systems so long as you do not backtrack. Other restrictions are that you (usually) must book the first sector in advance and cancellation penalties then apply. There may be restrictions on how many stops you are permitted and usually the tickets are valid for 90 days up to a year. An alternative type of RTW ticket is one put together by a travel agent using a combination of discounted tickets.

Circle Pacific tickets use a combination of airlines to circle the Pacific – combining Australia, New Zealand, North America and Asia. As with RTW tickets there are advance-purchase restrictions and limits to how many stopovers you can take. Typical prices are around US$1200 to US$2000.

You might not be able to include PNG on an RTW or Circle Pacific ticket but you can certainly get close, to Australia, Asia or the Pacific. Even adding on the sectors to/from PNG, an RTW ticket might work out cheaper than a direct fare. Flying into Australia, making your way through PNG and picking up the homeward leg in Indonesia, Singapore or elsewhere in Asia is possible on some tickets.

Buying a Plane Ticket

The plane ticket will probably be the single most expensive item in your budget, and buying it can be an intimidating business. There is likely to be a multitude of airlines and travel agents hoping to separate you from your money, and it is always worth putting aside a few hours or days to research the current state of the market.

Start early: some of the cheapest tickets have to be bought months in advance, and some popular flights sell out early. Talk to other recent travellers – they may be able to stop you making some of the same old mistakes. Look at the ads in newspapers and magazines, consult reference books and watch for special offers. Then phone round travel agents for bargains. (Airlines can supply information on routes and timetables; however, except at times of inter-airline war they do not supply the cheapest tickets.) Find out the fare, the route, the duration of the journey and any restrictions on the ticket.

(See Restrictions in the Air Travel Glossary.) Then sit back and decide which is best for you.

You may discover that those impossibly cheap flights are 'fully booked, but we have another one that costs a bit more...' Or the flight is on an airline notorious for its poor safety standards and leaves you in the world's least favourite airport in mid-journey for 14 hours. Or they claim only to have the last two seats available for that country for the whole of July, which they will hold for you for a maximum of two hours. Don't panic – keep ringing around.

If you are travelling from the UK or the USA, you will probably find that the cheapest flights are advertised by obscure bucket shops. Many such firms are honest and solvent, but there are a few rogues who will take your money and disappear, to reopen elsewhere a month or two later under a new name. If you feel suspicious about a firm, don't give them all the money at once – leave a deposit of 20% or so and pay the balance when you get the ticket. If they insist on cash in advance, go somewhere else. And once you have the ticket, ring the airline to confirm that you are actually booked onto the flight.

You may decide to pay more than the rock-bottom fare by opting for the safety of a better-known travel agent. Firms such as STA, who have offices worldwide, Council Travel in the USA or Travel CUTS in Canada are not going to disappear overnight, leaving you clutching a receipt for a nonexistent ticket, but they do offer good prices to most destinations.

Once you have your ticket, write its number down, together with the flight number and other details, and keep the information somewhere separate. If the ticket is lost or stolen, this will help you get a replacement.

Air Travellers with Special Needs

If you have special needs of any sort – you've broken a leg, you're vegetarian, travelling in a wheelchair, taking the baby, terrified of flying – you should let the airline know as soon as possible so that they can make arrangements accordingly. You should remind them when you reconfirm your booking (at least 72 hours before departure) and again when you check in at the airport.

To/From Australia
Air Niugini's Airbus flies between Sydney and Port Moresby three times each week, via Brisbane. The flight time from Sydney is about three hours, plus an hour's wait in Brisbane. There's a weekly flight between Cairns and Port Moresby on the Airbus and several others on a Fokker F28 'pocket rocket'. Qantas flies to Port Moresby three times a week from Sydney via Brisbane. Currently there are no direct flights between Cairns and Mt Hagen.

One-way economy fares and low/high season APEX return fares between Australia and Port Moresby are:

Departure Pt	One-way	APEX return
Sydney	A$778	A$940/1085
Brisbane	A$634	A$796/940
Cairns	A$378	A$489/536

The maximum validity of APEX tickets on this route is 45 days. The APEX seasons are complicated, but basically the high season is most of January, mid-April, mid-June to mid-July, mid-September to early October and most of December. As you might have guessed, Australian school holidays are a nice little earner for the airlines!

There isn't much discounting of tickets between Australia and PNG, but ask around and you might find something. STA and Flight Centres International are major dealers in cheap air fares, and it's worth contacting Air Niugini direct. Air Niugini has Australian offices in Sydney (☎ (02) 232 3100, fax (02) 290 2026); Brisbane (☎ (07) 229 5844, fax (07) 220 0040); and Cairns (☎ (070) 51 4177, fax (070) 31 3402). You can phone toll-free on 008 221 742.

To/From the Pacific
Solomon Airlines sometimes offers an interesting circle fare between Brisbane, Honiara (Dolomon Islands) and Port Moresby, but it's fairly pricey unless you can find a travel agent offering a special deal. Their direct flights from Honiara to Port Moresby costs about A$480 one way but sometimes there are specials. There is increasing bad-feeling between the governments of the Solomon Islands and PNG (due to Bougainville), so don't count on this route remaining open.

Island-hopping all the way from the USA requires careful planning as some connections only operate once or twice a week. Possibilities include Honolulu, Marshall Islands, Nauru, Honiara, Port Moresby; or Honolulu, Guam, Nauru; or Honolulu, Carolinas, Nauru; or Honolulu, Nandi (Fiji), Honiara. The tiny island state of Nauru is the focal point for a lot of these routes and Air Nauru has an interesting network to its Pacific neighbours.

Air fares on these Pacific routes are a bit of a puzzle since Guam-Honolulu and other routes between the USA and Micronesia are treated like US domestic routes, with nice low fares.

To/From Asia
Indonesia The short flight from Jayapura (K60) to Vanimo in PNG is currently the only air route between PNG and Indonesia, but there is talk of direct flights from Vanimo to Biak. This would be much more convenient, as from Biak you can fly to the USA.

Most other international flights out of Indonesia depart from Jakarta. There are flights from Jayapura to Jakarta most days for about US$440 (cheaper in Indonesia). You have to change planes twice, but you can do the trip in a day.

Note that you are not allowed to cross into Irian Jaya by land.

Travelling in Indonesia Once you're in Indonesia you can take advantage of that country's excellent air-pass deals – currently you can buy four flight coupons for US$350. There are also regular inter-island ferries. It might be possible to get a ticket written in Australia which will include stopovers in Port Moresby, other PNG destinations,

Jayapura and other Indonesian destinations such as Bali.

The most important thing to remember on arriving in Jayapura is you are no longer in PNG. Be on your guard, be prepared to be ripped off. Ask at the airport for the current official fare into the town, and don't be conned into 'chartering' the whole cab. If they won't be reasonable, and they usually

get more reasonable the longer you wait, simply walk 300 metres straight down the road from the terminal to the main road where there is a taxi station at the junction and taxis depart regularly.

The only reliable place in PNG to get rupiah (Indonesian currency) is in Port Moresby but don't get too much, you'll get a better price in Jayapura, but not at the

---

Air Travel Glossary

APEX APEX, or 'advance-purchase excursion' is a discounted ticket which must be paid for in advance. There are penalties if you wish to change it. PEX is a less limiting form of APEX, and many airlines are now offering even less restricted Excursion fares.

Baggage Allowance This will be written on your ticket: usually one 20-kg item to go in the hold, plus one item of hand luggage. Domestic flights in PNG have a limit of 16 kg, but foreign visitors can usually get away with 20 kg.

Bucket Shop An unbonded travel agency specialising in discounted airline tickets.

Bumped Just because you have a confirmed seat doesn't mean you're going to get on the plane – see Overbooking.

Cancellation Penalties If you have to cancel or change an APEX ticket there are often heavy penalties involved. Insurance can sometimes be taken out against these penalties. Some airlines impose penalties on regular tickets as well, particularly against 'no show' passengers.

Check In Airlines ask you to check in a certain time ahead of the flight departure (usually 1½ hours on international flights). If you fail to check in on time and the flight is overbooked the airline can cancel your booking and give your seat to somebody else.

Confirmation Having a ticket written out with the flight and date you want doesn't mean you have a seat until the agent has checked with the airline that your status is 'OK' or confirmed. Meanwhile you could just be 'on request'.

Discounted Tickets There are two types of discounted fares – officially discounted (see Promotional Fares) and unofficially discounted. The lowest prices often impose drawbacks like flying with unpopular airlines, inconvenient schedules, or unpleasant routes and connections. A discounted ticket can save you other things than money – you may be able to pay APEX prices without the associated APEX advance booking and other requirements. Discounted tickets only exist where there is fierce competition.

Full Fares Airlines traditionally offer first-class (coded F), business-class (coded J) and economy-class (coded Y) tickets. These days there are so many promotional and discounted fares available from the regular economy class that few passengers pay full economy fare.

Lost Tickets If you lose your airline ticket an airline will usually treat it like a travellers' cheque and, after inquiries, issue you with another one. Legally, however, an airline is entitled to treat it like cash and if you lose it then it's gone forever. Take good care of your tickets.

No Shows No shows are passengers who fail to show up for their flight, sometimes due to unexpected delays or disasters, sometimes due to simply forgetting, sometimes because they made more than one booking and didn't bother to cancel the one they didn't want. Full-fare passengers who fail to turn up are sometimes entitled to travel on a later flight. The rest of us are penalised (see Cancellation Penalties).

airport. See Lonely Planet's *South-East Asia on a shoestring* or *Indonesia – a travel survival kit* for more information. For information on Indonesian visas, see the Facts for the Visitor chapter of this book.

Elsewhere in Asia Air Niugini, in conjunction with Singapore Airlines, has weekly flights from Port Moresby to Hong Kong,

and two or three to Singapore. Unless you particularly want to visit Hong Kong, that routing is usually expensive. A Singapore to Port Moresby low-season Excursion return fare, valid for 45 days costs around US$1000. From Manila to Port Moresby on Air Niugini, in conjunction with Philippine Airlines, a 90-day Excursion return fare costs US$950. Both these fares are prob-

---

On Request An unconfirmed booking for a flight, see Confirmation.

Open Jaws A return ticket where you fly out to one place but return from another. If available this can save you backtracking to your arrival point.

Overbooking Airlines hate to fly empty seats and since every flight has some passengers who fail to show up, airlines often book more passengers than they have seats. Usually the excess passengers balance those who fail to show up but occasionally somebody gets bumped. If this happens guess who it is most likely to be? The passengers who check in late.

Promotional Fares Officially discounted fares like APEX fares which are available from travel agents or direct from the airline.

Reconfirmation At least 72 hours prior to departure time of an onward or return flight you must contact the airline and 'reconfirm' that you intend to be on the flight. If you don't do this the airline can delete your name from the passenger list and you could lose your seat. You don't have to reconfirm the first flight on your itinerary or if your stopover is less than 72 hours. It doesn't hurt to reconfirm more than once.

Restrictions Discounted tickets often have various restrictions on them – advance purchase is the most usual one (see APEX). Others are restrictions on the minimum and maximum period you must be away, such as a minimum of 14 days or a maximum of one year. See Cancellation Penalties.

Tickets Out An entry requirement for many countries is that you have an onward or return ticket, in other words, a ticket out of the country. If you're not sure what you intend to do next, the easiest solution is to buy the cheapest onward ticket to a neighbouring country or a ticket from a reliable airline which can later be refunded if you do not use it.

Transferred Tickets Airline tickets cannot be transferred from one person to another. Travellers sometimes try to sell the return half of their ticket, but officials can ask you to prove that you are the person named on the ticket. This is unlikely to happen on domestic flights, on an international flight tickets may be compared with passports.

Travel Agencies Travel agencies vary widely and you should ensure you use one that suits your needs. Some simply handle tours while full-service agencies handle everything from tours and tickets to car rental and hotel bookings. A good one will do all these things and can save you a lot of money but if all you want is a ticket at the lowest possible price, then you really need an agency specialising in discounted tickets. A discounted ticket agency, however, may not be useful for other things, like hotel bookings.

Travel Periods Some officially discounted fares, APEX fares in particular, vary with the time of year. There is often a low season and a high season. Sometimes there's an intermediate or shoulder season as well. Usually the fare depends on your outward flight – if you depart in the low season and return in the high season, you pay the low-season fare. ■

ably cheaper if bought in Singapore or Manila.

To/From Europe

You can put together a ticket taking you from Europe to Hong Kong, Manila or Singapore and connecting with an Air Niugini (see above) flight to Port Moresby there. A more complicated route would be to fly to Jakarta (Indonesia) and from there to Biak and Jayapura, from where it's a short hop to Vanimo in PNG.

Many people combine a visit to PNG with a holiday in Australasia or the Pacific. A cheap ticket to Australia (possibly a RTW ticket) plus an APEX return ticket between Cairns and Port Moresby might be the cheapest way to get to PNG from Europe.

There are a million-and-one deals on tickets from Europe to Australia and Asia, but check whether there are any good deals on flights all the way to PNG. Singapore Airlines flies from Europe to Port Moresby, and a low-season Excursion fare from London, valid for a year and with a stopover in Singapore might cost under £1100. Philippine Airlines (which flies from Manila to Port Moresby) doesn't seem to have particularly good deals on direct flights between Europe and Port Moresby, but it's worth checking out their specials between Europe and Australasia.

UK Trailfinders in west London produce a lavishly illustrated brochure which includes air fare details. STA also has branches in the UK. Look in the listings magazines *Time Out* and *City Limits* plus the Sunday papers and *Exchange & Mart* for ads. Also look out for the free magazines widely available in London – start by looking outside the main railway stations.

The Globetrotters Club (BCM Roving, London WC1N 3XX) publishes a newsletter called *Globe* which covers obscure destinations and can help in finding travelling companions.

To/From North America

There are four major alternatives: fly to Aus-

tralia, then on to Port Moresby; fly to Port Moresby via Guam with Continental; fly to Biak with Garuda then on to Jayapura and Vanimo in PNG; fly to Manila or Singapore then on to Port Moresby.

A return Excursion fare from Los Angeles (LA) to Sydney costs around US$1500 but there are often specials for less than US$1000. There is a lot of discounting on this route, so ask around. See the To/From Australia section for fares between Australia and Port Moresby.

Continental flies from LA to Port Moresby via Guam. The standard fare is US$995 one way, but there are various specials on return fares, such as US$1750 for a high-season APEX ticket and US$1500 in the low season.

You can fly with Garuda from LA to Biak on Wednesday, Friday and Sunday for about US$770 (cheaper in Indonesia and some LA travel agents offer excellent return fares). There are daily Garuda flights from Biak to Jayapura (US$77, probably cheaper in Indonesia). The Sunday Jayapura to Vanimo flight costs about US$60. This is the easiest way into the Sepik region, but check connections carefully, and remember that the international dateline will affect your calculations.

A one-way Excursion fare on Philippine Airlines from LA to Manila might cost under US$550, but the Manila to Port Moresby sector is expensive, especially if you buy it outside the Philippines.

The *New York Times*, the *LA Times*, the *Chicago Tribune* and the *San Francisco Examiner* all produce weekly travel sections in which you'll find any number of travel agents' ads. Council Travel and STA have offices in major cities nationwide.

The magazine *Travel Unlimited* (PO Box 1058, Allston, Mass 02134) publishes details of the cheapest air fares and courier possibilities for destinations all over the world from the USA.

Travel CUTS has offices in all major Canadian cities. The *Toronto Globe & Mail* and the *Vancouver Sun* carry travel agents' ads. The magazine *Great Expeditions* (PO

Box 8000-411, Abbotsford BC V2S 6H1) is useful.

SEA

Basically, entering PNG by sea is now difficult or impossible, unless you're on a yacht or a cruise ship.

To/From Australia

Unless you are a Torres Strait islander, it is illegal to island-hop between Thursday Island (known as TI to locals) and PNG. You can exit Australia from TI but you must go directly to PNG, usually Daru. There are plenty of fishing boats doing the trip, but no regular direct flights. You are allowed to island-hop as far as Saibai Island, just off the PNG coast, but from there you cannot exit Australia and enter PNG – you must return to Australia. These rules were once much flaunted but Australian patrols of the area have tightened up considerably and you're likely to be caught if you try to bend them. Non-Australians entering Australia this way can be charged with illegal entry.

To/From Solomon Islands

There was once a very interesting 'back door' route into PNG from the Solomons to Bougainville. This route is now used by the Bougainville Revolutionary Army to smuggle in supplies and by the PNG army on reprisal raids, so it's definitely out for the non-military traveller!

To/From Indonesia

It is possible but not legal to travel between Irian Jaya and PNG by sea, even the tempting little trip between Vanimo and Jayapura. If you do manage it you'll have problems with immigration.

Yachts

PNG is a popular stopping point for cruising yachties, either heading through Asia or the Pacific. If you ask around it's often possible to get a berth on a yacht heading off somewhere interesting. Often yachties depend upon picking up crew to help them sail and to help cover some of the day-to-day costs. The best places to try would be Port Moresby, Madang and Rabaul and Milne Bay, although you can quite possibly find yachts visiting at almost any port around the country.

TOURS

The two main PNG-based inwards tour operators are Melanesian Tourist Services and Trans Niugini Tours. Air Niugini also has packages. There are many other tour operators, most of which can offer packages. See the Activities section in the Facts for the Visitor chapter for names and addresses.

LEAVING PNG

There's a departure tax of K15 (this changes from time to time, both up and down). You have to buy a special stamp at a post office. If you've overstayed your visa, expect to pay a very hefty fine before they let you on the plane. People on yachts might be hit for a K100 per person 'customs clearance fee', especially at Samarai in Milne Bay.

Getting Around

AIR

Civil aviation was pioneered in PNG and there is no country that was more dependent on flying for its development. Even today, when a sketchy road network is beginning to creep across parts of the country, an enormous proportion of passengers and freight travel by air. Geographic realities continue to dictate this situation: the population is small and scattered, often isolated in mountain valleys and on tiny islands. Unfortunately, these factors also mean that flying is expensive. And, if you have limited time, it's virtually unavoidable.

Many towns grew up around airstrips, and there are still many important places where the arrival of a plane is the main entertainment for the day. People hang around airports the way they hang around railway stations in countries where trains still provide important transport links. How else are you to find out who is leaving town and who is arriving? The various airport callsigns are almost as well known as the town names. Perhaps you're flying from POM (Port Moresby) to WUG (Wau), down to LAE (yes, it's Lae, but the airport is 45 km away at Nadzab), then up to HGU (Mt Hagen) and TIZ (Tari), before heading to the Sepik strip of TBE (Timbunke).

Local Air Services

There are two main carriers on domestic routes and numerous small operations, some only for charter but some running scheduled passenger routes. The main outfits are Air Niugini (the national carrier) and Talair, with MAF (Missionary Aviation Fellowship – known to some as the Missionaries' Air Force!) the major small operator.

Air Niugini operates half a dozen Fokker F28s (jets), and De Havilland Dash 7s (big turbo-props) on its domestic routes. Talair once had a huge fleet of small planes but now operates only the slightly larger Twin Otters

and Bandeirantes. The MAF fleet is dominated by small aircraft. MAF, because it essentially supplies and transports missionaries rather than carrying passengers, has frequent and fairly regular flights but you'll have to hope there is room for you. There usually is.

You may come across the distinction between first-level, second-level and third-level airlines for the first time when you visit PNG. First-level describes a carrier that operates internationally (Air Niugini), second-level covers airlines that make the major domestic connections (Air Niugini and Talair) and third-level translates to mean an airline that operates between all the tiny towns and villages (MAF, Talair and many others).

Unfortunately the airline situation in PNG is more complicated than it once was. Air Niugini doesn't fly everywhere (its planes are too big for many strips) and Douglas, once one of the main third-level operators, has folded. To make matters worse, Talair has decided to concentrate on being an interprovincial airline. It has sold most of its smaller planes and has drastically cut the number of smaller strips it services.

Air travel is the lifeline of PNG so other operators are taking over the Douglas and Talair routes but some of them are shoestring outfits which might not last long, and getting firm timetables in much advance could be tricky. Many fly charters rather than scheduled passenger routes, and while you can often pay to go along on someone else's charter, this can take time (and beers) to arrange and isn't always possible. Most third-level operators are very approachable, though.

For the addresses of Air Niugini's overseas offices see the Getting There & Away chapter. Head-office addresses are:

Air Niugini
PO Box 7186, Boroko, Port Moresby (☎ 27 3555)

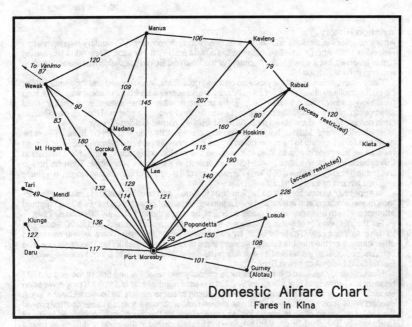

Domestic Airfare Chart
Fares in Kina

MAF
PO Box 273, Mt Hagen, Western Highlands
(☎ 55 1317)

Talair
PO Box 108, Goroka, Eastern Highlands (☎ 72 1240)

Some of the third-level carriers running passenger routes or regularly taking passengers along on charters are:

Islands Aviation
PO Box 717, Rabaul (☎ 92 2900, fax 92 2812)
New Britain, New Ireland and North Solomons

Airlink
PO Box 1930, Rabaul (☎ 92 1712, fax 92 1917)
New Britain, New Ireland, North Solomons and Lae

TransNiugini Airways
PO Box 3779, Boroko (☎ 25 6183, fax 25 4791)
Central Province (including Kokoda Trail strips); might expand into Simbu Province

Milne Bay Air (MBA)
PO Box 170, Port Moresby (☎ 25 2011, fax 25 2219)

Currently purely charter but expects to get a passenger licence and will be one of the larger operators.

Dovair
PO Box 205, Vanimo (☎ 87 1056)
Mainly Sepik area

Sandaun Air Services (SAS)
PO Box 206, Vanimo (☎ 87 1268/79, fax 87 1089)
Mainly Sepik area

Tarangau Airways
PO Box 292, Wewak (☎ 86 2203, fax 86 2820)
Mainly Sepik area

Northcoast Aviation
PO Box 12, Popondetta (☎ 29 7219)
Mainly Oro Province

MAF has bases (which operate fairly autonomously; not all have phones) in Anguganak, Goroka (☎ 72 1080), Mt Hagen (☎ 55 1317) (head office), Kawito, Madang (☎ 82 2229), Mendi (☎ 59 1091), Nadzab (Lae) (☎ 42 3804), Tari (☎ 50 8014), Telefomin, Vanimo (☎ 87 1091), Wewak (☎ 86 2500) and Port Moresby (☎ 25 2668).

Aviation History

After a couple of false starts and some ideas of exploring the country by Zeppelin airships, aviation arrived in 1922 when a small seaplane made a flight from Port Moresby. A few other pioneering flights followed, but it was the development of the Wau and Bulolo gold fields that really launched aviation in New Guinea.

Cecil John Levien, one of the pioneers on these gold fields, soon realised that they would never be successfully exploited as long as getting men and supplies up from the coast involved a long hard slog across difficult terrain, peopled by unfriendly tribes. After a number of unsuccessful attempts to interest Australian operators, Levien pushed through a proposal that his own Guinea Gold company should set up an air service, which they named Guinea Airways.

Their pilot, 'Pard' Mustar, had to do far more than just fly their first DH-37 biplane. First he arranged for an airstrip to be constructed at Lae (the local jail provided prisoners to build it) then he walked from Salamaua to Wau to supervise the airstrip construction there. Next he had to travel back to Rabaul where the DH-37 had arrived in pieces as sea cargo. Then he had to assemble it and fly to Lae – a 650-km journey, much of it over sea or unexplored jungle, in a single engined aircraft of less than total reliability.

In April 1927 Mustar took off on his first flight to Wau – and couldn't find it! He returned to Lae, took more directions and advice and tried again with an equal lack of success. Finally, on his third attempt and with an experienced guide on board, he made the first of many 50-minute flights.

For the next couple of years passengers and freight were shuttled back and forth. It cost £33 to fly up to Wau, only £10 to fly back, by comparison with K35 today. There were a number of other carriers on the run, but Guinea Airways were the most successful. Ray Parer was one who commenced operations with a DH-4 at much the same time, but lack of finance always held his Bulolo Gold Fields Aeroplane Service back.

Mustar quickly realised the need for more capacity and reliability and before the end of 1927 he went to Germany to buy a Junkers W-34 at the astronomical cost of £8000. It may have been expensive, but at the time it was the very latest thing in cargo aircraft and could lift over a ton. A second W-34 soon followed and with these aircraft Guinea Airways operated a service that proved the real possibilities of air transport just as convincingly as the much better publicised flights of Lindbergh or Kingsford-Smith. Wau became the busiest airfield in the world and more air freight was lifted annually in New Guinea than in the rest of the world put together!

Mustar left New Guinea, but in 1929 was called back to attempt a scheme that, to many people at the time, must have seemed like something in the realms of science fiction. He had to find a way of flying gold dredges weighing 3000 tons onto the gold fields! Mustar's answer was to dismantle the dredges and buy another Junkers, the G-31, a three-engined, all-metal monster which cost £30,000 and could lift three tons. In the early 1930s a fleet of these aircraft carried not just gold equipment, but also workers and even the first horses ever to be transported by air.

Throughout the 1930s more and more aircraft and operators came into New Guinea and the

---

Air Niugini and Talair (along with some of the smaller companies under Talair's wing) have computerised booking systems so bookings are usually quite efficient and can be made from anywhere in the world. Talair is linked to the Qantas system, so you can make bookings at any Qantas office. This level of sophistication does not apply to every PNG airport – some terminals can be more accurately described as sheds. Note that Talair and some of the smaller companies do not fly on Sundays.

Warning You have to check-in on Air Niugini's domestic flight an hour in advance of departure time. Take this seriously – half an hour before flight time they start giving seats to waitlisted passengers.

Aircraft The planes are small and fill quickly – many Air Niugini flights leave behind a long line of disappointed waitlist passengers. Book ahead and always reconfirm. If you're told a flight is full, it's often worth trying again – they don't always seem to end up that way. Travel can be more difficult during the Australian school holidays. Many expats bring their children up from their boarding fierce competition dramatically forced down the air freight rates. In 1931 regular services started between the gold fields and Port Moresby on the south coast.

Holden's Air Transport Services developed but was later taken over by Guinea Airways. The air service started by the island traders W R Carpenter & Co was longer lasting. In 1937 they absorbed Pacific Aerial Transport (originally formed by gold fields pioneer Ray Parer) and became Mandated Airlines Ltd (MAL).

In 1938 they started the first airmail service between PNG and Australia. Guinea Airways also expanded south into Australia operating a successful service between Adelaide and Darwin via Alice Springs using the ultra-modern, twin-engined Lockheed Electra.

Also during the '30s, pioneer missionaries proved that the aeroplane could be put to spiritual as well as secular use; possibly the first ever aerial mapping was conducted (in 1935); and aircraft supplied the prospectors and explorers who were opening up the final hidden parts of the country. One of the most spectacular forays was made by the wealthy American Richard Archbold who used a Catalina amphibian and discovered the Grand Valley of the Baliem in Dutch New Guinea.

The arrival of the Japanese in 1942 abruptly ended civil aviation. Most PNG-based aircraft were caught on the ground by the first devastating raids on Lae, Salamaua and Bulolo. The aircraft that survived made a final desperate series of flights to evacuate civilians away from the advancing Japanese.

When the war ended, aviation in PNG was a whole new story. In 1944 Qantas took over MAL's Australia-PNG connections and got their first toehold in the country. Guinea Airways were unable to obtain a licence to operate in PNG from the post-war Labor Government and Qantas became the dominant airline. Using DC3s and then DC4s Qantas started regular passenger services between Australia and PNG and during the '50s they built up quite an incredible fleet of aircraft for internal use. They operated everything from Beaver and Otter STOL aircraft, through DH-83 and DH-84 biplanes to Catalina, Short Solent and Sandringham flying boats. PNG was looked upon as a very useful training ground for pilots who would later fly on Qantas' international network.

In 1960 the Australian Government decided that Qantas should be a purely international airline and domestic services were handed over to Australia's domestic airlines, Ansett-ANA and Trans-Australia Airlines (TAA, now Australian Airlines) since PNG was considered to be part of Australia. MAL had been the main opposition to Qantas, swallowing smaller competitors such as Gibbes' Sepik Airways, but it was in turn engulfed by Ansett. TAA and Ansett-MAL operated turbo-prop Lockheed Electras and, later, Boeing 727s between Australia and PNG. Internally, they supplemented their DC3 workhorses with Fokker F27 Friendships in 1967.

Air Niugini was formed on I November 1973, almost immediately after the start of self-government, and took over Ansett's and TAA's PNG-based aircraft. Today Air Niugini, a very young airline with a very long pedigree, operates an Airbus 310 on international routes and Fokker F28s and De Havilland Dash 7s on its domestic routes. Talair, now the major third-level carrier, began as Territory Airlines Ltd (TAL) in 1952 and now has scheduled operations into 130 airports. ∎

schools and flights are heavily booked around Christmas, early February, late June and late September.

Remember that you may have to fly in *light* aircraft. If you do, flying out with a two-metre garamut drum tucked under your arm might be difficult. Not only is your baggage weighed (16 kg is the limit but 20 is usually accepted) – so are you.

You should really try to make at least one flight in a small aircraft while you're in the country – preferably somewhere up in the hills where flying can be a real experience. There are more than 450 licensed airfields so there

are plenty of opportunities – 18 could be described as second-level (large enough for F28s), while the rest are third-level (suitable for small aircraft only). TransNiugini Airways will take you along on their daily circuit of a number of spectacular mountain strips in Central Province for K195.

Unpredictable weather combined with mechanical problems and complex schedules can frequently lead to delays. If one plane is late at one airport the whole schedule can be thrown out. Considering the terrain, the airstrips and the weather, reliability is fair and the safety record is very good. The pilots are extremely skilful – keep telling yourself this as you approach flat-topped ridges masquerading as airports! Many young pilots are intent on building up their command experience so they can move on to a first-level airline, but others stay on because 'PNG has the best flying in the world'.

Discounts & Special Fares Talair no longer offers any discounts. MAF and some other third-level outfits offer student discounts of 25% (you must have current ID and they usually apply only to students under the age of 26 – the discount can be as much as 50% if you're under 18), but they don't really get into fancy discount structures. MAF also offers discounts of 25% to overseas volunteers with ID.

Air Niugini has a number of special deals. Given the high cost of air travel in the country, even travellers who don't usually pre-book air tickets might want to investigate them. These deals can and do change from time to time, so check before you leave home. See the Special Fares table.

ROADS

There is still a very limited network of roads around the country. The most important is the Highlands Highway, which is sealed from Lae to Mt Hagen, unsealed from Mt Hagen to Tari, and a 4WD track between Tari and Lake Kopiago where it ends. Madang is also connected to the highway.

Branching off the Highlands Highway are also a large number of secondary roads that go to numerous smaller places, such as Obura and Okapa in the Eastern Highlands; Chuave, Kegsugl, Kerowagi and Gumine in Simbu; Minj, Banz, Tabibuga and Baiyer River in the Western Highlands; Wabag,

---

Special Fares

Student Discounts Full-time students under 25 years of age get 25% off domestic fares (50% off if you're under 19). If you're making a booking outside PNG you need to have an International Student Concession Form, signed by the institution. You're also supposed to have one for booking flights within PNG.

Visit Papua New Guinea This must be booked outside PNG. You get four domestic flights for US$300, plus additional flights for US$50. This could be a huge saving but tickets, can only be bought in conjunction with a tour. There are other conditions – see a travel agent.

See Niugini These are booked outside PNG, in conjunction with certain advance purchase tickets to/from PNG (including APEX fares). You get 20% off domestic flights, and while you have to book flights before you arrive (well in advance), changes are permitted, with certain conditions. People seem to have no trouble getting the discount on tickets bought within PNG. Maximum stay 45 days.

Weekend Excursion Fares These round-trip tickets cost only 50% of the standard fare. You have to fly out on Friday or Saturday and back on Sunday or Monday. Unfortunately, only a certain number of discount seats are allocated to any one flight, and they're often booked out long in advance. These fares might apply only at certain times of the year. There are also good-value weekend packages which include accommodation.

Nambawan Fares These are probably the most useful fares for travellers, as they offer round-trip tickets at 50% discount. You have to stay a minimum of 14 and a maximum of 30 days, which allows plenty of time to explore your destination. You have to fly midweek. Like the weekend fares, these can be booked out, but it's less likely. You have to buy these tickets in PNG, from the town you'll fly from/to, in person. These fares might apply only at certain times of the year.

Hamamas Fares These offer 30% off round-trip fares, maximum 30 days, minimum seven days. Other conditions are similar to Nambawan fares. ■

Porgera, Kompiam and Kandep in Enga and Ialibu, Erave and Tambul in the Southern Highlands.

There are reasonable roads east and west along the coast from Port Moresby, along the north coast east and west of Madang, into the Sepik Basin from Wewak, and the Germans bequeathed excellent roads on New Britain and New Ireland. There is no road between Moresby and the Highlands or between Moresby and the north coast.

PUBLIC MOTOR VEHICLES (PMVs)

Wherever there are roads there will be PMVs. PMVs are one of the secrets to cheap travel in PNG and a very successful example of local enterprise. Thirty years ago they didn't exist, now they are indispensable. Most PMVs are comfortable Japanese minibuses, but they can be trucks with wooden benches, or even small, bare pick-up trucks.

Rural PMVs pick-up and drop-off people at any point along a pre-established route. You can more or less assume that anything with lots of people in it is a rural PMV, although officially they have a blue number plate beginning with P. In the urban areas there are established PMV stops (often indicated by a yellow pole or a crowd of waiting people). The destination will be indicated by a sign inside the windscreen or called out by the driver's assistant.

Stick your hand out and wave downwards and they will generally stop. PMVs have a crew of two: the driver, who usually maintains an aloof distance from the passengers; and the 'conductor', who takes fares and generally copes with the rabble. On most occasions the conductor sits up in the front next to the passenger-side window, so when the PMV stops, he's the man to ask about the PMV's destination. If it's heading in the right direction and there's a centimetre or two of spare space, you're on. You don't pay – yet.

If you're looking for long-distance PMVs, always start at the markets *early* in the morning. PMVs leave town when they're full (and I mean full) so if you're the first on board you can spend a very frustrating hour or two circling around looking for more passengers. Market days (usually Friday and Saturday) are the best days for finding a ride. On secondary roads, traffic can be thin, especially early in the week.

Costs

Not only is PMV travel cheap but it's also one of the best ways to meet the locals.

There are standard fares for PMVs. Ask your fellow passengers if you want to be certain what they are. If you are a student, try for a student discount; this won't always be forthcoming, but it can be generous when it is. In the towns you pay the conductor at the end of the trip after you've disembarked. If you tell the conductor where you want to go when you start, he'll let the driver know when to stop. If you make your mind up as you go, just yell 'Stop driver'.

In the country they quite frequently collect the fare either midway through the journey or 15 minutes or so before your final destination. It seems too many passengers were escaping into the bush without paying! Because of the general improvement in road standards and the fierce competition, fares have scarcely increased at all over the last few years.

Safety

Some expats say that PMVs are unsafe. Ignore these comments. You'll find that the people who are most hysterical about the dangers of riding on PMVs are the people who've never set foot in one. If the vehicle looks in pretty good shape and the driver does too, you are most unlikely to have any problems. Most drivers are very careful. They simply cannot afford to hit a stray person or pig (think of the compensation and the paybacks) let alone injure one of their passengers. You are not immune to armed hold-ups when you travel on PMVs in the Highlands but if you travel during the day and avoid pay afternoons (every second Friday) you're safer in a PMV than in a private car.

Make sure you get to your destination before dark and if you don't, ask the driver to deliver you to wherever you plan to stay.

CAR

Any valid overseas licence is OK for the first three months you're in PNG. Cars drive on the left side of the road. The speed limit is 50 km/h in towns and 100 km/h in the country.

Bear in mind the tourist office's recommendations if you are involved in an accident: Don't stop; keep driving and report the accident at the nearest police station. This applies regardless of who was at fault or how serious the accident is (whether you've run over a pig or hit a person).

Tribal concepts of payback apply to car accidents. You may have insurance and you may be willing to pay, but the local citizenry may well prefer to take more immediate and satisfying revenge. There have been a number of instances where drivers who have been involved in fatal accidents have been killed or injured by the accident victim's relatives. A serious accident can mean 'pack up and leave the country' for an expatriate.

Rental

It is possible to hire cars in most main centres but because of the limited road network (with the exception of the Highlands) you usually won't be able to get far. The major car rental organisations are Avis, Budget and Hertz. One or other of them will have cars in every major town, including on the islands of Manus, New Britain and New Ireland. There are also a few smaller, local firms that are sometimes cheaper than the internationals; they are mentioned in the appropriate chapters.

Costs are high, partly because the cars have such a hard life and spend so much time on unsealed roads. All rental rates with the big operators are made up of a daily or weekly charge plus a certain charge per km. In addition you should probably budget for insurance at around K15 a day. Typical costs and vehicles are:

Vehicle	Daily Rate	Km Rate
Mitsubishi Lancer	K54	K0.45
Mitsubishi Magna	K79	K0.55
Honda Accord	K84	K0.64
Mitsubishi Pajero 4WD	K88	K0.65

In addition, remote area surcharges of around K15 a day may apply. The Highlands are regarded as remote. The three main operators all have desks at Jacksons Airport, Port Moresby:

Avis
   PO Box 1533, Port Moresby (☎ 25 8429, fax 25 3767)
Budget
   PO Box 1215, Boroko (☎ 25 4111, fax 25 7853)
Hertz
   PO Box 4126, Boroko (☎ 25 4999, fax 25 6985)

BICYCLE

The Highlands Highway is probably out for cycling, because of the danger of robbery. Still, a mountain bike would be very handy on the Trobriands, around the Gazelle Peninsula (West New Britain) and, best of all, on idyllic New Ireland where there are two long, flat coast roads with little traffic. A couple of companies offer bike tours of New Ireland, and it might be possible to hire bikes in Kavieng.

HITCHING

It is possible to hitch-hike, although you'll often be expected to pay the equivalent of a PMV fare. In some places any passing vehicle is likely to offer you a ride. That is, *if* there is a passing vehicle. You're wisest to wave them down, otherwise it's possible they'll think you're a mad tourist walking for the fun of it. If your bag is light, it's also sometimes possible to hitch-hike flights from small airports.

WALKING

The best and cheapest way to come to grips with PNG is to walk. See some of the walks suggested in the Activities section of the Facts for the Visitor chapter. With a judicious mix of walks, canoes, PMVs, coastal ships and third-level planes PNG can change from a very expensive country to a relatively reasonable one.

Accommodation and food is normally available in the villages – meaning floor space, and sago or sweet potato – and once

Top: Carvings from the Blackwater Lakes region, East Sepik Province (RE)
Left: Sepik masks (TW)
Right: Malangan carvings from New Ireland Province (TW)

Top Left: Parliament Building, Port Moresby (JM)
Top Right: Looking across to Town from Hanuabada, Port Moresby (JM)
Bottom: Stilt village near Koki, Port Moresby (JM)

you're afloat or on foot you will spend very little money.

For detailed information on walking see the Lonely Planet book *Bushwalking in Papua New Guinea*. Your major costs will be paying for guides and porters, where they are necessary. Expect to pay them between K5 and K10 a day in addition to buying their food, providing sleeping gear and space and possibly some equipment.

SEA

There is a wide variety of interesting sea transport, from ocean-going vessels to canoes. You can plan your trip around Lutheran Shipping's passenger boats or you can just wait under a palm tree and see what comes along.

The main ways of getting around by sea are: large boats, small boats, charters and yacht crewing.

Large Boats

Basically there are boats taking passengers along the north coast between Oro Bay (near Popondetta) and Vanimo, and to the main islands off the north coast. There are no passenger vessels linking the north and south coasts or running along the south coast.

Most of the main cargo lines are very reluctant to take passengers on their freighters. However, if you make the right connections, usually via an expat in the shipping office or directly with a crew member at the docks, you'll often manage to get a berth or deck space. The major companies list their schedules in the Shipping Notes section of the *Post Courier*, so you'll at least have an idea of when and where to look for a boat.

Conditions on many freighters can be grim. It is essential to take your own food, and perhaps water. Your fare may include meals but these will amount to rice and tinned fish and may or may not be edible. At the very least, take fruit and drinks with you. If you're travelling deck class, a light sleeping bag or a bed sheet, a mat and a tent fly (for shade and shelter) will

be handy. Freighters often have schedules but they are very unreliable, due to delays in loading/unloading cargoes. Also, many ships won't take passengers if they have dangerous cargo (including petrol). They often won't know what the cargo will be much in advance, so you can't rely on travelling on a particular voyage.

Luckily, Lutheran Shipping runs a reliable, inexpensive and reasonably comfortable passenger-only service between Oro Bay and Wewak, with services out to New Britain.

Although there are a number of other smaller operations, some of the main shipping companies and their head offices are:

Coastal Shipping Company
  PO Box 423, Rabaul, East New Britain (☎ 92 2399, fax 92 2090)
Consort Express Lines
  PO Box 1690, Port Moresby (☎ 21 1288, fax 21 1279)
Lutheran Shipping
  PO Box 1459, Lae, Morobe Province (☎ 42 2066, fax 42 5806)
Pacific New Guinea Line
  PO Box 1764, Rabaul, East New Britain (☎ 92 3055, fax 92 3084)
PNG Shipping Corporation
  PO Box 634, Port Moresby (☎ 22 0420, fax 21 2815)

North Coast Lutheran Shipping has a virtual monopoly on passenger shipping along the north coast and services Oro Bay, Lae, Finschhafen, Madang, Wewak, Aitape, Vanimo and intermediate ports.

There are two passenger-only boats, the *Mamose Express* and the *Rita*, which run between Oro Bay and Wewak, with services from Lae to New Britain. The tourist class on these boats consists of air-conditioned seats and berths, and deck class has air-vented seats and berths.

Some people say that the difference in quality between the two isn't enough to justify paying the higher fare, although deck class can get very crowded and you might miss out on a bunk. Both classes have video 'entertainment', and you might want to

For the Lazy Shoestringer
The high cost of travel in PNG is exacerbated by the cost of transport, but it is possible to see most of the country without breaking the bank. The simplest way to do this is to walk, take local boats and canoes and stay in villages but for those who don't have the time or the stamina for this, there are alternatives.

The following suggestions don't include *any* walking or paddling and very little irregular local transport. Adding any of these opens up much more of the country.

Nor are the suggestions anywhere exhaustive – PNG has so much that's worth seeing. Almost all the major centres mentioned here are jumping-off points for some very interesting and often inexpensive places to stay – see the various sections in this book.

It would take much longer than the standard two-month visa allows to visit all the places mentioned here, and it's unlikely that you would want to – you'll be captured by somewhere magical along the way.

From Port Moresby you could fly to Kokoda (K51) and from there take a PMV to Popondetta (K5), where there are some inexpensive places to stay. From here, take a PMV to Oro Bay (K3) where a weekly Lutheran Shipping passenger boat sails to Lae (K21.50 deck class), Madang and Wewak.

From Lae, where the YMCA charges K12 for bed, dinner and breakfast, you could take a PMV to Wau (K5) and stay at the interesting Ecology Institute (K15). PMVs to Goroka from Lae cost K10, but you're better off taking a Lutheran Shipping boat to Madang (K21.50 deck class). There are some good places to stay in beautiful Madang, from K6 a night on Siar Island.

A PMV from Madang to Goroka costs about K20, but this should drop when a new road opens. In Goroka, a bed at the Lutheran Guesthouse costs K25, but it's an excellent place to stay, and the price includes a good breakfast and dinner. Once you're in the Highlands you can travel all the way to Tari or Kopiago by PMV (total fares from Goroka to Tari are about K30), and there are inexpensive places to stay all along the way, including guesthouses at Kegsugl (off the highway at the foot of Mt Wilhelm), several options in Mt Hagen, hostels in Mendi, and some very good choices in and near Tari.

avoid bunks near the video. There is a snack bar which serves soft drinks and pies, etc. You can get hot water to make tea or coffee, but you'll have to ask.

If you miss the boat you'll get a 50% refund on your ticket up to 48 hours after sailing, and nothing after that. Booking ahead might be necessary around Christmas.

Following is the schedule for Lutheran Shipping passenger-only boats along the north coast, but remember that it can change.

Note that some boats go on to New Britain from Lae, so you might have to change if you're going further east or west along the coast. Students are entitled to discounts, although whether this is 50% or 25% differs between booking offices.

Westbound

Port	Time	Day	Deck	Tourist
Oro Bay	1 pm (dep)	Tue	K21.50	K32.50
Lae	7 am (arr)	Wed		
	9 am (dep)	Wed	K21.50	K32.50
Madang	6 am (arr)	Thur		
	5 pm (dep)	Fri	K22.40	K33.80
Wewak	9 am (arr)	Sat		

Eastbound

Port	Time	Day	Deck	Tourist
Wewak	noon (dep)	Sat	K22.40	K33.80
Madang	6 am (arr)	Sun		
	9am (dep)	Sun	K21.50	K32.50
Lae	7am (arr)	Mon		
	7 pm (dep)	Mon	K21.50	K32.50
Oro Bay	11 am (arr)	Tue		

Through Rates

Route	Deck	Tourist
Lae-Wewak	K36.40	K54.60
Wewak-Oro Bay	K58.80	K88.40

Lutheran Shipping's passenger-carrying freighters run unpredictably between Oro Bay and Vanimo (and out to the islands), at fares slightly lower than those on the passenger-only boats.

Islands Lutheran Shipping has a weekly passenger-only boat sailing from Lae to Kimbe and Rabaul on Monday afternoon, arriving on Tuesday. To Rabaul deck class costs K34 and cabin K54.

Coastal Shipping has the *Lae Express*, a

You can fly from Tari to the Sepik (for example, to Timbunke for K98 with Talair) and from there take a motorised canoe (or wait for a passenger canoe) to one of the road-heads, from where you can travel to Wewak. Cheaper and easier (but not as interesting) is to take a Lutheran Shipping passenger boat to Wewak from Madang (K21.50 deck class). In Wewak you can stay at Ralf's for K9, and from here there are a number of ways to get onto the river. Cheapest is to take a PMV to Angoram (K6) and arrange a tour by motorised canoe there (about K70 a day), and stay in villages (K10 or less in Angoram, K5 or less elsewhere).

If you're going on to Indonesia, take a Lutheran Shipping freighter to Vanimo (K21 deck class). In Vanimo you can stay in a dorm at the Resort Hotel for K15. (It's probably better to fly to Vanimo (K86) from Wewak, as taking the freighter might mean a lot of waiting around.) The Sunday Air Niugini flight from Vanimo to Jayapura costs K60, or you can probably fly midweek with Sandaun Air Services for K65. Sandaun might soon be offering flights to Biak. Don't forget the K15 departure tax.

Of course, this route would miss some of the friendliest and most idyllic parts of PNG – Milne Bay and the islands, which are genuine, untouched Pacific paradises. You can hop around the coast on small boats to Milne Bay from Port Moresby, but that isn't for the truly lazy, so you might have to grit your teeth and fly to Alotau (K101). Once in Alotau there are fairly regular work boats to the Trobriand Islands (K20) and other groups. There are guesthouses in the Goodenough group but on the Trobriands you'll have to stay in villages, from about K10.

Lutheran Shipping and other lines take passengers to New Britain from Lae (K28 to Kimbe, K34 to Rabaul). Rabaul has some good places to stay, from K20 in town and less in nearby village guesthouses, one on the nearby Duke of York Islands (K5 from Rabaul). You can travel around the coast of New Britain on regular small boats. From Rabaul you can fly to Namatanai on New Ireland (K30). Make your way up the island, staying in the friendly villages along the way, to Kavieng, where there is a hotel (from K27 a double) and at least one island guesthouse (K30 or less).

Manus is accessible by Lutheran Shipping freighters from Lae (K40 deck class), Madang (K21) and less frequently by Coastal Shipping freighters from Rabaul (K46) or Kavieng (K32). Manus has a number of village guesthouses, including a couple on islands near Lorengau (from K10), where the freighters dock. ∎

passenger boat, running once a week between Lae and Rabaul via Kimbe. This boat has only just come into service so its timetable hasn't settled yet, but it will probably depart on Friday and take about 48 hours to Rabaul. Coastal's *Kimbe Express* also sails to Rabaul via Kimbe, departing on Friday arriving in Kimbe on Sunday and Lae on Monday. It's a mixed passenger/cargo boat, with deck-class accommodation only. The fare to Kimbe is K28 and Rabaul K34. Coastal's *Astro I* departs for Rabaul on Wednesday, running via the south coast of New Britain and stopping at Kandrian, among other places. This is not a passenger boat but there are a few cabins in which you can sometimes travel, for K80 to Rabaul.

Coastal also has freighters, unscheduled but running approximately fortnightly, sailing from Rabaul to Kavieng on New Ireland. The 18-hour trip costs about K35/50 in deck/cabin class. These boats sometimes continue on to Lihir Island and the other island groups off New Ireland's east coast. Other freighters run to Nissan Island and on to Buka approximately

weekly for K34, deck class. About once a month, Coastal has a boat from Rabaul to Manus (K46/90), via Kavieng.

Lutheran Shipping freighters depart Lae on Tuesday or Wednesday for Lorengau on Manus, usually calling at Madang either on the outward or the return voyage. Lorengau to Madang costs K21/26 in deck/cabin class; to Lae it's K40/47. The *Tawi* is operated by the Manus Provincial Government and plies between Lorengau, the outer islands of Manus, Wuvulu Island, Wewak and Madang. Theoretically, the *Tawi* makes about 30 voyages a year but it is often commandeered for government business so there is no real schedule and you could wait at least a month for it to show up. Lorengau to Wuvulu (K18) takes three days, and from there it's another day to Wewak (K28). The 24-hour voyage to Madang costs K17.

South Coast No freighters officially take passengers on the south coast. For unofficial berths try the shipping offices and docks in Port Moresby, where you'll also find small boats running to Gulf Province. Rambu Shipping is a small line which is reportedly worth approaching. You can village-hop east to Milne Bay, but it's probably best to start from Kupiano.

Small Boats

In addition to the freighters and passenger boats, local boats and canoes go literally everywhere. For these you have to be in the right place at the right time, but with patience you could travel the whole coastline by village-hopping in small boats.

Work boats – small, wooden boats with thumping diesel engines – ply the coast supplying trade stores and acting as ferries. They run irregularly but fairly frequently, and travelling on one will get you to some very off-the-track places. They aren't very comfortable and can be noisy and smelly, but for the adventurous there's no better way to travel.

Fares are low – for example, a two-day trip from Alotau in Milne Bay to the Trobriand Islands (overnighting on a tropical beach) will cost about K20.

If you're in a major centre ask at the big stores, as they might have a fairly set schedule for delivering supplies to the area's trade stores. Take your own food and water on these boats.

Around New Britain and other places there are slightly more regular coastal services in small freighters, and in some places mission boats run set schedules and will take passengers.

For shorter distances there are dinghies with outboard motors, often known as speedies or banana boats. These are usually long, fibreglass boats which are surprisingly seaworthy despite their bronco-like mode of travel, leaping through the waves. The cost of running outboard motors makes them very expensive if you have to charter one, but there will often be a speedie acting as a ferry (taking people to church or market) and the fares are reasonable. There are still canoes with outboards around, and you might even get to make a voyage in a sailing canoe on the south coast.

Tours

Melanesian Tourist Services runs the luxurious *Melanesian Discoverer* on cruises from Milne Bay to (and up) the Sepik, and you can take sectors.

Boat Charter

Many dive operators charter their boats, some for extended cruises. A cheaper alternative, if you're not looking for comfort and the chance to dive, is to try to charter a work boat. Chartering is definitely possible in Milne Bay and probably elsewhere, and between a group, of say five or six, isn't ruinously expensive.

Yacht Crewing

There are thriving yacht clubs in Port Moresby, Lae, Rabaul and Wewak and it is possible that you might be able to find a berth, if you have some experience. Yachts often clear PNG customs at Samarai Island in Milne Bay.

RIVER

There are a number of rivers that villagers use as 'highways'. These include the Sepik and some of its tributaries (including the April, May and Keram), the Ramu, the Fly and a number of other rivers that flow into the Gulf of Papua.

If you are prepared to rough it and live in the villages, it is possible to get around on inter-village canoes. The problem with this is that although they are relatively cheap they only run according to demand – there are no schedules. Traffic builds up from Wednesday through to Saturday because of people moving around for markets, but can be very quiet early in the week and nonexistent on Sundays.

If you are short of time, you can charter a motorised village canoe or boat, with a guide/driver. This is, however, expensive: probably somewhere between K10 and K20 per hour of running time (this is due to the high cost of operating two-stroke engines) plus a hire fee.

Paddling your own canoe (a dugout bought from a village) is most popular on the Sepik – see the Sepik chapter for a more detailed discussion of the options.

LOCAL TRANSPORT

Some of the larger towns have taxis, but they aren't common. Most places have PMVs (see the earlier Public Motor Vehicles (PMVs) section).

TOURS

See the Facts for the Visitor chapter for information on various tours in PNG.

River

On the Sepik some village guides will quote you an all-up daily rate for tours, including village accommodation, and this can be about K70 a day. See the Sepik chapter for more details on this.

There are also several tour boats cruising the Sepik.

Port Moresby & Central Province

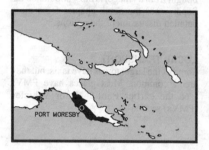

Land Area 29,940 sq km
Population 320,000

Central Province covers the narrow coastal strip along the south coast from the Gulf of Papua almost to the eastern end of the mainland, plus the southern half of the central mountain range. Port Moresby, the capital of PNG, is situated about halfway along the coast on a superb natural harbour. A rain shadow affects the city area and it is much drier than the rest of the country. The dry, brown, northern-Australian look of Moresby fades into the usual lush green as you move away from the capital, both along the coast and inland into the rugged Owen Stanley Ranges. In the dry season Port Moresby can suffer from extended droughts and there can be restrictions on water use.

HISTORY

There were two groups of people living in the Port Moresby area when the first Europeans arrived. They were the Motu and the Koitabu. The Motu were a seagoing people with an Austronesian language that has close links with other Melanesian and Polynesian languages. It seems probable that the Motuans were relatively late arrivals on the coast (possibly migrating from island Melanesia less than 2000 years ago) and they lived in harmony with the Koitabu who speak an inland, non-Austronesian language.

The Motuan people were great sailors and their impressive boats, *lakatois*, which were up to 15 metres long, were capable of carrying a large cargo and crew. They were rigged with one or two masts and strange crab-claw shaped sails.

The high point of the Motuan year was the annual *hiri* trading voyage – each Motuan village had a counterpart village in the Gulf region with which it traded clay pots for sago. The Motuans were not great farmers, perhaps because of the dry climate and

limited agricultural potential of the Port Moresby area, as well as their heritage, so they depended on Gulf sago for their survival.

Motu villages were built on stilts over the harbour. Hanuabada (meaning 'the great village') was the largest of their communities and still exists today, although in a considerably changed form.

The first European visit they received was in 1873 when Captain John Moresby, investigating the south coast of the mysterious island of New Guinea, sailed into the harbour. He spent several days trading with the villagers at Hanuabada and was very impressed with the people and their lives. In his diary he asked himself, 'What have these people to gain from civilisation?'

One year later the London Missionary Society established its first outpost and the missionaries were soon followed by traders, and 'blackbirders' who recruited indentured labourers and were little better than slavers. For a time the blackbirders' 'kanaka' labourers were as important an export as bêche-de-mer and pearl shell.

The island's interior remained largely unexplored and 'unclaimed' by Europeans as Britain had sufficient colonial problems to attend to without the addition of New Guinea. Finally, in 1888, under pressure from colonists in Australia and because of trepidation about the intentions of the

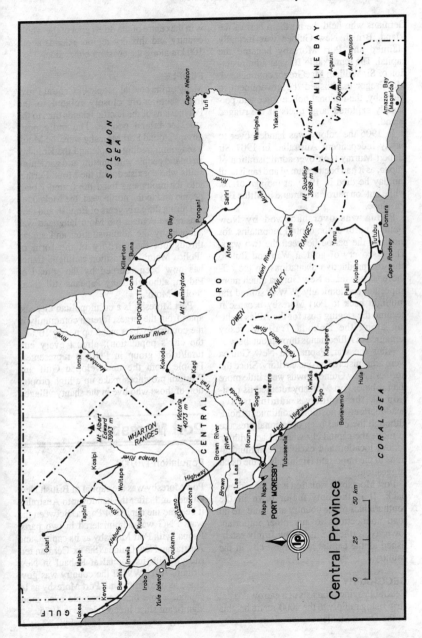

Central Province

Germans who held the northern half of the island, British New Guinea was formally claimed and Port Moresby became the capital. The remarkable 10-year administration of Sir William MacGregor commenced. MacGregor established the government in Moresby, the national police force and personally explored large tracts of the rugged island.

In 1906 the colony was handed over to newly independent Australia. In 1907 Sir Hubert Murray took over administration of Papua, as it had been renamed and ran it until the day he died in 1940, at the age of 78, while out 'on patrol' at Samarai in Milne Bay Province.

Papua was overshadowed by New Guinea, north of the central mountains, for much of the period between the two wars. The discovery of gold at Wau and Bulolo plus the productive plantations on the offshore islands made New Guinea much more important economically. WW II shifted the spotlight back to Port Moresby because it became the staging post for the Allies fighting along the Kokoda Trail. Moresby remained in Allied hands throughout the war.

After the war, Papua and New Guinea were administered as one territory. Since the northern New Guinea towns were little more than rubble, Port Moresby retained its position as the country's administrative headquarters – a position it continues to hold, although there has been occasional pressure to move the capital elsewhere. Lae, with its central location and excellent communications to the important Highlands, is the usual suggestion.

Port Moresby's isolation is its main drawback. It is the only major town in the southern half of the country and there are no road connections to any other important town. Nevertheless, it is now firmly established as the capital and largest city in the country.

GEOGRAPHY

Central Province consists of a narrow coastal strip rising rapidly to the 4000-metre heights of the Owen Stanley Ranges. Port Moresby is in the centre of the driest area of the whole country and this dry region extends about 100 km along the coast on either side.

PEOPLE

Many of the coastal people of Central Province seem more closely related to the Polynesians of the Pacific Islands than to the stockier inland people. The indigenous groups around Port Moresby were the Motu, a seagoing, trading people and the Koitabu, an inland people with hunting and gardening skills who coexisted with the Motu. Further into the mountains lived the feared Koiari people and to the north-west, the Mekeo.

During the early years of English and then Australian contact the Motu language was adopted by the administration and spread throughout the territory in the form of 'Police Motu'. Its position as lingua franca has now been usurped by the spread of Pidgin, although many Papuans still speak 'Police Motu'.

Port Moresby is a cosmopolitan city and apart from the largest foreign community in the country (expats make up nearly 10% of the city's population), almost every cultural/tribal group in PNG is represented. People from the undeveloped Gulf and Western provinces make up a high proportion of those who live in the shanty villages.

Port Moresby

Population 170,000

Port Moresby was the capital of British New Guinea and, after the handover to Australia, it became the capital of Papua. Between the wars PNG was administered in two parts, Papua, with Port Moresby as its capital, and Australian New Guinea (the ex-German territory), with its capital at Rabaul in New Britain. After WW II the country was governed as one entity with Port Moresby as its capital, a role that has become even more significant since independence in 1975.

Many people find 'Moresby', as it is

known locally, a rather dismal place. It is dry, hot and dusty for much of the year and that's only the start of its problems. People with cars may not find it annoying, but one of Moresby's biggest drawbacks is its amazing sprawl. It is not so much a city as a collection of widely separated suburbs. Architecturally and climatically, it resembles Australia's Darwin.

Moresby also suffers from a 'big city' syndrome – it attracts people in search of fame and fortune. Naturally many fail to find either and a large number end up living in squalid, unserviced squatter settlements. They contribute to Moresby's high crime rate, particularly the house-breaking (often with violence) that leads to fanatical security precautions. Razor wire, large dogs and private security guards are everywhere. The gloom is not all-pervading – there are interesting things to see and do around the city. At present, almost every visitor to the country is forced to go through Moresby and it is worth spending a couple of days looking around and acclimatising. It is, after all, an important part of the country.

Throughout PNG, knowing somebody can be enormously helpful, and this is especially the case in Moresby. If you do have an address, or you do know somebody, look them up! If you don't know anybody, try to meet people with similar work or leisure interests, or better still, contact them before you leave home.

If you still dislike Moresby, remember this important rule: never judge a country by its capital city.

Warning

Be careful. The crime rate is high, and the statistics for rape are particularly bad. As a general rule, do not walk around the streets at night as even in a group you can be vulnerable. If you are planning to 'hit the town', catch a PMV to your chosen venue, and catch a taxi home. Be especially wary on pay Fridays.

If you wouldn't walk around a tough neighbourhood in a big city at home, you won't enjoy walking around Moresby; if you live in a tough neighbourhood you'll know that most people are pretty friendly. You'll also know that most residents are as worried about crime as outsiders, and can offer advice. Meeting people – on the street, in Public Motor Vehicles (PMVs), wherever – is not only enjoyable but enhances your safety.

The basic rules are much the same as in any other dangerous area – beware of drunks and other crazies, and of young men (including young teenagers), especially in groups. Never leave any possessions unattended, and in crowded places be aware that occasionally there are pickpockets. Women should dress discreetly and should not go too far from other people and central areas of activity, even during the day. Above all, do not advertise your wealth. People dressed expensively or as obvious tourists might be targets for robbery. Unless you are staying at one of the top-end places, and perhaps even then, stay alert even when you get back to your hotel.

Walking up Paga Hill is all right during the day, especially at lunch time, but you would be unwise to go alone. Be careful walking past the shanty settlement on Three Mile Hill above Koki and behind Waigani around the golf club. Stay out of the shanty towns and Hanuabada unless you have a local guide; if you don't know what you are doing and where you're going, you can very easily get into trouble.

There are no problems with using PMVs or wandering around the markets – aggressively taking photos in the markets is another story.

Lastly, don't overreact! If you are careful, you would have to be extremely unlucky to have any problems.

Orientation

Getting your bearings in Moresby is no easy task as it spreads out around the coast and the inland hills. It takes a while to work out where things are. The hills mean that getting from A to B, a short distance in a straight line, may involve lengthy detours around the intervening terrain. Fortunately, PMVs run regular services between all areas of the city.

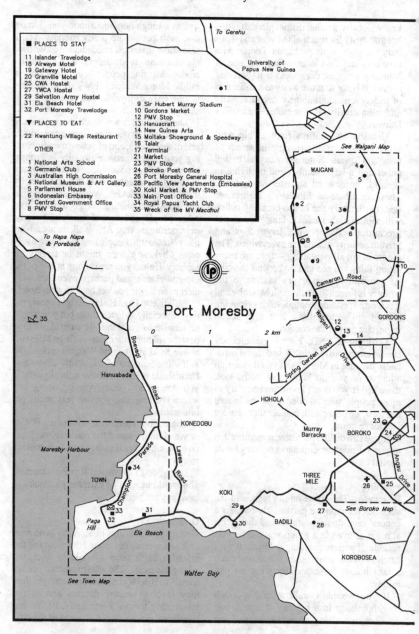

PLACES TO STAY
11 Islander Travelodge
18 Airways Motel
19 Gateway Hotel
20 Granville Motel
25 CWA Hostel
27 YWCA Hostel
29 Salvation Army Hostel
31 Ela Beach Hotel
32 Port Moresby Travelodge

▼ **PLACES TO EAT**
22 Kwantung Village Restaurant

OTHER
1 National Arts School
2 Germania Club
3 Australian High Commission
4 National Museum & Art Gallery
5 Parliament House
6 Indonesian Embassy
7 Central Government Office
8 PMV Stop
9 Sir Hubert Murray Stadium
10 Gordons Market
12 PMV Stop
13 Hanuacraft
14 New Guinea Arts
15 Moitaka Showground & Speedway
16 Talair
17 Terminal
21 Market
23 PMV Stop
24 Boroko Post Office
26 Port Moresby General Hospital
28 Pacific View Apartments (Embassies)
30 Koki Market & PMV Stop
33 Main Post Office
34 Royal Papua Yacht Club
35 Wreck of the MV Macdhui

Port Moresby

0   1   2 km

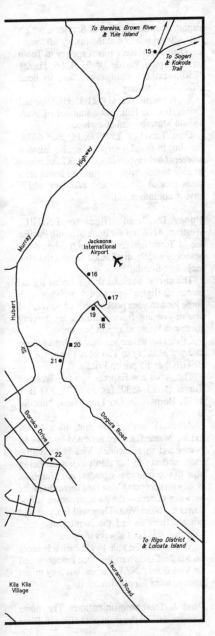

To Bereina, Brown River & Yule Island

15

To Sogeri & Kokoda Trail

Highway

Murray

Jacksons International Airport

16

17

19

18

20

21

St

Hubert

Boroko Drive

Dogura Road

22

To Rigo District & Loloata Island

Taurama Road

Kila Kila Village

The centre, if Moresby can claim such a feature, is on a spit of land which ends in Paga Hill and is usually known as Town. The centre has the majority of Moresby's older buildings, the shipping docks and wharves, most of the major commercial office buildings, the conspicuous Travelodge and a large Steamships department store.

If you follow the coast round to the north, past the docks, you'll come to the Sir Hubert Murray Stadium, then Konedobu (a government office centre), then Hanuabada (the original Motuan stilt village).

East from the Town, the main road runs alongside popular Ela Beach until you reach Koki where there are shops, the Salvation Army Hostel, the Koki Market and another, smaller stilt village. From Koki, the road divides into two one-way sections and climbs steeply up Three Mile Hill before dropping down to Boroko.

Boroko (also known as Four Mile – it is about six km from Town) has, in some areas, overtaken Town as the most important commercial and shopping centre. There are numerous shops, restaurants, banks, airline agencies and there's a new, efficient post office.

If you continue along the Sir Hubert Murray Highway you pass Jacksons International Airport (also known as Seven Mile). A few km past the airport the road divides, heading west to Brown River and east to the mountains, the Kokoda Trail and Sogeri.

The main intersection is at Boroko where there is a T-intersection between the Sir Hubert Murray Highway and Waigani Drive which runs out to the north-west. Waigani Drive takes you between the areas of Hohola (residential) and Gordons (industrial, with an excellent market) to Waigani (the sprawling government centre about four km from Boroko).

A little beyond Waigani you reach the University of Papua New Guinea campus. After the campus, one road turns west back to the coast (joining the coast road seven or eight km out from Hanuabada) and another continues to Gerehu, a fast growing residential suburb.

There are plans to build a freeway through Moresby but given the political scandals surrounding the previous government's attempts at getting it started, the completion date might be a long way off.

Information

Tourist Information There is a tourist information desk at the airport in the international arrivals area. It has a limited range of publications but hotel bookings can be made from there. The Papua New Guinea National Tourist Office (☎ 25 3316, PO Box 7144, Boroko) is in the Savings & Loan building at Waigani (see Waigani map). It may be worth giving them a call, or writing before you arrive; they do produce a Visitors' Guide, an annual Accommodation Directory and, in conjunction with Shell, a good map.

If you're in the Town and are desperate for information you could try the Department of Tourism office in ANG House but they aren't much help. (Don't go in the main entrance; turn left along the walkway and around the corner.)

Don't be hesitant about asking the locals for advice – 99% of the time they'll be friendly and helpful, even in Moresby, the big smoke.

If you're really stuck, you could call the Travelodge (☎ 21 2266) – the people at the front desk are helpful.

If you want assistance with your plans and itinerary, consider contacting Traditional Travel (☎ 21 3966, PO Box 4264, Boroko). They operate a number of adventure tours (day tours and rafting trips from Moresby, canoeing the Sepik, trekking the Highlands, etc) so they know a lot about the country. They also deal with a number of interesting village guesthouses. If you're not interested in tours, the staff are quite happy (for a moderate charge) to help you work out a personal itinerary. They have an information desk in the Travelodge.

Trans Niugini Tours, which runs the Bensbach, Karawari and Ambua lodges, also organise tours. Its head office is in Mt Hagen and it also has a booking office in Moresby (☎ 25 3829), in the Gateway Hotel at the airport. Melanesian Tourist Services, which runs several hotels and the luxury *Melanesian Discoverer*, has a travel agency in Town on Champion Parade (☎ 21 4766, fax 21 4750), near the main post office. Its head office is in Madang.

South Pacific Tours (☎ 21 3500), Davetari Drive, Togoba Hill, has a number of tours around Moresby and elsewhere.

Dove Travel (☎ 25 9800, PO Box 6478, Boroko) in Boroko serves Catholic mission workers (and anyone else) in PNG and might be able to help with information about missions around the country, many of which have accommodation.

Money The head offices for PNGBC, Westpac, ANZ and the Bank of South Pacific are in Town not far from each other, with branches widely distributed around the city, including Boroko.

The airport has a bank that opens for all incoming flights – probably! Arriving with some kina in your pocket isn't a bad idea. If you're coming from Australia try buying some at a Westpac airport branch.

Other than the airport branch, banks close at 2 pm Monday to Thursday (3 pm for the PNGBC) and 5 pm on Friday.

The American Express agent is Westpac Travel (☎ 25 4500, fax 25 1675, PO Box 1552, Boroko) in Ori Lavi Haus, Nita St, Boroko.

Amex, Diner's Club and, to a lesser extent, MasterCard are accepted by top-end places and some airlines. Visa is becoming more acceptable but don't count on being able to use it in many places. Air Niugini's policy on accepting Visa card seems to differ between offices – the Moresby town office currently takes Visa. They will tell you that other offices around the country also take Visa, but this isn't always true.

You should be able to get cash advances on MasterCard from Westpac branches and on Visa from ANZ branches, but they might have to telex for confirmation.

Post & Telecommunications The poste restante desk at the main post office in Town is efficient and reliable but, for many travellers, the post office at Boroko is much more convenient. At Boroko, go to the Registered Mail counter. Both these post offices have philatelic counters. The hours are from 8.30 am to 4.30 pm, Monday to Friday, and from 8.30 to 11.30 am on Saturdays.

There are phones outside Boroko post office, some coin operated and some card operated. There are no phones at the main post office in Town, but just inside the Steamships store next door are some coin and card phones – the supermarket is open every day.

You're less likely to have to queue at a card phone, and they are less often vandalised. Cards are available from post offices and some shops. Don't go overboard and buy the large denomination cards, as there aren't many places in PNG where you can use them. A reasonably long call to Australia will use up a K10 phone card.

Foreign Embassies Most foreign embassies are in Waigani. See the Facts for the Visitor chapter for addresses.

Books & Maps Excellent, detailed maps are available at the National Mapping Bureau in Waigani (☎ 27 6465, fax 25 9716, PO Box 5665, Boroko), open weekdays from 8 am to noon and from 1 to 3 pm. It has a full range of topographic maps of varying scales, as well as other specialised maps. Don't even think of bushwalking without getting a set of relevant topographic maps. If you fax or write to them, they'll send you a list of what they have in stock and you can order by mail. The Shell *Tourist Guide to PNG* (a map) is good value and is available from Shell petrol stations and the PNG Office of Tourism. Air Niugini also produces an excellent little map of the country.

There are several good places to buy books. The book section in the huge downtown Steamships department store has a varied selection, including guidebooks and Pidgin dictionaries. City News in the Morgoru Motu building on the west side of Steamships and the airport newsagent are both reasonably well stocked. The University of PNG and the National Museum are the best places to look for books on PNG.

It's worth visiting the Institute of PNG Studies in Angau Drive, Boroko; it sells publications by local authors and films, videos and recordings of traditional culture and music.

Libraries There's a small Port Moresby public library in Town on Douglas St next to the Big Rooster. The big National Library (an independence gift from Australia), at the University of PNG, Waigani, is an excellent library which houses a huge PNG collection. The National Archives, also at Waigani, houses an interesting collection.

All of them are open to the public.

Laundry The Agutoi chain has several laundromats around Moresby, two of which are usefully located for travellers: in Badili not far from the Salvation Army Hostel – next to the Mobil station on the next corner north; and in Lakatoi Arcade in Boroko.

Emergency The general phone number for emergencies (police, fire and ambulance) is 000. Note that this number doesn't apply elsewhere in PNG. The Port Moresby General Hospital (☎ 24 8200) is on Taurama Rd, Korobosea, not far from Boroko.

Port Moresby City

'Town', as it's commonly known, retains some sense of history, although there are few old buildings left, and characterless office blocks are now in the majority. Pacific Place (with a hemisphere on top), ANG House and the Travelodge dominate the skyline.

At the other end of Douglas St from the Travelodge is the PNGBC Bank, with some interesting, traditionally influenced decoration on the facade. Also check out the dugout canoe from the Gulf region which hangs from the ceiling. At about 25 metres long, it is said to be one of the largest canoes ever made. An inscription describes its ceremonial use.

The Parliament House and the National

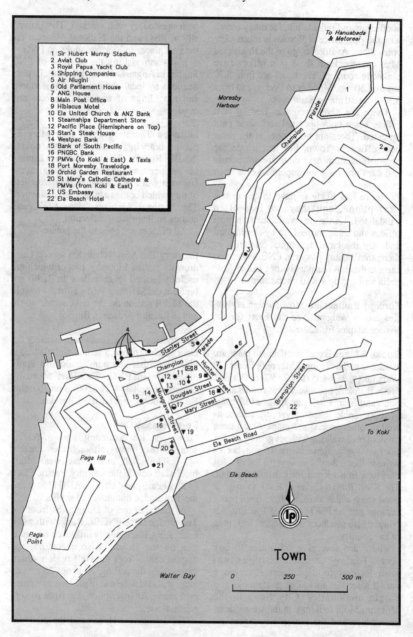

1 Sir Hubert Murray Stadium
2 Aviat Club
3 Royal Papua Yacht Club
4 Shipping Companies
5 Air Niugini
6 Old Parliament House
7 ANG House
8 Main Post Office
9 Hibiscus Motel
10 Ela United Church & ANZ Bank
11 Steamships Department Store
12 Pacific Place (Hemisphere on Top)
13 Stan's Steak House
14 Westpac Bank
15 Bank of South Pacific
16 PNGBC Bank
17 PMVs (to Koki & East) & Taxis
18 Port Moresby Travelodge
19 Orchid Garden Restaurant
20 St Mary's Catholic Cathedral &
   PMVs (from Koki & East)
21 US Embassy
22 Ela Beach Hotel

To Hanuabada
& Metoreai

Moresby Harbour

Champion Parade

Stanley Street
Parade
Champion
Hunter Street
Douglas Street
Musgrave Street
Mary Street
Brampton Street
Ela Beach Road

To Koki

Paga Hill

Paga Point

Ela Beach

Walter Bay

Town

0   250   500 m

Museum used to share a building just behind ANG House but the museum moved out to Waigani in 1977 and the parliament followed in 1984.

Paga Point, ends in a high hill – it's worth getting up to the top for the fine views over the town, the harbour and the encircling reefs. It's quite a popular spot at lunch times, but if you walk up, you would be wise to go in a group.

The oldest building still standing in Moresby is the **Ela United Church** in Douglas St between Steamships and the ANZ building. It was opened by the London Missionary Society in 1890 and is one of the city's last forlorn links with the past.

The main PMV stops in Town are on either side of Musgrave St south of the PNGBC Bank.

Hanuabada

Past the docks to the north lies Hanuabada, the original Motuan village. Although it is still built out over the sea on stilts, the original wood and thatched houses were destroyed by fire during the war. They were rebuilt in all-Australian building materials, corrugated iron and fibro-cement, and the surroundings are now littered with rubbish. However, it's still an interesting place and the people have retained many traditional Motuan customs.

Unfortunately it is not acceptable to wander around the villages if you are not a guest, or don't have a local guide. In some senses individual houses are more like single rooms in one great house, so if you wander around the walkways without knowing what you are doing and where you are going, you are certain to seriously offend people by invading their privacy.

The name Hanuabada is commonly used to describe six interlinked villages. In fact, Hanuabada correctly describes only one of the six villages that have grown together: collectively and officially they are known as the Poreporena villages.

Metoreai

The site for the first European settlement in Papua lies beyond Hanuabada on the ridge.

The building, which now belongs to the Ela United Church, was once the headquarters of the London Missionary Society and their first missionary, Reverend N G Lawes, arrived here on 21 November 1874. There's a stone cairn and a plaque to mark this event and another monument commemorates the pastors from the South Sea islands.

Ela Beach

Heading south down Musgrave St or Hunter St, you soon hit the long sandy stretch of Ela Beach. It's a popular spot for lazing on the sand but not much good for swimming, particularly at low tide, because the water is very shallow and weedy. There are also many black sea urchins – be careful where you step, the spines can be very painful. Windsurfing is popular.

St Mary's Catholic Cathedral is on Musgrave St, near Ela Beach, and has a Sepik haus tambaran-style front.

Koki

Ela Beach runs up to the headland at Koki, where there is a cluster of shops, the Salvation Army Hostel and Koki Market. There's also a stilt village, smaller and more 'suburban' than Hanuabada.

The Koki Market may not be the best market in the country, but it is an interesting spot. Saturday is the big market day although there's always plenty of activity. Koki Market is good for seafood; local fishers pull their boats up nearby. There are PMV stops on both sides of the road at the market. Until you know your way around, this is the best place to get off a PMV if you want to go to the Salvation Army Hostel.

The Girl Guides' Handicraft Shop is close to the market – see the Things to Buy section.

Boroko

Continuing up Three Mile Hill, past the YWCA, you come to Boroko (Four Mile). This is now the most important shopping centre, with a new post office, banks, airline agencies, a smallish market, several shopping plazas and a number of Chinese-owned

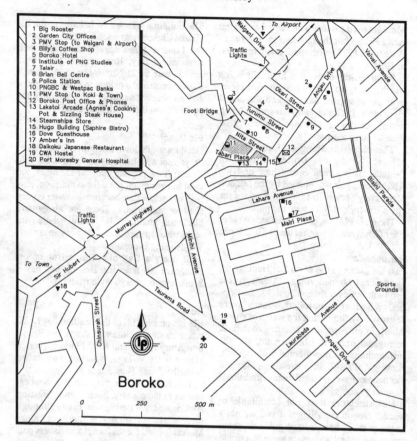

1 Big Rooster
2 Garden City Offices
3 PMV Stop (to Waigani & Airport)
4 Billy's Coffee Shop
5 Boroko Hotel
6 Institute of PNG Studies
7 Talair
8 Brian Bell Centre
9 Police Station
10 PNGBC & Westpac Banks
11 PMV Stop (to Koki & Town)
12 Boroko Post Office & Phones
13 Lakatoi Arcade (Agnes's Cooking Pot & Sizzling Steak House)
14 Steamships Store
15 Hugo Building (Saphire Bistro)
16 Dove Guesthouse
17 Amber's Inn
18 Daikoku Japanese Restaurant
19 CWA Hostel
20 Port Moresby General Hospital

Boroko

general stores. However, nothing matches the Steamships department store in Town.

There are also a number of restaurants and kai bars, and a few places to stay. There are even some human touches, like a square, a pedestrian mall and even a pedestrian overpass.

Boroko's success is due, in part, to its central position at the intersection of Waigani Drive and the Sir Hubert Murray Highway. Because of this it also has the largest PMV station which is well worth avoiding at peak hours. PMVs leave from both sides of the Sir Hubert Murray Highway (linked by the overpass).

Gordons

If you turn left into dusty Waigani Drive, instead of continuing out on the Highway towards Six Mile and the airport, you come to the main drag heading out to the government centre, the university and Gerehu. Gordons is on the right a couple of km from Boroko.

This is not an attractive part of Moresby, unless you like breweries and factories, but it is the home for PNG arts & crafts – see the Things to Buy section.

There's also the bustling **Gordons Market**, one of the largest and busiest in the country. It's open daily. In the clothing section, across the road from the main produce market, stalls sell cheap snacks, such as rolls with peanut butter or Vegemite for K0.20.

Gordons Market is the best place to catch PMVs for Bomana, Sogeri, etc. The market is just over one km east of Waigani Drive, down Cameron Rd, or a km north of the roundabout at the end of Spring Garden Rd. PMVs from Town which run to the market include No 4.

Waigani

Along Waigani Drive, past the Islander Travelodge on the left and about a half a km to the right, is the government centre. Most PMVs let you get off on the main road before continuing towards Gerehu, although at peak hours there will be a number marked 'W'gani' or 'Office' that will travel direct to the Central Government Office. No PMVs service the museum or the parliament.

On the corner of Waigani Drive and John Guise Drive is the new Sir John Guise Stadium complex, built for the 1991 South Pacific Games. This is a handy landmark if you've caught a PMV which doesn't run into Waigani proper, and from here it's a 500-metre walk to the offices.

Waigani has been dubbed 'Canberra in the Tropics' and there's more than a little truth in that description. There's a handful of flashy, modern buildings with a lot of empty space between them and the only way you can get around is by private car or on foot.

There are five main government buildings grouped together. The Haus Marea ('Pineapple' building) is the distinctively ugly high-rise near the corner of John Guise Drive and Kumul Ave. On the opposite corner, the first building you come to, Haus Tomakala, is a rather more innocuous high-rise that has a Chinese restaurant out the front and a couple of snack bars inside.

The three-storey Central Government Office, on the corner of Kumul Ave and Melanesian Way across from the Haus Marea, is home to the Immigration Section, a post office and an Air Niugini office. Be prepared for frustration if you want to extend your visa – see the Facts for the Visitor chapter for details. The National Mapping Bureau is behind the Central Government Office on Melanesian Way.

Parliament House The new parliament building was officially opened in 1984 with Prince Charles on hand. It's an impressive building, as it should be at a cost of K22 million. Built in a Maprik haus tambaran-style, it sits on a hill fronted by fountains, two km from the PMV stop on Waigani Drive. A taxi from Boroko costs about K10 or less.

The proceedings inside are interesting as they require simultaneous translations into English, Pidgin and Motu, the three main languages of PNG. Even if parliament isn't sitting it's worth a look inside, although you can't take photos. There's a small shop with some interesting books, and some cases displaying PNG's amazing butterflies. It's usually open from 9 am to noon and from 1 to 3 pm. There's a cafeteria with standard offerings under the front forecourt.

National Museum & Art Gallery The museum is not far from the parliament building. The displays justify the effort spent on reaching them and, as a further reward, the building is air-conditioned. There's a shady courtyard area in front, with wooden tables and seats, which is serviced by a most uninspiring (and often closed) snack bar. If you packed your lunch it would be a pleasant place to eat.

You'll need at least an hour or two to see the excellent displays covering the geography, animal life, culture and history of PNG. There are superb examples of masks, shields and totems, a magnificent Milne Bay outrigger canoe decorated in cowry shells, as well as exhibits on local foods and shells. A small courtyard has some (live) birds, lizards and, if the current incumbent is still alive, a tree kangaroo.

The museum is open Monday to Friday from 8.30 am to 3.30 pm and on Sunday from 1 to 5 pm. Admission is free. There is an

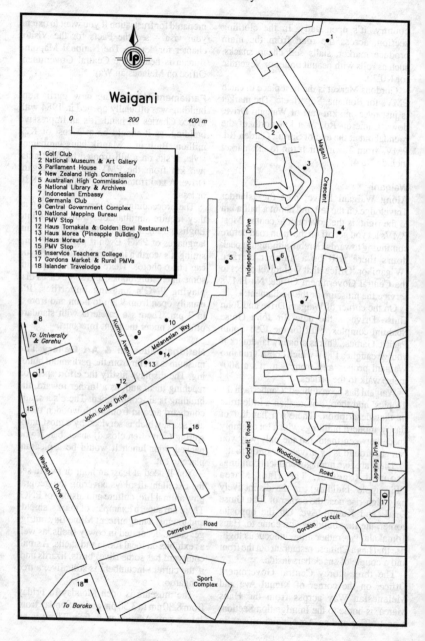

Waigani

200   400 m

1 Golf Club
2 National Museum & Art Gallery
3 Parliament House
4 New Zealand High Commission
5 Australian High Commission
6 National Library & Archives
7 Indonesian Embassy
8 Germania Club
9 Central Government Complex
10 National Mapping Bureau
11 PMV Stop
12 Haus Tomakala & Golden Bowl Restaurant
13 Haus Morea (Pineapple Building)
14 Haus Moruata
15 PMV Stop
16 Inservice Teachers College
17 Gordons Market & Rural PMVs
18 Islander Travelodge

Magani Crescent

Independence Drive

Kumul Avenue

Melanesian Way

To University & Gerehu

John Guise Drive

Waigani Drive

Godwit Road

Woodcock Road

Lapwing Drive

Cameron Road

Gordon Circuit

Sport Complex

To Boroko

interesting bookshop at the entrance. Although the selection of books is limited, there are publications about prehistory and culture that are hard to find anywhere else. The bookshop closes between 1 and 2 pm.

University of Papua New Guinea

After Waigani, you first come to the Administrative College, then to the attractive and spacious university. It's close to the main road and plenty of 'Gerehu' PMVs run by. The university has a good bookshop (to the right as you enter the main entrance) and a fairly extensive library. There is also a coffee shop (to the left of the entrance and the mural) with decent, good-value meals.

A bit further past the university are the Botanical Gardens, with a very fine orchid collection. Orchid cultivation is a big deal in Port Moresby and PNG as a whole. I managed to get myself invited to an orchid-fanciers' barbecue, but despite not knowing an orchid from a sunflower (well almost) I did not feel alone!

National Arts Schools

A little beyond the university entrance and on the opposite side of Waigani Drive, a normal suburban road leads to the National Arts School (☎ 25 5477, PO Box 5098, Boroko). It's less than half a km from the main road, easy walking distance from the university.

There are often people selling *buai* (betel nut) on the side of the road – for artistic inspiration perhaps? There are music, art and drama schools, and the students and staff are friendly and interesting. If you have a strong interest in any of these areas it would be worth getting in touch and checking it out.

The National Art School has a gallery that sells original paintings and prints. Some fascinating, vibrant fusions of modern and traditional art are produced and sold. The art gallery is next to the main car park.

Ask someone in the adjoining office to show you the prints they have for sale in addition to the works on display. Excellent quality colour prints by well known local painters like Kauage, John Mann and Akis

are sold for between K10 and K40; black and white prints are cheaper.

The National Music School (☎ 25 5477) has some outstanding students – don't miss an opportunity to see them perform. There are several groups and some play music around town.

The National Theatre School (☎ 25 2524) is on the opposite side of the road and there are occasional performances. Phone for information and while you're at it ask if anything is happening at the University Open Theatre.

Islands, Beaches & Reefs

In Moresby Harbour, off Hanuabada, the wreck of the Burns Philp cargo ship MV *MacDhui* can be seen just breaking the surface. It was sunk by Japanese aircraft in the early days of the Pacific War. Its mast now stands in front of the Royal Papua Yacht Club, and in the Burns Philp offices in Town is the Captain's report to the owners on how he came to lose the ship.

Many expats have boats and the yacht club is busy on weekends. If you play your charm cards right, you may get asked out for the day.

Manubada Island is used for weekend beach trips but beware – there is no shade. The **Bootless Bay** area (south-east of Moresby) and the other islands around the harbour are also popular.

Idler's Bay, on the Napa Napa Peninsula just east of Moresby, is a popular beach. It's a pleasant drive out beyond here to **Lea Lea**, a large coastal village which you get to by crossing the creek on a dugout canoe 'ferry' service. There might be a fee of K2 to use the beach. Napa Napa was once a nautical training centre and is now a fisheries research station.

Close to Napa Napa is **Lolorua Island** which is also known as Double Island because during WW II it was neatly chopped in two by a bomb. Also nearby, Gemo Island was established as a leper colony in 1937 but the colony was later moved to Laloki. **Tatana Island**, between Hanuabada and Napa Napa, is joined to the mainland by a causeway and has a village on the north-west side.

Basilisk Passage is the deep, narrow entrance to the harbour of Port Moresby and was named by Captain Moresby after his ship HMS *Basilisk*. Next to it is **Nateara Reef** on which the ship SS *Pruth* was wrecked in 1924. An attempt to sink it during WW II broke its hull in two. **Sinasi Reef** is a very beautiful reef outside the passage and is joined to **Daugo Island**, also known as Fisherman's Island. There are some very pleasant white sand beaches and it's a popular excursion from Moresby.

Activities

Clubs Clubs in PNG tend to have high membership turnovers so they can be hard to track down. You could start looking in a number of places: the Yellow Pages of the telephone directory, which has a far from complete list; *The Times'* 'What's on Where' section lists some club meetings.

The PNG Bushwalkers' Association has regular weekend walks, which would not only give you a chance to see something, but also to meet some nice people. Finding the current contact person might be tricky – Vladek Gontarez, who works in the Roads & Bridges section (☎ 29 2091) of the Department of Works might still be around. If not, someone at the Australian High Commission in Waigani might know who to contact.

The Hash House Harriers, the Hash House Harriettes and the Port Moresby Road Runners are popular in Moresby; they advertise their venues in Friday's *Post Courier* and the *The Times*.

It's reasonably easy to join boat crews if you hang around the Royal Papua Yacht Club. There are some serious yachties here who've done very well in international bluewater races. Water-skiing, scuba diving and game fishing are other activities which are organised from the yacht club. Hiri canoe races often take place along the coast.

Diving There are some good reefs and plenty of fish close to Moresby. Most diving is around the Tahira Marine Park or Horseshoe Reef. There are two small wrecks here, both scuttled in 1978; one is a 19½-metre government trawler/patrol boat and the other a 12-metre work boat.

The Dive Shop (☎ 25 4726, fax 25 4119) on Waigani Drive in Boroko rent equipment and can arrange dives and tours through Diveco (☎ 25 4466, fax 25 4418).

Tropical Diving Services (☎ 21 1768, PO Box 1745, Port Moresby) is at the Tahira Boating Centre on Bootless Bay, and they have regular dives. Nearby Loloata Island Resort (☎ 25 8590) also offers diving.

The Port Moresby Sub Aqua Club organises regular weekend dive trips to nearby reefs. Try contacting them through the Dive Shop.

Organised Tours Traditional Travel (☎ 21 3966, PO Box 4264, Boroko) runs a number of day and weekend trips around Port Moresby. It offers half (K35) and full-day tours (from K45) that include Parliament House, the Museum, Hanuabada, artefact shops and a drive out to Sogeri and the Varirata National Park. Weekend trips include a fly-in/fly-out trip to the Myola Lakes on the Kokoda Trail.

South Pacific Tours (☎ 21 3500), Davetari Drive, Togoba Hill, has slightly cheaper tours of Port Moresby – the one I took wasn't very good.

Festivals

In mid-June (the Queen's Birthday weekend) there is a Port Moresby show with spectacular displays of traditional dancing.

The Hiri Moale, held around the Independence Day celebrations in mid-September, celebrates the giant Papuan trading canoes which once plied the coast. The Hiri Moale sometimes seems to be more of an opportunity for Coke and Pepsi to battle it out than a cultural festival, but there are bound to be some events of interest.

Places to Stay

Places to stay are scattered around the suburbs and are generally pretty expensive. You'll find places near the airport, in

Boroko, Waigani, Koki, Ela Beach and the Town centre.

If you have a car, it doesn't matter where you stay, but if you are dependent on PMVs, Boroko is the most convenient location, followed by Koki.

Not much happens in Moresby on weekends, so it would be worth thinking about getting out to Yule Island, north-west of Moresby, where there is a convent guesthouse, or to Loloata Island, to the south-east, where there's a more expensive (but much more easily accessible) resort. There are also a couple of places on the way to Sogeri which are popular weekend retreats. See the Around Moresby section.

Places to Stay – bottom end

There is a shortage of inexpensive beds in Moresby, and you're strongly advised to book, well in advance and in writing if possible.

The *Salvation Army Hostel* (☎ 21 7683, PO Box 245, Port Moresby) is conveniently located in Koki near the market and on the main PMV route from Town to Boroko and the airport. This is a big residential complex, with one section kept free for travellers and other transient guests. Everything is well maintained (except the gas stove in the kitchen, which is sometimes exciting to light). Good-sized twin rooms with fan cost K25 per person (if shared), K40 for couples or K30 for a single. The 'Salvos' is central (you can walk into town, just) and you are likely to meet other travellers here, so it's a good place to get information.

The *CWA* (Country Women's Association) has a hostel, Jessie Wyatt House (☎ 25 3646, PO Box 1222, Boroko), on Taurama Rd across from the hospital. It's modern and very clean and there is a kitchen. Shared twin rooms cost K18 per person, with a key deposit of K8. Each room has a fridge and there's free tea and coffee. There are only six rooms so it's advisable to book ahead.

It's some way from the Boroko shopping centre. The easiest way to get there is by PMV. Most PMVs run to or from Town via Three Mile Hill and the Sir Hubert Murray Highway, but some detour to the east through Badili, Kila Kila Village, and Korobosea (running right past the CWA on Taurama Rd). Catch a PMV marked 'Kila Kila' and ask for the hospital. From the airport you can take No 10. The closest PMV stop is near the hospital's Gate 4.

The *YWCA Hostel* (☎ 25 6522, PO Box 1883, Boroko) is at the top of Three Mile Hill between Koki and Boroko. PMVs run past regularly between Town and Boroko. There are only a few rooms for visitors (men are welcome, which is not usually the case at YWCAs in PNG) otherwise it's all permanent residents. It costs K25 per person. The craft shop is worth looking at even if you're not staying. During the week there's a 10.30 pm curfew, at weekends 12 pm, but Moresby's nightlife is unlikely to make this a problem.

In Boroko, the Catholic *Dove Guesthouse* on the corner of Angau Drive and Lahara Ave, is an excellent place to stay. The rooms are self-contained, include cooking facilities, and cost just K20 per person.

The guesthouse, which has only a few rooms, is for clients of the attached travel agency (mainly church people) who are transiting Moresby, so it's often full. However, they'll take travellers for a night or so if they have the space. Another drawback is that you can usually check-in only during office hours, Monday to Friday, 8 am to 4.30 pm. For bookings, contact Dove Travel (☎ 25 9800, PO Box 6478, Boroko).

Apparently the *New Tribes Mission* (☎ 25 8201, PO Box 1001) in Boroko has rooms for K40.

There are various institutions which might have accommodation. The *University of PNG*, out on Waigani Drive, is most likely to have rooms during vacations, but try anytime. Contact the Warden of Students before 4 pm (☎ 25 1690); the office is upstairs in the central complex. The surroundings are pleasant and it's a good place to meet local people.

The *Institute of Applied Social & Economic Research* (☎ 25 3200, PO Box 5854, Boroko) which is on the left past the university, sometimes has rooms but it's a bit more expensive. The *Inservice Teachers College* (☎ 24 6500, PO Box 1791, Boroko) sometimes has accommodation, but you have to book in writing – write 'Hostel Booking' on the front of the envelope and address it to the principal.

Places to Stay – middle

Moresby's mid-range places are an odd assortment, much closer in style to the bottom-end than the top. Three of these are located very conveniently in Boroko.

The Civic Guesthouse, now called *Amber's Inn* (☎ 25 5091, PO Box 1139, Boroko), might be the first place you stay in PNG, and the spartan rooms might come as a shock – get used to it, this is a very good mid-range hotel by PNG standards. There is a pleasant garden with a small swimming pool and a pet hornbill whose squawk is heard intermittently throughout the day.

It's on Mairi Place just around the corner from Angau Drive in Boroko. They offer a free airport pick-up (although they forgot to collect me). Rooms with fans and very clean shared bathrooms cost from K39/59 for singles/doubles and K48/66 for triples/quads. Rooms with TV, air-con and bathrooms cost K63/79 a single/double. All these prices include breakfast but not the 2½% tax. There are sometimes evening barbecues, but otherwise dinner isn't great value.

Also in Boroko, but not as pleasant, is the *Boroko Hotel* (☎ 25 6677, fax 25 8532, PO Box 1033, Boroko) on Okari St. Singles/doubles cost K45/60 or K55/70 with bathroom. At the time of writing, the hotel had a special deal offering bed (with bathroom) and breakfast for K50. If you check in after 5 pm, ask about the standby rate. The rooms are reasonable and well-equipped, with air-con, TV and phone, but the large public bar is a popular boozing spot, and there's a bit of tension. There's also live entertainment on Friday and Saturday and sometimes mid-week, and things can get noisy, although given the lack of live bands in PNG this might be an attraction. The restaurant is reasonable, and the bar meals good value.

Apart from Amber's Inn, the best alternative is the *Granville Motel* (☎ 25 7155, fax 25 7672, PO Box 1246, Boroko). It's in Six Mile, only about a km from the airport but walking here might not be safe, certainly not at night. They can organise someone to pick you up, and most PMVs from the airport run through Six Mile.

The Granville was built for the Ok Tedi mine workers so the rooms are fairly spartan, but they're more than adequate and everything is clean. There's a pool, a tennis court, a *haus win* ('house wind' or open-air bar) and the meals are reasonable. Singles with shared bathroom cost K45, K52 with attached bathroom; doubles cost from K60, all plus 2½% tax. There are also some self-contained units with weekly rates.

In Town, the venerable old Papua Hotel finally went the way of many hotels in PNG, and burned down. There are plans for a five-star hotel on the site.

Places to Stay – top end

The prices at this end of the market are simply outrageous, but it seems there are people who will pay them. Add 2½% tax to all these prices.

The *Hibiscus Motel* (☎ 21 7983, PO Box 1319, Port Moresby), in Town on the corner of Hunter and Douglas Sts, is a new place in an older building. It makes it into the top-end category because of its prices, not its standards – a monstrous K70/90 for pretty ordinary singles/doubles with shared bathroom. A room with attached bathroom costs K100. If you stay for a few days they might give you their corporate rate, about 25% less. There is no restaurant, but meals can be ordered in. Similarly, they can probably arrange for someone to collect you from the airport.

The *Port Moresby Travelodge* (☎ 21 2266, fax 21 7534, PO Box 1661, Port Moresby) is the top-rated place to stay in Moresby. It's conspicuously located in Town at the corner of Douglas, Mary and Hunter Sts – right across from ANG House. Along with ANG House, it dominates the skyline. The rooms offer some appropriately stunning views over Moresby and the prices are similarly sky-high. Naturally the Travelodge offers all the features you'd expect – air-conditioning throughout, restaurant, bars, souvenir shop, conference facilities, swimming pool and entertainment. Room prices start at K165.

The Davara Hotel has been taken over by the Travelodge chain and is now the *Ela Beach Hotel* (☎ 21 2100, PO Box 813, Port Moresby). It is in a good location, looking out over Ela Beach, a short stroll from the town centre. Despite being refurbished, it still feels a little like an office building. There's a swimming pool and a popular bar and restaurant. Rooms cost K95 per person.

The *Islander Travelodge* (☎ 25 5955, fax 21 3835, PO Box 1981, Boroko) is in Hohola between the Waigani central government complex and Boroko. It's now part of the Travelodge chain and offers more space but less spectacular views than the Travelodge in Town. There's a health club out here. Rooms start at K135.

There are two places close to the airport. The *Gateway Motel* (☎ 25 3855, fax 25 4585, PO Box 1215, Boroko) is right by the airport – you see it when you walk out the doors. It would certainly be convenient for your flight out and the rooms are good, but you could be in any airport hotel in the world. Rooms cost from K115 to K165.

The nearby *Airways Motel & Apartments* (☎ 25 7033, fax 25 0759, PO Box 1942, Boroko) overlooks the airport from Jacksons Parade and provides top-quality facilities. Singles/doubles cost from K101/111, plus K15 for an additional person. There are also new serviced apartments for about K200 a day with lower weekly rates. There is an open-air bar overlooking the runways and a Greek restaurant.

A sports club with a gym and pool should be open by now, and they have planned some jogging routes around the area. Transport from the airport is provided (it's a 60-second drive!), or, during the day, you could walk down the road beside the Gateway Motel.

Places to Eat

There are more food alternatives in cosmopolitan Moresby than anywhere else in the country. This will be your last chance to eat Japanese, Greek or Italian food, but unfortunately you'll look long and hard for indigenous cuisine. Most restaurants are closed except at meal times and on Sundays they are often closed all day.

Places to Eat – bottom end

There are very few cheap, reasonably good quality places to fill the void between kai/sandwich bars and expensive restaurants. If you are on a tight budget and can't stomach the thought of a staple diet of greasy fish and chicken your best bet is to stay somewhere that has cooking facilities. Most of the kai bars close fairly early, so by about 7 pm your options have shrunk to the hotels, clubs and restaurants.

Tasty Bite is in the Steamships department store in Town, near the Champion Parade entrance, with another outlet deeper into the store. They have fresh pies and other snacks. Not far from Town, the *Royal Papua Yacht Club* sells snacks such as hamburgers for K2.50, and this is a nice place for a beer. Theoretically you have to be signed in by a member.

Boroko has a large selection of kai bars, but they're all pretty similar. The one outside the Boroko Hotel is open later than most. Note that the *McDonalds* opposite the PMV stop is a Chinese kai bar, despite the golden arches.

Still in Boroko, *Billy's Coffee Shop*, on Turumu St near the footbridge over the highway, is open until 4 pm on weekdays. The food is good and not too expensive. A two-cup plunger of coffee costs just K1, and there are snacks (toast with Vegemite is K0.80, a BLT sandwich is K2.20) and light meals. Another good place for a lunchtime snack is the sandwich bar in the arcade which runs beside the Boroko PNGBC bank. Prawn sandwiches are K2.20. Nearby, *Bib's Coffee Shop*, up the escalator in the Brian Bell Centre, serves breakfast all day for K4.50 and has snacks and meals.

In Koki, across the road from the Salvation Army Hostel is a shop selling reasonable kai and one or two Chinese dishes. You can sit down to eat. Also near the hostel is an Andersons supermarket where you can buy, for a price, many items that aren't sold in the less up-market places.

American-style fast food has arrived in Moresby in the guise of drive-in *Big Rooster*. There's one in Boroko on Waigani Drive, a short walk from Sir Hubert Murray Highway intersection, another in Koki on the main drag near the Salvation Army Hostel, and another in Town on Douglas St. They're not cheap but they're open till 8 pm and offer standard variations on the chicken-in-a-box theme, costing K2.30 for a 'snak-pak', K4.35 for a dinner box, and up.

There are a few kai bars around Waigani, but the best options are the snack bar under the forecourt of Parliament House, and the two on the ground floor of Haus Tomakala, opposite the Haus Marea.

The best-value place for a sit-down meal is the *University Coffee Shop* and it's also a good place to meet people. If you come in the main university entrance it's to your left past the mural. It's open Monday to Friday from 9 am to 3.30 pm and you can get a hot meal for about K2.50, as well as sandwiches and milk shakes.

Don't forget the markets. Gordons is the best, but Koki also has a good variety of fruit and especially seafood. There are a couple of smaller markets, including one at Boroko at the end of Okari St. Often the prices are clearly displayed, but even if they're not, you're unlikely to be ripped off. Bargaining is out.

Places to Eat – middle & top end

As well as the places listed here, it's worth checking out the various clubs, such as the *Golf Club* (☎ 25 5367) in Waigani, which often have relatively inexpensive meals, especially at lunch time. Many welcome visitors, although some have strict dress codes.

Town The *Green Jade* Chinese restaurant (☎ 21 4611) is now at the Royal Papua Yacht Club and is open for lunch and dinner most days.

The Travelodge's *Mala Mala Coffee Shop* is more like a restaurant than a coffee shop

and is open for breakfast, lunch and dinner. The food is good and the prices are not too bad. Big buffet breakfasts are pricey at K14 (although you won't need to eat again all day) but light meals and snacks are reasonable. On Friday and Sunday nights there's a sizzler dinner for K13 and a Saturday night buffet for K16. The Travelodge's up-market *Rapala Restaurant* has a good reputation (but a surprisingly small menu) and prices which aren't too bad – entrees are about K6 and a fillet steak is K20.

Stan's Steak House on the corner of Musgrave and Douglas Sts has seafood and steaks, with main courses starting at around K18. It looks a little run down but the food is reasonable. It's open weekdays for lunch and dinner. *Coyles Bistro* (☎ 21 2353) on the ground floor of Cuthbertson House is also meant to be OK.

Boroko Boroko has some excellent places to eat. *Agnes's Cooking Pot* (☎ 25 4013) is upstairs off Tabari Place. The entrance is in seedy Lakatoi Arcade but the restaurant is one of the nicer places in Port Moresby. The decor, service and food are all very good, as is the powerful air-conditioning. The owner, Luke Lucas, was once the PNG electoral commissioner, and some of the many 'Grassroots' cartoons (Agnes herself is a Grassroots character) on the walls refer to his run-ins with governments.

The food is mainly Indonesian and Filipino, with some Dutch-inspired dishes. Entrees are around K5 and main courses around K8. Ristaffel is available for K20 with a day's notice. Agnes's is open for lunch and dinner till 10 pm (11 pm for coffee).

Downstairs in Lakatoi Arcade, the *Sizzling Steak House* suffers by comparison with Agnes's, but it's a reasonable place with a large Chinese and Western menu. There's a two-course set menu for K9, and steak dishes cost from K10. Salads cost K4.50 and noodle dishes start from K4.50. It's open for lunch and dinner from Monday to Saturday. There are a couple of other mid-range Chinese places in the area, the *Marco Polo* on Tabari Place, near the highway, and the

Beijing, opposite the police station on Okari St. The *Bunga Raya* replaces the popular Rex, but isn't as good.

Back on Tabari Place, another good place for a meal is the *Saphire Bistro*, upstairs in the Hugo building, next to the post office. It's open for lunch most days and for dinner on Wednesday and Saturday, and has a big menu, including burgers from K4, good pizzas from K5, spaghetti from K6.50 and steaks for about K12. The salads are good value for around K4. It's German-run, so there are some dishes such as grillwurst and chips (K4.50) and kassler (K7.90). Downstairs in the arcade, *Saphire Smallgoods* has fruit and vegetables as well as a good range of delicatessen items.

The *Boroko Hotel* has a reasonable restaurant where most dishes are under K10, and bar meals are cheaper.

The *Tropicana Restaurant* (☎ 25 3841) is open for lunch and dinner daily, and offers good value set lunches on weekdays. It's in East Boroko on the corner of Karu St and Boroko Drive, across from the International High School. They have karaoke.

The *Kwangtung Village* (☎ 25 8997) on Boio St, East Boroko, has good food – the best Chinese food in Moresby it's said. It is moderately expensive and if you have driven to this place it is not a bad idea to tip the guy outside to watch your car.

Seoul House (☎ 25 2231) on the Sir Hubert Murray Highway a little north-east of Boroko has Korean barbecues daily.

Airport If you're not counting the kina too carefully and you've got an excuse for a special occasion (like a farewell dinner) try the *Airways Motel*. It overlooks the airport, and has an attractive open-air bar. This is an ideal spot to sip a drink on a balmy tropical night or wait for a flight – they have a TV-link to the airport which displays flight information.

Their *Bacchus Restaurant* is excellent, with a Greek-oriented menu. They've even got a traditional wood-fired oven to make the pitta bread. A meal will set you back around K25. If you are counting the kina, a meal in

their *Balus Bar* costs from about K8, and there's a lunch buffet on Wednesday and Friday for K18.

The nearby *Gateway Motel* has a pizza bar with some interesting offerings. Their *Mongolian Stirfry Restaurant* has lunch specials.

Other Areas *Spaghetti House* (☎ 25 9335) in Hohola is run by the honorary Italian Consul, and the food is, I'm told by an Italian traveller, 'real'. Also in Hohola, the *Islander Travelodge* has a pricey restaurant and a more reasonable coffee shop.

In Waigani, the up-market *Golden Bowl* (☎ 25 1656) is in front of Haus Tomakala and serves fairly pricey Chinese food daily except Saturday; the menu is large. The *Fortuna Seafood Restaurant* (☎ 25 1993) is off Waigani Drive, just north of Spring Garden Rd, at the Motor Sports Club.

The *Daikoku Japanese Steak House* (☎ 25 3857), above the Taurama supermarket, between Boroko and Three Mile on the Sir Hubert Murray Highway, is a popular place.

Entertainment

There is little public entertainment in Moresby (or PNG), with most socialising taking place behind the doors of clubs. *The Times* weekly newspaper has a useful 'What's on Where' page that lists films, discos, activities and clubs of all kinds.

There are often films at the University Theatre, especially on Saturday nights, for under K1. Try phoning the National Music School (☎ 25 5477) to see if there are any performances.

The Saphire Bistro, upstairs in the Hugo building in Boroko has live jazz or blues on Saturday from about 11.30 am (free) and on Wednesday night (K5). The Boroko Hotel often has live music.

Ask around before going to a pub or disco, as some are plagued by violence.

Things to Buy

PNG Arts is on Spring Garden Rd on the Gordons side of Waigani Drive, not far from Hanuacraft. These are two of the best artefact shops in PNG and a visit is a must. The range of items on sale is astounding, and prices aren't too bad.

Go there before you start travelling so you have an idea of what to look for and what to pay (discounting the considerable mark-up), and then visit again when you get back so you can buy what you missed. Both shops are open seven days a week (from 9 am to 5 pm Monday to Friday; 11 am to 4 pm weekends); and both will pack and ship your purchases overseas. You can buy a good booklet detailing the various styles of art & craft in the country for K6 at PNG Arts and probably at Hanuacraft as well.

There is a PMV stop on the corner of Spring Garden Rd; if you're coming from Boroko, Spring Garden Rd is before the roundabout. If you're having trouble finding a PMV to PNG Arts, ask for the Coca Cola factory, which is nearby.

The Institute for PNG Studies at the northern end of Angau Drive has some interesting tapes of traditional music for sale.

There are a number of other artefacts shops of varying quality – if you are keen, get to as many as you can – you never know where you will find the mask of your nightmares.

The YWCA at Three Mile Hill has some artefacts. The Girl Guides' shop in Koki has a small collection of crafts from various places around the country. The billums are good value. They also have an extensive postcard collection and books on the country, including guides and Pidgin dictionaries. The shop is closed on Sundays, but they also have branches in the Travelodge and Islander hotels that are open seven days a week. Profits go to the Girl Guides' movement.

Mr Tamboy, the caretaker at the Salvation Army Hostel, sometimes has billums for sale. You can also buy billums at Gordons Market, although one traveller reports paying more here than at PNG Arts.

Joseph Siyune sells his colourful paintings outside the Travelodge on Monday, Wednesday and Friday. A big one costs K30 and smaller ones are K10. You'll also find his paintings, and others, in Beyond Art, a contemporary gallery upstairs in the Hugo

building in Boroko. They also sell interesting T-shirts, cards, etc, and the prices are reasonable. The National Arts School also sells artworks.

Getting There & Away

Port Moresby is the hub for domestic and international air travel. There are numerous flights to major centres all over the country. If you want to fly to smaller places in Milne Bay (including the Trobriands), Gulf and Oro provinces, then Port Moresby will generally have to be your starting point. Some interesting flights to smaller places in the Highlands also originate here.

Although most travellers fly out of Moresby there are other ways to get to the rest of the country, although some of them are not exactly easy.

You could, for example, walk the Kokoda Trail to Popondetta then fly to Lae (K121) or catch a boat to Lae with Lutheran Shipping (K21.50 deck class). Or you could fly to Wau (K95) with Talair then either catch a PMV down to Lae, or walk to Salamaua, a short boat ride from Lae. Or you could get to Kerema by taking a PMV to Iokea, then a motor canoe to Malalaua (usually leaves Friday night and takes five hours), then catch a PMV to Kerema.

You might, if you're lucky, find a ship from Port Moresby right around the eastern end of PNG to the north coast. There are no passenger ships or freighters officially carrying passengers, which isn't to say that ingenuity and persistence won't get you a berth. You could travel by PMV to Kupiano and from there hop by village boats around the coast to Alotau. The further east you go, the friendlier the people become.

Air There is a K15 departure tax for all international flights.

If you want to get comparative schedules and prices for domestic flights, the best place to go to is the airport. The domestic airlines have separate offices and terminals at Jacksons Airport. Air Niugini is in the domestic departures hall; there's an inquiries window facing the street as well.

Next along is Milne Bay Aviation (MBA). Currently it only does charters but the company has applied for a passenger licence and when that comes through it will be one of the larger third-level airlines. The Talair and MAF buildings are further along. Trans-Niugini Airways (☎ 25 2211), a company servicing small strips in Central Province, is a fair walk further on towards the end of the runway.

Air Niugini also has an office in Town in Niugini Insurance House, on Champion Parade near the end of Hunter St. For domestic reservations and reconfirmations phone 27 3555; for international reservations phone 27 3444. Talair (☎ 25 5799) has an office in Boroko on Turumu St. If you don't find life at the MAF hanger try phoning 25 2668.

Qantas' head office (☎ 21 1200), a new building, is in Town behind ANG House. Continental Air Micronesia (☎ 21 4766), Singapore Airlines (☎ 21 3979) and Solomons Airlines (☎ 25 5724) are among the other international carriers with representatives in Moresby.

The prices for flights to most centres from Moresby are given in their appropriate Getting There & Away sections, but see the following table for an idea of straight fares from Moresby:

Destination	Fare	Airline
Alotau	K101	Air Niugini/Talair
Daru	K117	Air Niugini/Talair
Kavieng	K234	Air Niugini
Lae	K95	Air Niugini/Talair
Lorengau	K206	Air Niugini
Madang	K129	Air Niugini/Talair
Mt Hagen	K132/155	Talair/Air Niugini
Popondetta	K58	Air Niugini/Talair
Rabaul	K187	Air Niugini
Wewak	K180	Air Niugini/Talair

For getting around Central Province contact TransNiugini Airways (☎ 25 2211). It does a daily (except Sunday) 'milk run' around the tiny mountain strips in the Tapini area where missions, often French, are usually pleased to see visitors.

You can go along on the circular trip for K195. The fare to Woitape is K45; Tapini K65. On Monday and Thursday it flies to strips in the Kokoda Trail area. The fare to Kagi or Manari is K42. There are generally several flights on those days, depending on demand, but they start at around 6 am. It also does charters, as do several other companies.

TransNiugini Airways might also begin flights to Kundiawa and to the strip (currently closed) at Kegsugl near Mt Wilhelm.

Jacksons Airport Jacksons Airport, or Seven Mile as it is sometimes called, is a sudden introduction to PNG. The heat hits you the moment you step off the plane; slow-moving queues form for Customs formalities as you stand under slow-turning fans in the arrival shed; and when you're spat out into the car park you're surrounded by crowds – family groups patiently waiting in the shade, fierce looking young men with dreadlocks, tribespeople looking around in bemusement, sophisticated young office workers...

The airport has a bank that opens for incoming flights (normal banks close at 2 pm or 3 pm Monday to Thursday, 5 pm on Friday) and there's a snack bar, a well-stocked newsagent and offices for the three major car-hire companies. The Air Niugini counter is open Monday to Saturday from 5 am to 4 pm (yup, some of those early flights are a lot of fun) and on Sunday from 5 am to 7 pm.

In contrast to the arrivals hall, the international departure lounge is *air-conditioned* and has a duty-free shop and comfortable chairs, so it's worth going through immigration as soon as they let you – unfortunately, this is not all that long before the flight. You can't spend the night at the airport if you're catching an early-morning flight.

Towards the north end of the runway, near the Trans-Niugini Airways hangars, some of the taxiing area is still paved with pressed steel plate (PSP). PSP, slabs of interlinking plate, each small enough to be lifted by one person and holed for drainage, was developed and used during WW II to make instant roads and runways. All over the country you can see sheets of it used as fencing, drain covers, footpaths and just about anything else. It seems to be indestructible. Is PNG's most common 20th-century debris rusty pieces of PSP, or old shoes dangling from the power lines? It's a close call.

PMV Rural PMVs run to a limited number of destinations from Moresby – there are a limited number of roads! Most leave from Gordons Market. See the Around Port Moresby section for more information.

Sea There are no regular passenger boats sailing out of Moresby. Many of the large freighters *do* have accommodation facilities, but none of the shipping companies officially allow passengers. Asking around at the wharves or meeting someone who works for a shipping company (most offices are near the wharves) might get you a berth. If you want to go to the Gulf, ask around the smaller boats moored at the jetties north of the main wharf.

Heading east towards Milne Bay you might have better luck going to Kupiano and finding a small boat or canoe there. You're unlikely to find one running the whole distance, so allow plenty of time and be prepared to stay in villages.

Car Rental There are several rent-a-car places in Town. The three main operators all have desks at the airport.

Avis-Nationwide
    PO Box 1533, Port Moresby (☎ 25 8429, fax 25 3767)
Budget
    PO Box 1215, Boroko (☎ 25 4111, fax 25 7853)
Hertz
    PO Box 4126, Boroko (☎ 25 4999, fax 25 6985)

Costs are high and for a smallish car (say a Mitsubishi Lancer) you're looking at K54 per day plus K0.45 per km, plus insurance at around K15. Budget has an hourly rate (20% of the daily rate, plus K15 insurance), which could work out cheaper than taxis.

The Airways Motel at the airport offers guests a 20% discount on Hertz cars. The Granville Motel (☎ 25 7155), not far from the airport in Six Mile, offers slightly better

rates, with a Mazda 323 costing K43 a day plus K0.42 per km plus K15 insurance. Amber's Inn (☎ 25 5091) in Boroko also rents cars for a bit less than the major companies.

Getting Around

To/From the Airport Many places to stay will collect you from the airport if you arrange it when you make your booking. There are usually plenty of taxis hanging around outside the main terminal, the exception being early in the morning. A taxi to Boroko will cost between K5 and K10, to Koki K10 to K15 and to Town K15 to K20.

PMV departures are frequent between 6.30 am and 6 pm and a single journey anywhere in Town costs K0.40. PMVs don't enter the airport proper, but turn around at the end of the road before the flight tower. From the arrivals hall turn left and follow the road around to the right. See the following PMV section for some route numbers.

If you arrive after dark (that is, after about 6 pm), the only safe option for a newcomer is a taxi. It's much easier if you arrive in daylight, especially if you're a woman travelling solo.

Getting to the airport very early can be difficult. Consider staying nearby or book a taxi for the airport the night before. They usually show up, but often much later than you requested. They know the flight schedules and will race you to the airport and arrive with a comfortable two minutes to spare!

PMV Moresby has an efficient Public Motor Vehicle (PMV) service with frequent connections on all the routes between 6.30 am and 7 pm (usually a bit later). PMV fares haven't risen in years and the standard K0.40 for any trip in Moresby is great value. Pay the driver's assistant when you leave, but not with large bills.

Yell 'Stop, driver!' when you want to get off. In Town there are established stops indicated by yellow roadside poles. The main interchange point is in Boroko, which can degenerate to a complete shambles. Heading towards Town, PMVs stop near the dusty park; heading away from Town they stop near the pedestrian overpass. In Town, the main stops are towards the south end of Musgrave St.

The PMVs get very crowded at peak hours, and especially on Friday evenings when everyone is doing their weekend shopping, so it's worth avoiding them then, if you can.

Most PMVs travel along the Sir Hubert Murray Highway between Boroko (Four Mile) and Town, but some head east through Kila Kila Village (useful for the hospital and the CWA Hostel) and some head west through Hohola to Gordons or Gerehu, avoiding the traffic snarl around Boroko.

PMVs run set routes and have route numbers painted on the front. From the airport, No 5 runs down backroads to Boroko then down the Sir Hubert Murray Highway to Town, passing the YWCA Hostel and the Salvation Army Hostel in Koki. No 10 runs to Boroko, past the hospital and the CWA Hostel, down backroads to Koki and the Salvation Army Hostel, then into Town. No 15 runs to Boroko but not Koki. No 4 runs all the way from Hanuabada to Gordons Market. No 7 also runs to Gordons and past the turn-off to the Waigani government offices. No 11 runs from Boroko to Waigani.

As well as numbers, most PMVs also have destinations painted on the front. Outside peak hours (before 8 am and after 4 pm), few PMVs run directly to the Waigani government offices; those that do are marked 'Office' or 'W'gani Office'. At other times look for the PMVs marked 'Gerehu' that run along Waigani Drive past the government offices and the University to the suburb of the same name. They'll drop you off on the main road, a short walk from the offices. If you're going to Town, look for PMVs going to 'Kone' (Konedobu, the old government centre between Town and Hanuabada) or 'H'bada' (Hanuabada). PMVs to the airport usually show a '7 Mile' sign.

Taxi Taxis are readily available at the airport, the big hotels and on the streets. While many have meters, many of those meters don't work. Agree on a price before you get in, and be aware that there is some room for negotiation – don't let it get acrimonious, though. It's considered a bit stand-offish for men to sit in the back seat of a taxi. Loaloa Taxis (☎ 25 1118) is reliable. From Boroko it's about K8 to Waigani or Town and between K5 and K10 to the airport.

Most taxis are driven by Highlanders, as is most transport in Moresby, and they're generally nice guys. I started walking from the hospital to Boroko after dark, and a taxi driver stopped and insisted that he drive me because of the danger. I thought this must be a scam, but he wouldn't take any payment. Other taxis also gave me short rides for no charge.

Around Port Moresby

Moresby is the centre for a limited road network so there are a number of car or PMV trips you can make. There are also some interesting spots you can reach with short, relatively inexpensive flights. TransNiugini Airways is the most useful company for this region.

If you continue out on the Sir Hubert Murray Highway, past the airport and turn right just before the Moitaka Showground & Speedway, a sealed road takes you along the Sogeri Gorge up to the cool Sogeri Plateau, the beautiful Rouna Falls, Varirata National Park and the beginning of the Kokoda Trail.

If you continue past the Moitaka Showgrounds, the road becomes the unsealed Hiritano Highway and turns north-west through Brown River, passing several attractive riverside picnic spots, continuing past the turn-off to Poukama (where there's a ferry to Yule Island) and on to Bereina and Iokea.

To the south-east, the Magi Highway runs past Bootless Bay and the Loloata Island Resort and many fine beaches, continuing on to Kupiano.

SOGERI ROAD

The trip out to the Sogeri Plateau is one of the most popular weekend jaunts for Moresbyites. It's only 46 km all the way to

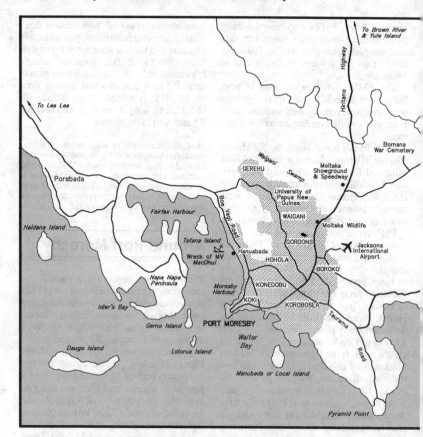

Sogeri, but there is quite enough to see and do to make it a full-day trip. You can get out there by PMVs which run regularly from Gordons Market and Boroko. The fare is K1.50. The road is surfaced to Sogeri and all the way down to the national park.

Head out of Town on the Sir Hubert Murray Highway and turn right about two km past the airport. There's a crocodile farm just before the turn-off and the Bomana War Cemetery is after the turn-off.

Moitaka Wildlife

A few km out of Moresby, before the turn-off

to Sogeri, is Moitaka Wildlife. Unless you make prior arrangements, it is only open to the public on Friday afternoons between 2 and 4 pm. This is also feeding time – crocodiles are hearty but infrequent eaters. The farm also has an enclosure of deer and some native animals and birds, including a raggiana bird of paradise which is quite an amazing show-off. Admission is K5.

Bomana War Cemetery

Not far past the turn-off to Sogeri is the large and carefully tended WW II cemetery where 4000 Australian and Papua New Guinean

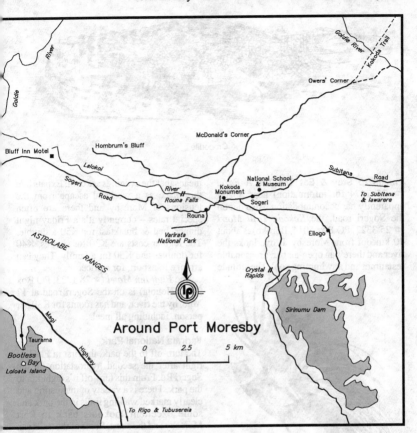

Around Port Moresby

0   2.5   5 km

soldiers lie buried. The American soldiers who died in PNG were generally shipped back to the USA for burial.

Sogeri

A few km past the cemetery, the road begins to wind up the Laloki River's gorge. Just past the turn-off to the Varirata National Park is a lookout point for the spectacular Rouna Falls – before the hydro-electric power plants were installed they were even more impressive. There are also good views back towards Moresby. You can have a look at the hydropower plants

and, just before reaching Sogeri, you pass the Kokoda Trail junction.

Apart from its cool climate (thanks to its 600-metre altitude), Sogeri has a pleasant Sunday market with a good selection of fresh vegetables. The road continues beyond Sogeri, via Crystal Rapids, a popular swimming spot, to Musgrave River and the Sirinumu Dam. At Crystal Rapids they charge K2 to enter with a car. If you walk in (it's not far) it's K0.30. The dam controls the water flow to the Laloki River which in turn supplies the Rouna hydroelectric station.

Crocodile

Places to Stay & Eat The *YMCA Farm* (☎ 25 7474 for information) near Sogeri apparently has accommodation. Also out on the Sogeri road, the *Kokoda Trail Motel* (☎ 25 3322, PO Box 5014, Boroko) is about 40 km out from Moresby. It overlooks the river and there's an open-air bar, a reasonable restaurant and a swimming pool. The altitude means that the evenings are cool. Expats like this place as a weekend escape from the tensions of Moresby and there are often special rates – currently it's a Friday night dinner, bed & breakfast for K50 a double. The regular costs are K30 for singles, K40 for doubles and K50 for a family. They can arrange transport, for a price.

The *Bluff Inn Motel* (☎ 28 1223, PO Box 9047, Hohola) is on the Sogeri road at 17 Mile, by the river, and has rooms for K80 per person, including all meals.

Varirata National Park

The turn-off to the park, the first in PNG, is right after the second hydrostation on the Sogeri Rd. From this turn-off it's eight km to the park. There is a variety of interesting and clearly marked walking trails in the park and some excellent lookouts back to Port Moresby and the coast. Some of the trails can be quite jungle-like – surprising considering the proximity to Moresby.

From June to November, in the early morning or evening, it is possible to see birds of paradise in a clearly signposted display tree above the circuit track.

Admission to the park, which is a popular picnic spot, is K1 per person, and a map of the walking trails is available at the park entrance.

Places to Stay It's possible to camp in the Varirata National Park but your belongings are not secure. There is, however, the *Varirata National Park Lodge* where accommodation costs a flat K40, whether there is one of you or a group. Bedding and cooking facilities

Bird of Paradise

are provided, but you must bring your own food and utensils. For further information phone the ranger-in-charge on 25 9340 or the National Parks Service's Assistant Secretary on 25 4247.

Hombrum's Bluff

A little way down the Kokoda Trail road, a smaller road branches off back towards Moresby running parallel to the Sogeri road but high above it on the top of the Laloki River canyon wall. It leads to Hombrum's Lookout which was used as a retreat for important military brass during the war. There are excellent views back towards Moresby.

HIRITANO HIGHWAY

The coast west of Port Moresby, which is connected by road all the way to Bereina, is the home of the Mekeo people who are noted for their colourful dancing costumes and face painting. On ceremonial occasions the men paint their faces in striking geometric designs.

You start to escape from the dry climate of Moresby by the time you get to Brown River,

a popular picnic spot about 40 km from Moresby. En route to the river you pass through teak plantations. You can get as far as Iokea by PMV.

Brown River

Brown River is a pleasant spot for swimming and a good place for quiet rafting, either on inner tubes or a rubber dinghy. Take the road up the river – it turns off the Hiritano Highway about a km before the bridge. It's best to have two cars, one to leave at the village by the turn-off and the other (preferably 4WD) to drive up the river to another village where you can leave the car right by the water. You then raft down to the bridge and drive back to get the second car.

The trip takes three to four pleasant hours. Don't be tempted to go downstream from the bridge – you can get tangled up in log jams and would, in any case, have trouble getting back to the bridge.

Yule Island

The missionaries who arrived at Yule Island in 1885 were some of the first European visitors to the Papuan coast of New Guinea.

Brown Falcon

Later the island became a government head-quarters, from which government and mission workers penetrated into the central mountains in some of the earliest exploration of the country. Today the government centre is on the mainland at Bereina but there is still a large Catholic mission and a Carmelite convent on Yule Island, where you can stay.

One of the early mission workers buried on Yule Island, M Bourgade, was one of France's top WW I air aces. You can still see his grave.

Place to Stay The *Carmel Convent* (☎ 25 8023 or book on 21 4953 in Moresby) still operates as a convent but they welcome visitors. You sleep in the original nuns' cells. Full board costs K50 per person, or you can cook your own food (fresh fish is available on the island) and pay K17.50/26 a single/double. There are plans for a backpackers' dormitory. It's a pretty place and worth the hassle of getting here.

Getting There & Away Turn off the Hiritano Highway approximately 38 km past Agu Vari. From the turn-off, which is signposted, you travel another 20 km to Poukama, where there is a car park (K1 per day) and a canoe to take you to the island (K1 per person).

Poukama is about 160 km (a three-hour drive) from Moresby. By PMV it's about 4½ hours and costs K5. A PMV (truck) leaves Gordons Market early but not every day.

There's an airstrip at Kairuku, the main village on the island, and TransNiugini Airways (☎ 25 2211) has some flights, mainly charters. Contact them to see if there is a vacant seat.

Hisiu

The *Hisiu Beach Resort* is an EC-funded project, where fully equipped bungalows cost K90 a day on weekends and K50 during the week. Hisiu is about 100 km north-west of Moresby. Book through Westpac Travel (☎ 25 4500).

MAGI HIGHWAY (Rigo Rd)

At Six Mile, instead of turning left to the airport, turn right onto Dogura road. As you're leaving Moresby the road passes through a shanty settlement. You have to slow down for speed humps in the settlement, making it a popular spot for hold-ups. The road circles round Bootless Bay to the small marina (Tahira Boating Centre) from which the ferry crosses to Loloata Island.

Loloata Island

Around 20 km from Moresby, Loloata Island in Bootless Bay is another popular weekend escape – midweek would be even better. A day trip to the Loloata Island Resort (☎ 25 8590, fax 25 1369, PO Box 5290, Boroko) costs K27, plus K5 each way for transfers to/from Moresby, and includes a big buffet lunch. The resort has snorkelling, fishing, sailboarding and diving facilities for hire. A wrecked, but intact, WW II Boston Havoc bomber is on the reef near the resort. For the truly lazy there is a bar and a fine collection of old *New Yorker*s. There's a licensed restaurant and the dinners are excellent.

It isn't a flashy place, but it's relaxed and a welcome escape from the tensions of Moresby.

To get there you drive out on the Rigo road (which meets the airport road in Six Mile) to the Tahira Boating Centre on Bootless Bay. None of the PMVs run all the way. The resort's ferry makes trips to the island at 8.30 am and 3.30 pm (5.15 pm on Friday).

The resort's comfortable accommodation, costs K80/140 a single/double with shared bathroom and K120/170 for rooms with bathroom, including all meals.

Along the Coast

A little further on there is a turn-off to **Tubusereia**, a big Motuan coastal village with houses built on stilts over the water. There are, unfortunately, few reminders of the attractive place it must have been. Corrugated iron, rusting car bodies and rubbish are the 20th-century additions.

The road continues past Gaire and Gaba Gaba, turns inland to Rigo and Kwikila, then back to the coast again at Hula on Hood Bay, another village close to the mouth of the Kemp Welch River. There are many fine beaches all along this road.

TAPINI & WOITAPE

If you want to get a look at the high country behind the coastal strip, or experience one of the most heart-in-mouth airstrips in PNG, or try a lesser known but extremely interesting walk then Tapini is a good place to go. It is a pretty little station at a bit under 1000 metres.

The airstrip is amazing. Carved into a hillside, it runs steeply uphill ending in a sheer face so you can only come in one way. When you leave downhill, the strip drops off sheer at the end. You've got a choice of flying or falling.

Walks in the Area

There are interesting walks around Tapini and most are not difficult. The Catholic Fathers bequeathed the whole area an excellent network of well-graded tracks which closely follow the contours (that is, they're not steep, a rarity in PNG). The tracks are wide, well-defined, and at one time took mule-trains. Several missions in the area have accommodation.

Lonely Planet's *Bushwalking in Papua New Guinea* details a number of these walks, and the Tapini Lodge and the Owen Stanley Lodge in Woitape can give you information.

There is also a rough road from Tapini to Guari where the once fearsome Kunimaipa people lived. In just 50 km, the road climbs up to nearly 3000 metres and drops down to about 700 metres. Guari is just an airstrip with no real village, but there are some nice walks in the valley below. You could do a circle trek out to the Kamali Mission.

June to October are the walking months, with June to August being the best.

Places to Stay & Eat

Near Woitape, the *Fatima Mission* has in the past accommodated travellers for about K5 a night but the Father is due to be replaced and his successor might not continue to

operate the guesthouse. Dove Travel or TransNiugini Airways in Moresby might have information on this. The only other formal accommodation in the area is very expensive, but staying at missions or in someone's home is a possibility. In Tapini, ask around for Daniel Rioro who might be able to help.

The small *Tapini Hotel* (☎ 29 9237, PO Box 19, Tapini) is near the airstrip and charges K115 per person, including meals. The *Owen Stanley Lodge* (☎ 25 7999) in Woitape is a small place charging K110/180 a single/double, including meals, snacks, guides for walks, fishing, etc.

Getting There & Away

Woitape is connected by a spectacular road to the coast and there are PMVs to Moresby most days for about K10. It's a long trip.

TransNiugini Airways (☎ 25 221, Port Moresby) flies from Moresby to both Tapini (K65) and Woitape (K45) daily except Sunday. This daily 'milk run' includes a number of tiny mountain strips where missions, often French, are usually pleased to see visitors. You can go along on the circular trip for K195.

Kokoda Trail

Mention walking tracks in PNG and the famed Kokoda Trail is the one most likely to spring to mind. This is a little unfair since the track is far from the most interesting walk in PNG, but its historical connections and its practicality are big attractions.

Linking the north and south coasts, the trail was first used by miners struggling north to the Yodda Kokoda gold fields of the 1890s, but it was WW II that brought it to the attention of the world.

Following the bombing of Pearl Harbor in December 1941, the Japanese made a rapid advance down the South-East Asian archipelago and across the Pacific, capturing New Britain and the north coast of New Guinea. The Japanese Navy's advance on Port

Moresby and Australia was dramatically halted by the Battle of the Coral Sea, but this only led to a new strategy.

The Japanese decided to take Port Moresby by a totally unexpected 'back door' assault. The plan was to land on the north coast near Popondetta, travel south to Kokoda and then march up and over the central range to Sogeri and down to Port Moresby.

They made one serious miscalculation: the Kokoda Trail was not a rough track that could be upgraded for vehicles, it was a switchback footpath through some of the most rugged country in the world, endlessly climbing and plunging down, infested by leeches and hopelessly muddy during the wet season.

The Japanese landed on 21 July '42 and stormed down the trail, battling an increasingly desperate Australian and American opposition. The Allies planned a last-ditch, defensive battle for Imita Ridge, within spitting distance of Port Moresby, and on 16 September this is where the Japanese, their supply lines hopelessly over-stretched, finally stopped.

They had failed to supply their troops by air, their plan to make the trail suitable for vehicles had proved to be unrealistic, and a man could barely carry sufficient food to get himself down the trail and back, let alone carry extra supplies for the front line soldiers. At the same time the Japanese were also being stretched to the limits at Guadalcanal in the Solomons, so they withdrew, with Port Moresby virtually in sight.

The campaign to dislodge them from Buna on the north coast was one of the most bitter and bloody of the Pacific War. If the two sides didn't kill each other, then disease or starvation did. The fighting was desperate and the terrain and climate were unbelievably hard.

It is impossible to comprehend the courage and suffering of the people who fought here, and it is no wonder the horrors of the Kokoda Trail and the Buna campaign have not been forgotten by either side. Never again did the Allied forces meet the Japanese

head-on during WW II. The policy for the rest of the war was to advance towards Tokyo bypassing the intervening Japanese strongholds. Rabaul in New Britain, for instance, was left alone and isolated while the front moved towards Japan.

The turn-off to the trail is just before Sogeri and there's a memorial stone at this junction. The road twists and turns and is rather bumpy, although quite OK for conventional vehicles (so long as it isn't raining).

At McDonald's Corner there is a strange metal sculpture of a soldier; this is where the road once ended and the trail commenced, but the actual trail now starts further on at Owers' Corner (there's a sign – sometimes!).

From Owers' Corner the trail is easy to follow and it heads straight down towards the Goldie River. You can stroll down to the river if you just want an easy taste of what it's like. On the other side of the river, the endless 'golden staircase' crawls up to Imita Ridge, the turning point for the Japanese. Beware of rascals.

It's also possible to fly in to strips along the trail; several are near village guesthouses.

WALKING THE KOKODA TRAIL

The Kokoda Trail is the most popular walking track in PNG. Although there are more interesting walks from a cultural point of view, there are good arguments in the trail's favour – the country it passes through is spectacular, its dramatic role in WW II provides an emotional draw, it is a practical link between the south and north coasts – and walking from one end to the other is a feat to be proud of.

The straight line distance from Owers' Corner to Kokoda is about 60 km but for the walker it is over 90 km, but this gives no impression at all of the actual difficulty. It's bloody hard work.

The trail is a continual series of ups and downs – generally steep, exhausting ups and muddy, slippery downs – over the whole trail you gain and lose 6000 metres (nearly 20,000 feet) of altitude.

Vine bridge on the Kokoda Trail

The walk can take as little as five (long) days, but it could easily be spread over 10, if you throw in a few rest days. There are between 40 and 50 hours of walking involved so most people average seven days. In 1986 Osborne Bogajiwai set a record of 28 hours, 14 minutes and 30 seconds.

Do not walk the trail during the wet season when the normally muddy trail is dangerously slippery and many rivers are high and hazardous to cross. The best months are usually August and September. Most people walk from south to north, but there's no reason not to do it the other way. It might even be easier, as walking from the south you encounter the hardest sections in the first few days.

As you may be starting to appreciate, the walk is no picnic, although anyone with reasonable fitness will be OK, so long as they stay within their limits (there are no prizes for speed) and have the right equipment. To get an idea of the fitness required, try walking up stairs carrying a 15-kg pack. One tour operator recommends that you be

able to do this for an hour before attempting Kokoda.

Information & Maps
Traditional Travel (☎ 21 3966) are likely to have the best information on the state of the trail and can help arrange guides.

Before you start out, contact the National Disaster, Surveillance & Emergency Service (☎ 27 6502; 27 6666 for emergencies) to inform them of your party's plans and get up-to-date information on the trail. The office is in Waigani, on the 3rd floor of Morauta House – turn left out of the lift. Don't forget to report in at the district office at Kokoda.

There are health centres (and radios) in Efogi No 1 and Kokoda. The TransNiugini Airways agents at Kagi and Manari also have radios.

Lonely Planet's *Bushwalking in Papua New Guinea* has a detailed description of the walk, and maps are available in Moresby from the National Mapping Bureau at Waigani. Do not leave without copies of the

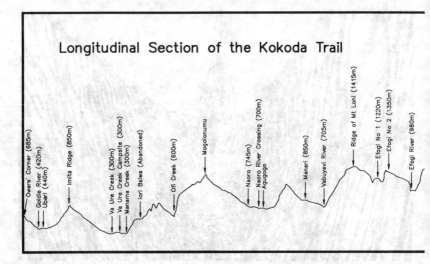

Longitudinal Section of the Kokoda Trail

Owers' Corner (685m)
Goldie River (420m)
Uberi (440m)
Imita Ridge (850m)
Va Ure Creek (300m)
Va Ure Creek Campsite (300m)
Manama Creek (300m)
Iori Baiwa (Abandoned)
Ofi Creek (600m)
Mogolonumu
Naoro (745m)
Naoro River Crossing (700m)
Agugogo
Manari (850m)
Vabuyavi River (705m)
Ridge of Mt Loni (1415m)
Efogi No 1 (1220m)
Efogi No 2 (1350m)
Efogi River (980m)

1:100,000 topographic maps for Kokoda, Efogi and Port Moresby, and the *Longitudinal Section of the Kokoda Trail*, which has useful descriptive notes and detailed sections of tricky areas. It's out-of-date but still essential.

Safety

The biggest dangers are the usual ones of trekking in rugged, remote country. If you get lost you run the risk of exposure, and the river crossings can be dangerous.

At both ends of the trail there has been a lot of rascal activity, and lone trekkers have had trouble on the trail itself, although this is unusual.

As usual in PNG, the way to minimise risks is to talk to local people and become accepted by them. A guide will help, and a guide from the local area is even better. Rascals almost always rob only the trekkers they have had advance warning about. If walking from south to north, it's vital that you arrive at Owers' Corner early and walk a fair distance that day. Similarly, make a long day's walk all the way into Kokoda rather than stopping for the night just short of the station.

Equipment

Local food can usually be bought in the villages, but you should bring your own supplies. Small trade stores at Naoro, Manari, Efogi No 1, Kagi and Kokoda sell the usual tinned meat, tinned fish and rice, but they are very unreliable. TransNiugini Airways (☎ 25 2211) flies twice weekly to most strips along the trail and you might be able to arrange for supplies to be flown in.

You'll need a comfortable pair of boots or a strong pair of running shoes. Grip is important. A tent, a fly or a large sheet of plastic is necessary to waterproof some of the shelters, or you might be stuck on the trail overnight waiting for a river to subside. Also, the itinerary suggested here includes at least one night camping. A compass and a camping stove are also recommended. Bring a bottle as you'll need to carry water along certain sections of the trail. It can get quite chilly, so bring a sleeping bag, and some kind of wet weather gear (even in the dry season). Make sure you take a comprehensive medical kit, and salt, matches or a cigarette lighter to detach leeches. The total weight of your pack should not exceed 15 kg.

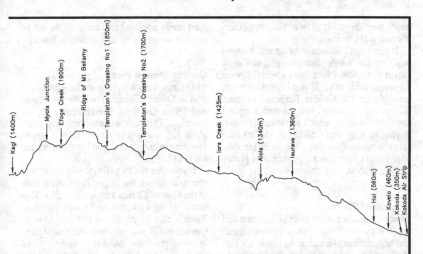

Guides & Porters

A guide might not be necessary, but you're strongly advised to take one, both because of the dangers of getting lost and because of the dangers of rascals. The best way would be to take different guides for different sections of the trail, so you always have someone with you who knows local people, but this might not be feasible. At least make sure that your guide comes from *somewhere* along the trail.

Having a porter might mean the difference between finishing the trail and giving up along the way. One porter between a few people might be a good compromise. Expect to pay a guide at least K15 to K25 a day (possibly a lot more), and a porter about K10 a day. You have to provide them with food and perhaps some equipment.

People do walk the trail alone, but you're strongly advised not to, as sections are quite isolated. The safest number of people is three or more (too many might mean problems with accommodation), which allows one person to stay with an injured trekker and one to go for help. Ask around the hostels in Moresby to see if you can meet other people planning to walk the trail.

Track Information

This is the itinerary suggested in Lonely Planet's *Bushwalking in Papua New Guinea*, which has detailed track notes:

Owers' Corner to Va Ure Creek Campsite (10 km, five hours) The campsite is about 1½ hours on from Imita Ridge.

Va Ure Creek Campsite to Naoro (17 km, nine hours) Naoro has a rest house.

Naoro to Efogi No 1 (19 km, seven hours) About halfway, there is a rest house in Manari village. There are two rest houses in Efogi No 1.

Efogi No 1 to Efogi Creek (12 km, 5½ hours) About 2½ hours past Efogi No 1 you pass through Kagi, where there's a good rest house. From Efogi Creek you can walk to Myola in about two hours.

Efogi Creek to Alola (17 km, 5½ hours) There's a guesthouse in Alola.

Alola to Kokoda (19 km, 5½ hours) The guesthouse in Kokoda is run-down and there have been robberies. People have stayed with the local policeman and with other locals.

Shortcuts

You could take a PMV from Moresby to the village of Madilogo. Doing this, you avoid the two hard days (possibly the hardest on the whole trail) it takes to walk from Owers' Corner to Naoro. It takes about two hours to reach the Kokoda Trail from Madilogo; from there it's 1½ hours to Naoro.

If you want a little taste of the trail without walking the whole distance, you can walk down to Goldie River from Owers' Corner in just an hour or so. If you have the energy, struggle up the Golden Staircase to Imita Ridge on the other side. Another option would be to fly in, walk a section and fly out. Flying to Kagi and walking to Manari (one day) or Naoro (two days) would be interesting. Myola also has an airstrip, but planes only land there on a charter basis.

Organised Tours
Many companies offer treks of Kokoda, and while they aren't cheap they do take care of the organisational hassles. As usual, it's Traditional Travel which gets the best feedback.

Places to Stay & Eat
There are basic guesthouses in many villages, and various shelters and campsites along the trail. Some of the guesthouses and shelters are small, so if you meet another party you might have to camp. Make sure you pay for village accommodation, even if you aren't asked. It's usually around K10 per person, with some of the better places charging more.

There's a good guesthouse at **Myola**, which is a bit off the main trail, and although it costs K25 for food and accommodation, it is recommended. The food is excellent, there are warm showers, the 'lakes' are interesting, there are trout in nearby streams and some interesting war relics. You can fly in (charters only) and this would make a great weekend escape from Moresby. It is necessary to let the people know you're coming as Myola

isn't really a village and there might not be anyone around. Talk to Traditional Travel.

Getting There & Away
PMVs run from Moresby to the start of the trail at Owers' Corner. They are infrequent and leave Gordons Market early in the morning. The 48-km (two-hour) trip costs about K3. It might be worth taking a taxi to Gordons to ensure that you get there in time for the PMV.

If you miss the early PMV, you could take one running out the Sogeri road and get off at the Owers' Corner turn-off (K1.50). This means a long walk, although you could hitch. There's also an afternoon PMV to Owers' Corner, but if you take this one you'll have to overnight there. Neither of these options are a good idea, however – see Safety earlier in this section.

PMVs from Gordons Market to the village of Madilogo leave twice a week, on Thursday and Sunday mornings, and return to Port Moresby the same day in the afternoon. The trip costs about K10.

Traditional Travel can arrange transfers to the start of the trail at Owers' Corner, but this costs K45 per person.

There are airstrips at Naoro, Manari, Efogi No 1 and Kagi, as well as Bodinumu and Naduli, two villages near Kagi. TransNiugini Airways (☎ 25 2211) flies from Port Moresby to most of these strips on Monday and Thursday, departing Jacksons Airport early in the morning. To Kagi or Manari the fare is K42. Talair or Northcoast Aviation (book through Talair) flies to Kokoda on Monday, Friday and Saturday for K51.

See the Oro Province chapter for information on transport at the Kokoda end of the trail.

Oro Province

Land Area 19,827 sq km
Population 105,000
Capital Popondetta

Oro Province (often called Northern Province) is sandwiched between the Solomon Sea and the Owen Stanley Ranges. It is a little-visited region of the country, but it is physically beautiful and there are a number of areas of interest. The northern end of the Kokoda Trail terminates at the village of Kokoda and from here to the coast, and around the beaches of Buna and Gona, some of the most violent and bitter fighting of WW II took place.

Oro Province's flag has a butterfly on it, as this is the home of the largest butterfly in the world, the Queen Alexandra Birdwing. You might think that you've seen some big butterflies in PNG, but these are monsters, with a wingspan of nearly 30 cm. The first specimen collected by a European was brought down by a shotgun! That butterfly, a little damaged, is still in the British Museum. The Queen Alexandra Birdwing is now a threatened species, for the usual reason – it lives on the top layer of rainforests, and the rainforests are vanishing. It feeds on a particular species of vine which is poisonous to most birds and animals, and the butterfly is poisonous as well.

HISTORY

Early European contacts with the Orakaiva people, who live inland as far as Kokoda, were relatively peaceful, but when gold was discovered at Yodda and Kokoda in 1895, violence soon followed. After the first altercation between the local people and miners a government station was established. The government's results weren't much better since the first officer was killed shortly after he arrived and made peaceful, or so he thought, contacts. Eventually things quietened down and the mines, which were initially some of the richest in Papua, were

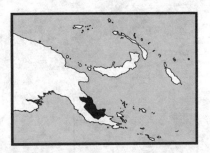

worked out. Rubber and other plantations superseded them.

The war arrived in the Oro area unexpectedly and dramatically in 1942. The Allied forces were just about to open a base in the area when the Japanese suddenly landed in late July '42 and immediately began to move to Kokoda from where they intended to climb up and over the Owen Stanley Ranges to take Port Moresby. This horrific campaign is covered in more detail in the introductory history section and in the Kokoda Trail section in the Port Moresby & Central Province chapter. As General Horii withdrew up the trail, lines of defence were drawn first at Eora Creek, mid-way along the trail, then at Oivi, on the road from Kokoda to Buna. Both were taken by the Australians after drawn out and bloody fighting. Horii drowned while attempting to cross the Kumusi River.

If the fighting down and up the trail had been bitter, the final push to retake the beachheads at Buna and Gona was nearly unbelievable. The Australian troops who had pursued the Japanese back up the trail were reinforced by American troops who came round the coast, but the Japanese held on suicidally. Although Kokoda was retaken at the beginning of January '43 it was the end of the month before Buna and Gona had fallen. The Japanese were not so much defeated as annihilated; it has been estimated

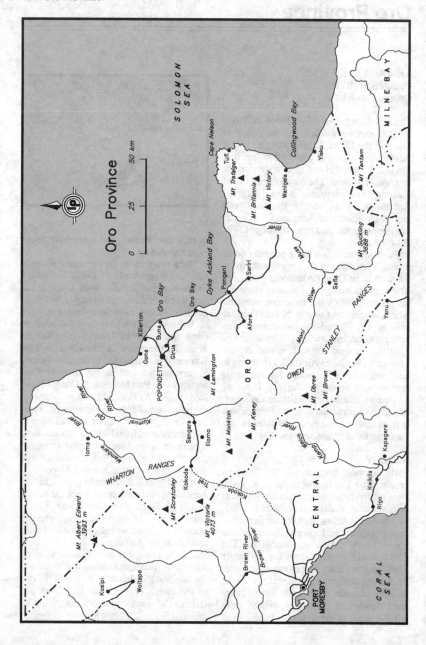

that of their total force of 16,000 men only about 700 survived.

There are many war relics scattered around the area, most of them considerably overgrown. At Jiropa Plantation, on the Buna road, there is a Japanese plaque commemorating their dead. Oro Bay, now the province's main port, was a major American base.

After the war, rebuilding the region was a difficult task as the damage was especially severe. Strangled by their supply difficulties, the Japanese troops had scoured the country for food, even eating grass and bark off trees in an often vain attempt to prevent starvation. The gardens and plantations were hardly back in operation after the war when Mt Lamington's disastrous eruption totally wiped out Higatura, the district headquarters, and killed nearly 3000 people. The new headquarters town of Popondetta has been established at a safer distance from the volcano.

GEOGRAPHY

The swamps and flatlands of the coast rise slowly inland towards the Owen Stanley Ranges then with increasing steepness to the peaks which stand at 3500 to 4000 metres at only 90 to 100 km from the sea. The only roads of any length in the province run from the coast inland through Popondetta to Kokoda where the famous trail starts. Mt Lamington, near Popondetta, is a mildly active volcano that, in 1951, erupted with cataclysmic force and killed nearly 3000 people. In the east of the province there are more interesting volcanoes near Tufi and a section of coast around Cape Nelson with unique tropical 'fjords' (their origin is volcanic rather than glacial) or *rias*.

ARTS

Tapa cloth, made by beating the bark from a paper mulberry tree until it is thin and flexible, is made in Oro Province. Natural dyes are used to make dramatic designs on the cloth. Only in the most remote parts is tapa cloth now worn by the local people. It is still made at Wanigela where distinctive clay pots are also fired.

GETTING THERE & AWAY

Oro Province is pivotal for shoestringers, or anyone who wants to make the most of sea travel in PNG. Taking the short flight across the Owen Stanleys to Kokoda (K51) and then PMVs to Popondetta (K5) and Oro Bay (K3) is the cheapest way to get from Moresby to the north coast of PNG. It would only cost a couple of kina more to fly direct from Moresby to Popondetta. You could, of course, walk the Kokoda Trail, but that would probably cost more. As a bonus, one of PNG's few excellent places to stay is in Popondetta.

Oro Bay is the easternmost port serviced by Lutheran Shipping's passenger boats, and from here you can head up the coast through Lae and Madang to Wewak, or Vanimo on a cargo boat. From Lae there are boats to New Britain, and from Madang you can pick up an irregular freighter to Manus Island. From Lae and Madang there are road connections to the Highlands, and from Wewak you can access the Sepik by road.

Heading in the other direction from Oro Bay it's possible (but time-consuming) to take small boats along the coast to Collingwood Bay, and perhaps from there to Milne Bay, from where boats run to the Trobriand Islands and the other island groups of Milne Bay Province.

The downside of all this is that Oro has suffered from an epidemic of PMV hold-ups and other robberies, especially between Kokoda and Popondetta. That has changed, at least for the time being, as the rascal gangs negotiated a surrender with the government in 1992. If you're worried about it, you can fly from Moresby direct to Popondetta (K58 on Air Niugini or Talair), which is still much cheaper than flying from Moresby to any of the other of the ports serviced by Lutheran Shipping's passenger boats. The short journey from Popondetta to Oro Bay is currently safe.

POPONDETTA

The district headquarters is not of particular interest except as a base to visit other parts of Oro Province. The town is currently experiencing a modest boom because of the huge Higatura oil palm project. There is a war memorial with an interesting map of the battle sites and a memorial to the victims of Mt Lamington in the town.

The rascal problem (hopefully solved by the amnesty and the surrender of most of the gangs) has produced the sort of aggressive adolescent graffiti (for example, 'Youth Run Wild', 'Ghetto Yut') common in the West but rare in PNG.

Popondetta is landlocked and inconveniently sited. The provincial headquarters are here because of the fate of the previous two – the one on the coast was invaded by the Japanese and destroyed, and the other, moved safely inland after the war, was destroyed by the eruption of Mt Lamington. The current site, a kunai grass plain, seems secure, but who knows? Rumour has it that the government is buying land at Oro Bay and plans to move the capital there.

The airport is 15 km south from town on the Oro Bay road, and Oro Bay, where the *Mamose Express* and the *Rita* dock, is 43 km from town. The town itself is spread along the highway. There are all the necessary basic facilities, including Air Niugini and Talair/Northcoast offices, banks and a few reasonable-sized shops.

There are the usual kai bars in town, none very appealing, although the one near the post office is Indian-run and has a few curries on the menu.

Locals will be able to point out to you the house used by Kokichi Nishamura when he is in PNG. This old man was a soldier here during WW II, and has since devoted himself to finding the remains of his comrades killed here and sending them back to Japan for proper burial.

Out of town near the airport is a picnic spot and swimming hole in a river (dug by a WW II bomb) which was once popular but is now rarely visited due to robberies. The local village used to charge a kina or two to visit. With Oro Province hopefully becoming safer, people might start to use it again. To get there from Popondetta, turn right off the highway onto a dirt track by a store just

before the entrance to the airport. Turn left onto a smaller track before the big, thatched Seventh day Adventist building and keep going. Total distance from the highway is about 1½ km.

If you plan to walk the Kokoda Trail from this end, see John Atkins at the Oro Guesthouse, as many trekkers stay there and pass on the latest information.

Basil Tindeba, from Buna, has been recommended as guide around the WW II sites in the area.

Places to Stay & Eat
There are some good places to stay in and near Popondetta, but the top-end *Lamington Hotel* (☎ 29 7222, PO Box 27) isn't one of them. It's becoming run-down and wouldn't be a bargain if the tariff (over K100) was halved. If there's a vacancy after 5 pm it will cost K70. The only restaurant in town is here.

Oro Guesthouse (☎ 29 7127, fax c/-29 7193, PO Box 2) is one of PNG's better places to stay, both for shoestringers and those with deeper pockets. It's comfortable, well-designed (although some rooms can be a bit noisy if people watch TV late at night) and extremely clean. A swimming pool and a *haus win* are planned. Good information about Oro Province and PNG in general is available, and the manager, John Atkins, has travelled widely. It's great to stay at a place where travel on a tight budget is regarded as normal! It's also nice to see that good accommodation in PNG can turn a profit without charging ridiculous amounts – although it does make you wonder why there aren't more places like this.

Many of the guests are government officials visiting Oro Province, and you can have some interesting conversations. Meals are simple but good, with a wide range of local vegetables. The ingredients are often the same as those used in village cooking but these meals taste a lot better.

There's quite a range of prices for rooms, although the rooms are basically the same, with fan and spotless shared bathrooms. Singles/doubles/triples cost K30/40/50, or

K40/60/80 with breakfast and dinner. Add another K3 to have a TV in the room.

If you're a student with ID you'll pay just K5 for a shared room. If you're a Youth Hostel member, or are a member of a backpackers' association (including the various Australian private enterprise hostel chains), or if you've walked the Kokoda Trail, or (maybe) if you are just an impoverished backpacker, you'll pay K8, also sharing. Anyone can camp for K3. Use of the kitchen costs K3 or you can buy breakfast for K4 and dinner for K6.

To get here from the town centre, walk down the main street away from the direction of the airport, and turn left when you get to the hospital's 'In' sign. Go past the park and it's the fifth house on the left. Coming from the PMV stop at the market, head back to the main road, walk towards town and take the first right after the high school.

Out of town, the *Christian Training Centre* (☎ 29 7384, PO Box 126), better known as the CTC, has cheap accommodation for groups who book in advance – it's primarily a conference centre. Their rates vary widely depending on what facilities you require, and whether you want meals, but it's good value. It's five km along the road to the airport, and a PMV costs K0.40. If you stay here or at one of the other religious centres nearby, ask about the village trails into town, which pass through forest and plantations.

Near the CTC, a short walk down a bumpy track that runs through the CTC grounds, is a nicer place, the *Franciscan Friary*, nestling in the rainforest. The Anglican monks lead a quiet but disciplined life, and conditions are spartan – you wash in the creek. While they have one or two rooms for visitors (male or female) they aren't really in the business of providing accommodation for travellers. Still, they are amazingly friendly, so you should be able to stay. Remember that you are a guest, not a customer. Camping is possible, and basic meals are available. Make a donation. There are many butterflies because the plants they feed on are grown here, and it's possible that you might see a Queen Alexandra Birdwing.

Further down the same track you come to a still nicer place, worth visiting even if you don't stay here. The *Sisters of the Visitation* are Anglican nuns, and their convent is devoted to meditation and retreats. The grounds are very beautiful and peaceful. It's possible that you may be able to stay here, but if you have the slightest inclination to party, stay well away.

The *Jonita Village Guesthouse* is also out of town. Coming from the airport it's a couple of km before the CTC, on the left just after the second one-lane bridge; there's a sign. The guesthouse, a very basic bush-material house, is deteriorating and may soon close down or fall down.

Things to Buy
St Christopher's Diocesan Office, just before the big open-sided Catholic Cathedral on the way into town from the airport, sells tapa cloth. You can sometimes buy it from the Vocational Centre; from Oro Guesthouse head down to the far end of the street and turn left.

Getting There & Away
Air The airport, 15 km from town, is officially called Girua and it's one of several wartime strips in the area. From the air you'll notice that the area around it is pocked with horseshoe marks – they're WW II gun emplacements.

The small terminal building has been torched.

The Air Niugini office (☎ 29 7022) in town opens at 8 am. Air Niugini has daily connections from Port Moresby to Popondetta and the short flight costs K58. Talair charges the same and the flight might be more interesting in a smaller plane.

Northcoast Aviation (☎ 29 7219), the Talair agent, has taken over a number of Talair routes in Oro Province, flying to Tufi (K64) and Kokoda (K51) five days a week and several other small strips.

Talair flies to/from Lae on Wednesday and Saturday for K121. One flight on Saturday is direct Lae – Popondetta – Gurney (Alotau), but the other Saturday flight and the Wednesday flight hop around the coast, stopping at Tufi (K64 from Popondetta), Wanigela (K64), Cape Vogel (K104), Raba Raba (K105), Wedau (K119) and Gurney (K127).

PMV PMVs aren't all that frequent so give yourself plenty of time if you're catching a plane or a boat. PMVs take about half an hour to get to the airport and about an hour to Oro Bay. It's possible that when you want to leave for Oro Bay, all the PMVs in town will have already left to pick up passengers from the boat.

You'll pick PMVs in town or on the main highway, but the market (walking out of town, first street on your left past the High School) is where most start from. PMVs for Kokoda (K5) and Oro Bay (K3) also stop at the Papindo supermarket in the town centre. A van to Buna (K2.40) leaves from the Price-Rite hardware shop, also in town. This isn't really a PMV, it's chartered by people from Buna to bring them into work, so there aren't many departures.

The road between Popondetta and Oro Bay is sealed and in good condition. Other roads in the area, particularly around the Higatura oil palm project are also good, but as you head to Kokoda the road becomes rough, although there are plans to seal it.

Sea Oro Bay, 43 km away on the coast, is the eastern turnaround point for Lutheran Shipping's weekly passenger-only *Mamose Express* and *Rita*, and there are also irregular freighters. Small boats for Tufi and other ports can also be found here. See the Oro Bay section for details. Lutheran Shipping has an agent in Popondetta, Robert Laurie Company (RLC) (☎ 29 7061, PO Box 77), on the main street a block or so beyond the hospital. They don't handle the passenger business but will be able to tell you about sailing dates for freighters. You buy tickets on the wharf at Oro Bay.

Getting Around

To/From the Airport No PMVs specifically service the airport, but you will get one on the nearby highway, heading either to Oro Bay or Popondetta. The fare from the airport to Popondetta is K1, or a negotiable K2 if you're dropped at the Oro Guesthouse. There aren't very many PMVs and they are particularly sparse on Sundays. Otherwise, one of the locals will probably help. This is one of those small airports where people gather to watch flights arrive, so there are usually plenty of vehicles.

Getting *to* the airport is trickier, but Popondetta is a small town and if you ask around you'll probably hear of someone flying out on the same flight who can give you a lift.

AROUND POPONDETTA

The country around Popondetta is very pretty, with stands of rainforest, kunai plains and huge tracts of oil palm. The dark aisles of oil palms are bathed in a deep green light, and look as mysterious as the depths of Indian temples. The tidy villages are bright with flowers and most of the houses are of traditional design and materials. There are lots of verandahs and *haus win*. The country is fairly flat, and there aren't many other places in PNG where you are inland but neither on a mountain nor in a swamp.

Oro Bay

This pretty bay has a new wharf complex, where the *Mamose Express* and the *Rita* dock. It's also where the oil from all those oil palms is loaded for export. The oil has to be heated so that it's sufficiently liquid to flow into the tankers. There's a village or two around the bay, and you could probably arrange to stay in one if you're waiting for a boat. A traveller suggests contacting Mr Lomas Orere in the trade store.

The hospital, across the bay from the wharf, has a dormitory which might be taken over by Popondetta's Franciscan monks – if it is, you might be able to stay here.

There are places to stay in a few of the villages around Oro Bay, such as the mission at Emo and the Baregi High School at Pongani. The *Ase Guesthouse* at Buna has been burned down, but ask around, as it might be rebuilt when the squabbling ends.

Getting There & Away Lutheran Shipping's *Mamose Express* or *Rita* leaves Oro Bay early Tuesday afternoon for the overnight trip to Lae (K21.50/32.50, deck/cabin class) and continues on as far as Wewak. There are also Lutheran Shipping freighters which take passengers on the trip, though less regularly and comfortably (K19/23 deck/1st class). Currently, there's a boat each week, arriving at Oro Bay on Wednesday and departing when the cargo has been loaded.

If you're going further than Lae, insist on buying a through ticket, otherwise you might be sold a ticket to Lae and have to buy another there, which works out to be considerably more expensive.

If you're heading east you can find small boats at Oro Bay. Ask around the village nearest the wharf. A work boat makes the overnight trip from Oro Bay to Tufi about twice a week, usually Monday and Friday, for K10. Moses, who works at Tau Traders in Popondetta (near the end of the cross street which runs off the main road at the Lamington Hotel), might have information.

Higatura Oil Palms

This British company owns some of the oil palm estates around Popondetta (many are owned by villagers) and the factory which extracts the palm oil. The network of good roads near Popondetta was made by the company for its trucks to collect the crop, those clumps of yellow-orange 'fruit' you see lying by the roadside. The factory (which stinks and pollutes the river) is a km or so down a dirt road from the village of Doublecross, about 10 km from Popondetta on the Kokoda road. Doublecross is so named because there are two river crossings here, but surely Doublecross Contractors could have thought of a more reassuring name!

A couple of km past the factory is **Sigura**, Higatura's company town. There's nothing much to see here, but it's an utterly orderly place, and surprisingly large. It has its own security force (with elaborate uniforms), school, hospital, sportsground, etc, and the houses come in different models depending on your position in the company. Electricity is generated by burning oil-palm husks.

AROUND THE PROVINCE
Kokoda

The road from Popondetta has brought Kokoda to within a couple of hours' drive (three by PMV). The Kumusi River is now crossed by a bridge near Wairopi (from 'wire rope' after the earlier footbridge). General Horii and hundreds of other Japanese troops died near here while crossing the river during the retreat from Oivi Ridge. The road climbs steeply over the ridge and then drops into the Kokoda Valley where the walking trail starts. The Owen Stanley Ranges rises almost sheer behind Kokoda.

The old trail was once used by miners walking from Port Moresby across to the gold fields of Yodda, only 13 km away.

For more information on the trail see the Kokoda Trail section in the Port Moresby & Central Province chapter.

The ranger will sell you a certificate for completing the trail!

Places to Stay Accommodation is available at the *Park HQ* for about K5 – see the ranger. There have been robberies here, and travellers have suggested staying in the police compound. Some food is available from the trade stores.

Getting There & Away A PMV to Popondetta costs K5 and takes nearly three hours. Flights to Moresby cost K51 with Talair. To Popondetta, sometimes via some small strips, it's K42 with Talair or North-coast Aviation.

Mt Lamington (Sumburipa)

The 1585-metre peak of Mt Lamington is clearly visible from Popondetta (there's a good view on the road into town from the airport) but the original headquarters was even closer, only 10 km from the volcano. Like many other volcanoes in PNG, Mt Lamington still shakes and puffs a little and the local residents paid no attention to a slight increase in activity in 1951. Then half of the mountain side suddenly blew out and a violent cloud of super-heated gases rushed down, incinerating all before it.

The entire European population of Higatura and many Papua New Guineans died – a total of around 3000 people. It was later estimated that the temperature stood at around 200°C for about a minute and a half and that the gas cloud rolled down at over 300 km/h. Nearly 8000 people, or 10% of the province's population, were left homeless. It took a number of years for the region to recover.

Mt Lamington has been fairly calm since then, and keen bushwalkers can climb it today. You start from Sasenbata Mission, a little way off the Kokoda road. Like most mountains the best time to reach the summit is in the early morning before the clouds roll in; there's a campsite on a ridge line. There is no crater atop Mt Lamington, but the views are excellent. Take water; there's none available near the top and it's thirsty work. Take care, too; it's still active.

A guide from a nearby village (for example, Duve) is almost essential to avoid hassles with local people.

Afore

This tiny town is on a high plateau. There are good walks in the area, which has been largely unscathed by the province's rascal problem. As is so often the case in PNG, it's strangers who cause the trouble, so making friends with people who live in the area is a good way of ensuring your safety.

In town there's a school where you might be able to stay, and surrounding villages will probably accommodate you for about K7. Sagarina Mission, most easily accessible on foot, is south of Afore and usually has accommodation.

Occasional PMVs run from Popondetta to Pongani but you might have more luck from Oro Bay. They aren't very frequent. From Pongani to Afore you might have to hitch; the road is rough.

Tufi Area

A suitably patriotic British sea captain named this scenic peninsula Cape Nelson after the legendary admiral and dubbed the three mountain peaks on the cape, Trafalgar (site of Nelson's naval victory over the French), Victory (his ship) and Britannia (she's the one who ruled the waves). The beautiful bay to the south he named Collingwood, after one of Lord Nelson's captains.

The cape was formed by an earlier eruption of its three volcanoes and the lava which flows down into the sea created the *rias*, 'fjords', for which it is famous. Unlike the Norwegian originals, the water is always warm and beneath the calm surface of the sheltered bays there is beautiful coral waiting to be inspected.

Tufi is one of PNG's best kept secrets. It is a spectacular place to visit and there are half-a-dozen pleasant, good-value guesthouses. The people are very friendly and English is widely spoken. If you can, go.

Further south, on Collingwood Bay, is **Wanigela**, where there's also good snorkelling. The market is supposed to be better than Tufi's. Although the guesthouse has closed down you might still be able to arrange canoe trips up the Murin River, and glass-bottom boat tours to the coral reefs can be arranged.

Yiaku village, east of Wanigela and quite close to the Milne Bay Province border, is a centre for the manufacture of clay pots and tapa cloth by the Maisin people. Nearly all the tapa cloth you see has been made in Yiaku, although other people make their own designs on the cloth.

Places to Stay & Eat The guesthouses at Tufi are all run by local clans and can be booked by writing care of the post office in Tufi. They lie between the villages of Angorogo and Sai. They all provide excellent local food, including superb seafood, and this is included in the tariff. All of them charge about K25 per person and arrange fishing and diving trips – I don't think it matters much where you end up staying. Outrigger canoes are the standard form of transport. It can get very windy between June and August.

Kofure Guesthouse is one km from the

airstrip and reached by outrigger canoe; the *Konabu Guesthouse* is on the point, a few minutes' walk to the sea; *Tainabuna Village Guesthouse* is an hour by canoe from the airport and has been recommended. The other places are the *Komoa* and *Jebo*.

There is no longer a guesthouse at Wanigela but the Anglican Mission can usually offer accommodation. See Duncan Kasocason or Father Amos. In Yiaku village see the mission or ask the local councillors.

Getting There & Away See the Oro Bay section for information on boats to Tufi. In Tufi ask for Mr Lei at the store; it's his boat that runs to Oro Bay. To travel between Tufi and Wanigela you can hire a small boat but the half-hour trip will cost about K25. In Wanigela see Max Gegeyo. If you wait, a boat taking passengers for much less will

probably turn up. It's a similar story on boats from Wanigela to Yiaku.

The air fare, with Talair or Northcoast Aviation, from Popondetta to both Wanigela and Tufi is K64.

You could perhaps continue eastwards by sea to Cape Vogel and Wedau in Milne Bay Province, but boats are not frequent and it's simpler to fly. From Tufi to Cape Vogel it costs K58 and Cape Vogel to Wedau is K75; Wanigela to Cape Vogel costs K37, Wanigela to Wedau K71. From Wedau a flight to Gurney (Alotau) costs K31. It's an easy four-day walk from Wedau to Alotau.

Talair flies from Lae and Popondetta to Gurney on Wednesday and Saturday via this route, and Northcoast Aviation flies from Popondetta to Tufi and Wanigela on weekdays.

Talair (or Northcoast) flies to Tufi (K115) and Wanigela (K107) from Port Moresby on Tuesday and Saturday.

Milne Bay Province

Land Area 14,000 sq km
Population 170,000
Capital Alotau

At the eastern end of PNG, the Owen Stanley Ranges plunges into the sea and a scatter of islands dots the ocean for hundreds of km further out. This is the start of the Pacific proper – tiny atolls, coral reefs, volcanic islands, swaying palms and white beaches. Yet, there is one big difference to the better known areas of the Pacific – there are virtually no tourists. The Trobriand Islands are the only place in Milne Bay Province with any sort of a tourist reputation, but it would be a very busy week if they had 20 visitors!

Because there are so few visitors, formal accommodation options are limited and often expensive. However, there are plenty of villages, missions, district offices, etc, and your novelty value usually assures you of hospitality. The quandary people find themselves in when encountered by a visitor is summed up by the expats I met who did have accommodation to let, but didn't have a clue how much to charge. They suggested a fairly high price, but then said that I'd better stay for a few days to see if I liked it before we talked about money!

All this could change rapidly, as the province is one of the world's more peaceful and beautiful places and it would only take a traditional landowner to cash in on his island by becoming a 'partner' with a foreign company for large-scale resort tourism to take over. Many people are worried about this, and while they are extremely friendly to the individual visitor, they are wary of mass tourism. One villager told me:

We dressed up in traditional costume and put on a sing-sing when the cruise ship arrived. Then it went away again. What did we get out of it? We don't want one tourist to set one foot on our island unless we invite them. Of course we *do* invite them; they are welcome, but as our guests, not the guests of some foreigner.

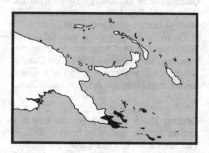

HISTORY

Before European explorers arrived, this area was known to other Pacific and Asian peoples. It has been suggested that the ceremonial canoes used by the people from the Louisiade Archipelago, the only plank-built canoes in the Pacific, are modelled on Chinese junks. There was so much pre-European contact, often hostile, that the aggression which European missionaries encountered isn't surprising.

The islands of Milne Bay Province were well known to early European explorers of the Pacific, and many of the islands still bear their names. The Louisiade Archipelago, for example, was named after Louis Vaez de Torres, who sailed through them way back in 1606, kidnapping 14 children and taking them to Manila in the Philippines to be baptised. In 1793 Bruny D'Entrecasteaux donated his cumbersome name to the island group further north and west.

In 1873, Captain John Moresby discovered the deep inlet which he named Milne Bay after Alexander Milne, the Lord of the Admiralty. Moresby had earlier landed on Samarai Island and named it Dinner Island after the meal he ate there; it must have been a memorable one. He also paused long enough to run up the flag and claim the whole area for Queen Victoria. The good queen, however, was not too keen on finding further places where the sun never set and his claim was repudiated.

Even before Moresby came on his empire-building expedition, there had been attempts at permanent European settlements; a mission was set up on Woodlark Island way back in 1847 but the islanders were extremely unenthusiastic about Christianity and the missionaries who survived their lack of enthusiasm soon departed. After Moresby's visit, traders and other missionaries followed and a thriving trade developed in pearl shells and bêche-de-mer, the large sea slugs which are a Chinese delicacy. The Milne Bay area also suffered from 'blackbirding', the forcible collection of 'voluntary' labour for Queensland sugar plantations.

In 1888, gold was discovered on Misima Island, the miners flooded in and, as in other parts of PNG, soon died like flies from the effects of disease, malnutrition and unfriendly natives. A later find on Woodlark Island eventually produced nearly $1½ million in gold at a time when the price was much lower than it is today. With all this passing trade, plus a major missionary station, the island of Samarai established itself as the major port and outpost in the region, a position it was to hold until after WW II.

Soon after the war spread to the Pacific, the Milne Bay area served as the stage for the turning point in the conflict between Japanese and Allied forces. In the Battle of the Coral Sea, the Japanese rush south was abruptly halted. Although this is regarded as a classic naval battle, the Japanese and American warships did not once come within 300 km of each other; the fighting was entirely conducted by aircraft. Some of the most violent dogfights took place high above Misima Island in the Louisiades. American losses were severe, but the Japanese fleet was crippled and never again played an effective role in the Pacific.

Despite this setback, the Japanese remained determined to capture PNG and in July 1942 they landed at Buna and Gona in Oro Province and pressed south down the Kokoda Trail towards Moresby. In August they made a second landing in Milne Bay, in an attempt to take the eastern end of the island. Again, as in the Coral Sea conflict, the Allies had advance warning and a strong Australian force was waiting for them. In addition, they landed at Ahioma, too far round the bay, and had to slog through terrible swamps to meet the Australians and attempt to take the airstrip. This blunder contributed to their total defeat, the first time in the war that a Japanese amphibious assault had been repelled. Active fighting did not again encroach on the Milne Bay area, but Milne Bay itself became a huge naval base that hundreds of thousands of military personnel passed through. Some of them came back again in 1992 to mark the 50th anniversary of the battle.

GEOGRAPHY

The mainland section of the province is extremely mountainous, for the eastern end of the Owen Stanley Ranges marches almost to the end of the island before plunging straight to the sea. The province has very little flat land.

Milne Bay itself is quite small compared with the size of the province, which extends right out to Rossel Island in the Louisiade Group.

It is the islands that are of greatest interest in Milne Bay Province and there are plenty of them – 160 named islands plus more than 600 islets and atolls and untold numbers of reefs waiting to trap the unwary sailor. Despite the province's relatively small land area, all those islands give it the longest coastline of any province.

The islands are enormously varied, from tiny dots barely breaking the surface of the sea to larger islands such as Fergusson and Goodenough in the D'Entrecasteaux Group. The highest mountain on Goodenough rises to over 2400 metres and there are so many other lesser peaks that, for its size, this is one of the most mountainous places on earth. By contrast, the Trobriand Islands are virtually entirely flat.

The islands are divided into six main

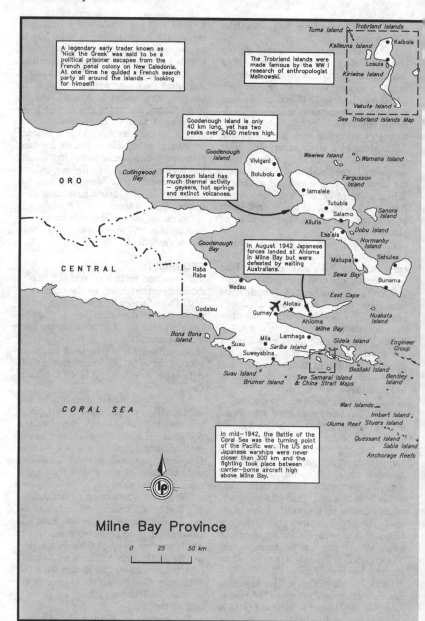

A legendary early trader known as 'Nick the Greek' was said to be a political prisoner escapee from the French penal colony on New Caledonia. At one time he guided a French search party all around the islands — looking for himself!

The Trobriand Islands were made famous by the WW I research of anthropologist Malinowski.

Goodenough Island is only 40 km long, yet has two peaks over 2400 metres high.

Fergusson Island has much thermal activity — geysers, hot springs and extinct volcanoes.

In August 1942 Japanese forces landed at Ahioma in Milne Bay but were defeated by waiting Australians.

In mid–1942, the Battle of the Coral Sea was the turning point of the Pacific war. The US and Japanese warships were never closer than 300 km and the fighting took place between carrier–borne aircraft high above Milne Bay.

Milne Bay Province

0   25   50 km

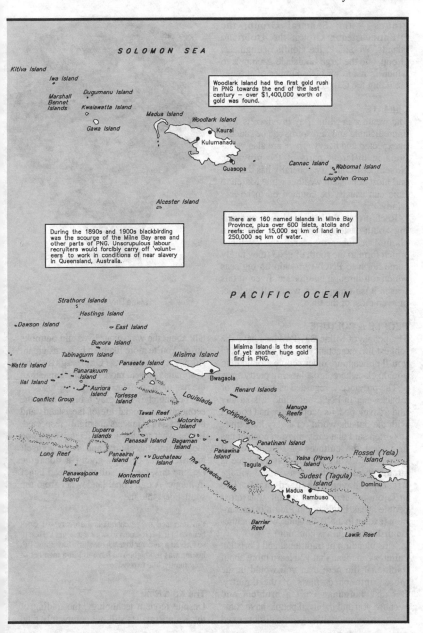

SOLOMON SEA

Kitiva Island

Iwa Island

Marshall
Bennet
Islands

Dugumenu Island

Kwaiawatta Island

Madua Island

Woodlark Island

Kaurai

Kulumanadu

Gawa Island

Guasopa

Woodlark Island had the first gold rush
in PNG towards the end of the last
century — over $1,400,000 worth of
gold was found.

Cannac Island

Wabornat Island

Laughlan Group

Alcester Island

There are 160 named islands in Milne Bay
Province, plus over 600 islets, atolls and
reefs: under 15,000 sq km of land in
250,000 sq km of water.

During the 1890s and 1900s blackbirding
was the scourge of the Milne Bay area and
other parts of PNG. Unscrupulous labour
recruiters would forcibly carry off 'volunteers' to work in conditions of near slavery
in Queensland, Australia.

PACIFIC OCEAN

Strathord Islands

Hastings Island

Dawson Island

East Island

Bunora Island

Tabinagurm Island

Misima Island

Panaeate Island

Misima Island is the scene
of yet another huge gold
find in PNG.

Watts Island

Panarakuum
Island

Ilai Island

Auriora
Island

Bwagaoia

Renard Islands

Conflict Group

Torlesse
Island

Louisiade

Tawai Reef

Motorina
Island

Archipelago

Manuga
Reefs

Duperre
Islands

Panasail Island

Bagaman
Island

Panawina
Island

Panatinani Island

Long Reef

Panaairai
Island

Duchateau
Island

The Calvados Chain

Yeina (Piron)
Island

Rossel (Yela)
Island

Panawaipona
Island

Montemont
Island

Tagula

D

Sudest (Tagula)
Island

Dominu

Madua

Rambuso

Barrier
Reef

Lawik Reef

groups – the Samarai Group, the D'Entrecasteaux Group, the Trobriand Islands, Woodlark, the Conflict (Engineer) Group, and the large Louisiade Archipelago which is made up of a number of groups, including the Calvados Chain.

CLIMATE

The weather in Milne Bay Province is very unpredictable and rainstorms can be sudden, unexpected and heavy. There are also variations in different parts of the province. November to January generally has the best and most consistent weather while March to June can usually be counted on to be less windy.

Reefs protect the islands when the prevailing south-easterly winds blow, but from about December to March the cyclones which form to the south of PNG (they rarely come north to PNG) can whip up big seas which roll through unimpeded. Even in this season it isn't rough and windy all the time, or even most of the time.

PEOPLE & CULTURE

The people of Milne Bay Province have the longest life expectancy of any in PNG, and you'll notice more older people around than you do elsewhere, most looking pretty spry.

The province is regarded as something of a backwater in PNG, but while it is largely underdeveloped, its people have had contact with the outside world for a very long time. It's often said that early mission contact has destroyed the cultures of PNG's coastal peoples, but while the mission influence is strong, local traditions remain and village lifestyles haven't changed much. The mission influence has meant that most people speak English and Pidgin is uncommon (except in the Trobriands, where neither English nor Pidgin is common).

This blending of traditional and Christian cultures can mean that you learn more about traditional life here than you would in the more 'untouched' parts of the country. Because language isn't a problem and because you and the local people have some things in common, it's easier to discover and

Milne Bay woman

talk about the ways your lives and outlooks differ. You're more likely to be a participant than an observer. (Once again, the Trobriands present more of a challenge than the rest of the province.)

The churches still play a big role in the economic and social life of the islands and the priests or ministers are highly respected. If you want to stay in a village it's a good idea to find the church and make yourself known there, perhaps giving a donation. Despite this, there is still widespread belief in magic. A traditional landowner from the south coast told me:

I'm intrigued by witchcraft and sorcery – I can't believe in it, but it seems to work. I thought I'd test it, so I asked a sorcerer to teach me spirit-travelling. But his fee was too high. You have to kill a member of your family. Too expensive.

The Kula Ring

Despite modern technology, the trading of the Kula Ring has still not completely died out although the sea voyages in outrigger canoes are unlikely to be as lengthy as in 'the time before'. This traditional, ritual, exchange of goods served to bind islands together. Two articles are traded in the ring – *bagi*, the red shell necklaces, and *mwala* decorated armlets made from cone shells.

The ring extends right around the province, including the Trobriands, Woodlark, Misima, the D'Entrecasteaux Group and around Samarai. The exchange between islands on the 'ring' is purely ritual, since the goods rarely go out of the ring and are always eventually traded on to the next island in the circuit. Eventually they get right back to their starting point, although this can take many years. The ring goods go in opposite directions – shell necklaces are traded clockwise, armlets anti-clockwise.

Today, traders on the ring sometimes make their voyages on board modern ships but elaborately decorated canoes are still used and villagers from every island still offer hospitality to their 'ring partners' from the next island on the circuit. At the same time as the ritual exchanges are made, other more mundane items are traded – pottery, food, baskets – but not with your 'ring partner'.

Mainland & China Strait

ALOTAU

The Milne Bay Provincial Government headquarters was transferred from Samarai Island to Alotau on the mainland in 1968, mainly because access to Samarai is only possible by sea and because the island was already crowded to its limits. Any further expansion had to be on the mainland.

The sleepy little town is spectacularly sited on the edge of Milne Bay. There's not actually a great deal to do here; you can't look at the view all day and there's not really anything else. It is, for most travellers, just the starting point for a trip to the islands, and it's the only spot to stock up on food and money.

As is common around the province, little Pidgin is spoken in Alotau; most people speak English, and most of them are very friendly. If you meet someone who speaks Pidgin they are likely to be a newcomer to the province. There are an increasing number of newcomers, partly due to the oil palm developments. This disturbs many locals – 'outsiders' equals 'criminals' for many people in PNG and this province is more insular than most.

There is talk of building a road to link Alotau with the south coast and Moresby, but many people don't want it. They would rather pay high freight charges than allow unrestricted access to their paradise. Still, although you hear some tut-tutting about the pretty pass to which things have come, the tension level in Alotau could hardly be lower. It's one of the most relaxed and hospitable towns in the country.

Across Milne Bay from Alotau is Discovery Bay, where Captain Moresby spent several days during his 1873 visit. The mysterious 'moonstones' in the hills behind this bay are, as yet, an unsolved archaeological riddle. There is very good fishing around Alotau.

Orientation

The commercial centre is laid out on a grid, with everything within a five-minute walk, basically around a single block. The new Masurina Centre passes for the town's shopping mall. Most housing and two of the three places to stay are in 'Top Town', a steep climb up the hill behind the commercial centre. The views are stunning. The bustling harbour is a short walk to the east of town. Further around is the Masurina Trading wharf and then the international wharf, where the big freighters dock.

Alotau's airport is Gurney, which is 15 km from town and surrounded by a massive oil palm development.

Information

There's a Milne Bay Tourist Bureau (☎ 61 1503, PO Box 119) and although it's not

really set up to deal with the public, it would be worth visiting if you want up-to-date information about some of the island guesthouses or want to make radio contact with them. Jennifer Varssilli, the Tourism Development Officer, is very friendly and helpful. The bureau is in the Commerce Department building, a small place to the left of the main government buildings, opposite the Westpac bank.

The major banks are represented and the shopping is adequate – you'll see the market on your right as you come in from the airport.

Harbour

The harbour is a colourful part of town, with boats from all over the province. You can easily entertain yourself for hours just watching the comings and goings – the fishers in the bay, and the brightly-painted island boats loading and unloading, all against the backdrop of mountains falling sheer into blue Milne Bay. Most of the boats seem to be in very good condition; about the only rusty scows are the derelict remains of the government fleet. For a birds' eye view of the harbour, walk up the steps in town to the hospital, take the right

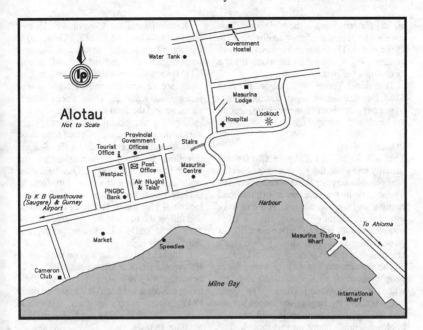

Alotau
Not to Scale

Government Hostel
Water Tank
Masurina Lodge
Hospital
Lookout
Provincial Government Offices
Stairs
Tourist Office
Post Office
Masurina Centre
Westpac
Air Niugini & Talair
PNGBC Bank
To K B Guesthouse (Saugere) & Gurney Airport
Harbour
To Ahioma
Masurina Trading Wharf
Market
Speedies
Cameron Club
Milne Bay
International Wharf

fork and keep going for a couple of hundred metres.

Alotau Harbour would be a good place to start if you had the time and the temperament for an unstructured, island-hopping expedition – the longer you sit and watch the more tempted you will be.

Activities

Swimming There isn't really a swimming beach in town; locals recommend the beach at the old Ahioma Plantation, on the old beach road a few minutes' drive east of town. PMVs run nearby.

Diving There is very good diving in and around Milne Bay. Rob Van de Loos runs Milne Bay Marine Charters (☎ 61 1167, fax 61 1291, PO Box 176) and he has a couple of purpose-built dive boats, the *Tania* (11 metres long, sleeps six) and the impressive new *Cheetan* (20 metres long, sleeps 10). His office is just past the high school; turn right off the airport road past the Mobil station. The *Cheetan* has an extensive touring programme and is usually pre-booked by groups, but the *Tania* might be available for charter at K435 a day. You might be able to arrange day dives in smaller boats.

Telita Cruises (☎ 61 1186, fax 61 1282, PO Box 303) has a good reputation and runs diving charters around the province and New Ireland.

Someone suggested that in China Strait, where the current is swift, it's worth just holding onto the anchor chain and watching what goes past – which can include three-metre tiger sharks.

Organised Tours The luxury *Melanesian Discoverer*, operated by Melanesian Tourist Services, runs tours between Madang and Alotau via the Trobriands. For details and schedule information contact Melanesian Tourist Services (☎ 82 2766, PO Box 707, Madang). Check the local paper (the fortnightly *Eastern Star)*, as the *Melanesian Discoverer* sometimes offers standby fares in the province. These are an expensive way of getting around, but might be worth it for a large dollop of luxury.

Traditional Travel (☎ 21 3966, PO Box 4264, Boroko) sail *wahagas* (traditional outrigger dugouts about 10 metres long) around the Louisiade Archipelago.

Places to Stay

The KB Mission's *Saugere Guesthouse* (usually known as the KB guesthouse) is the best place to stay for those on a budget. It's by the bay just before town, off the road running in from the airport. You can walk into town, although every time I tried someone would stop and offer me a lift. At present there is no electricity so there aren't any fans, but there's generally a sea breeze.

The guesthouse can fill up with church people (people from Kwato Island stay here when they're in Alotau). There isn't a phone but you could try ringing the tourist bureau and asking them to drop in and make a booking – don't count on this though. The guesthouse isn't especially cheap but it's the cheapest in Alotau: clean single rooms are K25 a night, or K40 with good meals of enormous size.

The *Government Hostel* has plain but decent accommodation for K45, including meals. Contact the tourist bureau to check they're not full of visiting Members of the Provincial Parliament. One traveller complained that the hostel was full of cheerful drunks when he was there.

The hostel is high on a hill in Top Town. To walk here from the town centre, go up the steps (they lead off the street that Talair and Air Niugini are on) which are the shortcut to the hospital, and take the left fork at the hospital. Further up the hill take the next left fork and keep going up past the water tank. Take the first right after the water tank, and the hostel is towards the end of the block on the left. There's no sign but there is a flagpole in the front yard. It's a very steep walk with a pack but there are great views of Milne Bay. A taxi costs about K4.

Downhill from the Government Hostel, *Masurina Lodge* (☎ 61 1212, PO Box 5) is the top place to stay in Alotau. Air-con singles/doubles in the main building cost K115/145, and across the street in four cottages are fan-cooled rooms with shared facilities for K85/120. These prices include all meals and the food is excellent.

They'll pick you up from the airport if they know you're coming. A taxi from town costs about K3, or you can walk. See the directions for the government hostel, but take the first road to the right, just below the water tank, after the second left fork. A slightly longer route takes you past a good lookout – take the right fork at the hospital and follow the road all the way around, past the lookout, and turn left just before the road turns sharply right.

It might be possible to stay on the coast at **Halowia**, east of Alotau near Ahioma, at Sebastian Miyoni's place. He runs a PMV along the coast road to Alotau, so ask other PMV drivers if he's in town. If there is accommodation it will be much cheaper than anything in town.

Places to Eat

The *Masurina Lodge* is your best bet in the evenings; let them know you're coming. For non-guests, breakfast is K5, lunch K7.50 and a three-course dinner is K10 – great value. On Friday night they put on an outdoor barbecue buffet for K7. The lodge is also the local watering hole and is a popular spot to down a few beers after work. Someone will probably give you a lift home if you're not staying here.

The *Screaming Tribesman Cafeteria* in the Masurina Centre is open during the day and sells sandwiches and snacks. The menu doesn't go far beyond kai bar standards but the atmosphere (and the air-con) makes the food palatable. If you have a meal you can buy a beer.

The *Cameron Club*, on the waterfront a little west of the town centre, is a pretty basic place, but you can buy meals and have a drink. Visitors are welcome, except perhaps on Friday nights when it's for members only, due to pay cheque-induced trouble.

Several shops around town sell the good wholemeal bread made by the Alotau Bakery.

Things to Buy

There are a few places to buy handcrafts, two of them in the Masurina Centre. Another shop, which is larger, is a little north of the main shopping centre. All have stuff from the Trobriands which is, predictably, cheaper there.

Getting There & Away

Air Gurney, Alotau's airport, is 15 km from town and getting to/from the airport is a bit of a problem. See the following Getting Around section. Gurney is named after Bob Gurney, an Australian who began flying for Guinea Airways in 1929 and was killed in action with the RAAF in 1942.

The strip can't take Air Niugini's F28 jets, so if you fly with them you'll be on a Dash-7, a very civilised plane, quieter and roomier than the jets.

Just like Rabaul, Lae and Madang, Alotau is convinced that it will be granted PNG's second international airport. The rumours are a bit more modest than the others, though,

so they might be true. It's said that Gurney will be upgraded to take F28 jets so Air Niugini can fly here from Cairns in Australia.

Both Air Niugini and Talair have offices in town: Air Niugini (☎ 61 1100, PO Box 3), Talair (☎ 61 1333, PO Box 73).

There are daily Air Niugini flights between Port Moresby and Gurney (K101) and on Wednesday and Saturday there are flights to/from Misima (K86). The Moresby-Misima fare is K136.

Talair is the most useful carrier for this region, with several interesting routes.

Talair's Alotau-Moresby flight (K101) is either direct (daily except Tuesday and Sunday) or via some small strips on the south coast of Central Province (Tuesday).

There are Talair flights from Gurney to Losuia on the Trobriands (K108) on Wednesday and Saturday, both connecting with flights to/from Moresby (K150 from Losuia).

The D'Entrecasteaux Islands are serviced by Talair from Gurney on Monday and Friday. The fares from Gurney are: Esa'ala (Normanby Island) K50, Sehulaea (Normanby Island, Thursday only) K57, Salamo (Fergusson Island) K51 and

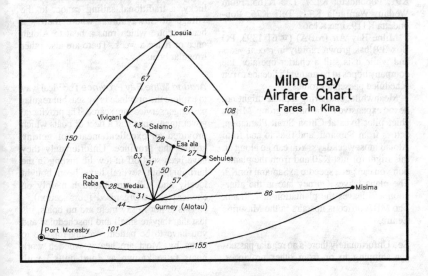

Milne Bay Airfare Chart
Fares in Kina

Vivigani (Goodenough Island) K63. The circuit route is flown in an anti-clockwise direction, for example, you can get from Esa'ala to Salamo (K28) but not the other way round.

To Misima Island, Talair flies from Moresby, both direct (K155, Saturday) and via Gurney (K86, Monday, Thursday and Friday).

You can fly with Talair between Gurney and Raba Raba (K44) daily except Tuesday and Sunday. This flight stops in Wedau (K31) but not on Thursday. From Raba Raba the circuit goes on to half a dozen inland strips on Monday. A similar circuit but including fewer inland strips is made on Thursday. On Friday the flight goes on from Raba Raba to Cape Vogel (K31 from Raba Raba, K35 from Wedau, K50 from Gurney) and from Cape Vogel flies direct to Moresby (K89). This flight comes back on the same route, also on Friday. Port Moresby to Wedau or Raba Raba is about K90.

On Wednesday and Saturday you can fly between Gurney and Lae, stopping at Wedau, Raba Raba, Cape Vogel and a number of other interesting places on the way. Fares from Gurney: Wanigela K87, Tufi K91, Popondetta K127, Lae K165. From Wedau: Wanigela K71, Tufi K75, Popondetta K119, Lae K156.

Milne Bay Air (MBA) (☎ 61 1393, PO Box 39) has grown rapidly in recent years and while it is still a charter operator, the company hopes to be granted a licence to run scheduled passenger routes.

Meanwhile, chartering a plane might not be too expensive if you have a group. MBA's chief pilot lives at China Strait Plantation, across from Samarai, and flies to and from Alotau most weekdays. You can go along on this flight for just K20 and from the plantation you can get a speedie to Samarai for K3. The plane leaves Gurney late in the afternoon and leaves the plantation at 7.30 am. The MBA office is upstairs in the Masurina Centre.

Sea Unfortunately there's no regular passenger shipping to or from other provinces, although there are freighters from both Moresby and Lae. None officially take passengers, but you might get lucky. Most are Consort Line (☎ 61 1318 in Alotau) vessels. Lutheran Shipping's north coast run only operates as far east as Oro Bay, although by small boats you can get from Oro Bay at least as far as Wanigela. From here you could fly to Wedau (K71) and walk to Alotau.

To/From Port Moresby Travellers with time to spare could travel from Moresby to Alotau in local boats, sleeping in villages. Thanks to Jim McKay for the following information.

You can travel by road from Moresby to Kupiano (where there's a guesthouse) by PMV from the Magi Highway turn-off (K8), and from there to Domara by PMV (K2). In Domara ask about accommodation at the store, and ask around for motorised canoes or work boats heading east. There are one or two most days travelling to Magarida, charging about K15 for the four-hour trip.

There's no accommodation in Magarida, a large village, but you should have no trouble finding somewhere to stay. From here you hop by motorised canoe or, if you're lucky, a traditional sailing canoe, to the village of Suwayabina, where there's a health centre which runs a boat to Alotau once or twice a week. There are also other irregular boats.

Around Milne Bay Province The ideal way to explore the province is by sea, but regular passenger services are scarce. The provincial government once had a fleet of boats which provided an excellent means of getting around the province. Unfortunately they have been sold off (a few lie rusting in the harbour), but several have been bought locally and still run, although mainly on charter (see the Organised Tours section).

This is not to say there are no boats, it's just that they're small and unscheduled and you have to be patient waiting for one to come by. Most are heavy, wooden work boats (also known as 'putt-putts') with central diesel engines. They're noisy, smelly and they roll a lot.

There are also the long, fibreglass outboard boats known as banana boats (or speedies), and thanks to the new diesel outboard motors they aren't nearly as expensive to run as they once were. Diesel outboards are very expensive to buy, however, so as yet not many people have them. If you charter one you're up for a lot of money, but some operate as irregular PMVs. They're very seaworthy and can safely carry a surprising amount of cargo, but they smash through the waves, so unless the sea is glassy smooth (which is unlikely) you'll be thrown around and probably get wet. Sit as far back as possible, and hold on tight!

Apart from hanging around the harbour (try the Masurina Trading wharf and the international wharf as well, and don't forget the small bay east of the market where banana boats often tie up) there are several other strategies if you want to get around the islands.

The Catholic Bishop will have the schedule of the *Morning Star*, an ex-government boat now touring the province's missions. This boat might give student discounts. The supermarkets will know about work boats carrying supplies, or contact Fifita Trading (☎ 61 1373), who supply many stores in the province. The *Arona*, another ex-government boat, sometimes does cargo runs and will take passengers. The captain lives on board, so see him if the boat is in harbour, otherwise contact Cameron Holdings (☎ 61 1007). Radio Milne Bay gives shipping information at 7 am and 7 pm.

Osiri Trading (☎ 61 1088) on Samarai runs a banana boat to and from the Masurina Trading wharf on Friday and Tuesday, and charges K8 for the trip in the smaller boat, K15 in the larger (it's faster). Four runs a week are planned. The tourist office will make a booking for you, or phone Ian Poole at Osiri.

A reasonable number of work boats run to Esa'ala and Salamo in the D'Entrecasteaux Group for about K10.

The two main trade stores on Kiriwina in the Trobriands run boats to Alotau approximately weekly, and charge about K20 for the two-day trip. These boats pass by the D'Entrecasteaux Islands and might be able to drop you off there.

There are a few charter options out of Alotau, expensive unless you have a group and not exactly cheap then. Both Telita Cruises and Milne Bay Marine Charters will charter their boats, although they are primarily dive outfits – see Diving in the Activities section earlier. The *Morning Star*, owned by the Catholic Church, is available for charter as well as doing regular mission runs. It costs K450 per 24 hours. The *Arona* can also be chartered, at K490. Contact Cameron Holdings (☎ 61 1007). See the Around Samarai section for information on the more basic but much cheaper *Georgina*.

One traveller's suggestions for exploring the province:

Spend a month going around Milne Bay Province, you don't have to be a millionaire with a yacht to enjoy the islands, coral, fish and villages. Work boats can be hired and you can go anywhere in a seven-metre work boat with a Yanmar diesel engine. With captain and crew on an extended charter they might cost well under K200 a day. There are hundreds in the province. Masurina Trading or the tourist bureau in Alotau could help arrange a charter. Boats are the PMVs of the province but if you cannot afford to charter one, just travel on them and pay the normal fare. Start by going from Alotau to Samarai, then on from there. A month can be spent in island hopping with no trouble. Just have plenty of time.

Another traveller suggests Salamo, on Fergusson Island, as a good starting point.

Walking It's possible to walk to Alotau from Raba Raba or Wedau. See the following North Coast section for details.

Getting Around

To/From the Airport Taxis meet most flights, but they charge K15 to get into town (that's a kina a km!), although you can share, and that's what most people do. PMVs run to town for K2 from the terminal or K1.20 from the nearby main road; most don't come in to the terminal. Allow yourself plenty of time if you're taking a PMV out to the airport. Masurina Lodge has free airport transfers for guests, but neither Air Niugini nor Talair have regular airport transport. Cadging a lift is the cheapest and easiest way.

PMV In town, PMVs heading for the airport can be found near the market; those going east stop near the PNGBC bank. The road continues east almost all the way to East Cape, the easternmost point on the PNG mainland.

Taxi & Car Rental Bay Cabs (☎ 61 1093) is the main taxi company and they also hire cars. Gilford is a nice guy who drives his own cab. He speaks good English, has a lot of local knowledge and won't rip you off.

NORTH COAST
Wedau Area
There are good beaches and reefs around the small settlement of Wedau. There's also a *Women's Guesthouse*, which charges about K25 for room and board. Nearby Dogura is worth a visit; there are views from the plateau, and there's a cathedral, but no accommodation. Gubanaona has also been suggested as a good place for swimming and snorkelling. Mt Pasipasi can be climbed in one long, hot day (take water!) and there are good views from the top.

Cape Vogel
Although I didn't see it myself, the tourist bureau recommended a village guesthouse at Bogaboga which charges about K15. It sounds good – first-hand reports will be gratefully accepted. Apparently, the attractions include bush trails, waterfalls, good snorkelling (including gear for hire) and artefacts for sale. Take your own food although there is a trade store. Contact the Milne Bay Tourist Bureau for more information.

Getting There & Away
Talair flies to Raba Raba, Wedau and Cape Vogel several days each week, from both Gurney and Lae. There are also flights from

Moresby. See the Alotau Getting There & Away section.

You can walk from Raba Raba or Wedau to Alotau, at least partly on a well used path that runs along the coast. There are plenty of villages along the way, which means that you will have no trouble finding somewhere to sleep, but also means that you should ask whether the water is fit to drink. Raba Raba to Wedau takes two days, and from Wedau to the tiny settlement of Taupota No 2 takes three easy days or two longer ones. From here, you can reach Alotau in a day by heading south across a low range but you'll need to take a guide for this section and there is a steep descent.

Alternatively, you can stay on the coast and walk from Taupota No 2 to East Cape, around the cape and back towards Alotau where you'll meet a road on which PMVs run. This section takes three days. For full details and maps see Lonely Planet's *Bushwalking in Papua New Guinea*.

SAMARAI ISLAND
The tiny (24 hectares) island of Samarai is in China Strait and is easily reached from Alotau, some distance around the coast on Milne Bay. Although Samarai definitely has seen better days it's a very pretty place in a very beautiful area.

A neat town covers most of the island, with plenty of big trees (although those which die aren't being replaced, sadly) and one or two tiny, sandy beaches. As an indication of how quiet the town is, Samarai people don't like Alotau because it's too big, too fast and there's too much traffic! A local told me that 'on Samarai you can get drunk and go to sleep under a tree and you'll wake up alive and with all your money'. It might be wise to be a little more cautious than that, but if you've ever wondered what life was like in a country town before cars were invented, Samarai is for you.

Samarai lies on China Strait, so named by Captain Moresby because he considered it would be the most direct route from the east coast of Australia to China. The island was long the provincial headquarters and the town predates Port Moresby. Before WW II it was the second largest town in PNG and one of the most attractive in the Pacific. During the war it was completely destroyed by the Australian administration, in anticipation of a Japanese invasion which never came.

The town's postwar reincarnation is in Australian country-town style, with lots of corrugated iron and cool verandahs along what passes for the main street. Well-mown grass grows on most of the narrow roads, and sleeping dogs lie undisturbed in the middle of them. Traffic isn't much of a worry, as there is only one car, rarely used, and the council's tractor to contend with. A road encircles the island but you can stroll right round it in half an hour!

Samarai's decline began in 1968, when the provincial government headquarters moved to Alotau, and when the international wharf closed in the '70s most businesses left. There are now only two or three expats on the island, from a peak of about 300. The old wharf, a big wooden structure, is now in terminal decay. People fish from it and kids dive off into the clear water. In a less civilised town the wharf would be closed and signs would forbid you to walk on it because of the rotten planks and beams.

1 Osiri Trading Wharf
2 Old International Wharves
3 Customs Wharf
4 Osiri Trading
5 Market
6 Memorial Hall
7 Tavern
8 Kinanale Guesthouse
9 Women's Guesthouse
10 Power House
11 Old Hospital (good views)
12 Police Station

Samarai Island

0   200   400 m

Information

Ian Poole, who runs Osiri Trading, the only big store left on the island, knows a lot about the area and is researching a history of Samarai. Wallace Andrew, owner of the Kinanale Guesthouse, is also a good source of local information, or you could try Sue Weekly, the manager of the women's guesthouse. For a more radical approach to the problems and politics of the area, talk to Perry Dotaona who is a member of SADA (Samarai Area Development Association). *Sada* means betel nut in a local language, and the group chose the name because it wanted 'hot, strong talk' (which betel nut produces) in defence of the islands' rights.

Things to See & Do

Be warned that there is absolutely no entertainment, except on Saturday when you can watch soccer or cricket on the sportsground. Other than that, you can walk around the island, climb the hill, have a drink in the tiny tavern, swim, watch other people swim, watch tropical fish swimming around the wharves, walk around the island again...

There is a monument to Christopher Robinson, the acting administrator who committed suicide in 1904. The inscription notes that he was an 'Able governor, upright man, honest judge. His aim was to make New Guinea a good place for white men'!

Festival

The Samarai Pearl Festival (some nearby villages grow pearls) has been defunct for some years, but there is talk of reviving it in 1993, probably in November or December. Last time it was held they had 9000 visitors – it must have been standing-room only on this tiny island!

Places to Stay & Eat

The friendly *Bwanasu Women's Association*

Guesthouse is on a hillside near the sportsground. It's airy and clean but fairly basic, and K42 for a dorm bed with meals isn't wonderful value. You might be within earshot of the town's electricity generator here.

Kinanale Guesthouse (☎ 61 1358, PO Box 88) is owned by Wallace Andrew, a local identity and entrepreneur (he's planning a handcraft shop and the island's only cafe), Kwato old-boy and grandson of a cannibal. The guesthouse is pleasant, with an open, beach house feel to it. It is by no means luxurious and the rates are high: K60 per person, including meals, K45 without. It's possible that the K45 rate could be stretched to cover more than one person, making the price reasonable.

Both of these places are booked out by groups from time to time – it's hard to believe, but Samarai styles itself as the 'conference centre of PNG'! If you're totally stuck for somewhere to stay, one of the churches might let you doss down in a hall or arrange a room in someone's house.

If you have a group, the most interesting place to stay is on the *Georgina*, an old, wooden work boat. See the Around Samarai section.

There are places to stay on islands around Samarai, and China Strait Plantation (☎ 61 1019 or contact MBA in Alotau) is planning to build self-contained bungalows sleeping about six people. These will be aimed at people who fly in on weekend packages with MBA and probably won't be cheap.

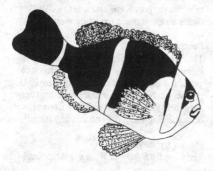

Getting There & Away

Osiri Trading has boats running regularly to Alotau, currently early on Friday and Tuesday mornings but two more runs are planned. In their smaller banana boat the fare is K8, in the larger boat it's K15. The trip takes 1½ hours or less. There's always the possibility that there will be no room for passengers (they take empty fuel drums to Alotau and bring back stock for the store), but that's unlikely. Osiri Trading will also charter banana boats but that's very expensive – how does K100 to Alotau sound?

Many local boats of all sizes, shapes and speeds ply back and forth between Samarai Island and Alotau – finding out about them means going to the wharves and persistently asking around. A work boat will cost less than a banana boat, although the trip will take four or five hours. There are also plenty of small boats and canoes travelling to nearby islands and further afield.

You can fly to Alotau with MBA from China Strait Plantation (nearby on the mainland) for just K20. See the Alotau Getting There & Away section.

A Consort Line (☎ 61 1088 on Samarai) freighter calls at Samarai about every three weeks on the run between Moresby and Lae. It doesn't officially take passengers, but if you get to know people on Samarai you might be introduced to the captain and get a cabin. There might also be other freighters. It's quite a sight to see a big ship looming over the town.

Pleasure yachts commonly clear PNG customs at Samarai, so it could be a good spot to pick up a ride, particularly between May and October. However, there are far fewer yachts now that there's a customs clearance fee of K100 for each person on board!

AROUND SAMARAI ISLAND

China Strait and the surrounding islands still have a reputation for witchcraft and despite the strong influence of missionaries, superstitions linger. Strange lights, ghost ships (ghost helicopters, for that matter!) and sirens (the singing kind) all crop up. Two

Top: Busy day on Samarai Island, Milne Bay Province (JM)
Left: Crashed Japanese fighter (Air Niugini)
Right: Alotau Harbour, Milne Bay Province (JM)

Top: Beach scene, Kaibola, Trobriand Islands (ML)
Bottom: Looking towards Cape Girumia, Wedau, Milne Bay Province (YP)

years after some people drowned in the strait, villagers were still chartering boats to search for the sorcerer who was holding their friends prisoner.

On **Kwato Island**, two or three km due west of Samarai, Charles and Beatrice Abel founded a non-hierarchical church in 1891. Kwato Mission functioned as a successful educational and boat-building centre, although it wasn't until the 1930s that the last of the nearby cannibal tribes was 'saved'. People who were brought up on Kwato are disproportionately represented in the upper echelons of PNG business. The mission's buildings survived the war (an order to destroy them was circumvented) and its boats were used to transport and supply Australian coastwatchers.

There was a decline in the 1970s, but the Kwato Church has now been officially recognised and receives some EC aid. There's sometimes a VSO volunteer working on the island. It may be possible to stay here, and a visit is worthwhile. Walk up to the church on top of the hill for good views. Wallace Andrew, owner of the Kinanale Guesthouse on Samarai, can probably tell you about boats to Kwato.

Tiny **Ebuma Island**, just one km off Samarai (you can see it from the wharves), has a house which is available for rent. This area gets so few visitors, however, that no-one is sure how much it costs. The house is currently a bit dilapidated and around K40 a night seems about right, but it's all pretty vague.

Ernie Everett grew up on Samarai and has lived on Ebuma since 1960, although he's currently staying in Alotau. His boat, the *Georgina*, is an old 12-metre work boat which sleeps five and is available for charter at K250 a day. That makes it comparable with accommodation on Samarai if there are a few of you, and also covers your travel costs. It isn't fast and it isn't flash, but it would be a great way to get around. The tourist bureau in Alotau or Ian Poole at Osiri Trading on Samarai might have information.

Doini Island, about 10 km south-east of Samarai, is a private island, on a 100-year lease signed in 1900. The only people living

here are a few workers on the coconut plantation and its expat manager, Tony Gallaway. There are no villages. The island is a decent size – big enough to get lost on (for a little while) – has a reasonable hill in the middle, walking tracks, plenty of reefs and sometimes surf at Clamp's Cove. The small white-sand beach near the manager's house is beautiful but plagued by sandflies.

There is a good two-bedroom guesthouse with electricity and potentially a stove and a fridge, but it has never been used by paying guests so no-one is sure how much it should cost. Phone Tony Gallaway (☎ 61 1441, PO Box 46, Samarai) after 6 pm to discuss accommodation.

Deka Deka, another tiny islet, is a popular beach and picnic spot as is nearby **Logea Island**. The small cluster of the **Wari Islands**, 45 km from Samarai, is another boat building centre and the people there are also fine potters.

On **Sideia Island** the Catholic Church has set up a sawmilling operation which enables villagers to harvest their own logs and sell them at a good price, rather than handing over logging rights to foreign companies. This has the added benefit of providing employment at the mill.

It should be possible to stay in villages on many of the islands in the area for K5 to K10, but mind your manners. Island people come in to Samarai to shop and to sell produce at the market (busiest on Saturday morning but never very busy), so ask around. A small sack of Trukai rice makes a good present for your hosts.

SOUTH COAST

The south coast of Milne Bay Province is the southernmost part of the PNG mainland, and it's beautiful, heavily forested country with very few services. The traditional landowners of the Suau area plan to open a guesthouse on Delina Island. For information, write to Ken Ah Chee, PMB Mogiriu, Suau via Samarai, MBP. The landowners are currently negotiating with logging companies, which they hope will build roads into the area.

Island Groups

D'ENTRECASTEAUX ISLANDS

The three comparatively large islands of the D'Entrecasteaux Group are separated from the north coast of the mainland only by a narrow strait. They are extremely mountainous and flying on the spectacular Talair flight between Alotau and Kiriwina in the Trobriands, you pass directly over them.

Whales, dolphins and dugongs are common in the area.

Normanby Island

Esa'ala, the district headquarters, is at the entrance to the spectacular Dobu Passage. It's a tiny place, with a couple of stores, a market and electricity for a few hours each day. However, there's a reasonable place to stay and a reef offering excellent snorkelling just offshore from the town. Trade boats from Alotau call at Esa'ala, but the airstrip is about an hour's drive away on a bad road.

In the middle of the south-west coast is Sewa Bay, used by Allied warships during WW II and a port of call for small inter-island ships today. There are strange, unexplained rock carvings around the bay.

Places to Stay & Eat The *Esa'ala Women's Guesthouse* is on the beach near the main wharf and charges about K20 a night. It's friendly and the food is good. Contact the district office (☎ 61 1217) for more information. There's apparently also a *holiday house* run by Tom & Val Inman (☎ 61 1209) who charge about K30 per person.

Dobu Island

In the passage is tiny, fertile Dobu Island where the Methodists established their first mission in the area; the mountains rise sheer on both sides of the strait. This island has a reputation for sorcery, but it's also fervently Christian. Simple village accommodation is easily available, and it's a beautiful place. However, Americans might want to be a little careful:

The Dobuans are firmly convinced that two boys have been shot by American yachties in recent years. Kids often load up a canoe with produce, slink out to a visiting boat and wait until someone takes notice of them. It is possible that trigger-happy tourists, frightened by strange black faces, shot the children and then scuttled their canoes and fled. Whether it really happened or not, the people believe it.

Bron Larner

Fergusson Island

Fergusson is the central island in the group and the largest in size. Although it is mountainous, it pales in comparison to nearby Goodenough. The highest mountain here is only 2073 metres high, with two other lower ranges from which flow the island's many rivers and streams. Fergusson's large population is mainly concentrated along the south coast. Fergusson is notable for its active thermal region – hot springs, bubbling mud pools, spouting geysers and extinct volcanoes. Thermal springs can be found at Deidei and at Iamalele on the west coast. There is a Methodist mission at Salamo on the south coast.

Salamo isn't a big place but it's the biggest town for some way, so there's a lot of boat and canoe traffic, especially for the Saturday market. It's not especially attractive but is a good base for travel around the island group and further afield.

Places to Stay & Eat There is a guesthouse at Salamo, charging about K15 a night, and in the mountains inland from here is the *Sebutuia Mountain Lodge*, built and run by a local village. Accommodation costs around K30, including meals.

Nadi, about 45 minutes by boat from Salamo, is a pretty village with good beaches. There's a guesthouse there, but bring your own mosquito net. Apparently the villagers will take you on strenuous but rewarding treks in the jungle. Jim Mackay, who supplied a lot of information on the D'Entrecasteaux Group, suggests that you let your guide walk in front, to deal with the spider webs across the trail. The spiders are 'as big as baseball mitts'!

Goodenough Island

The most north-westerly of the group, Goodenough is amazingly mountainous with a high central range that has two peaks topping 2400 metres. Quite something for an island only about 40 km long from end to end. There are fertile coastal plains flanking the mountain range and a road runs around the north-east coast through Vivigani, site of the major airstrip in the group. There's only an open shelter here – 'one of the less exciting places to spend 12 hours waiting for a plane that didn't show up', reported one visitor.

Bolubolu is the main station on the island, about 10 km south of the airstrip at Vivigani. In the centre of the island there is a large stone, covered in mysterious black and white paintings, which is said to have power over the yam crops. There are two or three mission stations on the island where you can probably stay.

Amphlett Islands

The tiny Amphlett Islands are scattered to the north of the main D'Entrecasteaux Group. The people here are part of the Kula Ring trading cycle and they make some extremely fine and very fragile pottery. By boat from Salamo it's about two hours and costs around K4 or K35 if you charter.

Getting There & Away

Talair flies to Normanby, Fergusson and Goodenough twice a week from Gurney. See the Alotau Getting There & Away section. A work boat from Alotau to Salamo on Fergusson or Esa'ala on Normanby costs about K10 and takes about 10 to 12 hours. Salamo probably sees the most traffic. From Salamo a boat to the Trobriands costs about K20 and takes about 12 hours; to Woodlark a boat costs about K30 and takes two days.

TROBRIAND ISLANDS

The Trobriand Islands lie to the north of the D'Entrecasteaux Group and are the most culturally interesting islands in the province. They are also very different, both culturally and geographically, from the rest of the province.

The group takes its name from Denis de Trobriand, an officer on D'Entrecasteaux's expedition. The largest of the group is Kiriwina, where the airstrip and district headquarters, Losuia, are situated.

The Trobriands are low-lying coral islands, in complete contrast to their southern neighbours, and they lack the other islands' spectacular scenery. There are some very good beaches and it's possible to stay in villages (essential if you're on a budget). The fishing is apparently also excellent.

There is almost no economic activity in the islands, apart from some sand-fish (bêche de mer) drying and trochus shell collecting. Trochus shells are exported to Europe where they are still used to make high-quality buttons. There's also some small-scale crocodile farming. Local lime, used with betel nut, is famed for its quality and is traded around the province.

While the Trobes are famous for their culture, and a visit here can be a highlight of your trip to PNG, be prepared for a completely different society to any other in the country. Some visitors arrive expecting an idyllic Pacific holiday then leave on the next flight out. Or try to – it isn't easy to change reservations on Kiriwina. Some people find the islanders unfriendly, and people certainly aren't always overjoyed to see you. However, if you don't treat people as museum exhibits you'll find them friendly enough.

Beware of the local sense of humour; practical jokes with the *dim dim* (foreigner) as the butt are greatly enjoyed. Teasing aside, the men are OK, if aloof, and the women friendly and courteous.

Communication is difficult as Pidgin is not common, although kids often know some English.

The only aggression I saw on the island was when a tourist ignored the people leading him away from a women's bathing place, and strode towards it, pulling out his camera...

People & Culture

The Trobriands were made famous after WW I by the work of Polish anthropologist

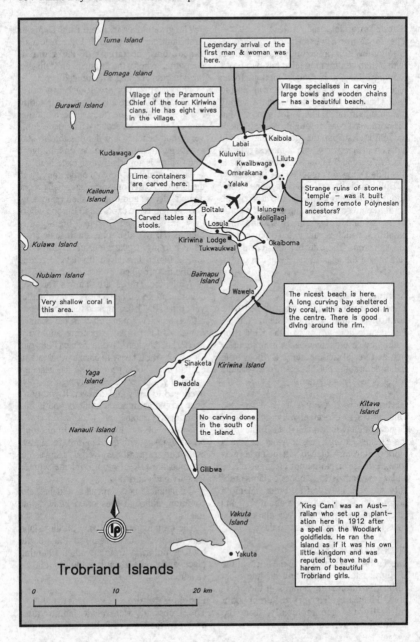

Legendary arrival of the first man & woman was here.

Village specialises in carving large bowls and wooden chains – has a beautiful beach.

Village of the Paramount Chief of the four Kiriwina clans. He has eight wives in the village.

Tuma Island

Bomaga Island

Burawdi Island

Kudawaga

Lime containers are carved here.

Kaileuna Island

Kulawa Island

Carved tables & stools.

Nubiam Island

Very shallow coral in this area.

Labai
Kuluvitu
Kwaibwaga
Omarakana
Yalaka
Boitalu
Losula
Kiriwina Lodge
Tukwaukwai

Kaibola
Liluta

Ialungwa
Moligilagi

Okaiborna

Strange ruins of stone 'temple' – was it built by some remote Polynesian ancestors?

Bairnapu Island

Wawela

The nicest beach is here. A long curving bay sheltered by coral, with a deep pool in the centre. There is good diving around the rim.

Yaga Island

Sinaketa   Kiriwina Island

Bwadela

Kitava Island

Nanauli Island

No carving done in the south of the island.

Gilibwa

Vakuta Island

'King Cam' was an Australian who set up a plantation here in 1912 after a spell on the Woodlark goldfields. He ran the island as if it was his own little kingdom and was reputed to have had a harem of beautiful Trobriand girls.

Yakuta

Trobriand Islands

0   10   20 km

Bronislaw Malinowski. Apparently, at the start of the war he was offered a choice of internment in Australia or banishment to the remote Trobriands. He sensibly chose the latter and his studies of the islanders, their intricate trading rituals, their yam cults and their sexual practices, led to his classic series of books – *Argonauts of the Western Pacific, Coral Gardens and their Magic* and *The Sexual Life of Savages*.

The Trobriand islanders have strong Polynesian characteristics and, unlike people in most other parts of PNG, they have a social system that is dominated by hereditary chieftains who continue to wield a tremendous amount of power and influence. The whole society is hierarchical, with strict distinctions between hereditary classes. It is a matrilineal society (not matriarchal) meaning inheritances are passed through the female side of a family. The chief's sons belong to his wife's clan and he is superseded by one of his oldest sister's sons.

The soil of the Trobriands is very fertile and great care is lavished on the gardens, particularly the yam gardens which have great practical and cultural importance.

The villages are all laid out in a similar pattern – which you can see most clearly from the air as you fly in or out of Kiriwina. The village yam houses form an inner ring, surrounded by sleeping houses, and the whole lot is encircled by a ring of trees and vegetation.

Yam house

Staying in Villages

The people are proud and fairly aloof, and they certainly know the value of a kina. They are adept at separating you from your money, and although outright theft is unusual you must keep a close eye on your gear and make sure you establish the price of *everything* in advance with the village chief. Nothing is free.

Apart from the islanders' expertise as traders (see the section on the Kula Ring) and the notion of reciprocal generosity, this attitude might partially be explained by the way the islands have, over the years, been poked and prodded by tribes of naive, insensitive anthropologists. I heard one story about a young anthropologist who was welcomed into a village, only to find himself making large financial contributions to feasts, ceremonies and this and that. No doubt he acquiesced in an attempt to ingratiate himself with the people. He lived happily until the day came when he ran out of money, and on that very day the tearful scientist was told to pack his bags!

You need to be fairly fit to cope with the rigours of village life, because although it may look like paradise, it is in reality pretty tough. There is a fair degree of overcrowding, hygiene leaves something to be desired, and the food is uninspiring. Taro, the basis of the villagers' subsistence diet, is like a stringy version of the potato. You

Local Customs

Yams Yams are far more than a staple food in the Trobriands – they're also a ritual, a sign of prestige, an indicator of expertise and a tie between villages and clans. The quality and size of the yams you grow is a matter of considerable importance. Many hours can be spent on discussions of your ability as a yam cultivator and to be known as a *Tokwaibagula*, a 'good gardener', is a mark of high ability and prestige.

The yam cult reaches its high point at the harvest time – usually July or August. The yams are first dug up in the gardens and before transport back to the village they must be displayed, studied and admired in the gardens. At the appropriate time the yams are carried by the men back to the village with the women guarding the procession.

In the villages the yams are again displayed, in circular piles, before the next stage takes place – the filling of the yam houses. Again there are extended rituals to be observed. Each man has a yam house for each of his wives and it is his brother-in-law's responsibility (in other words his wife's clan's obligation) to fill his yam house. The chief's yam house is always the first to be filled. So yams are not merely a food – they're also part of a complicated annual ritual and an important and ongoing connection between villages.

Sex Malinowski's weighty tomes on the Trobriand Islanders customs led to Kiriwina being dubbed with the misleading title: the 'Island of Love'. It is not surprising that such a label was applied by inhibited Europeans when they first met Trobriand women, with their free and easy manners, their good looks and short grass dresses, but it led to the inaccurate idea that the Trobriands were some sort of sexual paradise.

The sexual customs are different (some might even say, better) than in many other places, but they are not without complicated social strictures and normal human jealousies. Nevertheless, the place must be a Christian missionary's nightmare because there are fewer restrictions than usual.

From puberty onwards, teenagers are encouraged to have as many sexual partners as they choose – without guilt – until marriage, when they settle down with the partner who is chosen as suitable and compatible. Males leave home when they reach puberty and move into the village *bukumatula* or bachelor house. Here they are free to bring their partners back at any time, although preference is usually given to places with a little more privacy! Even married couples, subject to mutual agreement, are allowed to have a fling or two when the celebrations for the yam harvest are in full swing.

It is said that despite all this activity few children are born to women without permanent partners. Perhaps there are herbal contraceptives, although there are plenty of kids in all the Trobriand villages. The people do not believe there is a connection between intercourse and pregnancy – a child's spirit, which floats through the air or on top of the sea, chooses to enter a woman, often through her head. So much for the significance attached by Christians to the virgin birth!

All this apparent freedom has absolutely no impact on visitors. Freedom of choice is the basis of Trobriand life, so why would any islander choose some ugly, pale, *dim dim* (foreigner) who can't speak like a civilised human, doesn't understand the most basic laws and will probably be gone tomorrow?

Kula Ring Although the ring (see the People & Culture section at the start of this chapter) extends around many island groups in the province, Europeans usually equate it with the Trobriands – which pisses-off some of the much-studied Trobriand Islanders. Trobriands people sometimes block the ring to allow an accumulation of trade goods, then hold a big *uvulaku* (ring festival) which gives people an opportunity to display their wealth before trading it away again.

Cricket A much more modern custom, but just as colourful, is the unique sport known as 'Trobriands Cricket'. Supposedly introduced by missionaries as a way of taking the Trobriand islanders' minds off less healthy activities it's developed a style of its own, quite unlike anything the MCC ever had in mind. The mere fact that the Trobriands Cricket rule book contains absolutely no mention of how many players make up a team goes some way to explaining how it works. If there's a game scheduled while you're on the island, don't miss it! The dancing which accompanies the game completely defeats the missionaries' purpose.

I was told of tug-o-wars, also introduced by missionaries as good clean fun for the men. This was even less successful, as village girls assist their team by enticing members of the opposing team into the bush. Sometimes the rope is left entirely untugged, except for an old man at each end. ■

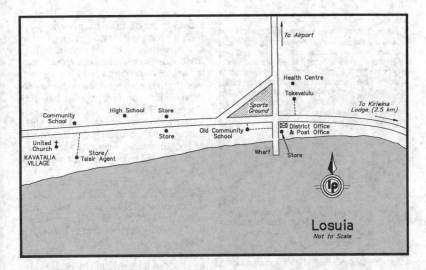

To Airport

Health Centre

Tokevalulu

To Kiriwina
Lodge (2.5 km)

Sports
Ground

Community
School

High School   Store

Old Community ●
School

☒ District Office
& Post Office

United ✝
Church

Store

KAVATALIA
VILLAGE

Store/
Talair Agent

Wharf

Store

Losuia
Not to Scale

must treat your water unless you are sure it has been boiled.

Having painted the bad side, I must add that people do stay in the villages, and for most it is a fantastic experience. Certainly you must be prepared to pay for what you use (hardly a shocking concept for good capitalist tourists), but you are also likely to meet friendly, interesting people and gain an insight (however limited) into an extraordinary culture.

Orientation

By far the largest island is **Kiriwina** and the airstrip is here. Most of Kiriwina is flat, although there is a rim of low hills (uplifted coral reefs) which run down the eastern side. The central plain is intensely cultivated, to the extent that there are no decent trees left, and it is hot and flat. The airport is here, and south of the airport on the coast is the main town, **Losuia**, a 15-minute drive away. North of the airport is Kaibola. The bay on the western side of the island is a huge expanse of very shallow water – so shallow that the canoes are punted along with poles. Towards the southern end of the island the eastern beaches are backed by beautiful

rainforest, and although they all have reefs they look out onto the open sea.

Information

There are very few facilities on Kiriwina or anywhere else in the Trobes.

Losuia, the only real town and generally known as 'the station', has a wharf, a couple of schools and churches, a police station, a health centre, a couple of government offices, a few small trade stores and that is about it. It's more like a sprawling village than a town.

The Trobes are not part of PNG's telephone network (although they might soon be), but you can make expensive calls on a radio phone at the post office. There is no bank, so you must bring all the cash you will need with you. If you plan to stay in the villages, make sure you bring small denominations. Kiriwina Lodge might change travellers' cheques for guests.

The fishing around the Trobriands is supposed to be very good, with September to April the best months.

June to August are the months when most cultural events take place. If you visit then, be a bit cautious, as things can get out of hand.

Some Interesting Things to Say

Malinowski, in his all-encompassing studies, makes a detailed foray into the Trobriands language. True to form it has a wide variety of sexual terminology including different ways of referring to male and female genitals depending on whether they're yours, your partners, or somebody else's. Just so you have your sexual terminology lined up before you get there, remember that it is:

Female	Male
my wiga	my kwiga
your wim	your kwim
her wila	his kwila

Since wila is pronounced 'Wheeler', my surname, to say the least, has a rather unfortunate translation. Once they had got over the sheer amazement that anybody could be so dumb as to call himself Wheeler (or *wila*) the girls at the Kiriwina Lodge took great pleasure in calling me *wila* as frequently as possible.

There's plenty of other fun to be had with the local language. If male readers would like something nice to whisper in your girl friend's ear try, *yoku tage kuwoli nunum, kwunpisiga* or when things get a bit heavier try *wim, kasesam!* Or for female readers, should you want to belittle some male just shout out *kaykukupi kwim*. (I've always had this urge to write an R-rated travel guide.) You can further enhance your questionable stock of Trobriand phrases at festivals during the yam harvesting season when islanders sing songs of amazing vulgarity known as *mweki mweki*.

Some Less-Interesting Things to Say

good morning	bwena kau kwau
good afternoon	bwena la lai
good night	bwena bogie
very good	sena bwena
very bad	sena gaga
yes/no	eh/gala
you/me	yokwa/yegu

How much is that (price)?	Aveka besa?
food	kaula
What is your name?	Yokwa amiyagam?
go away	kula
I am going to sleep.	Ye bala masisi. ■

Places to Stay & Eat – bottom end

Joseph Anang, a PhD student from Ghana, has established the *Tokevalulu Village Birth Attendants' Training Centre* near the health centre in Losuia. It's sort of a model village where courses are run for village midwives. There are five huts each sleeping two people and if there is a vacancy you can stay here for K20 a night. Bedding and mosquito nets are provided and conditions are very clean but basic – if you don't like this you won't cope at all in a village.

Look for Joseph here or at his home in town, near the old community school. He is due to leave in 1994 (having been on the island since 1988 – his will have been a hard-earned doctorate), and Tokevalulu might not survive his absence.

The government is considering building a *REST* (Rural Environmentally Sensitive Tourism) House, a low-budget place to stay near Losuia. If and when it is built it will cost about K10 a night.

Other than these, the only alternative for shoestringers is to stay in the villages, but this is not as easy as it sounds.

Villages Kiriwina Lodge arranges village stays for about K10 a night, including basic food, and will transport you (for a fee) to and from the village. To take advantage of this you have to stay at the lodge for a few nights, say when you arrive on Kiriwina and before you depart. Doing it this way might cost considerably more than arranging everything yourself but at least you won't be ripped off by the village and you will be guaranteed of transport back to Losuia in time to catch your flight, an important consideration on an island with little public transport and infrequent flights.

The villagers are well aware of what the Kiriwina Lodge charges for accommodation, and feel cheated if you pay too much less than you would there. North of Losuia it is possible to stay in some villages from about K10 a night. You must make the arrangements with the village chief. Make sure you know exactly what you're paying for, or you'll have endless small additions made to the bill. Two villages not far from the airport that have been suggested are Ialungwa and Omarakana. Another, apparently a 15-minute walk from Kaibola Beach, is Kapwapu, where the chief is Tobuguota. This village charges a very negotiable K20 a night including meals.

It's also possible to stay in villages south of Losuia although a chief in the area has apparently asked for a ridiculously high fee (K40 a night) and you must accept or leave. Not all are as unreasonable. Again, make sure you set prices in advance.

Places to Stay & Eat – top end
Kiriwina Lodge is the only formal accommodation on Kiriwina, and it is expensive and badly positioned. The legendary Kiriwina Hotel burned down and the new Kaibola Beach Resort went back to bush after the owner left hastily during problems with local landowners. A government-funded guesthouse being built on Wawela Beach simply disappeared after the local chief died.

Single/double rooms with attached bathroom at the lodge cost K72/99, including meals, laundry and airport transfers. This is slightly negotiable. Some of the rooms are to be upgraded to include air-con and TV, so prices will rise. The meals feature a lot of seafood and are reasonable; they'll seem like haut cuisine after a few days of village food.

Making a booking at the lodge is difficult, although it's usually not necessary. You could ask the Talair office in Alotau to contact their agent in Losuia, but it will take at least a day or two for your booking to be confirmed.

The lodge is on the coast, several km east of Losuia. It is on the lagoon side of the island and a small section of garden runs down to the water, which is, unfortunately, shallow, swampy and no good for swimming. A few small crocs are fattened up for slaughter in a pond. Sitting on the balcony, drink in hand, watching the outrigger canoes being poled across the bay and chatting to local people and expats as they come and go

is pleasant enough, up to a point. If you want to do any snorkelling, or see anything, however, you'll have to organise transport. See the Getting Around section.

Things to Buy
By far the best known artefacts in the province, although not the only ones, are the Trobriand carvings. Like other parts of PNG, certain villages tend to specialise in certain styles and types of carvings. In general, Trobriand carvings are more finely finished and have a more modern appearance than other PNG carvings. Curiously, it is only in the north of Kiriwina that the people carve.

The Trobriand Islanders are astute business people, so you should avoid rushing into any purchases. For a start, prices are definitely flexible and until you can judge quality you are at the vendor's mercy. There are always people hanging around the Kiriwina Lodge and the airport (when there are flights) so take your time and don't be bluffed. If you catch a vendor's eye you can come under quite a deal of pressure – be firm, good humoured and polite.

Bill Rudd, manager of the Kiriwina Lodge, has a good collection of carvings and other artefacts, most for sale. Check this out before you visit the villages so you have some idea of the quality and price to aim for. You might end up buying from him anyway, as his prices aren't unreasonable.

There are a variety of artefacts, ranging from bowls to walking sticks. The bowls – popular for use as salad or fruit bowls – often have decorative rims or flat surrounds carved like fish or turtles, with shells for eyes. Prices range from K5 for a small one up to K20 or more for large ones. The prices rise the further you are from the Trobriands.

Carved statues are usually delicate and elongated with curiously convoluted figures – a woman with a tree kangaroo perched on her head and a crocodile balanced on its tail behind her, for example. Intricately carved walking sticks, which are particularly well finished, are very popular. A big one could cost over K150, with smaller ones from around K25. There are also some squat little

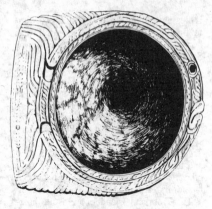

Trobriand bowl

carvings – particularly of coupling pigs. Occasionally there are some finely carved erotic scenes, but these are rarely seen. Some of these carvings are made from ebony, which is now very rare and comes only from Woodlark Island.

Stools are also made – solid circular ones with carved figures holding up the seats. A tiny one costs about K10, but the big stools are about K800 – plus the excess baggage charges you'll have to pay to get these monsters off the island. Three-legged tables are also popular. Lime containers made from decorated gourds, and chains carved from a single piece of wood are other items you may see.

Traditionally some of the best carving went into the magnificent canoe prows, particularly those used for the Kula Ring trading ceremonies. This *Massim* style of carving can also be seen on important yam house frontages.

Other than carvings, you can get shells and bagi (shell 'money'), although the latter is likely to be very expensive. The shell money is made on Rossel Island; it's meticulously ground shell discs with a diameter of about five mm strung like a necklace. If it's genuine, it will cost about K1 a centimetre – beware of plastic imitations. Doba (leaf money) is also still used as negotiable currency; it's a bundle of banana leaves with each leaf incised with patterns. The colourful grass skirts are also used as currency (they're worth K5-10) and make interesting buys.

You may be offered stone axe heads, but you should be wary of buying. Many of these implements are extremely old and there are controls on their export. If you do take these out of the country you may well be destroying important archaeological evidence.

Getting There & Away

Talair flies between Gurney (Alotau) and Losuia on Wednesday and Saturday for K108.

The Talair agent might be found somewhere in the vicinity of the small store near the United Church at the west end of the road which runs through Losuia. Technically, this area is called Oyabia, and the large village just beyond here is Kavatalia. In theory, the agency is open from 8 to 10 am on weekdays. There is no computer here, so don't expect to make complex bookings, get ticket refunds or anything of that nature.

The two main trade stores in Losuia run work boats to Alotau approximately weekly. One of the stores is owned by the Kiriwina Lodge people, so you could ask there. They charge K20 for the trip, which takes two days (anchoring by an island for the night) and passes by the D'Entrecasteaux island group. You can probably arrange to be dropped at the island of you choice. Take your own food and water.

Getting Around

Most of Kiriwina's main roads are now in fairly good condition, and you can now travel all the way down to the southern tip – this is yet another place in PNG where cycling would be a joy if there was a bicycle to ride.

The island's six PMVs run infrequently but cheaply – K0.60 should get you from Losuia to the north coast. Almost all private vehicles (there aren't many) operate as de facto PMVs. Otherwise, you'll have to walk, and this can get very hot. Make sure you carry water and have a decent hat.

You can organise tours and transportation using the Kiriwina Lodge's transport. This costs from K1 per km and can get expensive unless you can share costs – the cost of running a vehicle is very high. From Kiriwina to Wawela is around 20 km, to Kaibola is around 30 km and a day trip to either, with lunch, is K40, although there might be a discount for solo travellers.

Around Kiriwina

Going north from Losuia is 'inland' to the locals. This area has most of the island's roads and villages and consequently visitors, too. **Omarakana**, about halfway between Losuia and Kaibola, is where the island's Paramount Chief resides. You'll know you're there by the large, intricate, painted yam house not far from the road. The Paramount Chief presides over the island's oral traditions and magic and strictly maintains his political and economic power. He oversees the important yam festival and kula ritual.

Caves used for swimming and fresh water are found at Tumwalau, Kalopa, Lupwaneta, Neguya, Bobu, Sikau, Kaulausi and Bwaga. Large coral megaliths still exist and, together with designs on some ancient pottery, have linked the Trobes to possible early Polynesian migrations.

At **Kaibola** village there's a school and excellent swimming and snorkelling at this picture-postcard beach. In the village you can see traditional boats, fishing gear, shark-calling tools and other items. Ask one of the kids to take you to nearby Luebila village, past the neat gardens of yams, taro, bananas and tapioca.

About 1½ hours' walk from Kaibola is Kalopa Cave near Matawa village. There are several deep limestone caves housing burial antiquities and skeletal remains. Stories are told of Dokanikani, a giant whose bones are said to be buried with those of his victims in one of the caves. Also along the beach at Kaibola look for the little glow worms at night, clinging to the rocks along the shore.

The trip to Kaibola from Losuia takes about 30 minutes and covers nearly 30 km along the narrow, coral road. At Moligilagi near the east coast bring snorkel, mask and fins to explore the underwater caves. Be careful of logs; an underwater light is a good idea.

South of Losuia the road is even less frequently used and the population is smaller. **Wawela** village is on an excellent, curving sand beach edging a cool, deep, protected lagoon. On a falling tide beware of the channel out to sea from the bay, the current can be very strong. Local kids will sell you shells for about K0.50 (although collectors pay up to K500 for some of the rare shells found around the Trobes). Bring your own supplies; there is no store. The remains of a yacht that was wrecked on the reef in 1992 might still be there.

Further south, the road squeezes through thick jungle. At **Sinaketa** there are a couple of traditional kula canoes on the beach.

There are several islands off Kiriwina worth visiting for their 'tropical paradise' features, but getting to them is expensive. The fuel accounts for much of the cost and there isn't anything you can do about that except find a canoe. Kiriwina Lodge, as usual, is the most reliable place to find a boat. Their cheapest round trip costs about K80; negotiating hard you might get a local boat for K55. Of course, if you find a boatload of people who are already going somewhere you might be able to go along for a lot less. Labi Island is one of the nicest and is good for swimming. Kitava, a larger island east of Kiriwina, is also pretty. There's a good beach on the island about a km off the main wharf in Losuia.

WOODLARK ISLAND

Woodlark is east of the Trobriands and north of the Louisiade Islands. It takes its name from the Sydney ship *Woodlark* which passed by in 1836 although the local name is Murua.

The people of Woodlark Island are Melanesians similar to the people on the eastern end of the mainland. Their island is a continuous series of hills and valleys and is highly populated. Woodlark was the site of the biggest gold rush in the country until the later discovery of gold at Edie Creek near Wau. A form of 'greenstone', similar although inferior to the greenstone or jade of New Zealand, was also found here and made into axes and ceremonial stones.

Today the people are renowned for their beautiful wood carvings made of mottled ebony. Since there is less demand for their work than that of the more frequently visited Trobriands, due to their isolation, the carvings tend to be extremely well crafted. Kulumadau is the main centre although there is now an airstrip at Guasopa.

The Laughlan Group is a handful of tiny islands and islets 64 km east of Woodlark.

LOUISIADE ARCHIPELAGO

The Louisiade Archipelago received its name after Louis Torre's 1606 visit, but it was probably known to Chinese and Malay sailors much earlier as there are distinct traces of Asian heritage in the racial mixture. The name was originally applied to the whole string of islands including the group now known as the D'Entrecasteaux.

Sudest or Tagula Island

Largest island in the archipelago, Sudest had a small gold rush at about the same time as Woodlark. It consists of a similar series of valleys and hills, highest of which is Mt Rattlesnake at 915 metres.

Rossel Island

Most westerly of the islands – if you discount uninhabited Pocklington Reef – Rossel's rugged coastline ends at Rossel Spit which has had more than its fair share of shipwrecks. An airstrip was built here in 1980.

Misima Island

Mountainous Misima Island is the most important in the group with the district headquarters at Bwagaoia. Mt Oiatau at 1037 metres is the highest peak on the island. Misima too had a gold rush, although this took place between the wars, much later than on the other islands of Milne Bay Province. A major new gold and silver mine is now in operation.

During the brief span when Papua was a British colony rather than an Australian one, the people of Misima were thought of as the most dangerous and difficult in the country. Today Misima has about half of the total population of the archipelago.

The *Misima Guesthouse* (☎ 63 7001) in Bwagaoia is expensive and usually booked out by mine workers.

Getting There & Away Air Niugini flies to/from Port Moresby via Gurney (Alotau) on Wednesday and Saturday. The fare to Moresby is K136; to Alotau it's K86. Talair flies from Moresby, both direct (K155) and via Gurney (K86).

Calvados Chain & Conflict Group

The long chain of islets and reefs between Sudest and the mainland make navigation through the province an exacting and often dangerous operation. None of the islands are of any great size. To the west they terminate with the three islands of the Engineer Group.

Morobe Province

Land Area 34,500 sq km
Population 400,000
Capital Lae

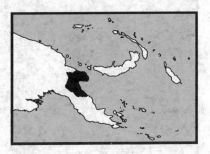

The province of Morobe curves around Huon Gulf and includes the mountainous Huon Peninsula. The provincial head-quarters, Lae, is its focal point and PNG's second largest city. The province's main river, the Markham, bisects the mountains with a broad, open flood plain. Morobe has the best road connections in the country. From Lae you can drive west to the High-lands along the Markham Valley, north-west to Madang, or south to the highland areas around Wau and Bulolo, the centre of the 1920s gold rush.

HISTORY

Some of the earliest remains of human civilisation in PNG have been found in this province; axe heads discovered at Bobongora by students of the University of PNG have been dated at 40,000 years old. It is believed the earliest settlements were in coastal areas. These early settlements were subsequently flooded by rising sea levels (post ice age) and therefore most of PNG's prehistory has been lost under the sea. However in some regions, like parts of the Huon Peninsula, these coastal areas have subsequently risen and exposed the remains of these early settlements.

The Leiwomba people occupied the Lae area and the Anga (once widely known as the Kukukuku, a term that was used by the coastal people and is now actively resented by the Anga) lived a nomadic existence in the central mountains in the Menyamya dis-trict, but their territory stretched through to the Gulf of Papua.

The first contact the coastal people had with Europeans came when the German New Guinea Kompagnie made an unsuccessful attempt to colonise the mainland.

In 1885 the Germans established their first settlement at Finschhafen, and soon started to disintegrate due to the effects of malaria, boredom, alcohol and various other tropical ills. These problems followed them along the northern coast and were only left behind (at least partially) when they transferred to the island of New Britain. The Lutheran Mission arrived when the company was at Finschhafen, but managed to hang on after it departed. Finschhafen is still a major Lutheran base.

After the Australian takeover Morobe became a fairly quiet place. Until the dis-covery of gold no one cared to disturb the regions' ferocious warriors. At Ho'mki (Outcrop of Rocks), by the Butibum/Bumbu River, large boulders mark the site of the last raid on Lae by hostile tribes from up the valley. This final clash, in 1907, killed 67 people.

The legendary prospector 'Sharkeye' Park is credited with the discovery of gold close to Wau in 1921. By the mid-1920s the gold hunters were flooding in, arriving at the port of Salamaua and struggling for eight days up the steep and slippery track to Wau, a mere 50 km away. As if the conditions of the track, the wet and often cold climate and tropical diseases were not enough, the miners also had to contend with hostile tribes. Frequent reprisal raids by angry miners hardly helped matters.

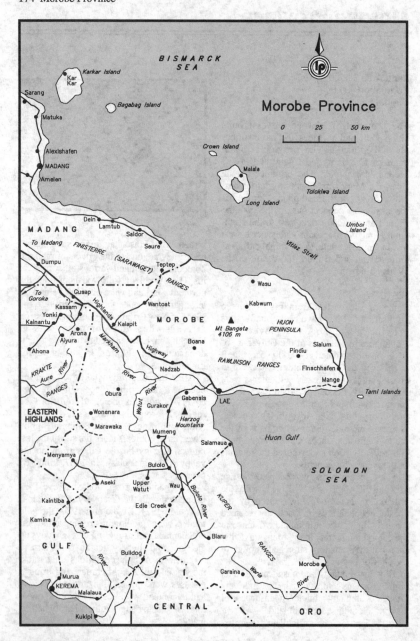

In 1926 a richer field was discovered at Edie Creek, high in the hills above Wau. Although miners made quick fortunes here and at the earlier Koranga Creek Strike, it soon became evident to the more far-sighted prospectors that to really squeeze the most out of these gold-rich streams, large investments and heavy equipment would be needed.

The rough trail from the port of Salamaua up to Wau, Bulolo and Edie Creek was totally unsuitable for transporting heavy equipment, so the New Guinea Gold Company took the brave step of flying in the equipment. An airstrip was prepared in Lae and a shuttle service began. At one time, more air freight was lifted in PNG than in the rest of the world put together!

The gold fields continued to be productive until after the war when the recovery rate started to drop, gold was pegged at an artificially low price (US$35 an ounce) and the costs of production increased. One by one, the eight huge dredges were closed down, the last one in 1965. Although many people still work the fields it is now a small-scale cottage industry.

Lae, or Lehe as it was originally spelt, was a tiny mission station before the gold rush. It soon became a thriving community clustered around its central airstrip in true PNG fashion. The history of the town and of aviation remained closely linked. In July 1937 the pioneer aviator Amelia Earhart took off from Lae on one of the final legs of a round-the-world flight and disappeared over the Pacific without trace.

The volcanic eruptions at Rabaul in 1937 prompted a decision to move the capital of New Guinea to Lae, but WW II intervened before the transfer was really under way. Lae, Salamaua and Rabaul became the major Japanese bases in New Guinea.

In early 1943, the Japanese, reeling from defeats at Milne Bay and the Kokoda Trail, their naval power devastated by the Battle of the Coral Sea, decided to make one more attempt to take Port Moresby. This time they attacked towards Wau, marching up over the mountains from Salamaua in late January 1943. Australian troops in Wau were quickly reinforced by air from Port Moresby and the Japanese advance was repelled.

The Battle of Wau was fought hand-to-hand after the ammunition ran out. Villagers watched the battle in much the same way that foreign researchers and voyeurs watch Highlands battles today.

A grim campaign to clear the Japanese from Morobe followed. It took six months to struggle through the mud and jungle to the outskirts of Salamaua. Australian troops landed on beaches 25 km east of Lae on 4 September and the next day a huge Allied force parachuted onto Nadzab airstrip, up the Markham Valley from Lae. Transport aircraft then flew vast numbers of men and huge amounts of materials in for the advance on Lae.

Salamaua was captured on 11 September and once Lae was surrounded it was easily taken on 16 September. Many Japanese escaped into the mountain wilderness of the Huon Peninsula and started on the incredible retreat that was to eventually end at Wewak.

Lae, Wau, Bulolo and Salamaua were all destroyed during the fighting and Salamaua was never rebuilt. Today it is just a tiny and very pretty village with a pleasant guesthouse. Although the gold was giving out and Papua and New Guinea were to become a united colony governed from Port Moresby, Lae soon had a new reason for existence.

The road between Wau, Bulolo and Lae was built during the war and work on a road along the Markham Valley from Lae into the Highlands commenced. The Highlands, unknown territory before the war, became the scene for major developments. Important coffee and tea industries were established and the crops were trucked down the Highlands Highway and shipped out from Lae. Lae became the major port and industrial centre in PNG and still has the most important road links into the interior.

GEOGRAPHY

Morobe is an arc of land surrounding the Huon Gulf; it's the hump in the New Guinea 'dragon's' back. The lofty Finisterre

(Sarawaget) Ranges form the spine of the Huon Peninsula; one of the most tangled and impenetrable rainforests in PNG blankets their lower slopes. The ranges march right down to the sea and pop up again as the backbone of the mountainous island of New Britain.

The mountains in the south-west are equally inhospitable. They are part of the central spine of the island and they rise higher and higher towards the centre. Between the two ranges there is the wide, flat, fertile Markham Valley which has become a major cattle-grazing area. Morobe also includes a number of volcanic islands between the Huon Peninsula and New Britain.

CLIMATE

Rainfall patterns vary dramatically throughout the province. Lae, Finschhafen and inland near Aseki are wettest from May to October, while around Wau and in the Finisterre Ranges this is the driest season.

PEOPLE

Curiously, there are many parts of Morobe which were virtually uninhabited when Europeans first arrived, including the fertile Wau and Bulolo valleys. The Leiwomba people, however, were long established in the Lae area and the Anga lived in the central mountains.

Anga girl

Frequently referred to incorrectly and offensively as the Kukukuku, the Anga averaged less than 150 cm (five feet) in height and were renowned fighters. They lived a nomadic existence interspersed with violent raids on more peaceful villages at lower altitudes – or upon each other. Despite the bitter climate in their high mountain homeland, they wore only a tiny grass skirt, like a Scotsman's sporran, and cloaks made of beaten bark, known as *mals*.

J K McCarthy, who between the two world wars made some of the first contacts with these people, describes them vividly in his book *Patrol Into Yesterday*. His contact even extended to an arrow in the stomach. The warriors are excellent bowmen who make up for their imperfect aim with an incredibly rapid delivery.

McCarthy also recounts their first sight of an aircraft: Men took turns at crawling underneath it to inspect its genitals, unsure whether the bird was male or female. Their first reaction to McCarthy was less confident. When the first white man arrived in an Anga village, many of these otherwise fearless people literally fainted.

Lae

Population 85,000

Lae is the second largest town in PNG. The city is well laid out, with plenty of trees and parks and once had a reputation as a garden city. Today, however, there are few places where the country's terrific potential and its problems are so startlingly obvious.

There's a touch of the Third-World city about parts of Lae, with fumey streets noisy with poorly maintained vehicles bouncing over potholes, and near-destitute people on the pavements. Brahaminy kites waft like scraps of umbrella cloth in the dusty air. Unfortunately, Lae lacks the usual Third-World compensations for this – you won't find street food or nightlife. Despite being on a dramatic harbour, the city turns its back on the sea and you have to make an effort to find a view. Looming mountains pull the eye, rather than the blue waters of the Huon Gulf.

Lae has a fearsome reputation for rascals, largely deserved, so there is no point staying any longer than you have to. Make your transport connections and go on to somewhere like Wau or Salamaua where things are less tense. That said, during the day you are unlikely to have problems if you keep an eye open and avoid lonely places. Bagsnatching is possible. The old Chinatown, at the eastern end of the city, is supposed to be especially dangerous. There is no problem with taking urban PMVs.

In two days of walking all around Lae I found almost everyone to be very friendly – I was even given coconuts to drink – but I also had the unnerving experience of being followed around the city centre for an hour by a guy who had the nerve to sit down beside me whenever I stopped. As I'd just changed a lot of money this was spooky. He disappeared when I spoke to a policeman, which was lucky as the policeman didn't want to know about it. The guy didn't *look* like a rascal, but as I didn't meet any other rascals in PNG I don't really know what they should look like.

Joe Branders

Warning

Be especially careful in Lae. Listen to the locals' advice. Do not wander around at night. Avoid wandering off by yourself; stay within sight and sound of other people. If you arrive at night, get your PMV driver to deliver you to wherever you plan to stay. The Botanical Gardens and Mt Lunaman are no-go areas for lone travellers, and even small groups.

There's no problem with using the local PMVs and most of the time people are friendly and helpful. I didn't see any violence or theft, but a couple of times the hair did prickle on the back of my neck.

A city with too many unemployed and disillusioned people is likely to have crime but it's also likely to have some interesting attitudes, as shown in this enigmatic graffiti:

Lost particles of Bumbu
Trying to search for something
And just walking up and down
The streets of sadness

Orientation

Lae is built on a flat-topped headland, although before the war the city was closer to the sea. The old airport, where the airlines have their offices, lies at the foot of the steep hill to the west of the town centre. Voco Point, where the shipping companies have their offices, is south of the airport. There's also a wharf at the end of Milford Haven Rd. Down here on the seaside flatlands are also a number of sporting venues, built for the 1991 South Pacific Games.

Huon Rd is the main through street, running in from the Highlands Highway, past the Eriku PMV stop and the main rural PMV stop, through the city centre (still sometimes known as Top Town) and connecting with Markham Rd, another major thoroughfare which leads down past the airport and Voco Point then runs out to Ampo and beyond.

Nadzab Airport is 45 km west of town, just off the Highlands Highway.

Information

Nane Winion is Morobe Province's Culture Officer (☎ 43 1758, fax 42 4745), and she is getting together tourist information on Lae and Morobe. As yet there isn't a lot of printed information available, but she's friendly and enthusiastic. Her office is in the Department of Sport, Culture & Liquor (!), in the northernmost block of the provincial government complex on Coronation Drive.

Lae is well supplied with all the major banks and shops, including sports stores (for snorkelling gear) and bookshops, such as Lo Gallam on 2nd St. There's a Coleman distributor on Coronation Drive opposite the provincial government offices, so you might be able to buy that vital doo-dad for your camp-gas stove. There's a good public library in town.

As well as Steamships and other supermarkets in the town centre, there's a useful cluster of supermarkets on the corner of Huon and Bumbu Rds, near the Eriku PMV stops. Anderson's and Papindo are the best.

The post office is efficient and opens at 8.30 am. There are public telephones nearby,

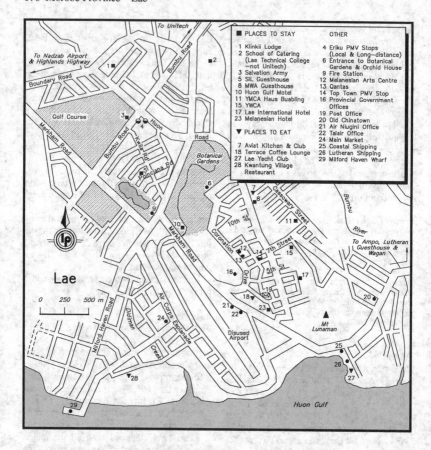

PLACES TO STAY

1 Klinkii Lodge
2 School of Catering
   (Lae Technical College
   —not Unitech)
3 Salvation Army
5 SIL Guesthouse
8 MWA Guesthouse
10 Huon Gulf Motel
11 YMCA Haus Buabling
15 YWCA
17 Lae International Hotel
23 Melanesian Hotel

▼ PLACES TO EAT

7 Aviat Kitchen & Club
18 Terrace Coffee Lounge
27 Lae Yacht Club
28 Kwantung Village
    Restaurant

OTHER

4 Eriku PMV Stops
   (Local & Long—distance)
6 Entrance to Botanical
   Gardens & Orchid House
9 Fire Station
12 Melanesian Arts Centre
13 Qantas
14 Top Town PMV Stop
16 Provincial Government
    Offices
19 Post Office
20 Old Chinatown
21 Air Niugini Office
22 Talair Office
24 Main Market
25 Coastal Shipping
26 Lutheran Shipping
29 Milford Haven Wharf

most of which work but all take only phone cards – the post office sells cards. There's a useful notice board outside the post office and a better one at the Bali news agency on Coronation Drive that advertises dances, club meetings, lost dogs, prams for sale and other useful things. Anderson's supermarket in Eriku also has a notice board.

Cars usually stop at pedestrian crossings in Lae, but don't take it for granted. If you're driving, be very careful of pedestrians who will expect you to stop.

For maps, see the Department of Surveying & Land Studies at Unitech (☎ 43 4950) or the the Department of Lands in the provincial government buildings in town.

There are several dentists in Lae. The only other places where you can find someone to deal scientifically with your gnashers are Moresby and Rabaul.

Botanical Gardens

These are the best botanical gardens in PNG. There are huge trees virtually smothered in vines and creepers, brightly coloured birds that call out raucously and electric-green lizards that scuttle through the undergrowth. The garden also boasts an exotic orchid collection that is theoretically open from 10 am to noon or 2 to 4 pm on the weekends, but don't count on the reliability of those hours.

Within the garden boundaries is the **Lae War Cemetery** with the graves of thousands of Allied soldiers who died during the last war. If the war seems distant and unreal, pay a visit and read some of the headstones. The names are frighteningly ordinary, many of their owners were extremely young, and the places where they died lie all around you.

Over the last few years there have been many vicious attacks on people in the gardens, even in broad daylight. Go with a decent-sized group and preferably with a local guide. There are more people around on weekends and it tends to be safer.

Markets

Lae has three markets. The main market on the west side of the airstrip is quite interesting. It has food and a few local curios. The Butibum market is a smaller, village market out of town on the Butibum road. The third market is the Kamkumsung market, just past the Bumbu Bridge on the way out to the Unitech. It serves the whole Kamkumsung suburb and surrounding villages.

Mt Lunaman

The hill in the centre of town – Mt Lunaman or, more correctly, Lo' Wamung (First Hill) – was used by the Germans and the Japanese as a lookout point. The Germans named it Burgberg or 'Fortress Hill', while the Japanese riddled it with caves and tunnels.

The current occupiers are rascals (no doubt they have given it a new name) and it is, once again, a no-go zone – unless you're in a car, with a group, in daylight and preferably with a local guide, it's not worth the trouble.

Unitech

The Matheson Library, at the PNG University of Technology (Unitech), is the largest library of technology in the South Pacific. The Duncanson Hall has 36 Sepik-style carved pillars and the coffee house is also built like a traditional haus tambaran.

Unitech also has an artefacts collection that includes many rare pieces. It's the only public collection of artefacts in Morobe Province. Unitech is about eight km from downtown Lae but you can easily get there on PMV No 11A or 11B.

Wagan

Eight km from town, across the Butibum River, Wagan is a small village near Malahang Beach which the Japanese used as a landing point. You must ask the villagers for permission to visit the black sand beach where the remains of the landing barge *Myoko Maru* are sinking into the sand.

Activities

The Bulai International Primary School on Huon Rd, north past the Eriku PMV stops, has a swimming pool that is open to outsiders on weekends for a small charge.

The Lae Explorers Club is active, with plenty of walks of varying standards, and you can rent some equipment. Membership is only K5, but you don't have to be a member on your first walk. The current contact person is John Clarke (☎ 42 6510) but that will almost certainly change. The Yacht Club would be a good place to ask for current information, or check the notice board outside the Bali news agency on Coronation Drive for notices advertising walks.

Niugini Diving (☎ 42 5692, PO Box 320) has regular Sunday dives, and two dives plus lunch costs just K45.

Organised Tours Morobe Tours (☎ 42 3647) operate air-con bus trips in and around the town. A two-hour tour taking in the local sites and history costs K50 and a full day tour is K75.

Places to Stay – bottom end

The *Salvation Army* is on the corner of Bumbu and Huon Rds near the Eriku PMV stops, one km or so from the centre, but there are no longer cheap rooms (see Places to Stay – middle). You might be able to sleep on the floor of the recreation hall for K2, along with a lot of other people.

The YMCA's big *Haus Buabling* (☎ 42 4412, fax 42 2654, PO Box 1055) on Cassowary St is a good place to stay; it's secure, cheap and near the city centre. It's also a good place to meet local people, as most of the 96 rooms are taken by long-term residents, mainly young working people (who can make a bit of noise). To get there, walk east on 7th St from Huon Rd and when 7th St turns right (you're now on Hawk St), turn left at the bottom onto Cassowary St. The YMCA is a little way along on your left; there's no sign.

This place became very run down a few years ago, but things have improved dramatically and it's now one of PNG's few accommodation bargains. Casual visitors have their own section, although solo women might be given a room in the women's wing. The rooms are very small (all are singles) and they can get hot as there is no fan. The shared bathrooms are clean enough, although due for renovation. The price (K12) includes breakfast and dinner.

Dennis, the chef, produced roast lamb with mint sauce the night I was there, and there was ice cream for dessert. Residents say that the meals tend to be more interesting around the beginning of the budget month, but that they are always good.

The *Lutheran Guesthouse* (☎ 42 2556, PO Box 80) is at Ampo on Busu Rd, opposite the Balob Teachers' College. Ampo (pronounced Umpo) is the main administration centre for the Lutheran Church and the colonial-style guesthouse buildings are about 200 metres on the right from the main road, set in green, attractive grounds. The shared rooms (two to five beds) are very clean, as are the bathrooms, and there are lounge rooms with coffee-making facilities. Bed & breakfast costs K25, with three good meals it's K33.

The guesthouse's priority is to look after people who are associated with the church, so although they welcome travellers, you may be unlucky and find it full, so phone first. As in other Lutheran guesthouses in PNG there are rules, but if you don't mind making a few concessions you'll meet some very friendly, interesting people in a calm, relaxing environment. The gates are closed between 10 pm and 6 am.

It's too far out of town to walk to the guesthouse, but PMVs are frequent. Catch one from the Top Town PMV stop on 7th St near Huon Rd. You want a 'Butibum' PMV (No 13A), but check with the driver's assistant that it goes to Ampo.

If you don't mind a walk, head down to the end of 7th St, where it meets the road to Ampo. Most PMVs departing from the cluster of shops here run past the guesthouse. This area, the old Chinatown, has a bad reputation for robberies so don't try walking here after dark.

Not great value as far as accommodation goes, but a good place to meet interesting and friendly people (as long as you don't act like an expat), is the *Morobe Women's Association* guesthouse (MWA) (PO Box 1468) on Huon Rd near 10th St. Both men and women can stay. Floor-space costs K2, dorm beds are K13 and the one double room (with a double bed) costs K20 per person. There are cooking facilities.

The women's association was founded by and for grassroots mothers and runs programmes to improve subsistence agriculture. Most of the association's members are rural women who stay at the guesthouse when they come to Lae. The manager, Mrs Gata Kalu, is worth talking to.

The *YWCA* has a hostel on 7th St between Huon Rd and Cassowary St, close to town. It's almost always full of permanent residents. They don't take men. If there's no-one there when you call in, try the YWCA centre (☎ 42 1691) on Huon Rd near the corner of Cassowary St.

There might be accommodation available in the *Unitech* student hostel during vacations. Check with the Director of Student Services (☎ 43 4377). There's also a very good guesthouse – see the following section.

The famous old Hotel Cecil, an establishment that became a South Pacific legend (it was featured in *Return to Paradise* by James Michener) is no more.

Places to Stay – middle

There is a guesthouse out at *Unitech* which is excellent value. It's a pleasant house rather than a hostel and there are only a few rooms (two singles, two twins and one double) which cost K35 each, whether there are one or two people in them. Breakfast costs K3 and a good dinner is K7.

The guesthouse is managed by an Australian academic, and it's also his home. People staying at the guesthouse can use the university's staff club which has cheap lunches, and dinner Wednesday to Friday from K3.50. To book, phone the Vice Chancellor's secretary (☎ 43 4201). Unitech is about eight km from downtown Lae, but there are plenty of PMVs running out here. Take No 11A or 11B.

The *Summer Institute of Linguistics* (SIL) missionary group run a guesthouse (☎ 42 3214, fax 42 5516, PO Box 342) on Poinsiana Rd, off Kwila Rd, which runs into Milford Haven Rd ('Milford Heaven' on one sign) opposite the Botanical Gardens. You could walk here from the Eriku PMV stops, although you might get lost entering this suburban maze from Bumbu Rd.

The guesthouse is clean and quiet, and smoking and drinking are banned. There are six rooms with shared bathrooms at K35/40, and six units which share a bathroom with one other at K40/50. There are cooking facilities and a very small swimming pool.

The *School of Catering* (☎ 42 6805), at Lae Technical College (not Unitech) on Milford Haven Rd, has four motel units. They look as though they were designed by a committee in the early '60s and are becoming shabby, but they are reasonable value at K45. They have air-con (the building gets very hot) fridges, toasters and electric kettles but no cooking facilities.

Meals are available during the week; on weekends you can eat in the student mess by prior arrangement. There's a small shop on campus. If you plan to arrive after hours or on a weekend, make sure you have the name of the person who is supposed to give you the key. If they aren't around, ask to see someone in Housekeeping.

The *Salvation Army* (☎ 42 2487, PO Box 259), on the corner of Bumbu and Huon Rds near the PMV stop, has closed its hostel and opened a 'tourist motel'. These bland twin rooms have attached bathrooms, fans, fridges and cooking facilities but cost K65!

Close by, on Klinkii St, which runs off Huon Rd, is *Klinkii Lodge* (☎ 42 6040, PO Box 192). The rooms are basic but clean enough. Rooms with shared bathroom cost K43/54; the two rooms with attached bathroom and air-con are K58/69, all including breakfast. Other meals are available. They'll take you out to the airport for K25.

Places to Stay – top end

The *Huon Gulf Motel* (☎ 42 4844, fax 42 3706, PO Box 612) is on Markham Rd in what must once have been a prime location, nestled into a corner of the Botanical Gardens and close by to the airport. Times change – the airport has closed and the gardens are dangerous to visit.

The motel looks a little forlorn, and while it's the cheapest of Lae's top-end places, paying K90/100 plus 7% tax for singles/doubles in what looks like a motel from the '50s seems ridiculous. If the price was lower it would be reasonable. If you arrive after 5 pm (and if you haven't already booked) ask about standby rates.

The *Melanesian Hotel* (☎ 42 3744, fax 42 3706, PO Box 756), is only a minute's walk from the town centre. It has everything you would expect, including a choice of bars and restaurants and a pleasant swimming pool. After 6 pm you must wear a shirt and trousers – enough said? There are 68 rooms costing K135 plus 7% tax. Meals are good but not cheap.

The top hotel in Lae is the new *Lae International Hotel* (☎ 42 2000, fax 42 2534, PO Box 2774), a few blocks from the town centre at the end of 4th St. It was, until recently, a gracious, old colonial lodge (it is still sometimes referred to as Lae Lodge) but it's now a modern and luxurious hotel. There's an excellent 25-metre pool and a *haus win* where they have a Friday night disco and a popular poolside lunchtime barbecue on Sunday. There's also a restaurant and a coffee shop. Rooms cost from K120/150 plus 7% tax, including breakfast.

Places to Eat

If you are not eating at your hotel, Lae has a small range of alternatives, particularly for snacks and light lunches.

The *Terrace Coffee Lounge* on 2nd St is good (there are even flowers on the tables) and it has excellent air-con. Omelettes are about K5, good coffee is K1.50. It's open 9 am to 5 pm on weekdays and on Saturday morning.

The Sandwich Bar, towards the south end of Coronation Drive has a good range of sandwiches and hot food. *Jako's Kai Bar* on 4th St is Indian-run and has some curries and sambals on the menu for about K3. *Lae Fish Supply* has more choices than the average kai bar and it's clean and cheap. A spring roll or a piece of fish costs K0.80 and a good serving of chow mein K1.60. *Bronco's*, on Coronation Drive between 7th and 8th Sts is a kai place with tables.

The most pleasant spot for a meal is the *Lae Yacht Club* which is down on Voco Point. It overlooks the water and they serve lunch every day and dinner Tuesday and Friday. The outside bar opens from 4.30 pm and there's no better spot to sit and watch the world go by – the beer is *cold*. Prices haven't risen in years, and a roast meal still costs K6 and something a bit fancier, like prawns, is K7. They also have cheaper snacks.

There are three Chinese places. The *Aviat Kitchen*, at the Aviat Club on Huon Rd, is a big Chinese restaurant open from 6 pm daily, with lunch on Sunday only. Soups cost from K3, salads K4, and most main courses are around K8. There are quite a few Western dishes on the menu, with steaks about K11. Be warned – they have karaoke.

Kwangtung Village Restaurant is run by the same people. The food is good but a little more expensive than at the Aviat Kitchen, but they have more seafood. It's rather inconveniently located on Mangola St, out beyond the market, on the other side of the airport. Lunch is served daily except Satur-

day and dinner every day. The *Apollo*, in town on 2nd St, is open for lunch and dinner on weekdays. There's a three-course lunch special for K5.50. Main courses range from about K7 to K14.

The *Huon Gulf Motel* and the *Melanesian Hotel* both have restaurants, with prices from about K12. The *Lae International Hotel* has an expensive restaurant, but the coffee shop isn't too bad, with spaghetti around K9 and steaks from K12. The hotel's Sunday lunchtime poolside barbecue can cost as little as K9.50 and the Friday night smorgasbord (K15) has been recommended.

Entertainment

Nightlife in Lae is largely restricted to the Lae International and the Melanesian hotels. The International usually has a disco on weekends and the Melanesian has a Wednesday night disco with dinner for K12.

If you want a taste of a true-blue Aussie pub, see if you can get yourself signed in at the Aviat Club on Huon Rd, open daily from 4 pm. Check out the various notice boards around town for dances, and read the *Post Courier*, which has a Lae supplement.

Things to Buy

The Melanesian Arts Centre (☎ 42 1604) on 8th St has a good collection of artefacts including many pieces from the Trobriands and the Sepik region. It's easy to walk past without noticing it; it's a weatherboard house next door to the Mobil station on the corner of 8th St and Coronation Drive.

Owned by Robyn Leahy, daughter-in-law of Mick Leahy, it's open Monday to Saturday, from 9 am to noon. Prices are similar to, maybe a little better than, those in Moresby and they will ship stuff home for you. The staff are friendly, helpful and knowledgeable. A buying day when local people bring in goods is interesting to see. Ask if one is coming up.

Morobe Arts & Handcrafts is in the building next door to the Melanesian Hotel and it has an interesting collection, including sand paintings. Walk down the passageway immediately in front of the drive and it is on your right. There's a good view over the harbour to the towering Herzog Mountains on the other side.

Small inexpensive crafts are also available from street sellers who spread their wares on the sidewalk around the downtown stores, particularly the Steamships store.

Getting There & Away

There's a wide choice of transport into and out of Lae, as Lae is the major centre on the north coast, the major north coast port, an important airport and the coastal access point for the Highlands Highway.

There are frequent air connections to all main centres, including to the islands, regular shipping services along the coast and out to New Britain and numerous PMVs running between the Highlands and Madang.

Air Lae's airport is at Nadzab, 45 km from town. This was an important airstrip during the war, and it is much more spacious than the old airport in town. Nadzab was used in the early '80s, but it proved so unpopular that in 1984 the town airport was re-opened, except for flights landing after 6 pm. Nadzab is now back in use but is still very unpopular. The problem, as you may have guessed, is transport to and from Lae. See the Getting Around section.

If you're heading for Madang you should seriously consider taking a PMV, which will cost a great deal less than a plane (it could cost a great deal less than just getting to Nadzab!) and take not much more time, once you add up the time taken to get to Nadzab, the check-in time, the flight time...

Lae is another town which confidently expects to be granted PNG's new international airport. Nadzab is big enough to be easily converted into an international gateway, but that's about all it has going for it.

The main airline offices are a short walk from the centre of Lae at the old airport. Air Niugini (☎ 42 3111) has frequent flights to all major centres, Talair (☎ 42 2630) destinations include the Wau/Bulolo region, Finschhafen, the Highlands, Port Moresby,

Northern Province and Milne Bay. MAF (☎ 42 1555) also has a base, and has flights around the region and up to the Highlands. The MAF office is in town on 2nd St, next to the Terrace Coffee Lounge.

PMV PMVs to Wau, Goroka and Madang leave Lae between 8 and 9 am every day; there are fewer on weekends. The main long-distance PMV stop is in Eriku on Bumbu Rd.

Sea There are frequent connections west along the coast as far as Vanimo and east as far as Oro Bay (Popondetta), and regular connections with New Britain and Manus Island. If any passenger-carrying freighters load (or expect to load en route) dangerous cargo such as petrol, they will not accept passengers. Usually they give a couple of weeks' notice, but not necessarily.

Lutheran Shipping (☎ 42 2066, 42 2823; fax 42 5806, PO Box 1459, Lae) and Coastal Shipping Services (☎ 42 3180, fax 42 1686, PO Box 1721) both have their offices and piers at Voco Point, a short walk from the airport near the Yacht Club. The Lutheran Shipping ticket office is open only from 8 to 8.30 am Monday to Friday and 8 to 9.30 am on Saturday. Get there early as there are queues. Tickets are sold up to a week in advance of sailing.

Other freight lines run to Lae but don't officially take passengers. You might have more success getting on a freighter by talking directly to the ship's captain rather than the office people.

Car Rental Avis (☎ 42 4929) and Budget (☎ 42 4889) have offices at Nadzab Airport. Hertz (☎ 42 5982) is on 9th St. Avis also has an office at the Lae International Hotel and Budget has an office at the Melanesian Hotel.

To/From Port Moresby Flights from Port Moresby climb up and over the central mountain range. In the old days you flew through, rather than over, the mountains. These days you whistle over the top in 45 minutes, but in an Air Niugini F28 you are still not too high to appreciate the dramatic geography.

Both Air Niugini and Talair have frequent flights to Moresby and the cost is K95. Talair also has a flight from Moresby to Wau, Monday to Saturday, also for K95. You could then catch the PMV down to Lae (K5), or walk three days to Salamaua and catch a boat (K6), or fly from Wau for K52.

Other alternatives from Moresby include: making your way to Kerema on the Gulf of Papua by PMV and boat then flying across to Lae with Talair (K94), walking the Kokoda Trail and flying from Popondetta for K121 or, more economically, catching the *Mamose Express* or the *Rita* from Oro Bay for K21.50/32.50 in deck/cabin class. It's very difficult to find a boat all the way from Moresby.

To/From Wau & Bulolo A Talair flight from Lae to Bulolo costs K45, and to Wau K52. The PMV fare from Lae to Bulolo is K4.50; to Wau it's K5. Flying between Wau and Bulolo costs K22. It is around 180 km by road to Wau and takes nearly four hours, although when the roadworks are completed the run will be quicker.

Most PMVs running this route are trucks and the ride can be rough. Try to sit near the front, and definitely not over the rear axle. There was a rash of PMV hold-ups on the Lae-Wau road in 1992. They seem to have died down, but ask around.

To/From the Highlands Talair flies to Goroka (K62) and Mt Hagen (K87) every day except Sunday. Air Niugini has no direct flights from Lae to the Highlands.

See the Highlands chapter for details on PMVs and the Highlands Highway. The PMV fare to Goroka is K10 and the distance is about 330 km. If you're lucky, you can sometimes deliver cars for Ela Motors (☎ 43 3655, PO Box 3182) who, for reasons best known to themselves, trust travellers (for a couple of days) with vehicles that would otherwise have to be transported. Boroko Motors (☎ 42 1144, PO Box 609), the Nissan franchiser, might do the same.

To/From Madang Air Niugini has a daily flight from Madang but doesn't fly *to* Madang on Monday or Thursday. The fare is K68.

The road is now pretty good and is sealed as far as Ramu. All up, it's about 360 km. When it is open, it can be covered by virtually any vehicle, but when it's closed (which now happens less frequently) even a 4WD won't get through. The problem is, as usual, the river crossings.

PMVs leave from the long-distance Eriku PMV stop around 8 am, cost K20 and take about six hours. After turning off the Highlands Highway, the road runs through a flat valley cultivated with the cane fields of the Ramu Sugar Refinery before climbing over the hills on the approach to Madang. Accommodation is usually available at the sugar refinery (☎ 44 3299) for about K58 or K69 for a double-bed double, with breakfast. A PMV from there to Madang costs about K10.

The boat trip is much more enjoyable and deck class costs about the same as a PMV. Lutheran Shipping's passenger-only *Mamose Express* and *Rita* service all the main north-coast ports. See the Getting Around chapter for a full schedule, but don't forget these things can change.

Currently, one of the boats leaves Lae for Madang every Wednesday morning and arrives in Madang on Thursday morning. It doesn't leave until late Friday, so you get two days in Madang, which is enough time to have a decent look around. Fares to Madang are K21.50/32.50 in cabin/deck class. The through fare to Wewak is K35/52.50, which includes overnight accommodation, with harbour views, in Madang!

Lutheran Shipping also operates less regular, slower and much less comfortable passenger-carrying freighters on the route. By comparison to the passenger boats they're not a bargain, but the trip is still enjoyable. Deck/1st-class fares are K18/23 to Madang and K32/38 to Wewak.

To/From New Britain Air Niugini has daily flights to Rabaul, costing K160. Airlink (book through Talair) flies to Rabaul on

Monday, Wednesday and Friday. The fare is the same but you get to stop at a number of small strips in West New Britain.

Lutheran Shipping has a weekly passenger boat (either the *Mamose Express* or the *Rita*) sailing to Kimbe and Rabaul from Lae on Monday afternoon, arriving on Tuesday. To Rabaul deck class costs K34 and cabin K54.

Coastal Shipping (Coastal) has the *Lae Express*, a passenger boat, running once a week between Lae and Rabaul via Kimbe. This boat has only just come into service so its timetable hasn't settled yet, but it will probably depart on Friday and take about 48 hours to Rabaul.

Coastal's *Kimbe Express* also sails to Rabaul via Kimbe, departing on Friday arriving in Kimbe on Sunday and Lae on Monday. It's a mixed passenger/cargo boat, with deck-class accommodation only. To Kimbe it's K28 and Rabaul K34. Coastal's *Astro I* departs for Rabaul on Wednesday, running via the south coast of New Britain and stopping at Kandrian, among other places. This is not a passenger boat but there are a few cabins in which, when available, you can travel for K80.

To/From Oro Bay The *Mamose Express* or the *Rita* sails from Lae for Oro Bay on Monday evening, taking about 18 hours. Deck/cabin-class fares are K21.50/32.50. There are also freighters.

To/From Other Destinations Talair flies to Finschhafen on Monday, Wednesday, Friday and Saturday for K68. A couple of these flights continue on to Lablab Mission and Siassi on Umboi Island.

On Monday and Friday there are Talair flights to Kerema (K94), via Menyamya (K60) and some interesting strips in Gulf Province.

Virtually all the Madang-bound boats call at Finschhafen. The fare on Lutheran Shipping's passenger boats is K11/16.50 in deck/cabin class.

The Lutheran Shipping cargo vessels run approximately weekly to Lorengau on

Manus, sometimes via Madang for K40/47 in deck/cabin class. Other cargo boats call in at Umboi Island approximately fortnightly.

There are frequent but irregular boats from Voco Point in Lae to Salamaua (K6, two hours) and other villages such as Labu Miti and Maus Buang near the Labu Lakes. You could also try for a small boat at the wharf at the end of Milford Haven Rd.

Getting Around

To/From the Airport Travelling the 45 km between Lae and Nadzab Airport is not easy if you don't have your own transport. Despite the signs in the terminal at Nadzab directing you to coaches, there are none.

Neither Talair nor Air Niugini have transport. Talair's excuse is that by law they can't carry the public in their staff vehicle because it isn't a registered PMV – which prompts the question 'Why not?'. Air Niugini *might* be able to take you out to the airport from their office in town, but only at 5 am, 8 am and 'lunch time'. All these times are hazy and you'd be unwise to rely on them.

There is an occasional PMV which comes into the terminal area, or you could walk the km or so out of the airport to the Highlands Highway and flag down a PMV there, but there are few after about 4 pm. Morobe Tours (☎ 42 3647) has a 'luxury minibus' which meets most flights, but paying K31 just to get into town from the airport is ridiculous.

If you're staying at one of the top-end hotels you can arrange to be picked up, but for a stiff fee. The only other option is to cadge a ride with a local. After the last flight has arrived (about 6 pm) you might be able to get a lift with the car hire people, and Air Niugini staff can also help the desperate but you might have to wait for hours before someone goes off duty. All in all, it's a shambles.

PMV PMVs around Lae cost K0.30. The local PMV stop in Eriku is on Huon Rd. The other local PMV stop (also known as the Top Town PMV stop) is on 7th St. There are now route numbers painted on urban PMVs but these are fairly vague.

Listen to the driver's assistant, who leans out the window and calls the destination and the names of stops in a semi-automatic, rapid-fire incantation. Even if you don't understand a word, people will point you in the right direction. You can't go too far in the wrong direction because the urban PMVs all have circular routes. Sooner or later you'll end up back where you started.

Taxi There are now very few taxis in Lae, due to hold-ups. People might tell you that taxis cruise the town centre, but I didn't see any. This is a nuisance as PMVs stop running early in the evening and walking at night is unsafe. The few taxis are mainly twin-cab pickups, and can sometimes be found at the Shell station (☎ 45 7339) on the road out to Unitech or you could try Jumi Taxis (☎ 42 4377). Don't count on a cab turning up.

AROUND LAE
The Labu Lakes, right across the Markham River from Lae, were used to hide ships during the war, but the maze of waterways and swamps are now only home to crocodiles. The beaches on the ocean side are beautiful and they are an important breeding site for the leatherback turtle, incredible reptiles that can live to a great age, weigh up to 500 kg and measure up to two metres in length.

Maus Buang & Labu Tali
From the end of November until early February, leatherback turtles come ashore along the beaches around Maus Buang and Labu Tali villages and dig deep nests where they lay up to 100 eggs, which hatch about two months later. This process is one of the most extraordinary sights in the world, and this is one of the few places where it can be witnessed.

Traditionally, the eggs are gathered by people from the villages, but over the years the demand for the eggs has increased to the point where the turtles are in danger of dying out. To both save the turtle and improve the villagers' very basic living standards, lecturers from Lae Unitech have convinced the people to set aside the three-km beach between the two villages for conservation.

As compensation for the lost food, Unitech has undertaken to raise money for the local school and other community facilities, including a guesthouse. The idea is that visitors will, in the long term, supply an alternative income for the villagers and provide them with an incentive to conserve the turtle population.

If you are fortunate enough to see the turtles, please make an effort not to disturb them; some human-being-type animals apparently have an overwhelming urge to torture them by shining torches in their eyes, riding them up the beach, poking them with sticks...

Places to Stay Until a guesthouse is built (and it's a long time coming), accommodation is on the floor of the school at Maus Buang. It's necessary to take food and sleeping gear. The K8 charge includes a guide to help you look for turtles, and the proceeds go to important local facilities and contribute to the conservation of the leatherback turtle.

Further along the coast is pretty **Busama** village, where there may still be a guesthouse, then Salamaua.

Getting There & Away Boats leave frequently from Voco Point in Lae – just go down to the point, ask around and wait. If you've waited too long, try the wharf at the end of Milford Haven Rd. The journey takes one to 1½ hours and costs about K3.50. It is also possible to get a boat across the Markham River and walk along the empty beaches. This takes four or five hours – watch out for crocodiles. Ask around in Lae or Salamaua about the current safety situation first.

Salamaua
The picturesque peninsula has little to indicate its role in the gold rush days when it was the largest town on the north New Guinea coast, or the part it played in WW II.

Today, two laid-back villages occupy the site: **Kela** and **Lagui**. Close by, there's excellent diving, good walks and a few interesting war relics. It's a popular place for Lae people to escape to, although the accommodation is now run-down.

The original town cemetery is disappearing under the bush, but it can still be reached by following a rough path that begins in the north-west corner of the school oval. This path also leads past a small reef which is good for snorkelling. Near the start of the path is the entrance to a Japanese tunnel. A steep path leads up the hill to four Japanese gun emplacements and there's a great view.

You can also visit Coastwatchers Ridge where Australians were stationed to report on Japanese shipping and troop movements and, if you want a full day's walk, Mt Tambu has spectacular views and a huge battlefield where the Australians met the Japanese advance towards Wau. Local guides are available.

Most people just relax, fool around with a snorkel and take in the scenery!

Place to Stay *Salamaua Haus Kibung* (☎ 42 3782 for information) was a good place to stay but has been taken over by the provincial government and is, surprise, surprise, falling into disrepair. The rates are supposed to be K20 per person but there are 'some problems with the water supply and the food' so they are charging only K10.

It's best to take your own food, but there is a local market near the school open from 7 to 8 am on Wednesdays and Saturdays where you can get fresh fruit and fish, and a trade store.

It used to be possible to stay in a bush hut at the Community School for about K5 and locals used to rent out huts for similar prices. Ask around to see if this is still the case.

Getting There & Away There's an interesting but tough three-day walk down from Wau – see that section for more details. Boats run from Voco Point or the Milford Haven Rd wharf in Lae and cost around K6. The local PMV boat is not entirely reliable but, most days, there will be something running,

probably leaving Salamaua early and returning from Lae in the afternoon.

It's possible to get off in other villages along the way, like Maus Buang, where you can watch leatherback turtles (see the previous section). You can walk from Busama to Salamaua along the beach in about five hours.

You could walk along the beach between Salamaua and Lae in about two days. Two major rivers must be crossed, the Buang and the Markham. You can wade across the first but you must definitely get a boat across the second.

Around Morobe Province

FINSCHHAFEN AREA

The town of Finschhafen was the German New Guinea Kompagnie's first, unsuccessful, attempt at colonising New Guinea. Between 1885, when they arrived there and 1892, when they moved west to Stephansort, the Germans had a miserable time and died like flies from malaria and assorted tropical ills.

They did not do much better at Stephansort and soon moved to Madang and then to Rabaul, where they finally found peace from the mosquitoes. Today Finschhafen is an idyllic, coastal town. The modern town of Finschhafen was moved from its original site after WW II. Little remains of the original town apart from one old Lutheran building, which is now used by holidaying missionaries. Its tower was once used as a lookout.

Towards the end of WW II the town was used as a staging post for American troops and vast numbers of GIs passed through. The war's abrupt end left them with millions of dollars of purposeless aircraft and equipment, so the whole lot was bulldozed into a huge hole. There are a number of well-preserved sunken ships and downed aircraft offshore. Niugini Diving (☎ 42 5692, PO

Box 320) can organise diving trips in the area.

Nearby **Malasiga** village was settled by Tami Islanders and it is possible to buy the famous Tami Island bowls – ask for the *stor bilong carving*. A reader suggests that on the way to Malasiga you visit the Ngasegalatu Church, which has some amazing carvings by David Anams.

The beautiful **Tami Islands**, south of Finschhafen, are only 12 km from the coast. The Tami Islanders are renowned for their beautifully carved wooden bowls. There is a village guesthouse. Malasiga is a good place to look for transport to get out here.

Places to Stay
Dreger Lodge (☎ 44 7050, PO Box 126) was built and is run by Dregerhafen Provincial High School, three km from Finschhafen. It consists of three chalets, each with room for four people and the cost is a fairly steep K25 per person. There are communal cooking facilities – no food is provided. There is good snorkelling nearby. There's a guesthouse at Logaweng Senior Seminary, and I heard talk of other places you can stay, so ask around.

In Sialum, on the coast about three hours' drive north of Finschhafen, there's apparently the *Paradise Spring Inn*, with rooms for about K60. The tourist office in Lae might have more information.

Getting There & Away
Virtually all Madang-bound boats call at Finschhafen. The fare on Lutheran Shipping's passenger boats is K11/16.50 in deck/cabin class.

Talair flies to Finschhafen on Monday, Wednesday, Friday and Saturday for K68. A couple of these flights continue on to Lablab Mission and Siassi on Umboi Island.

During the war a road was pushed through all the way to Finschhafen from Lae, but it has since disappeared. A road is being constructed now, mainly for new logging projects, but in a piecemeal fashion and major river crossings are liable to delay completion for many years. There's a road from

Finschhafen to Sialum and roads to Pindiu (50 km) and Wasu, past Sialum, are being worked on.

It's possible to walk to Lae from Finschhafen; students from Dregerhafen High School regularly do this walk. See the school principal for advice. The walk along the coast, sometimes on the beach, takes three days.

WAU & BULOLO
Wau (pronounced somewhere between 'wow' and 'wo') and Bulolo were the sites for New Guinea's gold rush of the 1920s and '30s, but the gold began to peter out by the start of WW II and the mines never got back into full swing afterwards. The construction of a road down to Lae on the coast during the war has encouraged the development of timber and agricultural industries. If you're interested in gold mining history, the mountains and their people and superb bird life, Wau and Bulolo are well worth a visit.

Many people still work small claims in the area and fossickers turn up the occasional nugget. Cash in your El Dorado at stores with the sign *Baim Gol Hia*.

A couple of the prewar dredges, weighing 2500 tons, all of which were flown in by the old Junkers tri-motors from Lae, can be seen near Bulolo. Between Bulolo and Wau the road winds through the deep Wau Gorge, crossing first Edie Creek and then Kotunga Creek – the two creeks which formed the basis of the gold rush activities.

Edie Creek is about 20 km from Wau by a winding, rather heart-in-the-mouth road. Mt Kaindi, towering behind Edie Creek, has a small hut – inquire at the Wau Ecology Institute about using it.

After the gold rush, the area's forests of Hoop and Klinkii pine were decimated by a logging company formed by the gold dredgers. Many of the bare hillsides riddled with erosion are the result of this, but others come from the deforestation which accompanied a more recent vegetable-growing project. This failed because settlers given plots by the government were attacked by locals.

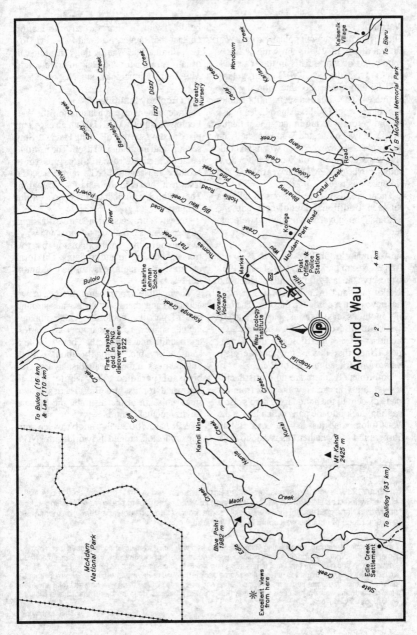

Around Wau

Warning

The big Namie open-cut gold mine near Wau closed down in 1990, throwing a lot of people out of work. This in turn caused a crime wave in the area. PMVs were regularly held up and houses became Moresby-style fortresses. The situation seems a lot calmer now but it would still be a good idea to ask around before walking in the area or taking a PMV between Lae and Wau, especially on pay Fridays. However, even when the hold-ups were common you would have been unlucky to be on a PMV that was robbed, and violence was rare.

There are also some tensions in the area between traditional landowners and the 'settlers' the government tried to relocate here.

McAdam National Park

This 20-sq-km park was established in 1962 to preserve the last virgin stands of Hoop and Klinkii pine and over 200 species of birds that have been recorded in the area. The bird life includes cassowaries, eagles and 10 species of bird of paradise. There are also orchids, ferns, butterflies and tree kangaroos. Note that this is not the McAdam *Memorial* Park, south-east of Wau.

Unfortunately, there are no tourist facilities yet, but you can view the park from the road adjacent to the boundary. There's also a walking track into the park which leaves the Wau-Bulolo road just as you enter Bulolo Gorge. Find out whether this is safe to walk before trying it. For further information contact the Ranger, National Park, PO Box 127, Bulolo. The Wau Ecology Institute can usually arrange for someone to drive you to McAdam National Park and back for K5.

Wau Ecology Institute

An independent research institution, the Wau Ecology Institute (WEI) is both an excellent place to stay (see the following Places to Stay section) and interesting in itself. The institute is dedicated to researching grassroots ecology and saving PNG's rainforests, the last great forests in the Asia-Pacific region. They publish a number of books on the flora & fauna.

Research projects include investigations of seed dispersal patterns by birds and ways of regenerating soil exhausted by too frequent burning off and cropping. This form of 'shifting' agriculture is still very common in PNG.

The institute's zoo is being enlarged to two hectares, and there's to be a walk-through bird of paradise enclosure. Other inmates include snakes, tree kangaroos, cassowaries, a crocodile and a hornbill. There will be a small entry fee, probably about K0.30. Several trees in the area are display trees for birds of paradise. The whole area is renowned for its bird life. There's also a small museum at the institute, the Somare Environmental Centre.

WEI has a **'butterfly ranch'**, which supplies collectors around the world with PNG's

---

Errol Flynn

In about 1930, a young, adventure-seeking Errol Flynn arrived in PNG and stayed three years. He first worked as a patrol officer, but was soon into trading, shipping and general hustling. Like so many others, gold caught his fancy. He did some prospecting and later, apparently, he managed a claim. Much of his time was spent in the Wau area.

I met a wacky, engaging, machinating Californian who had with him a treasure map he'd been given by an American old-timer and one-time New Guinea hand and soldier. This old guy, now living in California, had known Flynn and gave the guy I met a map indicating where to find Flynn's old gold stash. Apparently it fills an old tank's gun barrel and lies rusting along some track in the Wau area. Anyway, the fellow knew all about downed planes in the area and small village names and who knows? Only thing was he was broke and the visa department was on his case and Jesus this chewin' tobacco's gotta be better than that red stuff everybody's workin' on...

Mark Lightbody

astounding variety of insects. Butterflies are common around the institute because the plants they feed on are grown. Villagers earn money by selling insects to the institute, which sells them to collectors. The size and variety of the insects, both dead in the shop and wandering about the forest very much alive, is astounding.

The stick insect *eurycantha horrida* is just about the most creepy thing I have ever seen; the huge orb spiders, which seem to enjoy building their webs across paths, seem benign by comparison. The spiders are, I'm told, 'slightly' dangerous.

You can buy dead butterflies and insects: a magnificent blue emperor costs K4 and an impressive rhino beetle is K1. You can also buy insects at the Insect Farming & Trading Agency (☎ 44 5285) in Bulolo on Godwin St, uphill and to the left from the post office.

Another programme studies the area's medicinal plants. Some are grown at WEI and others are brought in by village people. Unfortunately, WEI doesn't have the money to properly evaluate the plants, they just find out the active ingredients.

There are many **interesting walks** in the area on local footpaths or through the neighbouring coffee plantations. It is a hard walk, up and over the hills north of Wau, to the Edie Creek area. Allow at least four hours to get there and three to return. Those planning longer treks in the area should talk to the people at WEI as they are knowledgeable, can help to find reliable guides and can often drive you to the trailhead.

There is a WEI field station at **Kolorong** where you can stay for K4. It's quite a way south of Wau off the Biaru road and getting there isn't easy, although WEI can organise someone to drive you there for K40. It's a beautiful area. Once there, a guide is necessary (one of the WEI workers is usually available) as the local clans don't like trespassers. This is a great area for **birdwatching**. The field station on Mt Kaindi has been closed because of local tensions, but you can still walk up the mountain (following the cleared path under the power lines) with one of the WEI workers. If no-one is going up when you want to, they'll find a kid to go with you – expect to pay a small fee.

The WEI can arrange birdwatching trips (especially to Biaru, a good area) or rent a vehicle to visitors, but this definitely depends on the availability of vehicles and staff.

War Wreckages

About a four-hour return walk to the south-east of Wau along a good path, there's a surprisingly intact B17 bomber. It was shot down by Zeros during the war. An upside-down DC3 with a jeep still inside is also said to be in the area.

Rafting the Watut River

PNG has countless rivers ideally suited for white-water rafting, but Sobek Expeditions pioneered rafting in this country on the Watut. Unfortunately, the last we heard was that expeditions on the Watut had become at best irregular because of problems with rascals. It's possible to raft all the way from Bulolo down to the Markham River.

Walking in the Wau Area

There is some good, if difficult, walking in the Wau area. One thing to inquire about is whether the clans in the area you plan on visiting are currently displeased with one another, that is, thumping each other.

These walks are 'adventures', not mere treks. Some Australian soldiers I met said the Black Cat was the hardest walk they'd ever done, mainly because the trail heads straight for its objective rather than following the less difficult ridges – a common problem with PNG trails. You walk straight up and straight down a lot. Guides are highly recommended and you should expect a hard slog and be properly equipped. Ask the people at WEI to recommend a guide. For full information on the Black Cat Track and other trails in this area see Lonely Planet's *Bushwalking in Papua New Guinea*.

Black Cat Track The Black Cat Track, which begins 14 km from WEI near Wandumi Forest Station, is the old gold miners' route between Wau and Salamaua. The path is in reasonable condition and it takes about three days of hard walking. Don't consider walking up from the coast.

The track reaches the lowlands by way of the Francisco River. The track between Buidanima and Wapali is hard. The remainder of the trail is generally easy to walk but there are numerous potentially dangerous crossings of the Bitoi River between Wapali and Mubo. Water is plentiful throughout the walk but there are no stores along the trail.

June, July and August are the best months, although May and September can also be quite nice.

Bulldog Track The old WW II Bulldog Track, intended to link Wau with the south coast, runs on from Edie Creek. The track never actually got to the coast – from Bulldog you had to travel by river. Since the war, the track has deteriorated and been cut by landslides and slips in many places. Good walkers, preferably with a guide, can walk to Bulldog in about three days from where you *may* be able to get a boat down river to the south coast. Serious planning is required and this walk should definitely not be undertaken lightly.

Lake Trist This lake south-east of Wau and a two-day walk from Wera Wera village, is apparently worth visiting and is stocked with golden carp. There is no village at the lake.

Places to Stay & Eat
The *Wau Ecology Institute* (WEI) (☎ 44 6218, fax 44 6381, PO Box 77) is one of the best places in PNG for budget travellers. It's a couple of km out of Wau on a hillside overlooking the town, so get a ride or ask your PMV to take you to the 'ecology' – you'll have a hard walk if you don't.

The institute undertakes a variety of research projects and they provide accommodation for visiting researchers, but they usually have room for travellers as well.

There's a useful book in which people write tips on travel in the area and all over PNG. Some of the comments about WEI are pretty churlish, possibly because some visitors arrive here direct from the First World (having made connections in Moresby) and aren't yet in Third World mode: 'there are too many people wandering around'; 'why no TV?'

There are many four-bunk rooms, where you'll pay K15 a night including breakfast, but they are sometimes booked out by groups so it pays to contact them in advance. There's also a new accommodation centre where beds in three-bed rooms cost K20. The new units have tea and coffee-making facilities and fridges. Wherever you stay you can use cooking facilities or buy meals; lunch is K5 and dinner K10. You're better off cooking your own. About 100 researchers a year use the facilities at WEI and there is separate long-term accommodation for them.

When you're at the WEI, ask about the *Elauru Village Guesthouse*. In cooperation with the WEI, the Elauru people have decided to opt for tourism and research rather than logging as a source of income, and their new guesthouse has been highly recommended. Accommodation costs K5 a night and there are very knowledgeable guides who will take you on excellent walks for K2. The guesthouse is in the Kuper Range, about two hours' drive from Wau. The WEI can take you there for K5.

About 25 km from Wau on the road to Bulolo and Lae, the big *Katharine Lehmann School* (☎ 44 6232, fax 44 6215, PO Box 81, Wau) has two and three-bedroom houses

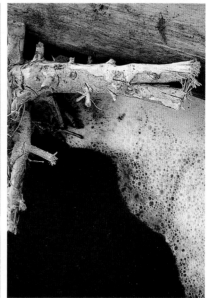

Top: Japanese bomber near Amron, Madang Province (JM)
Left: Karkar Island, Madang Province (JM)
Right: Black-sand beach at Malolo, Madang Province (JM)

Top: Siar Island, near Madang Province (RE)
Bottom: Spear fishing, Kranket Island lagoon, near Madang Province (RE)

which they let as holiday homes. You can do your own cooking (the charge is K25 per person), or you can eat with the students for K32. Meals might not be available outside term time. They have a car which you can rent for just K0.40 per km.

The *Pine Lodge Resort* (☎ 44 5220, PO Box 90) in Bulolo is owned by Melanesian Tourist Services, so the hotel is suitably luxurious. It is, however, on the market so things might change. There are 14 comfortable, furnished bungalows, each with a private balcony overlooking the Bulolo Valley. It has a swimming pool and aviaries in landscaped gardens. All this has a price: singles/doubles cost K105/130. It also organises tours to the surrounding district.

Also in Bulolo, there's apparently accommodation at the *PNG Forestry College* for K20 or K10 for students. To get there, head towards Wau on the main road and turn right at the market and keep going until you come to the plymill, where you turn right.

Remember that in Wau you're up at an altitude of about 1200 metres so come prepared for chilly nights.

Getting There & Away

Air Wau airstrip has nothing to remind you of its former level of activity. It's one of the steepest airstrips in PNG, falling 91 metres in its 1000-metre length. Very definitely one way!

Talair flies to Wau from Moresby, Monday to Saturday, for K95. Wau to Bulolo costs K22 and to Lae it's K52. Bulolo to Lae is K45. Other airlines fly in this area, but only on charters.

PMV Coming from Lae, several PMVs (trucks) leave from the Eriku long-distance PMV stop on Bumbu Rd fairly early in the morning, say before 9 am. In Wau, PMVs stop near the market and most going to Lae leave early. You can pre-buy a ticket to Lae at the store downhill and across the road from the market, and this PMV leaves at 7 am, costs K5.40 and runs nearly nonstop.

The pre-buy scheme was instituted as a hold-up deterrent, on the theory that rascals wouldn't bother to rob a vehicle which they know isn't full of people carrying K5 fares. This has the worrying implication that a potential haul of around K100 is worth the risk of a long jail sentence.

The road to Wau splits off the Highland Highway only a few km out of Lae. There are still long unsealed sections which are pretty rough but roadworks are underway. The road crosses the wide Markham River on a single lane concrete bridge, then twists, turns and winds up into the hills. Mumeng, around the mid-point, is the only town of any size that it passes through.

Walking Another way to get to Lae would be to walk to Salamaua (three days) and from there catch a boat to Lae (around K5).

MENYAMYA & ASEKI

Menyamya is in the heart of the old Anga country and is now a coffee growing centre; it's not particularly interesting in itself. Some people still wear traditional dress and the area has been recommended for walks.

The Anga used to smoke their dead and leave the mummified bodies in burial caves. They now practise Christian burials. It is possible to see some of these mummified bodies at Aseki, but the landowners' charge up to K15. Maybe the easiest cave to visit is near Koke village – walk around the airstrip, pass the Lutheran mission and keep going to Kalusa village. Here there's a trail to Koke, where you pay a fee to see the mummies and get directions to the cave.

The market days in Aseki are Tuesdays, Thursdays and Saturdays and at Menyamya, Mondays, Thursdays and Saturdays. You can see people in traditional dress, but ask permission before taking photos; they'll probably charge you.

If you have a less than enthusiastic welcome around here, it might be because some visitors haggle bitterly over prices for photos or accommodation, and some jerks have ripped-off villagers and PMV drivers. Morons like that often get their deserts in PNG (with a vengeance) but it makes life difficult for later visitors.

Walking in the Menyamya & Aseki Areas
For full information on the trails mentioned here see Lonely Planet's *Bushwalking in Papua New Guinea*. Guides and thorough planning are essential on these walks, as the country is remote and the inter-clan squabbles can cause problems.

Menyamya to Kerema This beautiful walk passes through the rugged heart of Anga country. Many people still wear traditional dress and life goes on much the way it always has.

June, July and August are the best months to walk although May and September can also be OK. The suggested itinerary takes eight days but you could shorten it to six by flying out of Kamina rather than walking all the way to the Kerema.

A guide is not necessary between Menyamya and Mbauyia, and between Didimaua and Murua. However, one is *essential* from Mbauyia to Didimaua. In Menyamya the district office or the Anga Development Authority can probably help you find someone reliable.

Food can be usually bought in villages along the trail and there are basic trade stores in Menyamya, Hawabango, Kanabea, Kamina and Kerema. There are unreliable trade stores in Murua and along the road between Meware and Wemauwa.

The first section, Menyamya to Mbauyia, basically follows a track on which patrol officers in the '70s rode motorbikes. A road, rarely used, links Kaintiba, Kanabea and Paina, a small village half a day's walk south of Kanabea. The rest of the track is narrower but easy to follow.

Between Mbauyia and Didimaua, the trail follows a difficult path through tough terrain and it's very hot and humid. It's the most difficult section of the walk and requires a fair degree of fitness. However, it's possible to bypass it by flying out from Kamina, half a day's walk due east of Ivandu.

From Didimaua another rough road is followed down to Murua Station. From here Kerema can either be reached by road or by motorised canoe down the Murua River.

Menyamya to Marawaka Expect five or six days of walking on this route. It takes you through the villages of Yagwoingwe, Yakana, Andakombe, Gwalyu, Yamuru and Wauko.

Places to Stay
If you want to stay up in the Menyamya district, contact the Anga Development Authority (☎ 44 0211) which has a guesthouse that costs K15. Meals are available.

Lutheran missionaries have established a basic guesthouse in Aseki costing K5 per night. It has a bucket shower, sink and pit toilet. In Aseki, you can stay with Giatulu and his family for K3 a night. Their very basic guesthouse is past the mission and across the river.

Getting There & Away
Air Talair flies to Menyamya on its Kerema-Lae run on Monday and Friday. From Menyamya the fare is K52 to Kerema and K60 to Lae.

There are no scheduled flights between Aseki and Wau, but if there are a few of you a charter (eg, with MAF) isn't too expensive.

PMV A road runs from Bulolo up to Aseki then on to Menyamya through some extremely rough and absolutely spectacular country. There are PMVs on the route, although they may not run every day; Bulolo to Menyamya costs about K10; from Wau it's about K12 but you'll usually have to change at Bulolo. In Bulolo, PMVs usually leave from the Wabu Trade Store. The road actually bypasses Aseki, so if you're going there make sure the driver knows so he can take you into the village.

ZUMIM
Still in Morobe Province, although a fair way up the Markham Valley on the Highland Highway, this small village to the left of the road, has an interesting local pottery industry where you can buy crudely fired pots.

SIASSI ISLANDS
The Siassi Group is between the mainland and New Britain. **Umboi Island** (Rooke

Island) is the largest with a total area of 777 sq km and a number of settlements. Siassi is the main village; there are two good boat anchorages at Marien Harbour and Luther. On the south-east side of Umboi is Lablab mission where there's a guesthouse.

Slightly north of Umboi is the sometimes violently volcanic island of **Sakar**, only 34 sq km in area. **Tolokiwa**, a little to the west, is wooded and inhabited but it too has a conical volcano, 1377 metres high. All these islands are in the volcanic belt which extends through New Britain and down to the north coast of New Guinea.

Getting There & Away
Talair flies to Lablab and Siassi on Umboi from Lae and Finschhafen. Lutheran Shipping passenger vessels sail to Lablab from Lae; their passenger-carrying freighters sail to Siassi. The fare on a local boat from Finschhafen to Siassi is about K5.

Madang Province

Land Area 28,000 sq km
Population 290,000
Capital Madang

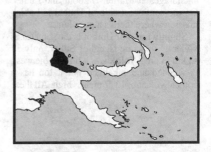

Madang Province consists of a fertile coastal strip backed by some of the most rugged mountains in PNG – the Adelbert and Schrader ranges to the north and the Finisterre Ranges to the south. Offshore are a string of interesting, and still active, volcanic islands. More or less in the middle of the coastal stretch stands Madang town – quite possibly the most beautiful town in the whole country, even, some claim, in the whole Pacific.

HISTORY

The Russian biologist Nicolai Miklouho-Maclay was probably the first European to spend any length of time on the mainland of PNG. He arrived on Astrolabe Bay, south of the present site of Madang, in 1871 and settled in for a 15-month stay before leaving to regain his health, which was badly affected by malaria. His interest in New Guinea led to two further, equally lonely visits.

Unlike many explorers who followed him, his relations with the local tribes were remarkably good and his studies still make fascinating reading. He was suitably amazed by the large, two-masted, sailing canoes of the Madang people and named the islands in Madang Harbour the 'Archipelago of Contented Men'.

The German New Guinea Kompagnie turned up 13 years later, but their stay, although longer, was rather less successful. As Maclay had found to his cost, the northern New Guinea coast was unhealthy and rife with malaria and the disease followed the Germans as they moved first from Finschhafen to Bogadjim on Astrolabe Bay and then on to Madang. If malaria didn't get them then Blackwater Fever usually did.

From 1884 to 1899 a total of 224 officials worked for the company, of whom 41 died and 133 either resigned or were dismissed. Gavin Souter's book *The Last Unknown* depressingly describes the sheer misery of working for 'the bloody bone' as the company became known.

On the point of failure, the German Government took over and moved to the healthier climate of Kokopo near Rabaul on New Britain, but the coast still has many German names and mission stations, although gravestones are almost the only reminders of the old company.

In WW II the Japanese soon took Madang, but after the recapture of Lae, Australian troops slowly and painfully pushed the Japanese along the coast to their final defeat at Wewak. The bitter fighting for control of 'Shaggy Ridge' and the route over the Finisterre Ranges to Madang, started in late 1943 and it took a full month to push the Japanese down to the coast and on towards Wewak.

Madang was virtually demolished during the war and had to be totally rebuilt. Even the old German cemetery bears scars from the vicious fighting. Madang's importance as a major north coast port, from where freight was flown up to the Highlands, was drastically changed when the Highlands Highway shifted business to Lae. Now that a new road has shortened the distance

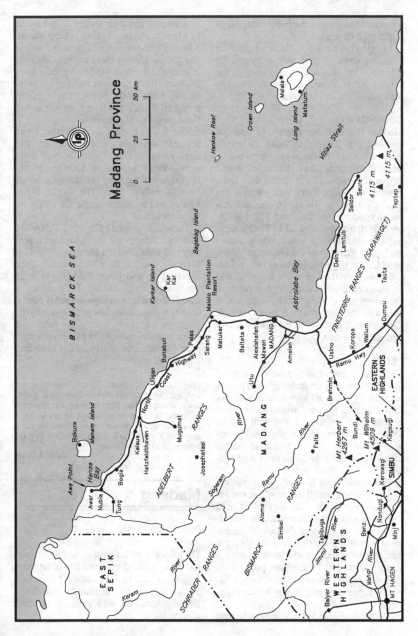

Madang Province

between Madang and the Highlands, things might pick up again.

Logging has since brought money into the town – a smoking pulp mill disfigures the harbour – but clear-felling is destroying the inland jungles and is threatening the province's bird and animal life.

GEOGRAPHY

Madang Province is composed of strips of lowland and mountain. Along the fertile coast, coconuts and cocoa have been grown since the German days. Inland, mountain ranges rise parallel to the coast then slope down to the Ramu River Valley which also parallels the coast. This is productive cattle country and home to the Ramu Sugar Refinery, which meets almost all of PNG's sugar requirements. Only a low divide separates the Upper Ramu from the Markham Valley, in which the Highland Highway runs to Lae.

Inland from the Ramu, the Bismarck and Schrader ranges rise to the highest peaks in the country, including Mt Wilhelm which stands on the border with Simbu Province. The volcanic islands off the coast are still periodically active.

PEOPLE

The diverse geographic nature of the province is reflected in the make-up of its people who can, by virtue of lifestyle, be broken into four distinct groups: islanders, coastal people, river people and mountain people. These groups are alike in physical appearance, apart from the small-statured Simbai tribes who inhabit the foothills of the Highlands.

Traditional dress is rarely worn, but the majority of people still live in villages and at a subsistence level. The coconut is used extensively, except in the mountains. Islanders depend on seafood; the coastal people grow a variety of different root crops, bananas and tropical fruits; the river people's staple is sago; and the mountain people base their diet on the sweet potato, although this is now supplemented by many Western vegetables.

The Manam islanders live around the base of a volcano and their society is dominated by a hereditary chief, known as the *Kukurai*. Although there are different language groups, the Manam clans are related to the people who live along the lower sections of the Ramu River, the north coast of the province and the lower Sepik. The artefacts produced on Manam Island are not unlike those produced on the Sepik.

There are even closer artistic links between the Ramu and the Sepik. The mighty Ramu is almost linked to the Keram, and thence to the Sepik, so there was probably extensive trade and cultural interchange for thousands of years. The way of life is similar, and the Ramu people are also great wood carvers.

The nearby coastal villagers of Yabob and Bilbil are famous for the earthenware pots they make and, like the Motuans of the Port Moresby district, they once traded these items far up and down the coast in large lalaoika (trading vessels). Their attractive houses are made from sago and toddy palms, usually without nails. The walls and fold-out windows are made from sago palm leaf stems tied into frames and panels with sago palm leaves, either intertwined or sewn into long shingles.

I had an insight into a culture, my own, when we visited a village. Our tour leader explained how 'these people don't understand time. They have day and they have night, they have the wet season and the dry season...' Meanwhile, the local drivers were wondering how much longer this guy would talk, as they had to be back at the hotel by 12.20 for another tour.

David A Court

Madang

Population 25,000

The title of 'prettiest town in the Pacific' may not be an official one, but has often been applied to Madang. The town is perched on a peninsula jutting out into the sea and is liberally sprinkled with parks, ponds and waterways.

The warm, wet climate and fertile soil lead to luxuriant growth and many of the huge trees, planted by the Germans, survived the war and still tower over Madang's gently curving roads (and house huge colonies of bats). A scatter of perfect islands around the town's deep-water harbour completes the picture.

Unfortunately, as in so many other towns in PNG, the beautiful rain trees are being severely lopped or cut down altogether. The reason is that they have a nasty habit of dropping their huge branches on people and property, but they aren't being replaced. Madang is now perhaps a less pretty town than Rabaul.

Madang is the most tourist-oriented city in PNG and this, fortunately, translates into a wide range of facilities but falls a long way short of being plastic. It is not, however, the place to come to if you want to see untouched local cultures. By far the greatest attraction is what lies beneath the surface of the sea. There are some excellent places to stay beside the sea, in all price brackets.

Until recently Madang seemed to be immune from rascal problems – people fondly imagined that it was just too beautiful for such things! Although there is nothing like the unfortunate atmosphere in Lae, and houses are not fortresses in disguise, it is wise to be a little cautious. Western swimming costumes should be worn with discretion. A local told me 'Madang is quite safe now, day and night', but by 'now' she meant since the troubles a month previously – the situation changes all the time.

Orientation

Madang is built on a peninsula; on the southeastern side, Coronation Drive faces across Astrolabe Bay to the beautiful Finisterre ranges and on the north-western side the town faces across the still waters of Binnen and Madang harbours to the airport and the palm-lined coast. The top of the peninsula on the north-western side faces the entrance to the harbours and Dallman Passage, which separates the peninsula from Kranket Island. The main shopping and business area is here,

at the end of the main road running the full length of the peninsula, Modilon Rd.

The airport, which is at least seven km from the main area of town (you have to cross the Wagol River and skirt Binnen Harbour), is not within walking distance. See the Getting There & Away section.

Information

The Madang Visitors Bureau (☎ 82 3302, fax 82 3540, PO Box 2025, Yomba) is on Modilon Rd at the intersection with Coronation Drive, near the provincial government offices. They produce a rather limited range of information on the province, but they will definitely be able to help you out if you have any queries. The Bureau is being incorporated into the cultural centre.

The shopping in Madang is not as extensive as in Lae, but you'll have no problems with essentials. There's a post office, banks and Air Niugini, Talair and Lutheran Shipping all have offices here. The third-level airline Island Airways (not to be confused with Rabaul's Islands Aviation) is based in Madang – book through Talair.

Melanesian Tourist Services (☎ 82 2766, fax 82 3543, PO Box 707), which runs the *Melanesian Discoverer* and a number of tours and places to stay in PNG, is based at the Madang Resort Hotel, where there's also a travel agency.

There's apparently a nightclub in town, not far from the Lutheran Shipping Wharf.

Cultural Centre

The centre, in Haus Tumbuna on Modilon Rd near the intersection with Coronation Drive, was a small but interesting museum – at the time of writing it was closed for expansion so it will definitely be worth visiting. There are statues, shields, spears, jewellery and musical instruments from the period of German occupation, and there are examples of contemporary carvings and paintings. There are also models of traditional local boats. The lalaoika, a one-masted canoe, and the *balangut*, a two-masted canoe, are beautiful vessels. They were used in trading fish and pottery along the coast. Lalaoika were once made at Bilbil village but they became obsolete with the arrival of roads, PMVs and outboard motors. One was built in 1977 for a royal visit, but it has since rotted away.

No-one is yet sure of the new opening hours, but the cultural centre will be open on weekdays and perhaps weekends.

Cemetery

In the centre of town, near the market, is the old German cemetery. Madang was the New Guinea Kompagnie's last attempt at a foothold on the mainland before they packed it in and moved to New Britain. The malaria in Madang Province was (and is) extremely virulent and this rather bleak little cemetery attests to that fact.

Market

The colourful and popular market is at its busy best on Saturdays. Apart from the vegetables and fruit, there is a section for handcrafts and artefacts. The local shell jewellery can be a bargain.

Parks & Ponds

Madang has some delightful parks and ponds – one of them liberally decked in water lilies – but all with ominous signs to warn you of crocodiles. Opinions differ as to whether there actually are any crocodiles left.

When the Germans decided, in 1904, to attack malaria by filling in the swamps around the town, thus creating these ponds, the locals did not take to forced labour. A plot against the Germans was stifled by the drastic action of rounding up the ringleaders and shooting them. They were buried on Siar Island in the harbour.

Coastwatcher's Memorial

This 30-metre-high beacon is visible 25 km out to sea, a reminder of those men who stayed behind the lines during the last war to report on Japanese troop and ship movements. The coast road from the memorial is one of the most pleasant in Madang, fringed by palm trees and poincianas and backed by the golf course with fine views across Astrolabe Bay towards the Rai Coast.

Activities

You can get out on the exceptionally beautiful harbour by yourself using local boats, or with a cruise.

Two islands that are commonly visited are Kranket and Siar; both are easily accessible for day trips. See the Around Madang section for more information; it's possible to stay cheaply on both these islands. Wherever you stay, you must take advantage of the harbour and the superb underwater scenery, whether through glass-viewing boxes, snorkelling or skin diving.

Swimming The small Lion's Reserve Beach, just north of the Smugglers' Inn, has excellent coral and tropical fish just a few strokes from the shore. It's not so good at low tide, however, when sea urchins and sharp coral wait for the unwary foot. Not far away there are two or three tiny bays with minuscule beaches along Coastwatcher's Drive near the end of Ixora Ave. You can also swim in the inlet by the CWA Guesthouse.

Other favourite – and much better – spots are Siar Island, Kranket Lagoon, Pig Island (an exceptionally beautiful little island, despite the name) and Wongat Island.

Snorkelling & Diving The snorkelling and diving are excellent, and the area is justifiably world famous. There is excellent visibility, superb coral, and if you're diving, many WW II wrecks. There is a wide range of different dive locations within 15 minutes of town and many more up the coast.

You can hire gear from Niugini Diving Adventures (☎ 82 2766, PO Box 707) at the Madang Resort Hotel, and they have some packages which include accommodation and dives. Snorkelling gear costs K10 a day and for K15 they'll take you along with divers, perhaps dropping you off at Pig Island. Skin diving gear costs K15 per day to hire and dives cost K30, less if you do a number of dives. Courses are also available.

If you are just snorkelling, have a word to them about possible locations. Other good places are Lion's Reserve Beach, Siar Island, the reef in the beautiful Kranket Lagoon, Pig

Island and around Sinaub Island. If you take a dugout out from Siar or Kranket to dive further from shore never do it alone. There are very strong currents in some places and the boat could easily drift away, leaving you stranded.

The Coastwatcher's Motel also offers diving and certificate courses.

You can hire snorkelling gear on Siar and Kranket islands for K4. Apparently, you can miss out on equipment at Siar, so you're probably best to rent in town.

A short drive north of town, the Jais Aben Resort (☎ 82 3311) specialises in diving. If you have a meal there you can use their facilities, including their swimming pool. They hire small boats and snorkelling gear. It's an interesting place that combines tourism and diving with facilities for serious marine research. See the North Coast Highway section, where there's also information on the Malolo Plantation Resort which also has diving.

Do-it-Yourself Harbour Cruises If you want to organise your own voyage around the harbour you can do it easily and cheaply. Wander down behind the Lutheran Shipping office, or just behind the Madang Club, and you'll find a ferry service that shuttles across to Kranket Island for just K0.30. It's irregular, but usually fairly frequent, and you could hardly do it cheaper. Sundays are quiet and the boat makes fewer trips.

Another method is to take a PMV to Siar village for K0.60 (you might be dropped on the highway and have to walk a few km to the village), then negotiate a ride across to Siar Island. It's only a short distance, but expect to pay at least K1. You can also find canoes for longer cruises.

A third alternative is to rent your own transport. Smith Keenan and Saimon Tewa on Siar Island hire canoes for around K5, and they are also available at Jais Aben Resort. Afternoons tend to get windy, stirring up waves and making it hard to paddle, but this is a great way to get around. Definitely take a T-shirt and suntan lotion: you can really fry out there!

Rooke's Marine (☎ 82 2325, PO Box 427) rent outboard boats for K80 a day, plus a deposit, or a little less if you drive yourself. The Jais Aben Resort has similar rates, and also a larger, faster and much more expensive boat suitable for groups.

If you're driving or paddling yourself, stay well away from Dallman Passage, the strait between Kranket Island and the mainland. This is the main shipping channel and some of the freighters hulking through are enormous. The same applies to the wharf area.

Organised Tours The Madang Resort's harbour tour departs every morning at 9 am and costs K25, with a minimum of two people. You get picked up from your hotel and taken to see the rusting wreckage of Japanese landing craft, Kranket Island where you can view the fish and coral formations through glass-bottomed viewing boxes, and Siar Island where you get a chance to wander around or snorkel for an hour or so.

The Coastwatcher's Motel has full-day tours to Kranket Island for K18 and harbour cruises for just K12. Smith Keenan, who runs a guesthouse on Siar Island, does a four-hour harbour tour for K15. Make sure you understand what you're getting.

Several places, including the Madang Resort Hotel and the Malolo Plantation Resort on the north coast, offer pricey tours of villages. If you haven't yet managed to see a sing-sing and don't plan on visiting areas of PNG where traditional culture remains strong, these tours could be interesting, but don't expect to find spontaneity.

There is plenty of bird life in the area (although the heavy-handed logging of the inland rainforest is threatening it) and Malolo Plantation Resort can take you to some good birdwatching places.

Places to Stay – bottom end
There are some good choices in Madang and the best is the *CWA Guesthouse* (☎ 82 2216, PO Box 154). Its location is excellent, not far from the town centre and on the harbour between the Madang Club and the Madang

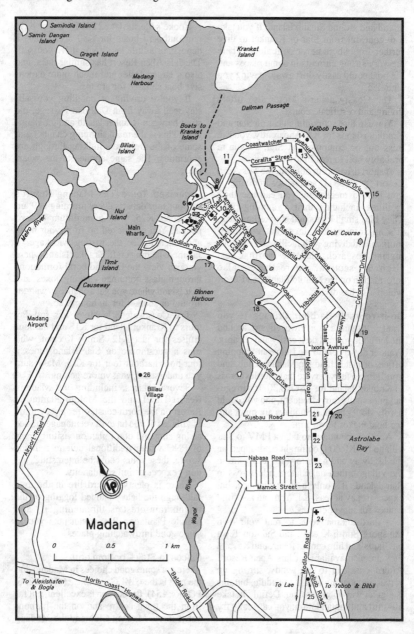

Madang

0   0.5   1 km

Resort Hotel, both good places for a meal and a drink. There aren't many beds so booking ahead is not a bad idea. The friendly woman who runs the place is only there from 8 am to noon but there's a live-in caretaker so you can turn up at any time. You'll probably meet other travellers here and there's a notice board.

There is a range of prices, from K16 in a shared room, to K31.50 for a single room (shared bathroom) to K42 for a self-contained family unit which sleeps up to four, but only two adults are allowed. No meals are served, but there are good kitchen facilities.

The *Lutheran Guesthouse* (☎ 82 2589, 82 2895 (AH), PO Box 211) on Coralita St, about midway between the Madang Resort Hotel and the Coastwatcher's Motel, is friendly, very clean and the rooms all have fans and attached bathrooms. It can get busy on weekends so it's worth booking ahead; solo travellers may be asked to share a room. The manager isn't always there but the caretaker lives-in, so you can arrive at any time.

Accommodation is K20 per person (including breakfast) and full board is K32. There's a kitchen. The guesthouse rents a car for K0.50 a km; this is comparatively good value, especially if you can get a group together. Bear in mind that this is a church guesthouse, despite Madang's resort-town atmosphere. Ask here about the cheaper *Lutheran Hostel*, although it's usually full of permanent residents and is pretty grubby.

The *Madang Resort Hotel* (☎ 82 2655, PO Box 111) has one backpacker room where a bunk bed costs K17. That's reasonable value if only one or two people are in the room, but any more and things become cramped. It's one of their older budget rooms with two double bunks in it, so while there's a TV, phone and attached bathroom, there's also air-con and you can't open the windows. You do get to use the hotel's pool. One big advantage of staying here is that you get a free ride to the airport, especially handy if you have an early-morning flight.

There is also an *SIL Guesthouse* (☎ 82 3254, PO Box 675), cheaper than the others at about K15, but located near the provincial government offices, a km or so from the town centre.

There are three other bottom-end alternatives within a few minutes of town, on Siar Island and Kranket Island. Siar Island has two competing village guesthouses and Kranket has a good hostel as well as more expensive accommodation. They're definitely worth considering and if you're planning to be in the area for more than a day or two, staying on one of the islands is almost obligatory – and cheap. See the Around Madang section. Smith Keenan, one of the guesthouse owners on Siar, is planning to build self-contained units on nearby Pig Island, a pretty place, which will cost about K15 per person.

Places to Stay – middle & top end
The *Madang Lodge* (☎ 82 3395, fax 82

3292, PO Box 59) is clean, comfortable and reasonable value. A notch or two above the bottom-end accommodation, it's still fairly spartan. It's on the coast on Modilon Rd not far from Smugglers' Inn. There's a rocky little cove where you can swim and snorkel. Singles/doubles with fan and shared bathroom cost K30/35, and rooms with bathroom and air-con are K40/50, plus K10 for each extra person. All prices include breakfast but not the 5% bed tax.

The *Madang Resort Hotel* (☎ 82 2655, PO Box 111) has a superb setting, looking over the harbour and across to Kranket Island. The hotel has a swimming pool and a haus win (open air) restaurant right by the water. There is a wide range of rooms and prices, ranging from K37 for budget rooms without sea views to over K200 for some of the waterfront bungalows. These prices are for single occupancy; add K10 for each extra person and 5% tax. What you get is what you pay for: the top end is luxury, self-contained waterfront bungalows; the bottom end (which is not too bad at all) is a motel-type room with a TV and coffee-making facilities. One of these is now reserved for backpackers.

The grounds are superb and include the Elizabeth Sowerby Orchid Collection and cages with cuscus, hornbills, cockatoos and other wildlife. Niugini Diving Adventures have their shop by the water, and there's a jetty for the *Melanesian Discoverer* which journeys to the Sepik and around Milne Bay.

Unfortunately, in the cheaper rooms there are hints of falling standards. This also applies to the other top hotel in town, *Smugglers' Inn* (☎ 82 2744, PO Box 303), which has long had a reputation as one of PNG's best hotels.

Smugglers' is built on the waterfront on Modilon Rd, where the open-air restaurant offers superb coastal views and breezes and an outdoor bar area juts out into the water. There's a swimming pool or you can snorkel at the Lion's Reserve Beach only 50 metres away. There are two categories of rooms, which cost a flat K55 and K70, plus 5%, whether there are one, two or three people in

them. The food is good – see the Places to Eat section.

The *Coastwatcher's Motel* (☎ 82 2684, fax 82 2716, PO Box 324) is on Coastwatcher's Ave, near the Coastwatcher's Memorial. It is a little characterless – it is a motel – but is newer and in better condition than the two main top-enders. All rooms are air-conditioned, have fridges, TVs and telephones. The motel also has a restaurant and a swimming pool. Singles/doubles range from K52/62 to K89/99, including light breakfast. The bar is a friendly spot for a cold beer and can get quite lively in the evenings.

The *Jais Aben Resort* is strongly oriented to diving and is about 14 km from Madang just north of Nagada Harbour. Further out is the *Malolo Plantation Resort*. See the North Coast Highway section for both.

Places to Eat

Steamships has the usual lunchtime sandwiches and fried food, and across the road in the market you can buy fresh produce. A drinking coconut costs about K0.10.

Jo Jo's Restaurant at the Madang Club offers good, plain food at low prices. Snacks cost from K1 and omelettes are just K2.50. A few meals are under K5, and Chinese meals start at K8. Steaks cost from K8 and seafood from K9. It's a relaxed, friendly place and is open daily from 11 am to 2 pm and 6 to 9 pm. Foreign volunteers working in the area often eat here. The rest of the Madang Club is similarly low-key, with snooker, darts and raffles the main entertainment. There's a good view of the harbour from the bar. Visitors are welcome, although getting into the snooker room might require some networking. The dress regulations ban singlets, but that's about all (and doesn't seem to deter members from wearing them). You can still see some old German steps near the club.

At the *Madang Lodge* lunch costs about K6 and dinner around K12.

At the *Country Club* (read golf club), along Coastwatcher's Ave, you can get cheap meals from Tuesday to Saturday and snacks like pies and sandwiches. You have to be signed in. It opens from 4 pm Monday to Friday and noon on Saturday and Sunday. There is also a bar, of course.

Consider spoiling yourself with a meal at the Smugglers' Inn or Madang Resort Hotel – it is quite a magical sitting out by the water on a balmy tropical night eating good food.

The restaurant at the *Madang Resort Hotel* is in a haus win by the sea and is open in the evenings only, except for Sunday when there's a K12.50 barbecue lunch. Main courses start at around K14, and for K16 you can have crocodile meat. There's a bamboo band most nights, and the hotel's main bar is here (open day and night for drinks and snacks) so you don't need to have a meal to enjoy a serenaded drink while looking out over the harbour.

The hotel also has a coffee shop, open for breakfast and lunch until 4 pm. An omelette, spaghetti or a steak sandwich will set you back K6. Pizzas are available from 10 am to 2 pm and 5 to 9.30 pm Tuesday to Sunday and they offer free delivery (☎ 82 2655). The various sizes of the 'supreme' model cost K6.50/10.50/14.50.

Smugglers' Inn has a similarly well-situated restaurant with good food and prices comparable to the hotel's, perhaps a little lower. Their restaurant is open for lunch as well as dinner, and the lunchtime prices are good value, with the seafood basket costing just K8.

The restaurant at the *Coastwatcher's Motel* offers good-value counter lunches from just K3 and dinners from K10; their Chinese steamboat is recommended.

Things to Buy

The clay pots from Bilbil village are the most interesting traditional local items. If you buy them, make sure they are very carefully packed as, like other PNG pottery, they are extremely fragile.

There are thriving artefacts workshops and marketplaces at Smugglers' Inn (where you can see a carver in action) and the Madang Resort Hotel, dominated by women from the Sepik and the Ramu. There are excellent selections of billums, shell jewellery and carvings. Don't rush into your purchases, and remember there is often a 'second price'.

Getting There & Away

Air The airport is about seven km from town, which is too far to walk unless you are very keen – see the Getting Around section for local transport details. Madang hopes to be granted PNG's second international airport, a hope shared by several other towns.

Air Niugini is at the airport (☎ 82 2255) and Talair (☎ 82 2946) has an office in town, which also handles Island Airways flights. MAF (☎ 82 2229) has a few flights in the province.

Air Niugini has flights from Port Moresby (K129), Lae (K68), Mt Hagen (K67) and Wewak (K90), and also has weekend packages offering fares from Port Moresby and accommodation in Madang. See the Getting Around chapter.

Talair flies to Goroka (K54) most days and less frequently to Kundiawa (K68) but no longer to any of the smaller strips around Madang Province. Island Airways (☎ 82 2601) flies to Bundi (on the way to Mt Wilhelm, K50), Saidor (east along the coast, K50), Karkar Island (K40) and many other small strips.

The flight from Goroka is very brief and quite interesting as you climb up and over the southern fringe of the Highlands, then over the Ramu Valley and drop down to the coast. Flying to or from Wewak, you can see the mouths of the Ramu and Sepik rivers as they meander and loop to the coast, joined by many tributaries.

PMV Madang is linked to the Highlands Highway by the Ramu Highway and roads run in both directions along the coast. The North Coast Highway runs nearly 250 km north-west, virtually to the mouth of the Ramu River, and south-east to Saidor.

There are PMVs on all these routes. PMVs for the north coast leave from near the big *pikus* (fig) tree on Bates Oval, behind the post office. All other PMVs leave from the market area, a block away. You might have to walk around for a while to find the right place to wait as they are not concentrated in one area.

Heading north, the PMV fare to (or near) Siar village is K0.60, Riwo/Jais Aben is K1, Alexishafen is K1, Malolo is K2 and to Bogia, near the end of the North Coast Highway, it's K6. Heading south, the PMV fare to Yabob village is K0.50, Bilbil village is K0.60, Usino is about K7 and Ramu Sugar is K10.

Sea Madang is on the main north coast shipping route that is so well serviced by Lutheran Shipping (☎ 82 2577, 82 2146; fax 82 2180, PO Box 789) on Modilon Rd.

Once again, the most important options are Lutheran Shipping's *Mamose Express* and *Rita*. Eastbound boats depart for Lae at 9 am on Sunday morning. Westbound, you arrive in Madang on Thursday morning and leave at 5 pm on Friday, so you get nearly two days in Madang, which is enough time to have a good look around. Tourist/deck-class fares from Madang to either Lae or Wewak are K21.50/32.50; Madang-Oro Bay through fares are K35/52.50.

Lutheran Shipping has several considerably less comfortable freighters that also call in to Madang on their way to west to Wewak and Vanimo, and east to Lae then Oro Bay or West New Britain. Deck/1st-class fares from Madang include: Wewak K19/23, Vanimo K29.50/35, Lae K18/23 and Oro Bay K19/23.

Occasional Lutheran Shipping freighters run to Lorengau on Manus Island for K21/26. The Manus Provincial Government's boat, the *Tawi*, runs irregularly from Lorengau to Wewak via Wuvulu Island, sometimes calling in at Madang.

A boat runs to Karkar Island daily from the Rab-Trad (Rabaul Trading) wharf, near Lutheran Shipping, stopping at Biabi (K6) and Kulili (K8).

Poromon Shipping used to take passengers on a freighter along the coast to the Sepik and upriver as far as Green River, but the company has been taken over by Lutheran Shipping which does not take passengers on the run. A great pity.

Car Rental Avis (☎ 82 2804) has a desk at the airport and at the Madang Resort Hotel and Budget (☎ 82 3044) operates from Smugglers' Inn. Lastly, the Lutheran Guesthouse (☎ 82 2589) rents a car for K0.50 a km.

To/From the Highlands The Ramu Highway joins the Highlands Highway at Watarais, and while the Ramu Highway is now quite OK, it can still be closed by floods. A new road is due to open which will cut across to the Highlands Highway from Dumpu, joining the Highway at Henganofi, midway between Kainantu and Goroka. This will make the trip much shorter and perhaps mean that there will be more PMVs running direct to Goroka – currently you usually have to change at Watarais. See the Highlands chapter for details on the Highlands Highway. PMVs leave from the Madang market.

There are currently some direct PMVs to Goroka for around K20 (almost all leaving Madang fairly early in the morning) and taking about seven hours. When the new road opens the time should be much less and the fare might drop too.

It's an interesting drive along the Ramu Highway, passing through many isolated villages, past beautiful mountain and jungle scenery. There are still some unbridged rivers to be fjorded. You also pass Usino, where you may be able to find shoestring accommodation (see the Inland section) and Ramu Sugar Refinery.

It is possible to walk from Brahmin Mission via Bundi (Island Airways flies there for K50) to Kegsugl, at the foot of Mt Wilhelm, where you can catch a PMV to Kundiawa in Simbu Province. This would probably take a minimum of four or five hot, hard days; it is much easier to walk down from Mt Wilhelm. See the Walking to Madang section under Simbu Province in the Highlands chapter.

To/From Wewak There are daily 40-minute flights with Air Niugini to Wewak for K90. Travelling on the *Mamose Express* or the *Rita*, you leave Madang at 5 pm on Friday and arrive in Wewak early Saturday morning. Fares are K27/18 for tourist/deck class. There are also freighters.

To/From Lae See To/From Madang in the Getting There & Away section in the Morobe Province chapter.

Getting Around
To/From the Airport All the middle and top-end places to stay in Madang (and the Jais Aben Resort) offer free airport transfers. You can also take a PMV into town from the small Rotary Park across the road from the terminal, but only during the day. The blue 'DCA' PMV definitely runs to town and there may be others. Most of the people in the park will be waiting for a PMV, so ask around. Taxis into town cost about K5 but make sure you agree on the price before you get in.

PMV There are frequent PMVs around Madang with a standard K0.30 fare in town. There are also plenty going further out – see the Getting There & Away section. The market is the PMV hub.

Taxi Madang Taxi Hire (☎ 82 2184) are reliable and a couple of kina will get you to most places in town; K5 should get you to the airport.

AROUND MADANG
Kranket Island
Kranket, just across the Dallman Passage from Madang town, is a large island with several villages and an absolutely beautiful lagoon. Once you're on Kranket Island you can wander around, swim, snorkel, or find somebody to take you further out on an outrigger canoe.

At the other end of the island, on the eastern side of the lagoon, there's a picnic area. As you cruise across the stunningly clear waters of the lagoon and approach the private jetty leading to immaculate lawns, it seems as though you're arriving at a $200-a-day resort. No. You pay only K1 to use the facilities provided by the owners, the Dum (pronounced 'doum') Clan, and the accommodation here is a bargain. The caretaker rents snorkelling gear for K4. The picnic area receives a fair number of visitors on weekends, but midweek it's quiet.

Places to Stay The *Dum Clan* also operates the lodges and hostel which adjoin the picnic area. The cheapest option is the *Hostel*, a large, clean house with four or five bedrooms, a pleasant lounge and a kitchen with a gas stove and refrigerator. It's much better than the average village guesthouse and a steal at K10 per person in shared rooms. Bring your own food.

Kranket Island Lodge (PO Box 800, Madang) consists of two well-built bungalows, both with private bathrooms, kitchens and hot and cold water. Each has a dining room, a bedroom with four or five beds, plus a large, furnished lounge room overlooking the water. The all up cost is K60 per night – and you really get all the comforts of home. You can book the lodge (but not the hostel) through the Madang Resort Hotel (☎ 82 2655) who will organise transfers.

Getting There & Away Small boats run to Kranket from near the Town Clinic, on an inlet behind the CWA Guesthouse, for K0.30 for the 10-minute ride. There are boats approximately hourly from 7 am to about 5.30 pm. They take you to the end of the island closest to Madang; the accommodation is right up the other end and it's a walk of about 45 minutes. You might be able to persuade the driver to drop you at the hostel for another K1 or so.

Biliau Island
There are three wrecked Japanese freighters and a small landing barge on Biliau Island, the large island right in the middle of the Madang Harbour. More Japanese barges can be seen further to the right. You can reach the

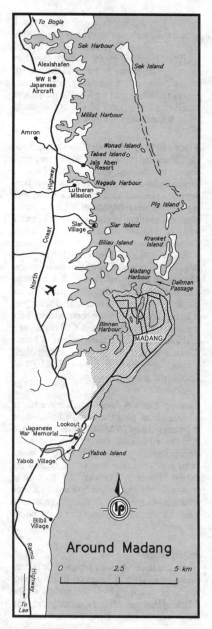

island by canoe while staying at Siar village or from the Madang Hotel.

Siar Island

Siar is a small island and is a popular spot for picnics, barbecues and snorkelling, and it's just a short boat ride from town. On the beach you can see some large chunks of aircraft wreckage and the totally rotted remains of a Japanese barge. With a fellow amateur aircraft expert we decided it was American, WW II of course, twin-engined, possibly a B-25 or a P-38. Any answers?

Somewhere on the island are the graves of those unfortunate victims of the anti-swamp-filling conspiracy. There are reefs on both sides of the island.

The best thing about Siar is the possibility of cheap accommodation, which allows you to make the most of the beach and reefs and learn something about village life.

Places to Stay Two local people have set up simple, basic accommodation for budget travellers. The conditions are not luxurious (there's no electricity on the island, for example), but they are adequate – even families stay. For some people this is a highlight of their PNG trip.

The men who run these two places are serious, even bitter, rivals in the competition to attract foreign shoestringers. The competition has kept prices very low, and it's possible that you could bargain if things are quiet. In a way, it's a pity that prices have stayed so low – another kina or two on the price of a bed and the standards might be higher.

Saimon Tewa (PO Box 887, Madang), contactable through the Madang Club (PO Box 2), is the originator and takes credit for the enterprise. His is the better-known place because it has been going for quite a while. It has the nicer beach and the facilities are OK. Unfortunately, Saimon has a somewhat disreputable reputation, but he has plenty of defenders as well as detractors.

Smith Keenan (PO Box 792, Madang), the upstart, lives nearby, and he has recently moved his guesthouse down to the beach, just like Saimon's. Smith and family are more reserved and pretty much leave you alone unless you make the effort.

Both places are airy bush-material houses with only a few dormitory rooms. Smith's place costs K6 a night and Saimon charges K8 with a little room for negotiation. Both prices include at least two meals a day, so it's an excellent deal. The fare is adequate, but it's worth bringing some of your own food for lunch or to supplement what can be a limited menu (rice and tinned fish).

You can *usually* rent a mask and snorkel although you're taking a chance on quality and availability – renting in Madang is a safer bet. Smith charges K4 for as long as you stay; at Saimon's place it's K4 a day. Smith rents canoes for K6 for your whole stay; Saimon's are a little more expensive. Smith will take you night fishing for K10 and I imagine that Saimon probably will too...

Getting There & Away Saimon drops in at the Madang Club almost daily to see if anyone wants to go to Siar Island. Smith does the same, but at the CWA Guesthouse and the Lutheran Guesthouse. Both charge K2 for the boat trip and it's a nice ride. Smith will pick you up from the airport if he knows that you're coming, but he doesn't have a phone so this is difficult to arrange.

Alternatively you can take a PMV to (or near) Siar village for K0.60 and catch a boat for the short ride from there, for at least K1. To get to the Jais Aben Resort for diving or a meal costs around K3.

Yabob Village
If you take Modilon Rd south out of town, shortly before the right turn to the airport and North Coast road, a road branches off left to Yabob village. You pass a lookout point and a Japanese war memorial on the way to this pretty little village. There's an island nearby, which you can easily arrange to visit by canoe.

Long before Europeans arrived in the area, Yabob was known for its fine clay pots which were traded far up and down the coast,

but unfortunately they have recently stopped making them.

Bilbil Village
This is another attractive village and pottery is still produced here. Take the first road on the left after the Gum River, off the Ramu Highway; this loops back to the highway. A PMV from Madang market costs K0.60.

Balek Wildlife Sanctuary
The sanctuary is currently closed, due to landowner squabbles, but ask around in Madang as it might reopen. Balek is to the right of the Ramu Highway if you're coming from Madang. The Sanctuary ends with the bitumen at the Gogol River. Backtrack to where the power lines cross the road and you'll see a sign.

Around Madang Province

NORTH COAST HIGHWAY
The road runs a long way north-west of Madang and will eventually reach all the way to Wewak. The tar stops at Malolo but beyond there it's in reasonable nick, although bumpy. The road already runs to the Ramu River although the last stretch is not too good and the final section from the Ramu to the Sepik is still a long way in the future. The road will meet the Sepik somewhere downstream from Angoram where vehicles will cross the river by ferry. A road already runs from Angoram into Wewak.

This would be a great road to cycle along. It's flat, mostly in reasonable condition and you're never too far from the beach. There are plenty of villages along the way where you should be able to buy coconuts to drink. Staying in villages for a few nights might allow the budget to stretch for a night of luxury at the Malolo Plantation Resort.

North Coast Diving
There's more good diving along the north

coast from Madang. An hour's drive brings you to a spot where the water drops off 60 metres only a stone's throw from the land. In 35 metres of water, the sunken wreck of the minesweeper *Boston* is a favourite dive. There's the wreck of US freighter *Henry Leith* near the Jais Aben Resort.

At the 'water hole' a lagoon is connected to the open sea by a large underwater tunnel. It's beyond the Malolo Plantation Resort and the enclosed lagoon has sand and is safe for children; it also offers dramatic snorkelling. At Bogia Bay there's a Japanese Zero fighter upside down in the water several hundred yards directly out from the jetty. Hansa Bay has some spectacular wreck dives.

Niugini Diving Adventures, Jais Aben Resort and the Malolo Plantation Resort all organise dives to Hansa Bay and other sites along the north coast.

Nobanob & Nagada

A little beyond the Siar village turn-off on the North Coast Highway, about 14 km from Madang, there are turn-offs to the left and right. The right-hand turn leads to the mission complex on Nagada Harbour. The left-hand turn leads up to Nobanob Mission out-station and was used as a Japanese lookout during the war. There is a fine view over the north coast, Madang and the harbour from up here. It's about a 20-minute drive to the lookout.

Place to Stay *Kristen Pres* (that is, Christian Press) has a big set-up on Nagada Harbour, across from Jais Aben Resort. It sometimes lets houses here, and it's good value – with a house sleeping four or five for about K20 a night or K130 a week. Phone Judy Bok (☎ 82 2035), leave a message and ring again next day for the reply.

Jais Aben Resort

About 16 km from Madang, off the main road, on the waterfront, the *Jais Aben Resort* (☎ 82 3311, fax 82 3560, PO Box 105, Madang) is a great place to stay and about the only up-market place in PNG not to have raised its prices since the last edition of this

book. The Jais Aben Resort specialises in diving and has equipment rentals and boat tours to good dive sites. A couple of km further north, 16 km from Madang, the site of the Japanese WW II strategic command headquarters is off to the left of the road at **Amron**.

Jais Aben has boats for hire from K80 a day and all water sports (except game fishing) are offered. This is apparently the only up-market place in the Madang area where you can snorkel off the resort. It has diving equipment and offers diving trips (snorkellers can go along for K10) and water skiing. You can also hire a canoe.

The resort features spacious grounds, self-contained units (half with their own kitchens), a swimming pool, restaurant and dive centre, all on the seafront. It's an attractive spot. They also provide facilities for serious marine research.

Most people buy a package that includes diving, but the rooms themselves go for around K55/65 for singles/doubles.

Lunches are good value, from at K2.50 to K8, and the dinner menu ranges from K8.50 to K15. Weekend barbecue buffets average around K8. If you buy a meal, you can use the facilities.

Getting There & Away The Jais Aben Resort people can arrange transport to or from Madang (whether or not you're staying at the resort) for K2.50, and they'll collect guests from the airport for nothing. You can take a PMV to the turn-off for K1; some PMVs run you all the way in to the resort, if not it's quite a walk. A taxi from town can cost K20! You can take a canoe from Siar Island for about K3.

Alexishafen

Alexishafen Catholic Mission is off the road to the right, 21 km north of Madang. Like so much of the area it was badly damaged during the war, although the old graveyard still stands as a firm reminder of the number of early missionaries who died for the cause. There is a fine teak forest along the North Coast Highway. The timber is totally unusable since the trees were riddled with shrapnel during the war.

A little beyond the mission you can see the site of the old mission airstrip, now virtually overgrown. The WW II Japanese airstrip is a little off the road to the left, between the mission airstrip and Alexishafen. The jungle has almost reclaimed it, and only the bomb craters and the odd aircraft wreck hint at the saturation bombing which destroyed the base. You can easily recruit a couple of kids from the villages to guide you around. The wreckage of one Japanese twin-engined bomber is only a wingspan away from the bomb crater which immobilised it. Closer to the North Coast Highway is the fuselage of an early Junkers mission aircraft.

Inland from Rempi, just north of Alexishafen, is **Baiteta** village, where Melanesian Tourist Services takes groups to see sing-sings. It might be worth visiting on your own, but then again the people there might be tired of camera-clicking outsiders.

Malolo to Hansa Bay

The road continues north to the old Malolo plantation, 42 km up the coast, where you'll find the **Malolo Plantation Resort**. The black sand beaches along the coast are the result of volcanic activity on Karkar and Manam islands. There's good swimming but watch out for the strong current which sweeps the coast. A traveller wrote that he had seen perfect surf at a beach near Bogia, but wouldn't say exactly where.

There are magnificent views of Karkar Island from Malolo Plantation Resort and further up the coast. Malolo is pronounced *Ma*lollo.

About 20 km on from Malolo there's a large Catholic mission at **Magiya**. Just beyond here there's a road leading inland about five km to **Aronis** village. About one km from the main village is an aid post, near which is Manubyai Cave, home to a colony of horseshoe bats. James is the keeper of the cave. Accommodation in Aronis can be arranged in Madang – see Places to Stay. Trans Niugini Tours sometimes brings groups here from Malolo and the villages

perform dances and show their medicinal plant gardens.

Bogia, 200 km from Madang, is the departure point for Manam Island. The road peters out a short distance before the mighty Ramu River. About 10 km beyond Bogia, towards Hansa Bay, is **Kabak** where there is a very nice beach at the old plantation. The reef at Kabak has plenty of colourful fish.

Hansa Bay is a popular diving spot past Bogia, where the wreckage of 35 Japanese freighters and US aircraft litter a shallow harbour. Although some are too deep to inspect without scuba equipment others are in only four to six metres of water. They've all been there since a US raid in November 1942. You can rent a dugout from a local village. Either go to the black sands beach at Awa Point or to the village of Sesemungam.

Get your guide to take you to the *Shishi Maru* – the upper deck is only six metres below the surface. Two anti-aircraft guns on the bow point towards the surface. Brass shell castings litter the deck and forward holds. Two fire engines are sitting in the hold, just before the bridge, where they were waiting to be unloaded. The *Shishi Maru* is about 60 metres long and would have been about 6000 tons. Before diving here ask the villagers for advice – there are sometimes sharks in the shallows.

Places to Stay & Eat On the site of the old Malolo of Madang Hotel and taking in a plantation, the *Malolo Plantation Resort* is part of the Trans Niugini Tours empire. A lot of work has been done to transform this into a very attractive place to stay. The North Coast Highway, which once ran between the hotel and the beach, has been diverted, and the new accommodation wing is superb. Two thousand orchids have been planted, there's a very good restaurant (main courses from K10 at lunch, K15 at dinner) and the staff are unusually friendly and competent. Tours in the area are available and there's a swimming pool and a tiny private island for picnics.

Accommodation costs K98 for a single or double, plus 5% tax. Airport transfers are

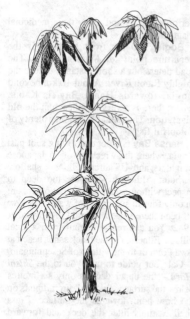

Cassava plant

K16 (a PMV would be K2) and day tours are K70.

The resort has a good relationship with the villages in the area (one of them cheerfully lent the resort its pet cockatoo the day I was there) so it's apparently safe to stroll along the beach at night – a real plus.

Scuba equipment can be hired for K15 a day and dives cost from K65 for two land-based dives, K90 for two boat dives. Snorkelling gear costs K8.50 a day.

Akia Aruah, on staff at the resort, has worked at the Baiyer River Sanctuary and knows a lot about birds. More importantly he knows where to find them, and if you go on one of the resort's early-morning tours you stand a good chance of seeing birds of paradise and many other species.

People sometimes stay with Caspar Didol at Aronis village, for K6 a night or K12 with meals. You can contact him at the provincial government offices in Madang (☎ 82 2966,

ext 50) and perhaps arrange a ride to Aronis. He's an articulate and friendly man, and his house is built of traditional materials, with split palm floors.

The Bogia Hotel has closed down (but is for sale so the new owners might re-open), so there's no formal accommodation in town, nor is there any at Hansa Bay.

Getting There & Away PMVs from Madang to Malolo cost K2. Bogia Company trucks go to Madang on Monday and Thursday and you might catch a ride with them either way. In Madang ask at Boroko Motors on Modilon Rd where they refuel before heading back. It's more than three hours' drive. You can also get to Bogia by PMV for K6. From Madang, PMVs leave from near the big fig tree at Bates Oval, behind the post office.

A traveller wrote that it's possible to get from Bogia to the Sepik. From Bogia take a PMV further along the coast to Boroi. Here, take a canoe (ask for Albert) to Watam, where there's a guesthouse. From Watam, near the mouth of the Sepik, there are infrequent passenger canoes up to Angoram.

INLAND

There are also some isolated and interesting places inland towards the Highlands. Stations in the area include the remote Bundi, wedged between Mt Wilhelm and Mt Herbert in some of the roughest country in PNG. Some of the people living in these areas are almost small enough to be termed pygmies. Dumpu was the base from where the attack on Shaggy Ridge was launched during WW II. The Ramu is one of PNG's great rivers, but it has never been popularised like the Sepik, although it is also home to wood carving cultures.

Usino

There is an interesting place to stay near Usino – low-key, village-style accommodation for about four people, not too far from the Ramu River. It's run by Martin, Kupile and their daughter Marianne. It's necessary to contact them in advance (Martin Borkent,

PO Box 230, Madang). Unfortunately, they don't have a phone, but if you have a contact number in PNG, Martin will ring you. The other option is to ask at the Lutheran Guesthouse in Madang; they'll probably have up-to-date information. B&B plus a light afternoon meal costs about K10.

Martin has been trading in the area for many years and knows it like the back of his hand. Visitors can explore the rainforests and swamps, which are full of wildlife, and the Ramu River is about a 1½-hour walk away.

To get to Martin and Kupile's camp, catch a PMV from Madang or Lae to Usino Junction for K7, then ask for 'camp bilong Martin'. There are two alternative routes, a main track which takes about 1¾ hours and a 'draiwara shortcut'. You'll need a guide for the shortcut.

Ramu Sugar Refinery

This is a major industrial development designed to make PNG self-sufficient in sugar. There is accommodation at the refinery and you can use the impressive sporting facilities that have been developed for the employees (golf, tennis, swimming). Singles/double-bed doubles cost K58/K69, including breakfast. Contact the administration office (☎ 44 3299).

Bundi & Brahmin

Bundi is about a six-hour walk from Brahmin Mission and Brahmin is about 25 km from the Lae-Madang road. A PMV from Madang to Brahmin costs K5 or K6 and takes about 1½ hours. Island Airways flies from Madang to Brahmin for K50.

There are a group of lodges at Bundi known as the *Mt Sinai Hotel*. The cost is around K12 per person and this includes dinner.

You can, if you're fit, continue walking from Bundi to Kegsugl, near Mt Wilhelm, and then catch a PMV to Kundiawa. See Walking to Madang in the Simbu Province section in the Highlands chapter.

Teptep

Over 2000 metres up in the rugged Finisterre Ranges, Teptep is a small, isolated village on the border of Morobe Province which is becoming popular as a base for walks in the area. Guides are necessary (local people are not keen on unaccompanied strangers blundering through their land) and cost K5 a day. May to October are the best months for walking.

There's a guesthouse at Teptep, charging about K8 per person and meals are available. Teptep is at an altitude where vegetables are grown, so the meals are good – if you choose the cheaper option. If you pay more (about K3) the menu is rice and tinned meat. Other villages in the area have more basic guesthouses. To book accommodation at Teptep, contact MAF in Madang (☎ 82 2229) or Lae (☎ 42 3804).

MAF flies to Teptep a few times each week for K65 from Madang or K47 from Lae. Island Airways (☎ 82 2601) also flies from Madang. You could walk in from Wantoat village, taking about two days. Wantoat can be reached by PMV from Kaiapit, on the Madang-Lae road in Morobe Province.

ISLANDS
Long Island

The largest of the volcanic islands, Long is 414 sq km in area and 48 km off the coast. It has two active craters, one of which contains a lake surrounded by crater walls up to 250 metres high. The population only totals about 600, but the island is renowned for its prolific bird life and the many fish which swarm around its reefs. Turtles come ashore to lay their eggs at certain times of year. Getting here isn't easy as there is no regular boat service. Island Airways flies from Madang (K90). A village guesthouse has apparently been built for visiting scientists.

Karkar Island

William Dampier, the English pirate-explorer whose visit to the west coast of Australia preceded Captain Cook's visit by nearly a century, made an early landing on the 362 sq km island. Later Lutheran missionaries had a hard time both from malaria and the inhabitants.

The island has a population of 25,000, a high school and 20 community schools. It's one of the most fertile places in the country.

A volcanic eruption temporarily evicted the missionaries, but they came back and today Karkar has both Catholic and Lutheran missions as well as some of the most productive copra plantations in the world. The volcanic cone is just two metres higher than Manam's at 1831 metres. The volcano erupted violently in 1974, leaving a cinder cone in the centre of the huge, original crater. It erupted again in 1979, killing two vulcanologists.

You can climb to the crater, taking a full day. After the 1979 eruption, climbing had to be authorised and you were accompanied by a vulcanologist. That has changed but you still need to get permission from whichever village you begin the climb from. This is partly for your own safety (no-one can search for you if they don't know you're there) and partly because the crater has religious importance for the villagers. Apparently the climb is easier from Mom village but there are better views if you start from Kavasob village. Be prepared for the intense heat of the sun bouncing off bare basalt and if it rains watch out for flash flooding.

A road encircles the island and it takes four hours to drive right round. You can also walk around the island, but treat the river crossings with great caution. When it rains on the mountain, water comes down the rivers like a wall. Some years ago some unwary Australians were killed crossing a river. Karkar also has good beaches and places for snorkelling.

The high school and the airstrip are at the government station at Kiaim, which is the closest thing to a town on the island. Kulili, where boats from Madang dock, is about 15 km away.

Places to Stay There is no formal accommodation on the island – in fact Madang shipping offices have signs warning

you of this. Niugini Diving Adventures at the Madang Resort Hotel can arrange for you to stay for about K30 and you don't have to go on one of their dives to do this.

People have stayed in villages, at the high school and at Gaubin Hospital (ask about this at the Lutheran Guesthouse in Madang).

Getting There & Away A boat runs to Karkar daily from Madang's Rab-Trad (Rabaul Trading) wharf, stopping at Biabi (K6) and at Kulili (K8). Kulili is about 15 km from the government station at Kiaim. There might also be faster and more expensive speedies. Island Airways flies to Kiaim from Madang for K40.

Bagabag Island

Bagabag, east of Karkar, encircles a sunken crater 36 sq km in area and is inhabited. During the war the Japanese used the 'fjord' to hide ships.

Manam Island

The island of Manam, or Vulcan, is only 15 km off the coast from Bogia. The island is 83 sq km in area and is an almost perfect volcanic cone, rising to 1829 metres. The soil is extremely fertile and supports a population of about 4000, but from time to time the entire population has to be evacuated as the volcano is still active. In 1992 it erupted again, with lava flowing for months down the north and east sides of the mountain and ash destroying gardens. At night the crater glows and occasionally spurts orange trailers into the sky. There is a seismological observatory on the side of the cone.

There is a German mission on the island. If you manage to make it to Manam you will enjoy an incredible welcome by the local people, particularly the children. Bring your own food and ask your boat crew for somewhere to stay. Boda village has been recommended. Recently, there have been some thefts from travellers – the modern world has arrived.

Getting There & Away Manam is 193 km from Madang and not easy to get to. Bogia is the normal departure point; take a PMV from Madang for K6. Apparently, government and private boats leave Bogia for Manam virtually daily for about K5, although there is no schedule so you might end up waiting a few days; check at the district office. Be careful with your possessions on the boats.

The Highlands

Land Area 65,248 sq km
Population 1,360,000

The great Highlands area, which is divided into five separate provinces (Eastern Highlands, Simbu, Western Highlands, Enga, Southern Highlands), is the most densely populated and agriculturally productive region of PNG. Strangely, it was the last part of the country to be explored by Europeans: the first Highlands tribes were not contacted until the 1930s. Until then, Europeans had thought that the centre of PNG was a rugged tangle of virtually unpopulated mountains. It was definitely a shock when a series of populated valleys, stretching right through the country, was discovered.

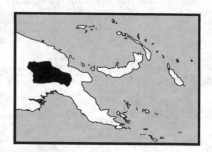

Little development occurred before WW II, which almost entirely bypassed the region, so it was not until the 1950s and '60s that the Highlands were really opened up.

Today, this is a dynamic and fascinating part of PNG. The people's lives are changing quickly, but many aspects of their traditional cultures remain, particularly in terms of social organisation. Clan and tribal loyalties are still very strong. It is possible to see dramatic sing-sings and warriors wearing ostentatious traditional dress, but in most parts of the Highlands, and especially in the main towns like Mt Hagen and Goroka, the people have taken on the trappings of the West – more particularly, *sekonhan klos* (second-hand clothes).

Although some individuals and even some tribes are exceptions to the rule, traditional dress and decorations are now most usually reserved for rare ceremonial or festive occasions, which, as a tourist, you will be very lucky to see. Some of the big hotels organise theatrical sing-sings, but these are usually rather sad and listless affairs.

The Highlands are not a lifeless, open-air museum specially designed for photographers, but home to a number of vital, rapidly changing cultures that are maintaining some things, adapting others, and adopting still more with wholehearted fervour.

The Highlands have the most extensive road system in the country, half-a-dozen major towns and a growing cash economy based on coffee and tea. Gold and oil, both in considerable quantities, are now bringing enormous wealth to a few areas, and are rapidly changing both the economy and the lifestyles of the peoples.

The countryside is dramatic and beautiful, with wide, fertile valleys, countless streams and rivers and endless, saw-toothed mountains.

HISTORY

Most of the Highland valleys were settled by about 10,000 years ago, and the presence of shells amongst archaeological deposits show that by this time people were also trading with the coast. Some sites that have been excavated date to much earlier.

Kuk Swamp in the Wahgi Valley (Western Highlands Province) has evidence of human habitation going back 20,000 years, but even more significantly there is evidence of gardening beginning 9000 years ago. This makes Papua New Guineans among the first farmers in the world. The main foods that were cultivated are likely to have been sago, coconuts, breadfruit, local bananas and yams, sugar cane, nuts and edible green leaves.

It is still uncertain when the pig and more productive starch crops (Asian yams, taros and bananas) were introduced but it is known that this occurred more than 5000 years ago, maybe as far back as 10,000. Domesticated pigs – which continue to be incredibly important, ritually and economically, in contemporary society – and these new crops were probably brought to PNG by a later group of colonists from Asia.

The sweet potato was introduced to the Indonesian Spice Islands by the Spaniards in the 16th century and it is believed Malay traders then brought it to Irian Jaya, from where it was traded to the Highlands. The introduction of the sweet potato must have brought radical change to life in the Highlands – it is still the staple crop. Its high yield and tolerance for poor and cold soils allowed the colonisation of higher altitudes, the domestication of many more pigs, and a major increase in population.

As with the rest of PNG, there was tremendous cultural and linguistic diversity. The largest social units were tribes numbering in the thousands and the area that a single group controlled was usually small. There were apparently no empires or dynasties. Despite the political fragmentation there were extensive trade links with the coast.

Evidence relating to the real history of the Highlands before the arrival of Europeans is extremely scarce, and it is unwise to assume that the situation that existed when the patrols entered the fertile valleys perfectly reflected the past. Highlands societies were certainly not static. It is difficult, for instance, to assess the impact of the introduction of the sweet potato. It is also known that some steel knives and axes had been traded from the coast in advance of the patrols, and this may well have changed patterns of labour and warfare in advance of the European invasion.

When the first Australian patrols arrived minor warfare between the tribes was common, but the number of fatalities was probably relatively low, in part because of the weaponry – bows, arrows and spears. Two of the most striking characteristics that were encountered were the intensive and skilful gardening (almost entirely the work of the women), and the fantastic personal adornment of the men, which was the most striking form of artistic expression.

The first direct European contact with the Highlands came as a result of the gold rush in the Wau/Bulolo region, which created speculation there would be more gold further afield. In 1930 Mick Leahy and Mick Dwyer set off south to search for gold in the region they believed formed the headwaters for the Ramu River. To their amazement the streams they followed did not turn north-west to join the Ramu, but led southwards through the previously undiscovered Eastern Highlands.

When they finally reached the Papuan coast they discovered that they were at the mouth of the Purari River. Rather than starting on the southernmost flanks of the Highlands the streams that formed the Purari started just the other side of the towering Bismarck Range from the Ramu (on the map, less than 25 km from the Ramu and around 80 km from the north coast) and ran through populated valleys all the way to the south coast.

In 1933 Mick Leahy returned with his brother Danny and this time they stumbled upon the huge, fertile and heavily populated Wahgi Valley. After an aerial reconnaissance they walked in with a large well-supplied patrol.

The first patrol built an airstrip at Mt Hagen and explored the area, but the hoped-for gold was never discovered in any great quantities. Jim Taylor, the government officer who accompanied this patrol, was one of the last direct links to those extraordinary times. He died peacefully at his farm outside Goroka, a PNG citizen, in 1987.

The film documentary *First Contact* includes original footage by Mick Leahy and is a priceless record of the first interaction between Highlanders and Europeans. See it if you can; the people at Haus Poroman, Ambua Lodge and the Madang Resort Hotel often screen it in the evening. The book of

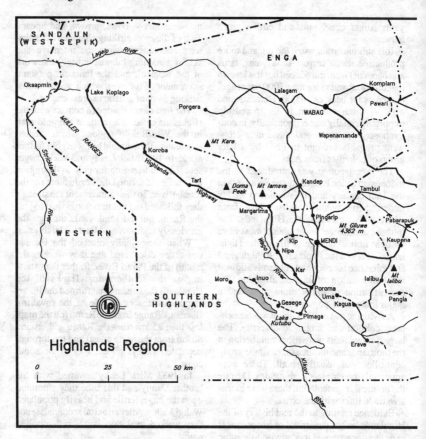

SANDAUN
(WEST SEPIK)

ENGA

Highlands Region

WESTERN

SOUTHERN
HIGHLANDS

0   25   50 km

the film is also available in the Highlands and around the world, and it's well worth buying.

Missionaries soon followed the miners and the government and missions were established near present-day Mt Hagen and in the Simbu Valley, near present-day Kundiawa. Two missionaries managed to get themselves killed and in response, a government patrol post was set up at Kundiawa and the whole Highlands area was declared a 'Restricted Territory' with controlled European access.

WW II intervened, and once again the mountains largely protected the Highlanders

from outside forces. It was the 1950s before major changes were really felt and many areas remained virtually unaffected until the '60s and '70s.

The construction of the Highlands Highway had a major impact on the area, as did the introduction of cash crops, particularly coffee. The Highlanders have adapted to the plastic age with remarkable speed, perhaps due in part to Western capitalism meshing with their existing culture; they have always understood the importance of landownership, and they are skilful gardeners and clever traders. Material wealth, while

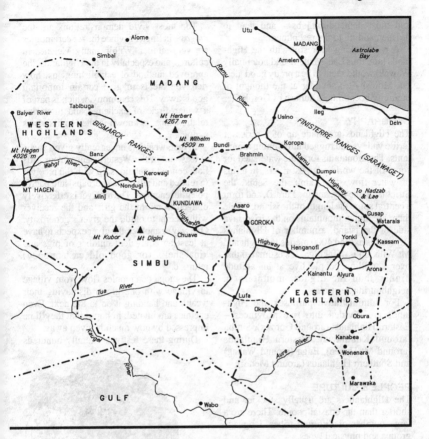

handled very differently to the way it is in the West, was still of crucial importance in establishing the status and wealth of a big man and his clan.

The dense population of the Highlands and the cultural differences between this and other parts of the country have caused more than a few problems. Ritual warfare was an integral part of life in the Highlands and to this day payback feuds (to revenge both real and imagined injuries) and land disputes can erupt into major conflicts.

Over the aeons the Highlanders and the coastal people have distrusted each other and this mutual suspicion still exists. The energetic Highlanders think that the coastal people are lazy and unfairly dominate government bureaucracies. The coastal people see the Highlanders as aggressive, their numbers as threatening and feel that the Highlands have had a disproportionate share of the development pie.

Population pressures have pushed many Highlanders out to other parts of the country in search of work, where they are often resented and held responsible for rascal activity. As is usual with immigrants, these 'expat' Highlanders often take on the dirtiest and most demanding jobs – and tend to prosper, adding to the resentment.

A road linking Moresby with the Highlands (and thus Lae, Madang and potentially Wewak) would seem to be a pretty good idea, but Moresbyites shudder at the thought of their city becoming 'a suburb of Goroka'!

GEOGRAPHY

The Highlands are made up of a series of fertile valleys and rugged intervening mountains. The mountains form the watershed for some of the world's largest rivers, in terms of water flow (the Ramu, the Sepik, the Strickland, the Fly, and the Purari), and form a central spine the length of the island. While there are higher mountains on the Irian Jaya side of the island, a number of Highlands mountains exceed 4000 metres in height and Mt Wilhelm is 4509 high. It's estimated that over a million people live at an altitude higher than the highest mountain in neighbouring Australia.

For administrative purposes, the Highlands are divided into five provinces – Eastern Highlands (around Goroka), Simbu (around Kundiawa), Western Highlands (around Mt Hagen), Enga (around Wabag) and Southern Highlands (around Mendi).

PEOPLE & CULTURE

The Highlanders are usually stockier and shorter than the coastal people. There are a large number of different tribes, language groups and physical types.

Mogas

If you need to be convinced that 'keeping up with the Jones' and accumulating and displaying wealth are not peculiarly modern preoccupations, a visit to the Highlands should soon do the job. Wealth is enormously important in establishing status and men of consequence in a village, the big men, are almost invariably men of affluence. Just being rich, however, is not enough – other people have to know you are rich. As a result, much of the ceremonial life of the Highlands is centred around displays of wealth – ostentatious displays.

The most vivid demonstrations are the *mogas* – in Enga Province the *tee* ceremonies are very similar. Within many Melanesian cultures, and especially in the Highlands, the approved method of establishing just how rich you are is to give certain important goods away. This ceremony, which is part of a wider circle of exchange and inter-clan relationships, is known in the Highlands as a moga.

In fact, wealth is never really given away, at least not in the Western sense. Your gifts both cement a relationship with the receiver (a related and allied clan perhaps) and pacify potential enemies. The receiver is effectively obliged to return the gifts and the receiver will attempt to outdo the giver's generosity. One way or another, the giver expects to have at least an equivalent number of pigs and kina shells (or good old cash money) returned.

The moga ceremonies flow from village to village with one group displaying their wealth and handing it on to the next. Even enemies are invited, in hopes that they'll be impressed by how much is given away.

During these festivals literally hundreds

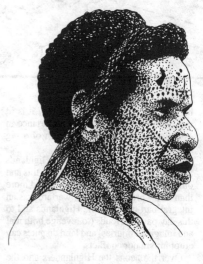

Highlands woman

of pigs are slaughtered and cooked and all present indulge in an orgy of eating. Each clan attempts to surpass their neighbours by producing as many pigs as possible. Some indication of the economic significance of these feasts can be gauged by the fact that a decent-sized pig is worth around K300 to K400 and a sow can be worth even more.

You'll see the ceremonial grounds where these feasts occur as you travel the Highlands Highway, especially past Mendi in the Southern Highlands. They are distinguished by a fenced quadrangle, covering up to an acre or so, surrounded by long houses (shelters where the guests sleep) with long pits dug in straight lines and filled with cooking stones (for cooking the pigs). Attempts to convince the Highlanders, many of whom live on the borderline of protein deficiency, that pigs could be rationed more sensibly, rather than used in this feast or famine manner, have been largely unsuccessful.

Bride Price

Marriage is another occasion that is used to prove just how much you can afford to pay: the bride's clan has to be paid a bride price by the husband's clan. Although local councils have tried to establish price controls, the going rate in the Highlands is now around 20 pigs plus K600 or more in cash and it's increasing.

Bride price varies throughout the country and is usually higher in the cities; in Moresby, the average is now more like K12,000, with wealthy people paying many times more. An interesting description of the tense negotiations to establish a bride price, and the related issue of prestige, can be found in Kenneth Read's book *The High Valley*.

The old shell money has been seriously devalued since European contact, both because it has become more readily available and modern currency has been widely accepted. Pigs still retain their value – a pig is not just food, it's the most visible and important measure of a person's solvency. Cassowaries are also extremely important in the Highlands although they're much less edible!

Huli man

Payback

Compensation claims may also make demands on a clan's wealth. An eye for an eye is the basic payback concept (it is virtually a greater sin to fail to payback than to have committed the initial wrong), but sufficiently large payments of pigs and cash will usually avert direct bloodletting. Pigs have traditionally been used to negotiate an end to conflicts of many kinds and naturally the government and the courts prefer this kind of solution.

In a society where the clan is of much greater significance than the individual a whole clan is held responsible for an individual's actions; in the case of a killing, revenge will be taken by the aggrieved clan, preferably by killing the murderer but, if that proves too difficult, anyone in the murderer's clan will do.

To this day, violence will often only be averted by very substantial financial compensation, whether or not Western-style justice has also been done. Car accidents are becoming an increasingly rich source of payback feuds.

Food

Women in the Highlands are highly skilled subsistence farmers, largely dependent on the sweet potato. This is grown in neat round mounds about a metre and a half in diameter (in the Wahgi Valley they're square). The mounds are fertilised with ashes and can have very high yields.

Bananas, sugar cane, greens and yams are also traditional crops which are now supplemented by many more familiar Western vegetables. Hunting is relatively unimportant, but the pig is vital, both for protein and as a symbol of wealth.

Sing-sings

Although these are not an everyday occurrence you should definitely try to see one while you're in the Highlands. Around Hagen they are still quite frequent, but finding where they are and getting to them can be a problem. Many parts of the Highlands are still inaccessible to vehicles, and the sing-sings are often in remote areas.

A sing-sing can be held for any number of reasons – it might be associated with paying off a bride price, a moga ceremony or even some more mundane activity like raising money for a local school or church. Whatever the reason, the result will be much the same – a lot of people, brilliantly costumed, singing and dancing. Take plenty of film if you're keen on photography.

Other Highland ceremonies you may come across are the courting rituals known as 'Karim Leg' (Carry Leg) or 'Turnim Head'. Ceremonially dressed young couples meet in the long houses for courting sessions where they sit side by side and cross legs (Carry Leg) or rub their faces together (Turn Head). While you may not get to see them 'for real', they are sometimes staged for tourists.

Highland Shows

During the 1950s, as the Highlands first came into serious contact with Europeans,

Sing-sing ceremony participant

the Highland Shows were instituted as a way of gathering the tribes and clans together and showing them that the people from across the hill weren't so bad after all. They were an amazing success and grew from the original concept of a local get-together into a major tourist attraction. As many as 40,000 warriors would gather together in the show arena in a stomping, chanting dance that literally shook the earth. Drums thundered, feathers swayed and dancing bodies glistened with paint, oils and pig grease. It was like nothing else on earth.

Unfortunately, the shows have suffered a serious decline. The Highlanders are increasingly sophisticated, so the curiosity-value of the gatherings for the participants themselves has declined, along with their pride in their traditional finery. In addition, with improved transport and better roads it is no longer such an effort to get from place to place, so people don't need to save up for an annual gathering.

Still, the shows go on and if you can see one, you're unlikely to be disappointed. It will certainly be one of the best available opportunities to get an overview of PNG's extraordinary cultural diversity. Mt Hagen and Goroka both have regular shows. The Goroka show is the better of the two, partly because it is more than just a chance for sing-sing groups to perform. There are agricultural displays, string band competitions and other exhibits. Still, attending either show is an amazing experience.

The shows used to take place on even numbered years in Goroka and on odd numbered years in Mt Hagen, most frequently in mid-August. The Mt Hagen show will probably become an annual event, with the Goroka show perhaps following suit and being held over the Independence Day weekend in September. Contact the National Tourist Office or the respective provincial governments for more information. Make sure you book accommodation as far ahead as possible if you will be in either town around the time of the festivities.

Arts

The Highlanders do not carve bowls, masks or other similar items; their artistic talents are almost always expressed in personal attire and decoration or in the decoration of weapons.

The best known weapons are probably the fine ceremonial axes from Mt Hagen. The slate blades come from the Jimi River area north of Hagen on the Sepik-Wahgi divide and are bound to a wooden shaft with decorative cane strips. They were never intended for use as weapons or tools.

'Killing sticks' from Lake Kopiago had an obvious and practical use: the pointed fighting stick is tipped with a sharpened cassowary bone to make a lethal weapon in close fighting.

THINGS TO BUY

Beautifully decorated bows and arrows are sold throughout the Highlands. Other traditional items you may see, sometimes for sale, are the fine kina shells made from the gold lip pearl shell. These can be expensive, around K20. Aumak (wealth tally) necklaces, which are made of bamboo rods and were used to record how many pigs the owner had given away, are also sold, but they're much cheaper than a kina shell. In the Western Highlands, kina shells are sometimes mounted on a board of red resin; at traditional wealth displays, such as the moga ceremonies, long lines of these are formed on the ground.

People also sell excellent basketry incorporating striking geometric designs (trays, baskets and so on) from stalls along the Highlands Highway, but once again they are not cheap, reflecting the amount of work that goes into creating them.

Hardly traditional, but extremely attractive nonetheless, coarsely woven woollen blankets, rugs, bedspreads and bags are available in several Highlands centres. Highlands hats are a necessary fashion accessory.

Ceremonial axe

GETTING THERE & AROUND
Air
Air Niugini and Talair have regular connections to and from Goroka, Mt Hagen, Wewak, Madang, Lae and Port Moresby. In addition there is a comprehensive third-level network around the Highland centres. The Highlands Airfare Chart details some of the connections and fares.

Talair's national headquarters is in Goroka (☎ 72 1240, PO Box 108) and has a larger range of flights to and around the Highlands than Air Niugini.

MAF has an extensive network to many out-of-the-way places and its headquarters is in Mt Hagen (☎ 55 1506, PO Box 273). If you're planning a walk, find out if and when MAF flies in your direction, just in case you need to take an easy way out. MAF flies twice a week to strips south and west of Hagen, and three times a week to strips in the Baiyer River and Jimi Valley areas. There's also a useful flight on Tuesday and Thursday which originates in Moresby and goes to Tari, returning via Aiyura and Mt Hagen. At Tari you can connect with flights originating in Telefomin and Kawito.

Remember that MAF flies small planes, so don't expect to get away with too much over the 16-kg baggage limit. Bad weather can play havoc with their schedules.

Road
The Highlands Highway The most important road in PNG starts in Lae and runs up into the central Highlands. Where the highway ends depends on your definition. As a decent road it now continues to Tari, in rougher condition to Koroba and in still rougher condition on to Lake Kopiago. The highway is now sealed as far as Mt Hagen and in parts between Hagen and Mendi. New branches off the main road are being developed, although their condition varies widely.

From Lae the road runs out through the coastal jungle then emerges into the wide, flat Markham Valley. Shortly after leaving Lae a road branches off to the left, crosses the wide Markham River and then twists up to Bulolo, Wau and Aseki. If you can, pause at the interesting pottery village of **Zunim**, about 130 km from Lae and 15 km past Kaiapit.

It's a rather hot, dull stretch to the base of the Kassam Pass where the road starts to twist, turn and climb. At the top of the pass

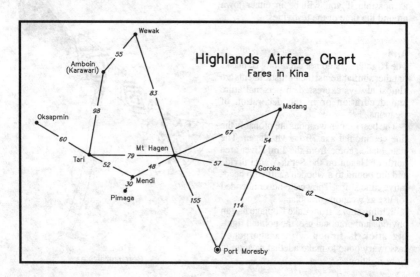

Highlands Airfare Chart
Fares in Kina

there are some spectacular lookout points across the Markham Valley to the Sarawaget Mountains. The road continues through rolling grass hills to Kainantu, the only reasonable sized town before Goroka.

The road up from Madang joins the Highlands Highway just east of Watarais, but a new road, which at the time of writing was near completion, should be open by now. This road, which joins the Highlands Highway at Henganofi, midway between Kainantu and Goroka, will cut a lot of distance and time from the Madang-Goroka trip. This should make Madang a better access point to the Highlands than Lae.

From Goroka the road continues through the valley to Asaro, then climbs steeply to the high (2450 metres) Daulo Pass, about 25 km from Goroka. It continues twisting, turning and generally descending all the way to Simbu Province and Kundiawa, about the mid-point between Goroka and Mt Hagen.

From Kundiawa the road descends to the Wahgi Valley and it's a fast run to Mt Hagen past the turn-offs to Minj and Banz. The road from Hagen to Mendi is spectacular; you skirt **Mt Giluwe**, PNG's second tallest mountain at 4362 metres, and go through some beautiful valleys. On good days you can also see Mt Ialibu to the south of the road. Along the way, you'll see some enterprising people selling woven walls of bamboo or pitpit leaves – sort of prefabricated housing. There are also likely to be some road-side stalls selling attractive, though expensive, basketry.

The road becomes even more interesting after Mendi, as you pass ceremonial grounds, a suspension bridge over the Lai River, and through the stunning **Poroma Valley**. It's a narrow gravel road in good condition, but you can't go too fast and you have time to soak in the views as you go through Nipa and Margarima. After Poroma you climb the 2900-metre pass overlooking the wide and fertile Tari Basin. It's then a quick run through the Huli's intensively cultivated gardens to Tari.

The road deteriorates after Tari and again after Koroba. If you're aiming for Lake Kopiago, you'll be lucky if you don't have to do some walking. There's very little transport, especially after Koroba: it's only an hour's drive or so to Koroba, but a two-day walk from Koroba to Kopiago. Beyond Kopiago it's definitely walking only. Koroba and Kopiago are small stations in very interesting areas.

Other Roads Between Goroka and Mt Hagen, the old highway parallels the new road for part of the distance. An old road also runs to Mendi from Mt Hagen, on the other side of Mt Giluwe to the new Mendi road. The new road runs through Kaupena while the old road goes through Tambul.

A reasonable road runs north from Mt Hagen through the spectacular Baiyer Gorge to Baiyer River and a good road branches off the Mendi road and continues on to Wabag and Porgera. From Wabag, there's a loop through Laiagam to Kandep and down to Mendi. It may not be passable due to washed out bridges and slides. From Kandep another branch goes down through Margarima, halfway between Mendi and Tari. This is not often used and its condition varies, though it's never great.

A new road from Mendi to Pimaga (for Lake Kutubu) should have opened by now.

There's a breathtakingly precarious road north from Kundiawa to Kegsugl if you're intending to climb Mt Wilhelm.

PMV PMVs are frequent between all the major centres. Just about all long-distance PMVs are comfortable, fairly new minibuses that make a trip quite pleasant – they're no hardship at all. There isn't a lot of space for luggage though, and if you have a large bag it may be on your lap most of the way.

On less important routes and over very bad roads, trucks are used as PMVs and these are somewhat more spartan.

PMVs generally make their first trip early in the mornings around 8 am, sometimes earlier. The best place to look for them is usually at the markets. Although there will often be some later in the day, their deadline for reaching a destination is sunset, which is around 6 pm; bear in mind that breakdowns can add unforeseen hours so give yourself some leeway if you have a deadline.

Many PMVs make return journeys within daylight hours, for instance they'll leave Lae early and leave Goroka for Lae around midday. PMVs meet a demand, so work out what the local people require. There will, for instance, be very early PMVs to get people to Saturday markets, and returning PMVs after the markets; there'll be PMVs between Kundiawa and Mt Hagen later in the day after people have had a chance to shop, and so on.

Your safest bet is to be early. In addition, it's not a good move to wander around Lae or most Highland towns at night looking for accommodation; try to arrive in daylight, but if you don't, get the PMV to deliver you to the place where you plan to stay.

Expats frequently criticise PMVs and rarely use them, but those who do find them comfortable, cheap and safe. The PMVs present a great opportunity to meet locals. Bad drivers are rare (I suppose they don't last) and most are surprisingly cautious. The following table shows approximate fares and journey times:

Route	Fare	Time Taken
Kainantu-Lae	K7	3 hours
Kainantu-Goroka	K4	1½ hours
Goroka-Lae	K10	4½ hours
Kundiawa-Goroka	K4	2 hours
Mt Hagen-Kundiawa	K4	2 hours
Mt Hagen-Goroka	K8	4 hours
Mt Hagen-Wabag	K5	3½ hours
Mt Hagen-Mendi	K10	3 hours
Mendi-Tari	K10	4 hours

When the new road connection to Madang opens, the trip between Madang and Goroka will be much shorter and cost about K10, assuming that there are direct PMVs on the route. Currently you usually have to change at Watarais and the total fare is around K20. It takes about seven hours.

Fares change, but over the past few years improved road conditions and competition have tended to counterbalance increased costs. Times are a different matter: if you get a straight run, times can be less than those

shown, but if you have numerous stops for passengers, or a flat tyre, they can be much longer.

Car You can drive yourself, at a suitably high price – see the Getting Around chapter. Rental firms often have restrictions on 'out of town' use, which particularly applies in the Highlands. An alternative is to deliver a car up to the Highlands from Lae. If your timing is right, Ela Motors in Lae may give you a vehicle to be taken to either Goroka or Hagen. If you do strike out with them, it would be worth trying others.

Although an early start and late finish, plus nonstop driving, could get you from Lae to Mt Hagen in a day (443 km), what's the hurry?

Because of the risk of being held-up by a roadblock manned by rascals, very few people drive at night. Roadblocks can even happen during the day, although this is not common. If you are forced to stop (don't unless you have to, and be very sceptical if you are waved down), don't panic. They'll just want your money. This warning is not intended to induce fear and loathing. Talk to people and they'll fill you in on the current situation: you are very, very unlikely to have any problems if you heed local advice. News travels very quickly and if there is trouble, it is usually part of a wider, well-known disturbance.

Walking The best way to see the Highlands is to walk – and there are networks of tracks everywhere. It is also possible to walk from the Highlands to the coast although with the exception of the route between Kegsugl and Madang, these routes are not for the faint-hearted.

Most tour companies (see the Facts for the Visitor chapter) have walks in the Highlands, but if you're reasonably well equipped, don't mind roughing it out and don't tackle anything too radical, there is no reason why you shouldn't do it yourself. This is a volatile, rugged area however, so it is important to talk to locals and local government officers, especially the *kiaps* (district officers) before you set out, and in most cases guides are necessary.

Eastern Highlands Province

Land Area 11,706 sq km
Population 340,000
Capital Goroka

The Eastern Highlands have had longer, more extensive contact with the West than other parts of the Highlands. The people have abandoned their traditional dress for day-to-day use, although you'll still occasionally see traditional dress at the Goroka market.

Their villages are recognisable for their neat clusters of low- walled round huts. The traditional design for huts includes two peaks to the roof. On each of these peaks is a tuft of grass, one from the owner's area and the other from a neighbouring area. These tufts talk to each other in the night, so you can hear your neighbour's secrets.

Although the province is heavily populated, the Eastern Highlanders are a less cohesive group than the people in other parts of the Highlands.

Goroka is the main town and is one of the most attractive places in PNG, a green, shady, well-organised city with decent shopping, transport and facilities. Kainantu, near the border with Morobe Province, is the second largest town.

The steep and rugged mountains of this province form the headwaters for two of PNG's most important river systems: the Ramu which runs parallel to the coast to the north-west, and the Wahgi and Aure rivers which run south and enter the Gulf of Papua as the Purari. The highest point is Mt Michael at 3750 metres, but most of the population lives between altitudes of 1500 and 2300 metres. There are large areas of rolling kunai-grass covered hills.

KAINANTU

The major town between Lae and Goroka, Kainantu is an important cattle and coffee production region. There was also some gold found in this area and very minor production still continues. The town is basically strung along the highway, 210 km from Lae and 80 km from Goroka. Evenings can be quite cool because the town lies at 1600 metres.

The Eastern Highlands Cultural Centre (☎ 77 1215, PO Box 91) which is on the Lae side of town on the highway, is well worth visiting. They sell reasonably-priced traditional crafts from the eastern Highlands, such as pottery and flutes, and there's a small museum and coffee shop. The centre also trains people in handcrafts like print-making, dressmaking and weaving. They're open from 8 am to 4.30 pm on weekdays and 9 am to 4 pm on weekends.

Places to Stay & Eat

The *Kainantu Lodge* (☎ 77 1021, fax 77 1229, PO Box 31) is on a hill overlooking Kainantu on the other side of the disused airfield parallel to the highway. It's signposted and is about a 20-minute walk from the PMV stop. It's quite a pleasant place, with a bar and a restaurant. Rooms in the new wing cost from K85/95 a single/double, in the old wing from K70/80 and with shared facilities K45/55. There are sometimes special offers, such as weekend rates, so check.

The *Salvation Army Flats* (☎ 77 1130) are a cheaper possibility, but ask first as their policy on renting to visitors fluctuates; certainly at times visitors have been most unwelcome.

Getting There & Away

PMVs from Lae to Kainantu cost K7 and take three hours, from Kainantu to Goroka they cost K4 and take about two hours.

AROUND KAINANTU
Ukarumpa

Adjoining a village of the same name, Ukarumpa is the PNG headquarters of the American-founded Summer Institute of Linguistics (SIL). It is about half an hour by PMV from Kainantu in the Aiyura Valley.

There are many expats, an excellent supermarket and the valley is a pleasant place for day walks. There's also a guesthouse (☎ 77 4651), one of the best in the country, which charges K20 per person or K35 with all meals. If there's space you'll have your own room.

SIL is a missionary organisation whose primary objective is to translate the Bible into every PNG language. The good side of this is that they do record many languages, some of which are dying out and might otherwise be lost. I suspect that their translations must be fairly free. The mind boggles when you wonder how they represent various things like camels, Romans and deserts, let alone the rest.

Other complications come to mind: in the Trobriands the people do not believe there is a connection between intercourse and pregnancy, which would rather spoil the impact of the virgin birth...

Yonki & the Upper Ramu Project

Situated 23 km from Kainantu, Yonki is the support town for the Upper Ramu hydroelectric project. Commissioned in 1979, the project was financed by a K23-million World Bank loan and supplies power for Lae, Madang and much of the Highlands. You can arrange a free tour of the project which is four km from the town.

Okapa

Okapa, south-west of Kainantu, is notable for the disease known as *kuru* which was unique to this area. No recent cases have been recorded. Kuru was dubbed the laughing disease since it attacks the central nervous system and the victims die with a peculiar smile. One particular language group was, apparently, decimated by kuru. It appears to attack women more often than men. It is thought there could be a correlation between this disease and ritual cannibalism of dead relatives.

Highland Handcrafts (PO Box 225, Goroka) is at Okapa, and sells, among other things, bark 'paintings'.

Okapa isn't a great town to be stuck in, but

about 15 km on from Okapa is the **Yagusa Valley**, where traditional culture is relatively intact. Here, the Highland Christian Mission (☎ 72 1881, PO Box 225, Goroka), has a guesthouse and two tree houses and welcomes visitors. The nightly cost is K18 or K28 with all meals. The mission is an American outfit and is apparently set on doing big things – there is hydroelectricity and a church is being built which will include an eight-metre revolving stage! First-hand reports are eagerly awaited.

An infrequent PMV from Goroka to Okapa costs about K6 and takes three or four hours, more after rain because of the very bad road. The wet season is from December to April.

GOROKA

The town of Goroka has grown from a small outpost in the mid-50s to its current position as a major commercial centre with a population around 25,000. It's still a typical PNG town clustered around the airstrip, but it's also spacious and attractive and conveys a sense of civic pride and community. There are several small parks and many tall pine trees.

The town is small enough to walk around and the atmosphere is much more relaxed than at Mt Hagen, perhaps because of a vigorously anti-rascal police chief. Along McNicholl St across from the Lutheran Guesthouse are several colonial-era houses in the 'Queensland' style, set in large gardens. Members of the judiciary live in them, and it's a sign of Goroka's relative safety that there is no apparent security – although maybe that's just because the police barracks are across the road.

At an altitude of 1600 metres, the climate is a perpetual spring – warm days and cool nights. Temperatures can drop to about 10° at night, especially in the dry season from May to November.

Information

The provincial government is hoping to establish a tourist bureau, but meanwhile the Bird of Paradise Hotel is the best place to get information. Bing Siga, the district ranger (☎ 72 2368, PO Box 657), should have information on the new national park planned for the Eastern Highlands, and can help with queries about Mt Wilhelm, which falls into his jurisdiction.

The town has an adequate range of facilities, including reasonable shopping, banks, a post office and the Raun Raun Theatre, an interesting performing arts complex. This is Talair's headquarters, Air Niugini and MAF also have offices here and the three major car rental firms are represented.

There's a council swimming pool just below Goroka Lodge that is open 9 am to 6 pm daily and costs K1. Be a bit careful walking between here and the town.

JK McCarthy Museum

McCarthy was one of PNG's legendary patrol officers and he wrote one of the classic books on New Guinea patrolling – *Patrol into Yesterday*. The museum that bears his name is off to the side of the airstrip, a reasonably lengthy walk from town. This is the only rival to the National Museum in Port Moresby, and it should definitely not be missed.

Among the exhibits, there are a variety of pottery styles, weapons, clothes and musical instruments, even some grisly jewellery, including a necklace of human fingers! Perhaps the most interesting feature is the fascinating collection of photos, many of which were taken by Mick Leahy when he first reached the area in 1933. There are also some relics from WW II, including a P-39 Aircobra left behind by the USAF after the war, which is behind the museum.

There is a shop with a selection of artefacts and handcrafts, including some striking modern paintings. It's open 8 am to noon and 1 to 4 pm on weekdays, 2 to 4 pm on Saturdays and 10 am to noon on Sundays. Admission is by donation and there is a K0.50 charge for taking photographs.

Market

Saturday is, as usual, the best market day. You'll see fruit and vegetables, rats,

possums, ferns, fungi, pigs and feathers. Despite all this, it's not as colourful as the Mt Hagen market.

Raun Raun Theatre

If you have a chance, it is well worth seeing a performance by the Raun Raun Theatre (☎ 72 1166, PO Box 118). This highly successful Goroka-based theatre company undertakes national tours and has also performed internationally to high acclaim. The theatre building itself is in the park opposite the market, a short walk from town, and it is an interesting and successful example of modern PNG architecture. Even if there isn't a scheduled performance, the company can often arrange a private, two-hour performance for K300. It is a bit expensive, but perhaps feasible if you get a large group together.

Mt Kiss Kiss Lookout

Wisdom St, beside the post office, leads to a track that climbs to an excellent lookout, Mt Kiss Kiss. It's a long, steep walk if you haven't got wheels, but the reward is an excellent view over the valley. Unfortunately, this has at times been off-limits to visitors because of rascal activity. Check the situation with a local.

Goroka Show

Goroka Show, the best of the Highland shows, is held over the Independence Day weekend (mid-September). Currently it's held in even-numbered years but might become an annual event. Goroka Show

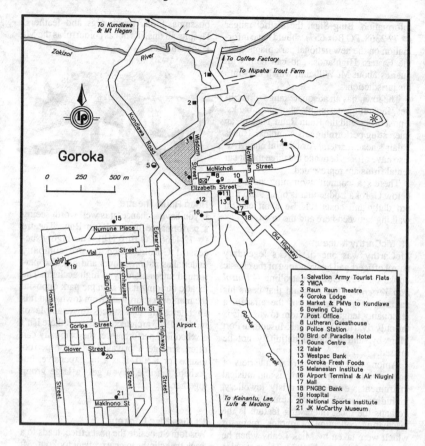

Goroka

0   250   500 m

1 Salvation Army Tourist Flats
2 YWCA
3 Raun Raun Theatre
4 Goroka Lodge
5 Market & PMVs to Kundiawa
6 Bowling Club
7 Post Office
8 Lutheran Guesthouse
9 Police Station
10 Bird of Paradise Hotel
11 Gouna Centre
12 Talair
13 Westpac Bank
14 Goroka Fresh Foods
15 Melanesian Institute
16 Airport Terminal & Air Niugini
17 Mall
18 PNGBC Bank
19 Hospital
20 National Sports Institute
21 JK McCarthy Museum

attracts (well, *hires*) more sing-sing groups than Mt Hagen's, and there are also bands and other cultural activities, as well as some elements of an agricultural show.

In 1992 the show included a sing-sing group from the Hagahai people, who discovered the rest of the world in 1984. This was their first public performance and they demanded a police escort all the way to Goroka – they had learnt that the new world was a big, bad place.

Accommodation in Goroka can be very scarce around showtime, with many places booked out months in advance.

Places to Stay – bottom end

The *Lutheran Guesthouse* (☎ 72 1171, PO Box 44), is right in the centre of town, behind the post office and is recommended. It's very clean, comfortable, convenient and friendly. Bear in mind that this is a church-run establishment and you will probably have to make some concessions. A bed, cooked breakfast and a good dinner costs K25; dinner is not available on Sunday, so the rate is K20 then.

Some people prefer the modern *National Sports Institute* (☎ 72 2391, fax 72 1941, PO Box 337) and it certainly is a good place to stay. Guests can take advantage of hot showers, satellite TV, tennis courts and other sports facilities.

There are 100 rooms at K14 per person, less with a student discount. Another K14 gets you three meals a day, but the Institute is about to take over the catering from an outside contractor so things might change. Check in at the office or, after hours, see Victor Simmons in room No 1.

It's a bit of a walk from the town centre, about a 20-minute walk from the post office, on Glover St near the museum. It's on the site of the old showgrounds (still used for the Goroka show), which are still shown on some maps.

The *YWCA* (☎ 72 1409, PO Box 636) is a residential hostel and is usually full, but they keep one room free for visiting women (only). It's a pleasant, cheerful place where you're likely to make a lot of friends. It's about 750 metres north of the post office.

The *Salvation Army Tourist Flats* (☎ 72 1218, PO Box 365) in McGrath St are a fair way from the town centre and they prefer to let by the week (K120), but they will let by the day (K25 per person). During the Goroka Show the rate rises to K30 per person and there is no single occupancy. The flats are becoming a little run-down, but they're quite OK and each has a stove, a fridge and attached bathroom. Two or four-bed flats are available.

The *Teachers College* (☎ 72 1039, 72 1257) sometimes has cheap rooms available, but it's a long way from town and not really worth the trouble.

Places to Stay – middle & top end

The *Bird of Paradise Hotel* (☎ 72 1144, fax 72 1007, PO Box 12) on Elizabeth St, in the centre of town, is the top hotel in Goroka, and it's one of the few hotels in PNG where paying K100-plus a night doesn't feel like a rip-off. All rooms have private facilities and all mod-cons, and cost from K110 a single or double, plus K15 per extra person. There are some excellent weekend specials on room rates – around 50% off. You can pay with Visa, MasterCard, Amex or Diners'.

'The Bird' has a pool, a couple of restau-

rants and two or three bars. There are squash courts and a gym for residents, and nonresidents can attend the evening aerobic classes for just K1.50. On Sundays, there are often informal volleyball games by the pool.

Goroka's other hotel, *Goroka Lodge* (☎ 72 2411, fax 72 2307, PO Box 2), runs a very poor second behind The Bird, although it is considerably cheaper. In the lodge section very small, spartan rooms with shared bathroom cost K39/48/54 a single/double/twin, and better-equipped rooms with attached bathroom in the motel section are K75/85 a single/double. Meals are available and on Sunday there's a barbecue; some nights there's a disco. The Lodge is a bit of a walk from the town centre, down and up a couple of steep hills, but you can get them to fetch you from the airport.

Places to Eat

By far the best places to eat are at the Bird of Paradise Hotel. The open-air *Deck Bar* is a good place to hang out and is open from 10 am to 10 pm. Meals, snacks, tea and coffee are available. At lunch there's a buffet where you can help yourself to a wide range of salads for just K3.50 and there are various other inexpensive dishes. At dinner, steaks are under K10 and fish & chips are K8. On Wednesday night there's a Reef 'n' Beef buffet for K17. The Bird also has the good, but expensive *Lahani Room* restaurant. Men will need to wear long trousers.

The *Bena Vista Restaurant*, behind the airstrip across from the Aero Club, is a popular place with main courses costing about K10 at lunch and K15 at dinner. There's also a bar, and it's worth having a beer to see the views.

Spices, in the shops at street level under The Bird, is open during the day and sells excellent snacks. Other than these there are the usual kai bars and meals at the *Goroka Lodge*. The food at the Lutheran Guesthouse is excellent but only for guests. *Goroka Fresh Food* sells a good range of produce.

Things to Buy

Some artefacts are sold from the footpath near the Bird of Paradise Hotel. If you've just arrived in the Highlands, this is an opportunity to buy that essential item of clothing, a Highlands hat. In recent years there has been an influx of baskets in all shapes and sizes, once a handcraft only of the Mendi area. Something as big as a laundry basket might cost K80, but prices are negotiable. Tell the seller that if the basket you want is still unsold at the end of the day you'll make an offer. There are a lot of other things, such as billums, spears, bows and arrows and necklaces, none cheap but all negotiable.

Across from the Bird of Paradise are a pricey artefacts shop and the Christian bookshop, which also has a few souvenirs. Other artefacts are sold in the lobby of the Bird of Paradise.

The Prison Rehabilitation Shop, in the low wooden buildings behind the police station, sells carvings.

The art department at the Goroka Teachers College produces and sells prints, paintings and so on using Western tools and traditional concepts. They also have some artefacts for sale.

Getting There & Away

Air Talair (☎ 72 1240) has its national headquarters at the airport and they have a travel agency here. Air Niugini (☎ 72 1211) and MAF (☎ 72 1080) also have offices at the airport.

Air Niugini has daily flights between Goroka and Moresby (K114), but their only other direct flight from Goroka is to Mt Hagen (K57) once or twice a week.

Talair flies to Mt Hagen (K57), Wewak (K98), Vanimo (K176), Moresby (K114), Lae (K62) and Madang (K54) most days. In Mt Hagen you can connect with flights to Tari (K130 from Goroka), the Sepik and other destinations. There's a weekly flight to Kundiawa (K34).

PMV The main PMV station is at the market, but if you're going to Lae or planning to stay at the Sports Institute, you may find the PMV stops on Edwards St, parallel to the airport, more convenient. There are PMVs to Lae (K10, four or five hours); to Kundiawa (K4);

to Mt Hagen (K8, around four hours); and to Madang (about K20). You currently have to take a Lae-bound PMV and change along the way, but a new road will make the journey much shorter and cheaper.

Car Rental Budget (☎ 72 2858) is in West Goroka, Hertz (☎ 72 1710) is at the Bird of Paradise Hotel and Avis (☎ 72 1084) is at the Air Niugini terminal. Apparently Avis will give you a discount if you book ahead through Air Niugini.

The Lutheran Guesthouse (☎ 72 1171) has a car which can usually be hired, for K2 an hour plus K0.40 a km.

Getting Around

It's easy enough to walk around Goroka and, consequently, there don't seem to be any taxis or urban PMVs.

AROUND GOROKA

You can arrange visits to coffee plantations or coffee processing plants around Goroka. Try to line up a trip with a coffee buyer; some of them can speak English and it is an interesting way to visit a Highlands village.

The Bird of Paradise Hotel runs various day tours in the area, for a minimum of two people, including one to visit the Asaro mud men for K25 per person. A botanist from Mt Gahavisuka Provincial Park sometimes calls in at the Lutheran Guesthouse on Friday evening to see if anyone wants to take his K15 tour.

Nupaha Trout Farm

About five km north-east of Goroka on a 4WD track (which continues on from Greathead Drive in North Goroka), this trout farm offers you the chance to catch and eat fish. You don't have to achieve the former to enjoy the latter, as you can buy freshly caught and cleaned fish for K2 and there's a barbecue to cook them on. Accommodation, in round houses, has recently been completed and will cost in the vicinity of K60 a night. For more information contact Robin Kosi (☎ 72 1855).

There was also a trout farm at Kotuni,

about 15 km out of Goroka; it has closed but there's a possibility of it starting up again.

Lufa

Lufa is south of Goroka and is a good base for climbing Mt Michael, named after those two original Highland 'Michaels': Mick Dwyer and Mick Leahy. There is a cave near Lufa with some interesting prehistoric cave paintings.

Bena Bena

About 10 km out of Goroka on the old road to Kainantu (it must have been a hard trip once) is the village of Bena Bena, which was until recently a centre for hand-loom weaving. The weaving seems to have stopped and the main sight in the area is the Rothman's tobacco factory. After seeing gammune twist tobacco rolled you can take a swim in the nearby river. The manager will guide you around the factory and point you towards the river. Start from Goroka early so you have time to get back before dark.

Mt Gahavisuka Provincial Park

This is an area of around 80 hectares set in beautiful mountain scenery. It is 11 km from Goroka and one km higher, and is reached by a 4WD road (dry weather only) that turns off Highlands Highway on the Mt Hagen side, opposite the Okiufa Community School (look out for the sign).

The park includes a botanical sanctuary, where exotic plants from all over PNG have been added to the local, orchids and rhododendrons. There are clearly marked walking tracks and a lookout at 2450 metres with a spectacular view. Facilities include picnic shelters, two orchid houses and an information centre. There is no admission fee. You can contact the ranger on 72 2368.

Asaro Mud Men

Many years ago, so the story goes, the village of Asaro came off second best in a tribal fight. Someone at Asaro had a bizarre inspiration and the revengeful warriors covered themselves with grey mud and huge mud masks before heading off on their inevitable

payback raid. When these ghostly apparitions emerged from the trees, their opponents scattered.

The mud men recreate this little caper for tourists, but unfortunately it has become rather commercialised and dull. The number of mud men appears to be in direct proportion to the number of kina-paying tourists. Mud men tours are arranged by the Bird of Paradise Motel for K25 per person, and by Trans Niugini Tours and Haus Poroman in Mt Hagen.

One traveller wrote that Komiufa, about five km from Asaro on the Highlands Highway, was a good place to see, very briefly, the mud men. Payment of K10 could persuade four men to don their masks and dance around for a couple of minutes.

Daulo Pass

The road out to Hagen is fairly flat through Asaro, but it then hairpins its way up to the 2450-metre-high Daulo Pass. The Pass is cold and damp but the views are spectacular, particularly if you're heading down from the pass towards Goroka. This has become a notorious spot for rascals to stop and rob vehicles. Very few attempt the trip after dark.

Simbu (Chimbu) Province

Land Area 8476 sq km
Population 195,000
Capital Kundiawa

Travelling west from Goroka, the mountains become much more rugged and the valleys become smaller and less accessible. Some of the highest mountains in PNG are in this region, including Mt Wilhelm, at 4509 metres, the highest of them all.

The province's name is said to date to the first patrol into the area. The story has it that steel axes and knives were given to the tribespeople and that the recipients replied that they were *simbu* – very pleased. The area was accordingly named Simbu, which was temporarily corrupted to Chimbu, and finally changed back to Simbu.

Despite its rugged terrain, Simbu Province is the most heavily populated region in PNG. The Simbu people have turned their steep country into a patchwork quilt of gardens that spreads up the side of every available hill. Population pressures are pushing them to even higher ground – to the detriment of remaining forests and, consequently, the birds of paradise. As in Enga Province, most people speak a similar language, and Simbu-speakers make up the second-largest language group in PNG.

Kundiawa, the provincial capital and site of the first government station in the Highlands, has been left behind by Goroka and Hagen. It has a spectacular airstrip, but its attractive location, on steep hillsides, may well have inhibited its development.

The Simbus have a reputation for being avid capitalists who keep a good eye on their coffee profits and also for being great believers in the payback raid. Minor warfare is still common in the Simbu region and aggrieved parties are all too ready to claim an eye-for-an-eye. In Kundiawa, check out the painted signboard at the police station, which depicts a tribal battle with the police not doing terribly much to stop it...

The old customs are breaking down, but at one time all the men in a village would live in a large men's house while their wives lived in individual round-houses – with the pigs.

KUNDIAWA

Although it's the provincial capital, you can cover most of Kundiawa in half an hour – and you won't be much better off for your efforts. There's a PNGBC bank, a post office, some rather limited shopping and that's about it. Most people go straight through to Mt Wilhelm, Goroka or Mt Hagen. One of the main problems is the absence of reasonably priced accommodation. If you're heading for Mt Wilhelm, try to get to Kundiawa early in the day to ensure that you don't get stuck there overnight.

There is a tourist officer, whose office is next to the Simbu Women's Resource Centre (see Places to Stay for directions). He has very little printed information but can probably help with queries about climbing Mt Wilhelm. He has no direct phone number, but can be contacted through the provincial government switchboard (☎ 75 1155) – he rang me back within half an hour!

The Simbu Women's Handicraft Shop is in the strip of government offices down the side road opposite the main government offices complex. There is very little stock.

Many people have enthused about rafting on the Wahgi River near Kundiawa, but unfortunately no operators are currently offering it, partly because they have had groups harassed by rascals. Ask around the local and foreign tour operators to see if anything has started up again. The scenery is excellent: the river goes through deep chasms, under small rope bridges and there are several good stretches of rapids and waterfalls.

There are a number of caves around Kundiawa that are used as burial places. Other large caves, suitable for caving enthusiasts, are only a few km from Kundiawa while the Keu Caves are very close to the main road near Chuave. The Nambaiyufa Amphitheatre is also near Chuave and is noted for its rock paintings.

Places to Stay & Eat

There are only two places to stay in Kundiawa and neither is cheap. The up-market Simbu Lodge suffered the fate of many hotels in PNG and burned down, and the *Kundiawa Hotel* (☎ 75 1033, PO Box 12), now fills the top-of-the-market niche. Unfortunately, although its prices reflect this status, K56/78 for singles/doubles with attached bathrooms, its quality doesn't. Even so, as the only hotel in town it can be full.

The only other alternative is the *Simbu Women's Resource Centre*, where the people are friendly and the prices high – K35 per person in a seven-bed room! No meals are available but there are cooking facilities. Follow the road past the hotel and the government offices, and turn left onto a muddy

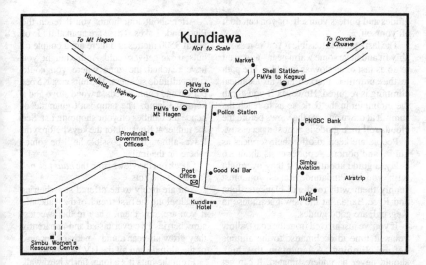

track as you go down the hill. It's a pink building.

The kai bar diagonally opposite the post office is reasonable, with fried rice for K1.20 and fish for K0.80.

Getting There & Away
Air The airport is quite spectacular as it's on a sloping ridge surrounded by mountains. Air Niugini (☎ 75 1273) has a weekly flight to/from Moresby (K113) and Talair has direct flights to Moresby (K113), Goroka (K34) and Madang (K68) about once a week. Simbu Aviation took over many of Talair's local routes, but might not still be in business. TransNiugini Airways (☎ 25 2211 in Moresby) might fill the breach.

PMV The fare to Goroka is K4, to Mt Hagen K4 and Kegsugl (for Mt Wilhelm) K5, and each of these sectors takes around two hours. PMVs for Kegsugl leave from the Shell station; others stop on the highway near the police station.

MT WILHELM
Climbing to the 4509-metre summit of Mt Wilhelm is, for many people, the highlight of their visit to the Highlands. On a clear day you can see both the north and south coasts. Even if you don't intend to tackle the summit, it is well worth staying near the base, from where you can explore the area and walk some of the way up the mountain.

While you're in the Mt Wilhelm area a visit to **Niglguma** village or **Gembogl** is worthwhile. You can walk to Gembogl from Kegsugl in a couple of hours and on the way you pass through half a dozen villages, including Niglguma. Gembogl has suffered the inroads of corrugated-iron construction, so Niglguma is more interesting.

Climbing the Mountain
Although this is a popular climb, it's quite hard work, especially if your exercise lately has been climbing into PMVs and sitting in boats. Allow yourself plenty of time to get used to the altitude before you start.

There are a number of ways of tackling the climb, depending on your wealth, health and available time: you can go with a tour company (talk to Traditional Travel or Niugini Tours) who will provide a guide, porters, food and equipment; you can hire guides and porters yourself; or you can do it all yourself.

The last option is feasible if you're reasonably fit and have some warm gear – and want to go as fast or as slow as you like. The path to the summit is marked and no technical climbing is required. However, if you climb the mountain in the dark, so as to reach the summit at dawn and see the views before the clouds roll in, a guide is almost a necessity.

People are keen to offer their services as guides and porters. A porter costs about K6 a day, a guide about K12. If they overnight with you at Pindaunde Lakes you must supply them with food and blankets. John and Rose Banda, at the new guesthouse in Kegsugl, are good guides.

If you've just arrived from the coast, allow yourself time to acclimatise to the altitude before climbing. A mountain this high should never be underestimated. It can get very cold on top and can easily become fogbound and even snow. Climbers (and guides) can suffer from altitude sickness, sunburn and hypothermia. See the Health section in the Facts for the Visitor chapter. It is vital that you have sufficient food and warm clothing and that you assess the weather and your physical state realistically. You would be most unwise to tackle it alone. In addition, make sure you have a hat and sun cream (you burn deceptively quickly at high altitudes), water containers (there's no water on the last stretch past the lakes), a torch with a spare globe and strong batteries, gloves and candles. Cooking gear might be useful – check in Kegsugl whether there are still utensils at the lake huts.

You might be confronted by a traditional landowner who asks for a fee of a few kina to climb the mountain. He is within his rights.

The first stage of the climb entails walking up to the Pindaunde Lakes from the high school and disused airstrip at Kegsugl. The track takes off from the top end of the airstrip. After climbing fairly steeply through dense rainforest, the track turns into the Pindaunde Valley and continues less steeply up the hummocky valley floor.

After about four hours you'll reach the Pindaunde Lakes. These are at an altitude of about 3500 metres and there are a couple of huts; it can get very cold. At this height, you have reached the zone where you could suffer altitude sickness. The huts cost K5 per person and contain beds, a wood stove and a kerosene lamp. The lamp isn't guaranteed, hence the candles on your shopping list. See the ranger at Kegsugl for the keys before you leave, although it's possible he'll be somewhere on the trail.

Check out the views from the *haus pek pek* (toilet) at the huts.

You are likely to be offered strawberries for sale along the first stretch of the walk, and if you are, buy them. They're the sweetest strawberries I've ever tasted and apparently they grow all year round – perhaps because of the altitude and all the UV radiation.

From the huts it's a long, fairly hard walk to the summit, taking about five hours. Some walkers reckon it is better to spend a day acclimatising at the lake huts and exploring the area before attempting it. After the lakes, water is difficult to find, so carry your own. It can become very cold, wet, windy and foggy at the top. The clouds roll in soon after dawn so it is wise to start from the huts as early as possible – maybe 1 am! – hence the torch on your shopping list. The ascent and descent will probably take you all day (coming down to the huts takes about three hours), but some people do go all the way back to Kegsugl (about 2½ hours from the huts).

Places to Stay

Herman, whose guesthouse near Kegsugl was a haven for backpackers, has gone back to Germany but Johnny Kail Dor, Herman's brother-in-law, has taken over the guesthouse and charges about K10 a night. He's friendly and helpful and might be a source of strawberries! Good meals are available.

There is also a good new guesthouse near the airstrip, run by Henry Agum. It's very clean and a bed costs K10 a night. There are cooking facilities. Both places can arrange guides and porters.

A new place is due to open, a bit more up-market than these two. Bob Ward (☎ 72 1315, Port Moresby) is building a hostel near the start of the trail to the huts and plans to charge K50 per person with meals or K25 without.

There used to be a good guesthouse in Niglguma village, at the junction of two streams on the Kundiawa-Kegsugl road, past Gembogl, but it burnt down. Let us know if it has been rebuilt.

Getting There & Away

Kegsugl, at the foot of the mountain, is about 57 km from Kundiawa along a road that has to be seen to be believed. You can get there by irregular PMVs that cost K5 and take a couple of hours. They leave from the Shell service station in Kundiawa. The Bundi road branches off to the right over a bridge, just before Kegsugl. The airstrip at Kegsugl, once the highest in PNG at 2469 metres, has been shut down.

WALKING TO MADANG

The turn-off for the Bundi road, and the trek to Brahmin (and Madang) is between Gembogl and Kegsugl. You turn right over a bridge, instead of left to Kegsugl. You can walk right down to Madang – but most people catch a PMV at Brahmin.

It's a relatively easy trek, though hot, because you follow a 4WD track. Some vehicles have apparently gone through. A reasonable pace would get you to Madang in three fairly long days. Bring your own food, although you can get meals at Bundi.

The first stretch is largely up-hill and there are very few villages. The first village you come to is **Pandambai**, where there's a store, and a missionary lives here. Next along is **Bundikara**, where there's an attractive waterfall and you can apparently stay in the village. There are great views from lookout points along the way. Some people take about five hours to get to Pandambai; others get to Bundikara in the same time.

From Bundikara it's 3½ hours to **Bundi** where there is a group of lodges known as the *Mt Sinai Hotel*. These cost K10 per person with breakfast, about K18 for full board. The meals are good. From Bundi it's 2½ hours to War, which is just after a suspension bridge and from War it is a 3½-hour climb to Brahmin Mission. A PMV from Brahmin to Madang costs K5 or K6 and takes about 1½ hours. Brahmin is about 20 km from the Lae-Madang road.

Western Highlands Province

Land Area 8288 sq km
Population 340,000
Capital Mt Hagen

Continuing west from Simbu Province you descend into the large Wahgi Valley. Although almost half the province was restricted or uncontrolled until the '60s, traditional dress is now rarely worn. You will still see some of the older men dressed traditionally, especially for market days and sing-sings.

Mt Hagen is the provincial capital and although it is not particularly attractive it does have the somewhat out-of-control energy of a frontier town. The surrounding countryside is worth exploring.

The province's terrain varies between swamps just above sea level and a number of peaks that are over 4000 metres high, including Mt Giluwe at 4362 metres and Mt Hagen at 4026 metres. Forest only remains on the mountain slopes and the valleys and lower hills are grass covered. This is the result of human activity: shifting (slash-and-burn) cultivation and hunting fires. Gardens and stands of casuarinas are scattered through the hills and large tea and coffee plantations now dominate the most fertile valley floors.

The men usually have beards and their traditional clothing is a wide belt of beaten bark with a drape of strings in front and a bunch of tanket (or tanget) leaves behind. The leaves are known, descriptively, as *arse-tanket*. The women can be just as decoratively dressed, with string skirts and cuscus fur hanging around their necks.

Today, that attire is usually reserved for sing-sings and bright lengths of printed cloth and T-shirts are more likely to be the everyday wear. Naturally, traditional dress is more likely to be seen in the smaller towns and villages than in main towns. At sing-sings both sexes will have beautiful headdresses with bird-of-paradise plumes and other feathers.

The Wahgi people keep carefully tended vegetable gardens and neat villages, often with paths bordered by decoratively planted flowers, ceremonial parks with lawns and groves of trees and colourful memorials to deceased big men.

Sing-sings are still an integral part of life and you should make every effort to see one. This is, unfortunately, not all that easy to do, but keep an ear to the ground, especially if you're walking through the region.

BANZ & MINJ

These two small towns are mid-way between Kundiawa and Mt Hagen in the Wahgi Valley; Banz is a few km north of the

A typical Highlands village

Highway and Minj is a few km south. It's an attractive area, but other than that there is little to attract the traveller, unless you want to use the excellent golf course at Minj.

Places to Stay

In Minj, *Tribal Tops* (☎ 56 5538, PO Box 13) is operated by Tribal World who also run the Plumes & Arrows Hotel in Mt Hagen and the Sepik International in Wewak. It is surrounded by a high wall, and has an attractive garden and swimming pool. Like the other places in the chain, it is liberally decorated with Sepik art, much of which is for sale (it ain't cheap). Singles/doubles are K83/104, but it might be possible to arrange cheaper packages – see Plumes & Arrows in Hagen.

The hotel in Banz seems to be concentrating on beer sales.

Getting There & Away

A PMV from Hagen to the Minj turn-off is K2 and a further K0.20 will get you to the town centre, such as it is.

MT HAGEN

This is the provincial capital for the Western Highlands, and although it is now commercially more important than Goroka, it is not nearly as attractive. It lies 445 km from Lae and 115 km from Goroka.

Mt Hagen was just a patrol station before WW II, but in the last 20 years, with the opening of Enga and the Southern Highlands, it has grown into a unruly city with over 40,000 people living in town and nearby. It's quite a shock to find a PNG city where the streets are packed with people.

Hagen can sometimes be quite tense; there's a 'wild west' feel to the place. Payrolls for many businesses in the region now go by helicopter because trucks are ambushed so often.

Aside from the rascal problem, the more traditional tribal warfare continues, exacerbated by the value of coffee and the over-population of the best land. Most people will know which areas to avoid at any given time. Don't walk around at night.

The town acquired its name by a rather

roundabout route. It is named after nearby Mt Hagen, which in turn was named after a German administrator, Kurt von Hagen.

In 1895 two Germans started off on a badly planned and ill-fated attempt to cross the island from north to south. They were murdered by two of their carriers, although one wonders if they would have survived the trip in any case. The carriers later escaped from custody. In the subsequent hunt for them, von Hagen was shot and killed near Madang in 1897; he was buried at Bogadjim.

Rascalism can work in your favour. Someone told me how he left his luggage in an Air Niugini office while he checked out hotels, but found the office closed for the weekend when he returned. He explained his problem to a group of young men who were hanging around. A few minutes later all hell broke loose – crashing glass and alarms going crazy. A guy ran up with his luggage, gave it to him and said, 'You can go now – quickly!'

Information

The Department of Lands & Surveys at the end of Kuri St has a good selection of maps, although they are less likely than the National Mapping Bureau in Moresby to have complete stocks. All the main banks have branches, as do the airlines. This is the headquarters for MAF.

Forster's Newsagent on Hagen Drive has a good collection of books and stationary. Ask around about the Mt Hagen Bushwalking Club, which is currently dormant.

Market

The Saturday market is one of the biggest and most interesting markets in PNG and, if you're lucky, you will still see some people in traditional dress. You're unlikely to see plumed headdresses, but you may notice young men with leaves, feathers or flowers in their hair as a more subtle continuation of the tradition. Snapping a picture of anyone is likely to be followed by a demand for money – it's always best to ask permission first.

It is even rarer for women to dress traditionally than it is for men, but they make up for this with the sheer brightness of their dresses and billums. Add a brilliant kerchief,

several flowing scarves in various colours, traditional facial tattoos and you have a striking sight.

Don't forget to look at what is for sale; aside from a superb range of fruit and vegetables, there are pigs and, when I was there, a cassowary tightly trussed up in lengths of bamboo.

Mt Hagen Show

Although the Mt Hagen Show is not as big as the Goroka Show, it's definitely worth seeing – it's an experience you won't forget.

Make sure you arrive early in the day, say before 8 am, to see the groups dressing and putting on impromptu performances for the people who can't afford a ticket into the grandstand. These are powerful and vigorous – even ribald – compared with the more formal stuff dished up for the dignitaries in the arena.

Birdlovers might be relieved to know that there isn't a general slaughter just before showtime; most of the feather headdresses and costumes are extremely valuable heirlooms, and many are hired for the occasion.

If the politicians can be believed, Mt Hagen Show will become an annual event from 1993, held on the third weekend in August. It might not be up to the politicians, however, as the show is organised by a local committee, with a big contribution from Trans Niugini Tours, and if they make a loss there isn't much incentive to continue.

As a visitor, you will be expected to buy a grandstand ticket. The price is high (K25) but without this contribution the show couldn't be held. All those groups have to be transported to Mt Hagen and accommodated there, and they are competing for some fairly large prizes. Also, paying the entry fee gives you the opportunity to stroll around the arena in a sea of colour and noise unlike anything on earth. It's astounding. When and if a fence is built around the showground, everyone will pay an entry fee of only a few kina.

The showground is quite a way from town, beyond the airport. You can get there by PMVs and on foot, but hitching a lift on showday isn't difficult.

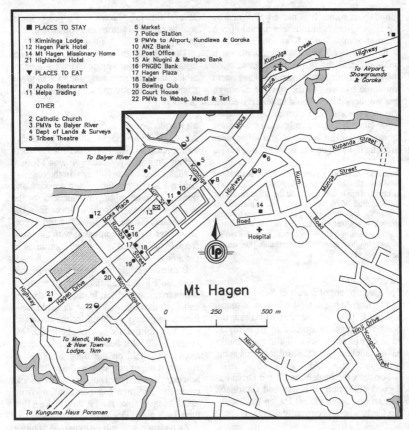

■ PLACES TO STAY

1 Kimininga Lodge
12 Hagen Park Hotel
14 Mt Hagen Missionary Home
21 Highlander Hotel

▼ PLACES TO EAT

8 Apollo Restaurant
11 Melpa Trading

OTHER

2 Catholic Church
3 PMVs to Balyer River
4 Dept of Lands & Surveys
5 Tribes Theatre

6 Market
7 Police Station
9 PMVs to Airport, Kundiawa & Goroka
10 ANZ Bank
13 Post Office
15 Air Niugini & Westpac Bank
16 PNGBC Bank
17 Hagen Plaza
18 Talair
19 Bowling Club
20 Court House
22 PMVs to Wabag, Mendi & Tari

Mt Hagen

0   250   500 m

To Balyer River

To Airport, Showgrounds & Goroka

To Mendi, Wabag & New Town Lodge, 1km

To Kunguma Haus Poroman

Organised Tours

If you plan to stay at Ambua Lodge near Tari, you may be able to ride up with a Trans Niugini Tours (☎ 52 1438, fax 52 2470, PO Box 371, Mt Hagen) vehicle, which will give you a chance to stop along the way. Its head office is on Kongin St behind the hospital and quite a walk from town. It has tours around the area and to see the mud men of Asaro. Haus Poroman (see the Places to Stay section below) also arranges tours.

Places to Stay – bottom end & middle

The *Kunguma Haus Poroman* (☎ 52 2722,

fax 52 2207, PO Box 1182) should not be missed, no matter what budget you're travelling on. It's clean, comfortable and an interesting place to stay. This is a good place to meet other travellers and to get information, especially on the Highlands. It is very relaxed and friendly but also very competently run. I was there over the Mt Hagen Show weekend and despite an overflow of guests the extraordinary hospitality didn't waver for a second. Why aren't there more places like this?

It's usually just called Haus Poroman, which means 'house of friends'. Near Kunguma village, about seven km from

Top: Mt Wilhelm, PNG's highest mountain, Simbu Province (YP)
Left: Traditional houses, near Mendi, Southern Highlands Province (RE)
Right: Whagi Valley near Mt Hagen, Western Highlands Province (JM)

Mt Hagen Cultural Show, Western Highlands Province (JM)

town, it perches on a ridge, with superb views across Hagen and the valley to the mountains.

Keith & Maggie Wilson, the owners, or Liz, the manager, will give you a lift out from town for K7. Phone Haus Poroman or, during the day, go to its office in town at the Tribes Theatre on Kumniga St.

The original lodge, built in traditional bush materials, is now the dining and lounge area, with an open fire, a well-stocked library and a range of videos (some made by Maggie) about PNG. Accommodation with shared facilities for singles/doubles costs K31/42, in well designed traditional round houses; with attached bathrooms it's K47/62. There is also a dormitory hut for backpackers (you'll need a sleeping bag) which costs K12.50 per person. New facilities are being added, so check current options and prices.

Maki the hornbill flies around the place, and there are other birds and animals, including a rare white cuscus, in a small zoo. And there's an extremely large and rather too friendly dog.

There are plenty of things to do in the surrounding area: there's a marked trail through the rainforest; you can visit the nearby village and watch traditional crafts being made; make a three-hour trek through the Nebilyer Valley, through forest and past villages to the Leahy's coffee plantation; make a one-day walk to the huge Kum Caves (K25 with a guide) or search for gold at Kuta Ridge (K8 with a guide).

Day tours further afield, such as to Baiyer River Sanctuary (from K30 per person, minimum K80) are also available. Haus Poroman is now organising various longer tours, including trekking and Sepik expeditions.

If you decide to stay in town there are a number of reasonable options.

The *Mt Hagen Missionary Home* (☎ 52 1041, PO Box 394) is across from the hospital, which is a short walk from the market. The home is friendly and very clean, but it's no longer particularly cheap, with beds in a shared room costing K33, or K40 for a double room, both including breakfast. Volunteers get a discount.

Kimininga Lodge (☎ 52 2399, fax 52 1834, PO Box 408) is on the Goroka side of town, about 10 minutes' walk from the centre, past the market. If you are coming from Goroka by PMV get off before you get into town. There are three classes of rooms: Class A – K67/77 for singles/doubles with bathroom; Class B – K42 for singles with common bathroom and K54 for doubles with bathroom; Class C – K29/40 for pretty basic singles/doubles in the old wing with common bathroom. Backpackers pay K10 for a bed in a shared B-class room. All prices include a light breakfast and good meals are available at reasonable prices. The A-class rooms are comparable to those at Plumes & Arrows Inn, although the overall atmosphere isn't as good.

The top-end *Plumes & Arrows Inn*, near the airport, has bunk beds for K30.

Pretty much as a last resort, you could try the *New Town Lodge* (☎ 52 2872, PO Box 1006), on the highway about a km past the Highlander. It's very spartan and can get noisy, but it is clean and friendly. Some PMVs run past, but walking out here at night could be unsafe. Small rooms are K40/45 a single/double, including breakfast.

Places to Stay – top end

The *Highlander Hotel* (☎ 52 1355, fax 52 1216, PO Box 34) is at the west end of the main street, not far from the town centre. It has two wings and rooms in either wing have private facilities and tea or coffee-making equipment. The newer rooms have all mod-cons. Rooms range in price from K92 to K135. The Highlander is surrounded by pleasant gardens with a heated swimming pool; it's quiet and peaceful, but a little colourless. If you arrive after 5 pm (and haven't already booked) ask about standby rates.

The *Hagen Park Motel* (☎ 52 1388, fax 52 2282, PO Box 81) is rather more noisy and active and starting to look a little run-down. The rooms here are quite large: a budget room costs K45 and B-class room (the same room with TV and coffee-making facilities) costs K75/85 a single/double. A-class rooms are K85/95. The food is also a bit cheaper than at the Highlander.

The *Plumes & Arrows Inn* (☎ 55 1555, fax 55 1546, PO Box 86) is a bit inconvenient for town, but is only a five-minute walk from the airport. It has a high stockade fence and it feels like a fortress, but there are some attractive gardens and a swimming pool inside. This is the headquarters for Tribal World, a company that organises up-market tours in the Sepik region and around the Highlands. A-class rooms are K135 a double, B-class are K82/103 a single/double and there are backpacker beds for K30.

Places to Eat

The food at *Kunguna Haus Poroman* is excellent. A light breakfast costs K4 and a big full breakfast is K7. Lunch is K2.50 to K7 and dinner is K15. Traditional mumus are sometimes organised and backpackers can cook for themselves.

A full breakfast at the *Highlander Hotel* costs K10.75, and main courses are around K18. There's a Wednesday night buffet dinner for K18.

The *Plumes & Arrows Inn* has good food, with decent snacks for K4, main courses about K9 at lunch and K15 at dinner. A pot of tea will set you back K4, though. The very pleasant lounge/dining room area has Sepik art for sale.

Other than the hotel dining rooms there are a few choices. In Hagen Plaza, the *Plaza Coffee Shop* has sandwiches, omelettes, milk shakes and so on – lunch costs from K2.50. The patio is a good place to regroup after pounding the streets of Hagen – check out the hungry tortoises in the pool. It's closed on Sundays and after 4 pm.

The *Apollo* Chinese restaurant is open daily for dinner and for lunch on weekdays. The K5.50 three-course lunch special is good value; most main courses are about K8.

Melpa Trading, in the centre of town on Hagen Drive, is a cut above the usual kai bar, and there are tables on the footpath. It stays open until about 7 pm daily.

Getting There & Away

Air The airport is at Kagamuga, about 10 km from town. Air Niugini (☎ 52 1183) and Talair (☎ 52 1347) have offices in town and MAF (☎ 55 1506) has its headquarters at the airport.

Air Niugini flies to Moresby (K155) at least daily, but its flights to other parts of the country aren't very frequent. They include Madang (K67) on Monday, Friday and Saturday, Wewak (K83) and Vanimo (K137) on Wednesday, Goroka (K57) on Thursday and Saturday (to, not from Goroka), and from (but not to) Tabubil (K99) on Thursday. There are no direct Air Niugini flights between Mt Hagen and Lae.

Talair has an extensive network of flights, and flies daily (except Sunday) to Wewak (K83) and Vanimo (K137), Goroka (K57), Lae (K87), Madang (K67), Mendi (K48), Tari (K79) and Tabubil (K137). You can make connections to Moresby (K132) and other places.

MAF flies twice weekly to literally dozens of third-level airstrips. If you're planning a walk, and want to know where along your route you could bail out, or how you could make some shortcuts, go and talk to them.

PMV PMVs heading east, to Simbu and Goroka, leave from the market. Those heading west, to Mendi and Tari, leave from the highway near the Dunlop building. Wabag-bound PMVs (K5) can usually be found here as well; some continue on to Porgera (K14). There are regular connections to Mendi (K10, three to four hours), Kundiawa (K4, about two hours) and to Goroka (K8, four hours). PMVs to Baiyer River (K3, around 1½ hours) leave from the corner of Moka Place and Kumniga Rd.

Car Rental Hertz (☎ 55 1522), Budget (☎ 55 1260) and Avis (☎ 55 1350) have representatives.

Getting Around

To/From the Airport The airport is about 10 km from town. Most places to stay will collect you. A PMV from the airport to town costs K0.60, sometimes more coming the other way. Walk out of the terminal, turn left and walk down to the small group of shops (if you went straight ahead you'd get to the Plumes & Arrows Inn), where PMVs stop. Most PMVs stop at the market, with a few going through town along the highway. Other than these there are few PMVs in Mt Hagen.

Taxi The Timstar Travel Service (☎ 52 2933) in Hagen Plaza has a taxi.

BAIYER RIVER
The 120-hectare Baiyer River wildlife sanctuary is 55 km north of Mt Hagen and it *used* to be one of the best places in the Highlands to visit and to stay. Sadly, it is now quite run-down and has become unsafe. The lodge has closed, at least temporarily – when it was open it cost K10 a night and there were student discounts. This situation could change; ask Haus Poroman which still does tours when it's possible, and you could try phoning the sanctuary's superintendent on 52 1482. There's a K1 entry fee to the sanctuary.

If you visit, and everything has been maintained in the intervening period, you'll find the largest collection of birds of paradise in the world, nature trails through the forest, display trees used by wild birds of paradise. Don't forget birds of paradise moult between January and March.

There are many animal and bird enclosures dotted around the rainforest and some good picnic spots. Not only are there birds of paradise, but also hornbills and parrots. There are some cassowaries, but they're in cages – a good thing, too, because they're downright mean looking! They also have a large collection of possums and tree kangaroos.

A garden has been established with special plants to attract butterflies – over 84 species, including the famous Ulysses, have been sighted.

Getting There & Away
Haus Poroman makes day tours (from K30 per person, minimum K80) when it's feasible, and if the situation improves some of the other operators might start tours again. A PMV from the corner of Moka Place and Kumniga Rd in Mt Hagen costs K3. On the way you pass through the spectacular Baiyer River Gorge. The PMV trip takes about 1½ hours and would be safer than driving yourself.

Enga Province

Land Area 10,790 sq km
Population 195,000
Capital Wabag

Beyond Mt Hagen to the north-west the roads deteriorate and the country is less developed although, as elsewhere in the Highlands, coffee is an important local industry. This situation is changing, especially with the development of the giant gold and silver mine at Porgera in the west. Porgera produces more gold than any other in the world outside South Africa, although other mines in PNG are vying for the title.

Even in the '60s much of this region was still virtually independent from government control, and it was a part of Western Province until 1973. Control may have arrived, but tribal warfare can still occur. You may occasionally see circular, fenced areas filled with green and purple *tanget* bushes. These are the burial places of victims of tribal fighting.

Wabag is the provincial capital but it is still more an outlying town to Hagen than a major centre in its own right. The province is made up of rugged mountains and high valleys and the main rivers are the Lai and the Lagaip. The people are fragmented into small clans, but the Enga language-group covers most of the province and Engas belong to the largest single language-group in PNG. Some tribes have close similarities with the people of the Southern Highlands.

Enga had a very bad reputation for rascals, and while that seems to have died down, tribal fighting and other friction caused by 'outsiders' working at the mine can cause problems.

It can get very cold in Enga, so come prepared.

WABAG

From Mt Hagen the Wabag road starts out in the same direction as the Mendi road, then branches off north-west. It climbs over the Kaugel Pass, which is nearly 3000 metres high, before Wapenamanda.

Wabag has a large cultural centre in the valley that cuts the town in two. It's open from 9 am to 4 pm on weekdays and has an art gallery and museum. The gallery has a workshop where you can see young artists making 'sand paintings', the principal artwork on display in the gallery. Different coloured sands are mixed with glue and applied to a hard surface, usually plasterboard, with striking visual effect. The adjacent museum has a large number of war shields, wigs and masks from many parts of PNG as well as Enga Province.

Places to Stay & Eat

The *Malya Hostel* (☎ 57 1108, PO Box 237) is a short way out of town on the road to Mt Hagen and is run by the provincial government. Rooms cost K50, including breakfast; lunch is K5 and dinner K8. It isn't in great condition. Not far from the Malya Hostel is the *Teachers' Transit Hostel*, which charges K20 a night; a good dinner costs about K10 and breakfast is K5.

The *Kaiap Orchid Lodge* (☎ 52 2087, PO Box 193) is some way out of Wabag. About 2700 metres above sea level, it is built from local bush materials and is surrounded by gardens, with more than 100 species of orchids and 13 species of rhododendron. There are walks you can do in the local area and, with luck, you may well see birds of paradise.

It's a friendly, informal place with a bar, lounge, a log fire and good food. Unfortunately, tribal fighting closed the lodge in late '92, and although it is expected to re-open we don't have current prices. It used to be very good value, at about K20 for a bed and meals for around K8. From Wabag, you can either ring the lodge and get picked up (if

no-one answers go to Kol Trading in town, which is run by the same people). You can also get here by catching a PMV from Wabag to Sari village, a couple of km from town along the road to Laiagam, and from there making a tough but pleasant two-hour walk on the road up to the mountain ridge. Before you do this check that the lodge is open and that the area is safe.

Getting There & Away

A PMV from Mt Hagen to Wabag costs K5, and it's about K4 from Wabag on to Laiagam. The scenery on the three to four-hour trip from Hagen to Wabag is magnificent and the road is now sealed most of the way. The road to Porgera has been upgraded for gold-mine traffic and is now good.

Although the roads are no longer much of a deterrent to visiting Wabag, the tribal fighting in the area might be. Ask around before making the trip. Enga Province is officially dry and there are roadblocks where your pack might be searched for alcohol. The people doing the searching don't always identify themselves as government officers and can be aggressive. Keep goodies like personal stereos out of sight, and argue (politely) if it's suggested that you might want to give a present.

AROUND WABAG

Wabag to Mendi

If you have a sturdy 4WD you can continue beyond Wabag to Laiagam and down to Mendi. It's hard going and the road from Laiagam to Mendi is often closed between Kandep and Mendi due to poor road conditions and washed away bridges. If it is closed, you have an interesting 54-km walk along the highest road in PNG ahead of you. It may be possible to stay at the mission about halfway along the road at Pingarip.

Laiagam

Laiagam has the National Botanical Garden with a huge collection of orchids.

Kandep to Margarima

There's a road from Kandep to Margarima,

about halfway between Mendi and Tari. It runs through magnificent scenery with extensive marshes and high mountains, inhabited by many relatively isolated people. The road is often washed out so transport can be hard to find. You'll probably have to walk.

Lake Rau

Lake Rau is a crater lake at nearly 3000 metres in the centre of Enga Province. It's a day's walk from Pumas, above Laiagam and you will need a guide.

Southern Highlands Province

Land Area 25,988 sq km
Population 290,000
Capital Mendi

The Southern Highlands are made up of lush, high valleys between impressive limestone peaks. This region is particularly beautiful and traditional cultures thrive, especially in the Tari Basin, with many people retaining their traditional ways and dress. The headwaters of some mighty rivers, the Kikori, Erave and Strickland among them, cross the province and Mt Giluwe, 4362 metres high, is the second tallest mountain in PNG.

This most remote region of the Highlands is still relatively undeveloped, although big oil and gas finds near Lake Kutubu and a huge alluvial gold mine at Mt Kare are rapidly changing that. Even in the past, it was at the end of the trade route from the Gulf of Papua to the Highlands.

Beyond the Wahgi/Hagen area, both to the south-west past Mendi and north-west around Wabag, is the country of the 'wigmen' – these are the Huli, the Duna and a number of other tribes whose men are famous for the intricately decorated wigs that they wear. The proud Huli men of the Tari Basin, in particular, still wear their impressive traditional decorations. The Huli are the largest ethnic group in the Southern

Highlands with a population of around 40,000 and a territory exceeding 2500 sq km.

The Huli do not live in villages, but in scattered homesteads, dispersed through immaculately and intensively cultivated valleys. The gardens are delineated by trenches and mud walls up to three metres high, broken by brightly painted gateways made of stakes. These trenches are used not only to mark boundaries and control the movement of pigs, but also to secretly deploy large troops of warriors in times of war. As usual, the women do nearly all the work, while the men concentrate on displaying their finery. War was and to some extent still is a primary interest of the men.

The Mendi area is now the most developed part of the Southern Highlands (although the Tari area has more attractions and services for travellers) but it was not explored by Europeans until 1935 – these early explorers called it the Papuan Wonderland. It was 1950 when the first airstrip was constructed and 1952 before tribal warfare was prohibited. Not unnaturally the Mendi tribes turned their energies to attacking government patrols who were still fighting them off as late as 1954. The discovery of the beautiful Lavani Valley in 1954 set newspapers off with high-flown stories about the discovery of some lost Shangri-la.

The Southern Highlands is starting to attract caving expeditions as the limestone hills and the high rainfall is ideal for the formation of caves. Some caves of enormous depth and length have already been explored and it is a distinct possibility that some of the deepest caves in the world await discovery in this region.

CULTURE
Wigs

The striking decorative wigs that distinguish the wigmen are made from human hair. The hair is usually the wigman's own, supplemented by hair 'donated' by wives and children, who are consequently often short-haired. The whole design is held together by woven string. It is possible to tell which tribe

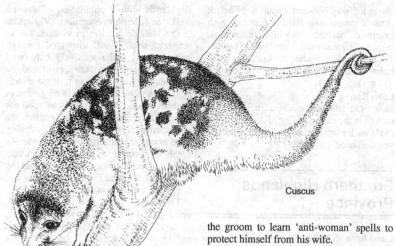

Cuscus

a man comes from by the way he wears his hair or decorates it.

The Huli wigmen cultivate yellow ever-lasting daisies especially to decorate their wigs and they also use feathers and cuscus fur. They often wear a band of snakeskin on their foreheads, a cassowary quill through their nasal septa and their faces may be dec-orated with yellow and red ochre.

Flutes similar to Pan pipes are a popular form of entertainment.

Brides in Black

Mendi brides wear black for their wedding – they are coated in black *tigaso* tree oil and soot and they continue to wear this body colouring for a month after the wedding. The tigaso tree oil comes from Lake Kutubu and is traded all over the area.

During this time neither the bride or the groom work, nor is the marriage consum-mated. This gives the bride time to become acquainted with her husband's family and for the groom to learn 'anti-woman' spells to protect himself from his wife.

Throughout the Highlands, women are traditionally distrusted by men, who go to extraordinary lengths to protect themselves and maintain their status. Sexual relations are not undertaken lightly. Contact with women is believed to cause sickness, so the two sexes often live in separate houses and the men often prefer to cook their own food. Boys are usually removed from their mothers' houses at a very young age.

Women travellers should bear these customs in mind, because in many places they are still strictly upheld. Violence against PNG women is widespread.

Widows in Blue

A dead man's wife, daughters, mother, sisters and sisters-in-law, coat themselves with bluish-grey clay while in mourning. The wife carries vast numbers of strings of the seeds known as 'job's tears'. One string a day is removed until eventually, with the removal of the last string, the widow can wash herself of her clay coating and remarry. This is usually about nine months after the death.

Women's Houses

The walls of women's houses are about four metres high, with kunai thatched roofs and walls of pitpit cane on the outside. The women sleep in semi-circular sleeping rooms at each end of the house, and the pigs sleep in stalls along one wall. The sitting and cooking area is in the centre.

Long Houses

Long houses known as *haus lains* are built along the sides of Mendi ceremonial grounds and used as guesthouses at sing-sings and pig kills. They can be up to 150 metres long, although 70 metres is the usual length and they are built beside stone-filled pits where the pigs are cooked.

Warfare

Land ownership is highly complex and very important, so disputes over land are often at the root of conflicts. In general, people inherit land rights, not just from their parents, but from any known ancestor. All the descendants of a woman who planted a tree might have rights to its fruit; and people will probably have rights to a number of widely scattered pieces of land.

Fighting arrows are carved from black-palm and are traditionally tipped with human bone. The tips were made from the forearm of a male ancestor so that his spirit could 'guide' the arrow to an enemy. Although casualties are fairly rare in traditional warfare, the men are fine bowmen and can shoot over long distances. They also carry bone daggers carved from the leg bone of a cassowary. Fights are still quite common.

Face Decoration

Imbong'gu girls paint their faces red and their lips white for sing-sings. Their heads are crowned with a great range of bird feathers, including several raggiana bird-of-paradise feathers. The wigmen wear their wigs and blacken their faces with soot, whiten their beards and eyes and colour their lips and noses red.

MENDI

Despite being the capital of the Southern Highlands, Mendi is just a small town, built around an airport. It shelters in a long green valley, surrounded by beautiful limestone peaks. It has a population of around 6000 and, although it can supply all essentials, there is not much to keep you hanging around. It's really just the starting point for a trip to the Tari Basin or to Lake Kutubu.

Friday and Saturday, when tribespeople crowd into town, are the best times to visit Mendi, although it can be rough on pay weeks.

The big oil project near Lake Kutubu is changing the face of the Mendi area. Oil began flowing through the pipeline down to the Gulf of Papua in 1992, and the Chevron company is fulfilling its agreements with the local landowners, the Foi and Fasu people, which include building a road from Mendi to Pimaga and eventually on to Moro, the company headquarters near the north-west end of Lake Kutubu. The Moro airstrip will be upgraded and given to the government, so more flights will go there in future.

Information

Mendi has Westpac and PNGBC banks, a handful of shops, supermarkets and kai bars, a post office, a hotel and, being a provincial capital, a lot of government offices where it's difficult to find anyone at their desks.

If you're heading to Lake Kutubu, call in at the Foi Diagaso Oil Company (☎ 59 1328, fax 59 1305), near Mendi Motors, to arrange meals and accommodation at the Pimaga guesthouse or Lake Kutubu Lodge. This company belongs to the Foi people and handles their side of the Chevron development, as well as running the accommodation.

There used to be a small museum, and there is talk of re-establishing it. Ring the Department of Commerce & Tourism (☎ 59 1033) to see if anything has happened. There's an artefacts shop near Mendi Motors on the other side of the main road, that sells hand-loomed products, baskets and weapons. It's not cheap, but the wares are of reasonable quality; it's open 9 am to 3 pm Monday to Wednesday, 9 am to 4 pm Friday and 9 am to noon on Saturday. A much better shop is in a village on the Hagen road, about

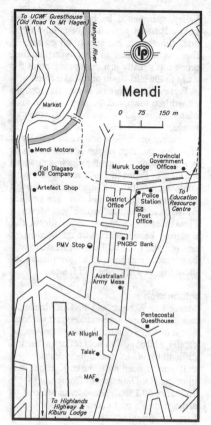

Mendi

0   75   150 m

To UCWF Guesthouse
(Old Road to Mt Hagen)

Mangani River

Market

Mendi Motors

Foi Diagaso
Oil Company

Artefact Shop

District
Office

Muruk Lodge

Provincial
Government
Offices

Police
Station

Post
Office

To
Education
Resource
Centre

PNGBC Bank

PMV Stop

Australian
Army Mess

Pentecostal
Guesthouse

Air Niugini

Talair

MAF

To Highlands
Highway &
Kiburu Lodge

an hour from Mendi. Mendi dolls make a good buy, although they are now rarely in the traditional designs, which had religious significance. Expect to pay at least K20.

From the town centre there's a shortcut down to the market and the main road on a steep dirt path but it's almost impossible to walk with a pack after rain.

The Menduli Book Store is apparently a good place to buy books.

Australian Army engineers are helping with road-building projects in the area, and they have a club in town. It's quite formal, very 'army' and doesn't really cater for vis-

itors, but if you think you can pass muster it's a pleasant place to damage your liver.

Places to Stay & Eat

The *Pentecostal Guesthouse* (☎ 59 1174, PO Box 15) is in town, not far from the airport. There are only a few rooms and church workers have priority, so it's sometimes full. The rooms are small but clean enough and there are cooking facilities. It costs K8 for a bunk bed or K15 for a room to yourself (if available). If this is full, check out the *Training Centre* across the road, which is cheap but very run-down.

The *Educational Resource Centre* (☎ 59 1252) also has reasonable-value rooms with meals and cooking facilities.

The *UCWF Guesthouse* (☎ 59 1062, PO Box 53) is a 20-minute walk from town and costs K10 in a shared room or K15 per person in a twin room with attached bathroom. UCWF stands for United Church Women's Fellowship, and this is a new incarnation of the Menduli Guesthouse but it's no longer great value. You can't cook there and dinner costs K15. To get there, walk out onto Old Hagen Rd past Mendi Motors, take the left fork after the bridge, pass the turn-off to the large Menduli Trade Store and it's further up the hill on your right, near the hospital.

Southwest Airlines has a guesthouse for their crew where you might be able to stay if you're stuck for a bed – ask at the airport. I also heard of a guesthouse at Wendia village, K0.50 by PMV from Mendi along Old Hagen Rd. Margaret, who works at the UCWF Guesthouse, might have information.

Muruk Lodge (☎ 59 1188, PO Box 108) is the revamped version of the old Mendi Hotel. It's comfortable and has a licensed restaurant. Singles/doubles are K75/95. The food is reasonable, although the steak sandwich I bought (K6) contained the toughest meat I've ever gnawed.

A few km south of town, on the Highlands Highway just beyond the turn-off into Mendi, *Kiburu Lodge* (☎ 59 1077, fax 59 1350, PO Box 50, Mendi) costs about the same (K75/85) but is much nicer. The 12 rooms are in quasi-traditional style (they have thatched roofs) and the lodge has pleasant grounds and views. It is owned by the Kiburu people but is managed by Melanesian Tourist Services, based in Madang. Tours of the area are available, ranging from treks to helicopter flights.

Getting There & Away

Air Talair and Air Niugini (☎ 59 1233) fly between Mendi and Tari for about K50, and Port Moresby for K136. Talair flies to Mt Hagen (K48), and while Air Niugini will sell you a ticket to Mt Hagen, you have to fly via Moresby and it costs K236! Most other Talair destinations involve making connections.

The Talair agent is Southwest Airlines (☎ 59 1031), at the airport. Southwest is also a third-level operator, flying mainly charters but with a regular passenger flight to Pimaga (K30), an access point for Lake Kutubu. MAF might also fly there. MBA (Milne Bay Air) flies to Moro, the Chevron headquarters an hour's walk from the west end of the lake, for K52. From here to Tage Point (for Lake Kutubu Lodge) it's K25 by boat if you charter, or K5 if there's a boat going to the lodge.

I took a PMV from Tari to Mendi and a Talair flight from Mendi to Mt Hagen. The flight went via...Tari.

PMV PMVs run back and forth between Mt Hagen and Mendi with reasonable regularity, taking three hours or so and costing about K10. The road to Tari goes via Nipa and is a spectacular four-hour drive costing K10. The new road to Pimaga and on to Moro should be completed by now, and there will presumably be PMVs running this route. The Foi Diagaso Oil Company will have the latest information.

Car Rental Mendi Motors might have cars to hire.

LAKE KUTUBU

South of Mendi, Lake Kutubu has some of the Highlands' most beautiful scenery and an excellent lodge. According to legend the lake was formed when a fig tree was cut down by a woman looking for water. Whatever the tree, its trunk, branches or roots touched, turned to water. The lake is beautiful, the surrounding country is home to friendly people who still live a largely traditional life – currently changing fast because of the Chevron oil development. Butterflies and birds of paradise are common. You can swim in the lake and visit local villages or just soak up the beauty and peace.

The lodge is a local initiative and profits are being channelled into agricultural projects and community services. Chevron is assisting with the upgrading of the lodge and the development of a national park in the area.

One of the reasons why the Foi people built the lodge was to control visitors. They are still quite traditional, and segregation is maintained between the sexes – this segregation, among other things, was undermined by travelling couples who stayed in the villages. (The men's houses are impressive buildings 150 to 200 metres long, built on stilts.) The lodge means that the people can now more easily accept visitors on their own terms, and maintain their privacy.

If you visit Lake Kutubu, remember you are a guest of the people and tread carefully – try not to damage this beautiful spot. Do not try and stay in the villages – this would defeat the purpose of the lodge. It is OK to swim in Western costume at the lodge, but elsewhere you should swim in a lap-lap. Women should not wear shorts. Ask before you take photos or enter buildings.

The big Lake Kutubu oil project has changed the character of this area somewhat, and local people are used to dealing with (or hearing exaggerated stories about people dealing with) oil workers with fat wallets and expense accounts. Some prices asked to cross bridges or just walk across land can be outrageous, but getting angry won't help.

Walking to Lake Kutubu

If you have the time and inclination, the ideal way to get here would be to walk in from

Nipa and fly out from Pimaga. Both methods end up costing much the same. See Lonely Planet's *Bushwalking in Papua New Guinea* for detailed descriptions of these walks, and a couple of alternatives, including walking to the lake from Tari.

Lately, people have found that charges asked in this area, for crossing bridges, staying in villages, guides, etc, have risen enormously. This is probably due to the amount of oil money around.

From Pimaga You can fly between Mendi and Pimaga with MAF or Southwest Airlines (☎ 59 1031) for K30. There are a couple of places to stay in Pimaga: a guesthouse owned by the Foi people (who also run Lake Kutubu Lodge) and a cheaper council guesthouse. From Pimaga you could walk about 22 km on a dirt road to the south-eastern tip of Lake Kutubu and an attractive village called Gesege (but check in Mendi that the new road hasn't altered this routing). This takes about four hours and a guide isn't necessary. From Gesege you catch a canoe to the lodge at Tage Point for anything up to K45! If the people at the lodge know you're coming they'll make arrangements for a boat and you'll pay about K5.

From Pimaga it might be possible to arrange a walk all the way down to Kikori in Gulf Province.

From Nipa The alternative is a fairly hard three-day walk from Nipa, on the Tari-Mendi road. Go to Nipa and the Tiliba Mission where Jim Slaughter can recommend guides, or you can walk three hours to Ungubi where Pastor Tom may also be able to organise a guide. A guide costs from K10 a day and you supply the food. It's an interesting walk that crosses several large rivers.

The start of the trail is at Halhal, about five km west of Nipa and accessible by PMV along the Highlands Highway (1½ hours, K4).

The suggested itinerary is: Halhal to Ungubi, 1½ hours walking, stay at Pastor Tom's Place; Ungubi to Sagip, six hours, stay in hut (people have taken 11 hours on

this leg); Sagip to Yalanda, four hours, stay at Yalanda rest house; Yalanda to Tage Point, three hours, stay at Lake Kutubu Lodge.

The sections between Ungubi and Yalanda involve some steep ascents and descents on rocky paths and it's hard going. A traveller describes the trail as 'wet, steep, slippery, leechy, snakey and isolated – absolutely fantastic but hugely tough'! You'll need a guide for these sections, and possibly another from Yalanda to Tage Point. You provide food for the guide. Village stays en route cost at least K10 a night.

Places to Stay & Eat
The comfortable *Lake Kutubu Lodge*, on a ridge overlooking the lake, is attractively designed and constructed from bush materials. Prices have risen quite a lot lately, and might rise further – there are hopes of a tourist boom. Currently, you pay K60 for the first night, then K55 for full board. There's also a backpackers' bunk house, where a bed costs K8 a night or K12 if you need sleeping gear (mattress, pillow, mosquito net). Meals are available, costing K8 for breakfast, K9 for lunch and K15 for dinner. To book, contact the Foi Diagaso Oil Company (☎ 59 1328, fax 59 1305) in Mendi. If you don't book there might not be anyone here when you arrive.

If you're cooking for yourself it's best to bring at least some food, although you can often buy things from the lodge and Kutubu's perfect climate means there is never a shortage of fresh fruit and vegetables.

The lodge has a motor canoe and they arrange tours to some of the beautiful rivers and waterfalls that run into the lake. The cost depends on how much fuel is used, but will probably be around K20. Fishing trips can also be arranged – women fish by day, men by night.

Getting There & Away
The new road from Mendi to Pimaga means that you will probably be able to go most of the way there by PMV. That takes some of

the adventure out of a visit to Lake Kutubu, but it makes getting here a lot easier.

MBA flies from Mendi to Moro for K52, the Chevron headquarters near the west end of the lake, and from there a boat to Tage Point costs K25 if you charter or about K5 if there's a boat going to the lodge anyway. It's a bit of a walk, under an hour, from the airstrip to the lake. See also the Walking to Lake Kutubu section earlier.

TARI

Tari is the main town for the Huli wigmen and the centre for the beautiful Tari Basin. The main attractions are the people and the surrounding countryside, but there's a PNGBC bank (which can shut down unexpectedly), a post office, a few large but basic stores, a hospital and, of course, an airfield. The town really is just the airfield plus a handful of buildings.

The Tari area went through a boom with the Mt Kare alluvial gold rush in the late '80s, but the main winners were SP Brewing, helicopter companies, Toyota dealerships and the top hotels in Moresby. About the only grassroots to benefit were prostitutes. Things have since quietened down but a big mine is being established by Australia's CRA and there are still plenty of individual miners hoping to strike it rich.

There's a tiny museum in a stockaded compound and most of the items in the small display are for sale. The place is a sort of old men's home, and a couple of nice old guys will show you around and accept your donation. The covered structure in the compound is the grave of a former provincial premier, and you'll see similar (but usually smaller) structures all around the Tari area – people live under thatch but when they die they get corrugated iron to keep the rain off.

Saturday is the main market day, but there are smaller markets between Wednesday and Saturday.

The kai bar at J & S Traders (behind the PNGBC) is better than the one at the supermarket and sells good chips. The Huli Bakery, next to the market, sells buns, tea and coffee.

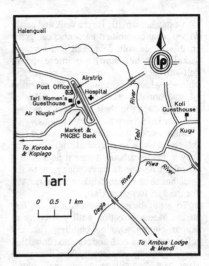

Tari

0   0.5   1 km

Places to Stay & Eat

Despite the small size of the town, the Tari area boasts some excellent places to stay.

In town is the *Tari Women's Guesthouse* (☎ 50 8030) where a bed in one of the small bunkrooms costs K15 or K8 for students. There's a kitchen. As is usual at women's guesthouses, you might meet some articulate and politically aware women. Men can stay too. There's a *haus kai* in the same compound but it seems to have closed.

If you're stuck for a bed see Chris Rose in the airport office who lets a room at K70 a night.

About four km east of town, an interesting walk past traditional villages and gardens, is the small *Koli Guesthouse* (PO Box 74, Tari). A bed costs just K5 a night and you can cook your own food or pay K3 for a vegetarian meal or K5 for one with meat. If there are a few of you they'll put on a mumu. Accommodation is in a fairly basic hut built from traditional materials, but there is solar power and hot showers are available. There's also a nearby stream for washing. Walks in the area and village accommodation can be arranged here. Highly recommended.

This place is worth visiting even if you

don't stay here, partly for the walk and partly to see what committed gardeners can grow in this fertile soil. John Vail and his wife Jukali (it's her land) are interested in self-sufficiency and are testing plants and animals which might improve the nutrition of traditional diets. The sheer variety of things growing in their garden is amazing, and there are sheep and other animals.

John works at the hospital in Tari a few days each week, so you could drop in on your way to the guesthouse to see if he's there – he might be able to carry your pack to the guesthouse on his motorbike after work. Ask for the Tari Research Unit.

To get to the guesthouse, head out of Tari in the Mendi direction until you come to Kupari church, a yellow building. Take the left turn at the church and continue down this road, ignoring side roads. You'll cross a river, pass Piwa village and eventually climb a small hill. A road leads off to the left but keep going straight ahead a short way and the guesthouse is through the blue gate on your left. If you're coming by PMV from the Mendi direction, ask to be dropped at Kupari Church. There are plenty of people coming and going along the road, some in traditional dress, and most of them are very friendly. However, it isn't recommended that unaccompanied women make the walk, at least until you are known in the area.

Perhaps the nearest equivalents to the *Ambua Lodge* would be some of the famous African game park lodges. At 2100 metres, the lodge has a superb view of the land of the Huli below and a refreshing mountain climate. The dining/lounge/bar is the kind of place you could relax in for hours just watching the clouds roll by. There's even an outdoor spa.

Guests are accommodated in individual, luxury, bush-material huts. Every hut has a great 180° view and they are surrounded by flower gardens with a backdrop of mossy forest. It is a little incongruous to find such opulence in such rugged circumstances, but it's certainly impressive.

Needless to say, it isn't cheap. Single/double/triple rooms cost K141/182/207 a

night, breakfast is K11, lunch is K13 and dinner K27. Transfers from Tari are K12 each way. Day tours are K70 and other tours are available. The birdwatching near here is excellent.

They show a *First Contact* video every night. There are also some pleasant walks that have been put in through the forest to a couple of nearby waterfalls. Ambua is operated by Trans Niugini Tours (☎ 52 1438, fax 52 2470, PO Box 371, Mt Hagen) who also run the Karawari and Bensbach lodges.

If the price is a worry, you can get a taste of all this a lot cheaper – there's a basic *Wilderness Hostel* with cooking facilities, costing K15 a night. You'll need a sleeping bag. Maybe they were having a bad day when I called in, but it didn't seem that backpackers got a particularly warm welcome. The lodge is off the main Tari-Mendi road, and occasional PMVs run past. It's about 45 minutes to Tari by PMV.

Getting There & Away

Air Air Niugini flies between Port Moresby and Tari on Monday, Wednesday and Friday via Mendi (but not in both directions), and on Sunday direct, for K153. Talair flies between Tari and a number of strips, including Moresby (K153), Mt Hagen (K79), Mendi (K52), Oksapmin (K60), Telefomin (K85), Amboin (Karawari) (K88) and Wewak (K151).

MAF flies to many strips in the area, including Kopiago (K38) and Oksapmin (K63), but to get to April River you'll have to charter a plane. Tarangau Airways, a Wewak-based company which flies to many Sepik strips, flies to Telefomin for K111 and Timbunke for K130.

PMV PMVs can take a while to collect enough passengers to leave Tari, but it's best to get to the market early in the morning if you're heading in the Mendi direction. PMVs to Mendi cost K10 and take four hours. PMVs also run from Tari to Koroba (K3). Beyond this, most transportation is by plane or foot, although the roads have been pushed through to Lake Kopiago. There are actually two roads from Koroba to Kopiago, both likely to close after rain and traffic is light. People from Kopiago sometimes come to the Tari market, so see if you can get a lift back.

KOROBA

This is a small station, still pretty much at the end of the road. Near the community school is the Huli Cultural Centre, with displays on Huli housing styles and artefacts for sale. Market days, when there will probably be more transport in and out, are Wednesday and Saturday.

There are apparently many caves in the area. Ask at the high school for a guide on the weekend.

In Hedemari, midway between Tari and Koroba, is the bush-material *Lakwanda Lodge* (PO Box 103, Tari), where you can stay for K15 a night. A PMV from Tari costs K1.50 for the 40-minute ride. Trans Niugini Tours sometimes sends people here, so things are a bit better organised than in some villages. Some food is available but you'd be wise to bring some of your own. There are good walks in the area and the guesthouse can provide a guide for about K5 a day and accommodation in other villages for K5. There's also the possibility of rafting on a nearby Tagari River. This is an interesting area, well worth visiting for the scenery and the culture.

KOPIAGO TO OKSAPMIN

From Lake Kopiago, you can walk to Oksapmin in West Sepik Province in four or five days. Just getting to Kopiago from Koroba can mean walking, as the road is rough and there are few vehicles. If you walk, it will take about two days.

There's a mission guesthouse about three km from Kopiago and a more basic council guesthouse in town.

Kopiago to Oksapmin is a hard and potentially dangerous walk, so don't undertake it unless you are pretty fit. The walk passes through the spectacular Strickland Gorge, a staggeringly rugged and awe-inspiring stretch of country – so it's worth the effort.

The tracks are very steep and slippery, even in the dry season, which is definitely the best time to walk. Guides are essential; expect to pay them around K5 per day.

This route assumes that the Strickland bridge has been rebuilt – that seems to be taking a long time, so it might not be. If not, see the route suggested by Tom Cutrofello.

On the first day, you walk from Kopiago to Kaiguena where there is a village guesthouse, or on to Waip where there's also accommodation. Day two takes you on a hard 10-hour walk from Kaiguena through beautiful rainforest to Yakona where there is a haus kiap. On day three you can either walk from Yakona to Gawa in one very hard 10 or 12-hour day or break the walk by camping at the Strickland River.

It's a steep and dangerous three hours down the Strickland Gorge to a bridge across the river. You can camp in a cave near the bridge.

The next stretch is to Gawa where there is a small hut you can use. It's a steep, unshaded, uphill walk that takes six to eight hours. If you overnight at the river you can start early in the morning and avoid the worst of the heat. The last day's walk is a reasonably easy three hours to Oksapmin. There's an Agricultural Centre at Oksapmin run by the Peace Corps and you can stay in the guesthouse. See Lonely Planet's *Bushwalking in Papua New Guinea* for more details.

Tom Cutrofello, who worked with the Peace Corps in Kopiago, suggests a different itinerary which avoids the Strickland: Kopiago to Yakona (10 hours through forest); Yakona to Ambi (nine hours through a beautiful valley); Ambi to Wire Bridge (eight hours, passing through the village of the Hewa people then crossing the Laiagam River by raft (K5), then to the Om River, crossed by a wire bridge – here there are old kiap houses where you can stay, although you might have to untie ropes to get in); Wire Bridge to Oksapmin (seven hours straight up, tougher than Mt Wilhelm, then three hours down to Oksapmin).

If you are really keen, you can continue walking to Tekin, Bak, Bimin and down to

Olsobip in Western Province, or to Telefomin.

Talair flies from Oksapmin to Green River on the Upper Sepik for K73, to Telefomin for K33 and to Vanimo for K109. MAF flies between Kopiago and Oksapmin for K30. See the Sepik chapter for more information on Oksapmin and Telefomin.

The Sepik

Land Area 79,000 sq km
Population 380,000

This chapter is divided into three sections: East Sepik Province, Sandaun (West Sepik) Province and, although the Sepik flows through both provinces, The Sepik & its Tributaries, which includes riverside towns and villages.

The Sepik region is quite possibly the most fascinating area of PNG. There are islands, a long stretch of open coastline with good beaches and some rugged mountain ranges. It is the mighty Sepik River, however, that commands the most attention.

The Sepik (pronounced 'sea-pick') is one of the largest rivers in the world in terms of annual water flow and although it is rivalled in size by the Fly River in the south of the country it is far more significant as a means of communication and in terms of its cultural and artistic heritage. The region is a centre for thriving artistic skills.

The Sepik has the same relevance to PNG as the Congo to Africa and the Amazon to South America. River-boating down the Amazon is an amazing experience, but people say the Sepik is even better. Do it!

HISTORY

Very little archaeological evidence has been found to shed light on the early history of these provinces. Since most people are likely to have lived along shifting rivers or the coastline (which has flooded since the last ice age) it is unlikely much will ever be found. The area was, like other parts of PNG, fragmented into numerous different language groups and clans, and violence between these groups was commonplace. Most languages are spoken by fewer than 2000 people. The main language group of the Middle Sepik is Ndu (with over 10,000 speakers), in the Maprik area there are 30,000 Abelam speakers and along the coast

around Wewak there are around 35,000 Passam speakers.

The Sepik's first contact with the outside world was probably with Malay bird-of-paradise hunters; the feathers from these beautiful birds were popular long before European ladies of society had their fling with them during the last century. The first European contact came in 1885 with the arrival of the Germans and their New Guinea Kompagnie. Dr Otto Finsch, after whom the German's first station – Finschhafen – was later named, rowed about 50 km upstream from the mouth and named the river the Kaiserin Augusta, after the wife of the German Emperor.

During 1886 and 1887 further expeditions, using a steam boat, travelled 400 km upriver and then, when the river was higher, 600 km. These early expeditions were soon followed by more mercenary explorers, traders, labour recruiters and missionaries.

The Germans established a station at Aitape on the coast in 1906 and in 1912-13 sent a huge scientific expedition to explore the river and its vast, low-lying basin. They collected insects, studied the tribes and produced maps of such accuracy that they are still referred to today. Angoram, the major station in the lower Sepik, was also established at this time, but the arrival of WW I put a stop to activity for some time.

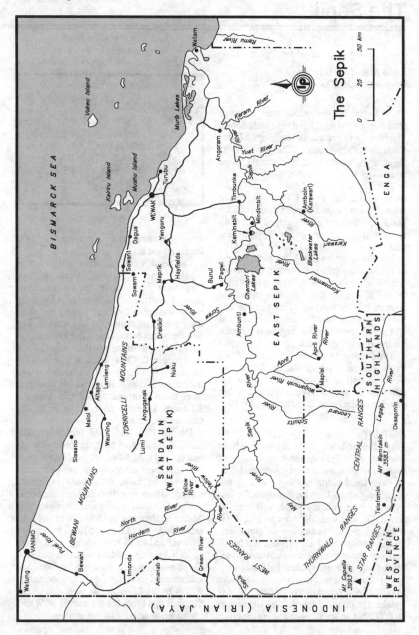

The Australian administration of New Guinea suffered from very tight purse-strings and an area like the Sepik, with little economic appeal, was pushed to the end of the line. The station at Ambunti was established in 1924 and in the early '30s a small flurry of gold rushes in the hills behind Wewak and around Maprik, stirred further interest. Then WW II arrived and once more development and exploration of the Sepik went into reverse.

The Japanese held the Sepik region for most of the war but the struggle for control was bitter and prolonged. As the Australian forces pushed along the coast from Lae and then Madang, the Japanese steadily withdrew to the west. In early '44 the Americans seized Aitape and an Australian division started to move west from there. When a huge American force captured Hollandia (Jayapura in Irian Jaya today) in April '44, the Japanese 8th Army was completely isolated.

The enormous number of rivers and the extensive coastal swamps made the fight along the coast a drawn out struggle. It was over a year later, in May '45, before Wewak fell and the remaining Japanese troops withdrew into the hills behind the coast. Finally, with the war in its last days, General Adachi surrendered near Yangoru. He was so weak he had to be carried on a chair. The formal surrender took place a few days later on 13 September '45 at Wom Point near Wewak. Of 100,000 Japanese troops only 13,000 survived to surrender.

Since the war, government control has been re-established and extended further upriver although the uppermost limits of the Sepik are still amongst the most unchanged and isolated parts of the country. It has been a touchy area ever since the Indonesian takeover of Dutch New Guinea, although the border was jointly mapped and marked in 1968. On several occasions large numbers of refugees have fled into PNG.

In 1984 more than 100 Melanesian soldiers in the Indonesian Armed Forces deserted to the OPM (the Irian Jayan rebels) sparking a major Indonesian operation, which in turn drove over 10,000 Papuans into PNG. Years later these refugees, and those that have come both before and since, remain a political football. Only a small number have shown any interest in returning to Irian Jaya, so the PNG government has belatedly decided to settle them permanently. Unfortunately for the refugees PNG doesn't have the necessary funds, and Australia has refused to help. In the meantime they live in extremely basic conditions in camps close to the border: Blackwater, near Vanimo, and Green River, near the Sepik River, are two of the largest camps.

GEOGRAPHY

The Sepik River is 1126 km long and is navigable for almost that entire distance. It starts up in the central mountains, close to the source of the country's other major river, the Fly, which flows south. The Sepik flows in a loop, first west across the Irian Jaya border, then north on the Indonesian side before turning east across the border again. It then runs through two PNG provinces: Sandaun, with its capital at Vanimo, and East Sepik, with its capital at Wewak.

At its exit from Irian Jaya, the Sepik is only 85 metres above sea level and from there it winds gradually down to the sea; a huge, brown, slowly coiling serpent. It has often changed its course leaving dead-ends, lagoons, ox-bow lakes or huge swampy expanses that turn into lakes or dry up to make grasslands in the dry season.

As an indication of its age and changing course, along much of the river there is no stone or rock whatsoever within about 50 km of its banks. Villages often have 'sacred stones' that have been carried in from far away and placed in front of the village haus tambaran (spirit house).

The inexorable force of the river often tears great chunks of mud and vegetation out of the river banks and at times these drift off downstream as floating islands – often with small trees and even animals aboard. There is no delta and the river stains the sea brown for 50 or more km from the shore. It is said that islanders off the coast can draw fresh water straight from the sea.

For much of its length, the Sepik is bordered by huge expanses of swamp or wild sugar cane known as *pitpit*. Further inland there are hills and eventually the Sepik climbs into wild mountain country near its source. Between the river and the coastal plain the Bewani and Torricelli Mountains rise to over 1000 metres.

There are no natural harbours on the whole Sepik region coastline.

CLIMATE

June to October is the driest time in most of the Sepik, but it's December to March around Wewak and November to January around Telefomin. You can expect drenching rain at any time on the river.

ARTS

Traditional art was closely linked to spiritual beliefs, indeed Sepik carvings were usually an attempt to make a spirit visible and concrete, although decorations were also applied to practical, day-to-day items, like pots and paddles.

Carving is now rarely traditional – it is now more likely to be a mixture of traditional motifs, the individual's imagination, and commercial good sense. (Sound familiar Michelangelo?) Originally each village had its own distinctive style, but a pan-Sepik style is now emerging.

Carving has become a vital part of the river's economy and without it some villages would probably cease to exist. In many river villages it is literally the only significant source of cash, which is needed for clothes, store food, education, petrol, utensils... Coffee is grown in the Maprik region, but on the river there are no cash crops, no paid employment and rarely any agricultural surplus.

If a group arrives in a village, a market will materialise instantly. Considering the amount of labour and skill that goes into a carving the prices are very low. Depending on the size and quality of the piece, prices vary – you can buy hooks and carvings for as little as K1, a mask for K5, all the way up to K40 and more.

Bargaining in the Asian sense is unknown and is considered rude. The people are proud and it is not wise to denigrate someone's carvings. You can, however, ask for a 'second price', or just walk away wistfully. There are no prizes for taking a villager down.

As you will soon discover, if you are a keen collector, you can very quickly end up with a lot of very heavy *diwai* (wood). Bear in mind that the airlines have baggage limits and particularly in the case of light aeroplanes there simply may not be room for a three-metre statue! Although the airlines seem to be fairly flexible, there just isn't much room for flexibility on the smaller planes. Air Niugini, however, has special freight rates for flying artefacts from Wewak to Moresby.

You must also bear in mind the PNG Government's restrictions on exporting some items, and import restrictions in your country of origin and any other country you may be visiting on your way home. See the Customs section in the Facts for the Visitor chapter.

Sea mail is the cheapest way to get a lot of wood home, but will take at least three months and possibly much longer. Also, you can't mail (sea or air) anything longer than one metre. Air mail is very expensive. The other alternative is to have the item shipped home through a cargo agent. This isn't all that cheap as the smallest space you can buy is a cubic metre and you will have to make packing crates. There is also a great deal of paperwork, as carvings which are shipped (as opposed to mailed) need export clearance from the National Museum in Port Moresby.

GETTING THERE & AWAY
Air

The standard way to get to the Sepik is to fly to Wewak from Mt Hagen, Madang or from Jayapura (Indonesia) via Vanimo. The direct flight from Jayapura to Los Angeles is no longer operating, but Garuda (the Indonesian international airline) flies from Jayapura to Biak every day and you can pick up a flight

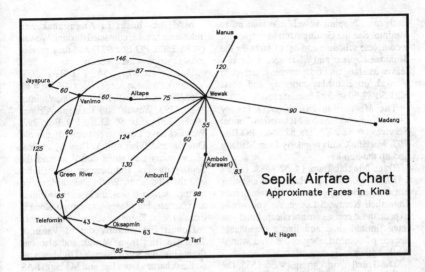

Sepik Airfare Chart
Approximate Fares in Kina

from Biak to Los Angeles. Sandaun Air Services in Vanimo might also fly to Biak.

Note that there is now an Indonesian Consulate in Vanimo and a PNG Consulate in Jayapura, both of which issue visas.

Air Niugini flies between Madang and Wewak every day of the week for K90. There's a flight to/from Mt Hagen (K83) on Wednesday and Sunday which goes through Wewak and on to Vanimo (K87 from Wewak), continuing to Jayapura (K60 from Vanimo) on Sunday only. A flight from Manus Island (K120) arrives in Wewak on Wednesday, and a flight to Manus departs on Sunday. Many of these flights originate and terminate in Moresby (K180).

Talair has a daily (except Sunday) flight between Mt Hagen (K83) and Wewak. The outward flights often continue on to Goroka and Madang; the inward flights often continue on to Vanimo (K86 from Wewak). On Monday, Wednesday and Friday there are flights to/from Tabubil for K156. Talair no longer flies to many of the small strips in the region. The main Talair route of interest as a 'back door' entry to the Sepik is the Tari-Amboin (Karawari)-Timbunke (K98) circle on Monday, Wednesday and Friday. There

are also weekly flights from Tari to Oksapmin (K60) and Tari to Telefomin (K85).

The third-level airlines offer some flights into the Sepik, but remember that these are usually unscheduled and many are charters on which you have to hope for a spare seat.

MAF flies to many strips, including Oksapmin from Tari for K63, and from Oksapmin to Kopiago for K30.

Tarangau Airlines (☎ 86 2203, fax 86 2820, PO Box 292, Wewak) also has flights into the Sepik from other areas: Oksapmin-Ambunti (K86); Tari-Karawari (K99); Tari-Mt Hagen (K111); and Tari-Timbunke (K130). Sandaun Air Services (SAS) (☎ 87 1268/79, fax 87 1089, PO Box 206, Vanimo; ☎ 86 2793 in Wewak) also flies in from other places, and you can often fly to Jayapura from Vanimo with them for K65, usually midweek. They might also be offering flights to/from Biak – if you don't want to visit Irian Jaya this would be a great way to get to/from PNG.

Sea

Wewak is the most westerly port for the trusty *Mamose Express* and *Rita*, but other

Lutheran Shipping vessels continue on to Vanimo. See the Getting Around chapter for a complete schedule and list of fares for the *Mamose Express* and *Rita*; one of the two leaves Madang on Friday evening, arrives in Wewak on Saturday morning and costs K21.50/32.50 in deck/tourist class.

The *Melanesian Discoverer*, a luxury cruise ship operated by Melanesian Tourist Services (☎ 82 2766, fax 82 3543, PO Box 707, Madang), sails regularly from Madang and up the Sepik.

Trans Niugini Tours (☎ 52 1438, fax 52 2470, PO Box 371, Mt Hagen) has a similar but smaller boat, the *Sepik Spirit*, which runs from their Karawari Lodge. As you would expect, these cruises are not cheap, but if you have limited time and like a reasonable degree of comfort, they could be a worthwhile option.

The Tribal World group (☎ 56 1555, fax 55 1546, PO Box 86, Mt Hagen) has plans for cruises on the Sepik, probably less luxurious and considerably cheaper than the other two. Ask at the Sepik International Beach Resort in Wewak.

The *Tawi*, which is operated by the Manus Provincial Government calls at Wewak on its irregular voyages between Manus, Wuvulu, Wewak and Madang. See the Manus Province chapter for details.

For an interesting route from Madang to Angoram, see the Malolo Plantation Resort to Hansa Bay section in the Madang Province chapter.

GETTING AROUND
Air
Talair flies between Vanimo and Wewak (K86) daily except Wednesday and Sunday. There is a direct flight and, most days, one via Aitape (K80) and some isolated airstrips in the Bewani and Torricelli mountains.

The various third-level operators also do this flight, in even smaller planes than Talair's. This is much more enjoyable than streaking over the top in a F28 and some of the landing strips are really interesting! Talair no longer flies to many of the smaller strips in the region.

MAF has bases in Anguganak and Telefomin that are contacted through Wewak (☎ 86 2500, PO Box 977) and they service most airstrips at least weekly.

Dovair (☎ 87 1056, PO Box 205, Vanimo), Sandaun Air Services (SAS) (☎ 87 1268/79, fax 87 1089, PO Box 206, Vanimo; ☎ 86 2793, Wewak) and Tarangau Airlines (☎ 86 2203, fax 86 2820, PO Box 292, Wewak) have taken over many of the old Douglas and Talair routes. They fly to most of the many tiny strips dotted around the Sepik provinces, and there are some flights into the Highlands. While these airlines do have passenger routes, many of their flights are charters, but passengers can go along if there's room. There are set passenger fares.

Dovair flies mainly out of Vanimo; Tarangau flies from Wewak and also has flights into the Sepik from the Highlands, as well as charters from Lae and Madang. SAS is based in Vanimo but flies all over the region and also to the Highlands and elsewhere. Nigel Lang, the chief pilot, is very helpful.

Planes belonging to the New Tribes Mission, based in Maprik (☎ 88 1258) but with an office in Wewak (☎ 86 2407), fly to some very out-of-the-way places. The organisation is a little wary of outsiders but the missionaries seem friendly enough. New Tribes is an American fundamentalist outfit and has had run-ins with people concerned about its attitude to, and impact on, local cultures.

Fares on the third-level operators can vary quite a lot, so ask around. Remember that many of these flights are irregular charters, and there will have to be a spare seat for you to go along. Fares from Wewak are:

Destination	Fare
Aitape	K75
Ambunti	K60
April River	K88
Green River	K124
Hayfields	K37
Karawari	K55
May River	K105
Oksapmin	K115
Porgera	K111

Telefomin	K130
Timbunke	K40
Vanimo	K84
Wuvulu	K97

Fares from Vanimo are:

Destination	Fare
Aitape	K60
Ambunti	K84
Green River	K60
Karawari	K160
May River	K90
Telefomin	K125
Timbunke	K85
Oksapmin	K133
Wewak	K84
Wuvulu	K80

Sea
Lutheran Shipping's somewhat basic cargo freighters continue on to Vanimo from Wewak for K21/K26 in deck/cabin class, half that to Aitape. There might be one boat a week but there might not. 'Deck class can be OK. Food, of a kind, is available on board and you eat with the captain – which is no special thrill as he eats where everyone else eats!', reports one traveller.

River
There is a wide range of methods for getting out on the big, brown Sepik and its tributaries. There is no right way or wrong way; the factors to consider are your finances, available time, and last, but not least, your capacity for roughing it. The spectrum of travellers ranges from the dedicated shoestringers who buy canoes and paddle from village to village, to those who rely on hitching rides with village canoes, to those who prefer a tour using motorised canoes, and at the luxury end, those who stay on a cruise ship or at a comfortable lodge. See Getting Around in The Sepik & its Tributaries section for a more detailed discussion of the options.

Roads
The road links in the Sepik provinces are quite limited, but where there is a road there will be PMVs. The roads are rough, even the road to Angoram and this is, in relative terms, a good, all-weather road. The roads to Pagwi and Timbunke are real teeth rattlers and in the wet they must be a nightmare, sometimes impassable. When they are dry, conventional vehicles will survive, but 4WD is essential after rain. The North Coast Highway runs west to Aitape and a little beyond.

PMV
Except on major routes like from Wewak to Angoram and Maprik, PMVs are quite infrequent. Starting very early and being relaxed about arrival times is more important than ever. The PMVs are usually trucks and are often very crowded. Hitching is possible – most private cars act as de facto PMVs anyway – so if you're waiting on the side of the road, wave down anything that comes by (thumbing is unknown). You may well be expected to contribute the equivalent of a PMV fare, but you'll also meet some exceptionally generous people.

Car Rental
You can hire from Hertz and Avis in Wewak, but remote area surcharges apply. This means a 4WD utility (a ute to Australians, pick-up to Americans) costs around K90 a day, plus K0.63 a km, plus insurance.

East Sepik Province

Land Area 43,000 sq km
Population 280,000
Capital Wewak

East Sepik Province is much more developed than its western counterpart and includes the most visited and heavily populated sections of the Sepik, as well as several large tributaries. Wewak, the provincial capital, is a thriving, important commercial centre, separated from the Sepik Basin by the Prince Alexander Range.

WEWAK
Wewak is an attractive town where you can

happily spend a day or two in transit to the Sepik or Irian Jaya. Apart from good shopping and some reasonable accommodation options, there's an attraction that is rare for PNG coastal cities – golden sand, backed by the proper swaying palm trees, right next door to town. Beautiful beaches stretch all along the coast.

Wewak is built at the foot of a high headland that overlooks the coast and nearby islands of Kairiru and Muschu. Cape Wom, to the west, is the place where General Adachi finally surrendered to the Allied forces near the end of WW II. To the east is Cape Moem, an army base.

The hills behind the town climb steeply, so you don't have to travel far to enjoy a very good view.

Orientation

The headland overlooking Wewak is largely residential, although the New Wewak Hotel is here. The main commercial area is at the bottom of the hill behind the beach. The rest of town stretches eastwards towards the airport which is about eight km away. Like a number of other PNG towns, Wewak is irritatingly spread out; fortunately, there's an excellent PMV system.

Note that the intersection of Boram Rd with the road leading down to the main wharves and the provincial government offices, is referred to as Caltex, despite the fact that the service station on the corner is now of the Shell persuasion.

Wewak is not a particularly well-sheltered harbour. There's a small wharf for local fishing boats and canoes, right by the town centre, and a longer one for larger ships to the east of the Sepik International Beach Resort, midway along the bay formed by Wewak and Boram points; the main coastal road does a loop around it.

Information

There is a tourist officer (☎ 86 2663) in the provincial government's Department of Culture & Tourism, but the office is not really set up for dealing with the public. They might be able to tell you if there are any cultural events in the area, and advise you about getting to places like Cape Wom and Kairiru Island.

Ralf Stüttgen (see the Places to Stay – bottom end section) has lived in PNG for 25 years and is an excellent source of information about the Sepik. However, unless you stay at his place (and anyone planning a trip on the Sepik should), at least offer to pay for his time – people treat him as a sort of amateur consultant on everything from buying masks to establishing fish farms, and that doesn't pay the bills.

Although Wewak is much more relaxed than Lae, it is not without its problems, so you should exercise a moderate degree of caution. There are some quite large squatter camps and some accompanying crime. You are not likely to have any problems during the day and most people are particularly friendly and helpful. Walking around at night would be asking for trouble, and women should not go off alone. Discretion should be used when swimming in Western costume, but the beach in front of the Sepik International is fine.

All the banks and airlines are represented, and this is the spot to stock up for a Sepik expedition. If you're going on to Irian Jaya get some rupiah (Indonesian currency) in Moresby, as the banks here occasionally have small amounts, but don't carry a permanent stock.

The post office closes for lunch between noon and 1.30 pm.

The local Hash House Harriers run on Mondays; ask around at the Yacht Club. Someone will take you along and after the run there's food and drink.

Things to See

Near the main wharf the rusting remains of the MV *Busama* are rotting away in the sand. Further down at Kreer, on the road to the airport, there's a market and the wooden hulk of a Taiwanese fishing junk that was seized a few years ago for infringing PNG's coastal fishing limits. On the beach between Kreer Market and the hospital are some rusting

Japanese landing barges. There are apparently some Japanese tunnels on Mission Hill.

There are five markets, in descending order of importance: Taun (at the end of the main street), Dagua (good for PMVs, not far from town), Kreer (on the airport road, just before it turns inland), Nuigo (not very interesting) and Chambri (really just an artefact stall on Boram Rd).

The view from the hills behind the town is superb. Those staying at Ralf Stüttgen's guesthouse don't have to go any further than their bedroom window to see it, but if you are staying in town it's worth the trip. The deep, jungled valleys up here are reserved by the nearby villages for hunting, so while they would be good for walks you should always ask permission first.

Here and elsewhere around Wewak you'll notice large nets spread across clearings on ridge-tops. Flying foxes (bats) fly through these gaps because the clearings seem to be the lowest point to cross the ridge, fly into the net, become entangled, and end up in the cooking pot.

There's decent snorkelling along the outer edge of the reef in the harbour. Much of the Sepik coastline is unprotected, so in season, from September to January, there can be surf, including board-rideable waves to the east towards Turubu. Dabiar Beach at Forok village has been recommended.

War Wreckages Wewak's most vivid legacy of the bitter fighting in WW II is the bomb craters that pockmark the area. They are still visible around the Boram airport runway and the now disused Wirui airstrip (closer to town).

As in other places in PNG, there are an enormous number of bits and pieces from the war scattered around Wewak. These include unexploded bombs, and every now and then someone burning the bush to make a garden sets one off. The replacement of Wewak's water mains took longer than expected, as the excavators kept encountering bombs. Infantry equipment, mainly Japanese, is a fairly common find.

Near the Sepik International there's a serene and simple Japanese/PNG Peace Park. At Mission Hill there's a Japanese War Memorial; the remains of the many troops buried here in a mass grave were later exhumed and returned to Japan. Someone in the know could lead you to old gun emplacements.

Places to Stay – bottom end
Ralf Stüttgen's (☎ 86 2395, PO Box 154) place has become an institution, and every budget traveller that visits the Sepik ends up staying here. It's a great place for meeting all sorts of weird and wonderful people, and getting up-to-date information on the river. It's fairly basic, and completely chaotic, with all sorts of people and children virtually hanging from the ceiling of a small house.

Ralf is a German expat (now a citizen of PNG) and he knows the Sepik. If you can pin him down for a conversation he has a wealth of anecdotes and facts – he's kept pretty busy delivering kids to and from school, cooking, shopping, painting the house – and answering questions about the Sepik. There's also an excellent multilingual travellers' notebook, to which I am indebted.

He can squeeze about 10 people into two bunkrooms, and I'm sure he'd make room for more. It's a homely, friendly place and it only costs K9 per night. A big breakfast is K2, a scratch lunch K1 and dinner K3. There's also an endless supply of coffee.

It's on the ridge overlooking the coast, just below a radio mast (the area is called Tower because of this), on the right-hand side of the main road running to the Sepik, about 15 km from the centre of town; less from the airport. Although this makes it a bit inaccessible it also means there are great views, and it is (at 400 metres elevation) markedly cooler than in town. It's too far to walk but it's on the main Sepik road so there's plenty of traffic.

If you're expected (and only if), Ralf will pick you up. He can then explain the system with the PMVs (No 14, 16 or 19 to Kreer Heights for K0.30, then hitch or take a rural PMV to Tower for K0.50). He goes in and out of town so frequently you can often get a ride with him anyway; free if it's one of his

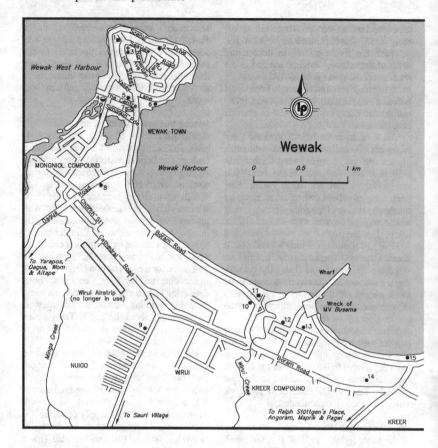

regular trips or for K3 if he's making a special trip for you. If you're ringing to book a bed and an airport pickup, 7 am and 7 pm are the best times to try.

Ralf's is a good spot to start your Sepik trip because all the PMVs go right past. This means you don't have to hang around the markets, and you can sit under the shady tree at the bottom of Ralf's driveway and enjoy the view while you wait. Even if you miss the early morning PMVs you'd stand a good chance of getting a ride in the early afternoon.

There are a few other places, none as cheap as Ralf's, such as the *SIL Guesthouse* (☎ 86 2416) in Kreer Heights which charges K20 per person, and K5 for airport pickups. In town, not far from the Sepik International, you may be able to stay with Peter Ulai.

Places to Stay – top end

There are two hotels in Wewak. One on Hill St, on the Wewak headland above town, and one right beside the beach. The Wewak Motel has closed down.

The *New Wewak Hotel* (☎ 86 2155, 86 2554, PO Box 20), right at the top of the hill overlooking the sea, has 16 singles and 17

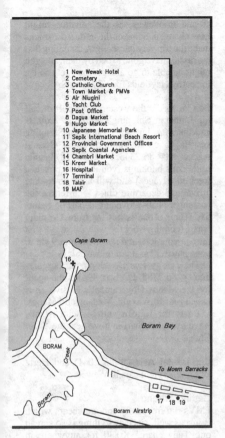

1 New Wewak Hotel
2 Cemetery
3 Catholic Church
4 Town Market & PMVs
5 Air Niugini
6 Yacht Club
7 Post Office
8 Dagua Market
9 Nuigo Market
10 Japanese Memorial Park
11 Sepik International Beach Resort
12 Provincial Government Offices
13 Sepik Coastal Agencies
14 Chambri Market
15 Kreer Market
16 Hospital
17 Terminal
18 Talair
19 MAF

Cape Boram

Boram Bay

BORAM

To Moem Barracks

Boram Airstrip

twin rooms, some air-con, some with fans. Singles/doubles/triples are K47/73/98. It's a friendly place but while some renovation has been done it's still a bit run-down. Japanese guidebooks list this place under another name and there might be a few other names floating around.

The *Sepik International Beach Resort* (☎ 86 2388, PO Box 152) is three km round the bay from town towards the airport, with an enormous wooden crocodile encircling the swimming pool and Sepik carvings at the entrance. It has the best location if you're interested in being right on the beach – it's

only a couple of steps into the sea from the rooms at the front – but this can be a distinct disadvantage if there's a surf running and you're trying to sleep.

It's worth visiting just to see the carvings that have been incorporated in the interior, including a magnificent crocodile bar. They have masks for sale, and local people gather to sell their trinkets every afternoon. You could spend a pleasant couple of hours alternating between beach, bar and artefacts.

There are three classes of rooms, becoming more expensive the further you are from the beach. All can sleep three people, maybe more. C-class is pretty ordinary and you share bathroom facilities – K50 for the first person plus K10 for each extra person; B-class has fans and private facilities – K80 plus K20 for each extra person; A-class has air-con – K110 plus K12 for each extra person.

The hotel is run by the Tribal World group which also has hotels in Minj and Mt Hagen, and organises tours around the region, including the Sepik.

Places to Eat

There aren't too many options apart from the hotels and the standard kai bars in the shopping centre. You can get some snacks at the *Yacht Club* and on Friday from 4 to 7 pm they have good meals.

At the *New Wewak Hotel*, breakfast costs K6, lunch K7 and dinner around K10.

The *Sepik International Beach Resort* is a popular local eating place at lunch and dinner (although it sells meals all day) and it's a good place for a beer. There is an extensive and reasonably priced snack menu, with scones and coffee for K2 and steak sandwiches for K5. A main course at lunch will be around K12 and K15 at dinner.

The Garamut Supermarket has an excellent hot bread kitchen, where you can fill up on delicious fresh cakes and soft drink for less than a kina.

Things to Buy

A group of traders set up a market at the Sepik International after about 4 pm. They sell jewellery and smaller pieces that are fairly commercial, but there is occasionally something interesting. It's worth a look.

There's also a small stall on Boram Rd with attractive, though expensive, billums and a few carvings. If you're coming from town, it's just off Boram Rd on the left, before the turn-off to the Sepik and Ralf's place. It's known as Chambri Market.

Getting There & Away
Air Wewak is a major hub for air transport around the Sepik, and has frequent connections to Madang, Vanimo and the Highlands. The main Air Niugini office (☎ 86 2233, PO Box 61) is in town and Talair (☎ 86 2012, PO Box 47) also has offices in town and at the airport.

See this chapter's introductory Getting There & Away and Getting Around sections for information on flights to/from Wewak.

PMV Roads run west along the coast as far as Aitape, through the Torricelli Mountains and into the Sepik Basin. The markets are, as always, the best places to get PMVs, particularly Dagua. If you're going to the Sepik, Ralf Stüttgen's place is also a good spot to start. They leave early, but to Angoram you can often get PMVs in the early afternoon.

Most PMVs have numbers painted on the front. The number on the left-hand side refers to the route they are running, in theory, anyway. Always ask. No 1 takes the west coast road to Aitape, No 2 the Angoram road, No 3 the Maprik-Pagwi road. The number on the right-hand side gives an indication of how far along that road they run, eg, a No 2-4 will get you all the way to Angoram, a No 2-1 won't. A No 3-8 or higher should run to Pagwi.

Times and fares from Wewak include: Angoram (two hours, K6); Timbunke (three hours, about K8); Maprik (2½ hours, K7); Pagwi (at least four hours, K13). These times can stretch a lot after rain.

Warning The Wewak-Maprik road has seen a lot of PMV hold-ups lately and you are advised to think twice about using it. Ask

around in Wewak, as the situation might have changed. Some of the trade store trucks make the trip very late at night, assuming that the rascals have gone to bed by then, and you might be able to go along. You can also fly to nearby Hayfields for K37 with SAS.

Sea Wewak is the westernmost port of call for Lutheran Shipping's *Mamose Express* and the *Rita*, but other Lutheran Shipping vessels go on to Vanimo. Sepik Coastal Agencies (☎ 86 2343, PO Box 118) handle Lutheran's bookings (you can buy tickets a week in advance) and will have up-to-date arrival and departure times – currently, the passenger boats arrive and depart on Saturday. Their office is not far from the main wharf (coming from the wharf take the first turn on your left) and it's open from 9 am to noon and 1.30 to 3 pm on weekdays.

The nearby Lus Development Corporation (☎ 86 2788, PO Box 494) is the agent for the Manus Government's elusive *Tawi* which runs to Wuvulu, Madang and Manus.

Boats for Kairiru and Muschu islands leave from the wharf in town near the Yacht Club.

Car Rental Avis (☎ 86 2041) and Hertz (☎ 86 2023) rent cars in Wewak.

Getting Around
PMVs run frequently and are cheap, which is just as well, since everything is so spread out. They charge K0.30 for anywhere in town. There are major PMV stops at all the markets and one opposite the post office. A few run all the way along Boram Rd, but they are more frequent along Cathedral Rd. They run right past the airport – you can see the road and a shelter from the terminal. If you're going to Ralf's, get off at Chambri Market and start walking up the Sepik Rd. Try hailing any passing vehicle.

The PMVs stop at dusk, which can mean you can be stuck at the airport, especially if you come in on the Air Niugini evening flight. The best solution is to let someone know you're coming – all the accommodation places can arrange for someone to pick you up from the airport. There are no taxis.

AROUND WEWAK

There are some good beaches for swimming and diving at **Cape Moem**, past the airport, but the cape is an army base so you have to get permission to enter from the commanding officer (☎ 82 2060). Get a PMV to Moem Barracks, then walk a km or so along a dirt road to the right. Unless you're a keen diver, it's not really worth the effort.

At Brandi High School, to the east of Cape Moem, the students have built a traditional village within the school grounds. There's also a collection of Japanese war relics.

Cape Wom

Cape Wom, about 14 km to the west of Wewak, is the site of a wartime airstrip and this is where the Japanese surrender took place. There's a war memorial flanked by flag poles on the spot where Lieutenant General Adachi signed the surrender documents and handed his sword to Major General Robertson on 13 September 1945. On the west side of the cape there's a good reef for snorkelling and a nice stretch of sand for swimming. It would be a very pleasant place for a picnic and there are good views across to the islands.

Unfortunately, Cape Wom is not safe to visit unless there are a lot of other people there, which means a sunny weekend. There's no transport all the way there, so you'll have to hitch; again, this is easiest when lots of people are going there. You could catch a PMV at Dagua Market bound for Dagua (a small village further to the west) and get off at the turn-off to the cape (there's a small village known as Suara). From the turn-off it is a hot three-km walk.

The gates are open from 7 am to 6.30 pm; there's a ranger at the gates and you pay a small fee to enter.

Kairiru & Muschu Islands

These two islands are just off the coast from Wewak. Kairiru sounds particularly interesting. It is heavily forested, rises to nearly 800

metres and the western end is volcanic – the sea has apparently broken into an active crater at Victoria Bay, where there's good snorkelling. There are hot springs, waterfalls and, at the north-eastern end of the island, two big Japanese guns. It's an untouched place (it is reserved as a hunting ground and there are no inland villages) and a good escape from Wewak.

Places to Stay There are apparently places where you can stay with local people for about K5. Take your own food. On Kairiru Island, Joe & Edwick Sareo have been recommended – see Godfrey Sareo at the Bana store next to the PNGBC in Wewak. St Xavier or St John's schools might have accommodation. On Muschu Island there's the *Niarpop Guesthouse*, costing about K10 a night.

Getting There & Away The *Tau-K* goes between Wewak, Muschu and Kairiru on Tuesday and Thursday or Friday. It arrives in Wewak about 9 am and leaves around 2 pm – don't rely too heavily on these times. The journey takes about two hours and costs K2 to Muschu and K5 to Kairiru. It docks at the wharf across the road from the post office. On the beach nearby there are often small boats and canoes. If you can get a lift as a passenger the fare is low, but chartering costs at least K50.

MAPRIK AREA

Maprik town itself isn't a great place, but the area, in the Prince Alexander Mountains, overlooking the vast Sepik Basin, is very interesting. It is noted for the Abelam peoples' distinctive haus tambarans, their yam cult and their carvings and decorations.

The population around Maprik is quite dense and there are many small villages, each with a striking, forward-leaning haus tambaran, a unique architectural style that has been echoed in such modern buildings as the National Parliament. The front facade of the Maprik haus tambarans is brightly painted in browns, ochres, whites and blacks and in some cases they are 30 metres high.

Inside, the carved spirit figures are similarly treated.

Yams are a staple food in this region and they also have cultural significance – you will see them growing on their distinctive, two-metre, cross-like trellis. Harvesting entails considerable ritual and you may see yam festivals or sing-sings during the July/August harvest time. The woven fibre masks, which are the region's most famous artefacts, were originally used in a ceremony where the yams were decorated like human beings, establishing a ritual link between the clans and their crops.

There are some interesting back roads between Maprik and Lamu linking villages, some with spectacular haus tambarans and good carvings, and you can walk between villages. Ask permission before entering villages and then see the headman. Ask before taking photos, and don't assume you can wander into the haus tambaran at will, especially if you're a woman. Haus tambarans were traditionally exclusively an initiated man's preserve, although these days the rules are sometimes bent for Western tourists.

Places to Stay

The Maprik Waken has closed down, but there's a *Haus Meri* (women's house – men can stay too) which charges about K5. Ask for Lucy Goro. It used to be possible to stay at Maprik High School two km from Hayfields, towards Pagwi, but it closed indefinitely in 1987 due to rascal activity.

Several travellers have enjoyed staying with Noah Washun in **Kimbangoa** village, near Maprik, for K6. He's friendly, knowledgeable and can show you around the area.

Getting There & Away

From Wewak the road climbs up and over the Prince Alexander Mountains then continues 132 km to Maprik. Maprik is actually eight km off the Wewak-Pagwi road; the junction is called Hayfields, where there is a petrol station, a couple of trade stores and an airfield. A PMV from Wewak to Maprik costs K6, Maprik to Pagwi K4, or you can get one direct to Pagwi. The last stretch to Pagwi goes across the Sepik flood plain, and it would be very hard going in the wet.

The road to Wewak has been plagued by hold-ups, and you might want to fly in to Hayfields, near Maprik. Third-level operators such as SAS have irregular flights from Wewak (K37) and Vanimo (K83).

Roads will eventually link Lumi with Aitape. A road already continues from Maprik to Lumi, although missing bridges and deep rivers can make it hazardous. 'Always get out and walk the crossing before trying to drive across', suggested one visitor, 'or join the Lumi yacht club'. A road link to Ambunti is also planned.

Sandaun Province

Land Area 36,000 sq km
Population 145,000
Capital Vanimo

Sandaun (formerly West Sepik) is so named because it's in the north-west of PNG – it's where the sun goes down. The province is little developed, but agricultural activity in the Telefomin district and timber development around Vanimo, the provincial capital, have nonetheless brought rapid change.

VANIMO

Vanimo is on a neat little peninsula that is reminiscent of Wewak. The similarity continues because there are beautiful beaches on both sides. It is however, much smaller and quieter, with invariably generous and hospitable people. In Vanimo everything is within walking distance, but I'd no sooner start out on foot than someone would offer me a lift! In PNG smaller is better.

Vanimo is only 30 km from the Indonesian border so it is virtually within earshot of the trouble that sporadically flares up between the Indonesians and the Irian Jayans. The last influx of refugees was in 1984 and these people are still a major, sometimes resented, presence in town. Their camp is at Blackwater 20 km to the east. The situation along the border is now quiet.

The town has all the essentials: there are Westpac and PNGBC banks, a post office, a couple of reasonable supermarkets and a couple of places to stay, one with backpacker accommodation. Since late '92 there has been an Indonesian consulate in Vanimo (☎ 87 1371/2, fax 87 1373, PO Box 39), which issues one-month visas in a day.

If you're adequately protected from the sun and carry some water along, you can do a pleasant two-hour walk around the headland. You're bound to find some good spots to snorkel. There's another good walk west along the beach from the airport. After about 40 minutes you come to a limestone headland draped with vines; wade around it to the beautiful beach on the other side. There's a rusting Japanese landing barge just offshore.

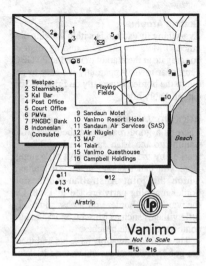

1 Westpac
2 Steamships
3 Kal Bar
4 Post Office
5 Court Office
6 PMVs
7 PNGBC Bank
8 Indonesian Consulate
9 Sandaun Motel
10 Vanimo Resort Hotel
11 Sandaun Air Services (SAS)
12 Air Niugini
13 MAF
14 Talair
15 Vanimo Guesthouse
16 Campbell Holdings

Playing Fields

Beach

Airstrip

Vanimo
Not to Scale

Places to Stay & Eat

The *Vanimo Resort Hotel* (☎ 87 1102, fax 87 1131, PO Box 42) is the Narimo Hotel by another name. It is nicely sited on the eastern side of the peninsular, right next to the beach, with a fine view. Prices range from about K50/60 a single/double (including breakfast), and there are rooms for backpackers where a bed costs K15.

The new *Sandaun Motel* (☎ 87 1000, fax 87 1119, PO Box 35) is better but more expensive, at K95/130. The beer is very cold and meals in the restaurant are good, costing from about K10.

The *Vanimo Guesthouse* might have closed – if not, pretty basic rooms cost about K35.

Getting There & Away

Air Air Niugini and Talair fly from Wewak to Vanimo for K86. The various third-level operators also do the trip, and it's slightly cheaper on Sandaun Air Services (SAS) (☎ 87 1268/79, fax 87 1089, PO Box 206). It's much more interesting to fly in a small plane, because the views are great and on some flights land at Aitape (K60) and some interesting strips in the mountains.

On Sunday, Air Niugini flights continue from Vanimo on to Jayapura (K60) and return the same day. SAS often have midweek flights to Jayapura (K65), and they might be flying to Biak on Tuesdays.

From Jayapura there are daily flights to Biak (US$77 if the ticket is bought outside Indonesia), from where Garuda flies to Los Angeles on Wednesday, Friday and Sunday (US$770, but probably less if you buy the ticket in Indonesia). If you're leaving PNG remember to buy a K15 departure tax stamp at the post office.

Dovair (☎ 87 1056, PO Box 205) and SAS fly to many small strips. A flight from Vanimo to Green River costs K60, to Ambunti K84, May River K90, Timbunke K86.

Sea Lutheran Shipping's somewhat basic cargo freighters continue on to Vanimo from Wewak; one or the other makes the voyage most weeks for K21/26, deck/cabin class; and half that price to Aitape. In Vanimo you get tickets at the wharf prior to departure. Don't count on arriving in town in time for the Jayapura flight – there are inevitably delays.

Getting Around

Everything in Vanimo is within walking distance. PMVs to the surrounding district congregate at the market or near the PNGBC bank near town. Apparently it's easy to get out to the border, especially on Fridays. You can probably hitch.

AROUND VANIMO

There is a good road along the coast from Vanimo to the Irian Jaya border which is marked by the PNG patrol post of Watung. Here you can see one of the 14 markers which the joint Australian-Indonesian border mapping party erected in 1968. On the way to the border you'll pass some tidy little villages such as Muschu and Yako and some superb white beaches.

The road to Bewani is passable and there are good views and several waterfalls.

AITAPE

Aitape is a tiny town that has retained evidence of its long, by PNG standards, colonial history. The Germans established a station here in 1905 and the jail they built in 1906 still stands above the town. It was used by the Japanese during the war.

There are some bits of aircraft wreckage near the wartime Tadji airstrip, the first place captured by the Allies in their advance on the Sepik district. In 1974, 48 dumped aircraft were counted and in a six-week operation

many of them were shipped back to the USA for eventual restoration and display at an aircraft museum in California. A Japanese war memorial is between the town and the Santa Anna Mission.

The offshore islands, about 15 km from the coast, are interesting.

Tony Friend, who works in the district office, has been suggested as a source of information on the area.

Places to Stay

There are rooms at the *Aitape Hotel* (☎ 87 2055, PO Box 72); a single or double costs K90 in the new section or K70 in the old. Cheaper accommodation might be available at the Catholic Mission.

Getting There & Away

A road links Wewak to Aitape. It's rough, without much traffic and it can be impassable in the wet season. Infrequent PMVs run from Wewak. Talair has stopovers daily on the way to/from Vanimo (K68) and Wewak (K86) except Wednesday and Sunday. The third-level operators might have cheaper flights.

TELEFOMIN

The remote and tiny station at Telefomin was only opened in 1948 and it's still one of the most isolated places in the country. However, fundamentalist missions have hit

---

The PNG-Indonesian Border

The border between PNG and Indonesia (Irian Jaya) is a typical example of good colonial thinking. A ruler-straight line was drawn across a totally unknown area of the world, with no regard for who might be living near it, or on it. There have been a whole series of Dutch-English, Dutch-German, Dutch-Australian and most recently Indonesian-Australian attempts to define exactly where the border is and today it is pretty clear just which unfortunate villages straddle the line.

For many years, PNG villages near the border were under much more Dutch influence than Australian for Hollandia was close while Wewak was a long way away. Many people close to the border still speak Bahasa Indonesian, the lingua franca of Dutch rule. Apart from their other insecurities, villagers within 32 km of the border on the PNG side are not allowed to grow coffee or raise cattle due to fears of diseases being spread across the border and eventually reaching the productive PNG coffee and cattle industries. Further south in the Sepik region the high Star Mountains of Irian Jaya continue across the border to form the watersheds for both the Sepik and Fly rivers. ∎

the area's culture hard and a new mine is completing the rapid transition. Traditional dress is now rare.

Baptist Mission has established a museum with wicker masks, arrows and displays of local flora & fauna. There is a coffee shop run by some volunteers and this would be a good spot to get information about accommodation. There are some dramatic caves in the Oksapmin Valley – guides are necessary.

Places to Stay

There's an expensive mission guesthouse near the station. In **Drolengam** village, about a 20-minute walk south of the airstrip there's apparently a guesthouse, run by Robinok and Solumnot who charge K5 a night. There is other village accommodation in the region, but talk to the district officer-in-charge. Some of the missions in the region accept visitors, but advance notice is a very good idea.

Getting There & Away

Talair flies between Tari and Tabubil on Friday, via Oksapmin (K60 from Tari, K63 from Tabubil) and Telefomin (K85 from Tari, K37 from Tabubil). The fare from Telefomin to Oksapmin is K43. There are direct flights to Tabubil from Mt Hagen, Wewak and Moresby, but none connect with the Tari flight. You might be able to make connections if you fly to Tari from Mt Hagen (K79) or Moresby (K153), but check.

MAF has an extensive network in the area. On Tuesday and Thursday MAF flies from Moresby to Tari, and you can make connections to many small strips from this flight.

Tarangau flies from Telefomin to Wewak for K157, to Tari for K111 and to Tabubil for K31. SAS flies from Wewak and Vanimo (K125).

It is possible to walk from Oksapmin in five days, but this is very tough and should not be undertaken lightly. Guides are necessary.

OKSAPMIN

Although it was only established in 1962 this remote station is now seeing a fair bit of development and changing quickly. Oksapmin is the main centre for people around the area where Southern Highlands Province meets Western and Sandaun provinces. This is a beautiful region with the Om and Strickland rivers and their spectacular valleys. The climb from the valley floor to the ridges is 3000 metres in some places. It's driest in November and December, but it can be very wet anytime.

The area's name derives from its two main clans, the Ok and the Min.

Places to Stay

It is possible to stay in villages around the area, but you should contact the district officer-in-charge first. There's an Agricultural Centre at Oksapmin run by the Peace Corps where you can stay, and a guesthouse at **Tekin**, two hours' walk away (10 km). Both charge about K10 a night.

Getting There & Away

If you were really keen, you could continue walking to Tekin, Bak, Bimin and down to Olsobib in Western Province, or to Telefomin. There's a road link to Tekap, a three-day trail to Framin (where there's an aid post), and another two or three days to Telefomin. Don't attempt this without a guide and make sure you contact the police or the district officer-in-charge before you set out. It's another tough five-day walk to Lake Kopiago – see the Highlands chapter for more information.

MAF flies to Tari for K63 and Kopiago for K30, and may have other useful flights in the area. SAS flies irregularly from Wewak (K115) and Vanimo (K133).

AROUND OKSAPMIN

There are now trade stores in the area with the usual tinned fish, rice, sugar and so on. The district is becoming important for the vegetables it grows and supplies to the Ok Tedi mining project not too far away. Other cash crops like coffee have also been introduced. This was a protein-deficient area and even spiders, grubs and beetles were eaten

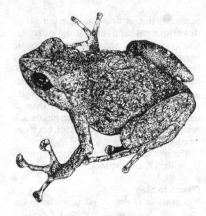

before the ubiquitous *tin fis* (canned fish) was introduced. In the evenings you can still sometimes see torches around the valleys as women search for frogs, mice and snakes.

An interesting circular walk can be made through the villages around Oksapmin to the west and back along the Arigo River. North of town there are very few people but around town and to the south in the five high valleys of Bimin, Bak, Tekin, Teranap and Gaua there are over 10,000 people. For the most part their homes and gardens are at about 2000 metres. There's a sub-district office in the Teranap Valley.

Bimin is the most isolated of the valleys though it does have an airstrip. Gaua, too, is isolated, but it is only a few hours' walk over the mountains south of Teranap office. The other three valleys are linked by a 32-km road from Teranap to Tekin, up the valley to Tekap through the gap to Bak Valley and down to Daburap. This is known as the Opiago road. Eventually it will run down to the Strickland, go up the valley of the Tumbudu River and to Lake Kopiago.

The Highlands Highway will eventually extend all the way to Oksapmin. Hopefully by then the Strickland Valley and Gorge will have been designated as a National Park.

Both the Om and Upper Leonard Schultz valleys now have two airstrips and three aid posts, but they are still very isolated. Baptist Missions are found in Telefomin and Tekin

and Seventh Day Adventists have moved into the Om River area.

Socially, the entire district is different to the Highlands. There are no ceremonial exchanges and no bride price transactions. 'Big Men' don't exist in the same way and there are few leaders of any lasting duration. The societal system is based on sharing, with power more or less distributed equally. Traditionally, wars were rare and small in scale and sorcerers held the most power. Male and female initiation, along with platform burial and certain forms of dress, have virtually died out, and traditional dress is now only worn on special occasions.

The people in the Oksapmin area are known as having a shame rather than a guilt culture. When people for any number of reasons are shamed they often blame themselves. Apparently a very high percentage of deaths is attributable to suicide. Difficulties in marriage and problems with witches are major causes, but the most important reason was bereavement. Family members used to kill themselves at the loss of loved ones, but this no longer occurs.

Modern development and the problems caused by men leaving to work in other districts and then returning home have resulted in difficulties and disillusionment for people in the region, but it remains quiet and peaceful.

Sheldon Weeks of The University of PNG has collected and edited various studies of the area into *Oksapmin, Development & Change*, available inexpensively at the university in Moresby. This work supplied much of the information for this section.

The Sepik & its Tributaries

The mighty Sepik reverted to its local name when the Australians took over from the Germans and Kaiserin Augusta had her name withdrawn from the river. Some people say 'Sepik' means 'great river', but nobody is

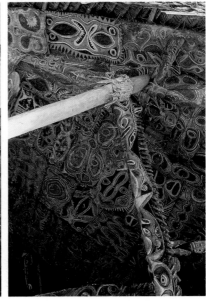

Top: Mendam Village, Murik Lakes, East Sepik Province (ML)
Left: Chambri Lakes, Middle Sepik (TW)
Right: Painted bark ceiling (ML)

Top Left: Sepik woman in mourning (ML)
Bottom Left: Construction in Palambei, Middle Sepik (TW)
Top Right: River scene (Air Niugini)
Bottom Right: River bridge in Timbunke, Middle Sepik (ML)

certain. There are few exploitable natural resources so the Sepik has attracted little development, despite the relative density of the population. On the surface, most villages still appear relatively untouched by Western influences and the art is still vigorous and unique, although rarely traditional.

The art itself makes a visit worthwhile. The scale of the river, the impressive architecture of haus tambarans, the beautiful stilt villages, the long canoes with their crocodile-head prows, the bird life, the flower-clogged lakes, the misty dawns and spectacular sunsets make a visit unforgettable.

Nowadays, however, there are many Western influences. The Sepik peoples have a dynamic, living culture, not a museum culture, so change, both good and bad, is not surprising. Western clothing is the rule and the impact of the missions has been profound. Although in some villages there has been a revival of traditional ceremonies, including male initiation, this is alongside, or somehow mixed with, Christianity and Western-style education. Many of the young men leave the villages and if they survive the shanty towns in the cities and return, they bring with them both visible and invisible baggage. Travellers and artefact buyers have also left changes in their wake.

Although the Middle Sepik in particular is one of the most frequently visited parts of the country it is not by any standards crowded with tourists, and you are unlikely to be in a village at the same time as any other traveller. You may see the odd group sweeping past in a canoe or river boat, and perhaps a trader or missionary, but that will be about it. Only a small but steady number of travellers stay in the villages, especially independently.

Bear in mind that although in photos Sepik villages look idyllic the photos do not show the heat and humidity (which can be extreme), the mosquitoes (which can be unbelievably numerous and vicious), the village food (which is, at best, monotonous and tasteless), or the housing conditions (which in terms of Western comforts are basic). Nor do they indicate the rewards of travelling at your own pace, meeting the people and experiencing such a rich and fascinating culture!

As a general rule, you're best not to try and do too much. Resist the urge to cast yourself as a heroic explorer. Although there are differences between the villages' carving styles, their organisation and appearance does not change significantly.

Rather than exhaust yourself paddling for

Frill-neck Flycatcher

days in the middle of a huge monotonous river you would be better off to give yourself time in a village, preferably a bit off the beaten track, so you can establish relationships and get a feel for the people's lives. This is difficult if you're looking at the world through a fog of sunburn, mosquito bites and exhaustion. Two or three villages on the Middle Sepik will be quite enough for most people, and many people find they enjoy themselves more when they get off the main river.

In order to see a lot of the Sepik you must either grit your teeth and spend a considerable amount of money, or have plenty of time and persuasive ability – see the Travel on the Sepik section. There is road access to the Sepik at only three points: Angoram on the Lower Sepik, and Timbunke and Pagwi on the Middle Sepik. The alternative is to fly in to airstrips like Amboin on the Karawari River, or Ambunti on the Upper Sepik. The most artistic villages are concentrated on the Middle Sepik and the most spectacular scenery is on the lakes or tributaries. If you want to see a reasonable amount of the river at not too considerable a cost, Angoram or Pagwi are the best bases to use although Timbunke and Ambunti are also worth considering.

The Upper Sepik extends from the river's source to just below Ambunti, the Middle Sepik covers from above Pagwi to just before Angoram and the Lower Sepik is the final section from Angoram to the coast.

WHEN TO GO

June to October is the dry season, with the main wet season being December to April; most rain falls in January and February and the river level starts to drop after April. The region gets over 72 cm of rain a year, so it can rain anytime. Temperatures and humidity can be high, but it's usually pleasant on the river, where you're more likely to get a breeze.

The dry season is the best time to visit, since the mosquitoes are less numerous. By August the river level can drop significantly, and this may make negotiating some tributaries and barats difficult. In the dry season the Chambri Lakes can get very smelly: they shrink, fish die and weed rots. The people start gardening in June (when there is little likelihood of floods) and they harvest vegetables from September to November (which must be a relief from sago).

WHAT TO TAKE

Whether you're going in a dugout canoe or on a cruise boat, you must carefully plan what to take. If you're travelling independently the issue becomes vital.

You need light cotton clothes – light enough not to be too hot, long enough to protect you from the sun and heavy enough to prevent mosquito bites (they'll bite through fine cheese-cloth). You'll appreciate being able to tuck a long pair of pants into

socks to protect your ankles from probing proboscises, especially in the evenings.

A broad-brimmed hat, sun cream, sunglasses and insect repellent are essential. People talk about their insect repellents on the Sepik with much the same professional interest that travellers in India bring to bear on their stomach condition, but all the major brands seem to work.

A swimsuit is worth packing, although it won't be much use if you're staying in a village since most villagers are very prudish. For men a pair of shorts will be appropriate, women may find a laplap best. Tennis shoes that you don't mind getting wet and muddy are ideal footwear; thongs or sandals are nearly as good.

Bring plenty of film if you're a photography freak and binoculars if you're interested in birds. Make sure this sort of equipment is in a bag or case that is at least rain and splash-proof, preferably fully waterproof. A rain-cape is a good multipurpose tool (ground sheet, cargo and person protector), and in the wet season, or if you burn easily, an umbrella would also help.

Wewak and Vanimo are the only places in the area where you can change money. Make sure you have plenty of small denomination notes – especially K2 and K5 – as village people rarely have change.

Staying in Villages

Those staying in villages will need a torch (flashlight) for night excursions. It's ideal if the torch casts a wide beam, because you may need it for cooking at night. Take a spare globe and batteries. Candles are useful.

It is essential to sleep well if you're going to survive the heat, food and mosquitoes in good humour. That means you must have a mosquito net (nets will probably be supplied for tour groups) and a sleeping mat. There is an art to organising a mosquito net, but first you must ensure that it is large enough to allow you to sleep without touching the sides (a two-person net gives you much more room, if you're large it's essential) and the mesh size must be very fine (around one mm). A well-ventilated inner section from a hiking tent is ideal, as it also gives you a bit of privacy. Good mosquito nets are available in Wewak for K5 to K15. There are also some useless nets on sale, so check them out carefully. Don't buy the circular type which hangs from one central point.

You will need a supply of cheap string or twine so that you can suspend the net from handy beams and walls. Sepik long houses have no internal divisions, so your net becomes your bedroom. If you've hung a net and you're not using it, drape the sides across its roof. Make your entry as swiftly as possible, tuck the bottom edges of your net underneath your mat, and then make sure you've killed any *natnats* (mosquitoes) that have come in with you. The mat is not just an optional extra. The floors of Sepik long houses are made of the outer casing of a palm, which is smooth, springy, airy, and definitely not mosquito proof. The mat will also be very useful as a cushion in your canoe.

You must take at least some food. Although there are infrequent trade stores they usually only sell tinned meat and fish, rice and tobacco. The local people will often offer you a meal (not always), but most of the year this will only consist of *saksak* (sago) and *makau* (smoked fish). The sago is, in most forms, vaguely suggestive of tasteless Plasticine and the smoked fish, while good, quickly loses its appeal. Coconut and banana (the starchy, cooking type) can liven the picture a little, and there are taros and introduced vegetables late in the dry season. An English traveller with a taste for rice pudding recommends pouring condensed milk over your rice.

It is an unbelievably monotonous diet, and you will be hard pushed to look that smoked fish in the eye for the 10th consecutive meal. If you do eat the locals' food and have nothing else to give in return, you should pay a kina or so per meal. Instead of paying, however, the best idea is to have packet soups, biscuits, jam and other Western-style food that you can share and trade. If you stay with families, there will always be a cooking fire, but if you end up in a haus kiap you'll need some sort of stove.

Many villages have rats, and while they won't bother you in your mosquito net, they will eat through bags to get at your food. A tin, such as an old powdered-milk tin, is very handy for storing those noodles and beef crackers.

Villages often have rainwater you can drink, and it's handy to have a water bottle. The Sepik water may look a bit muddy, but it's quite OK, so long as it hasn't been taken directly downstream of a town. The volume of water is so huge and the number of people living alongside is so small that there aren't any problems. However, water in the lakes and backwaters is suspect, especially when the level is low. If you want to be absolutely confident take along some purification tablets.

Make sure you have some good maps. The river changes quickly, however, so they are all out of date. An ox-bow becomes the main stream, or the main stream becomes an ox-bow very quickly, and smaller channels can be blocked by floating islands. *Wewak, the Gateway to the Sepik* is a reasonable map and it is available in Wewak at the Christian Bookshop or Ralf's for K2; the spelling is more accurate than most.

If you're going on one of the tributaries, I suggest getting some detailed topographic maps at the National Mapping Bureau in Moresby. Although their detail on the river will not be much help, mountains don't change quite so quickly, so you should still be able to orientate yourself.

There are aid posts along the river, but you should have a medical kit to cope with emergencies. It's easy for a mosquito bite to become infected for instance, and if you are planning a long trip, you should research how to identify and treat malaria.

POINTERS

The Sepik people can be fairly indifferent, even suspicious, when you first meet them. Younger men particularly, often adopt a tough-guy image. It can take a while to get beyond this barrier.

Perhaps this is partly due to pushy travellers who rush in, grab a pile of carvings, struggle bitterly to save every toea and leave without making any contribution. And I'm not just talking about money, but being friendly, taking time to talk, sharing food and maybe even a song.

The Sepik is not some sort of anthropological zoo, and you cannot pass through as an anonymous observer. To the villagers, an outsider is a potential friend, but also a potential enemy. If you are to have a safe and enjoyable time you must meet people and relate to them on their terms. An American traveller reckoned that Sepik people are 'just like people from LA'!

Try to behave in accordance with local customs – watch and learn. Dress and act conservatively, taking your cue from people around you. If you're in a village and want a swim, ask when and where the locals bathe; there will often be separate times for men and women and it is extremely rude to watch or take photos. Most Sepik villages are rigidly patriarchal.

Western men should be cautious about talking to women – you'll often embarrass them and may cause jealousy – talk to middle-aged men. And Western women should be cautious about talking to men – this may be misinterpreted – talk to the women. It is always difficult to read peoples' characters, but watching their faces and learning their names will be a good start. Don't over use their name in normal speech.

Don't argue or haggle over prices, it is considered rude. Bargaining is not a normal part of a business transaction the way it is in Asia and elsewhere. Above all, never belittle the item in an attempt to lower the price.

There may well be a 'second price' but if the vendor doesn't like you, you'll never be offered it. Also, if the vendor is acting on behalf of someone else, they might not be able to change the price. If you think a price is too high or if you can't afford something, express polite regret and slowly walk away, maybe glancing back.

Try to arrive in a village well before dark, maybe mid-afternoon, so you have plenty of time to find somewhere to stay and get yourself organised. Apart from the fact that it's difficult to do things in the dark, the mosquitoes come out at dusk and doing anything but sitting by a fire is torture.

Involving people in what you are doing is a good idea. For example, if you ask for advice on the best place to moor your canoe, the people who show you might feel some responsibility for the canoe's safety.

It is immensely preferable to stay with a family, rather than isolated in a haus tambaran or haus kiap. It will be more enjoyable and more secure. You'll often have to ask to stay with a family, and if the village seems determined to have you sleep in an empty house, say that you're afraid to sleep alone. Ask adults (men if you're male, women if you're female) about accommodation, not kids.

Villagers go to bed early, perhaps as early as 8 pm, but if you sit up late they'll feel obliged to keep you company. They also get up early and complete many jobs before the day is too hot. If you ask what people plan to be doing the next day you might be invited along on a fishing or hunting trip.

The amount you are expected to pay for accommodation varies. This is compounded by the fact that in many places, especially the more remote, you don't actually *pay* for accommodation, you give a gift to the people who have shown you hospitality. Of course, a gift is expected and some people will want more than others, but discussing the price of accommodation in advance could well be considered bad manners.

Somewhere around K5 is usual, often less on the Upper Sepik, plus a couple of kina for food, if you don't have anything to trade. Tinned food, band-aids and aspirin make welcome gifts, and one budding entrepreneur collected *kaurie* (cowry) shells from a beach near Madang and used them as gifts for Sepik carvers.

You will normally be expected to pay the man of the house, but this is not always the case. Because it's a gift you are giving, make it a whole note rather than a handful of coins, and give it nonchalantly. In purpose-built accommodation, such as a village guesthouse, there is likely to be a set fee, generally higher than you'd pay to stay in someone's house.

An exception to the idea of giving gifts is when you take a photo of a cultural item or event – this will be a fee, usually K2 or less but sometimes more if the people receive a lot of visitors, or if they receive none. Here you will be paying a fee. Ask before you take photographs.

Never take a picture of or in a haus tambaran (even if it is only under construction) before gaining permission from the men who are inevitably sitting around underneath.

The nearest equivalent in Western society is a church, so you should show respect. Ask before you enter, even the ground floor, and remove your hat. Women may not be allowed to enter, especially upstairs, although this rule is usually bent for Westerners. Sometimes there will be a charge (usually K1 or so).

On the Middle Sepik you will usually be able to find someone who speaks a little English – often one of the children – but in most cases you will be very restricted in your communication without some knowledge of Pidgin. Beyond the Middle Sepik, Pidgin will be even more important.

Finally, remember that it isn't necessary to cover a lot of territory. You can have just as interesting a time staying in one village for a week as you would spending long, hot days paddling down the river.

SAFETY

Basically, it is safe to visit the Sepik, but you should be a little cautious and use your brains. Once you are out on the river you are a long way from help. There have been reports of robberies, and although these are rare, most locals don't like to travel alone.

You do have to watch your belongings, so you are best off leaving non-essentials like passports at somewhere like Ralf's place in Wewak. A pile of interesting things left in your canoe while you go for a wander will soon disappear.

Never display wealth, and that includes personal stereos, jewellery, even fashionable clothes. Alcohol is the number one motivation for robbery in rural PNG, so if you carry it don't show it.

Although you might be safer travelling in a group (of Westerners), you will inevitably be perceived as a group rather than as individuals, which will make it harder to make friends with villagers – which in turn increases the danger. Once you have made friends in a village it is highly unlikely that you will have any problems there, and you will be given help and information.

Mixed groups of men and women will always be safe to approach, but you should be sceptical about small groups of men. Several homosexual attacks on lone male travellers, after they have trustingly paddled ashore in response to a friendly greeting, have been reported. There have also been stories of children threatening to tip canoes.

Be aware of the strict segregation of the sexes among Sepik people. Men should talk to men in a village, women to women. Women should *never* drink alcohol with men. Couples should not show physical affection.

There are still crocodiles on the Sepik, although they are hunted heavily and are very leery of human beings. Their territories do not extend any great distance from the edge of water – you are most at risk if you are a long way from human habitation, within 20 or 30 metres of a river, at dusk, and you have returned to the same spot several times.

A number of people have been bitten by snakes, mostly at night stumbling around in the dark – take a torch and in long grass flick the ground ahead with a handy stick. Check the location of the toilet, which will be a separate shack a short walk away, and the layout of the washing place in daylight.

Women Travellers

A woman who travelled on the middle Sepik recommends making eye-contact with every woman you meet. As she was with a male guide, the village women found the situation initially confusing but she mixed almost exclusively with women in the villages and was usually accepted.

She recommends having a reason for being in a village, such as studying gardens or houses. Many village women resented the fact that she was allowed into haus tambaran (which was taboo for them) and this created a barrier.

TRAVEL TO THE SEPIK

See this chapter's introductory Getting There & Away and Getting Around sections for information on air travel to the Sepik. See the Wewak section for information on PMVs to Angoram, Timbunke and Pagwi, the only road-access points.

TRAVEL ON THE SEPIK

There are several ways to travel on the river: village canoes – you go along as a passenger in someone else's canoe; do-it-yourself canoes – you buy a canoe and paddle it yourself; motorised canoes – you charter a canoe and a guide/driver; and tours on one of the boats cruising the river. There are no longer any passenger-carrying freighters on the Sepik.

Village Canoes

The cheapest, most time-consuming method of travel is to rely on inter-village, PMV-type canoes with outboard motors and to stay in the villages.

There is a reasonably constant movement of boats along the river, with people trading, going to markets and visiting friends and relatives. Predictably, the movement of these boats is entirely unpredictable. You may have to wait many days for someone heading in your direction, and without a reasonable grasp of Pidgin you will find it very difficult to make your intentions clear. There will often be a complete (deliberate?) lack of understanding and people will pressure you to charter a canoe (very expensive) and then load it up with assorted cronies anyway.

If you do get a ride it will be very cheap: around K2 to K3 per hour. The best time is Wednesday or Thursday, when people are going to market. Absolutely no boats at all came by on the Friday afternoon or Saturday when I was waiting in Mindimbit and Sunday isn't much better. This is partly because of religion. Some of the Sepik villages (Suapmeri, Mindimbit, Angriman) are Seventh Day Adventists – their sabbath is Saturday and is strictly upheld. Similarly, the Catholics don't travel on Sundays.

The bottom line is that you need a lot of time and patience to travel this way – and even then you just may not have any luck.

Do-it-Yourself Canoes

You can buy a small dugout canoe and paddle yourself. This can be very physically demanding. It is not always easy to find a canoe in reasonable condition for sale at a reasonable price and you will need to have enough time to be open-ended with your plans.

Beyond the obvious advantages of being independent, there are also disadvantages aside from the physical demands. You will only be able to paddle downstream (the current is too strong to fight), and your view of the wide brown river with high grass crowding to its banks, will soon become monotonous. Much of the really beautiful scenery is up the tributaries away from the Sepik flood plain. Without a translator you may well miss out on worthwhile explanations, and because the river changes course so quickly, some of the most important villages are now quite a distance inland – without a guide you could easily miss them. Look for coconut palms – they almost always indicate human settlement.

Ambunti is a reasonable place to buy canoes; it's difficult to buy canoes around Pagwi, but the nearby villages are more helpful.

Prices vary greatly depending on your negotiating skills and the canoe's condition. Make sure you know whether paddles are being included in the deal, and think in terms of paying K20 to K60 for a canoe. Don't pay too little, or the canoe will probably sink, although that fate has also befallen travellers who paid a lot.

It takes a month of hard work to make a decent-sized canoe. They are an essential tool for the villagers, so usually they'll only want to palm one off if they no longer need it or they can make a profit (that is, the canoe will be old, leaky and expensive). You must check the condition of the canoe carefully. Small cracks can be sealed with mud, but large ones may be a problem.

Depending on your competence with a canoe, you may consider having an outrigger attached (someone in the village should be able to do this at a moderate cost), or even joining two canoes together (although this will slow you down).

Although there are no rapids, manipulating an unwieldy dugout in a five-knot current can be quite challenging.

You must keep your eyes open for floating debris (which can be chunks of riverbank the size of small islands), and for the occasional whirlpool – these aren't big enough to do any damage unless you are caught off balance.

The river is wide enough in places to have quite big waves, maybe up to a metre. The locals paddle standing up, but I don't recommend trying this with your gear on board.

We've heard of several travellers having disasters with their canoes, often on the first day or two of paddling. Once you've bought a canoe find someone to show you how to manage it. Any leaks in the canoe might become apparent while you're learning, and you'll have an expert on hand to show you how to patch them. One traveller suggested taking along a guide for the first day's paddling.

Take along something to bail out the canoe. As well as leaks, downpours can swamp you. A trick that is worth remembering is to lay some sticks across the bottom of the canoe to make a raised base. Use this to keep your luggage out of the water that inevitably pools in the bottom. A traveller has suggested using banana leaves to cover your luggage when (not if) it rains.

Travellers have suggested the Green, May and April rivers as good places to start, but all these are fairly strenuous expeditions, not to be undertaken lightly. It takes at least 10 days solid paddling from Green River to Ambunti and around a week from April River. From Ambunti it takes a solid week to Angoram.

One thing you notice when talking to people about their travels on the Sepik is the differing experiences they have had and the different advice they give.

Some say you travel faster in the middle of the river (the current is stronger); others point out that you can save many km by cutting corners close to the banks. Some recommend one paddle shape, others another. Some say that the Upper Sepik is *the* place, others that it definitely isn't. A few became incredibly bored after a day or two, a few have found things rather too exciting. Most agree that you get very dirty, although some don't think that this is a drawback. The most consistent comment, though, is 'Do it!'

Motorised Canoes

You can hire motorised canoes, especially in Ambunti, Pagwi, Angoram and to a lesser extent Timbunke, where there are an increasing number of local entrepreneurs who hope to make their living this way.

This is much more expensive than paddling, but can work out your own itinerary and travel upstream, and the driver doubles as guide. Depending on the driver, this could be good or bad. There are a few rogues who do their very best to rip you off, and some virtually force you to do what they think you want to do, entirely disregarding what you say you want to do!

Hiring a canoe will be more feasible if you have a decent-sized group – you may be able to organise this at Ralf's in Wewak. Most of the motorised dugouts comfortably hold six or seven people and their luggage – they can be over 20 metres long. This kind of trip also entails staying in villages, although an honest and friendly guide will make life a bit easier and more interesting than if you do it by yourself.

If you charter a canoe you also have to pay for the driver to return to his base, whether you go or not. It is, however, much cheaper to travel downstream with a full load, as the petrol (also known as *benzin*) consumption will be considerably reduced. Petrol will be the largest single component of your expense – it's K3 or more per gallon, and you can't negotiate your way around that.

There are several ways hire is computed: a per person charge; a daily rate for a driver and canoe including petrol, which is usually around K60 to K80; or a daily rate for a driver and canoe excluding petrol, which is around K35 to K45. The hourly running costs are around K10 to K20. To get from Ambunti to Angoram would be a five to seven-day trip and could vary between K300 and K600. Some of the more organised guides quote all-up daily rates which include food, accommodation and incidentals like entrance to haus tambaran and photo fees.

These costs may seem outrageous, but if you subtract the petrol component and break them down on a daily basis they make sense: K10 for the canoe; K15 for the motor (these are expensive and take a fair battering, pay less for a 15 hp motor); K10 for a driver/guide. These figures will vary depending on your negotiating skills. You will also need to stock up with food, and be equipped to cope with life in the villages.

If you are paying for petrol on top of daily hire, ensure your driver fills up before you start (petrol is much more expensive away from the road heads): 15-hp engines are recommended as they are faster and economical. Don't pay in advance for anything except petrol and check the price and quantity delivered. It's possible to hire flat-bottomed boats in Angoram and they're worth considering if you want to move quickly. They're much faster than a canoe, especially if the river is chopped up by wind – they plane over the top.

As a rule of thumb, bearing in mind that all sorts of factors can have an influence, travelling downstream in a large canoe takes about 1½ hours' running time from Ambunti to Pagwi, about six hours from Pagwi to Timbunke, and five hours from Timbunke to Angoram. You can probably add at least 30% for going upstream. A boat is twice as fast. Again as a rule of thumb, thirty minutes in a motor canoe equals two or three hours' paddling.

You're not going to be superbly comfortable in a canoe but the biggest drawback is uncertainty – you can arrive at the river and find there are no canoes available and have to hang around for days.

Guides There are plenty of people with motorised canoes who will be only too happy to take you on a Sepik tour. You will probably need a couple of days at the beginning of the trip to negotiate a reasonable rate and to find a reliable driver. Talk to as many locals as possible (store owners, district officers, police) and try and build up a picture on who is trustworthy, the going hire rates, how long a journey will take, and how many gallons of petrol will be used.

A lot of so-called guides are just village people who happen to be on the spot when a traveller with a wad of cash comes along looking for a motorised canoe. There's no reason why you shouldn't have a great time with one of these instant guides, but there's always the risk that you'll be stuck with someone who doesn't know what he is doing.

There are a few guides with excellent reputations.

Joseph Kone can be contacted in Ambunti, either through Ambunti Lodge (☎ 88 1291) or PIM (☎ 88 1303). Kowspi Marek is also contactable through PIM in Ambunti, but he usually runs tours from Pagwi.

Cletus Smank Maiban in Angoram has been guiding artefacts buyers on the river for nearly 30 years. Steven Buku is another big name, but he is now working at the Sepik International Beach Resort in Wewak – he might be able to recommend a guide.

Alois Mateus, manager of the Ambunti Lodge, can help organise trips, as can Joe Kenni in Angoram.

There are plenty of other honest and competent guides, but these are names which crop up over and over again in travellers' letters.

Organised Tours

Depending on where you want to go and your ability to strike a bargain, it may not be much more expensive to join a tour.

A number of companies organise groups who travel in large motorised dugouts, and stay in the villages. Prices vary considerably. It would be worth writing to all these people in advance to get an idea of up-to-date costs and options.

See also the Motorised Canoe section above, as some of these operators are becoming more professional in their approach and are offering packages, some of which you can pre-book.

In between the local operators and the tour companies is Ambunti Lodge (☎ 88 1291, fax 86 2525, PO Box 248, Wewak; PO Box 83 Ambunti), which can prearrange fairly inexpensive tours.

You could also try Ralf Stüttgen – see the Wewak Places to Stay section.

Traditional Travel
  PO Box 4264, Boroko (☎ 21 3966)

Haus Poroman
  PO Box 1182, Mt Hagen, PNG (☎ 52 2722, fax 52 2207)
Tribal World
  PO Box 86, Mt Hagen (☎ 55 1555)
  Some tours, and also possibly a regular boat trip along the river.
Melanesian Tourist Services
  PO Box 707, Madang (☎ 82 2766)
  Operator of the luxury cruise boat, *Melanesian Discoverer* that travels the length of the river.
Trans Niugini Tours
  PO Box 371, Mt Hagen (☎ 52 1438)
  Operator of luxury Karawari Lodge and the *Sepik Spirit* river boat.
  Some tours involve staying in villages.
Niugini Tours
  100 Clarence St, Sydney, Australia 2000 (☎ 290 2055)

Haus Poroman and Traditional Travel offer the cheapest tours, with village stays, and Trans Niugini Tours also have some packages aimed at backpackers, but none of the tours are particularly cheap. But they do take you to places it would be difficult to find yourself, and they do operate to reasonably certain schedules. If you have limited time and want to visit some of the more remote tributaries, this option is worth considering.

Travel Times

The travel times given in this chapter should be used as very rough indicators only. There are many variables that can significantly alter times: the length of a canoe, the weight of cargo, the size of a motor, the skill of the driver, the number of stops you make, how hard and efficiently you paddle, whether you get lost, the height of the river, whether there's a head wind and whether there's any wind at all (chop considerably slows down most canoes).

The river flows between three and five knots per hour so travelling upstream is slower and more expensive (more fuel is needed) than travelling downstream. Although the locals can paddle upstream it is unrealistic for Westerners to consider doing so.

The motor canoe times given in this chapter are for a large canoe (12 metres) with a 25-hp motor and a full load travelling

Sepik Glossary

Barats These are artificial channels that are built as shortcuts across loops in the river (sometimes saving many arduous miles of paddling) to link adjoining lakes to the river or, when the river's course changes, a village with the river.

Haus Tambarans Tambarans are spirits so the haus tambaran is the house where they live – or at least where the carvings that represent them are kept. You may also hear them referred to as 'spirit houses' or 'men's houses', since only initiated men (and tourists) are allowed to enter. Once upon a time a woman who ventured inside met instant death – and although Western women are usually allowed inside, times have probably not changed for the village women.

Every clan has to have a spirit house and although they may have lost some of their cultural importance they are still very much the centre of local life. On the Sepik, men while away the day lounging around in the cool shade underneath, carving, talking or just snoozing. On the Blackwater Lakes during the nine month leadup to their initiation, the initiates live in the upstairs section of the haus tambaran, and are only allowed out at night when the rest of the village has gone to sleep.

Haus tambaran styles vary: the high, forward leaning style of the Maprik region is probably best known, but some on the Sepik are equally spectacular. They can be huge buildings on mighty, carved piles, 40 or 50 metres long with a spire at each end stretching 25 metres into the air. When the missionaries first arrived some zealous individuals burnt down haus tambarans to destroy the village 'idols'. One brave district officer actually took the commendable action of charging a missionary with arson and these days a more enlightened attitude is usual.

Head Hunting The Sepik people were once fierce and enthusiastic warriors, but with the arrival of Europeans the frequent inter-village raids came to an end. Traditionally, no man could take his place in the tribe until he had killed – it didn't matter who, an old woman or a small child was just as good as a rival warrior. The skull was brought back and hung in the haus tambaran and the warrior was then allowed to wear an apron of flying fox skin as a mark of distinction. No haus tambaran was erected without a human skull under every post. Some of them had a lot of posts.

Initiation In most villages the traditional initiation for young men is no longer practised, but in a surprising number of places it has been re-established – Michael Somare, PNG's first prime minister, underwent initiation on the Murik Lakes. Sometimes there is a significant departure from strict forms of the ceremony, particularly in the amount of time initiates are trained, and the skin-cutting may be carried out over a number 'operations'.

After a long period of confinement, training and education the initiation ceremony culminates in a skin-cutting ceremony. The initiates' arms, shoulders and upper bodies are patterned with cuts. These cuts are between one and two cm long, quite deep (they don't just break the skin) and arranged in swirling patterns. The cuts are now most usually made with a razor blade, in place of the traditional bamboo knives, and the whole process takes about an hour. Clay and ashes are rubbed in to the cuts to ensure they heal as raised keloid scars – like crocodile scales. During the ceremony the haus tambaran is totally shielded off by a high fence and the drums, flutes and bull roarers play continuously.

Makau The most commonly caught fish on the Middle Sepik is the Makau, a small fish similar in size and shape to a bream. They are smoked over a pottery hearth for preservation, then wrapped in banana leaves and cooked. They make good eating and are the usual accompaniment to the sago pancake. They seem to be prolific and they are netted in large numbers by the women. I was told that fish (perhaps only makau?) were introduced to the Sepik by the Germans – does anyone know?

Natnat This is Pidgin for mosquito. The Sepik variety isn't particularly big or vicious, but they make up for this with their numbers. Walking through Suapmeri one morning I looked up to see the back of the person in front of me completely black with hitchhikers.

They aren't a problem while you're in the middle of the river, but once you're on the banks they descend in hoards. They are particularly bad in the evenings. The dry season (July to November) is much better than the wet, which is impossible to imagine. The mosquitoes are not such a problem once you get up the tributaries, either. Higher altitudes, cooler weather and faster flowing water might explain it, although the Blackwater Lakes seem particularly free.

The Sepik people have developed a number of strategies to cope. The simplest is to wave a plaited fan/whisk, an action that soon becomes completely reflex. Perhaps the greatest contribution the West has made is the cotton mosquito net. Before these were available finely woven wicker baskets, which must have been unbelievably hot, were used. The other technique is to drive them away with smoke. Special aromatic, smoky woods are used (if possible) and fires are lit under the long houses, so the smoke can drift up through the floor. This makes the long houses smoky, as well as hot, but anything is better than the mosquitoes. Wherever people sit around, fires are lit. The Sepik is the only place I have been where smoke from a fire hasn't followed me – and the only place where I wanted it to!

Penis Gourds In the Upper Sepik region men traditionally wore a long, decorated gourd on their penises, and not much else. Western clothes have now been adopted. Some villages on the Middle Sepik sell penis gourds to tourists.

Pitpit is a wild sugar cane that crowds up to the bank of the river and grows up to three metres high. Much of the Middle and Lower Sepik is densely lined with this monotonous weed.

Puk Puk is Pidgin for crocodile. Crocodiles still have enormous cultural and economic importance on the river. In their initiation rites, young men are scarred so that it looks like they have crocodile scales on their arms, legs and trunk. Incisions are made in patterns, and mud is rubbed in to make raised scars that men wear with pride. The process must be unbelievably painful, although the initiates are somehow trained to cope.

Crocodile heads are still carved on the prows of the handsome Sepik dugout canoes. And, of course, crocodiles are still one of the most important sources of cash for the Sepik villagers.

Crocodiles are still very important commercially although it is now illegal to take ones over seven feet (two metres) – the illegal size is actually determined by girth, not length. A seven-foot crocodile is about 50 cm (20 inches) in girth. The skin from a good condition saltwater crocodile can be worth K6 an inch (in girth), a freshwater only K4. Below 25 cm (10 inches) they're worth much less. Many villages have crocodile farms, but they're generally not grown beyond 1½ metres (4½ feet) in length as they take a long time to grow larger than that. The complete hide must be presented for sale, so you can't cheat on the maximum size limit by cutting the skin down. Crocodiles are edible, but only the tail is palatable – the rest is very sinewy. According to the connoisseurs it has a sort of fish-meat taste. Crocodiles won't bite underwater so villagers catch them by feeling in the mud with their feet – I wouldn't want to test that theory! Many are caught in fishing nets.

Saksak is Pidgin for sago, which is the staple food for the Sepik people, and in fact for people who live throughout the swampy areas of PNG.

The preparation of sago is a long process and the end result is neither very appetising nor very nutritional. It is basically pure starch, but in a land where it is often too swampy to grow anything else, it is vitally important. Certainly there is no shortage of it, since sago palms grow prolifically. On the Sepik, dry sago is usually mixed with water and fried into a rubbery pancake, although it can be boiled into a gluey porridge. Mixed with grated coconut it becomes quite palatable, but by itself it is almost tasteless. Supplemented with bananas, vegetables or fish it will keep you going.

The sago palm is a very ancient food source and it is difficult to imagine how and when it was discovered. First, a sago palm (which looks just like any other palm tree to me) is cut down, the bark is cut away and the pith is chipped and pounded out, producing what looks like fibrous sawdust. That's the men's contribution. Next the women knead the pith in a bark funnel with a rough filter, draining water through the pith to dissolve the starch. The starch-laden water is collected (often in an old canoe) and the starch settles in a orange, glutinous mass at the bottom.

Salvinia Salvinia Molesta, to give this water weed its full name, once threatened the entire Sepik system with ecological disaster. It could well have forced the depopulation of the region, but it is now, fortunately, under control. Salvinia originated in Brazil, has small, fleshy fan-like leaves and can double in size in two days. You will see small chunks of it floating down the river and anybody who has spent time on the river will be able to point it out to you.

When it was introduced to the Sepik it went wild. In the early '80s it covered 60% of the Lower and Middle Sepik's lakes, lagoons and barats, often forming a mat too thick for canoes to penetrate, isolating villages and preventing fishing. Herbicides were clearly inappropriate, and it grew much faster than it could be cut.

The solution was to introduce a weevil, Cyrtobagus. The adult feeds on Salvinia's buds and the larvae burrow through the plant which dies, becomes water-logged and sinks. Wide distribution of the weevil began in 1983. The results were dramatic, and within months Cyrtobagus was winning the war – and it still holds the upper hand today. ∎

downstream in good conditions. Canoe times are for solid paddling. As a general rule, 30 minutes in a motor canoe equals two or three hours' paddling. Add about 30% for upstream times. Flat-bottomed aluminium boats are much quicker, especially in windy conditions.

UPPER SEPIK

Above Ambunti the villages are smaller and more spread out. The people have had less contact with Western tourists and are often friendly and hospitable, although clumsy or downright rude foreign visitors have created bad feeling in some places.

This is not helped by the fact that many villagers have no real understanding of the value of money, so prices can be erratic. It's not a bad idea to take presents, such as salt, cigarette papers, tobacco, photos of your country, simple toys for kids, etc.

People might be bemused by foreigners who have no apparent reason for being there – you aren't a missionary and you aren't looking for oil, so what are you up to?

There is not nearly the same concentration of artistic skills that you find on the Middle Sepik, but it is still an interesting area – traditionally, different villages had their own cult or focal point for the spiritual world.

Natural historians will find this the most exciting part of the river. From Ambunti the river narrows and the land it flows through becomes more hilly with denser vegetation. In many areas trees grow right down to the water's edge. Large vessels can travel a day or two from Ambunti, but beyond this the twisting river is suitable only for small boats.

There are few artefacts after Yessan and there is a long uninhabited stretch between Tipas and Mowi (perhaps two days paddling) although there are hunting lodges where you can stay, at relatively frequent intervals.

The Upper Sepik is more isolated than the Middle Sepik, since there are no roads, so a visit requires detailed planning. You should definitely bring your own food. If you want to buy your own canoe, a village up here would be a good place to start.

Villages around here tend to move, and there are lots of deserted villages. Names of villages also change.

Green River

This is a subdistrict station, close to the Sepik River in Sandaun (West Sepik) Province, due south of Vanimo and very close to the Irian Jaya border. It's about a three-hour walk to the river, but there is a road and you may get a lift.

You can fly from Wewak to Green River for K124 with Tarangau or from Vanimo (K60) with Dovair, or from Vanimo (K60) with SAS.

There are also links to Telefomin (K90) and Oksapmin (K123). This has been suggested as a starting point for a canoe trip, but you will be undertaking a major project; something like 10 days solid paddling to get to Ambunti.

Swagup

Well off the main stream, east of the April River, Swagup is the home of the insect cult people, who are still fairly isolated and have their own language. Their unique art usually incorporates the figure of a sago beetle, dragonfly, praying mantis or other insect. The ferocious reputation these people earned in former times lives on.

There are many crocs in the many swamps around here, and the people are great hunters.

Maio & Yessan

The people here have a yam cult, but they have been heavily influenced by missionaries. This area is quite swampy and marshy.

Maliwai

This village is on a small lake off the river. Going up the river one encounters many villages known for their specialised religious cults.

Here the cassowary figures prominently in myth and is carved into most things, regardless of function. It is customary to cut off a finger joint when there is a death in the family.

Yambon

Not far from Ambunti, Yambon has good art and an interesting haus tambaran.

Ambunti

Ambunti is an administrative centre of no great interest, but there is an airstrip and a couple of reliable people who hire out motorised canoes, so this is one of the best potential places to start a trip.

As in Angoram on the Lower Sepik, there are plenty of river guides and motorised canoes available here. Joseph Kone, a highly recommended guide, runs tours out of Ambunti. Kowspi Marek, another respected guide, can be contacted here but he usually runs tours out of Pagwi. Other guides recommended by travellers include Bonny Simbakwa.

See what Alois Mateus at the Ambunti Lodge can offer and ask around at the stores. Often the owners have been around for a while and can offer good advice.

In general, canoes are cheaper to buy here than around Pagwi. If you're having problems it might be worth hiring a motorised boat for a day – you *may* be able to find something in a nearby village.

Places to Stay & Eat The *Ambunti Lodge* (☎ 88 1291, PO Box 83, Ambunti) has simple but clean singles/doubles at K20/35. Backpacker beds cost K10. Breakfast, lunch and dinner are available for K3.50, K4.50 and K9.50; beer is available at the lounge for K2.50. In the lounge area, there are numerous Sepik artefacts on the wall.

The lodge runs half and full-day canoe trips, and they can put you in touch with a guide for longer journeys.

Perhaps better is the *PIM* (Pacific Island Ministries) guesthouse, also known as *The Akademi* (☎ 88 1303, fax 88 1290, PO Box 41), which has singles/doubles for K20/40. There are cooking facilities.

St Joseph's Training Centre (☎ 88 1263, PO Box 84) has a guesthouse where you can stay for K10. There's also the *SSEC Guesthouse*, in a house once used by missionaries, which charges K10 a night.

Across the river is the *Apan Guesthouse*, a bush-material building where basic accommodation costs K5 a night. Take your own food. If there are people from Apan in town they'll paddle you across for K0.50, or someone will come and pick you up for K1. It's about half an hour by canoe.

Several people around town will let you stay in their houses, such as Alphonse Maua, who also has a motorised canoe.

Getting There & Away There is no road link. MAF, SAS or Tarangau fly to Ambunti from Wewak most days for about K60.

SAS also flies to/from Vanimo (K84) and MAF has a couple of flights a week to/from Mt Hagen. The Tarangau agent is Joseph Ouyoumb; contact him care of St Joseph's School (☎ 88 1263).

When you can find one, a communal canoe costs about K5 to Pagwi. Travel times to Pagwi are: one hour motor, six hours canoe.

Malu

This village, near Ambunti, is interesting for its variety of fruit trees and flowers.

Avatip

Although this is the largest village on the Upper Sepik, it's not very interesting. The Germans burnt it down twice and the old carving skills have been totally lost. The men's house is a dull place.

The village has three initiations, the second of which is involved with the yam cult while the third is only for old men. Debating is of great importance. They debate to try to find the meanings of names, information which the owners of the names are very reluctant to part with.

MIDDLE SEPIK

The middle Sepik region starts just below Ambunti and finishes just short of Angoram. This is regarded as the 'cultural treasure house' of PNG and almost every village has a distinct artistic style, although these styles are now tending to merge. The villages themselves are very similar so there is no pressing

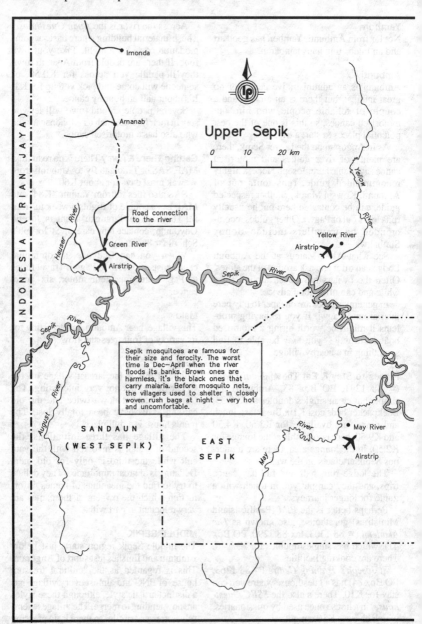

Upper Sepik

0   10   20 km

INDONESIA (IRIAN JAYA)

Imonda

Amanab

Hauser River

Road connection
to the river

Green River
Airstrip

Sepik River

Yellow River
Airstrip

Yellow River

Sepik River

August River

Sepik River

Sepik mosquitoes are famous for
their size and ferocity. The worst
time is Dec–April when the river
floods its banks. Brown ones are
harmless, it's the black ones that
carry malaria. Before mosquito nets,
the villagers used to shelter in closely
woven rush bags at night – very hot
and uncomfortable.

SANDAUN
(WEST SEPIK)

EAST
SEPIK

May River

May River
Airstrip

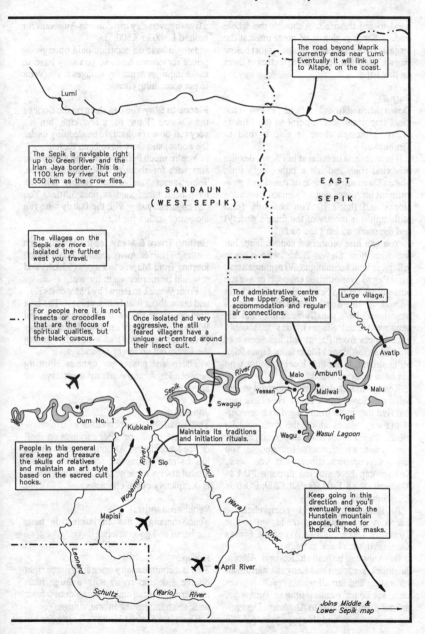

The road beyond Maprik currently ends near Lumi. Eventually it will link up to Aitape, on the coast.

The Sepik is navigable right up to Green River and the Irian Jaya border. This is 1100 km by river but only 550 km as the crow flies.

SANDAUN
(WEST SEPIK)

EAST SEPIK

The villages on the Sepik are more isolated the further west you travel.

The administrative centre of the Upper Sepik, with accommodation and regular air connections.

Large village.

For people here it is not insects or crocodiles that are the focus of spiritual qualities, but the black cuscus.

Once isolated and very aggressive, the still feared villagers have a unique art centred around their insect cult.

Avatip

Sepik River

Maio
Ambunti

Yessan
Maliwai
Malu

Swagup
Yigei

Oum No. 1

Kubkain

Maintains its traditions and initiation rituals.

Wagu
Wasui Lagoon

People in this general area keep and treasure the skulls of relatives and maintain an art style based on the sacred cult hooks.

Sio

Wogamush River

April River

Mapisi

Keep going in this direction and you'll eventually reach the Hunstein mountain people, famed for their cult hook masks.

Leonard

April River

Schultz
(Wario) River

(Wara)
River

Joins Middle & Lower Sepik map →

need to see them all. Although the whole middle Sepik region is of great interest the largest concentration of villages is just below Pagwi. It is possible to visit a number of them on day trips.

Pagwi

Down the road from Hayfields, Pagwi is the most important access point to the Middle Sepik, although there is also a road to Timbunke.

There is little of interest in Pagwi, despite this vital role, and it's a rather ugly little place. There are a couple of run-down government buildings and galvanised iron trade stores and that's it. You can buy food (although it is mostly of the tinned variety) and the mark-up isn't too bad.

You can hire motorised canoes here, but use discretion. Steven Buku, whose home village is Yenchenmangua, 30 minutes away from Pagwi by motorised canoe, is one of the best guides on the Sepik. He now works in Wewak at the Sepik International Beach Resort and isn't usually available, but his nephew, Daniel Singavi, runs reasonably priced tours from Pagwi and has been recommended. Aldonus Mana from Japandai, a bit upstream, is another local operator who has been recommended.

Kowspi Marek, a highly respected guide, helps run Sepik Spies Tours. He offers four and five-day tours from Pagwi to more out-of-the-way places along the river and its tributaries for about K66 per person per day, usually with a minimum of four people. You can set your own itinerary if you want. Kowspi can be contacted through PIM in Ambunti (☎ 88 1303, fax 88 1209, PO Box 95, Ambunti).

An interesting and fairly comprehensive three-day tour could be made out to the Chambri Lakes, down river as far as Kaminabit, then back to Pagwi.

Day trips can be made to Korogo. Aibom, Palambei, Yentchen and Kanganaman are all interesting and are all within reach. It takes about six hours' running time to Timbunke, and another five hours to Angoram. Depending on your stops and side trips you could do

a five to seven-day trip down to Angoram for around K300 to K500.

People have on occasion paid outrageous prices for canoes here, so you may have to make inquiries at nearby villages if you want to get something cheaper.

Places to Stay You can sleep on the floor of the Council House for a few kina, but it's very run-down (you might be sleeping *under* the house) and there have been thefts.

You're much better off finding a family to stay with for about K5. Benjamin Jericho, Tobi, James Yambai and Jimmy Janguan have been mentioned as possibilities. You can apparently stay with the family who run the petrol station for K3.

Getting There & Away See the Maprik Area Getting There & Away section. It is a rough journey from Maprik to Pagwi (53 km) and it would be murderous in the wet.

From Wewak to Pagwi by PMV costs K13 and takes about four hours, at least. The best time to catch PMVs back to Maprik and Wewak is very early on Saturday mornings (4 or 5 am); there's a trickle of traffic during the week, but nothing on Sundays.

There are passenger canoes running between Pagwi and Ambunti most days, for about K5.

Japanaut

This small village specialises in trinkets – little black masks or other carvings on shell or seed necklaces. Although every village has its own distinctive style there is also almost always some strange little item which is completely out of character.

Yenchenmangua

Yenchenmangua has an interesting haus tambaran and good artefacts.

Korogo

This is a commercially oriented village right on the side the river, with a huge haus tambaran. You can make a pleasant two-hour walk to an interesting inland village.

There is a *Korogo Village Guesthouse* but

it is unsupervised and people staying there have been robbed and even assaulted. If you can persuade a local to stay there with you it will be safer. Try Cletus Yambun.

Travel times from Pagwi are: ½ hour motor, three hours canoe.

Suapmeri

Variously misspelt as Swatmeri and Sotmeri, Suapmeri is famous for its mosquitoes, less so for its carvings. There is little for sale, although the village was famed for its orator's stools. I was told the mosquitoes take the pleasure out of carving! Despite all this, it's an attractive village and it is at the entrance to the Chambri Lakes.

You may be able to stay with a friendly family; ask for James Yesinduma. James knows everyone who lives on the river and speaks reasonable English.

It is very difficult to find your way through to the Chambri Lakes along the weed-filled barats, but James will arrange a guide for a couple of kina. Rather than backtrack to Suapmeri, you can follow a channel that brings you out just above Kaminabit, but only if the water level isn't too low.

Travel times from Korogo are: ½ hour motor, three hours canoe. To Aibom in the Chambri Lakes: 1½ hours motor, nine hours canoe. If you can get a communal canoe from Pagwi it will cost around K4.

Indabu

This is a good place to buy carvings and billums, as few people come to this small, friendly village. People have stayed at Steven Buku's house for K4.

Yentchen

An hour by motorised canoe from Suapmeri, you can stay here in a big, clean haus tambaran for K5.

The two-storey haus tambaran was copied from photographs taken at the turn of the century by German explorers of the one standing at that time. The top floor is only for initiates, the rest of the men stay downstairs. You climb upstairs between the legs of a graphic female fertility symbol, getting blessed in the process.

Yentchen is noted for its wickerwork dance costumes – figures of crocodiles, pigs, cassowaries and two-headed men.

Palambei

You can't see the village proper from the river and it can be easy to miss. There are two or three huts and there may be some canoes on the bank. It's a hot 20-minute walk along a barat (dry in the dry season), but it is worth the effort because the village is beautiful. Built around several small lagoons, which are full of flowering water lilies, there are also two impressive haus tambarans at either end of a ceremonial green. The ruined buildings, including a haus tambaran close to the green, were bombed by the Allies in WW II.

Stones, which must have been carried many km, have been set up in the glade. There are also two virtuoso garamut drummers who will bring their hollow-log drums to life in an intricate duet. The village women make the best billums I saw on the river.

Travel times from Suapmeri are: 1½ hours motor, nine hours canoe.

Kanganaman

A brief walk from the river, this village is famous for the oldest haus tambaran on the river. It has been declared a building of national cultural importance and is being renovated with help from the National Museum. It is a huge building with enormous carved posts.

Kaminabit

Kaminabit is not a particularly attractive village, not least because of the large lodge. There are, however, some good carvings. The lodge is used by a number of tour groups, including Trans Niugini (the Karawari and Ambua people) and is usually opened only for them. There is also a guesthouse in another Western-style building and costs about K5. Ask for James Minja or Anton Bob. Dominic and Francesca have been recommended by several travellers.

Travel times from Aibom are: one hour

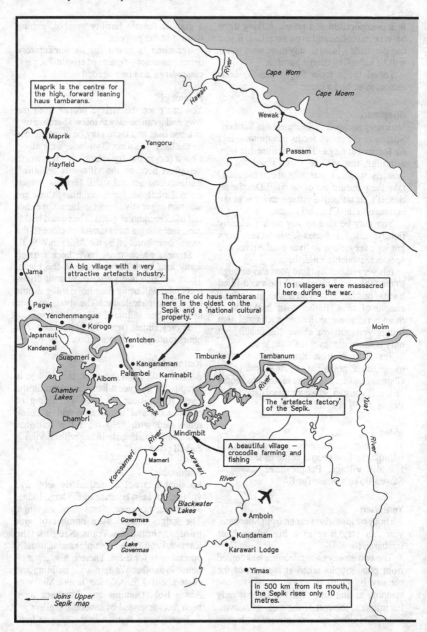

Maprik is the centre for the high, forward leaning haus tambarans.

A big village with a very attractive artefacts industry.

101 villagers were massacred here during the war.

The fine old haus tambaran here is the oldest on the Sepik and a 'national cultural property.'

The 'artefacts factory' of the Sepik.

A beautiful village – crocodile farming and fishing

In 500 km from its mouth, the Sepik rises only 10 metres.

Joins Upper Sepik map

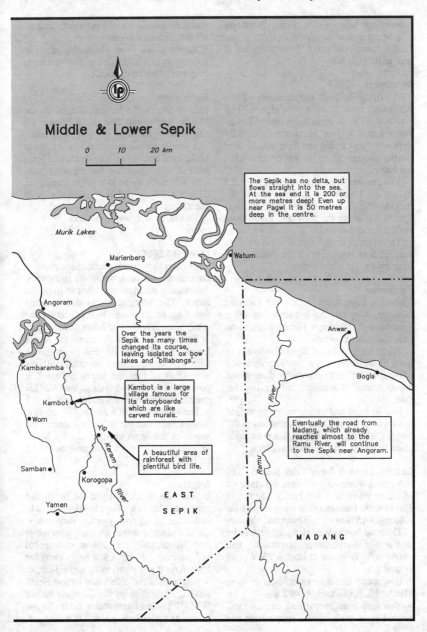

Middle & Lower Sepik

0   10   20 km

Murik Lakes

Marienberg

Watum

Angoram

Anwar

The Sepik has no delta, but flows straight into the sea. At the sea end it is 200 or more metres deep! Even up near Pagwi it is 50 metres deep in the centre.

Kambaramba

Bogla

Over the years the Sepik has many times changed its course, leaving isolated 'ox bow' lakes and 'billabongs'.

Kambot is a large village famous for its 'storyboards' which are like carved murals.

Kambot

Wom

Yip

Eventually the road from Madang, which already reaches almost to the Ramu River, will continue to the Sepik near Angoram.

A beautiful area of rainforest with plentiful bird life.

Samban

Korogopa

EAST

SEPIK

Yamen

MADANG

Keram River

Ramu River

motor; six hours canoe. From Palambei: 1½ hours motor; nine hours canoe. If you find a communal canoe from Suapmeri it will cost about K3.

Mindimbit

The village is near the junction of the Karawari and Korosameri rivers. The Korosameri leads up to the beautiful Blackwater Lakes region. Mindimbit is entirely dependent on carving and there is some nice work, though there is no proper haus tambaran.

You can stay with a friendly family for K5 or so; ask for Peter Bai. They live in the downstream section of the village, which is spread out along the bank and a half-hour walk from end to end.

Travel times from Kaminabit via the river are: 2½ hours motor; or via the shortcut: one hour motor, six hours canoe.

Timbunke

This is a large town with a big Catholic Mission, hospital and a number of other Western-style buildings. There are also some impressive long houses.

Trans Niugini Tours' *Sepik Spirit* calls in here, so while there is a lively appreciation of the depth of the tourist wallet, there is also a good range of artefacts and carvings for sale.

People have had problems trying to find somewhere to stay, and the mission is not helpful. The primary school is a reasonable place to stay but isn't always available.

Getting There & Away Talair flies the Tari – Amboin (Karawari) – Timbunke circle on Monday, Wednesday and Friday. The fare to Tari is K98. Tarangau flies from Wewak for K40 and SAS flies from Wewak and Vanimo.

The road link to Wewak would be murder in the wet, maybe even impassable, and traffic is fairly sparse at best. A PMV costs around K8.

If you can find a communal canoe from Mindimbit, it will cost about K2.

You can hire motorised canoes; ask around at the trade stores. People have had

problems getting out of Timbunke; communal canoes aren't frequent.

Travel times from Mindimbit are: one hour motor; six hours canoe. Travel time to Angoram: four hours motor.

Tambanum

This is one of the largest villages on the Middle Sepik, and fine, large houses are strung along the bank for quite a distance. The people are renowned carvers. Margaret Mead lived here for an extended time. Cletus Maiban from Angoram has relatives here, who will probably be able to put you up, or there's a pricey and not especially good guesthouse.

Travel time from Timbunke: ½ hour motor.

LOWER SEPIK

The Lower Sepik starts a little upstream from Angoram and runs down to the coast. Angoram is the most important town on the Sepik. The Marienberg Mission station which has been operated by the Catholics for many years is about two hours downstream.

Near the mouth of the river, the Murik Lakes are vast semi-flooded swamplands, narrowly separated from the coast. Villages along this part of the Sepik are smaller, poorer and generally have had less Western contact than many in the middle region.

The vast volume of water and silt coming down means that the landscape around the mouth of the Sepik changes rapidly. Many villages here are only a few generations old, built on new land.

Angoram

If you want to see some of the Sepik and experience life in a village but don't want to undertake a long river journey, Angoram is the best place to come. It's easily accessible from Wewak and there are plenty of beautiful and interesting places a few hours away (or a few days if you want) by motorised canoe.

Angoram is the oldest and largest Sepik station, established by the Germans before WW I. It is the administrative centre for the Lower and Middle Sepik and is a pleasant,

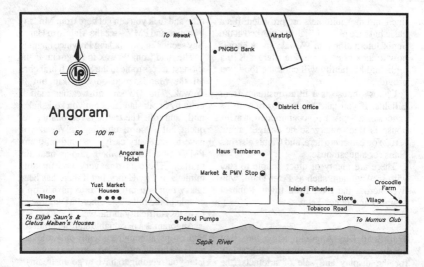

Angoram

0   50   100 m

To Wewak
PNGBC Bank
Airstrip
District Office
Haus Tambaran
Market & PMV Stop
Angoram Hotel
Yuat Market Houses
Village
Inland Fisheries
Store
Crocodile Farm
Village
Tobacco Road
To Elijah Saun's & Cletus Maiban's Houses
Petrol Pumps
To Mumus Club
Sepik River

sleepy place with a bit of frontier town atmosphere in the 'colonial' centre, giving way to a large traditional village straggling along the river. Lately the station's sleepiness has been disturbed by helicopters flying to and from a nearby oil rig.

The town centres on a large, grassy area which was a golf course for the expats who once lived here.

You cannot change money in Angoram, although there is a PNGBC bank and a small Westpac agency. There are a couple of reasonable trade stores.

On the riverbank west (upstream) of the town centre are a number of large, deserted houses. These belong to Yuat people who use them when they come into Angoram on trading trips. The main village is further along from here. In the dark, watch out for the deep ditches running down to the river. Heading along the river in the other direction, down Tobacco Rd, you come to a crocodile farm. At the far end of Tobacco Rd is the basic Mumus Club, the only place in town where you can get a cold beer, at least until the hotel re-opens.

'Shanghai' Brown Ominously perched

right at the end of the rarely used airstrip is a tiny graveyard. Amongst those buried there is the legendary labour recruiter 'Shanghai' Brown who, according to his headstone, 'died in 1956 of Blackwater'. He features briefly in Colin Simpson's book *Plumes & Arrows*.

Places to Stay The *Angoram Hotel* (☎ 88 3054, PO Box 35) is a rambling, fibrocement building. It's currently leased by the oil company, but even if it again becomes available to the public it's pretty poor value at about K60 per person, although there is air-con. Joe Kenni, the owner of the hotel, is an important local figure and enthusiastically promotes tourism in the region, organises tours and rents river transport.

Elijah Saun and Cletus Smank Maiban, who are in competition, offer both accommodation and motorised-canoe trips. They are very different men. Elijah, a carver, is large and patriarchal, with a craftsman's methodical competency. Cletus is quieter but his family is lively and he has an extensive knowledge of the Sepik.

Elijah's house adjoins his carving workshop on the riverbank. Mattresses, pillows, linen and mosquito nets are provided. It's a basic but nice place. Elijah has worked at the Sepik International in Wewak, so he knows how to look after guests. He charges K10 a night and his family will cook the food you provide.

Cletus's house is a little upstream from Elijah's. If you take his boat or one of his canoes on a Sepik trip, accommodation at his house is free, otherwise he charges about K10. You can camp here, and Cletus also has plans for a guesthouse.

There are plenty of other people to stay with in Angoram, such as Peter Dimi, who lives across the river from town, Raphael Maimba and James Yabu.

Things to Buy Angoram has a large but nearly derelict haus tambaran, built solely for the display and sale of artefacts (the *Melanesian Discoverer* sometimes calls here). It is pretty run-down but there are plans to resurrect it. Items from all along the Sepik are sold in the haus tambaran when a boat comes in, but they aren't stored there, so you'll have to ask around to see them.

There are a few carvers' workshops in the village along the river, one of the biggest belonging to Elijah Saun. His own carvings are worth seeing (he helped carve the bar at the Sepik International in Wewak) and he also sells various pieces for other people. In the workshop are two massive wooden fish, Uandumoi and Pangadumoi, which relate to the Creation story of Elijah's clan. They were carved by his father. Here and elsewhere in Angoram you'll find the famous (but large and heavy) Kambot storeyboards; elsewhere on the river (other than in Kambot) they are scarce.

Getting There & Away Scheduled flights no longer call at Angoram; if you can get a seat on a charter it will cost K35 to Wewak.

Eventually Angoram will be connected with Madang – slightly downstream from the town a barge will cross the river and a road will be put through to the Ramu River. With time and luck you can get here from Madang by canoe and PMV – see the Malolo to Hansa Bay section in the Madang Province chapter.

The road from Wewak to Angoram is the shortest access route to the Sepik. It branches off the Maprik road only 19 km out of Wewak. The 113 km, all-weather road is good by Sepik standards but you still shake, rattle and roll. The traffic is reasonably frequent, but if you're returning to Wewak you have to start very early – around 6.30 am. PMVs cost K6 and their stop is near the market. There is one very comfortable minibus, run by Henry, but if there has been heavy rain you might have to push it up a couple of the hills. The other PMVs, trucks, have less difficulty in the wet.

Angoram is a reasonable starting point for Sepik trips, although it is really only relevant to those hiring motorised canoes (sooner or later you're going to have to go upstream).

Elijah Saun and Cletus Smank Maiban also compete as river guides. Cletus is much more experienced, having guided artefact buyers for nearly 30 years. On some trips he undertook the buying himself. He is an excellent guide, with good contacts all along the Sepik. If he is not available his sons, especially Jeffery, can take you on the river. Cletus has several motors of different horsepower, a couple of canoes and an aluminium boat. He charges around K40 a day plus petrol. To get to Ambunti in three days with plenty of sightseeing costs about K250, including accommodation, plus the petrol to get Cletus home. This price applies even for a group of four or five.

Elijah is a relative newcomer to the game but he is very reliable. His canoe has a canopy, an innovation he designed.

Other people in Angoram offer motorised-canoe trips, notably Peter Dimi, who lives across the river. Jimmy Bagu has also been recommended. You can also arrange trips through Joe Kenni, whose house is next to the hotel.

Travel times by motor upstream from Angoram are: Tambanum (four to five hours); Timbunke (five to six hours); Pagwi (nine hours).

Around Angoram

A good day trip is south on the Keram River to **Kambot**, stopping at either Magendo or Chimondo on the way. These villages are familiar with outsiders and there are no great art bargains, but the river is narrow, winding and the banks are crowded with luxuriant growth. Further south on the Keram is **Yip** station, and south from here there is beautiful rainforest with plenty of birds, especially around **Korogopa** and **Yamen**, on a Keram tributary.

A day trip from Angoram to **Kambaramba** and the beautiful lagoons nearby costs about K70. Further south on a tributary is **Wom**, a village built among grass lanes.

Kambaramba is an unusual village in several ways. Built in swamp land, all buildings must be up on stilts. Out the front of most houses is a large balcony which in times of flood must house the pigs, chickens and dogs.

Because there is no arable land the village had to come up with their own economic solution. Which they did. The women became prostitutes. The government and no doubt the missionaries rather frown on this and there have been moves to relocate the town to higher ground. But home is home and people seem reluctant to go – one factor may be that there are no mosquitoes here for some reason.

Mark Lightbody

You can also make day trips to the **Murik Lakes** – they're about three hours away – or stay overnight at **Mendam**. **Watam**, on the coast near the mouth of the Sepik and usually accessible from the main river, apparently now has a guesthouse. The seafood here is supposed to be wonderful.

TRIBUTARIES & LAKES

The Sepik River can become monotonous as it winds through its vast, flat plain, with pitpit crowding up to its banks. The most spectacular scenery is on the tributaries and the villages are generally smaller, friendlier and less visited. In most cases you have to travel quite a distance upstream and this means you either have to fly in or use a motor canoe. Most of these areas are more traditional; you should plan your journey with some care and bring food of your own.

May (Iwa) River

May River is a small town more than halfway from Ambunti to the Irian Jaya border. There's an airstrip and mission settlement and it's possible to begin a river trip at this point.

Canoes can be bought for around K30. The locals and missionaries will discourage you from going alone. The local guides don't like to go alone either – they travel in pairs and ask at least K10 each a day. The villages in this area are not often visited and relationships between them are not always amicable but it could be a great trip.

Talk to the people at MAF or Ralf's in Wewak; they might be able to give you the names of people to contact in the area. It's not a good idea to arrive unannounced and expect to be accommodated. SAS flies here for K105 from Wewak or K90 from Vanimo.

April River & Wogamush River Area

Life on these tributaries continues more traditionally than on the main river with initiation rites and various social taboos and systems still intact. Both are good for birdwatching, with the Wogamush perhaps better.

For accommodation contact the Evangelical Mission, CMML, PO Box 72, Wewak in advance.

Although there aren't many spare canoes, you might be lucky enough to find one. Expect to pay around K50. There are villages at regular intervals and it takes about 21 hours of paddling to get to the Sepik – three or four days. The river splits 2½ hours after Bitaram and the left fork is the quicker route to the main river. From the junction it will take you another three or four days to get to Ambunti.

One traveller recommends not paddling yourself on the April River without a guide, or when it's in flood. His canoe overturned and he lost everything – he reports that walking barefoot for two days through the jungle, eating soggy beef crackers isn't much fun!

It is possible to fly to April River from Tari, although you might have to hitch a lift on a charter. Talk to the people at MAF. Tarangau and SAS fly from Wewak via a number of Sepik strips for about K90.

Wasui Lagoon

Also known as Wagu Lagoon, after the main village, this is a beautiful place, with many birds. The Hunstein Range is behind Wagu and there is beautiful rainforest. You can stay at the Wagu aid post for K5 or see Lucas Kiaui who might be able to help you.

Chambri Lakes

The Chambri Lakes are a vast and beautiful expanse of shallow water (they partially dry in the dry season, making things pretty smelly and the water unfit for drinking untreated). It's difficult to find your way in, as floating islands can block the entrances. James Yesinduma at Suapmeri can organise a guide for a couple of kina. Rather than backtracking via Suapmeri you can continue east and come back out on the river just above Kaminabit, if the water is deep enough.

Indagu is one of the three villages that make up Chambri. There is a haus tambaran here with a huge collection of carvings – mainly in the polished Chambri style. There are also many ornamental spears. **Aibom**, another village on the lakes, is noted for its pottery. The distinctive Aibom pots sell from only a kina or two and the pottery fireplaces used all over the Sepik are made here.

If you're looking for somewhere to stay, ask for Anscar Kui at Aibom, who may be able to help you to stay at the mission. Jimmy Maik of Kandangai village, Kandangai, PO Box 106, Maprik, has accommodation.

From Pagwi, the shortest way into Chambri is via Kandangai, but if the water level is low you won't be able to get through.

Travel times from Suapmeri to Aibom are: 1½ hours motor canoe, one day canoe; from Aibom to Kaminabit: one hour motor canoe, six hours canoe. It is possible to catch a village boat to Kandangai from Pagwi most

days of the week (between 3 and 5 pm) for around K5.

Karawari River

The Karawari runs into the Korosameri (which drains the Blackwater Lakes) and then into the Sepik just near Mindimbit. For the first hour or so the banks are crowded with pitpit but the jungle soon takes over and the river becomes more interesting, with wide sand bars (in the dry), interesting bird life, occasional crocodiles and attractive villages.

Amboin

For those with the money, the *Karawari Lodge* (Trans Niugini Tours, (☎ 52 1438, PO Box 371, Mt Hagen) at Amboin is recommended. It's a luxury base for exploring the Sepik. Built with bush materials and with some of the atmosphere of a haus tambaran, the lodge has dramatic views across the Karawari River and a vast sea of jungle. There are 20 twin rooms all with panoramic views. The cost is K141/182 a single/double, plus K12 for transfers from the airstrip. Meals are extra, K11 for breakfast, K13 for lunch and K27 for dinner. Day tours are K70. You can get through some money here!

Amboin is usually reached by air and from there you travel a short distance up the river to the lodge. Talair flies from Tari (K88) on Monday, Wednesday and Friday, Tarangau flies from Wewak (K55) and SAS flies from Wewak and Vanimo (K160). The lodge river trucks will take you to nearby villages like Maraba, Marvwak and Simbut – where the traditional Sepik-style tree houses are still used. There are also tours that utilise the lodge at Kaminabit and some that stay in the villages. Sing-sings and re-enactments of the Mangamai skin-cutting ceremonies are all part of the deal. They also organise special tours for bird-watchers to the Yimas Lakes.

Korosameri River

Mameri, about 40 minutes by motor canoe from Mindimbit and just before the turn-off to the Blackwater Lakes, has some of the most accomplished, dramatic and expensive carving I saw; make sure you see some of Ben's work. He will also be able to organise somewhere to stay. Day tours of the Blackwater Lakes from here cost around K50.

Blackwater Lakes

To enter the Blackwater Lakes is to enter a vast water world where villages are often built on stilts and the people pole their canoes through shallow, reed-clogged lakes. The bird life is fantastic. As you get higher, away from the Sepik, the temperatures become cooler and the mosquitoes become fewer. The closer you come to the mountains, the more spectacular the scenery becomes. Lake Govermas is covered in water lilies and surrounded by low hills, mountains, dense forest and three beautiful villages. It is impossible to find your way around the myriad of channels without a guide.

Tour boats now come to the lakes and you might find that prices are higher than reasonable in some places.

Sangriman This is an attractive, friendly village built on the edge of a reed-filled lake, but there are few artefacts. It may be possible to stay in the Youth Movement Hut.

Travel times from Mindimbit are: about 1½ hours motor canoe.

Kraimbit There is a new haus tambaran and the locals are welcoming.

Govermas A place of dream-like beauty, Govermas also has one of the most impressive haus tambarans in the region and some excellent carving. It's about 1½ hours by motor canoe from Sangriman. If you get as far as this it's worth going on further to see **Lake Govermas** and the village of **Anganmai**, on top of a hill. On a tributary at the very south of Lake Govermas is **Mariama** village, where there's a good haus tambaran. Dennis Worry will take you around in his motorised canoe and you can stay at his house.

Someone told me the perhaps apocryphal story of a Japanese anthropology student who arrived in a remote Sepik village. The people didn't know what to make of him, but they speculated that he came from the country where radios were made. To test this theory they gave him a broken radio – he repaired it. Some months later he was visited by his supervisor. The student hadn't done much study, he hadn't learned the local language, but he had a thriving radio repair business.

Gulf & Western Provinces

Land Area 134,000 sq km
Population 190,000

The two west Papuan provinces are amongst the least developed in the whole country. The coastline is broken by a series of river deltas, and huge expanses of swamp run inland before rising to the foothills and then the mountains of the Highlands. In the far west the border with Irian Jaya runs north through the open expanses of seasonally flooded grassland. Two of the greatest rivers in the country, the Fly and the Strickland, run for almost their entire length through Western Province.

HISTORY

The coastal people of the provinces have had a long history of contact with outside influences. The annual Motuan trading voyages along the south coast, known as the *hiri*, were still a regular feature long after the establishment of Port Moresby. The Motuans traded pottery for the gulf region's prolific sago. There were also trade links to the Highlands. Due to their easy access from the sea the coastal villages were also the hunting grounds for representatives of the London Missionary Society who were in operation from the early 1880s.

In 1827, Durmont D'Urville surveyed part of the north-east coast of New Guinea and in 1842 he returned in HMS *Fly* to chart the western side of the Gulf of Papua. He discovered the Fly River and decided a small steam-powered boat could travel up this mighty river far into the interior of the country.

It was some years before this idea was put into action, but when the controversial Italian explorer Luigi D'Albertis did make his second and most successful trip up the Fly in 1876, he quickly made up for lost time. In his tiny steamer, the *Neva*, he travelled over 900 km upriver, far further into the unknown interior of New Guinea than any

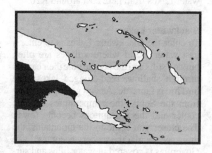

previous explorer. He returned from this epic voyage with a huge collection of botanical specimens, insects, artefacts and even painted skulls from village spirit houses.

However, his methods for appropriating his collection and his relationship with the villagers have coloured subsequent opinions about D'Albertis. He was a great believer in the philosophy of shooting first and asking questions later and he travelled up the river with a huge arsenal of fireworks, rockets, gunpowder and dynamite. At the slightest sign of any difficulty with the locals he was inclined to launch off fusillades of dynamite loaded rockets! It was certainly not sheer chance that led to so many of his artefacts being found in strangely 'deserted' villages.

When he returned to the Fly in 1877 he found the villagers much readier to attack him than on his previous expedition. He did not manage to penetrate so far upriver and along the way he lost five of his Chinese crew, one of whom, it would seem, died at his hands.

Many of D'Albertis' 'difficulties' appear to have been self-inflicted, but later missionaries also had their problems although the best known case, that of the Reverend James Chalmers, was also partially his own fault. Chalmers, one of the earliest missionaries in New Guinea, had been involved in some of the first expeditions into the interior, and was a highly respected man. Yet somehow, after 25 years in the country, an act of sheer stupidity led to his death and that of at least 50 others.

In 1901, Chalmers visited Goaribari Island on the Papuan Gulf and his boat was besieged by hostile tribesmen. He eventually managed to persuade them to leave the boat by promising to come to their village in the morning. He must have known that the people were practising cannibals, all too ready to execute captives in their *dobus* (men's houses), and any sane man would have departed immediately. Yet next morning, Chalmers, another missionary, a friendly chief and nine local mission students, went ashore – perhaps looking for some sort of martyrdom. They quickly found it, for all 12 had their skulls crushed with stone clubs and were soon cooking up nicely in a sago stew.

The rest of his crew managed to escape and retribution from Port Moresby soon followed. When the government ship *Merrie England* arrived at Goaribari the bill for the islanders' missionary meal was rather more than they might have expected. At least 24 were killed in their first encounter with white justice and 12 dobus were burnt down.

A year later Chalmers' skull was recovered and all might have been allowed to settle down had not Christopher Robinson arrived in Moresby in 1903 to become temporary administrator. Robinson decided another visit to Goaribari to recover the skull of Oliver Tomkins, Chalmers' assistant, was in order. As on the first punitive expedition, the visit quickly turned into a massacre and somewhere between eight and 50 villagers were killed. When Robinson returned to Moresby he found Australian public opinion violently against his over-reaction and early one morning, before the official enquiry had commenced, he stood beside the flagpole in the garden of Government House and put a bullet through his head.

Although the Gulf and Western coasts were well charted and the Fly, Strickland and other major rivers were soon comprehensively surveyed, it was not until the late 1920s that the mountains north of the coast were explored. In 1927 Charles Karius and Ivan Champion set out to travel upriver from Daru, near the mouth of the Fly, to cross the central mountains and then to go down river on the Sepik to the north coast. Their first attempt failed when they ran out of supplies while trying to find a way through the jagged limestone mountains. A year later they managed to complete their journey, one of the last great exploratory expeditions. In complete contrast to D'Albertis, they did not fire one shot in anger on the whole trip.

Exploration apart, not much happened in the region – there proved to be little agricultural potential due to the frequent flooding. Today there is a massive gold and copper mine, Ok Tedi, high in the central mountains near the border with Irian Jaya, but a very large percentage of the population continues to migrate to other areas, either temporarily or permanently, in the search for work.

GEOGRAPHY

The border region with Irian Jaya is composed of vast, open, seasonally flooded grasslands to the south, rising up into the mountainous backbone of the country. The Fly River starts from high in this central divide and turns south-east towards the sea where it ends in a huge, island-filled mouth. The Strickland River, nearly equal in size, joins the Fly about 240 km from the coast.

Despite its size the Fly does not have the same interest for visitors as the Sepik: it is much more difficult to visit and there is not so much to see. Villages are usually some distance from the river, because it tends to flood so far over its banks. In 800 km to the sea the Fly River falls only 20 metres, it flows (slowly) through 250,000 sq km of swampland where mosquitoes appear to be the most successful inhabitants.

From the mouth of the Fly, eastwards to the Purari River, the Gulf of Papua is a constant succession of river deltas, backed by swamps which run 50 to 60 km inland. East of the Purari the land rises more rapidly from the coast, is less subject to flooding and more heavily populated.

The Turama, the Kikori, the Purari and the Vailala are just some of the great rivers that flow into the swampy, delta land of the Papuan Gulf. Nor is the water just at ground level, the dry climate of Port Moresby and Central Province gets progressively damper as you move west around the Gulf. When you get to Kikori in the centre of the Gulf the annual rainfall is an astounding six metres! May to October are the wettest months, if you're interested in rain.

PEOPLE & CULTURE

The people of the delta land build their houses on piles high above the muddy river banks. As the rivers change their courses they frequently have to move their villages. Each village is centred around the men's longhouse, known as a *dobu* or *ravi*, in which weapons, important artefacts, ceremonial objects and the skulls of enemies were stored. Men slept in the longhouse, women in smaller, individual huts outside.

Today the longhouses are no longer so culturally important; the Gulf people have been bombarded with Christianity for nearly a century and much of their culture and many traditions have been lost – including cannibalism.

Cannibalism had ritual and religious importance, but it is also possible that it was provoked by the endemic protein deficiency of the area. As on the Sepik and the Ramu, the main food is sago, the tasteless, starchy food produced from the pith of the sago palm. There is no shortage of sago, which grows prolifically in the Gulf area, so nobody starves, but where sago is the staple food, severe protein deficiencies are common. Although the villagers supplement their diet with whatever fish they can manage to catch and the small quantity of vegetables their inhospitable land will allow them to grow, this deficiency remains a serious problem today.

Angry protests were once made to the Dutch colonial officials about 'their head-hunters' poaching across the border into British New Guinea. The Tugeri people, whose land once spread across both sides of the border, were ferocious head-hunters, who believed they had to collect a head for every child born. But a head was no good unless it had a 'name' to pass on to the child. So their unfortunate victims had first to be persuaded to say something before they were despatched. Presumably even 'don't do it' was good enough.

In the hills behind the coastal swampland live the Anga people, a sparse and scattered tribe once erroneously called the Kukukuku, whose territory stretches right across to the south-eastern Highlands in Morobe Province. They raided villages on the south coast just as often and just as violently as on the north. The last major Anga raid took place at Ipisi near Kerema just before WW II. Today there is a government station at Kaintiba in the heart of their land and all is fairly peaceful.

The Kiwai people, who live on the islands in the mouth of the Fly, are noted for their seagoing abilities and their interesting dances. They have close cultural links with the Torres Strait islanders off Cape York Peninsula in Queensland, Australia.

Arts

There are few artefacts created in Western Province now – the kundu drums of Lake Murray are very rare and the Kiwai people do not often carve – but art is still strong in the Gulf region. Unfortunately, when the missions first arrived in the Gulf area their attitude towards local culture was considerably less enlightened than it became later. Along with abandoning their spiritual beliefs and giving up head-hunting the Gulf villagers were also pressured to halt their artistic pursuits and in some cases the missionaries actually persuaded them to burn and destroy their best work. Old artefacts still in existence today are zealously protected.

In the Gulf region, from the mouth of the Fly around to Kerema, seven distinct artistic styles have been categorised. Once upon a time the men's longhouses in the delta villages were veritable museums and although there are no 'fully furnished' spirit houses left, there is still a busy trade turning out figures, bullroarers, *kovave* masks, headrests, skull racks (every home should have one) and *gope* boards.

Gope boards are elliptical in shape, rather like a shield, and incised with brightly coloured abstract patterns or stylised figures. Once upon a time warriors were entitled to have a *gope* board for each act of bravery or to celebrate each successful conflict. Boards were often cut from the curved sides of old canoes and a board from your vanquished enemy's own canoe had particular significance, transferring some of its previous owner's strength to the victor.

Hohao boards are similar in their original role to gope boards, but can be recognised by their squared off edges, coming to a point at the top and bottom. These were particularly prevalent around Ihu and Orokolo at the eastern end of the Gulf, but greater affluence in this region has caused the skill to virtually die out. It was also in this area that the Hehevi ceremonies once took place, a cycle of rituals and dramatic rites that took a full 20 years to complete. The ceremonies have been halted for 50 years now and the huge masks which were used in dances have also disappeared.

GETTING THERE & AROUND
Air
Air Niugini has an office in Daru (☎ 65 9058, PO Box 161). There are Air Niugini flights

between Moresby and Daru (K117) on Monday and Friday. On Thursday there's a circular flight from Moresby to Tabubil (K189), Mt Hagen (K99 from Tabubil) and back to Moresby.

Talair, the main carrier in the two provinces, has offices or agents in Daru (☎ 65 9039, PO Box 10); Kerema (☎ 68 1196, PO Box 90); Kiunga (☎ 58 1107, PO Box 135); and Tabubil (☎ 58 9288, PO Box 547).

Talair flies to Kerema from Moresby (K113) daily except Sunday (Taliar doesn't fly anywhere on Sundays). On Monday, Wednesday, Friday and Saturday, the outward flight from Moresby calls at small coastal towns including Malalaua (K96 from Moresby).

From Kerema, there are daily flights to a number of places in Gulf Province: Ihu (K33), Baimuru (K65), and Kikori (K91). On Monday and Friday there are flights between Kerema and Lae (K94), via some interesting mountain strips: Kamina (K32), Kanabea (K35), Kaintiba (K39), and Menyamya (K52). Making you way around the coast to Kerema then flying to Menyamya (from where there are PMVs to Lae) would be an interesting way of getting to the north coast from Moresby.

Talair flies between Moresby and Daru (K117) daily, and from Daru to several strips in the south of Western Province, including Bensbach (K108). There are daily flights between Daru and Kiunga (K127).

From Kiunga you can fly with Talair to Moresby (K189), Tabubil (K55), Mt Hagen (K137) and several smaller strips. From Tabubil there are flights to Wewak (K156), Telefomin (K37), Tari (K101) and connections to other strips around the country, including Moresby (K189).

MAF has extensive but irregular services around these provinces. There is an MAF agent in Tabubil (☎ 58 9025).

Sea
There are no passenger vessels sailing between Moresby and the Gulf and none of the major freight lines officially take passengers. Your nautical options are limited to

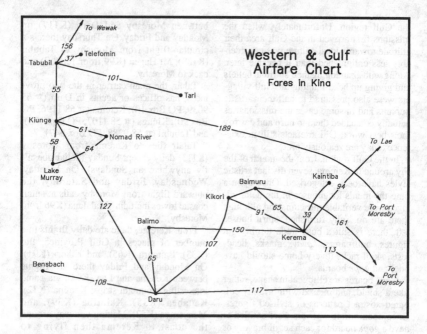

Western & Gulf Airfare Chart
Fares in Kina

To Wewak
156
37 — Telefomin
Tabubil
101
55
Tari
Kiunga
61 — Nomad River
189
58
64
Lake Murray
Baimuru
Kaintiba
94
Kikori
127
91 65 39
To Port Moresby
Balimo
150
161
65
107
Kerema
113
Bensbach
108
To Port Moresby
Daru
117
To Lae

finding a smaller cargo boat out of Moresby. Gulf-Delta Shipping (☎ 25 4422) in Moresby sounds like a good place to start looking, or try the wharves. Village-hopping in smaller boats or canoes is definitely possible if you have time.

River

About the only regular boats going up the Fly are the ore-barges from Ok Tedi. Unless you have contacts, getting a lift on one is almost impossible, as you would first have to get to the mother ship anchored in the Gulf, wait until a barge arrived and then negotiate a trip.

It would be an interesting trip and the barges are apparently comfortable, although note that the Fly, despite the huge volume of water coming down, does occasionally strand the barges. One crew was finally picked up a couple of months after their barge had run out of river, and the crew had established a fine vegetable garden around their vessel!

Other Transport

The Hiritano Highway from Moresby now goes as far as Iokea (pronounced 'yoh-kea'), and you can get there by PMV. There's a mission here where you can stay. From Lavare, a couple of km west of Iokea, you can catch canoes to Malalaua for K10 (five hours). The trip through the swamps to Navara is very interesting. Apparently, it is also possible to go direct by canoe to Kerema from Iokea for K20. There is a road link between Malalaua village (which is about two km from the river) to Kerema and there are PMVs for K3. It is also possible to walk along the coast from Iokea at low tide; government-funded ferrys take people across the rivers; if they're on the opposite side, light a fire to attract their attention. Canoes may not operate during the wet season. People are very friendly – one traveller reports that it took him days to get to Kerema, not because of any shortage of canoes, but because people insisted that he stay the night with them.

People have walked into Menyamya (north in the Highlands) from Kerema, but this would definitely not be a picnic stroll. You could also fly to Kaintiba and walk from there, picking up road transport into Lae. See the Menyamya/Aseki section in the Morobe Province chapter.

GULF PROVINCE
Kerema
This tiny government headquarters town of 3000 people is stationed in Kerema mainly because it has a drier climate than Kikori. Facilities are limited, but there is a PNGBC bank and a sketchy road network, including a link to Malalaua. It is also possible to travel by boat upriver from Kerema. Kerema is not a destination, but a place to go through.

Places to Stay The *Elavo Inn* (☎ 68 1041, PO Box 25) might still have accommodation. Don't expect too much. The Catholic mission near the market apparently has decent rooms, and cooking facilities for about K20.

Around Kerema
Malalaua Malalaua can be reached by air, or a combination of PMV and canoe from Moresby. This is the southern end of the WW II Bulldog Track which goes through to Edie Creek near Wau. Walking from this end would be extremely difficult; first you'd have to get upriver to Bulldog, and then you'd have a very difficult uphill walk to Edie Creek. Most of the few people who undertake this difficult trek come from the other direction (from Wau).

Ihu Ihu is the main station between the delta-country and Kerema and it will be the centre for the proposed Purari River power project. A road runs most of the way to the Purari and it is surrounded by beautiful bush. Canoes apparently travel between Ihu and Baimuru and from Baimuru to Kikori, although they may not operate between January and September. There's a tractor road along the beach from Ihu to Murua.

Places to Stay There are a couple of basic places to stay in Ihu, but we don't have first-hand reports on either of them. Contact the Division of Commerce, Culture & Tourism in Kerema on (☎ 68 1084 for information.

Kamina This is a beautiful place, between Kerema and Kaintiba – it's a difficult but interesting two-day walk to Kaintiba, through villages which have retained their traditional culture. Guides are available for about K5 a day.

Kaintiba Kaintiba, in the mountains behind the coast, is in Anga country. There is good walking in the area with frequent villages. Many are within a day's walk of each other and many have some sort of mission where you can put up. The going rate at most of these country missions is around K15, including meals. You can walk from Kerema, or fly with Talair for K39. From Kaintiba it is a tough though interesting walk to Aseki and Menyamya, which are linked by road to Lae. See the Morobe Province chapter.

Kikori & Baimuru
These two major delta-country towns are set well back from the coastline. Kikori is one of the oldest stations in Papua but Baimuru is now the larger of the two. Both have small

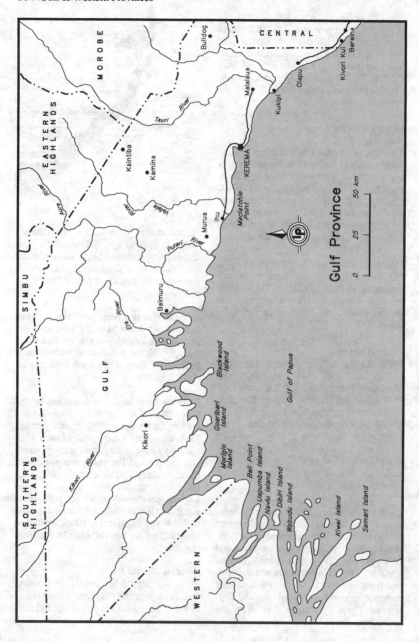

airstrips and it is possible to get from one to the other by boat through the maze of waterways. There are some interesting villages along the way.

The old Gulf Hotel in Kikori closed down a few years ago but you can try the *Kikori Guesthouse* run by the Kikori District Office.

WESTERN PROVINCE
Daru

The main town for Western Province is Daru, on a small island of the same name close to the coast. It used to be a pearl and bêche-de-mer trading port and it is still a busy port with a growing fishing industry. Daru is the town from which the skins of crocodiles, caught in Western Province, are exported. There's a PNGBC bank.

There is not much of interest for travellers and it's not a very attractive place. It's becoming run-down and overcrowded. Apparently a local airline donated prizes for a competition: the first prize was one week in Daru, the second prize was two weeks in Daru!

Place to Stay The *Daru-Wyben Hotel* (☎ 65 9055, fax 65 9065, PO Box 121) is the only place to stay. For rooms with fans, TV and private bathrooms it costs K90/95 a night. The food is good and features excellent seafood. If they know you're coming they'll collect you from the airport.

Balimo

This relatively large missionary town is inland from Daru, on the Aramia River. The hospital here is supposed to be one of the best in the country. One of the nearby villages specialises in carvings, which can be bought in town. For accommodation try the mission or ask at the district office about staying in the Cultural Centre.

Bensbach

Only a few km from the Indonesian (Irian Jaya) border, Bensbach Wildlife Lodge is the premier tourist attraction in Western Province – for premier (well-off) tourists! The mouth of the Bensbach River forms the border between PNG and Irian Jaya, but the border runs due north while the river bends off north-east into PNG territory. This area is a vast expanse of grassland and swamp, lightly populated due to the effects of heavy head-hunting in earlier years.

What it lacks in people it makes up in wildlife – the area is alive with animals and birds, many of them amazingly fearless since they have had little contact with man. The Dutch introduced Rusa Deer into West New Guinea in the 1920s and, untroubled by natural predators, they have spread far into PNG – there are over 20,000 Rusa Deer west of the Bensbach in PNG territory. Wallabies, wild pigs and crocodiles are also prolific and the bird life is quite incredible. It's a photographer's paradise. Keen fishers will also enjoy themselves since the Bensbach River is renowned for the size and number of its barramundi, which feature frequently on the menu at the lodge.

Pelicans at Bensbach

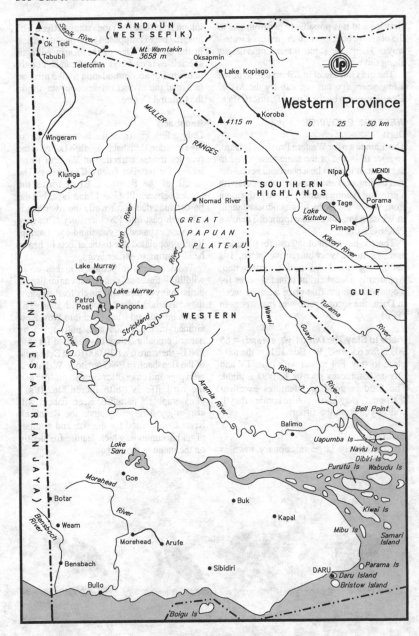

Place to Stay The *Bensbach Wildlife Lodge* is near Weam, 96 km north of the river mouth, on the east bank of the Bensbach River. The low-lying lodge is built of local materials and has 12 twin rooms, flanking a central bar, lounge and dining room. The rooms are simple, fan cooled rather than air-conditioned (unnecessary in the generally cool climate), and have a refrigerator in each room. The basic cost per person per night is K120, including meals and transport. Bookings are made through Trans Niugini Tours (☎ 52 1438, fax 52 2470, PO Box 371, Mt Hagen) and other travel agents.

The lodge might not operate between December and March, when the fish are out at sea.

Ok Tedi

Ok Tedi is a huge gold and copper mine, which was developed in some of the most rugged country and difficult circumstances imaginable. It has not been without controversy, both in terms of its impact on people and the environment. Until the Porgera mine in Enga Province was developed, Ok Tedi was the largest gold mine outside South Africa.

The area's remoteness, in the Star Mountains near the Indonesian border, created special problems and solutions as well as very odd juxtapositions. Local men wearing only penis gourds worked beside gigantic modern cranes and bulldozers.

The mammoth undertaking essentially involves chewing up a gold-topped copper mountain with a little silver thrown in. The Australian company BHP and the PNG Government are the two main shareholders.

Operations were meant to begin in '84 but a tailings dam, designed to trap waste by-products, collapsed in '84 making a hell of a mess, raising further environmental concerns and doubts about the project's engineers and planners, as well as costing a fortune to fix up.

The PNG government was forced to accept a plan for a new interim tailings dam, despite strong misgivings over its environmental impact. According to local and international environmental groups, those misgivings were well-founded, and the Fly is becoming polluted. This could have disastrous result for fish, not only in the river but all over the delta, an important breeding area for fish in this region of the South Pacific.

In order to service the area, a town had to be built. The town, **Tabubil**, has a post office, a hospital, a pharmacy and a good supermarket. The main supply centre is at **Kiunga**, south of the site on the Fly River. There are Westpac and PNGBC banks in both Tabubil and Kiunga. There is accommodation, but few tourists turn up.

Roads have been cut through virgin jungle from Kiunga to Tabubil and the mine. Barges take the treated ore downstream to the delta where it is transshipped to waiting cargo vessels.

Places to Stay In Tabubil, *Hotel Cloudlands* (☎ 58 9277, fax 58 9301, PO Box 226) has singles/doubles with air-con and TV for about K105/125, less without air-con, and some more basic singles with air-con but shared facilities for about K50 – women might not be allowed to (or want to) stay in the cheaper rooms.

The *Kiunga Guesthouse* (☎ 58 1188, fax 58 1195, PO Box 20) has rooms for K110/154, including meals and laundry. There might still be cheaper old rooms for about K60.

Lake Murray

Lake Murray, in the centre of the vast Western Province, is the biggest lake in PNG; during the wet season it can spread to five times its 400-sq-km dry season area. There is a crocodile research station at the lake. Nomad, to the north, is one of the most remote and inaccessible patrol stations in the country.

New Britain

The island of New Britain, the largest of PNG's offshore islands, offers a strange contrast between its two provinces. East New Britain (ENB) Province ends in the densely populated Gazelle Peninsula where there has been lengthy contact with Europeans and, due to the high fertility of the volcanic soil, the people are among the most affluent in the country. The southern part of the province, around Pomio, is much less developed.

In complete contrast, the other end of the island, West New Britain (WNB) Province, is comparatively sparsely populated, little developed and did not come into serious contact with Europeans until the 1960s.

For most visitors, New Britain will mean Rabaul – the beautiful harbour city on the Gazelle Peninsula with its dramatic, sometimes too dramatic, cluster of volcanoes.

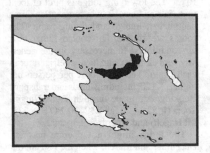

HISTORY

It is now believed that people have lived on the PNG islands for at least 30,000 years, and there is evidence of trading on New Britain 12,000 years ago.

The Tolai people, now the major ethnic group in ENB, originally came from New Ireland. They took the Gazelle Peninsula from the Baining, Sulka and Taulil people a few centuries before the Europeans arrived. Although the Tolai have a distinct language, they share many customs and physical characteristics with the New Irelanders. The Tolai were a warlike people and there were frequent inter-clan battles.

Early explorers from Europe spent much more time around the northern islands than they did around the mainland. William Dampier, the swashbuckling English pirate-adventurer-explorer, was the first to land in the area. He arrived early in the year 1700 and named the island New Britain when he sailed around the east coast of New Britain and New Ireland. Although he proved New Britain was an island, separated from the New Guinea mainland by Dampier Strait, it

was not until 1767 that Phillip Carteret discovered that Dampier's St George's Bay was really St George's Channel when he sailed through it, proving New Ireland was actually a separate island.

A hundred years passed with only occasional contact although many whalers and other sailors passed through St George's Channel and sometimes paused for water or to stock up with provisions. Then, in the 1870s, traders started to arrive, often in search of copra. In 1875 the legendary Methodist missionary Dr George Brown showed up and with six Fijians, set up the first mission station in the Duke of York Islands, which are in St George's Channel.

Brown could hardly be faulted for lack of energy; apart from working flat out on converting the heathen he also found time to be a keen amateur vulcanologist, a linguist, a scientist, an anthropologist and managed a fair bit of local exploring. While his reception was not the best and only one of his Fijian assistants survived the first turbulent years, Brown more than merely survived, and left as a respected, even loved, man.

In 1878 a Mrs Emma Forsyth arrived from Samoa, started a trading business at Mioko in the Duke of York Islands and took the first steps towards her remarkable fame and fortune (see the separate section). In 1882 Captain Simpson sailed in on HMS *Blanche* and named the harbour where the town of Rabaul now stands after himself and the bay after his ship. Two years later the Germans, thoroughly beaten by malaria and the climate on the north New Guinea coast, moved their headquarters to Kokopo on New Britain, naming it Herbertshohe.

In 1910 the Germans moved round the bay to Rabaul's present site. The name means mangrove in the local dialect, for the town site was in the middle of a mangrove swamp. The Germans did not have long to enjoy what soon became a very beautiful town: when WW I arrived, Australia invaded New Britain in order to take the German radio station at Bita Paka. The first six Australians to die in the war lost their lives in this action, along with one German and 30 PNG soldiers. A larger contingent of Australians also died when their submarine mysteriously disappeared off the coast during the attack.

For the rest of the war, things carried on much as before. Since Australia was in no position to take over the efficiently run and highly profitable German copra plantations, the Germans were allowed to keep on operating under close military supervision.

At the end of the war however, the unfortunate planters all had their plantations expropriated and the planters were shipped back to Germany. They were compensated, as part of the war reparations agreement, in German marks, which soon became totally worthless in the bout of hyper-inflation suffered by Germany in the early '20s.

One doubly unfortunate individual made his way back to New Britain, started again from scratch and once more built up a thriving plantation. Unfortunately, he neglected to take out Australian citizenship and in WW II his property was expropriated again.

Between the wars, Rabaul continued on its busy and profitable way as the capital of Australian New Guinea, until nature decided to shake it up a little. ENB is the most volcanically active area of the country and nowhere is this more evident than in Rabaul. Blanche Bay, Rabaul's beautiful harbour, is simply the flooded crater of an enormous volcano that is over three km wide. The cataclysmic eruption that formed what is now the harbour took place aeons ago, but the Rabaul area has had many more recent upheavals – as the string of volcanic cones around the rim of the super crater indicates.

Sputterings and earthquakes are an everyday occurrence in ENB and it takes more than a little shake to upset the citizens of Rabaul. In 1971 a major quake was followed by a tidal wave that temporarily swamped the city centre, but the last disastrous upheaval took place in 1937.

There was plenty of warning: minor quakes became increasingly frequent and sea water boiled and dead fish floated to the surface around Vulcan, a low lying island in the harbour that had appeared after an 1878 eruption. When Vulcan suddenly erupted, 500 Tolais who had assembled on the island for a festival were killed. Eruptions continued all night; 27 hours later when they finally ceased, the low, flat island was a massive mountain joined to the mainland.

The harbour was coated in yellow pumice stone and everything was covered in a film of ash and dust, brought down by a violent thunderstorm that accompanied the eruptions. But that was not all: Matupit started to fume and then erupted for three days. Months later, when the town had been restored, Matupit continued to rumble and cough.

Government minds soon turned to thoughts of transferring the New Guinea capital to a safer site. The mainland had barely been touched when Australia took over German New Guinea, but now it was much more widely explored and the gold rush in Wau and Bulolo had prompted development. Accordingly, the decision was taken to transfer the headquarters to Lae. The move had barely commenced when WW II arrived in Rabaul. Its impact was even more dramatic than that of the volcanoes.

After the Japanese attack on Pearl Harbor it was obvious that Rabaul would soon be in danger; women and children were evacuated by the end of December 1941, but there were still about 400 Australian civilians in the town when a huge bombing raid on 22 January

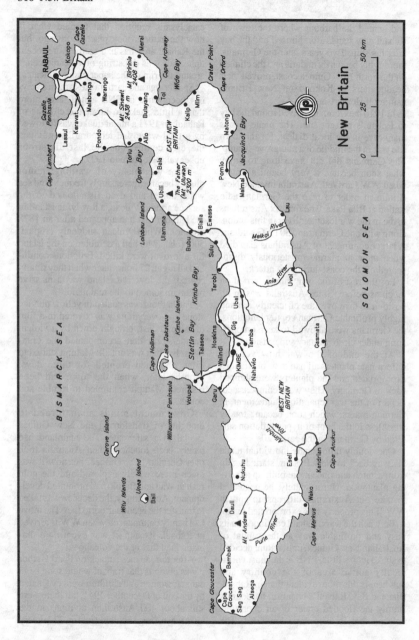

heralded the coming invasion. The following day a small contingent of Australian troops was completely crushed by a Japanese assault. Those who managed to escape found themselves cut off in the jungle and isolated from the New Guinea mainland where, in any case, the Japanese had already captured Lae and Salamaua. In an amazing feat of endurance, patrol officers based in New Britain (including the legendary J K McCarthy who retells the operation in his book *Patrol Into Yesterday*) shepherded the surviving troops along the inhospitable, roadless coast to the southern tip of the island where a flotilla of private boats undertook a mini Dunkirk and rescued 400 of the 700 men who had survived.

The civilians left behind in Rabaul were not so fortunate – not a single one was ever heard from again. It was later established that they were loaded onto a prison ship, the *Montevideo Maru*, and drowned when the ship was torpedoed by an American submarine off the Philippines while it was on its way to Japan.

The Japanese intended to use Rabaul as a major supply base for their steady march south, but the tables were soon turned. With their defeat at Guadalcanal in the Solomons, at Milne Bay and Buna on the New Guinea mainland, and with their naval power shattered in the Battle of the Coral Sea, they were soon on the defensive and Rabaul was made into an impregnable fortress. They dug 500 km of tunnels into the hills, a honeycomb of interconnecting passages used for storage, hospitals, anti-aircraft guns, bunkers, gun emplacements and barracks.

At the peak of the war 97,000 Japanese troops and thousands of POWs were stationed on the Gazelle Peninsula. They had even imported 800 Japanese and Korean prostitutes. The harbour was laced with mines and the roads were camouflaged with trees. And the Allies never came.

MacArthur had learnt the lesson of Guadalcanal and Buna where the bitter fighting had led to enormous casualties on both sides. Never again did the Japanese and Allied forces meet head-on; bases like Rabaul were

simply by-passed. The Japanese air force was unable to compete effectively with Allied air power and over 20,000 tons of bombs rained down upon the Peninsula keeping the remaining Japanese forces underground and impotent. When the war ended they were still there, trapped in a bastion that may well have been invulnerable, but was never put to the test.

Rabaul was utterly flattened. Photographs taken just after the Japanese surrender show Mango Ave, the main street in Rabaul, marked only by occasional heaps of bricks. Over 40 ships lay at the bottom of the harbour, and it took two years just to transfer all the troops back to Japan.

Rabaul soon bounced back, although the evidence of the war is still readily seen. The hills are riddled with tunnels (although many are sealed up for safety's sake), remnants of barges, aircraft, guns, cranes and other military equipment litter the area and the harbour bottom is carpeted with sunken shipping. Even today you hear stories of people finding Japanese tunnels and arms caches.

The transfer of the capital of New Guinea from Rabaul to Lae did not have the negative impact that had been feared, partly because after the war Papua and New Guinea were administered as one territory from Port Moresby.

The Tolai people have a relatively high level of education and economic wellbeing, but their bounteous peninsula is heavily populated so there are considerable land pressures. These problems are compounded by the large percentage of land that was bought from the Tolais by the Germans and is still owned by Europeans.

After the war, as concepts of self-government developed, land become a major issue and discontent rose to a fever pitch. Many Tolais wanted all land bought from them in the German days, when they were considerably less sophisticated in their dealings with the west, to be returned. A political organisation, known as the Mataungan Association, sprang up with the aim of subverting the Australian-managed local councils and self-government programmes. The Tolais wanted self-government, but on their own terms; they successfully boycotted the first pre-independence election and then demanded their own Mataungan leaders be given power. The problem has not gone away, but it is not currently a central issue.

Rabaul's volcanoes have not, however, been so cooperative. In 1983 Rabaul seemed to be heating up for a repeat of the 1937 eruptions and by early '84 the town was ready for an instant evacuation. At one point women and children were sent away and aircraft were actually standing by. The threatened eruption failed to eventuate, but the situation highlighted, once again, the town's precarious position.

GEOGRAPHY

New Britain is a long, narrow, mountainous island. It is nearly 600 km from end to end but at its widest point it is only 80 km across. The central mountain range runs from one end of the country to the other. The interior is harsh and rugged, split by gorges and fast-flowing rivers and blanketed in thick rainforest. The highest mountain is The Father (Mt Uluwan) an active volcano rising to over 2300 metres. The north-eastern end of the island terminates in the heavily populated, highly fertile and dramatically volcanic Gazelle Peninsula, with the three peaks known as The Mother (Kombiu), North Daughter and South Daughter.

New Britain lies across the direction of the monsoon winds so the rainy season comes at opposite times of the year on the north and south coast. From December to April the mountain barrier brings the heavy rain down on the north coast, while in June to October it is the south coast that has the rain. Rainfall varies widely around the island, at Pomio on the south coast it averages 6500 mm a year (over 20 feet of rain!) while in relatively dry Rabaul it is only 2000 mm annually, with May to October the driest months. Pomio once had over a metre of rain in one week.

The island is divided into two provinces: East New Britain (ENB) with its capital at Rabaul, and West New Britain (WNB) with its capital at Kimbe.

PEOPLE

The Tolai people are the major ethnic group in ENB and number about 80,000, although it is believed they arrived from New Ireland only a few centuries before the Europeans. The Baining, Sulka and Taulil people, who predated the Tolais' invasion, fled into the mountains.

There are probably four or five thousand Baining people left, living mainly in the Baining Mountains south of Rabaul. They still perform their spectacular fire dances, costumed in huge, Disney-like masks. If you are lucky enough to be in Rabaul when a fire dance is on, usually at Gaulim, it is an experience not to be missed. Ask the tourist office, or phone Ulatawa Plantation (☎ 92 1294), where there are sometimes fire dances. Their main income comes, sadly, from selling their land, usually at ridiculously low prices.

As elsewhere in PNG, aid organisations are trying to set up community-based logging and sawmilling operations. This will help the Baining people financially and also discourage the sale of their land and, hopefully, prevent its devastation by foreign logging companies.

The Mokolkols, a group of nomads who even after WW II continued to make murderous raids on coastal villages, were far fewer in number. It was not until 1950 that the government finally managed to capture a handful of these people, even though they lived within 100 km of Rabaul! After a spell in the big city, the captives led government officers back to the rest of their clan – there were only 30 in all.

When the first missionaries arrived, the Tolai were still a pretty wild bunch and inter-clan warfare was common. They are a matrilineal society (not to be confused with matriarchal), which means that a child belongs to its mother's clan, not father's. A clan's property is looked after by the senior male, but the land is inherited by one of the man's sister's sons, and his own sons inherit land held by his wife's brother.

The Tolai don't live in villages as such. Rather, family groups live in hamlets and when the children marry they usually leave to start their own settlement nearby.

Authority was wielded by big men who won their prestige through wealth or military prowess and a male secret society played an important role in village life, organising ceremonies and maintaining customary laws. Ceremonies featured leaf-draped, anonymous figures topped by masks – the *tumbuan* and *dukduk*. A lawbreaker who found a tumbuan at his front door would mend his ways, or else! They are still taken quite seriously, and a tumbuan is still not a pleasant thing to find at your door. There are definite tumbuan and dukduk 'seasons', from about Easter to October. If you're lucky enough to see a ceremony you'll agree that 'comparing a sing-sing to a tumbuan dance is like comparing musical comedy to grand opera'. The

Tumbuan

Duke of York Islands are 'home' to many tumbuan and dukduks.

Shell money, or *tambu*, retains its cultural significance for the Tolai and is still displayed at traditional ceremonies. It is distributed at *kututambu* ceremonies. Little shells, similar in shape to cowries, that are obtained from WNB, Manus and the North Solomons are strung on lengths of cane and bound together in great rolls called *loloi*. You can still see people using tambu to make small purchases at Rabaul market. It takes a dozen shells to equal K0.10.

Kuanua, the Tolai language, is spoken by two-thirds of the people in ENB. Kuanua for 'good afternoon' is *ravien*; for 'good evening' it's *marum*. Although there will always be someone around who speaks English, Pidgin will come in handy in rural areas. If things get to the stage where you're counting on your fingers, note that many village people do it 'backwards' – showing five fingers means zero, showing four means one, etc.

Bananas are a staple food for village people. A powerful banana spirit was once a staple drink, but now there's a fine of K1000 for making it.

At one time, Rabaul had a very large Chinese community but many Chinese left after independence and Rabaul's Chinatown is a shadow of its former self. There are also many Papua New Guineans from the less affluent Highlands and Sepik regions, who have been imported to do the boring, unskilled work on the copra plantations that the Tolai are not interested in.

East New Britain Province

Land Area 15,500 sq km
Population 185,000
Capital Rabaul

RABAUL
Population 15,000
Lying at the rim of a huge, flooded volcanic

caldera, the provincial capital vies with Madang for the title of most beautiful town in PNG – or even the Pacific. It may not have Madang's beautiful waterways and parks, but it does have dramatic volcanoes towering over it on all sides, and the beautiful Simpson Harbour. Laid out in grid style, the streets are wide and clean and just about everything is within walking distance. People are very friendly.

There is probably more to do and see around Rabaul than any other town in PNG. You can climb volcanoes, inspect war relics and dive some of the best coral and wrecks in PNG. There is also a better choice of hotels and restaurants than you will find in almost any other town.

Despite all this and a relatively large population, Rabaul is a sleepy town – the local TV news is a tape of the previous day's Port Moresby news!

Unfortunately, Rabaul is threatened by Matupit Volcano, right at the town's edge, beside the airport. Since a scare in 1984, however, there has been no major activity or threat. The situation is closely monitored, so do not hesitate to visit – the locals are quite blasé about the occasional *guria* (tremor). The country around Rabaul is lush and very beautiful, although it's hardly virgin jungle. Most of that was wiped out in the 1937 eruption and the growth you see today is mainly Tolai 'gardens', usually cocoa shaded by palms.

Information

Rabaul is one of the few places in PNG with a tourist office (☎ 92 1818, fax 92 2696, PO Box 385). It's on Park St, east of Mango Ave, and there's also a notice board at the airport with hotel addresses and information about current events. They have a good supply of pamphlets and maps, and they are helpful and friendly. They also have information on forthcoming cultural events, festivals, singsings and the like and may be able to arrange transport to them. Their hours are 8 am to noon and 1 to 4 pm, Monday to Friday.

The town is well serviced with shops, a post office, hire cars – and an excellent market. The major banks have branches and Rabaul is the headquarters for Coastal Shipping and Pacific New Guinea Lines.

There are payphones at the telephone exchange on Malaguna Rd, west of Mango Ave.

Anderson's Supermarket, near the wharves at the corner of Malaguna Rd and Pethridge St, has the biggest range.

The Harbour & Surrounds

The harbour is magnificent and it still services the rusting tramp freighters which wander along the coastlines of New Britain, New Ireland, the Solomons and among all the islands in between. The market should not be missed.

In the little park, towards the market end of Mango Ave, by the town and Gazelle area maps, stands the grinding wheel from Port Breton. In 1879 a crazy French Marquis and real estate speculator despatched naive shiploads of would-be colonisers and farmers to Port Breton on New Ireland. The mill stone no doubt gave credence to their hopeless dreams of broad acres of wheat. See the New Ireland Province chapter. Nearby there's a small statue of a small dog. No-one could tell me why.

Across from the Rabaul Community Hostel on the waterfront there's a memorial to the Rabaul prisoners who died on the *Montevideo Maru*.

The Market

The Rabaul market, or *bung* ('meeting' in Kuanua), is the best and most colourful in PNG, and Saturday is the best day to visit. You'll see a wider selection of fruit and vegetables (in larger quantities) than anywhere else in PNG. Scattered among the food stalls are bamboo combs, wicker baskets, shells and shell jewellery. Check out the hand-rolled cigars; they look crude but the aroma had this ex-smoker twitching. The market is open daily except Sunday and is on the corner of Malagura and Causuarina Aves.

The New Guinea Club

The club was built just before the war, gutted

during the bombing and subsequently rebuilt to its original plan. It is one of the very few buildings in PNG that survives with any sense of history intact, or any genuinely interesting European architectural style. There are some fascinating old photos on the walls, and as you wander around under the high ceilings and slow-moving fans it's easy to be transported to a long gone South Pacific. Not only is it interesting, but it also has cold beer, good food, billiard tables and reasonable accommodation.

War Museum

A tiny war museum is opposite the New Guinea Club on the corner of Central Ave and Clarke St and is open 8 am to 3.30 pm, Monday to Friday, 10 am to 2 pm on Saturdays. Admission is K0.50. The museum is housed in Admiral Onishi's war time command bunker.

Outside there's a lightweight Japanese tank, an anti-aircraft gun and a field gun. Inside there's a collection of odds and ends – in two control rooms; Japanese maps can still be seen on the walls. There are also some interesting photos of Allied raids on Japanese ships in the harbour and a photo of Mango Ave at the end of the war shows just how complete the destruction was. This was the bunker where Admiral Yamamoto spent his last night before being shot down over Bougainville.

A larger museum has opened near Kokopo – see the Around Rabaul section.

WW II Relics

There are countless tunnels and caverns in the hillsides around Rabaul. Many of them are now closed, but a knowledgeable local guide can still take you around some amazing complexes. There are over 500 km of Japanese-built tunnels around the Gazelle Peninsula.

Near the golf course on Sulphur Creek there is a big Japanese gun. There is an anti-aircraft gun near the Vulcanology Observatory (one of many) while on the waterfront a scuttled Japanese ship was filled with cement and became a wharf.

Beside the Rabaul airport runway there's quite a mass of Japanese aircraft wreckage scattered among the palm trees. Follow the road past the strip. Just after it curves off to Matupit village take the dirt road on your right. You're unlikely to have to guide yourself as the local kids have a thriving business showing visitors to the remains. Careful you don't end up with too many guides – even at K0.10 a time they soon mount up!

There are two main chunks of wreckage. First you'll come to the fuselage midsection and part of the wings of a bomber, then a little further along the much more complete wreckage of a Betty Bomber – the tail section lies upside down behind it. The rising sun is still clearly visible underneath the wing. Various bits of engines, nacelles and undercarriage lie scattered around. As well as lots of Japanese aircraft wreckage the plantation also has lots of mosquitoes so come prepared or get bitten.

German Residency

Nothing remains of the old German residency apart from the stone gateposts and the crumbling staircase. The site offers fine views from a ridge that overlooks Rabaul in one direction and out to the open sea in the other. And those two little cement footpaths from the car park to the two lookout points? Built for Missis Kwin's last visit to PNG.

Orchid Parks

The Rabaul Orchid Park overlooks the town from up the hill towards the old German residency. There are many indigenous orchids, including a number of varieties that grow in the branches of frangipani trees. There's also a collection of parrots and New Britain cockatoos, a large and hungry crocodile and a couple of cassowaries. The park is worth visiting but it can be hard to find unless you ask directions.

Out at Kokopo there's another orchid park, near the golf course.

Japanese War Memorial

Overlooking the harbour a few km out of town on Namanula Hill Rd is the Japanese

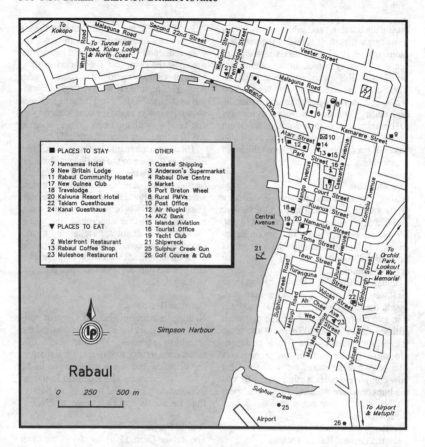

PLACES TO STAY
- 7 Hamamas Hotel
- 9 New Britain Lodge
- 11 Rabaul Community Hostel
- 17 New Guinea Club
- 18 Travelodge
- 20 Kaivuna Resort Hotel
- 22 Taklam Guesthouse
- 24 Kanal Guesthaus

▼ PLACES TO EAT
- 2 Waterfront Restaurant
- 13 Rabaul Coffee Shop
- 23 Muleshoe Restaurant

OTHER
- 1 Coastal Shipping
- 3 Anderson's Supermarket
- 4 Rabaul Dive Centre
- 5 Market
- 6 Port Breton Wheel
- 8 Rural PMVs
- 10 Post Office
- 12 Air Niugini
- 14 ANZ Bank
- 15 Islands Aviation
- 16 Tourist Office
- 19 Yacht Club
- 21 Shipwreck
- 25 Sulphur Creek Gun
- 26 Golf Course & Club

Rabaul

Simpson Harbour

0   250   500 m

War Memorial, the main Japanese memorial in the Pacific. It's worth visiting for the views. PMV No 7 gets you there, or it's about K8 by taxi. Near the memorial is a huge kapok tree.

Activities

Diving Underwater ENB is just as spectacular as above water. Frank Butler's Rabaul Dive Centre (☎ 92 1100, PO Box 400), behind the Shell Gazelle Autoport on Malaguna Rd, has all the necessary equipment (including snorkelling gear for K12) and can also organise diving courses and

tours around the district. Their daily dives cost K50 with equipment and they'll take along snorkellers for K25.

The Kaivuna Resort Hotel gives discounts on accommodation to people who do the Centre's dive course (K350). There's also diving available with Dive Rabaul at Kulau Lodge. Both Taklam Guesthouse and Ulatawa Plantation plan to offer diving and snorkelling. See the following Around Rabaul section for information on dive sites.

Trekking The rugged and beautiful Baining Mountains offer some excellent trekking possibilities. Grassroutes Ecotravel (☎ 92 1756, PO Box 710, Rabaul) has guided treks in the area. Bruno Letong will probably be the guide, and he's a nice guy with a lot of knowledge about the culture, flora & fauna of the area. Grassroutes offers other possibilities, including village stays on Watom Island and treks in the south of New Ireland departing from Rabaul.

Contact Grassroutes or ask the tourist office for more details. Grassroutes is a new venture, and the name has already changed once (from REST), so if it seems to have disappeared keep asking – there might be a new name.

Organised Tours Paivu Tours (☎ 92 2916, PO Box 44) has a number of tours around town and the Gazelle Peninsula.

The cheapest and best way to see the region is to head off on the reasonably-priced PMVs. You can't really get lost – when you get to the end of the road, just turn around and come back again!

Festivals

Each year towards the end of July, the Rabaul Frangipani Festival is held. This is a pleasantly small-town affair, with fireworks, a parade (showered with flowers dropped by a plane) and various functions. The festival celebrates the blooming of the area's many frangipanis, which were the first flowers to reappear after the 1937 eruption.

Around October or November (it varies) Tolai Warwagira Festival is two weeks of sing-sings and other events. Currently it is held on odd-numbered years but that might change.

Places to Stay – bottom end & middle

The best known Rabaul cheapie is the *Rabaul Community Hostel* (☎ 92 3598, PO Box 409), on the corner of Atarr St and Cleland Drive. It is excellently located near the town centre and across from the harbour but it is becoming run-down and the prices have risen considerably.

Singles/doubles cost K30/45, including meals. The food is straightforward and OK,

but you must turn up on time if you want to be fed. The rooms are spartan but reasonably comfortable although there are no fans and they can be hot. Chinese-hotel style, the walls don't reach the floor or ceiling so noise (and there is plenty) tends to travel.

If you want a bit more luxury, but still at a reasonable price, the *Kanai Guest Haus* (☎ 92 1955, PO Box 510) is a clean, comfortable and very friendly place. You're likely to meet other travellers here. Singles/doubles are K30/40, or K20 per person sharing, with shared bathroom and kitchen facilities – coffee, tea and milk are supplied. It's more like a converted house than anything else (although it started out as a trade store) so there are only four immaculately clean rooms, all with fans.

It's a popular place and is sometimes full, but they can usually squeeze everyone in. The only disadvantage is that it's on Wee St which is a bit of a walk from town, but it's not far from the main PMV route between the market and the airport. Moana Gangloff, the friendly manager, will pick you up from the airport if you're expected, and can often drive you to other places around town. If you stay for more than a few days you might be able to negotiate a lower room rate.

On the corner of Vulcan St and Kombiu Ave, the recently opened *Taklam Guesthouse* (☎ 92 3078, fax 92 3043) is closer to the town centre than Kanai but is as yet nowhere near as pleasant. Taklam was also once an old trade store and charges K25 per person, mostly in shared three-bed rooms or K35 per person in the one air-con room. They plan to offer tours, diving and snorkelling. If you can't find anyone at the guesthouse, go across Vulcan St to the video store and ask there. If *that's* closed, go down the driveway on the right to the house behind the shop.

The *New Guinea Club* (☎ 92 1801, 92 2325, PO Box 40) in the middle of town is a classic, well-kept, colonial building. To get to the rooms you go through the billiard room which has three beautiful, antique tables. There are 10 rooms at K35/40 for singles/doubles, including breakfast and laundry. There are discounts if you stay a

Banana palm

week. Lunch and dinner are also available at reasonable prices and you needn't be a member, or male, although there is some degree of formality. There's a bar, two lounges and satellite TV.

On the corner of Kamarere St and Kombiu Ave the *New Britain Lodge* (☎ 92 2247, PO Box 296) has singles/doubles/triples with fans for K36/42/63. Rooms with air-con are K50. There's nothing flash about the shared bathroom facilities. The downstairs rooms are a bit like cells and although the upstairs rooms are OK, they're not as pleasant as those at the Kanai or the New Guinea Club.

Out of town near the Kulau Lodge Beach Resort, Kabakada village is setting up the first *Grassroutes Haus*. The Grassroutes project aims to help villages establish and run tourist accommodation, as well as running tours. This is good for the villages and it's great for visitors, as the type of accommodation planned is just what PNG lacks – quality low-cost places built in traditional styles. There will be electricity, good water and probably meals available. A

number of huts are planned, something like Asia's *losmen*. The nightly charge will be about K10. Kabakada was a good choice for the first guesthouse, as it's near Rabaul but on a beautiful bay where you can swim. With Kulau Lodge's bar, restaurant and watersports facilities a short walk away, this would be an ideal place to laze away a few days.

From Rabaul, Kabakada is about 12 km and 15 minutes by PMV (No 5, K0.60). Contact Grassroutes Ecotravel (☎ 92 1756, PO Box 710) or the tourist office for the latest information, and also ask whether the Grassroutes Haus planned for Mioko on the Duke of York Islands has been built.

For a completely different experience you could try *Ulatawa Plantation* (☎ 92 1294, fax 92 1197). This old plantation is about 40 km from Rabaul, inland from Vunapope. It's about 200 metres above sea level, so the nights are cooler and the days a little less humid than on the coast.

It's a beautiful place, with immense manicured lawns, several thousand orchids, a *benetii* (cassowary) called Vanessa and avenues of big old rain trees. The trees were planted by the Germans, and Ulatawa is on the site of their botanic gardens and zoo. There's still a good chunk of indigenous forest and the manager, Max Henderson, plans to re-establish the gardens. The deer which once roamed the area might have been the reason for the Gazelle Peninsula's name. The Bainings people sometimes hold fire dances on the plantation.

Accommodation is in self-contained huts (most still under construction at the time of writing), costing about K40 to K80 per person, including some meals. The food is excellent, and there's a bar and a swimming pool (built in a WW II bomb crater). It's a 15-minute drive to the coast and dive courses are planned.

To get here from Rabaul phone to arrange a lift with the truck that goes to town most days, or take PMV No 2 to Buai Corner and walk the rest of the way. Phone for directions first. If you walk in you'll probably be met by three very large dogs.

Places to Stay – top end

Probably the best top-end place to stay isn't the most expensive. The *Hamamas Hotel* (☎ 92 1999, fax 92 1927, PO Box 214) is new, central and pleasant. It's on Mango Ave near the corner of Kamarere St. Singles/doubles are K62/77, with suites costing K90.

The *Travelodge* (☎ 92 2111, PO Box 449) is on the corner of Mango Ave (the main street) and Namanula St. All the rooms have air-con and private facilities (but no views, as the building faces away from the harbour) and cost K115 plus 3% tax. There is a swimming pool and a restaurant. Whether you stay here or not, drop in to look at the photographs of the results of the 1971 tidal wave.

The *Kaivuna Resort Hotel* (☎ 92 1766, fax 92 1832, PO Box 395) is only about 100 metres away from the Travelodge on the other side of Mango Ave. There are 32 assorted rooms, all air-con with private facilities. Singles/doubles cost K99/110 plus 3% tax. There is a restaurant, swimming pool and a top floor open-air bar area where counter-style lunches are available. The bar is very pleasant for an evening drink and the food is good. There are discounts on accommodation here for people who do a course with the Rabaul Dive Centre.

About 12 km out of town and on a beach is *Kulau Lodge Beach Resort* (☎ 92 7222, PO Box 65), across Tunnel Hill on the North Coast Rd. It has a range of accommodation in a very pleasant garden setting: up-market huts with bathroom, TV and fridge are K86 or K450 a week; self-contained townhouse-style units cost K140 a night or K735 a week. Add 3% tax to these prices.

The restaurant is good (see Places to Eat) and there are often dances or discos on weekends. You can hire windsurfers, at a pricey K17 for half an hour, and there are also paddle-boats. Fishing trips can be made and there's a dive shop – Dive Rabaul (☎ 92 2317) – where a dive costs K28, including tank and weights.

By PMV (No 5, K0.60) Kulau is about 15 minutes from Rabaul.

Places to Eat

Rabaul has a good range of restaurants. Unfortunately, the famous Changs restaurant has vanished, along with most of Chinatown, but there are still a few Chinese places left. The *Waterfront*, near the harbour on Pethridge St, is moderately priced, has good food and is open for lunch and dinner on weekdays and Sunday, for dinner only on Saturday. You can get takeaways.

Cookie's *Muleshoe Restaurant* is on Ah Chee Ave, near Kanai Guest Haus and is open for lunch and dinner Monday to Saturday. You can get breakfast from 9 am; bacon and eggs are K5. It's quite basic but there is a bar and the food is reasonable, with main courses from K7.50. The servings are large – choose the small size unless you're very hungry.

There's another Muleshoe, in town on Kamarere St, but this one is a kai bar.

Right in the middle of town on Mango Ave near the post office, the *Rabaul Coffee Shop* is a relaxed and quite reasonably priced restaurant, with snacks and meals – and a bar. Burgers are K6, salads K6, grilled fish K8.50 and steaks K10. It's open 9 am to 2 pm and from 6.30 pm until late every day except Sunday.

Nearby is *Vibbies Kitchen*, an above-average kai bar where you can sit down to eat. *Hennessey's Bake Shop*, also on Mango Ave but near the ANZ bank has a few tables out on the footpath where you can eat pastries and cakes as well as the usual kai-bar fare.

At lunch time or in the early evening you can get excellent-value meals at the various clubs and out-of-town guests are always welcome (you may have to sign in). The *New Guinea Club* has good-value counter meals and the *Rabaul Yacht Club* (on Mango Ave near the Kaivuna Resort Hotel and Travelodge) has lunches from K4 on weekdays and dinner of Friday night. The *Golf Club* has meals on Wednesday, Friday and Saturday (lunch only).

For a big night out, Rabaul residents head across to the *Kulau Lodge Beach Resort* (see Places to Stay for directions), to dine romantically on the waterside. Despite the good food and atmosphere prices aren't too high, with fish from K9, steaks from K10 and lobsters K16.

The top-end hotels/motels all have their own licensed restaurants. Chinese food is available at the *Hamamas Hotel*, and as well as a restaurant, the *Travelodge* has take-away pizzas. Shoestring backpackers will find that the food in the Rabaul Community Hostel is quite adequate, edible and filling. And cheap!

If you're staying at Kanai Guest Haus, the kai bar at the small supermarket across the road sells above-average food, including excellent quarter-chickens for K1.50.

Entertainment

All Rabaul's discos are open Thursday to Saturday and charge about K5 entry. The disco at the Hamamas Hotel is popular but just what the atmosphere is like will depend on whether there are any visiting dignitaries in town, as official functions often monopolise the disco. The Gym is near the Kanai Guest Haus (a little too near if you are staying at the Kanai) and is much more basic but probably more fun, if you mind your manners. Whispers Disco, in town on Mango Ave, was closed during the 1992 elections because it was a security risk...

Rabaul boasts at least two recording studios, and a lot of the country's pop music is recorded here. Despite the number of bands around, live music is hard to find but it's worth looking for. Seeing a band here is a lot less nerve-wracking than in Moresby.

An interesting Sunday morning activity is to head out of Rabaul and find a village church. The singing is magnificent (the Tolai are noted singers), with the different brands of Christianity favouring different styles. Because of inter-village rivalry, adjacent villages usually have churches or missions of differing denominations, so you can browse.

Things to Buy

Tolai culture is mainly expressed in singing and dancing, so there are few traditional artefacts available around Rabaul, although shell necklaces and bracelets are sold in the market. Most carvings you will see are either modernistic or local interpretations of other PNG styles. You might come across strange pre-Tolai stone carvings, some ancient and not to be exported, and some modern reproductions.

Rabaul Souvenirs, in the arcade in front of the Travelodge, has pieces from all over PNG and a good selection of Bainings firedance masks, worth a look even if you don't want to buy one. They have postcards, too, and the shop is open weekdays, Saturday morning and on Sunday from 10 am to 2 pm.

Nearby there's a popular little market where people spread out their wares in the evening. Hidden away in their bags, waiting to be whipped out at the slightest sign of interest, are a Rabaul speciality – wooden salt and pepper shakers in the shape of male genitals.

For some very interesting modern carving it's worth visiting Emmanuel Mulai in Ratongor village, on the north coast road a few km west of Kulau Lodge. Emmanuel's father and grandfather were carvers and his interpretations of Tolai beliefs are powerful. Especially striking are the *ingiat* (sorcerer) masks which protect houses from evil. These cost about K50 and are large, but Emmanuel can pack for export. There are also smaller, cheaper items.

To get there, take PMV No 5 and get off at Ratongor church. The track up to the village is across the road from the church and Emmanuel's house is near the top of the hill. Take the first right fork, the next left, and the next two rights. It's best to visit on the weekend, although on Sunday morning everyone will be at church.

Getting There & Away

Air People in Rabaul say that the government is about to announce the construction of an international airport on the Gazelle, to be operational by 1995. However, people in several other places in PNG are convinced that *their* area will get an international airport soon, and they can't all be right. Still, Rabaul must have a strong claim.

Top: Strickland Gorge, Sandaun Province (YP)
Bottom: Overlooking the Tauri Valley, Gulf Province (YP)

Top: Looking across Simpson Harbour, Rabaul, New Britain (TW)
Left: Sculpture by Emmanuel Mulai, New Britain (JM)
Right: WW II aircraft wreck, Rabaul, New Britain (TW)

The current runway, too short for big jets, is near town on a spit of land running into Simpson Harbour. The approach is highly spectacular since Matupit Volcano is in a direct line from the end of the runway. Aircraft have to make a sharp turn as they approach and you might get a whiff of sulphur on the way in.

If there is any threat of volcanic disturbances, flights can be booked for days in advance. Even without threats, flights out of Rabaul are often heavily booked so make sure you reconfirm and check in early.

Air Niugini has an office at the airport (☎ 92 1222, PO Box 120) and on Mango Ave. Rabaul is on their main island route that links Manus, New Ireland and New Britain (see the New Ireland Getting There & Away section), but it is also linked at least once daily to Port Moresby, usually via Hoskins (WNB) and Lae.

Fares from Rabaul are: Hoskins K80, Kavieng K79, Lae K160, Manus K153 and Moresby K187. Air Niugini also has some good value weekend packages – see the introductory Getting There & Away chapter.

Talair no longer flies to New Britain. Two companies cover most of New Britain and New Ireland: Airlink (☎ 92 1712, fax 92 1917), the Talair agent, and Islands Aviation (☎ 92 2900, fax 92 2812), not to be confused with Island Airways, a Madang company.

Both have offices at the airport and in town, on Vulcan St (Airlink) and on Park St (Islands). On a few of their routes these airlines offer return fares which are less than two one-way fares – a rarity in PNG.

Airlink flies to Lae (K160) on Monday, Wednesday and Friday, and both airlines have frequent services to Buka (North Solomons) (K122) and Nissan Island (K111).

Both airlines fly to Namatanai on New Ireland (K30) at least daily except Sunday. Flights usually continue on to Londolovit on Lihir Island and some days to Boang in the Tanga Group.

On Wednesday, Islands Aviation flies from Rabaul to Kavieng via Namatanai, Boang, Londolovit and Mapua on Tatau Island in the Tabar Group. The flight goes on

to Emirau and Mussau in the St Matthias Group, back to Kavieng then direct to Rabaul. On Friday the same route is flown but in the reverse order. On Wednesday and Friday, Airlink has a direct flight from Rabaul to Kavieng, continuing on to Emirau then returning to Kavieng and Rabaul.

Airlink has a weekly flight to Manga and Silur, in the south of New Ireland, and Islands Aviation flies once a week to Manga, continuing on to Malekolon on the Feni Group.

Fares from Rabaul on either airline are: Namatanai K30, Manga K54, Silur K59, Malekolon K84, Boang K65, Londolovit K74, Mapua K81, Kavieng K79, Emirau K148 and Mussau K162.

Towns in both East and West New Britain are serviced by frequent flights by both airlines. Some fares from Rabaul are: Bialla K90, Hoskins K80, Kandrian K130, Uvol K117 and Jacquinot Bay K89.

Sea Rabaul is one of the most important ports in PNG but, as elsewhere in the country, the downturn in the copra and cocoa industries has meant that fewer freighters are sailing, and those that do are rarely on scheduled routes.

The most important company to look for is Coastal Shipping (☎ 92 2859, fax 92 2090, PO Box 423) on the main wharves. Coastal has a few passenger-carrying cargo boats and are the agents for Lutheran Shipping.

Coastal's booking office is upstairs in a building just north of the main wharf and warehouse – take the outside staircase where the sign says Coastaco Marine. The office is open Monday to Saturday and Sujeeva Sawatura, the busy but helpful wharf operations manager, can answer most questions.

The other big cargo lines (for example, Pacific New Guinea Line (☎ 92 3055)) no longer regularly carry passengers, but there's always a chance you'll get on a boat if you speak to someone at the wharves. You will see other boats moored along the waterfront and if you want to get off the beaten track, asking around at the wharf is likely to be more fruitful than inquiring at the offices.

To/From Lae Coastal Shipping (Coastal) has the *Lae Express*, a passenger boat, running between Lae and Rabaul via Kimbe. This boat has only just come into service so its timetable hasn't settled yet, but it will probably depart Rabaul on Monday and take about 48 hours to Lae.

Coastal's *Kimbe Express* also sails to Lae via Kimbe, departing on Tuesday afternoon and arriving on Friday. It's a mixed passenger/cargo boat, with deck-class accommodation only. To Lae it's K36. Coastal's *Astro I* departs for Lae on Sunday, running via the south coast and stopping at Kandrian, among other places. This is not a passenger boat but there are a few cabins in which, when available, you can travel for K80.

Lutheran Shipping (book at Coastal) has a weekly passenger boat, either the *Mamose Express* or the *Rita*, sailing from Rabaul direct to Lae on Wednesday afternoon, arriving on Thursday. Deck class costs K34 and cabin K54.

Elsewhere For small boats running regular services around the Gazelle Peninsula and further afield, see Bismarck Tugs (☎ 92 3160). Their Dawapia wharf is south of main wharves. Their boats, including the *Cuddles*, are small and conditions are cramped and basic, with only deck-class accommodation. Still, going along on the voyage to Gasmata on the south coast (three days, K40) or to Ulamona (two days, K21) on the north coast would be a good way to see some small ports.

Coastal has freighters, unscheduled but running approximately fortnightly, to Kavieng on New Ireland. The 18-hour trip costs about K35/50 in deck/cabin class. These boats sometimes continue on to Lihir Island and the other island groups off New Ireland's east coast. Other freighters run to Nissan Island and on to Buka approximately weekly for K34, deck class. About once a month there's a boat to Manus (K46/90), via Kavieng.

Small boats to the Duke of Yorks leave from south of the main wharves in the afternoon, charging K5 for the one-hour trip. Many more leave from Kokopo. On Satur-

day there are fewer boats and you'd be lucky to find any on Sunday.

The *Taleo Tambu* (☎ 25 1974, fax 25 2920), a large, luxurious sailing catamaran, sometimes makes cruises in the Rabaul area as well as longer cruises in the South Pacific. At about US$300 a day per person it's out of the reach of most, but people who have tried it say that it compares with anything in the world.

Car Rental There are several car rental places, including Avis (☎ 92 1131), Budget (☎ 92 1008) and Blue Star (☎ 92 2063), which is a local company and has the cheapest rates. The office is in the mall on Mango Ave in front of the Travelodge.

You can hire taxis by the day for K80 or K60 for half a day.

Getting Around
PMVs are cheap, safe and fairly frequent, not only in Rabaul but all over the Gazelle Peninsula, which has a very good network of roads, many sealed. There's a fair amount of traffic and hitching is relatively easy.

PMV PMVs cost a flat K0.30 to anywhere in town – those with '8' painted on the front are urban.

Rabaul's new rural PMV depot is just off Malaguna Rd, near the market. PMV No 1 runs out along the coast past the Karavia barge tunnel (K0.50) and Kokopo (K1) to Bita Paka War Cemetery (K2.50). No 2, running the 60-odd km to Warangoi (K3) and No 3 to Vunadidir (K1) and Toma (K2) offer the chance to see the inland of the Gazelle and perhaps a glimpse of the Baining Mountains. PMV No 4 runs to Keravat (K1.60); No 5 runs across Tunnel Hill (a beautiful ride) and along the north coast road, passing Kulau Lodge (K0.60); No 7 runs up to Namanula Lookout (K0.30) and to Matupit (K0.40) and Talwat (K0.60).

Taxi There are only a few taxis. The fare to the airport should be around K3 to K5. Getting a taxi, especially early in the morning, can be a hassle as they are without radios. If you have a flight early in the morning it's best to catch a PMV; the big hotels have courtesy buses, as does the Kanai guesthouse. During the day, taxis can usually be found at the airport and parked along the waterfront park with the drivers fast asleep.

A taxi from Rabaul to Mamanula Lookout should cost K7; to Kokopo is K25.

AROUND RABAUL

Three roads lead out of Rabaul, connecting to the excellent bitumen road network around the Gazelle Peninsula. The roads are another legacy of the German days when they were laid out to connect their productive plantations. One road, a continuation of Vulcan St, leads out south-east by the airstrip (and the city dump) to Matupit Island from where you can get canoes across to Matupit Volcano.

The road to the north coast exits Rabaul via Tunnel Hill – during the German days it actually did go through the hill in a tunnel, but it was later opened out to a cutting. The third road continues to skirt the coast round Blanche Bay to Kokopo and beyond. Other roads turn inland from the Kokopo road, including the Burma road which climbs up and over the original huge crater rim on its way to Coastwatcher's Lookout and further inland.

If you have driven around the coast to Kokopo or Vunapope it's worth driving home on the inland roads. You can make your way back to Rabaul from Bita Paka but there's a more direct route which branches off the coast road at Vunamami, on the Rabaul side of Vunapope. There are good views of the Baining Mountains near Vunadidir.

Some huge *pikus* (fig) trees tower over the landscape. I was variously told that the trees were planted by Queen Emma, and that the Tolai invaders (several centuries earlier) built their villages around the trees and used them as watchtowers. The trees seem big enough to comfortably accommodate a village up in the branches, *Swiss Family Robinson* style.

Beaches

There are no good beaches in the harbour; the best places for swimming are on the north coast or further round Blanche Bay. Once you find a good beach don't assume that it's public property. Nearly all land in PNG, including beaches, is owned by someone, and with the density of population on the Gazelle, most land is used for something. Beaches are often of religious significance, so always ask before swimming.

Near the Japanese Barge Tunnel, Touman Resort is a village-run picnic area where you can swim. You might be charged a small fee if there's anyone there to collect it. Pilapila Beach, just across Tunnel Hill, is a popular beach spot and close to town. Ratung Swimming Resort (another picnic area) is a bit further along the north coast road on the way to Kulau Lodge. PMV No 5 runs past it. Nonga, also on the north coast, has a beach. There's also a good, white-sand beach at Submarine Base – you'll be charged K1 to use it.

Some of the best beaches are round the corner from Cape Gazelle and quite a drive from Rabaul.

Diving & Snorkelling

In the harbour, 10 of the 54 Japanese shipwrecks from WW II are accessible although some of them are quite deep. Many of them went down during one raid on 2 November, 1943. Also in the harbour are a couple of plane wrecks and reef walls. Right in Rabaul, at the end of Turanguna St, just beyond the swimming pool, there's a modern wreck – a small fishing craft which foundered only about 20 metres from shore. It's the home for many colourful, small fish and you can snorkel right through the main holds.

Submarine Base is an incredible place for snorkelling and scuba diving – the coral shelves gently away from the beach until there's a vertical reef wall that drops about 75 metres. Swimming over the incredible drop feels like leaping off a skyscraper, but not falling. The Japanese used to provision submarines here during the war. There's a K1 fee to dive or swim here.

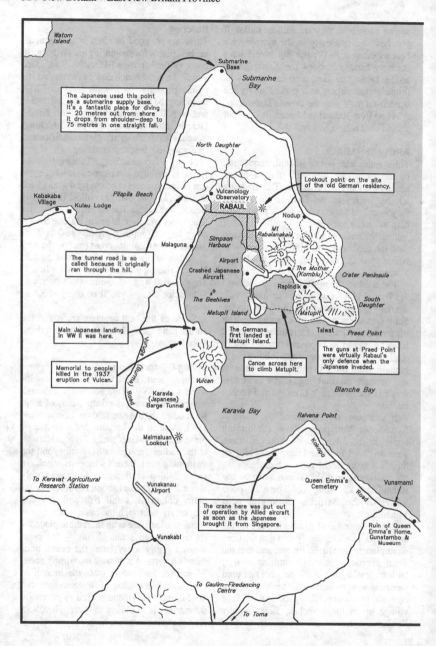

Watom Island

Submarine Base

Submarine Bay

The Japanese used this point as a submarine supply base. It's a fantastic place for diving – 20 metres out from shore it drops from shoulder–deep to 75 metres in one straight fall.

North Daughter

Vulcanology Observatory

RABAUL

Lookout point on the site of the old German residency.

Nodup

Kabakaba Village

Kulau Lodge

Pilapila Beach

Mt Rabalanakaia

Malaguna

Simpson Harbour

The tunnel road is so called because it originally ran through the hill.

Airport

Crashed Japanese Aircraft

The Mother (Kombiu)

Crater Peninsula

Rapindik

South Daughter

The Beehives

Matupit Island

Matupit

Main Japanese landing in WW II was here.

The Germans first landed at Matupit Island.

Talwat

Praed Point

The guns at Praed Point were virtually Rabaul's only defence when the Japanese invaded.

Canoe across here to climb Matupit.

Memorial to people killed in the 1937 eruption of Vulcan.

Vulcan

Blanche Bay

Karavia Bay

Ralvana Point

Karavia (Japanese) Barge Tunnel

Malmaluan Lookout

To Keravat Agricultural Research Station

Vunakanau Airport

Queen Emma's Cemetery

Vunamami

The crane here was put out of operation by Allied aircraft as soon as the Japanese brought it from Singapore.

Vunakabi

Ruin of Queen Emma's Home, Gunatambo & Museum

To Gaulim–Firedancing Centre

To Toma

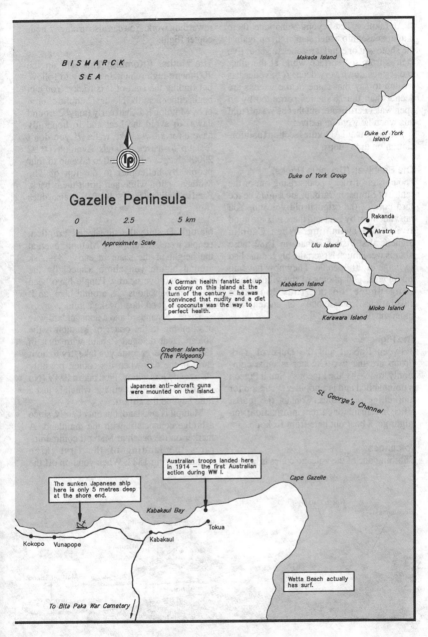

BISMARCK
SEA

Makada Island

Duke of York
Island

Duke of York Group

Gazelle Peninsula

0   2.5   5 km

Approximate Scale

Rakanda
Airstrip

Ulu Island

A German health fanatic set up
a colony on this island at the
turn of the century – he was
convinced that nudity and a diet
of coconuts was the way to
perfect health.

Kabakon Island

Mioko Island

Kerawara Island

Credner Islands
(The Pidgeons)

Japanese anti–aircraft guns
were mounted on the island.

St George's Channel

Australian troops landed here
in 1914 – the first Australian
action during WW I.

Cape Gazelle

The sunken Japanese ship
here is only 5 metres deep
at the shore end.

Kabakaul Bay

Tokua

Kokopo   Vunapope   Kabakaul

Watta Beach actually
has surf.

To Bita Paka War Cemetery

At Takubar, just beyond Vunapope, there is a Japanese ship which sank right up against the shore – at one end it reaches to about five metres from the surface while at the other end it goes down very deep. A traveller has written to say that some of the wrecks are deeper than the 20 metres permitted by an open water certificate, but that he wasn't told this when he went on a dive.

See the Rabaul Activities section for information on dive shops.

The Beehives (Dawapia Rocks)

The cluster of rocky peaks rising out of the centre of Simpson Harbour are said to be the hard core of the original old volcano. You can visit them by boat and there is some good diving and swimming. When Captain Blanche first visited Rabaul in 1882 these islands were much larger; the bigger one had a village of 200 people. They now have no inhabitants. Old photos of the village huddling under the tall rock look like illustrations from a book of ancient and apocryphal traveller's tales.

The Pigeons

Between Rabaul and the Duke of York Group are the two Credner islands, commonly known as 'the Pigeons'. Small Pigeon is uninhabited and is a popular excursion for snorkelling or picnics. Contact the tourist office in Rabaul for current information; you might get a boat out here from Kokopo.

Volcanoes

Climbing one of the volcano cones is hot but rewarding work. You can also arrange a helicopter flight.

The Mother ((Kombiu) The path up the 700-metre-high mountain is easy to follow, but finding the start of it is tricky. You can begin either near the Nodup Catholic church or by Motolou Rd. Start early (maybe around dawn) to avoid the heat and to hopefully have clear views. Take water. If you don't feel up to a trek, Islands Aviation (☎ 92 2900) charges a flat K160 to take up to four people by helicopter to the top of The Mother, wait a while and bring them back. Pacific Helicopters (☎ 92 2198) also does trips.

Matupit Despite the threatened eruption, people were still climbing Matupit, even at the height of the scare in early '84. Ask around before you climb, especially the people who live nearby. People have been killed by poisonous gas around here, so it might be a good idea to take a guide.

There's a standard and a nonstandard way of climbing to the crater of Matupit – the volcano that deluged Rabaul with dust in 1937. Whichever route you take, try to do it early in the day when it's cooler, possibly clearer and less windy. First take a PMV (No 7, K0.40) to Matupit village which is just a little beyond the airport.

Matupit is an island, but only barely, since a bridge connects it with the mainland. A marker on the beach at Matupit commemorates the landing of the first three missionaries in 1882. When you hop off the

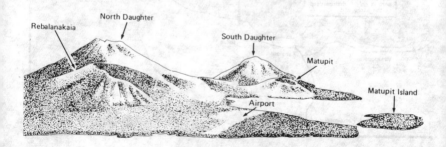

PMV you'll probably be pounced on by someone willing to paddle you across to the base of the cone. If not, you'll have to make your way down a small track to the beach.

Make sure you negotiate the price for the canoe ride. The usual charge is K2 for the canoe and K2 for each paddler – there might be two. If it's very windy canoes can't make the trip, but people will show you a road route.

You're dropped off on the beach from where a clear path runs up to the crater, or more correctly craters, since Matupit has a number of them. A km or so along the beach there's a small Japanese freighter at snorkelling depth. From the beach it's less than a half hour's steady (and hot and sweaty) climb to the crater rim. There's a firmly anchored rope leading down to the bottom of the crater should you want to inspect Matupit from within. It's still mildly active with foul, sulphur-smelling smoke billowing out at various places.

You can follow the craters' rim around in either direction although you can't do a complete circuit since there's a great gash in the rim around the back. It's worth clambering around clockwise towards the highest point, for although Matupit is not the highest cone around the harbour the view from up there is very fine indeed. It's one of those places where you wish you had a camera that could take 360° pictures.

When you've finished looking around you can stroll back down to your canoe or try the alternate descent by following the crater rim right round to the back of the cone and beating your way down through the bush to the coconut plantations and on to the Praed Point road where you can grab a PMV. The path is much steeper and less clearly defined than on the harbour side route. I got down by going around anticlockwise then slithering down a steep trail – hard work. I wouldn't recommend trying to ascend that way, although a PMV driver could probably point out a path that skirts the bottom of the volcano.

There is also said to be a volcano beside Matupit, under water in the harbour. There are rumours that the sea floor has risen a metre.

Around the foot of Matupit you might see megapodes (a type of wildfowl with, as the name says, big feet). Megapodes incubate their eggs in large mounds, and the geothermal heat in this area is ideal for them. Similar hatching systems are employed by other birds, but they rely on the heat generated by the rotting plant matter in the mound. Matupit's megapodes use sand.

Hot Springs & Mt Rabalanakaia Not far from the airport, right at the beach, are some hot springs, but they're too hot for bathing – it's really boiling water. To get there turn left past the airport. Follow the road to the end of the sealed part and turn right. A footpath leads down to the beach and the springs. The village here is Rapindik and the beach is known as Bubbly Beach. The red colour of the beach is due to the iron which precipitates from the boiling water.

From Rapindik village, you can climb the steep path up the side of Mt Rabalanakaia, but since the path is not very clear you should ask directions from the people at Rapindik. From the crater rim you can climb down to the floor of the crater where there are gas vents and sulphur deposits.

Vulcan When Vulcan erupted so disastrously in 1937 there was a small cargo ship passing through the narrow channel between the island of Vulcan and the mainland. Today this ship is high and dry and 70 metres from the sea since Vulcan heaved itself out of the water and is now joined to the mainland. It juts out over a small river and its tanks are still full of oil.

Vulcanology Observatory The road to the Vulcanology Observatory, on the slopes of North Daughter, turns off the Tunnel Hill road and climbs up to the top of the old crater rim, overlooking Rabaul. It is the main vulcanological station in PNG and there's a good view. There are tunnel entrances off the road. Visitors are not usually admitted to the observatory.

Praed Point

If you turn left off the Matupit road, just after passing the airport, a dirt road will take you through coconut plantations, passing between Matupit and South Daughter, through Talwat village to Praed Point. There are a couple of coastal guns at Praed Point – when the Japanese invaded they were virtually the only defence Rabaul had, but they weren't used. They're of 15-cm and 10-cm calibre and the smaller one still traverses.

Around here there are a number of Japanese-built gun covers, occupied today by bats, and a few wartime concrete blockhouses. Fish traps extend out into the water. On the other side of the road, as you skirt round Matupit, there is a small, peaceful, Japanese war memorial. PMVs along this road are quite frequent.

Karavia Barge Tunnel

A few km out of Rabaul, on the Kokopo road, a sign points towards the Japanese barge tunnel. A long passage cut into the hill houses a number of Japanese barges used, some say, to carry supplies around the coast at night. Others say they were just held in readiness for emergency use and were never actually operated. Either way they would have been winched down to the sea on a long track as the tunnel is a considerable height above sea level.

There's an admission charge (anything from K0.50 up to a few kina) to the tunnel

which is said to contain five barges, lined up nose to tail. Without a light it fades into darkness beyond the second barge and the back three are totally invisible. The first one is badly rusted and the second is little better, but the back three are said to be in reasonable condition. Parallel tunnels were used to house supplies and as offices.

A little further around the bay is the wreckage of a huge crane which the Japanese towed here from Singapore. It was bombed as soon as it arrived and was never actually used. Also nearby, along the road towards Kokopo, there are seven more large Japanese tunnels used for storing patrol boats.

Malmaluan Lookout

Malmaluan Lookout, formerly known as Coastwatcher's Lookout, is just off the Vuruga (Burma) road, which turns away from the coast a couple of km out of Rabaul towards Kokopo. It offers one of the best views in the area – you look out over Vulcan, the harbour and to the volcanoes beyond Matupit Island. It's well worth the PMV ride – bring your camera.

Kokopo Historical & Cultural Centre

This new museum at Kokopo will concentrate on the culture and history of East New Britain. It is still getting its collection together, but there is already a fair range of items relating to WW II. As well as the usual interesting photos and trivia of wartime, there's part of the American B17 bomber, 'Naughty But Nice', complete with its 'figurehead' soft-porn painting. It's in remarkably good condition for a painting that lay in the jungle for many years until it was retrieved by a surviving crew member.

In the grounds there are a few (live) birds and animals on display, along with some Japanese military hardware.

The museum is near the Ralum Club, a little way from Kokopo village, and is open from 8 am to 4 pm on weekdays, closing for lunch between one and two, and from 1 to 5 pm on weekends. Admission is K1.

A small German cemetery with the graves

of men from the first German expedition in the area and from German colonial times is near Kokopo – get directions at the museum.

Queen Emma Relics

Very few traces of Queen Emma remain in the Rabaul area. Her stately residence, Gunantambu near Kokopo, was destroyed during the war – all you can find today is the impressive staircase which led from the Kokopo waterfront up to the house. The view she must have enjoyed is still magnificent. The staircase is near the Kokopo museum.

Her *matmat* (cemetery) is a couple of km back towards Rabaul and is signposted. It overlooks the Rabaul-Kokopo road. All that remains of Queen Emma's grave is a cement slab with a hole in the centre – her ashes were stolen shortly after she was buried. The gravestone of her brother, and of her lover, Agostino Stalio, are in much better shape; the latter with a romantic inscription:

Oh for the touch of a vanished hand
and the sound of a voice which is still

About 1½ km north is her brother-in-law's, Richard Parkinson, cemetery, which is even more overgrown. It's called Kuradui after his plantation, but only the tombstone of Otto Parkinson, who committed suicide in the early 1900s, remains standing.

Richard Parkinson is nowhere near as well known as his flamboyant sister-in-law, but he wrote some of the earliest works on New Guinea island anthropology and natural history, a book titled *Thirty Years in the South Seas* and was an enthusiastic botanist who planted many trees in the Rabaul-Kokopo area. His grave is near Parkinson Point.

Vunapope

Just beyond the town of Kokopo, Vunapope is the Catholic Mission centre and one of the largest mission establishments in PNG. Vunapope is pronounced as if it ended in a 'y' and means 'place of the Catholics'.

The Catholics arrived in New Britain in 1881, only a few years after the pioneering Methodists, and at first established themselves at Nodup, on the north coast across from Rabaul. They soon moved round to

Queen Emma

Queen Emma was one of those larger than life people destined to become legends in their own lifetime. Emma was born in Samoa of an American father and Samoan mother. Her first husband disappeared at sea and in 1878 she teamed up with Thomas Farrell, an Australian trader, and started a trading business at Mioko on the Duke of York Islands. She was an astute business-woman and she soon realised that a plantation on the rich volcanic soil of the Gazelle Peninsula would be an excellent investment.

With her brother-in-law Richard Parkinson, who conveniently happened to be a botanist, Emma acquired land at Ralum, near Kokopo, and became the manager and owner of the first real plantation in New Guinea. When Thomas Farrell died he was succeeded by a steady stream of lovers.

By the time the Germans arrived in New Britain, Emma had extended her little empire to several other plantations, a number of ships and a whole string of trade stores. She made astute use of her American citizenship to avoid possible German take-overs. Emma built a mansion called Gunantambu (you can still see the regal stairway to the front door today) and entertained like royalty. She had her own wharf where she met guests, accompanied by her friends and servants, dressed in the finest clothes Europe could provide, then took them up to the mansion to dine on imported food and champagne.

'Queen Emma' may have been a joke at first, but it was soon a name she had earned. For many years Emma was faithful to her lover Agostino Stalio, who is buried just outside Rabaul, but after his death she married Paul Kolbe. He died in Monte Carlo in 1913 and Emma herself died a few days later. Her empire fell apart soon after she was gone and her fine home was destroyed during WW II. ∎

Vunapope near Queen Emma's plantations and built an impressive cathedral, destroyed in WW II.

Bita Paka

Bita Paka War Cemetery is several km inland, the turn-off is a little beyond Vunapope. It contains the graves of over 1000 Allied war dead, including many Indians who came to the Rabaul area as POWs captured in Singapore. There are also memorials to the six Australian soldiers killed in the capture of the German WW I radio station at Bita Paka, to the crew of the Australian submarine that disappeared off the New Britain coast in the same operation, and to the civilians who went down with the *Montevideo Maru*.

Keravat

South-west around the north coast road from Kulau Lodge, Keravat has the Lowland Agricultural Experimental Station where research is carried out on coconuts, oil palms, cocoa, coffee and fruit trees. There is also a forestry department. This is a good place to learn something about all those weird and wonderful tropical fruits which can look so daunting in markets.

Nearby is Vudal Agricultural College.

DUKE OF YORK ISLANDS

The Duke of York Group is about 30 km east of Rabaul, approximately midway between New Britain and New Ireland. Duke of York Island is the largest in the group, but there are also a cluster of smaller islands. This was the site for the first mission station in the area, the place where Queen Emma started her remarkable career, and it is also blessed with some beautiful white-sand beaches, lagoons, reefs and scenery. There are a couple of places to stay and transport is easy to find.

In the wet season you might see whales passing through St George's Channel (which separates the Duke of York Group from New Ireland).

Port Hunter, at the northern tip of the main island, was the landing point for the Rever-

end Brown in 1875 and the site of his first mission. You can still see the crumbling chimney of his house, overlooking the entrance to Port Hunter's circular bay. Near the beach is the cemetery where most of his assistants ended up.

Mioko Island, where Emma & Thomas Farrell established their first trading station, is a small island off the other end of Duke of York Island. Mioko Harbour is a large stretch of sheltered water between Mioko and Duke of York.

Kabakon Island, closest of the group to Rabaul, has a rather curious history. A German health fanatic named Engelhardt established a nudist colony here in 1903. He was soon dubbed Mr Kulau (Mr Coconut) by the locals for not only did he consider nudism was the path to perfect health but he supplemented it with a diet of nothing but coconuts. At one time he had 30 or more followers on the island, but coconuts must get boring, even with nude bodies added, and he died alone just before WW I.

The Duke of Yorks are the haunt of dukduks and tumbuans, and there are special areas set aside for them, often on beaches. You might not be allowed in these areas, especially if you are female, so always ask before swimming.

Places to Stay

There is a guesthouse on Ulu Island, which is run by the United Church. Contact the tourist office or SPAN Enterprises (☎ 92 1952) in Rabaul. The guesthouse is small and run-down and K10 is pretty steep for a dorm bed, intermittent electricity and water, and lots of mosquitoes.

On the other hand, Ulu Island is a very nice place. No meals are available at the guesthouse and although there's a basic trade store on the island it's best to bring your own food unless you can live on a diet of noodles, biscuits and the occasional fish. You need to be a little hardy to stay here. One traveller said that after staying on Ulu he understood why Queen Emma moved from the Duke of Yorks to the mainland, but that he had had a good time:

This island gives so many things: pleasant and unpleasant wildlife, wonderful beaches and snorkelling, Melanesian culture, friendly people canoeing by on their way to the gardens, plantation workers from all over PNG... I had a very good time there, although my health could not put up with all the fleas and mosquitoes. In one line: I'd go back to Ulu again.

Jürg Furrer

The similarly basic accommodation on Mioko Island, off the south end of Duke of York Island, was closed at the time of writing but was expected to re-open, perhaps as a new Grassroutes Haus. Ask at the Rabaul tourist office for the latest information.

Getting There & Away
Airlink (☎ 92 2899) sometimes flies to Rakanda airstrip on Mioko Island for K26 but most people go by small boat. From Rabaul there are a few boats in the afternoon, charging K5 for the one-hour trip, but boats are more frequent from Kokopo (near Leong's store and petrol station) and the fare from there is K3. There are fewer boats on Saturday and fewer still, if any, on Sunday.

WATOM ISLAND
Watom Island is an extinct volcano cone and site of one of the earliest settlements in New Britain. Archaeological finds here have been dated to 600 to 500 BC. The island is also a good place for walking or snorkelling; it can be reached from Kulau Lodge or Nonga beach, near Nonga hospital. It's possible to stay in villages, either independently or on a tour with Grassroutes Ecotravel.

West New Britain Province

Land Area 21,000 sq km
Population 135,000
Capital Kimbe

Surprisingly, considering the high level of development and many places of interest in East New Britain (ENB), the rest of the island is relatively untouched and little developed.

This province sums up the polarised nature of travel in PNG – you can spend a great deal of money staying at a hotel in Hoskins or Kimbe, and more by travelling around the province by plane; or you can travel by basic coastal boats and hope to find somewhere to stay in villages. There are also rugged and virtually unexplored mountains for the insanely adventurous. Luckily, there's also the Walindi Plantation Resort, which is not cheap but does offer high-quality accommodation and outstanding diving.

Most development is around the Williamez Peninsula where the roads are concentrated. The rest of the island – away from the Gazelle and Williamez peninsulas, plus the stretch of coast around Stettin Bay – is largely virgin rainforest. Oil-palm plantations are making inroads, and with labour recruited from all over PNG, especially the Highlands, there is some tension between locals and outsiders.

KIMBE
Population 4800
About 40 km from Talasea and the same distance from Hoskins, Kimbe is the provincial headquarters and a major centre for oil palm production. Oil palms are three times more efficient in the production of oil than coconuts but require a much larger investment for processing. The projects in West New Britain (WNB) have been resoundingly successful and have led to further developments in other provinces of PNG, notably Milne Bay and Northern.

In Kimbe there's a hospital, post office, shopping centre, PNGBC bank, and a daily market. Try contacting the Division of Commerce (☎ 93 5233, fax 93 5298, PO Box 427, Kimbe) for further information on the province. This is one of those phones which are never answered, so you might have better luck contacting one of the places to stay.

Places to Stay
The *Palm Lodge Hotel* (☎ 93 5001, PO Box

32) is adjacent to the beach, a short walk from town. It's reasonably well equipped but very pricey – K80/90 for fan-cooled singles/doubles, K90/110 with air-con.

It may be possible to stay at the United Church or camp at the police station.

Getting There & Away
A number of ships, including Lutheran Shipping's passenger vessels, call in at Kimbe on the voyage between Lae and Rabaul – see those sections. Kimbe Bay Shipping Agents (☎ 93 5154, PO Box 27) in town should have information on these and other boats. There's also a government boat which makes an irregular 10-day voyage from Kimbe to Pomio, stopping in many small ports along the way. From Pomio you could pick up a boat to Rabaul.

The coastal road runs from Talasea through Kimbe to Hoskins where you will find the main airport in WNB. From Talasea to Kimbe or Kimbe to Hoskins by PMV costs about K2.

HOSKINS
This small town is a major logging and oil-palm production centre. The oil-palm project is between Hoskins and Kimbe at Mosa and the company estate is surrounded by smaller plots worked by migrants from all over the country. Palm oil is used in the manufacture of soap and margarine. There are a number of extinct volcanoes in the area surrounding Hoskins – some with textbook perfect cones – and a short distance inland, at Koimumu, there's an active geyser field.

Places to Stay
The *Hoskins Hotel* (☎ 93 5113, PO Box 10) is also known as Palm Lodge Hoskins. It's close to the airport. Singles/doubles with fan are K60/80 and with air-con you pay K80/100.

Getting There & Away
This is the main airport for WNB, with Air Niugini, Islands Aviation and Airlink flights; there's at least one flight to the mainland each day. Fares from Hoskins include:

Rabaul K80, Lae K115, Port Moresby K140, Kandrian K50, Bialla K44 and Witu K72. Air Niugini has some good value weekend packages with accommodation at Walindi Dive Resort. See the Getting Around chapter.

A PMV from Hoskins to Kimbe costs around K2.

TALASEA & THE WILLIAMEZ PENINSULA
The pretty little town of Talasea looks across the bay with its many islands from Williamez Peninsula. The peninsula is an active volcanic region; there are even bubbling mud holes in Talasea. Lake Dakataua, at the end of the projection, was formed in a colossal eruption in 1884.

On Pangula Island, across from Talasea, there is a whole collection of thermal performers (geysers and fumaroles) in the Valley of Wabua. The name means 'Valley of Hot Water' and is only a short walk from the shops. In the hills behind Talasea are the wrecks of two US bombers, one of them a B-24 Liberator. Both are in reasonable condition.

Talasea is a centre for the manufacture of shell money. Obsidian (volcanic glass) from here is believed to have been traded from about 3000 BC until recent times. It went from New Britain to New Ireland, Manus and the Admiralty Islands or even further afield, and was used in knives, spears and arrows.

Tribes inland from Talasea used to bind their babies' heads to make them narrow and elongated. Other tribes near Kandrian used Malay-style blowguns to hunt birds and fruit bats. The wooden 'darts' are shot through a long bamboo tube.

Places to Stay
The *Walindi Plantation Resort* (☎ 93 5441, PO Box 4, Kimbe) is between Kimbe and Talasea on the east side of the peninsula. The plantation itself is a large, privately-owned oil palm plantation, right on the shores of Kimbe Bay, and there is a group of attractive and comfortable thatched bungalows.

Kimbe Bay is fringed by volcanic mountains, some of which are still active.

Apart from the superb natural surroundings, which are stunningly beautiful, the main attraction is the diving, which has many people raving about clear water, volcanic caves draped in staghorn coral and reef dropoffs. Fishing trips and day tours are also organised. All meals and accommodation are K140 per person per day in a bungalow, or K110 in a room with shared bathroom, and a return transfer to Hoskins costs K30. Two dives per day cost another K80, including equipment hire.

Apparently the *Kautaga Guest Haus*, on a small island off the west side of the peninsula, has closed down.

AROUND WEST NEW BRITAIN PROVINCE

Mt Langila, on Cape Gloucester at the southwestern end of the island, is still active and hiccups and rumbles every few months.

There used to be a guesthouse at Bialla, charging about K50 per person, but we've had reports that it has closed.

There are several places to stay in and near **Kandrian**. The *Kandrian Guesthouse* (PO Box 14, Kandrian) is in town and charges K25/45 a single/double. Breakfast is K3, lunch K8 and dinner K10.

The new *Akanglo Guesthouse*, five minutes by boat from Kandrian, should have opened by now, but we don't know how much they plan to charge. It's apparently in a beautiful location.

There's also the *Awa Guesthouse*, another new place, which is 45 minutes by boat from Kandrian. The Department of Commerce (☎ 91 7305) in Kandrian can arrange boats and will have more information.

Pomio has been noted for its beliefs, similar to the cargo cult, that the land would be turned into some sort of earthly paradise.

The Kimbe islanders, off the Williamez Peninsula, are expert sailors and canoe builders who live on the islands but tend gardens on the mainland.

The **Witu Islands**, west of the Williamez Peninsula, are about 80 km off the coast and are of volcanic origin. Unea has a peak 738 metres high while Garov, the largest island, has a beautiful bay formed when the sea broke into its extinct crater. Pirates once used the bay as a hideout.

During the first 10 years of this century a smallpox epidemic virtually wiped out the people on these fertile and quite heavily populated islands.

New Ireland Province

Land Area 9500 sq km
Population 90,000
Capital Kavieng

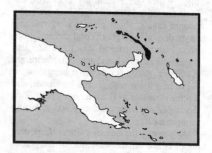

New Ireland is the long, narrow island north of New Britain. It's a beautiful and friendly place but little known and rarely visited, yet it has one of the longest records of contact with European civilisation. European explorers sailed through St George's Channel, which separates New Ireland from New Britain, from the early 1600s, and St George's Bay, near the south-east tip, was a popular watering spot for early sailing ships in the region. Later, the Germans developed lucrative copra plantations and the first extensive road network in PNG.

Perhaps the nicest thing about New Ireland is that it's safe – or no more dangerous than the rest of the world. There are infrequent incidents of lawlessness (the locals blame people from outlying islands) but you would have to be very unlucky to be caught up in one. In rural areas you will have no trouble meeting people and once you do, your safety is all but guaranteed. In Kavieng, the big smoke, be a bit careful at night, especially pay nights. It is claimed that there are no poisonous snakes on New Ireland.

New Ireland Province also includes a number of offshore islands. The major island is New Hanover, also known as Lavongai, off the north-west end. Well offshore from the east coast are the Tabar, Lihir, Tanga and Feni island groups. Further to the north-west is the large island of Mussau in the St Matthias Group and the smaller islands of Emirau and Tench.

The name New Ireland translates into pidgin as *Niu Ailan* – which translates back into English as New Island.

HISTORY

Archaeological finds near Namatanai suggest that New Ireland was inhabited 30,000 years ago.

At the same time as they chanced upon the Admiralty Islands in 1516-17, the Dutch explorers Schouten and Le Maire 'discovered' New Ireland, although they did not know it was an island. Later, in 1700, the flamboyant British buccaneer-explorer William Dampier, sailed through the Dampier Straits between New Britain and the mainland and named St George's Bay between New Ireland and New Britain – thinking they were both one island. It was nearly 70 years before Carteret sailed into Dampier's St George's Bay and discovered it was really a channel and New Ireland was separate to New Britain.

It was in 1877 when the first missionaries arrived, always an important milestone in PNG. The Reverend George Brown, stationed in the Duke of York Islands between New Britain and New Ireland, arrived at Kalili during that year, crossed over to the east coast and after some suitably hair-raising adventures, moved back to safer climes. Not long after, the amazing Marquis de Ray saga took place near the south-east corner of the island.

Despite its inauspicious beginnings, New Ireland soon became one of the most profitable parts of the German colony of New Guinea. Under the iron-handed German administrator Baron Boluminski, a string of copra plantations were developed along the

The Marquis de Ray & Cape Breton

The story of the colony of Cape Breton and the Marquis de Ray is one of the most outrageous in the saga of European colonisation in the Pacific. The Marquis had never set foot on New Ireland, yet on the frail basis of a ship's log he contrived to sell hundreds of hectares of land to gullible, would-be settlers at the equivalent of about $0.40 an acre. He raised no less than $60,000 (an amazing sum for 1879) on the basis of his flimsy prospectus. Unfortunately, many of his colonists paid with their lives as well as their savings.

The Marquis had advertised Cape Breton, near Lambom Island off Cape St George, as a thriving settlement with fertile soil, perpetual sunshine and friendly natives. In actual fact there had been no preparation at all and the settlers were dumped into a tangled jungle where the rainfall was so heavy that, even today, there has been virtually no development. And the Reverend George Brown, an early visitor to this part of New Ireland, had found the natives far from friendly.

With only three weeks' supplies and such useful equipment as a mill for an area where grain would never grow, the settlers soon started to die like flies. It's anyone's guess whether malaria or starvation took the larger toll but the Marquis helped things along by sending supply ships from Australia with useful cargoes like cases of note-paper or loads of bricks. Not to mention three more shiploads of naive land-buyers from Europe.

Eventually the pitiful survivors were rescued by Thomas Farrell and his wife Emma, who later became famous as Queen Emma. Much of the equipment abandoned on the beaches of Cape Breton was used to construct her magnificent mansion near Rabaul. Although most of the rescued settlers were sent on to Australia, one 16-year-old did eventually become a successful plantation holder – but on New Britain not New Ireland. The grinding stone for the Cape Breton grain mill can still be seen in a park off Mango Avenue in Rabaul and some parts are in Kavieng. The crazy Marquis ended his days in a lunatic asylum in France. ■

east coast and a road system, which was long the envy of other parts of the country, was constructed.

Boluminski died of heatstroke before the Australian takeover, and although his road (it still bears his name) was gradually extended, in other respects the island simply marked time. When WW II spread to the Pacific, New Ireland fell almost immediately and Kavieng was subsequently developed into a major Japanese base, although never a rival to Rabaul. Most of the Australians in Kavieng managed to escape but those who chose to stay behind as coastwatchers were gradually captured as the Japanese extended their control over the island.

Like Rabaul, the Japanese held the island right until the final surrender and, again like Rabaul, although the Allies made no attempt to retake New Ireland they inflicted enormous damage. Kavieng, the main Japanese base, was comprehensively flattened, and the Boluminski Highway and its adjoining plantations were severely damaged – the Japanese used it to move supplies down the coast and across to Rabaul. Extensive re-development since the war has restored the productive copra plantations along the highway and coffee, rubber and timber industries have also developed. Kavieng is also an important fishing port and has a major, Japanese-developed, tuna fishing base.

GEOGRAPHY

Note that the north-east coast is generally called the east coast, and the south-west the west. Anything south of Namatanai is known as the south.

New Ireland is long, narrow and mountainous. For most of its length the island is only six to 10 km wide with a high spine falling straight to the sea on much of the west coast and bordered by a narrow, but fertile, coastal strip on the east coast. It is along this strip that the efficient New Ireland copra producers are based. The highest peak in the Schleinitz Ranges is just under 1500 metres. In the centre of the island is the high, cool Lelet Plateau. The island bulges out at the south-eastern end and the mountains of the Hans Meyer Ranges and the Verron Ranges

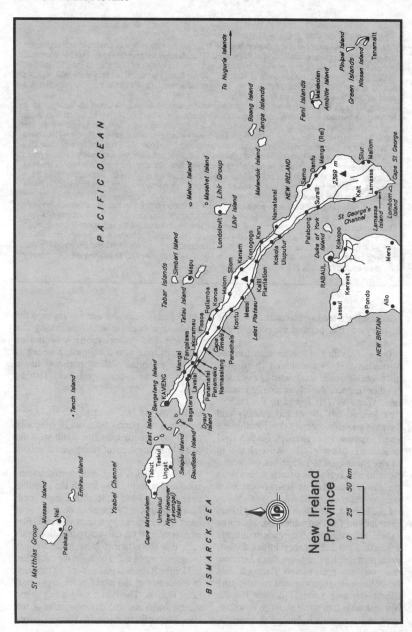

New Ireland
Province

are somewhat higher: the tallest peak reaches 2399 metres. Despite the narrow channel that separates this part of New Ireland from New Britain there is no comparable volcanic activity in New Ireland.

PEOPLE & CULTURE

The people of New Ireland are Melanesian, with some cultural affinities with the peoples of New Britain. About 20 different languages are spoken, two of which don't belong to the Austronesian family. In rural areas there will usually be someone who speaks English, but many people speak only pidgin.

Dance is an important part of New Ireland culture, with around 50 different styles.

Many villages, especially on the west coast, have a *haus-boi* (a fairly offensive colonial-era name, but it's the one commonly used), which is something like a men's club. In some villages female guests are welcome to enter but it's best to ask first. Sometimes there is no actual house, just an area defined by a stone wall, but there will usually be a forked branch, through which you must step to enter.

Malangan Carving

Twenty years ago it was widely reported that the art of malangan carving had completely died out. Now there has been a modest revival and there is at least one group of carvers. This group began after an American collector prompted Hosea Linge, the son of a famous carver, to resurrect the craft. You can find him, and his carvings, at Libba, a small village about 22 km before Konos.

On Masahet Island, a beautiful little isle near Lihir, with a population of less than a thousand, the Catholic mission church has posts carved into malangan, as does the airport terminal building in Kavieng. Panamecho, a village on the west coast, has some old malangan carvings.

Other places of interest for artefacts on New Ireland are Lamusmus on the west coast and Lihir Island where shell money is still made.

Shark Calling

New Ireland, especially the west coast between Konogogo and Kontu, is the centre for the art of shark calling. Because of the documentary film *The Shark Callers of Kontu*, that village attracts what little attention the west coast gets. The other west coast villages are a bit put out about this, so you won't find people shy about their shark calling prowess.

Certain men have the ability to 'call up' sharks, although there is no special right to do so, despite some clans claiming the skill for themselves.

The shark is called to the canoe, by voice or with a coconut- shell rattle, where it is snared in a noose. Attached to the noose is a propeller-shaped piece of wood which acts as a drag and slows down the shark as it tries to swim away. Eventually, the shark tires and is speared or bludgeoned into submission. Even after this experience, your average shark displays a lively resentment at being hauled out of the water. Getting a two-metre shark into a canoe can be pretty exciting.

Shark motifs feature in the material

Malangan

Malangan is the practice of making totemic figures to honour the dead. Malangan also refers to the figures themselves, and also to the gatherings and feasts where the figures are made. A malangan feast marks the end of the mourning period, and also provides an opportunity for the sharing of traditional knowledge.

The arrival of Christian missionaries and cash cropping nearly destroyed malangan and today the culture is strong only in the Tabar islands and a few areas on New Ireland's east coast.

Only one man in a tribal group has the right to carve or display the malangan and this was a matter of considerable prestige. The complex masks are the best known malangan, but there are also several other types, some not carved but woven from vines. ■

culture, and some people 'own' particular sharks.

Shows

Shows in New Ireland Province aren't the major events they are in the Highlands, but they are worth seeing. Unfortunately the dates can change, catching even the tourist office unawares.

The Kavieng Show is the biggest in the province and has been held in February, over the Provincial Government Day long weekend. This might change to bring the date closer to Rabaul's Frangipani Festival (late July). Lihir Island Show is in August or September.

KAVIENG
Population 5000

Kavieng is a somnolent little town – the very image of a Somerset Maugham south sea island port. There's nothing much to do here, but it's a very nice place to do nothing much.

The town has sea on three sides so there are often cool breezes. Rain falls all year, but May to November are the driest months.

Orientation & Information

The town centre is Coronation Drive, which has the hotel and the club, the Air Niugini office, the post office and the banks (PNGBC and Westpac). The nicest part of Kavieng is the harbour drive, a gently curving road, shaded by huge trees, with most of Kavieng's points of historical interest dotted along it. Most of the few shops are north of Corona-

tion Drive, clustered around Tong's Supermarket.

The big island across the harbour is Noosa, with a narrow passage separating it from Noosa Lik on the left. Left of Noosa and Noosa Lik is Nango Island.

The New Ireland Tourist Bureau (☎ 94 1449, fax 94 2346, PO Box 103) is on Coronation Drive near the post office, and although there is little printed information the staff are friendly and knowledgeable. Kavieng (and New Ireland for that matter) is the sort of place where everyone knows everyone else, so it's relatively easy to get good information. In the same building is the Department of Culture, where you can see a few malangan artefacts.

A small artefact shop is intermittently open at the airport. There are some good malangan masks but they're expensive – about K100 – as they are 'used' ceremonial masks. There are also some cheaper items. While at the airport check out the malangan carved columns. The new terminal building was opened with an impressive ceremony which included *kolup taina* dancing, on top of tall poles. There's apparently a video of the ceremony somewhere in town.

PMVs around town cost K0.40. Some run out to the airport.

Harbour Drive

If you walk south from the Coronation Drive intersection with Harbour Drive you come to a small local market and, on your left, a gentle grassy slope leading up to the District Commissioner's residence. The slope, with

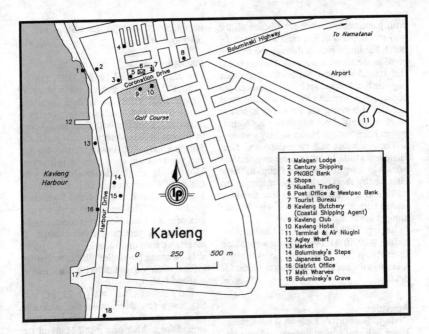

1 Malagan Lodge
2 Century Shipping
3 PNGCB Bank
4 Shops
5 Niuallan Trading
6 Post Office & Westpac Bank
7 Tourist Bureau
8 Kavieng Butchery
  (Coastal Shipping Agent)
9 Kavieng Club
10 Kavieng Hotel
11 Terminal & Air Niugini
12 Agley Wharf
13 Market
14 Boluminsky's Steps
15 Japanese Gun
16 District Office
17 Main Wharves
18 Boluminsky's Grave

Kavieng

a jumble of paving stones along each side, is all that is left of the imposing stairway to Boluminski's residence.

The legendary German administrator's home was destroyed during WW II and the far less imposing District Commissioner's residence was built on the same site. A few other stones and bits of paving can be seen on top of the ridge. Further along this waterfront ridge is a large Japanese gun still pointing futilely out to sea.

Down at the shoreline a small, inconspicuous workshop houses another New Ireland relic – the castings to hold the stone, grinding wheel for a mill for the Marquis de Ray's ill-fated project. The wheel itself is in Rabaul but the castings are in remarkably good shape with their date of manufacture, 1852, clearly visible.

The main wharf area looms up next, followed by an ugly shark proof swimming enclosure. Across the road, and another 100 metres along, is the old cemetery with Boluminski's grave, marked by a plain cross, taking pride of place.

The Harbour & Islands

Kavieng has a large and very beautiful harbour. If you aren't feeling energetic you can get a good view of the harbour from (and have a drink on) the sandy beach in front of the Malagan Lodge.

The fishing enjoys a good reputation, particularly game fishing, if that's your blood sport. The Kavieng Hotel can arrange charters. Keep your ears open in the lodge, hotel or club and you may get a chance to invite yourself along for a fishing trip. If not, then a wander along the waterfront should turn up a banana boat bound for somewhere or other. There are more or less fixed charges for trips out to various islands or you can arrange a charter or a 'drop me off, pick me up later' trip.

A good place for the latter would be the idyllic little island of **Edmago**. A tiny dot with palm trees, a white-sand beach all the way round and beautiful clear water over the coral. Finding a way in through the shallow coral to the shore is not easy. Further out is the island of **New Sulaman** – another popular local picnic spot where you can see copra being prepared by a handful of local families. **Lisinung** (or Paradise) **Island** is another beautiful dot and there's accommodation here. See the Places to Stay section.

The sea between New Ireland and New Hanover is full of islands, most tiny, and it is possible to get from Kavieng to New Hanover by short hops. If you're tempted to do this in a canoe remember that there are strong currents, and you'd be wise to take along a guide and a good chart.

Raging Thunder, based in Cairns, Australia (☎ (070) 31 1466), has sea-kayaking tours from Kavieng. See the Activities section in the Facts for the Visitor chapter for details.

Activities

Diving, Surfing & Fishing The Kavieng Hotel will rent you equipment and take you to the area's excellent dive spots, but only if you are qualified – they don't run courses. One dive is K30 or it's K90 for the whole day. There are some war wrecks (including a midget submarine) but the plentiful, varied and large fish are the main attraction here. You might get to hand-feed sharks.

When the north-westerlies blow, between November and February, the big swells sometimes produce good surf near Kavieng, but it breaks on a reef so only the experienced should tackle it. Nearby islands also have big waves.

The game fishing around Kavieng is apparently excellent.

Organised Tours Contact Air Niugini or the New Ireland Tourist Bureau for information on a number of interesting tours of New Ireland from three nights to a week, some involving accommodation in village guesthouses. Traditional Travel (☎ 25 3966, Port Moresby) has cycling tours, as does Grassroutes

Ecotravel (☎ 92 1756, Rabaul), as well as other tours and treks.

Places to Stay

The *Kavieng Hotel* (☎ 94 2199, fax 94 2283, PO Box 4), once a drowsy place, is now a little more lively and there's a renovation and extension programme underway. Doubles with fans and shared bathroom in the old section cost just K27. This is good value, but the rooms are due for renovation so prices might rise. Motel-style singles/doubles/triples with fridge, TV and air-con cost K75/85/95. The hotel now has a pool and a pleasant garden area. The main bar, with a good mix of expats and New Irelanders, can be noisy but is generally calm enough. If there's a dance on in Kavieng it will probably be at the hotel. See Places to Eat for information on the hotel's stupendous seafood buffet.

The *Kavieng Club* (☎ 94 2027, PO Box 62), just a few doors down the road, also offers rooms and is a fun place to hang around for a drink or a meal. Many of the island's 'befores', expats of 20 to 35 years duration, regularly drop by for a cold beer or a game of darts. (Darts rule No 3 states that team captains will be held responsible for any brawls...)

Membership of the club costs K25, but casual visitors can be signed in by a member. The club is a good place to hear stories or maybe line up a ride to somewhere else on the island.

Beneath the club is a very large Japanese bunker. To investigate bunkers of another sort you can pay K2 for a round of golf on the club's nine-hole course. Clubs can be borrowed.

The buildings are a bit run-down but are gradually being renovated. There are seven self-contained rooms with fridge, TV and tea/coffee-making facilities. Singles/doubles with a fan cost K42/64 and those with air-con cost K48/70. Meals are available. If you stay more than a few days you might get a discount; the monthly rent is K600 per person.

The top place to stay is *Malagan Lodge* (☎ 94 2344, PO Box 238), owned by the provincial government and currently managed by one of PNG's better-known expats, Barry Walker – The Phantom. The lodge is new, pleasant and beautifully situated right on the harbour, with its own stretch of beach. Rooms with air-con cost K110 and with fan they're K95. Amex, MasterCard and Visa are accepted.

Lisinung Island, 15 minutes by fast boat from Kavieng, is a couple of hundred metres long, palm-covered (with a patch of jungle which is home to megapode wildfowl), secluded and quiet. The only people who live here are the caretaker, Timon, and his family. Two simple but high-quality units have been built and a few more are planned, and at K30 per person it's a good deal. You can hire a canoe, fish, swim off the white-sand beach or snorkel on the reef. There is no generator to disturb the peace, but there is solar lighting and a kerosene fridge. You can hire the whole island if you want. Contact the Kavieng Hotel for bookings.

There are also more basic guesthouses on Limalum and Mansawa islands.

Places to Eat

Smoked fish is sold in the market for K0.50. It can be a little dry, but with some lime or lemon it's pretty good. The kai bar at *Tong's Supermarket* is better than many. Mud-crab fans should note that Kavieng's crab season is August and September, when there are some monsters available. Lobsters can cost as little as K3 if you buy in the market.

Why do Air Niugini pilots like Friday night stopovers in Kavieng? Because of the seafood buffet at the *Kavieng Hotel*. For just K12.50 you are let loose on an incredible array of crabs, lobsters, oysters (the biggest I've seen), prawns... Less spectacular meals are available other nights.

The *Kavieng Club* serves three meals a day, seven days a week and the food is reasonable in quality and price, with most main courses under K10. The limited menu has mainly seafood and Chinese dishes but they will cook dishes to order if you give advance notice.

Malagan Lodge has a reasonable restaurant with great views across the harbour.

Getting There & Away

Air There are plenty of Air Niugini flights to Kavieng but the schedule is quite complex.

There are flights *from* Moresby via Hoskins and Rabaul on Monday, Tuesday, Thursday (not Hoskins), Friday and Sunday (not Hoskins); via Lae, Madang and Manus on Tuesday; and via Madang, Wewak and Manus on Sunday.

There are flights *to* Moresby via Rabaul and Hoskins on Tuesday, Wednesday, Friday, Saturday and Sunday (not Hoskins); via Manus, Madang and Wewak on Thursday; and via Manus, Madang and Lae on Sunday.

Some fares from Kavieng are: Lae K207, Madang K183, Manus K106, Moresby K234, Rabaul K79 and Wewak K194. Air Niugini has some good value weekend packages.

Islands Aviation (☎ 92 2900, Rabaul) has some useful services in the area. Every day except Sunday there is at least one flight between Rabaul and Namatanai, usually continuing on to Londolovit on Lihir Island.

On Wednesday, Islands flies from Rabaul to Kavieng via Namatanai, Boang Island in the Tanga Group, Londolovit on Lihir Island, and Mapua on Tatau Island in the Tabar Group. The flight goes on to Emirau and Mussau in the St Matthias Group, back to Kavieng then direct to Rabaul. On Friday the same route is flown but in the reverse order. On Monday there's a flight from Rabaul which stops at Manga, in the south of New Ireland, and continues on to Malekolon on the Feni Group and Boang, returning the same day. You can fly from Manga to Rabaul but not the other way on Thursday.

Fares from Rabaul are: Namatanai K30, Manga K54, Malekolon K84, Boang K65, Londolovit K74, Mapua K81 and Kavieng K79. Fares from Namatanai are: Boang K35, Londolovit K35, Mapua K42 and Kavieng K75. Fares from Kavieng are: Mapua K50,

Londolovit K72, Boang K98, Emirau K74 and Mussau K83.

Airlink (☎ 92 2899 in Rabaul) flies at least twice daily, except Sunday, between Rabaul and Namatanai. On Wednesday and Friday there is a direct flight from Rabaul to Kavieng, continuing on to Emirau then returning to Kavieng and Rabaul. Fares are the same as Islands'.

Road The Boluminski Highway, which runs 270 km from Kavieng to Namatanai and for about 80 km beyond Namatanai, is sealed as far as Poliamba (near Konos) and in good condition as far as Namatanai.

There is, however, little public transport running the whole way between Kavieng and Namatanai. If you do find a PMV running the whole way the trip will cost under K20, but it's more likely that you will have to take vehicles, either PMVs or hitched lifts, from village to village. There isn't much traffic but provincial government vehicles charge up and down the coast fairly frequently. Travelling this way it should be possible to do the trip in a day – a private car can do the trip in about five hours. There's a mail truck which runs to Namatanai on Tuesday and returns to Kavieng on Wednesday, but it doesn't run every week.

It's best to ask around Kavieng. Someone is bound to know someone who can give you a lift. Coming from Namatanai might be more difficult but you won't get into too much trouble. If you get stuck along the way, there are a couple of places to stay (see the East Coast section), and staying in just about any village is possible.

If you want a lift from Kavieng up to Lelet Plateau, ask around in the market as most vegetables sold here are grown on Lelet and there are regular trucks.

Sea The Consort Express Line has freighters running weekly between Kavieng and Lae via Kimbe, and they take passengers. It's one night to Kimbe (K31) and two to Lae (K46), deck class only. They usually depart on Sunday. The Consort also has boats making the overnight trip to Rabaul (K37) but there is no fixed schedule. Consort's agent in Kavieng is Century Shipping (☎ 94 2239), opposite Malagan Lodge. There's no sign.

Coastal's freighters also call in at Kavieng but they don't have a fixed schedule. There is a boat to Rabaul approximately fortnightly and one to Manus Island approximately monthly. Approximate fares in deck/cabin class are K35/50 to Rabaul and K32/80 to Manus. The Coastal agent can sometimes be found in the Kavieng Butchery on Coronation Drive. If he isn't there ask around at the main wharf.

From the small Agley wharf, near the market, banana boats and work boats run to the nearby islands, including a weekly boat making the overnight trip to Tatau, main island in the Tabar Group (K10), and two boats each week to New Hanover Island (K8). It takes about six hours by small boat to Mussau Island.

Car Rental The Regent garage, next to Malagan Lodge, hires 4WD vehicles but they're expensive. You can get a driver, too. Outside Kavieng and Namatanai the price of petrol can be monstrous – around K3 a litre! Diesel is scarce outside the two main towns.

Bicycle Both coasts of New Ireland offer outstanding cycling, with good, flat roads, little traffic and plenty of water, fresh and salt, to cool off in. If you cycle across the island be very careful coming down the steep crossings. Unless you know how to adjust brakes so they work well, it's safer to walk down.

Traditional Travel in Port Moresby and Grassroutes Ecotravel in Rabaul have bike rides up the west coast. These are not cheap but are well worth it. There are also plans to hire out bikes, probably from Kavieng, although at the time of writing it hadn't been decided just who would do it. Ask around.

EAST COAST
The east coast is more developed than the west, but that just means that there are more pretty little villages, generally on clear rivers. Running most of the length of the east

coast is the Boluminski Highway, one of PNG's best roads, although it carries only light traffic.

New Ireland's autocratic administrator, Herr Boluminski, built a road that was not rivalled on the mainland until well into the 1950s. When WW I cut short the period of German rule the Boluminski Highway already ran 100 km out of Kavieng along the east coast. Under the Australians it was gradually extended and it now reaches about 80 km beyond Namatanai to Rei, before petering out into a 4WD track. The road is now sealed from Kavieng to the Poliamba oil palm project, near Konos.

Boluminski built the road by forcing each village along the coast to construct and maintain a section. On his tours of inspection, Boluminski would summon the villagers to personally push his carriage over any deteriorated sections and woe betide these villagers if repairs were not underway when he returned.

The highway was (and is, where it's unsealed) paved with *koronos*, crushed coral, a fine surface for an unsealed road although the glare is rather hard on the eyes in bright conditions and when it's wet it acts like grinding paste on car tyres.

Almost all the way along, the east coast is one continuous copra plantation – in places cocoa trees fill the gaps between the palms. You'll notice that some of the palms are twisted into a corkscrew shape, the result of a disease. Rubber plantations in varying states of prosperity are also interspersed along the route.

There are many villages built beside the road, often right on the palm-fringed beach. Visitors to New Ireland are few, and outsiders quickly become an interesting diversion. People are friendly, waving and shouting as you drive by, gathering around if you stop. Note how many of the locals have blonde hair – some due to dietary deficiencies, some to an odd genetic strain, as in the Highlands, and sometimes due to good old bleach.

Nearly every village is built near one of the many streams that run down from the central mountains. These streams are cool,

clean (except perhaps at the height of the dry season) and delightfully clear and refreshing. Stopping at these to join the villagers in a drink and a dip can make the trip to Namatanai a very pleasant day. It would be good to walk along either coast road from one village to another; they're often within a few km of each other on the east coast.

Cross-Island Roads

There are several roads crossing from the east coast to the less visited west coast. Although some of these trans-island roads can be rough or even impassable for conventional vehicles during the wet, none of them are very long. It's a narrow island! From north to south, the crossings are:

Fangalawa to Panamafei The Fangalawa crossing runs from near Panamafei village on the west coast to the east coast a few km on the Kavieng side of Lakuramau. It's in good condition but crosses the Schleinitz Ranges and is very steep, so much so that some of it is sealed for safety.

Poliamba to Panachais This track might be impassable even in a 4WD vehicle (it's one of the roads imperfectly built by a logging company) but it would make an excellent and easy walk. The track runs through spectacular jungle-covered limestone gorge. At Panachais there's a community school where you could probably find accommodation. There might also be accommodation at Poliamba. From the sawmill, past (coming from Kavieng) the oil palm project's administration centre , take a dirt road running off the highway to the right. Follow this road through the oil palm plantation for a km or so and when the new road turns hard left, keep going straight on. Shortly after this take the left fork.

Karu to Konogogo This crossing is also steep and the road isn't in great condition. Take it slowly.

Namatanai to Uluputur/Labur Bay Beginning at Bo, near Namatanai, this is the least hilly of the crossings. From the west coast it should be possible to find a boat to the Duke of York Islands, although you might have to wait a day or so if you don't want to charter the whole boat.

Down the East Coast

In **Matanasoi** (or Liga) village, about five km along the highway from Kavieng airport a little pathway leads off the road to a limestone cave filled with crystal clear water. During WW II the Japanese used this grotto as a source of drinking water. There are various underground passages supposedly leading to another pool, but you can't explore them or swim here because it's an important village water resource.

The big Commonwealth Development Corporation oil palm project at **Poliamba** has created a new town and there's a guesthouse here. It's supposedly only for people connected with the project but you might get a room for about K35. See the administration office.

Libba village, just before Konos, is a good place to look for malangan carvings. **Konos** itself is the approximate halfway point to Namatanai and the only major village along the road. It's also the loading point for timber ships, which collect logs from the project operating from a little beyond Konos all the way to Namatanai. The foreign logging companies pay as little as K5 for a huge rainforest tree, and their promises of building good roads – and maintaining them – are often broken. Also, judging by the size of some of the logs, they are clear-felling rather than managing the forests.

Pinis Passage, just on the Namatanai side of Konos, is a small, popular beach.

The turn-off to Lelet Plateau is just after Malom village, about 30 km south of Konos.

Beyond here the road climbs a couple of times and occasionally deteriorates a little, but in general it continues to hug the coast all the way to Namatanai and beyond. Although there are many fine stretches of white sand, backed by the obligatory palm trees, the swimming is mostly not so good because the water is very shallow and rocky until it suddenly drops steeply away.

Karu

This small village is on both the highway and the coast about 30 km before Namatanai and a few km after a crossing to the west coast. If you're asking for directions to Karu, stress that you want the village, not the plantation or the 'development'. There's now a village guesthouse here, and it's a pleasant spot for a stay of a day or two. The guesthouse is a new building, basic but pleasant, built by Thomas Molis, who also runs the adjacent trade store. He's a friendly man and plans to charge about K10 a night. There's no electricity but the beds are comfortable and the sheets are clean. Meals can be arranged.

The paintings and carvings in the church are creations of Kou, who has gone on to local fame as a singer.

Jacob, the village's pet *kokomo* (hornbill), once belonged to an Australian expat so if you're white you might find yourself with a friend. Watch out for that *big* beak!

A few hundred metres across from Karu Bay from the village is the small **Mumu Island** (also known as Mumugas Island), which the traditional owners have proclaimed as a conservation area. Turtles come ashore to lay their eggs around the end of July. It's a beautiful place and good for picnics and swimming. You can get across in a canoe for about K1.

One side of Karu Bay is a depot for the logs which are being ripped out of New Island, waiting to be loaded onto ships.

Namatanai

A quiet little place, midway down the coast but near the end of the good road, Namatanai (population 800) is the second-largest town on New Ireland but you won't find much more here than a hotel, a supermarket and a few stores. It was until recently a much prettier place, but all the big old rain trees were cut down after one of them fell on a policeman.

With Rabaul only 15 minutes away by air,

Namatanai is a convenient point of entry to New Ireland.

Namatanai was an important station in German days and the Namatanai Hotel is on the site of the old German station house. You can find the graves of Dr Emil Stephan, the German administrator, and Mrs Scheringer, wife to another German official from pre-WW I days, in the picturesque old graveyard down the road from the National Works compound on the other side of the airstrip.

Just before you enter the town from Kavieng the road goes through a deep cutting; the old road winds off below it and down on the shore there is a jumble of Japanese tanks and guns which were bulldozed off after the war. From the road you can only see one rusting tank – you have to clamber down the steep cliff face to see the whole pile of them, although the cliff is being used as the town dump and the tanks are disappearing under garbage. It is said their engines still contain oil. About 20 km before Namatanai, there is the mid-section of a Japanese bomber sitting by the roadside.

Places to Stay The *Namatanai Hotel* (☎ 94 3057, PO Box 48) has an easygoing atmosphere. It's right down by the waterfront, near the new wharf. There are only a few rooms; singles/doubles in the old section go for K45/90, in the new section K65/90 or K75/150 with air-con. Meals are available.

St Martins *Catholic Mission*, uphill from the town centre, had accommodation but at the time of writing the guesthouse was being rebuilt. When it re-opens, beds (perhaps for women only) will be about K10.

The council's guesthouse has been taken over by a second-hand clothes store. You might be able to find a bed at the sawmill a few km out of town.

Getting There & Away Both Islands Aviation and Airlink make the 15-minute flight from Rabaul at least daily, Monday to Saturday, for K30. You can also fly to Kavieng and the Eastern Islands from Namatanai – see also the Kavieng Getting There & Away section. To walk into town from the airport,

turn right out of the terminal then take the next two left turns. It's not far.

There may be boats from Rabaul, via the Duke of York Islands, to the west coast a short distance by road from Namatanai.

See the Kavieng section for information on road transport.

WEST COAST

If you thought that the east coast was idyllically laid-back, friendly and beautiful, wait until you try the west coast. About the biggest hassle on the west coast is the number of times you have to smile and say *monin* and *apinun*.

A road, also of crushed coral in parts, runs along most of the coast and it carries even less traffic than the east coast highway. For most of the way – from the Fangalawa crossing down to Konogogo village – it's in good condition, but a 4WD (or, better still, a bicycle) is usually necessary because rivers have to be fjorded. Some of them are bridged but that can make things even more difficult, as the riverbanks at the ends of the concrete bridges are sometimes washed away. If you're driving be very careful. In the wet season even a 4WD will have trouble with the river crossings.

The rivers are astoundingly clear and fresh, and many are crammed with freshwater prawns and fish. If you walk or cycle you'll find fjording them a delight, in the dry season, anyway.

There are some plantations and a couple of logging depots but most of the villages rely on fishing and gardening. With many west coast people living near rainforest this is a good place to find out about bush food, which is available in abundance if you know what to look for. Between Konogogo and Kontu shark calling is practised.

There are no formal places to stay on the west coast, but visitors are such a rarity you should have no trouble finding a place to sleep in a mission, school or village house. While you probably won't have to pay for this you should always leave a gift of about K5 – K10, plus some money or food if you have been given meals.

The population density is lower here than on the east coast, but there are still plenty of villages. Listed below are some of the larger ones. Very basic food (rice, noodles, tinned meat or fish) can usually be bought in these villages, but don't count on it.

From the crossing near Karu village and heading north up the coast, you come to **Konogogo**, known locally as Kono. There's a basic store here and a Catholic school where you can usually stay. The headmaster speaks good English.

From here the undulating road runs to the big **Kalili Plantation**, where the country becomes flatter. This area gets nearly five metres of rain a year, falling all year round. Just north of the plantation's harbour there's

Fruit bat

a mission. The road crosses several rivers in this area; be careful of washouts at the ends of the bridges.

Further north is **Messi village**, under the lee of a jungle-covered limestone escarpment. About 300 adults live here, and many more children, making it an unusually large village for New Ireland. There's a basic medical aid station here.

In this area the ground is covered with water-rounded black stones and pebbles – it looks like a Japanese formal garden. Perhaps the escarpment was once the sea-shore and

the land below the sea-bed, and Messi villagers do say that their ancestors once lived over the escarpment but moved down to the shore. Their gardens are still on top of the escarpment and it's a tough but rewarding climb. People are always coming and going so it's easy to find someone to show you the best way up.

There is no village guesthouse, but you should have no trouble finding somewhere to stay as there's a school and a mission. The stream on the northern edge of town is where people bathe; women near the beach and men near the road. It's cool, clear and fast-flowing.

The escarpment continues on nearly to **Kontu village**, where the famous shark callers live. Between Messi and Kontu there are many rivers, some of which must be fjorded. Kontu is smaller than Messi but it's still a reasonable size. Men might be invited to stay in the haus-boi; women might be granted male status. Shark-calling implements are kept in the haus-boi.

From Kontu the road wanders inland a little and rises through some spectacular rainforest. There are fewer rivers to worry about but the road is dirt rather than crushed coral and can be slippery in the wet. It's a little rutted but still in quite good condition. At **Cape Timeis** the road runs near clifftops from where there are stunning views down to the sea below and along the coast.

Further on, past Namasalang, you come to Panamafei village and the Fangalawa crossing to the east coast. North of here the coastal road deteriorates.

LELET PLATEAU
This high plateau (over 1000 metres) is a very different place from the steamy coast. The climate is cool enough to grow vegetables and can get quite chilly. It's rolling country and there are no rivers; perhaps that is why rain magic is practised.

Apparently there's an enormously deep cave, as yet unfathomed, and there are bat caves near Mongop.

The villages up here – there are only four – are larger than those on the coast. As yet there is no commercial accommodation but there is talk of a guesthouse being built. If you visit Lelet, take some rice and perhaps a live chicken (preferably white) as a gift for your hosts.

There's now a road leading up to Lelet. Turn off the highway just after Malom village, about 30 km south of Konos. Because there are a fair number of trucks bringing vegetables down, you should be able to arrange a lift. Try asking around Kavieng market. Walking up is another possibility.

THE SOUTH

The southern 'bulge' of the island is still relatively isolated because the roads are not too good. The rugged mountains and heavy rainfall further complicate things. The people in the south are similar to the Tolais of East New Britain, but are less sophisticated than the other New Irelanders who have long been linked by the coast road.

There is a move to list the impressive Weitin Valley on the World Heritage register, as it is a rare rift valley – the point where two tectonic plates (the Pacific and Indian Ocean plates) meet. There are also a couple of high-altitude lakes.

Getting Around

Air There are airstrips at Manga and Silur which receive at least one flight from Rabaul. Currently there are no flights from Namatanai.

Road Along the east coast you can continue in a conventional vehicle from Namatanai through Samo to Danfu and from there to Rei by 4WD. It's possible, with great effort, to walk, canoe and boat right around the southern tip of the island. Logging companies are building roads in the south, especially on the west coast, but if they are anything like their roads on the rest of the island they might not last long. The road already goes south to Palabong and will extend to Wapi.

Walking On the way south from Namatanai, Samo is where the road used to start getting

really rough. After Warangansau village there is a big hill to Manga and the road is almost deserted after this point. There is a mission and an airstrip at Manga and plantations at Muliana and Manmo, just after Muliana village. After Manga you come to Maritboan Plantation. There is a small plantation near the end of the road.

From the end of the road in Rei it takes about two days to Srar village – ask the way from the villagers. From Srar to Maliom is fairly easy – a good, well cut path. After Maliom the paths get difficult and some sections of the coast can only be negotiated by canoe. Canoes are reasonable to hire and easily obtained. There is a path across the southern part of the peninsula or, if you are lucky enough to pick up a boat, you can go around to Lambom Island by the cape.

Cape St George is worth seeing, if you can fix it up. Canoes from Lambon to Lamassa are easy to find and there is a path from there all the way to Palabong – although it is better

The Johnson Cult

The people of New Hanover are best known for their brave attempt to buy the US President, Lyndon Johnson. When the first House of Assembly elections in PNG were held, the New Hanover voters decided, quite reasonably, that if this was democracy and they could vote for whoever they liked they might as well vote for Lyndon Johnson.

New Hanover went 'all the way with LBJ', but when the American President showed no sign of taking up the island's cause the islanders decided to take more direct action. They refused to pay their taxes and instead put the money into a fund to 'buy' him. They raised quite a large sum but even this example of Texas-style capitalism failed to bring the man to New Hanover.

Eventually the Johnson cult died out and the events were all but forgotten. Until someone on the island started selling Johnson outboard motors. Well, you can imagine... ■

to get a canoe from Kabisalao to Wapi. The road is meant to go from Palambong to Wapi, but the timber companies have been slow.

Grassroutes Ecotravel in Rabaul have treks around the south.

NEW HANOVER

The island of New Hanover (or Lavongai) is the second largest island in the province, a mountainous, isolated island with productive copra plantations on the volcanic soils of its coastline.

EASTERN ISLANDS

There are four island groups strung off the east coast of New Ireland – Tabar, Lihir, Tanga and Feni. They are only 30 to 50 km offshore and clearly visible from the coast. The islands are all quite beautiful and their inhabitants are great canoeists.

Tabar is thought to be the original home of the malangan carvings and ceremonies and traditional culture here remains strong. The Feni Islands are covered in dense, steamy jungle, and conform to the popular idea of 'primeval forest', and there are geysers to complete the picture.

Huge gold deposits have been found on Lihir Island and a big mining operation has begun. The only problem is that the ore is in the centre of a collapsed volcano caldera and the deeper they drill the hotter it gets. Gold has also been discovered on the Tabar Group.

Perhaps more interesting than Lihir are the nearby coral islands. These remote places have had little contact with the world, but the friendly villagers welcome travellers.

Even further out are the Nuguria Islands, composed mainly of uninhabited atolls. There is great diving and snorkelling here and there's apparently accommodation. The problem would be getting there.

Places to Stay

There is no organised accommodation on any of these islands so they are very much places for travellers with open-ended schedules who want to stay in villages. On the Tabar Group, men can probably stay in a haus-boi, but the strength of the traditional culture means that women are unlikely to be allowed to. It's best to arrange this with Noah Lurang, cultural officer in Kavieng, who comes from Tabar. There's a Catholic mission on Lihir where you can probably find a bed, but it's two hours by road from the airport and doesn't have a phone. You can, however, get there direct from Namatanai by an irregular boat.

Getting There & Away

There are a number of airstrips on the islands, most serviced by Islands Aviation or Airlink (see the Kavieng Getting There & Away section) and it is also possible to get out to them by local shipping services. There are boats running fairly frequently from Konos to Tatau Island in the Tabar Group, and some from Kavieng to Tatau. From Namatanai there's an occasional boat running to the mission on Lihir for about K5.

ST MATTHIAS GROUP

The islands of Mussau, Emirau and Tench

are some distance north-west of New Ireland; they put up a determined resistance to the European invasion. Tench was the last 'uncontrolled' part of the New Ireland region.

During the war there was an American base at Emirau with a larger force than the entire present-day population of the group. The people build fine, large canoes without outriggers, which can carry 30 or more people. Tench is also famous for woven mats. These islands and New Hanover make up the sub-province of Lamet – the name comes from the first letters of Lavongai (New Hanover), Mussau, Emirau and Tench.

Islands Aviation flies to both Emirau and Mussau; Airlink flies to Emirau. See the Kavieng Getting There & Away section.

Manus Province

Land Area 2100 sq km
Population 27,000

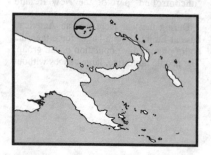

Manus is the most isolated and least visited province in PNG. It consists of a group of islands known as the Admiralty Islands plus a scattering of low-lying atolls. Manus Island, which gives the province its name, is the largest of the Admiralty Islands.

HISTORY

No significant archaeological research has been undertaken on Manus, so it is uncertain when the first settlers arrived and where they came from but they have probably been there for 10,000 years.

The islanders were sophisticated mariners and fishers with an extensive trade system. Their large sea-going outrigger canoes were up to 10 metres long, with two or three sails, and their fishing methods included fish traps and kite fishing. Trade linked the islands in the face of their geographic dispersion and the 26 different languages and dialects spoken in the region. The main social unit was the clan, and warfare between clans and tribes was commonplace.

A Spanish sailor, Alvaro de Saavedra, made the European discovery of the island in 1527, but although various Dutch and English explorers came past in the 17th and 18th centuries it was not until the late 19th century that serious contacts were made. Carteret, an Englishman, dubbed the islands the Admiralty group in 1767 and they were annexed, along with the rest of New Guinea, by Germany in 1885. German law and order, however, did not arrive on Manus until 1911. Some Spanish touches remain – the airport is on an island that is still called Los Negros.

Manus is a rugged, relatively infertile island and this, combined with the fierce independence of its inhabitants, encouraged the German and Australian colonisers to leave it pretty much alone. The Germans did plant coconut plantations on some of the

islands, but serious change did not arrive until WW II – and then it was pretty dramatic.

The Japanese occupied Manus in April 1942. In February 1944 American and Australian forces recaptured the island, causing a great deal of damage to villages, for the construction of a huge base to counterbalance the Japanese forces at Rabaul. Dock facilities were built around Seeadler Harbour and an airstrip capable of handling heavy bombers was built at Momote.

Untold millions of dollars were lavished on the base and at times as many as 600 Allied ships were anchored in Seeadler Harbour. All in all, a million Americans and Australians passed through. A year after the war ended, the Allies had gone, but not before they had scrapped everything. Not surprisingly, this display of Western technology and profligacy had quite an impact on the local people, an impact that anthropologist Margaret Mead described in her book *New Lives for Old*.

After the war a remarkable movement led by Paliau Moloat, put paid to old Manus. Although it was first treated simply as a cargo cult, it is now recognised as one of PNG's first post-war independence movements and as a force for modernisation. The movement brought together the diverse tribes of the islands in unified resistance to

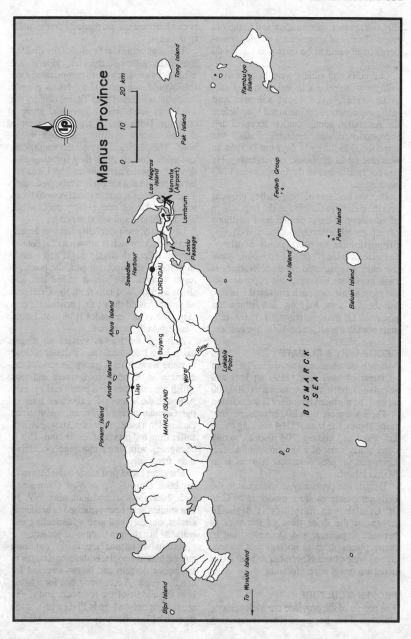

Manus Province

the Australian administration and to the old ways. It also had a significant religious component and came to be known as the Paliau Church.

Old cults and rituals were thrown over, villages were rebuilt in imitation of European styles, even local schools and self-government were instituted long before the Australian administration accepted that independence was inevitable. Paliau was imprisoned in the early days but in 1964 he was elected to the House of Assembly. He has not held a seat in the independent PNG parliament.

Perhaps because of their trading prowess and their early realisation of the importance of education, Manus people hold positions of responsibility throughout the country, disproportionate to their small numbers. Because of Manus' fragile economic base, the money repatriated by these workers is most important. Coconuts and copra are still the most significant cash crop on the island, but there is some logging, and fishing has potential. Of the approximately 35,000 citizens born in the province, 7000 live outside.

GEOGRAPHY & CLIMATE

Manus is the smallest province in PNG, both in terms of land area (2100 sq km) and population, but it has a vast sea area (200,000 sq km). Its northern boundary is the equator.

There are more than 200 islands, ranging from Manus, the largest (104 km long by 28 km wide) and highest (704 metres), to tiny coral atolls, most of which are uninhabited. Lorengau, the provincial headquarters, is on Manus Island.

Despite the proximity to the equator, the daily temperatures are a moderate 24°C to 30°C, although humidity is high. In Lorengau the drier time of the year is between September and December, but in many places there is no real wet season. Strong winds from November to March can make sea travel uncomfortable.

PEOPLE & CULTURE

The people of the province are Melanesians, although there has been some intermixing with Micronesians, particularly on the atolls to the west.

The population can be artificially divided into three, although the clan, village and tribal links are much more complicated than this would suggest. The Manus people (sometimes referred to as Titans) occupy the south and south-west islands and share a common language, Titan. These people depend entirely on fishing for their livelihood. The Matangol live to the south, east and north, and although they fish they also depend on some agriculture. The Usiai are inland people and are exclusively gardeners. There is further specialisation between those who make canoes, nets, pottery, coconut oil, obsidian blades and wood carvings.

Obviously, such specialisation was dependent on trade, which is known as the Kawas system. Although ritual, magic and friendship played an important part, the practical result was that the Manus traded fish and shells for sago and taro from the Usiai and all groups traded their own particular speciality. The obsidian blades from Lou Island were especially important.

Although the Kawas system no longer exists in its traditional form it does continue in some ways. This is partly because of the distribution of land, reefs, rivers and seas which are inherited on a patrilineal system. Although the Manus were allocated some of the German-planted coconut plantations they, and to a lesser extent the Matangol, still suffer from a shortage of fertile land. This is changing, with inter-marriage occurring more frequently.

Margaret Mead first studied the Manus in her book *Growing up in New Guinea* and came back for a second look after WW II. Her studies have been criticised in academic circles, but they still give a fascinating and readable insight into traditional society.

Extensive tattoos are fairly common among Manus people, with some designs in the public domain and others reserved for certain people. A common place for a tattoo is in the middle of the forehead, and if you see someone elsewhere in PNG with a tattoo there, it's likely that they come from Manus.

Top: Tolai sing-sing near Rabaul, New Britain (JM)
Bottom: Jacob the Kokomo, Kuru Village, New Ireland Province (JM)

Top: Village kids, (West Coast), New Ireland Province (JM)
Left: Malangan carving, Kavieng airport, New Ireland Province (JM)
Right: Shark caller and equipment, (West Coast), New Ireland Province (JM)

Despite its relative poverty, Manus has a good education system, and it shows – you can have some interesting conversations here. Four years of secondary schooling are compulsory, and students unable to attend the few secondary schools in the province use the radio 'School of the Air'. The facts almost match the theory, with over a third of the population having received at least six years of schooling. English is widely spoken, even in remote villages.

Carving has virtually died out in the province although the people of Bipi Island still do some – you can see examples in the Lorengau council office. Wooden bowls, stone spears and arrow heads were produced on Lou Island and shields and spears decorated with shark's teeth were produced on the North-Western Islands. Dancing is the most popular form of cultural activity.

MANUS & LOS NEGROS ISLANDS

Only two degrees south of the equator, Manus is a steamy, sleepy place, with inland jungle on the central limestone hills which rise to about 700 metres. There are many sharp ridges and streams. Los Negros is volcanic and rather more fertile than the main island.

Very few visitors come to the Manus and there are few tourist-oriented services.

Orientation & Information

The airport is at Momote on Los Negros Island and a good road serviced by PMVs connects it with the provincial capital, Lorengau, 27 km away on Manus. A bridge crosses the narrow Loniu Passage.

Lorengau (population 3900) is the provincial capital and the only town of any size on Manus, but it's still a small place. The town straggles along a nice bay, with the provincial government at one end and the market and main wharf at the other.

The tourism department (☎ 40 9361, fax 40 9218) is in the provincial government buildings. See if the planned booklet on Manus has been produced yet; if not Ronald Dipon, the friendly and enthusiastic tourist officer, will be able to give information.

Cyril Fitzgerald, the Avis agent, is also a good source of information.

There are both PNGBC and Westpac branches in Lorengau.

Lorengau has the only hospital in the province (there are many aid posts), and I met its sole doctor in Lae airport, making complex connections to get to Wuvulu – to perform a post mortem.

You'll find payphones at the post office but Manus is not yet part of the PTC's satellite network, so phone calls to and from the island can involve shouting.

Things to See & Do

There are the remains of the US base at Lombrum (now home to a much smaller PNG navy coastal patrol) and rusting relics scattered around. You can see some from the bridge across Loniu Passage. Seeadler Harbour, ringed by small islets and reefs, is very beautiful.

A crocodile farm is planned for Salamei, on Los Negros. Crocs are still fairly common on and around Manus, so take care.

Good places to swim include Salamei Beach, Rarah Island, a couple of km from Lorengau, and Tulu village, along the coast and accessible by boat from Lorengau and Andra Island. There is a waterfall and fresh water pool on the Lorengau River about five km upstream from town.

Manus is a shell-collector's paradise. Ron Knight senior has a good library of shell books, and at the Kohai Lodge you can see some shells on display. The vivid shells of the unique Manus Green Snail are featured on the provincial flag.

Buyang, a village in the centre of the island, has been suggested as a place where you might see traditional dancing. **Worei**, in the south near the coast, is on a river you can make canoe trips. There's apparently a guesthouse near Lokabia Point.

With all of the north coast bordered by a reef, the diving around Manus is superb, and by no means all of the sites have been explored. Visibility is reputed to be up to 60 metres and there is a fantastic variety of sea-life, with many large fish, as well as some wartime wrecks. Whales are sometimes seen from January to March.

Ron Knight (☎ 40 9159/9323, PO Box 108) is an experienced professional diver, although he isn't a registered instructor. He will take groups diving and hire them equipment (bring your own regulator), but you must be qualified. You'll find his store on a road leading to the waterfront near the market. A day's excursion with five dives costs K120, or you can hire equipment for K40 and find your own boat or hire one of his, which range from speedies to a new 30-footer. There are also overnight and longer trips, camping on islands or staying in villages. The dives offered sound very interesting, such as unexplored underwater caves, Manta Ray Passage on the isolated Hermit Islands, spectacular drop-offs, underwater volcano cones...

Places to Stay & Eat

On Los Negros, not far from the airport, the *Momote Tavern* (☎ 40 9061, PO Box 196) is undergoing renovations, so the price, currently K35 a room, will rise.

Campbell's Guesthouse has burned down so there is no inexpensive accommodation in Lorengau, although Ron Knight might be able to arrange discounts for people who dive with him, and perhaps tents. There are guesthouses on nearby islands – see the Islands Near Manus Island section.

Kohai Lodge (☎ 40 9004, PO Box 100) is on the main road into town, a km or so before the shopping centre. It's a pleasant and friendly place, on a low hill to catch the breezes. Motel-style singles/doubles with attached bathroom and fan cost K70/85; rooms with air-con in self-contained two-bedroom units are K75/90, all with breakfast. The fan rooms are much nicer. There's a lounge bar, where there are some books to read, and a restaurant serving lunch for about K6 and dinner from K10. They will collect you from the airport.

The *Lorengau Harbourside Hotel* (☎ 40 9093, PO Box 89) has a resort-style main building but most accommodation is in prefabricated huts, with a few larger motel-style units. A pool is planned and there's a small craft shop. The quality of accommodation is higher than at Kohai Lodge and the hotel is more centrally located, near the market, harbour and shopping centre, but it's surrounded by the only high fence in town and feels a little out of place on this easy-going island. All rooms have attached bathrooms and air-con, and the prices range from K80/95 to K90/103. The dining room serves little seafood; most dishes are of the meat-and-three-veg variety, with steaks costing from K12. Airport transfers are K15.

Tourism in Manus is being actively encouraged and village guesthouses may be opened on Manus and some of the outlying islands. At present, accommodation can be found at village social clubs or private houses. The rates are negotiable, but you won't have to pay more than K10 for a room at a village club. Take some food, partly so you can repay the local hospitality.

Getting There & Away

Air Air Niugini has regular flights but they are not all that frequent so plan ahead. See the Kavieng (New Ireland) Getting There & Away section for the schedule. Fares include: Port Moresby K206, Kavieng K106, Lae K145, Madang K109, Wewak K120.

The airport is one of PNG's less organised. People do get bumped off flights (I heard of a flight that left half an hour early to avoid a confrontation with unsuccessful passengers) and luggage gets misdirected. Reconfirm well in advance at the Air Niugini office in Lorengau (☎ 40 9092) and arrive at the airport with plenty of time to spare.

Sea A Lutheran Shipping freighter departs Lorengau on Friday for Madang, taking 24 hours and costing K21/26 in deck/cabin class, or Lae, 48 hours, K40/47. Coastal Shipping runs about once a month between Rabaul (K46/90) and Manus, via Kavieng (K32/80).

The *Tawi* is operated by the Manus Provincial Government and plies between Lorengau, the outer islands of Manus, Wuvulu Island,

Wewak and Madang. Theoretically, the *Tawi* makes about 30 voyages a year but it is often commandeered for government business so there is no real schedule and you could wait at least a month for it to show up. Lorengau to Wuvulu (K18) takes three days, and from there it's another day to Wewak (K28). The 24-hour voyage to Madang costs K17. All accommodation is deck class and you should take your own food. Some beds are available but conditions can be very cramped, especially while the *Tawi* is travelling along the Manus Island coast. You can get information from the Marine Office, a red building near the Neruse wharf (behind Steamships), which is where the *Tawi* docks. The office is open daily and the people are helpful.

Getting Around

PMV The road system is being extended, and it's possible to drive from Lorengau to the south coast and several inland villages. PMVs (trucks) cover the road network, including to the naval base at Lombrum and airport at Momote. There aren't many PMVs, however, and you should try flagging down any vehicle.

Car Rental The Avis agent is Cyril Fitzgerald (☎ 40 9207, PO Box 253, Lorengau), who generally meets incoming Air Niugini flights. His office in Lorengau is near the Harbourside Hotel. Avis charges the usual high rates, plus a K15 a day remote area surcharge. Cyril also hires older 4WD vehicles for a flat K80 per day, and these might be more useful than cars if you're exploring on the rough roads.

Sea 'Speedies' (small boats with outboard motors) come and go all the time, and you can often go along as a passenger. This is by far the cheapest way to get around, but it can be time-consuming. There are also larger work boats which take passengers. In Lorengau, speedies are usually found in the bay near the creek mouth; work boats usually dock at Neruse wharf, but try the main wharf as well.

You can charter canoes with outboards or,

Outrigger canoe

more common these days, speedies. The boat will cost only about K40 a day with a driver, but petrol is expensive and you'll pay another K10 to K20 an hour for running costs, depending on the size of the engine. If you charter one for 10 days you could make an interesting trip right around Manus. If the south-east winds are blowing you might have to stick to the north coast; the south coast if the north-east is blowing. The fishing is great, particularly along the north coast in the Seeadler Sea. There are guesthouses on some of the northern islands like Andra and Ahus, but on others you can arrange to be put up by asking your captain.

From November to March, strong winds can make travel in small boats uncomfortable and even impossible.

ISLANDS NEAR MANUS ISLAND

On **Andra Island**, north-west of Lorengau and K5 by speedie, there's a good village guesthouse. The nightly charge is K10 and you have to take your own food but the friendly Andra people will cook it for you and might be able to add fish and shell-fish. You can hire canoes on Andra and, as the island is on the reef which runs along the north coast of Manus, it's a good place to snorkel. You don't need to book. There isn't a phone on the island but if you want more information go to the provincial government offices and see the tourist officer or find Paula Nakam in the Health Department. Andra is her home island.

A more up-market guesthouse is being built on **Ahus Island**, near Andra but a little closer to Lorengau. It will cost about K35 per person. Contact Ron Knight in Lorengau for more information.

Lou Island (pronounced 'low') is an old volcano and is particularly fertile and beautiful. There are hot springs. Lou was once an important source of obsidian (volcanic glass used for tools), which was traded through the south-west Pacific. In Rei, the main village, there's a guesthouse charging about K10 a night. About four speedies run from Lorengau each day (fewer or none on Sunday). It takes about 1½ hours and the

fare is about K15. The crossing can be very choppy.

There's a village guesthouse planned on tiny **Pam Island**, south of Lou, from where you can get a boat. East of Lou is the **Fedarb** group, which includes beautiful **Sivisa Island**. About 15 km north of Sivisa is **Tilianu** atoll, inhabited by seafarers who apparently still use large canoes with sails. Dive parties camp here, and about the only food available is lobsters...

WUVULU ISLAND

Wuvulu is less than 200 km from Wewak and is according to all descriptions the perfect tropical island. There are no rivers or creeks discharging into the sea so the water is incredibly clear, and visibility can be around 50 metres.

The diving and snorkelling is superb, with coral, and sharks. Apparently, the islanders are mainly Seventh Day Adventists, who don't eat sea turtles, so there are many around. May to July are supposed to be the best months for diving. One traveller suggests that you keep a close track of depth and time if you dive here.

The Wuvulu islanders are closely akin to Micronesians and still make distinctive canoes, some large enough to hold 40 people. There are two villages on the island, Aunna (sunrise) and Onne (sunset).

Places to Stay & Eat

Wuvulu Lodge (PO Box 1071, Wewak, East Sepik Province) has accommodation for 12 people at about K40 for full board. The meals are good, and there's diving equipment for hire. Onne has a guesthouse, which charges about K10 for basic accommodation and around K1 for good meals.

Getting There & Away

Wuvulu is very difficult to get to, although that could be part of the attraction. There are no longer any scheduled air services, and the only regular boat going there is the Manus government's *Tawi*, but that isn't very regular. Or reliable – one traveller reports heading off from Wewak on the *Tawi* but returning a couple of days later because the captain couldn't find Wuvulu! Perhaps that's understandable, as the island is marked 'position approximate' on some charts. Food such as rice can run short on Wuvulu, because of the unreliable boat service.

People from Wuvulu who work in Wewak occasionally club together to charter a plane for a visit home, and you might be able to join in. Rose Johnson, who works at Air Niugini, comes from Wuvulu and might have information. If there are a few of you, taking your own charter from Wewak or Vanimo (cheaper) might not be too expensive.

There is talk of developing dive packages including the Walindi Dive Resort (West New Britain), Kavieng (New Ireland) and Wuvulu, so ask around. Sea New Guinea

(☎ (02) 267 5563, fax (02) 267 6118, 100 Clarence St, Sydney 2000, Australia) might have information.

OTHER ISLANDS

The other islands in Manus Province are principally low-lying coral atolls where coconut palms are virtually the only thing that will grow. The main group, scattered hundreds of km north-west of Manus, are known as the **North-Western Islands**. The people are fine canoeists and, as there are no suitable trees on their tiny islands, they are said to construct their ocean-going canoes from logs that have floated down the Sepik and out to sea.

Bipi Island, off the western end of Manus, is famed for its fine carvings.

North Solomons Province

Land Area 9400 sq km
Population 165,000

The islands that comprise the North Solomons (Buka, Bougainville and a scattering of smaller atolls) are more closely related to the neighbouring, independent Solomon Islands than they are to much of PNG – just as the name suggests. The major island, Bougainville, is green, rugged and little developed, yet it provides a very considerable portion of PNG's gross national product from the massive open-cut copper mine at Panguna – at least it did until the Bougainville Revolutionary Army closed down the mine.

Due to the rebellion on Bougainville and the PNG government's blockade of the island (see the following History section), visitors are not permitted, and it will be a long time before the situation returns to normal. Buka Island has suffered less, but you should still be cautious about visiting, even if it is legally possible.

This chapter is included in case the situation improves, but that seems unlikely in the next few years. Even if Bougainville is made safe enough for the mine to re-open it's unlikely that the rest of the island's infrastructure, heavily damaged in the fighting and by the rebels, will be quickly repaired. Many people were herded into 'care centres', so even villages will have to be re-established. Prices will be sky-high, travel will be restricted and there will be a lot of guns and angry people around.

HISTORY

It is not known from where, or when the first settlers arrived on Bougainville. It is possible that the present dark-skinned Melanesians who inhabit the island first settled as long as 30,000 years ago.

Bougainville acquired its very French name from the explorer Louis Antoine de

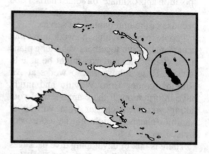

Bougainville who sailed up the east coast in 1768. Near the narrow passage which separates Bougainville from Buka he came across natives paddling long, artistically carved canoes. They greeted him with cries of 'Buka, Buka' which Bougainville promptly named their island. Actually, *buka* simply means 'who' or 'what' – a very reasonable question to ask! Of course Bougainville was not the first European to drop by; Torres passed by in 1606.

A hundred years later, Catholic missionaries attempted to set up a station at Kieta. They were driven away on their first attempt, but they were more successful the second time around. Bougainville and Buka were considered part of the Solomons group, which was a British possession, until 1898, when they were traded to Germany. The Germans added them to their New Guinea colony and set up copra plantations along the coast, and in return the British had their ascendancy over Vavau in Tonga and the other islands in the Solomons confirmed. Australia seized the North Solomons, along with the rest of New Guinea, at the start of WW I. The Bougainvilleans, however, had a reputation for being 'difficult' and although the island was thoroughly explored by the Australian administration, by the start of WW II the only development was still on the coast.

In mid-1942 the Japanese arrived, swiftly defeated the Australians, and held most of the island until the end of the war. Buka in the north became an important air base, Shortland Island (part of the Solomons) was a major naval base and Buin, at the southern tip of Bougainville, was an equally important base for ground troops.

Australian coastwatchers scored some notable successes on Bougainville, particularly during the battle for Guadalcanal. Jack Read, a district officer, and Paul Mason, a plantation owner, retreated into the jungle after the Japanese occupation. Read watched over Buka Passage, near his former station, while Mason set himself up near Buin in the south. Bomber aircraft from Rabaul and bound for Guadalcanal passed over Buka and Buin and the fighters were based right at Buka, allowing the coastwatchers to give the Allied forces a two-hour warning of impending air strikes. This knowledge gave the Allies a tremendous advantage in what many regard as a crucial battle – a turning point in the Pacific war. Miraculously, Paul Mason and Jack Read both survived, despite determined efforts by the Japanese to track them down.

In November 1943, American troops captured the west coast port of Torokina and, in 1944, Australian forces started to fight their way south towards Buin. Fortunately, the war ended before they came into direct confrontation with the main Japanese force. Nevertheless, the cost of the war in Bougainville was staggering. Of 80,000 Japanese troops only 23,000 were finally taken prisoner: 20,000 are thought to have been killed in action and the remaining 37,000 died in the jungles of disease and starvation.

After the war Bougainville returned to normal – a mixture of quiet, subsistence farming and fishing villages and a few plantations. The district headquarters was transferred from Kieta to Sohano in Buka Passage but found its way back to Kieta in 1960.

Then, in 1964, a major copper discovery at Panguna revolutionised Bougainville. Over K400 million was invested in the development of the mine and its ancillary operations. A new town, roads, a power station and a port were all constructed from scratch. And thousands of workers from around PNG and the world descended, bringing with them a cash economy and all its attendant vices. The district headquarters is now at Arawa, the main dormitory town for the mine. The mine was developed by Bougainville Copper Ltd (BCL), a subsidiary of Australia's CRA, itself a subsidiary of the British Rio Tinto Zinc.

Secession & War

In the lead-up to independence, Bougainville was a strong part of the push for an independent grouping of the Bismarck Archipelago islands. That plan quickly faded, but around 1975 strong Bougainville secessionist movements sprang up, with Father John Momis as one of the leaders. Partly to offset this pressure, the North Solomons was granted provincial government, and the 'me too' reaction from the rest of the country has seen PNG burdened with all those provincial governments.

Meanwhile, the Panguna mine went ahead, huge royalties flowed to the landowners and the PNG government, expat enclaves were established and everything seemed rosy.

However, a new generation was growing up. A small group of traditional landowners was doing very well out of the mine, but not much community development was taking place. Nor, it was claimed, were these landowners even the legitimate recipients of the royalties, and anyway, the environmental destruction caused by the mine was affecting many more people than those directly compensated for it.

Many people had been against Panguna in the first place, and there was a growing feeling that the people had been cheated in the initial negotiations with CRA – that in their innocence they had signed away their land without realising the consequences, and they had not been given enough money for doing so. Criticism of CRA's parent company in Richard West's influential book

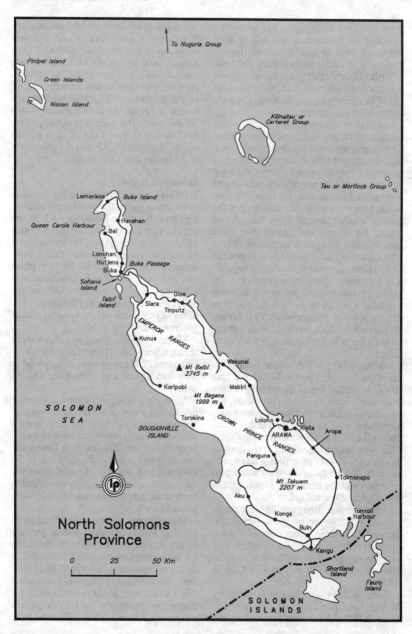

To Nuguria Group

Pinipel Island

Green Islands

Nissan Island

Kilinailau or
Carteret Group

Tau or Mortlock Group

Lemankoa *Buka Island*

Hanahan

Queen Carola Harbour

Bel

Lonohan
Hutjena   *Buka Passage*
Buka

*Sohano
Island*

*Taiof
Island*

Dios

Siara

Tinputz

EMPEROR RANGES

Kunua

Wakunai

*SOLOMON
SEA*

Mt Balbi
2745 m

Koripobi

Mabiri

Mt Bagana
1999 m

Torokina

Loloho

CROWN PRINCE

Kieta

*BOUGAINVILLE
ISLAND*

ARAWA

Aropa

RANGES

Panguna

Mt Takuam
2207 m

Tolmonapu

Aku

Tonnoli
Harbour

Konga

Buin

**North Solomons
Province**

Kangu

0   25   50 Km

*Shortland
Island*

*Fauro
Island*

*SOLOMON
ISLANDS*

River of Tears, also fuelled fears about foreign control of PNG's economy and an apartheid-style situation developing. Sean Dorney, in his excellent book *Papua New Guinea*, says that the rebels later wore T-shirts printed with 'River of Tears'.

In 1987 the Panguna Landowners' Association was formed, lead by Pepetua Sereo and Francis Ona, as an alternative to the previous group who were seen as puppets of BCL. It demanded better environmental protection, huge back-payments of profits from the mine and US$10 *billion* in compensation.

Not surprisingly, these demands were not met, and in 1988 the Bougainville Revolutionary Army (BRA) began to sabotage the mine. Relations between the police sent to protect the mine and the locals deteriorated sharply. Several politicians, including the premier, were beaten-up by police, and the police and workers from other parts of PNG came under attack from the BRA.

Increasing attacks on mine workers resulted in the mine closing altogether in late 1989. This was an enormous blow to the PNG economy, although Ok Tedi and the new Highlands gold mines have meant that it was not a disaster.

After the mine closed a state of emergency was declared, the PNG army moved in and the conflict spread to the rest of the island. Whole villages were moved into so-called care centres, outside areas of BRA control. To make sure the people moved, the army burned their villages and stories about rape and murder by the army flooded out of Bougainville. The Panguna issue had become a civil war.

In 1990, the international concern about human rights violations and the hopelessness of a war which was costing many lives on both sides lead the PNG government to simply give up on Bougainville, withdrawing all its forces and instituting a blockade.

The blockade resulted in great hardship to the people of Bougainville. News from the island since then has been highly unreliable, but it seems likely that the BRA has been committing some atrocities of its own.

Paius Wingti won the 1992 elections partly on a platform of solving the Bougainville problem, but his solution has been to simply send back the army. The situation remains confused and the blockade is still in force.

The BRA has evaded the blockade by bringing over supplies from the nearby Solomon Islands, and the PNG army has caused international tensions by raiding suspected BRA bases in the Solomons, killing a few innocent people in the process.

The PNG army now controls most of Bougainville's main centres but the BRA still controls large areas of jungle. Francis Ona has offered to surrender if it is negotiated under church supervision, but Wingti has rejected this and calls for the unconditional surrender of the rebels. Still, it seems that the leaders might eventually reach an agreement.

Unfortunately, that won't help solve what has been a major problem all along – the angry young men with guns. The PNG army probably doesn't have the resources to hunt them all down and the politicians certainly don't have the will – things would get very much nastier than they have been if the army tried to defeat the BRA in a no-holds-barred war.

If most members of the BRA don't go along with a negotiated surrender, an ugly little guerrilla war could boil along almost indefinitely.

GEOGRAPHY

Bougainville is about 200 km long and 60 to 100 km wide and covered in wild, generally impenetrable jungle. There are two major mountain ranges – in the south the Crown Prince Ranges and in the north the higher Emperor Ranges. The highest mountain is Mt Balbi at 2745 metres; Balbi is an active volcano, like its smaller and more spirited cousin Mt Bagana, and is visible from both coasts. The coastal areas are extremely fertile and most of the population is concentrated along them.

Buka, in the north, is separated from Bougainville by a channel only 300 metres wide and a km long. Tidal currents rush through the passage at up to eight knots. In the south Buka is hilly, reaching 400 metres at its highest point. Buka is generally low-lying, apart from this southern hill region, and very wet – annual rainfall is over six metres. There are many coral islands off its south and west coast.

PEOPLE

The people of Bougainville and Buka are often collectively referred to as Bukas and the early German colonisers favoured them due to their energy and abilities. The Bougainville people are instantly recognisable anywhere in PNG due to their extremely dark skins, said to be the blackest in the world. There are 19 different languages on Bougainville.

The Bougainvilleans' relative affluence has, like the Tolai of East New Britain, led to a reluctance to perform the dull work on copra plantations and copra-labourers are imported from other parts of the country. Many people, however, still live in bush-material villages and depend on shifting agriculture for their food.

The Bougainvilleans are proud of their traditions and culture and, despite the strong influence of the church, are determined to retain them. Always ask permission before entering a village and then ask to see the head man.

Fishing

People on the islands north-west of Buka Passage still occasionally fish by the unique kite and spider web method. A woven palm leaf kite is towed behind a canoe and a lure, made of a wad of spider webs, is skilfully bounced along the surface of the sea. Garfish, leaping at the lure, get their teeth entangled in the web and are then hauled in.

ARTS

Apart from intricately woven Buka baskets, there are few artefacts still made on Bougainville, although prior to the arrival of the missions, many elaborate carvings were kept in men's houses.

Buka baskets are made from jungle vine. The variation in colour is made by scraping the skin off the vine. They're amongst the most skilfully made baskets in the Pacific, but with prices up towards K20 they're strictly tourist items and are rarely used for food holders as they were originally intended.

KIETA & ARAWA

Kieta and Arawa, virtually contiguous, have been severely damaged and remain off-limits.

Orientation

Coming north from the airport you first go through Toniva, a suburb of Kieta, then Kieta, which is now virtually a suburb of Arawa, and then 10 km east (over the Kieta Peninsula) Arawa, the main town.

Four km north-west of Arawa is Loloho on Arawa Bay. This is the port to which the copper concentrate was piped down from Panguna, the site of the power station and home to many of the mine workers. There's an attractive beach. The mine itself is high in the mountains, often shrouded in cloud and rain, about 28 km drive south-west from Arawa.

Place to Stay

The new *Kieta Hotel* was torched, but the staff quarters are intact and could take guests as soon as the blockade is lifted. Prices will be very, very high.

BOUGAINVILLE COPPER – PANGUNA

High in the centre of Bougainville is one of the world's largest artificial holes – Bougainville Copper's gigantic open-cut mine at Panguna.

A geological expedition discovered copper reserves at Panguna in 1964 and by 1967 the size of the deposit was known to be large enough to justify cutting an access road from Kobuna. Progress from that point was rapid: in 1969 construction of the mining project started, advance sales of copper were made, the temporary road was upgraded and port facilities were constructed. At the peak period for construction, before the mine started commercial operation in 1972, 10,000 people were employed.

Before it was closed by the BRA, 4000 people worked for Bougainville Copper and approximately one in five were foreigners.

BUIN

Buin, in the south of the island, has suffered less damage than Kieta/Arawa, but it's still off-limits. Buin is extremely wet from November to April. It is here that the finely made Buka baskets are woven – not, as the name might suggest, at Buka Island in the north. During the war Buin was the site of a very large Japanese army base and the area is packed with rusting relics of the war.

The extensive Japanese fortifications came to nothing because the Australians landed north of Torokina and moved south, instead of making the frontal attack the Japanese had expected. You can see much wreckage at Lamuai and on the Kahili Plantation which you can walk to from Buin.

Before the troubles there was a district office, a couple of trade stores, a PNGBC bank, and an interesting, bustling market, with many people coming from the Shortland Islands in the Solomons to sell fish.

Getting There & Away

There's a good unsealed road from Aropa south to Buin. It's an attractive, interesting drive of about three hours. You can complete a circuit and come back through Panguna if you have your own transport, but the road fjords several fast-flowing rivers, which would be pretty tough going after rain.

AROUND BUIN

Apart from the formidable base the Japanese developed, there were plans for resettling a huge number of civilian Japanese in the area – at a place called Little Tokyo. There were plans to develop some village guesthouses in the area, including at the beautiful Tonnoli Harbour.

If you take the road straight through Buin, you come to an intersection; turn right to head back to Arawa through Siwai and Panguna, left to Malabita village or straight ahead for Kangu Beach. If you head for Kangu Beach, keep driving for 10 to 15 minutes until you spot a small overgrown bunker on the right and a track just past it. This goes through to an open area with a couple of pill boxes and a gun pointing forlornly out to sea. The beach is a long stretch of sand, with islands hovering on the horizon. If you don't turn off to Kangu Beach, you come to the little cove where the open boats from the Shortland Islands pull in and past that you come to a collapsed bridge and an attractive village.

Admiral Yamamoto's Aircraft Wreck

The most historically interesting wreck in the area is the aircraft of Admiral Isoroku Yamamoto – the man who planned the attack on Pearl Harbor. On 18 April 1943 he left Rabaul in a Betty Bomber, accompanied by a protective group of Zeros. He did not realise that the Japanese naval code had been broken by the Americans and that US fighters would be waiting for him near Buin. As his aircraft approached the south of Bougainville the US P-38s pounced, shooting down Yamamoto's aircraft and scoring an enormous psychological victory over the Japanese.

The wreckage of Yamamoto's Betty still lies in the jungle, only a few km off the Panguna-Buin road. It is well signposted, near the village of Aku, 24 km before Buin, and a path has been cut through the jungle from the road. It's a one-hour walk. Unfortunately, there's a bitter feud between the landowners, who tried unsuccessfully to sell a wing to Japan, and the government, who stopped them. As a result, access to the plane is either completely blocked, or it costs about K20 per person, depending on the mood of the local big man.

In 1968, only 400 metres from the Buin-Kangu Hill road, an American Corsair fighter was discovered, where it had crashed in November '43, its pilot still in the cockpit. Just down the beach from the hill itself is a Catholic mission whose small plantation contains three more bombers.

NORTH TO BUKA

There's a rough road running up the east coast of Bougainville from Kieta to Kokopau on the Buka Passage. Not all of the rivers are bridged so this is a 4WD adventure. On the way you can stop at Wakunai where spears and other traditional weapons can be bought at the Wakunai Marketing Coop. From Wakunai you can make a three-day trip to climb Mt Balbi, 2743 metres, the highest mountain on Bougainville. From the summit of this extinct volcano you can see Mt Bagana (1999 metres) the most active volcano in PNG.

BUKA PASSAGE

The narrow channel that separates Bougainville from Buka is steeped in history and legends and packed with beautiful islands. It's also thick with fish just waiting to be hauled out. Sohano Island, in the centre of the passage, was the district headquarters from just after the war until 1960. There was a guesthouse on the island and a free government ferry. Nearby Tchibo Rock features in many colourful local legends.

Saposa was a popular picnic spot and an old meeting ground on the island is marked by traditional carved posts. Various war relics, including the wreckage of a Japanese fighter in the mangrove swamps, can be seen around Sohano. The current flows through the Buka Passage extremely swiftly and the pontoon that crosses the passage charged K6 per vehicle. There was a market at Buka Passage on Wednesday, Friday and Saturday and a number of Chinese trade stores.

Place to Stay

The *Buka Luman Guesthouse* (☎ 96 6057), PO Box 251, Buka Passage, on Sohano Island used to be the District Commissioner's residence. It's on Sohano Island in the passage, reached by the free ferry.

BUKA

Population 20,000

A crushed coral road runs up the east coast of Buka Island, connecting the copra plantations. Construction of the road caused some local strife between the local council and the

locally organised Hahalis Welfare Society, centred around Hanahan. Both of them insisted that road construction was their prerogative and members of the society refused to pay the head tax. Even more colourful was their Hahalis baby farm in the '60s which had a certain flavour of organised prostitution about it. Read John Ryan's *The Hot Land* for the full story.

Hutjena, in the south-east, is the main town and site for the Buka airstrip. Queen Carola Harbour, on the west coast, is the main port on Buka.

Place to Stay

The *Buka Lodge* (☎ 96 6057), PO Box 251, Buka, is in the town of Buka.

Getting There & Away

Airlink (☎ 92 1712, fax 92 1917) and Islands Aviation (☎ 92 2900, fax 92 2812) have frequent services to Buka and some of the outer islands from Rabaul. Coastal Shipping (☎ 92 2859, fax 92 2090, PO Box 423) has freighters to Buka and Nissan Island approximately weekly for K34, deck class.

OUTER ISLANDS

There are a scattering of islands far away from Bougainville and Buka which, nevertheless, come under North Solomons jurisdiction. Some are as easily accessible from New Ireland as from the North Solomons.

Nuguria (Fead) Group

The 50-odd islands in the group have a total area of only five sq km and a population of not much over 200 Polynesians. They are about 200 km east of New Ireland and a similar distance north of Buka.

Nukumanu (Tasman) Islands

Nukumanu is the largest island in the group with an area of less than three sq km. They lie about 400 km north-east of Bougainville and much closer to the extensive Ontong Java Atoll in the Solomon Islands. The population is about 300 Polynesians.

Kilinailau (Carteret) Group
Only 70 km north-east of Buka they comprise six islands on a 16 km circular atoll. The population of about 900 are Buka people who appear to have supplanted earlier Polynesian inhabitants.

Tau (Mortlock) Group
About 195 km north-east of Bougainville the ring-shaped reef has about 20 islands, virtually mid-way on a line drawn from the Carteret to the Tasman Islands. The population of around 600 is predominantly Polynesian.

Green Islands
The Green Islands are on an atoll about 16 km by eight km which lies approximately 70 km north-west of Buka. Nissan is the large elliptical island and the smaller ones lie within its curve. Nissan and Pinipel Island, a little further north, are the only islands in the group which are inhabited. Total population is about 3200.

The textbook-perfect atoll was totally evacuated during WW II and a large American airbase was operated here. After the war vast quantities of supplies were dumped and thousands of drums of fuel were sold at only US$0.13 a litre. There was no shortage of war surplus material in New Guinea.

Getting There & Away
Coastal Shipping (☎ 92 2859, fax 92 2090, PO Box 423) has freighters to Nissan Island approximately weekly for K34, deck class. Airlink (☎ 92 1712, fax 92 1917) and Islands Aviation (☎ 92 2900, fax 92 2812) might fly here.

Index

THANKS

Thanks to all the following travellers and others (apologies if we've misspelt your name) who took time to write to us about their experiences of PNG.

To those whose names have been omitted through oversight – apologies – your time and efforts are appreciated.

Lon Abbott (USA), Zoara Alfandari (Isr), Eden Aminoffe (Isr), B Andersen (DK), Traxler Andreas (A), Nick Askew (AUS), Jonatan/Michal Assaf (Isr), John Atkins (PNG), Sean Banville (UK), Anat Barak (Isr), John Barnard (AUS), Andrew Bartley (UK), Bob Bates (PNG), Marc Batschkus (D), Erez Bendet, Ellen Benjamin (USA), Andre Bergstrom (S), Michael Biltoft (AUS), Inge Bollen (D), Andrew Bolton (AUS), Craig Boutlis (AUS), Chris Bradley, Jens Bruun (DK), Guy Buchanan (AUS), Mitchell F Bunkin (USA), Frank Butler (PNG), Jeff Butt (AUS), Magdalen Carroll, Paul Chatterton (AUS), Richard & Theresa Crislip (USA), Tom Cutrofello (USA), Andre D'Cruz (AUS), Donald J Daniels (PNG), Karen Davidson (PNG), Saskia de Jonge, William de Prado (USA), Captain Denis (PNG), Harold Down (AUS), John & Anne Eddison, Nati Elinson (Isr), Shy Eran (Isr), Henrik Eriksen (DK), Howard Evans (USA), David M Filkins (USA), John Fitzgerald (PNG), Dr Peter Freeman (UK), Bob Fuller (AUS), G P George (UK), Don Gilder (PNG), Don Gilder Jnr (USA), Bo Girst (PNG), B Gitterman (USA), Silvia Gonzales (Sp), Noah Goodis (C), Rich Gregory (AUS), Richard Gregory-Smith, Yanny Guman (PNG), Robert Hallam (UK), Sr Molly Hargadine (PNG), Josje Hebbes (NL), Diana Hollingsworth, Rick Hudson (USA), John Hunter (USA), Brendon Hyde (AUS), Rick Jali (USA), Lucas Kawage (PNG), Kevin O Kelly, Danny Kennedy (PNG), Robert Kennington (NZ), Jesta Koning (NL), Deborah Koons (USA), Ortwin Krause (PNG), Jan Krupnick (USA), Bron Larner (PNG), John Lawrence III (USA), K Lawson (PNG), Tim Lee (UK), Xavier Lefaure (F), Steve Lewis (AUS), Avi Lugasi (Isr), Jim Mackay, Andrew Martin (PNG), Erna & Harold Mazeland (NL), Gerry McGrade (PNG), Brendan McGrath, Peter McLean, Mon & Brian McNamara (AUS), Alain Menager (Fr), Joy Merrett (PNG), John Miles (UK), Paul Millis (UK), R Mireba (PNG), Shirin Moayyad (PNG), Claire B Moran (UK), Dominique Moroni (CH), David Mortimer (AUS), Dennis Morton (UK), Debe Moskowitz (USA), Mrs D Naman (UK), Daniel Nuitten (B), Edgar O'Neill (PNG), Donal O'Sullivan (IRL), Matt Oldfield (UK), Nancy Opperman (USA), Larry Orsak (USA), Larry Orsak, Elizabeth Owers (AUS), Peter Parks (UK), Vicki Pauli (AUS), Alex Peachey (AUS), Vin Pellegrino, Nitsan Penso (Isr), Steven Philp (PNG), Tsri & Dzdia Piran (Isr), Sylvie Ple (F), Dan Pool (USA), Aihi Poreni (PNG), Dianne Portelance (USA), Lynette Regan (AUS), Ehud Reiter (USA), Martin Reynolds , Jim Reynolds (USA), Ofir Ronen (Isr), Karen Rosenjweg (C), Karen Roseryweg (C), Heidi Sanchez (USA), Dr Sanjay Sathed, G F Scheuermann (C), Ross Seager (AUS), Simon Shillater (UK), Tiana Sidey (UK), Mr Bonny Simbakwa (PNG), Robyn Slarke, Stephen Bruce Smith (AUS), David Sparks, Greg Stathakis (USA), Scott Stengel (USA), D M & J Steven (PNG), Judy Stoel, Ralf Stüttgen (PNG), Rose Tarere (PNG), Frank Taylor (AUS), Jesper Thorup (DK), Jacob Timmer (NL), Steve Tomlinson (AUS), Jim Torresen (N), Sepik Express Travel PNG (PNG), John Vail, Angus Vail (AUS), Ron Vanden (C), Kurt von Rosador (D), Dr Jurg Wassmann (CH), Elizabeth Waters (USA), Richard White (USA), Aarn Whitehouse (AUS), Heidi Wilhelmstroop (AUS), Mr & Mrs S Wilkie, Mr A S Wilson (PNG), Stuart Worboys

A-Austria, AUS-Australia, C-Canada, CH-Switzerland, D-Germany, DK-Denmark, IRL-Ireland, Isr-Israel, N-Norway, NL-Netherlands, NZ-New Zealand, PNG-Papua New Guinea, Sp-Spain, S-Sweden, UK-United Kingdom, USA-United States of America.

Keep in touch!

We love hearing from you and think you'd like to hear from us.

The Lonely Planet Newsletter covers the when, where, how and what of travel. (AND it's free!)

When...is the right time to see reindeer in Finland?
Where...can you hear the best palm-wine music in Ghana?
How...do you get from Asunción to Areguá by steam train?
What...should you leave behind to avoid hassles with customs in Iran?

To join our mailing list just contact us at any of our offices. (details below)

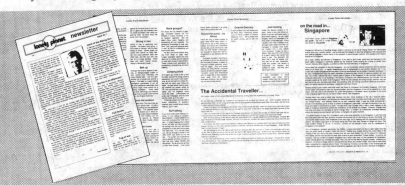

Every issue includes:

- *a letter from Lonely Planet founders Tony and Maureen Wheeler*
- *travel diary from a Lonely Planet author - find out what it's really like out on the road*
- *feature article on an important and topical travel issue*
- *a selection of recent letters from our readers*
- *the latest travel news from all over the world*
- *details on Lonely Planet's new and forthcoming releases*

Also available Lonely Planet T-shirts. 100% heavy weight cotton (S, M, L, XL)

LONELY PLANET PUBLICATIONS

Australia: PO Box 617, Hawthorn, 3122, Victoria (tel: 03-819 1877)
USA: Embarcadero West, 155 Filbert Street, Suite 251, Oakland, CA 94607 (tel: 510-893 8555)
UK: Devonshire House, 12 Barley Mow Passage, Chiswick, London W4 4PH (tel: 081-742 3161)

Guides to the Pacific

Australia – a travel survival kit
The complete low-down on Down Under – home of Ayers Rock, the Great Barrier Reef, extraordinary animals, cosmopolitan cities, rainforests, beaches ... and Lonely Planet!

Bushwalking in Australia
Two experienced and respected walkers give details of the best walks in every state, covering many different terrains and climates.

Islands of Australia's Great Barrier Reef – a travel survival kit
The Great Barrier Reef is one of the wonders of the world – and one of the great travel destinations! Whether you're looking for a tropical island resort or a secluded island hideaway, this guide has all the facts you'll need.

Melbourne city guide
From historic houses to fascinating churches and famous nudes to tapas bars, cafés and bistros – Melbourne is a dream for gourmands and a paradise for party goers.

Sydney city guide
A wealth of information on Australia's most exciting city; all in a handy pocket-sized format.

Fiji – a travel survival kit
Whether you prefer to stay in camping grounds, international hotels, or something in-between, this comprehensive guide will help you to enjoy the beautiful Fijian archipelago.

Hawaii – a travel survival kit
Share in the delights of this island paradise – and avoid some of its high prices – with this practical guide. Covers all of Hawaii's well-known attractions, plus plenty of uncrowded sights and activities.

Micronesia – a travel survival kit
The glorious beaches, lagoons and reefs of these 2100 islands would dazzle even the most jaded traveller. This guide has all the details on island-hopping across the north Pacific.

New Caledonia – a travel survival kit
This guide shows how to discover all that he idyllic islands of New Caledonia have to offer – from French colonial culture to traditional Melanesian life.

New Zealand – a travel survival kit
This practical guide will help you discover the very best New Zealand has to offer – Maori dances and feasts; some of the most spectacular scenery in the world; and every outdoor activity imaginable.

Tramping in New Zealand
Call it tramping, hiking, walking, bushwalking, or trekking – travelling by foot is the best way to explore New Zealand's natural beauty. Detailed descriptions of 20 walks of varying length and difficulty.

Rarotonga & the Cook Islands – a travel survival kit
Rarotonga and the Cook Islands have history, beauty and magic to rival the better-known islands of Hawaii and Tahiti, but the world has virtually passed them by.

Samoa – a travel survival kit
Two remarkably different countries, Western Samoa and American Samoa offer some wonderful island escapes, and Polynesian culture at its best..

Solomon Islands – a travel survival kit
The Solomon Islands are the best-kept secret of the Pacific. Discover remote tropical islands, jungle covered volcanoes and traditional Melanesian villages with this detailed guide.

Tahiti & French Polynesia – a travel survival kit
Tahiti's idyllic beauty has seduced sailors, artists and traveller for generations. The latest edition provides full details on the main island of Tahiti, the Tuamotos, Marquesas and other island groups. Invaluable information for independent travellers and package tourists alike.

Tonga – a travel survival kit
The only South Pacific country never to be colonised by Europeans, Tonga has also been ignored by tourists. The people of this far-flung island group offer some of the most sincere and unconditional hospitality in the world.

Also available:
Papua New Guinea phrasebook.

Lonely Planet Guidebooks

Lonely Planet guidebooks cover every accessible part of Asia as well as Australia, the Pacific, South America, Africa, the Middle East, Europe and parts of North America. There are five series: *travel survival kits*, covering a country for a range of budgets; *shoestring guides* with compact information for low-budget travel in a major region; *walking guides*; *city guides* and *phrasebooks*.

Australia & the Pacific
Australia
Bushwalking in Australia
Islands of Australia's Great Barrier Reef
Fiji
Melbourne city guide
Micronesia
New Caledonia
New Zealand
Tramping in New Zealand
Papua New Guinea
Bushwalking in Papua New Guinea
Papua New Guinea phrasebook
Rarotonga & the Cook Islands
Samoa
Solomon Islands
Sydney city guide
Tahiti & French Polynesia
Tonga
Vanuatu
Victoria

South-East Asia
Bali & Lombok
Bangkok city guide
Myanmar (Burma)
Burmese phrasebook
Cambodia
Indonesia
Indonesia phrasebook
Malaysia, Singapore & Brunei
Philippines
Pilipino phrasebook
Singapore city guide
South-East Asia on a shoestring
Thailand
Thai phrasebook
Vietnam, Laos & Cambodia
Vietnamese phrasebook

North-East Asia
China
Mandarin Chinese phrasebook
Hong Kong, Macau & Canton
Japan
Japanese phrasebook
Korea
Korean phrasebook
Mongolia
North-East Asia on a shoestring
Seoul city guide
Taiwan
Tibet
Tibet phrasebook
Tokyo city guide

West Asia
Trekking in Turkey
Turkey
Turkish phrasebook
West Asia on a shoestring

Middle East
Arab Gulf States
Egypt & the Sudan
Egyptian Arabic phrasebook
Iran
Israel
Jordan & Syria
Yemen

Indian Ocean
Madagascar & Comoros
Maldives & Islands of the East Indian Ocean
Mauritius, Réunion & Seychelles

Mail Order

Lonely Planet guidebooks are distributed worldwide. They are also available by mail order from Lonely Planet, so if you have difficulty finding a title please write to us. US and Canadian residents should write to Embarcadero West, 155 Filbert St, Suite 251, Oakland CA 94607, USA; European residents should write to Devonshire House, 12 Barley Mow Passage, Chiswick, London W4 4PH; and residents of other countries to PO Box 617, Hawthorn, Victoria 3122, Australia.

Indian Subcontinent
Bangladesh
India
Hindi/Urdu phrasebook
Trekking in the Indian Himalaya
Karakoram Highway
Kashmir, Ladakh & Zanskar
Nepal
Trekking in the Nepal Himalaya
Nepal phrasebook
Pakistan
Sri Lanka
Sri Lanka phrasebook

Africa
Africa on a shoestring
Central Africa
East Africa
Kenya
Swahili phrasebook
Morocco, Algeria & Tunisia
Moroccan Arabic phrasebook
South Africa, Lesotho & Swaziland
Zimbabwe, Botswana & Namibia
West Africa

Central America
Baja California
Central America on a shoestring
Costa Rica
La Ruta Maya
Mexico

North America
Alaska
Canada
Hawaii

South America
Argentina, Uruguay & Paraguay
Bolivia
Brazil
Brazilian phrasebook
Chile & Easter Island
Colombia
Ecuador & the Galápagos Islands
Latin American Spanish phrasebook
Peru
Quechua phrasebook
South America on a shoestring
Trekking in the Patagonian Andes

Europe
Dublin city guide
Eastern Europe on a shoestring
Eastern Europe phrasebook
Finland
Iceland, Greenland & the Faroe Islands
Mediterranean Europe on a shoestring
Mediterranean Europe phrasebook
Poland
Scandinavian & Baltic Europe on a shoestring
Scandinavian Europe phrasebook
Trekking in Spain
Trekking in Greece
USSR
Russian phrasebook
Western Europe on a shoestring
Western Europe phrasebook

The Lonely Planet Story

Lonely Planet published its first book in 1973 in response to the numerous 'How did you do it?' questions Maureen and Tony Wheeler were asked after driving, bussing, hitching, sailing and railing their way from England to Australia.

Written at a kitchen table and hand collated, trimmed and stapled, *Across Asia on the Cheap* became an instant local bestseller, inspiring thoughts of another book.

Eighteen months in South-East Asia resulted in their second guide, *South-East Asia on a shoestring*, which they put together in a backstreet Chinese hotel in Singapore in 1975. The 'yellow bible' as it quickly became known to backpackers around the world, soon became *the* guide to the region. It has sold well over half a million copies and is now in its 7th edition, still retaining its familiar yellow cover.

Today there are over 100 Lonely Planet titles – books that have that same adventurous approach to travel as those early guides; books that 'assume you know how to get your luggage off the carousel' as one reviewer put it.

Although Lonely Planet initially specialised in guides to Asia, they now cover most regions of the world, including the Pacific, South America, Africa, the Middle East and Europe. The list of *walking guides* and *phrasebooks* (for 'unusual' languages such as Quechua, Swahili, Nepalese and Egyptian Arabic) is also growing rapidly.

The emphasis continues to be on travel for independent travellers. Tony and Maureen still travel for several months of each year and play an active part in the writing, updating and quality control of Lonely Planet's guides.

They have been joined by over 50 authors, 48 staff – mainly editors, cartographers, & designers – at our office in Melbourne, Australia and another 10 at our US office in Oakland, California. In 1991 Lonely Planet opened a London office to handle sales for Britain, Europe and Africa. Travellers themselves also make a valuable contribution to the guides through the feedback we receive in thousands of letters each year.

The people at Lonely Planet strongly believe that travellers can make a positive contribution to the countries they visit, both through their appreciation of the countries' culture, wildlife and natural features, and through the money they spend. In addition, the company makes a direct contribution to the countries and regions it covers. Since 1986 a percentage of the income from each book has been donated to ventures such as famine relief in Africa; aid projects in India; agricultural projects in Central America; Greenpeace's efforts to halt French nuclear testing in the Pacific and Amnesty International. In 1992 $45,000 was donated to these causes.

Lonely Planet's basic travel philosophy is summed up in Tony Wheeler's comment, 'Don't worry about whether your trip will work out. Just go!'